MW00624308

A Union Against Unions

MINNESOTA HISTORICAL SOCIETY PRESS

A UNION AGAINST UNIONS

The Minneapolis Citizens Alliance and Its Fight Against Organized Labor, 1903–1947

William Millikan

First edition.

www.mnhs.org/mhspress

Manufactured in the United States of America

10 9 8 7 6 5 4 3 2 1

♾ The paper used in this publication meets the minimum
requirements of the American National Standard for Information
Sciences—Permanence for Printed Library Materials, ANSI Z39.
48-1984

International Standard Book Number
0-87351-398-3 (cloth)

Library of Congress Cataloging-in-Publication Data

Millikan, William.
    A union against unions : the Minneapolis Citizens Alliance and
    its fight against organized labor, 1903–1947 / William Millikan ;
    introduction by Peter Rachleff.
        p. cm
Includes bibliographical references and index.
ISBN 0-87351-398-3 (alk. paper)
        1. Citizens Alliance of Minneapolis—History.
        2. Union busting—Minnesota—Minneapolis—History.
        3. Labor unions—Minnesota—Minneapolis—History.
        I. Title.

HD6519.M6 M55 2001
331.88′09776′579—dc21
                                                    00-052544

To Emily

Contents

Introduction

Peter Rachleff

ON THE EVE OF THE ANNUAL Labor Day holiday in September 2000, Human Rights Watch, an internationally respected non-profit, non-governmental organization, released a 217-page report, "Unfair Advantage: Workers' Freedom of Association in the United States under International Human Rights Standards." Based on field research in nine states, the report detailed widespread labor rights violations across regions, industries, and employment status. It described how thousands of workers are fired from their jobs each year for trying to organize unions, while millions of workers in agriculture, domestic service, and temporary employment are excluded from labor laws that are supposed to protect workers' organizing rights. "The cards are stacked against workers in the United States," said Kenneth Roth, executive director of Human Rights Watch.[1]

Human Rights Watch was hardly alone in its contentions. The Century Foundation, an independent, non-profit research institution founded in 1919 as the Twentieth Century Fund, reached similar conclusions. An "Idea Brief," issued in August 2000 and entitled "Labor Organizing as a Civil Right," states: "American society has more economic inequality than most other major industrial democracies . . . because our unions are weak—and our unions are weak because it is relatively easy to fire workers who attempt to organize a union." According to the federal government's own statistics, 24,000 workers were fired for trying to organize unions in 1998, the last year for which data is available.[2]

The anti-union environment within the United States violates this nation's own expressed ground rules. The basic labor law, the National Labor Relations Act of 1935 (also known as the Wagner Act), states unequivocally: "Employees shall have the right to self-organization, to form, join, or assist labor organizations, to bargain collectively through representatives of their own choosing, and to engage in other mutual aid or protection." Similar standards are affirmed by various international resolutions which have been endorsed by the U.S. government. For instance, the International Convention on Civil and Political Rights, ratified by the U.S. in 1992, declares: "[E]veryone shall have the right to freedom of association with others, including the right to form and join trade unions for the protection of interests."[3]

How is it that the country that most identifies itself with the values of "rights" and "freedom" can be cited by one of the world's most respected NGOs as a flagrant violator of the letter and the intent of international law? We need look no further than Bill Millikan's carefully written and painstakingly documented *A Union Against Unions* to find answers to this question. This book takes us for an extensive historical journey which, in the end, deposits us once again in the present, now well-informed about a subject that affects millions of Americans yet is never discussed on the front page of the newspaper or on the TV and radio news. Employer resistance to workers' efforts to organize themselves into unions has been a well-kept secret in Minnesota and across this country, although it has been a consistent and dominant theme in American industrial relations.[4]

A number of historians and industrial relations scholars have speculated about the sources of American employers' determined anti-unionism. Some have suggested that its roots lie in "proprietary capitalism," where business owners also function as managers and resist each and every effort to impinge on their decision-making domain, their "right to manage," whether it comes from workers, the government, or financial institutions. Others have argued that frontline managers, whether they hold a stake in the ownership of the business or not, oppose workers' efforts to shift what Carter Goodrich in the 1920s called the "frontier of control," that invisible dividing line where managerial authority ends and workers' capacity to make decisions begins. Some scholars have even suggested that American employers and managers have been so fixated on control that they have undercut their own profits. Still others have insisted that managerial control is the only way to protect profitability in the long run. Whatever the rationale, however, most scholars have agreed that rare has been the employer who has not perceived a union of his own workers to represent a threat to his authority *and* to his bottom line, a threat that must be overcome.[5]

Employer anti-unionism has been a prominent feature of the American industrial relations scene since workers began to organize, and it has remained significant throughout the nineteenth and twentieth centuries (and will remain so, most likely, well into the twenty-first). This has been true except for brief periods when specific historical circumstances ranging from economic conditions to political conjunctures have enabled workers to install institutions and legal protections that have forced employers to deal with unions rather than seek to eradicate them altogether. A long view of American history suggests that these periods of worker success have been the exception rather than the rule, but it also suggests that employers have had to struggle to keep the upper hand in their relationship with their employees, that this has been a frequent and difficult struggle, and that they have relied typically not only on their own direct economic power but also on their command over the political power of the government. That workers have ever succeeded in imposing their will suggests that it could possibly happen again.

The early nineteenth century saw the birth not only of the industrial revolution but also of the labor movement and, with it, the beginnings of employer resistance to worker organization. From newspaper composing rooms and print shops to shoe shops and carpet factories, employers turned to the courts to argue that unions were "conspiracies" that sought to interfere with and restrain their trade. While judges were sympathetic to the employers' charges, juries were not always so inclined. By the mid-1830s, legal precedents were being established that by organizing into a union workers were not automatically participating in an illegal "combination," and that by withholding their labor in a strike they were not automatically guilty of seeking to "damage" their employer's business.[6]

Having fended off these legal challenges, workers proceeded to organize a panoply of unions in the 1830s, 1840s, and 1850s. However, these fledgling organizations proved little able to withstand the persistent trend of the industrial revolution to turn skilled labor into unskilled labor and of national markets to take the place of local markets in which small unions might have been effective. Employers, politicians, newspapers, and minstrel performers also undercut the ideological rationale underlying unions by contrasting the "free labor" of the industrializing North to the slave labor that typified the plantation South. By the Civil War, unions were losing the economic and ideological battle as ranks closed around Abraham Lincoln and the federal government and the foremen and supervisors who became Union Army officers.[7]

Workers' impetus to organize was renewed in the years after the Civil War, and they reached out to form national associations. Though activists hoped that Reconstruction might bring such labor reforms as the eight-hour day along with the breakup of the planter monopoly of land and wealth in the South, they were to be bitterly disappointed by the emergence of nationally organized corporations who used their political influence along with their economic power to bowl over union challenges to their hegemony. In a revealing irony, the last federal troops that had protected African American political rights in the South were withdrawn in the summer of 1877 only to be sent to put down railroad strikes that were sweeping the middle of the country. The troops had been pulled out of the South as part of the backroom bargain that had resolved the contested 1876 presidential election in favor of Republican

Rutherford B. Hayes in exchange for Hayes' commitment to end the Reconstruction "experiment" in the South. Railroad workers were striking against the third round of wage reductions their employers had instituted during the national depression which had begun in 1873. The depression was the most severe economic "panic" yet to grip industrial America, and the strike wave that began in the summer of 1877 was the most militant challenge to capitalist authority yet mounted by the labor movement. National guardsmen and federal troops fired on crowds of workers from Martinsburg, West Virginia, and Pittsburgh to Chicago and St. Louis. Dozens of strikers and strike supporters died. The strike was broken and the labor movement's threat was stifled.[8]

The labor movement rebounded in remarkably short order. The continuing industrial revolution, public hostility to the rise of corporate power, and popular fears about the havoc wrought by economic depressions motivated workers, farmers, and even small businessmen in the 1880s and 1890s to challenge the direction of American society, from the level of an individual workplace to the workings of the national marketplace. Labor organizations of diverse forms and dynamics played key roles in these movements, from the local assemblies of the Knights of Labor to the industrially structured American Railway Union, headed by Eugene V. Debs. These movements faced responses from American employers commensurate with the threats they represented, and the results, while less violent than in 1877, were equally destructive of the labor movement.[9]

In the mid-1880s, a formerly secret, even underground, labor organization called the "Noble and Holy Order of the Knights of Labor" sprang onto the national scene in a series of major strikes. In 1881, telegraphers who belonged to the Knights struck Western Union, and, in 1883, railroad worker members struck Jay Gould's Southwest Railroad system. Both strikes were successful, and interest in this new organization spread. Between 700,000 and 1 million workers joined in 1885 and 1886, inspired by these earlier struggles and determined to win the eight-hour day nationwide. The Knights organized mutual insurance, co-operatives, reading rooms, drama troupes, and independent political party formations as well as workplace organizations, and they offered a vision of mutuality and cooperation as an alternative to the dominant ideology of competition and individualism. Their struggles came to a head in May 1886 in Chicago when their activists sought to bring out on strike the largely immigrant workforce of America's biggest factory, the McCormick Harvester Works, as part of the movement for the eight-hour day. When police broke up a union rally on May 4, a bomb exploded, killing several police, and the police opened fire, killing several demonstrators. The Chicago leadership of the Knights were then arrested and charged with murder. They were convicted, and several were executed. Newspapers around the country ran headlines accusing the Knights of "terrorism," and the organization broke apart and faded away. Employers resistant to labor organization were learning the value of propaganda, of molding public opinion.[10]

On the heels of the Knights' defeat, a new labor organization burst onto the scene, seeking to unite all railroad workers. Founded in 1889 by railroad fireman and union magazine editor Eugene V. Debs, the American Railway Union (ARU) learned from the Knights' experience with solidarity as a force among workers and sought to institutionalize it among all railroad workers, regardless of their crafts or home cities. When the American economy slid into another major depression in 1893, the ARU came forward to oppose rail management's intention to impose wage cuts. In April 1894, in a strike that spread from Montana to St. Paul, the ARU forced James J. Hill's Great Northern Railroad to rescind its announced wage reductions. Months later, railroad shop workers in the company town of Pullman, Illinois, joined the ARU and called for the organization's assistance in their efforts to resist wage cuts that had not been accompanied by rent reductions. Debs' call for a boycott of all trains that included Pullman sleeping cars soon turned into a nationwide railroad strike. At this point, Richard Olney, the Pullman Company's attorney and former attorney general of the United States, convinced the federal government to seek an injunction against the strike because it was interfering with the shipment of the mail. Armed with the first-ever federal injunction against a strike, the Pullman Company insisted that Debs call off the strike. When he refused, he was cited for federal contempt of court, arrested, and imprisoned for the next eighteen months. The strike was broken and the union fell apart. Employers were learning how to use the federal courts to break up unions.[11]

Two decades later, the Loewe Company used the Sherman Anti-Trust Act to destroy the Danbury, Connecticut, Hatmakers Union. When the union's 1907 strike had been defeated by the use of strikebreakers, the union had called a boycott on the company's hats in a last-ditch effort to win its members' jobs back. But the company sued the union under the terms of the Sherman Anti-Trust Act, claiming that the union was a monopoly that sought to impose its will on the company. When the company won the case in 1914 and was awarded the triple damages allowed by the law, the judge seized the homes of 140 union members and announced his intent to have them auctioned off, the proceeds going to their former employer. Sam Gompers and the American Federation of Labor saved the day. They ran a campaign asking each and every union member in the country to donate one hour's wages to a fund that would be used to buy back the homes and return them to their owners. While the AFL campaign did indeed succeed, the union was broken and employers, again, had learned how useful the federal courts could be.[12]

It was also at this time—the era in which *A Union Against Unions* begins—that employers were learning the value of being organized themselves. This process was complicated, as it seemed to contradict the basic capitalist principle of competition and their instincts about managing their own affairs. Ironically, if nineteenth-century unions had had no other effect, they had taught employers the value of organization, not merely providing role models but also because they were palpable threats to employer hegemony. Beginning in the 1890s, employers experimented with diverse combinations, some within local markets, some within national industries, some on an even broader basis. Across the country, out of the soil of the industrial scene, sprang the National Founders Association, the National Metal Trades Association, the National Association of Manufacturers, the National Civic Federation, local chapters in city after city, and local civic and commerce associations. Some of these organizations briefly experimented with negotiating "trade agreements" with unions as a means to keep costs predictable and to limit union incursions into their decision-making arena. This was especially critical to employers in industries that were undergoing rapid technological and organizational change and yet were still dependent upon a supply of skilled labor.[13]

When unions proved unwilling to remain within the limited parameters that these trade agreements had staked out for them, employers reaffirmed their commitment to their own collective organization and raised high the flag of the "open shop," aiming to exclude unions entirely from their businesses. From the early years of the twentieth century through World War I, managers across the country, including the Twin Cities, as Millikan shows, asserted and defended their right to run their factories without interference from their workers and their workers' unions. In the face of strikes, tight labor markets, and militant union leaders, employers used their new self-organization to propagate to the public an ideology of "individual freedom" for workers, to initiate training programs that would teach values as well as skills, to create employment bureaus to recruit and place non-union workers, and to underwrite "intelligence gathering" (i.e., espionage) within labor organizations. They accused labor organizations of being "socialist" and "communist" in their orientation and filled newspapers with fears of "threats to democracy." Across the country, the results were impressive.[14]

Although World War I disrupted the employers' juggernaut, it was but a temporary interruption. The gains that workers and unions made in the brief years of a tightened labor market and an interventionist government proved to be ephemeral. With nearly one-quarter of all the workers in the U.S. striking at some point, 1919 was a year of showdown from coast to coast. Employers revitalized their organizations, revived their employment bureaus, bewailed the "red menace" posed by unions, recruited African American strike-breakers from the South, and, in extreme cases, solicited the intervention of the National Guard. Every major strike between 1919 and 1922 was broken. By 1920, Millikan tells us, there were 500 local "open shop" associations in 240 cities in forty-four states. Employer resistance to unions in the postwar years had coalesced into an "open shop" movement according to the dictates of the "American Plan." It coupled the big stick of the National Guard and strikebreakers with an array of carrots. Employers introduced "corporate wel-fare" programs for their non-union workers, providing such benefits as vaca-tions and pensions and even promotions linked to long-term employment, recreational activities and social organizations, and employee representation plans (also known as company unions). The entire employer package was stunningly successful, as unions shrank into an ever smaller and ineffectual niche over the remainder of the decade.[15]

The Great Depression of the 1930s pulled the rug out from under what had begun to look like an employers' paradise. Not only did workers organize themselves into unions on a scale never before seen in the United States (some 8 million joined up), but the federal government shifted from its *laissez faire* stance of the 1920s (which allowed businesses to pursue their own policies) to an interventionist orientation whose agenda was shaped by popular pres-sures from the unemployed, workers, farmers, and small businessmen. In 1934, mass strikes in Toledo, San Francisco, and Minneapolis signaled labor's turning point. In 1935, new unions began to emerge and support each other around the idea of industrial unionism, that all workers at a given employer's workplace should organize together rather than separating out the skilled craft workers. Union literature appeared in the diverse languages of the heav-ily ethnic workforce, and union organizers opposed racism and urged the in-clusion of African Americans and other workers of color. The new movement created its own institutional form in late 1935 when the Committee for In-dustrial Organization (later the Congress of Industrial Organizations) came together outside of the American Federation of Labor, and it found a new and effective tactic in the sit-down strike, which swept factories, mills, packing-houses, and mines in 1936 and 1937. Far from sending in the National Guard to break these strikes, the federal government and many state governments notified employers that they would have to deal with these unions rather than break them openly, as they had in the past. In 1935, Congress passed the Na-tional Labor Relations Act, which established a legally sanctioned path to union recognition. Although challenged in the courts, it was upheld in mid-1937 by the U.S. Supreme Court, and it became the law of the land. The "open shop" era was over.[16]

But employer determination to manage their businesses with minimal interference persisted unabated. In Minneapolis, as Millikan shows, and across the country, employer organizations turned their attention to devising means to soften the impact of these developments on their rights to manage and maximize their profits. Although some of their favorite tactics, such as company unions and the use of the National Guard at critical junctures, had been taken away, they still had access to many sources of strength. Institutions that they had built and nurtured to train new generations of workers outside of the context of union rules and loyalties, like the Dunwoody Institute in Minneapolis, were as secure as ever. Newspapers, ministers, and politicians could still be counted on to trumpet employer concerns with labor radicalism. If anything, now more than ever, anti-communism was becoming an important ideological weapon. Most importantly, the employers' political friends, the likes of Hjelmer Myre and Joseph Ball in Minnesota and their counterparts in other states, could be counted upon to introduce legislation at the state and federal levels that could contain the union challenge to management, limit union tactics like the sit-down strike, and encourage unions to keep their expectations and practices within narrow parameters. Employer organizations like the Minneapolis Citizens Alliance could change their public image and even their names while advising diverse employers how to lessen the damage that unions might inflict on their freedom to manage their workplaces and to rake in their profits.[17]

This process was fostered by a series of contingent historical developments, shifts in the political and economic contexts within which labor-management relationships took shape. The spread of unionization slowed in the late 1930s, when the economy slumped precipitously. Though all of the 1930s is—and was—known as "the Depression," there had been a period of prolonged economic recovery (though still with employment levels below those of the late 1920s) between 1934 and 1937, which is when unions made the lion's share of their progress in the decade. The "second trough," which began in the summer of 1937, threw millions of workers back out of work and onto relief rolls and brought union organizing to a crunching halt. It coincided with a political backlash against Roosevelt and his programs, which led to Republican successes in the congressional and state elections of 1938. Union gains within particular industries—General Motors within auto manufacturing, General Electric within electrical products, and U.S. Steel within steel fabrication—as well as regional breakthroughs in the Midwest and New England faced the threat of becoming isolated islands rather than beachheads from which further organizing might spread. Key individual firms like Ford, Westinghouse, and Republic Steel solidified their opposition to unionization, while employer organizations within local regions, such as the South, and local markets, such as Minneapolis, sought to hold union gains to their early 1937 levels. In Minnesota, as Millikan shows, and in other states, they promoted state legislation that confined union breakthroughs and limited their political and economic power.[18]

World War II provided additional steps on this path toward containing the threat represented by union growth. While unions did add 4 million members during the war years (to a base of 10 million), employers and their organizations succeeded in limiting union power. Thousands of union activists—organizers, shop stewards, local officers—left their grassroots bases to join the military. Government-promoted "union security" and "maintenance of membership" clauses made millions of workers, many of whom were southerners and women who had not been touched by the labor upheaval of the 1930s, members of unions without their undergoing union organization, orientation, education, socialization, or involvement. They were made members on paper, their dues were deducted from their paychecks, and they experienced the union as yet another institution that shaped their lives. The government's "cost-plus" defense contracts enabled employers to pay generous overtime wages and made the shop floor itself much less a center of conflict over workloads and speed. Employers offered unions productivity-based wages, in exchange for which unions backed off on resistance to technological and organizational changes in the workplace. Most contracts included "management's rights" and "management prerogatives" clauses, in which unions divested themselves of the authority to challenge managerial decisions in areas other than those that were spelled out clearly in the contract. All these "other" matters, including decisions to invest—or disinvest—capital in whatever forms, were assumed to be management's prerogative to control.[19]

When unions sought to increase their voice in the direction of postwar American society, they found themselves opposed not only by employers big and small, but also by the government. A strike wave in 1945 and 1946 sought to secure workers' positions in an uncertain American economy by raising wages across the board and limiting price increases. They faced ferocious opposition from unionized as well as non-unionized companies, in the union strongholds of the Midwest and Northeast as well as the South, and from Democrats as well as Republicans. Not only did the strikes fall far short of the unions' goals, but they were followed by the passage of the Taft-Hartley Act of 1947, which amended the National Labor Relations Act by adding a list of "unfair labor practices" by workers—sympathy strikes, secondary boycotts, and closed shops. Taft-Hartley also allowed states to pass "right-to-work" laws, which picked up on employer organizations' crafted language of workers' "freedom" to *not* belong to unions and required unions to sign affidavits certifying that none of their officers were "communists" (a term that was undefined in the legislation). Disastrous consequences were nearly immediate. "Operation Dixie," the CIO's campaign to break into the South, collapsed, as did a white-collar workers' organizing drive in banks and offices in the North. Eleven national unions refused to sign the affidavits and were expelled from the CIO, and other unions scrambled to pick up their members. Implosion rather than expansion became the order of the day for the labor movement, as employers solidified their control over their workplaces, their industries, and their labor markets.[20]

Though the era of the "open shop" was over, employer resistance to unionism had only temporarily been replaced by employer tolerance of unions. This tolerance was very conditional. It depended on unions remaining within the narrow limits of legally sanctioned collective bargaining—which especially meant no incursions on managerial decision-making and no threats to the structuring of corporate profits—and on the U.S. and U.S.–based firms enjoying a hegemonic position within a global pattern of economic growth which meant expanding profits. For the better part of a generation, from the 1950s through the 1970s, such a truce held sway in American industrial relations. That unions and workers had paid a high price for their share of the bargain would not become clear until corporate management tore up this "social contract" in the mid-1970s and returned to an overtly anti-union stance. At that point, unions found themselves miserably hemmed in and limited by their own participation in the system in which they had been tolerated for a generation.[21]

Beginning in the mid-1970s, American employers decided that their engagement in the global economy, on the one hand, required that the scope of their decision-making not be restricted in any way by union representation of their workers and, on the other hand, made possible a wholesale deunionization of their enterprises through plant closings, relocations, downsizing, outsourcing, the replacement of strikers, and the outright blackmail of employees. Aided by a veritable army of lawyers and consultants and encouraged by various employer organizations, employers dusted off their open shop pedigrees. For the last quarter of the twentieth century, they waged what former United Auto Workers' Union president Doug Fraser called a "one-sided class war."[22]

This employer offensive—which might well be named the fourth "open shop drive" of the twentieth century—faced an opposition that fought one battle at a time, and, typically, lost. The halls and walls of labor history are decorated with the names and stories of the vanquished of the 1980s and 1990s—the Professional Air Traffic Controllers; Phelps-Dodge; Hormel; International

Paper; the *Chicago Tribune*; Caterpillar; Staley Corn Processing; and the Detroit Newspapers. Union membership as a percentage of the U.S. workforce fell from 23 percent to less than 14 percent, while the majority of the workers employed in coal-mining, auto manufacturing, meat-packing, and steel fabrication became non-union.[23]

Yet unions still have a presence in American society. They have more than 13 million members, are particularly effective in some sectors and industries, such as public schools, auto manufacturing, and the postal service, and are struggling under new leadership to rebuild their influence in workplaces, communities, and our country's political life. The "New Voice" leadership team headed by John Sweeney, Richard Trumka, and Linda Chavez-Thompson, elected to AFL-CIO office in 1995, has encouraged unions to devote one-third of their sizeable resources to organizing. Some unions have responded, and they have enjoyed some success. In 1999, for instance, 74,000 home health aides in Los Angeles won recognition as part of the Service Employees International Union (SEIU) in the biggest union-organizing victory since the 1930s. Indeed, in that same year, for the first time since Ronald Reagan fired the air traffic controllers in 1981, union membership grew rather than shrank. Organizations like Human Rights Watch and the Century Foundation would not be exploring issues of violations of unions' organizing rights if the labor movement were not putting pressure, once again, on employers. And so the conflict—which predates and postdates this book—persists.[24]

At this point, you might be wondering: "If this is such a 'one-note' story, if employers have always resisted unions, plain and simple, why should I find this book interesting?" I have many elements of an answer, and I want to mention just a few of them before putting you in Bill Millikan's capable hands.

In the first place, as I suggested at the outset, while this might be a consistent story in American history, it is one that is not well known. Diverse sources—newspapers, magazines, business and governmental histories, television and films—have remained silent on this score, and most mainstream history books used in the schools have taken their cue from these "recorders" of history. Furthermore, anti-union employers, as Millikan shows so well, have spun their own smokescreens of ideologies and myths about freedom and individualism, covering over their actions in pursuit of their own material interests. These smokescreens have also affected the telling and retelling of history.

For Minnesotans, it is important to understand the array of prominent families and central institutions that have been implicated in the employer project of eradicating or containing workers' unions. *A Union Against Unions* points to the involvement of prominent business and political leaders in anti-union campaigns, from funding to design to implementation. Similarly, such vaunted local institutions as the Dunwoody Institute, the Blake School, the Minneapolis Institute of the Arts, and the Walker Art Center are revealed to have stood somewhere other than above the fray when class struggles have erupted in the Twin Cities. If we are to understand our own communities, we must come to grips with this history.

A Union Against Unions also demonstrates that these elements of Minnesota's history have been intimately bound up with national history. At times, Twin Cities business leaders took their cues from anti-union activists prominent on the national scene. At other times, it was the Twin Cities business leaders themselves who were setting the tone and the pattern for national developments. At no time, it is important to recognize, were Twin Cities business leaders moving against the grain of national practices. In this sense, one might argue, they were part of a class, a class that communicated with, set agendas for, and defended the interests of its members. At critical moments, these interests were diametrically opposed to those of their workers, not just in the Twin Cities but across the United States.

By making readers aware of the range of tactics used by Minneapolis employers to resist unions—selective firings and blacklists, court injunctions, the police and the National Guard, anti-communism and "red-baiting," the ideologies of worker "freedom" and "individualism," vocational education, employment bureaus, infiltration and espionage, company unions and labor-management "cooperation" structures, the exacerbation of conflicts within and among unions, the passage of anti-union legislation, and more—Bill Millikan cautions us to look closely at the world around us today. One cannot read this book without becoming a more astute viewer of and listener to the news, a more skeptical reader of the newspapers, and a more determined pursuer of alternative sources of information.

Bill Millikan has achieved all this in a well-written, painstakingly documented tome. This book has been more than a decade in the making, which is reflected not only in the richness of its sources but also in the carefulness of its argument. I suspect that many readers will have their eyes opened by *A Union Against Unions*, and quite a few will not like what they see. But all will recognize the remarkable achievement that this book represents.

NOTES

1. Human Rights Watch, "Unfair Advantage: Workers' Freedom of Association in the United States under International Human Rights Standards," (August 31, 2000), available at http://www.hrw.org/reports/2000/us-labor/findings/htm, p. 1–2. Human Rights Watch has investigated accusations of human rights abuses around the world since 1978.

They have issued reports on fourteen African, ten South American, ten Asian, ten Middle Eastern, and twenty-five European countries, as well as several reports on different issues within the United States.

2. The Century Foundation, "Labor Organizing as a Civil Right," Idea Brief no. 15, (August 2000), available at http://www.tcf.org, p. 1. Also see *What's Next for Organized Labor? The Report of the Century Foundation Task Force on the Future of Unions* (New York: The Century Foundation Press, 1999). The 24,000 figure is given in the Human Rights Watch press release announcing the publication of "Unfair Advantage." See also National Labor Relations Board, *Annual Report for FY 1998* (Washington, D.C.: U.S. Government Printing Office, 1999).

3. Section 7, National Labor Relations Act, 49 Stat. 449 (1935); "International Covenant on Civil and Political Rights," December 16, 1966, 999 U.N.T.S. 171 (art. 22).

4. The only comparable study is Howell J. Harris, *Bloodless Victories: The Rise and Fall of the Open Shop in the Philadelphia Metal Trades, 1890–1940* (New York: Cambridge University Press, 2000), which appeared in the fall of 2000.

5. Philip Scranton, *Proprietary Capitalism: The Textile Manufacture at Philadelphia, 1800–1880* (New York: Cambridge University Press, 1983); Carter Goodrich, *The Frontier of Control* (New York: Harcourt, 1920); Alfred Chandler, *The Visible Hand: The Managerial Revolution in American Business* (Cambridge, Mass.: Belknap, 1977); David Noble, *Forces of Production: A Social History of Industrial Automation* (New York: Knopf, 1984).

6. John R. Commons et al., eds., *A Documentary History of American Industrial Society* (Cleveland: Arthur H. Clark Company, 1910); Edmund E. Witte, "Early American Labor Cases," *Yale Law Journal* 35 (1926).

7. Alan Dawley, *Class and Community: The Industrial Revolution in Lynn* (Cambridge: Harvard University Press, 1976); Eric Foner, *Free Soil, Free Labor, Free Men* (New York: Oxford, 1971); David Roediger, *The Wages of Whiteness* (New York: Verso, 1991).

8. David Montgomery, *Beyond Equality: Labor and the Radical Republicans, 1862–1872*

(New York: Knopf, 1967); Montgomery, *Citizen Worker: The Experience of Workers in the U.S. with Democracy and the Free Market in the Nineteenth Century* (New York: Cambridge University Press, 1993); Jeremy Brecher, *Strike! The True History of Mass Insurrections in American History* (Boston: South End Press, 1999 [1972]), chapter 1: "The Great Upheaval," pp. 13–38.

9. Herbert Gutman, *Work, Culture, and Society in Industrializing America* (New York: Vintage, 1977).

10. Brecher, *Strike!*, chapter 2: "May Day," pp. 39–68; Bruce Nelson, *Beyond the Martyrs: A Social History of Chicago's Anarchists, 1870–1920* (New Brunswick, N.J.: Rutgers University Press, 1988); Rob Weir, *Beyond Labor's Veil: The Culture of the Knights of Labor* (University Park: Pennsylvania State University Press, 1996); Leon Fink, *Workingmen's Democracy: The Knights of Labor and American Politics* (Urbana: University of Illinois Press, 1983).

11. Nick Salvatore, *Eugene V. Debs: Citizen and Socialist* (Urbana: University of Illinois Press, 1982); Brecher, *Strike!*, chapter 3: "The Ragged Edge of Anarchy," pp. 69–114.

12. Loewe v. Lawlor, 208 U.S. 274 (1908) and Lawlor v. Loewe, 235 U.S. 522 (1915); David Bensman, *The Practice of Solidarity: American Hat Finishers in the Nineteenth Century* (Urbana: University of Illinois Press, 1985).

13. Bruno Ramirez, *When Workers Fight: The Politics of Industrial Relations in the Progressive Era, 1898–1916* (Westport, Conn.: Greenwood Press, 1978); David Brody, *In Labor's Cause: Main Themes in the History of the American Worker* (New York: Oxford, 1993); George E. Barnett, "National and District Systems of Collective Bargaining in the United States," *Quarterly Journal of Economics* 26 (1912); Albert K. Steigerwalt, *The National Association of Manufacturers, 1895–1914* (Ann Arbor: University of Michigan Press, 1964); Clarence E. Bonnett, *Employers' Associations in the United States* (New York: MacMillan, 1922); Margaret Loomis, "National Founders' Association," *Quarterly Journal of Economics* 30 (1916); Sidney Fine, *"Without Blare of Trumpets": Walter Drew, the National Erectors'*

Association, and the Open Shop Movement, 1903–1957 (Ann Arbor: University of Michigan Press, 1995).

14. David Montgomery, *Workers' Control in America* (Cambridge: Cambridge University Press, 1979), chapter 3: "Machinists, the Civic Federation, and the Socialist Party," pp. 48–90; Jeffrey Haydu, "Trade Agreement Versus Open Shop: Employers' Choices before World War One," *Industrial Relations* 28 (1989); Marguerite Green, *The National Civic Federation and the American Labor Movement, 1900–1925* (Washington, D.C.: Catholic University Press, 1956); Harris, *Bloodless Victories.*

15. Joseph McCartin, *Labor's Great War: The Struggle for Industrial Democracy and the Origins of Modern American Labor Relations* (Chapel Hill: University of North Carolina Press, 1997); David Montgomery, *The Fall of the House of Labor: The Workplace, the State, and American Labor Activism* (New York: Cambridge University Press, 1987); James Barrett, *Work and Community in the Jungle: Chicago's Packinghouse Workers, 1894–1922* (Urbana: University of Illinois Press, 1987); David Brody, *Labor in Crisis: The Steel Strike of 1919* (New York: Lippincott, 1965); Colin J. Davis, *Power at Odds: The National Railroad Shopmen's Strike* (Urbana: University of Illinois Press, 1997); Mark Perlman, *The Machinists: A Study in American Trade Unionism* (Cambridge: Harvard University Press, 1961); Robert W. Dunn, *The Americanization of Labor: The Employers' Offensive Against the Trade Unions* (New York: International Publishers, 1927); Allen M. Wakstein, "The Origins of the Open Shop Movement, 1919–1920," *Journal of American History* 51 (1964).

16. Staughton Lynd, ed., *"We Are All Leaders": The Alternative Unionism of the Early 1930s* (Urbana: University of Illinois Press, 1996); David Brody, *Workers in Industrial America: Essays on the Twentieth Century Struggle* (New York: Oxford, 1980); Farrell Dobbs, *Teamster Rebellion* (New York: Monad, 1972).

17. Colin Gordon, *New Deals: Business, Labor, and Politics in America* (New York: Cambridge University Press, 1994); Karl Klare, "Judicial Deradicalization of the Wagner Act and the Origins of Modern Legal Consciousness," *Minnesota Law Review* 62 (1978); Christopher L. Tomlins, *The State and the Unions: Labor Relations, Law, and the Organized Labor Movement in America, 1880–1960* (New York: Cambridge University Press, 1986); Harris, *Bloodless Victories,* chapter 11: "The New World: Accommodation and Adjustment, 1936–1939," pp. 405–32.

18. Millikan's study, particularly his analysis of the "Stassen Labor Relations Law," pp. 349–62, is the best historical treatment of this long overlooked topic. Some additional insight can be gained from James Matles and James Higgins, *Them and Us: Struggles of a Rank and File Union* (Englewood Cliffs: Prentice Hall, 1974); Harry A. Mills, ed., *How Collective Bargaining Works: A Survey of Experience in Leading American Industries* (New York: MacMillan, 1942); Robert R. R. Brooks, *As Steel Goes: Unionism in a Basic Industry* (New Haven: Yale University Press, 1940); Sanford M. Jacoby, *Employing Bureaucracy: Managers, Unions, and the Transformation of Work in American Industry, 1900–1945* (New York: Columbia University Press, 1985).

19. These wartime experiences are most powerfully conveyed in Harriette Arnow's novel *The Dollmaker* (New York: Avon, 1999). For more analytical treatments, see Martin Glaberman, *War-time Strikes* (Detroit: Bewicked, 1980) and Nelson Lichtenstein, *Labor's War At Home: The CIO in World War II* (New York: Cambridge University Press, 1982).

20. Nelson Lichtenstein, *The Most Dangerous Man in Detroit: Walter Reuther and the Fate of American Labor* (New York: Basic, 1995); Elizabeth Fones-Wolf, *Selling Free Enterprise: The Business Assault on Labor and Liberalism, 1945–1960* (Urbana: University of Illinois Press, 1994); Michael Goldfield, *The Color of Politics: Race and the Mainspring of American Politics* (New York: The New Press, 1997); Steve Rosswurm, ed., *The CIO's Left-Led Unions* (New Brunswick, N.J.: Rutgers University Press, 1992); Barbara Griffith, *The Crisis of American Labor: Operation Dixie and the Defeat of the CIO* (Philadelphia: Temple University Press, 1988).

21. Michael Goldfield, *The Decline of Organized Labor in the U.S.* (Chicago: University of Chicago Press, 1987); Kim Moody, *An Injury to All: The Decline of American Unionism* (New York: Verso, 1988); Paul Baran and Paul

Sweezy, *Monopoly Capital* (New York: Monthly Review Press, 1966).

22. Douglas Fraser, letter of resignation from the Labor-Management Advisory Committee, July 19, 1978, quoted in David Gordon, *Fat and Mean* (New York: Free Press, 1996), p. 205.

23. Peter Rachleff, *Hard-Pressed in the Heartland: The Hormel Strike and the Future of the Labor Movement* (Boston: South End Press, 1993); Barbara Kingsolver, *Holding the Line: Women in the Great Arizona Mine Strike of 1983* (Ithaca: Cornell University Press, 1988); Brecher, *Strike!*, chapter 9: "American Labor on the Eve of the Millenium," pp. 305–61; Kim Moody, *Workers in a Lean World: Unions in the International Economy* (New York: Verso, 1997).

24. Ray M. Tillman and Michael S. Cummings, eds., *The Transformation of U.S. Unions: Voices, Visions, and Strategies from the Grassroots* (Boulder: Lynne Reinner, 1999); Gregory Mantsios, ed., *A New Labor Movement for the New Century* (New York: Monthly Review Press, 1998); Kate Bronfenbrenner et al., eds., *Organizing to Win: New Research on Union Strategies* (Ithaca: Cornell University Press, 1998); Jo-Ann Mort, ed., *Not Your Father's Labor Movement* (New York: Verso, 1998).

Acknowledgements

THE UNSUNG HEROES of this book work in the acquisition department of the Minnesota Historical Society. Without the vast business collections of MHS, the story of the Minneapolis Citizens Alliance would never have been revealed. The acquisition of CA papers by Lucile Kane in 1963 was particularly critical. When new important sources were donated to MHS during my research, I was quickly informed by research supervisor Debbie Miller, and I was allowed access to materials before they were available to the public by Mark Greene, head of manuscripts acquisitions.

In addition to publishing the book, the MHS Press and research department have encouraged and financially supported this project from its inception fifteen years ago. Jean Brookins, Debbie Miller, and Ann Regan realized the importance of this research and expressed their faith in my ability to complete this project both verbally and with a series of research grants. My determination was also buoyed by the acceptance of several of my articles by Mary Cannon and Anne Kaplan for publication in *Minnesota History*.

As an independent scholar, I have had very few contacts with other labor and business historians. However, in the earliest stage of research (this project began as research for a novel), I met Peter Rachleff at a screening of *Labor's Turning Point*. He has been an enthusiastic supporter of my research and a sounding board for my ideas ever since. In the isolated world of the independent scholar, he has been an essential friend.

Finally, I would like to thank Big George, whom I never met, for raising the Gherity sisters while he toiled away his life on the drop forge at Minneapolis Moline. It was his hatred of the bosses that ultimately seeded my mind with the necessity for writing *A Union Against Unions*.

Prologue:
The Battle of Deputies Run

AT 3:30 A.M. on Tuesday, May 22, 1934, the army of the Citizen's Alliance (CA) of Minneapolis stirred in its temporary barracks in the Studebaker Garage in the city's downtown. The determined businessmen of the CA, along with their lawyers, doctors, and trusted employees, had half an hour to eat breakfast before reporting for duty.

The commerce of the city had been shut down by a strike of the radical Teamsters union. In a desperate effort to move trucks, the CA, an association of Minneapolis employers that had suppressed labor unions since 1903, had recruited the "cream of Minneapolis citizens to establish law and order." Over five hundred of these newly appointed sheriff's deputies clutched their billy clubs and waited for Colonel Watson and Major Harrison to give them their orders. The veterans of the previous day's bloody hand-to-hand combat at least knew what to expect—a thousand ferocious workers charging at them with swinging clubs. The new recruits naively thought they were assembled simply to convoy trucks.

At 4:00 A.M., Colonel Watson quickly organized his untrained troops into nine-man squads, each one under the command of a volunteer with military experience. In order to stiffen the resolve of his men and to avoid a repeat of the previous day's defeat, Watson paired each squad with a uniformed Minneapolis policeman. To the surprise of many of the men, Watson deployed all sixty squads in the market district, primarily in the area from Fifth Street to Seventh Street between First and Third Avenues North. Police Chief Johannes, working closely with the CA, assembled over three-quarters of the city's police force in the same area. By 4:30 the force of more than 1,500 men was in position, ready to repel the striking truck drivers and keep the streets of Minneapolis open for business.

Watson and Johannes directed their men to break up any large concentrations of strikers, to stop the movement of cars and men into the market, and to search for and confiscate any weapons. Several squads patrolled the alley in front of the Gamble-Robinson Company, the site of Monday's battle, to prevent any infiltration of picketers across the railroad tracks west of the market. To the north, at Fifth Street and Second Avenue, Squads Number Four and Forty-three stopped cars and searched for lead pipes and clubs. Between 5:00 and 11:00 they turned twenty men over to the police department for arrest.

On the corner of Seventh Street and Third Avenue, the southwest corner of the market, a force of fifty deputies assisted a police sergeant in stopping and inspecting automobiles. When crowds of bystanders gathered, they were moved away from the northeast corner of the intersection. One half block north of Central Labor Union (CLU) headquarters, near the Butler Brothers Building, Squad Number Forty-one was instructed to permit no automobiles or pedestrians to pass through their lines. These orders were obeyed, although there was little activity in the early morning hours. Close cooperation between the police and the CA's army was temporarily maintaining the security of the market district.

By mid-morning, however, the crowd congregating in front of CLU head-quarters had swelled to block off First Avenue. The police established a line across the north end of the block in an attempt to keep the sidewalks on Sixth Street open. By 10:00, the small contingent of police faced a belligerent crowd of several thousand union supporters. Further attempts to clear the sidewalks were prudently abandoned. Men in the front ranks of the crowd now openly brandished gas pipes. As the anger of the mob increased, a steady barrage of eggs, stones, and bricks rained down on the nervously waiting force of 150 deputies. The police, afraid of inciting an out-of-control riot, maintained their position without interfering in the crowd's bombardment. The harsh threats and vicious insults of the mob finally incited several deputies to break rank and attack the nearest tormentors.

Several of the hecklers stood out in the memories of the beleaguered businessmen. One "battle axe" of an elderly woman harangued the deputies for several hours, exhorting the strikers to charge the "Special Rats!" Partially hidden under her coat, a baseball bat hung from her wrist. Whenever the police line neared a deputy sheriff, the woman would step out of the crowd and attempt to club the deputy. She even raised her bat to strike a woman walking by, but was restrained by nearby strikers.

Squad Number Forty-one nicknamed an older male heckler "Banjo Eyes," noting that, "if he had ever taken a bath, the shock would have been too great for him." He approached the deputies, leaned up against them, and said, "What have you got those clubs for? Hit me here!" Then he would remove his hat and point to the side of his head. He yelled incessantly, "Hit me here, come on! Hit me here!" Despite the increasing friction between the crowd and the deputies, the police made no attempts to remove the hecklers or to disarm the "battle axe."

By 11:30, the mounting tension of the confrontation had reached the boiling point. Union organizer Walter Franks realized, however, that a direct attack against a police line might provoke gunfire and lead to a tragic defeat. To gain control of the marketplace, the union forces needed to separate the special deputies from the Minneapolis police. Strikers approached the police with an offer to defuse the potentially violent situation: the strikers would disperse if the police would order the special deputies to move down Sixth Street to Second Avenue. If any fighting did take place, the strikers would attack only special deputies. The police, eager to avoid a repeat of the previous day's violent battles, quickly accepted the offer. Minutes later, the deputies lounging around the northeast corner of the market watched the huge mob disperse behind them. Sensing that the crisis had passed, two members of Squad Number Forty-one ducked into the Percansky Restaurant and ordered a lunch that they would never eat.

Union leaders had very different plans. Earlier that morning, the police had allowed a union reconnaissance team to tour the marketplace and observe the disposition of the CA's army. In order to guard all approaches to the market square, Colonel Watson had spread his troops thinly across the entire district. A large, fast-moving attack could quickly mop up one special deputy patrol after another.

Following their battle plan, several thousand angry pickets retreated south on First Avenue to Seventh Street, where they wheeled and marched west toward the railroad tracks. Reinforced by three truckloads of armed strikers, the force met a small police line stretched across the corner at Seventh Street and Third Avenue between the Weisound Malt & Beer Company and the Minneapolis Anoka & Cuyuna Range Railroad passenger depot. While the twenty-three police officers briefly stalled the march, the special deputies posted on the northeast corner of the intersection were advised to flee into the market. Leaderless and outnumbered fifty-to-one, the businessmen quickly retreated from the battleground. One deputy overheard a well-dressed striker comment, "We are getting the rats down in the hole where we want them."

Three squads watched nervously from the alley in front of the Gamble-Robinson Company as the mob "broke loose and came down Third Avenue like a bunch of hyenas." As the pickets rushed down Third Avenue at a run, the special deputies retreated into their alley. Within minutes, shouts of "here they come" were heard from in front of Ryan Potato Company on Third and Sixth Street. CA director Arthur Lyman yelled to several squads and led them forward to defend the corner. As the crowd swept down Third Avenue, "they appeared to be beyond any sense of reason and were certainly one hundred percent in a wild rage." The real battle for control of the Minneapolis market district was about to begin.

A mass of several thousand angry strikers poured into Sixth Street in the next ten minutes, filling the street and even covering the awning roof on the market side of the street. The CA's army retreated under an aerial bombardment of bricks, bottles, fruit boxes, sticks, two-by-fours, and steel rods. Deputies, cut or bleeding or unconscious, were dragged off the street as the strikers overtook the retreating army. In vicious hand-to-hand fighting, more deputies were clubbed to the ground by hoses, lead pipes, baseball bats, and iron hooks. When an injured deputy still displayed his badge, he was clubbed until he was unconscious. Bloodied deputies crawled or were dragged into the buildings lining Sixth Street or rolled under vehicles in a desperate attempt to escape the ferocity of the strikers. One deputy realized that the truck drivers "took a terrible grievance towards us and were angered beyond mad men."

As the strikers bore down on them, one of the deputies shouted above the din at nearby police officers: "For God's sake get your gun out. They are going to kill us!" The police officer, however, made no effort to stop the charging crowd. Although the police did not retreat, they were not attacked by the strikers. The battle surged around them as if they weren't there. Not one officer raised his club or drew his gun. The strikers passed the word to "lay off the police." It was clear to the beleaguered army of the CA that a deal had been struck. Despite Police Chief Johannes's determination to break the strike, his officers had tacitly agreed to step away from the confrontation and allow the strikers to batter the businessmen's army into submission. One deputy noticed that the "police department were enjoying the situation as much as the rioters."

As the CA's army retreated down Sixth Street, Arthur Lyman, vice-president of American Ball Company and a CA director, rallied twenty deputies to help the men in the front lines escape. "Give the poor chaps a chance," he called. Within minutes Lyman was trapped in the frenzy of swinging clubs. A small, sickly-looking man in dirty coveralls struck him on the head. Dazed, Lyman was thrown over an automobile and worked over with clubs and fists. His unconscious body dropped to the street by the alley, lying there until an improvised ambulance could pick him up. Still unconscious, Lyman lay across the laps of six other wounded men as they rode to the hospital. His skull badly fractured, the sixty-year-old executive was never to regain consciousness.

Isolated, without any leadership, vastly outnumbered, and viciously outfought by the strikers, the demoralized deputies broke ranks and ran to protect themselves. One squad fled up a stairway off of Sixth Street and barricaded themselves on the second floor. Realizing the futility of returning to the battle, they disposed of their clubs and shields and snuck away two at a time. In the melee on the street, the police advised badly beaten deputies to drop their badges and flee. A truck of reinforcements, dispatched from CA army headquarters, arrived and unloaded, but police officers immediately ordered them back into the vehicle. Colonel Watson's efforts at military strategy were far too late. At Klingelhutz and Martinson Produce, deputies were waved inside and secreted on the third floor, where they could watch the last deputies retreating past First Avenue. Down the street at Naus Brothers Fruit Company, Mr. Strate hid over fifty deputies on the second floor, where they watched their compatriots in the street run for their lives.

In less than one hour, the battle of Deputies Run was over. The streets of Minneapolis belonged to the ferocious strikers of Teamsters Local 574, led by a small, dedicated group of Trotskyite truck drivers. The businessmen of the city licked their wounds and regrouped for a long war of attrition.

NOTE

This account of the battle of May 22, 1934, is based primarily on twenty-six pages of reports by special deputies in the CA's army, Frank P. Leslie Papers, MHS. Leslie was treasurer of the Republican State Central Committee. Interview of Totten P. Heffelfinger by Charles Walker, C. Walker Papers, MHS.

A Union Against Unions

1 An Ideology Takes Root

AS THE NINETEENTH CENTURY ENDED, Minneapolis had become the industrial, transportation, and financial center for the Northwest. The foundation for the Northwest's prosperity rested on the agricultural production of Minnesota, North and South Dakota, and Montana. With the Northwestern wheat crop expected to exceed 750 million bushels, Minneapolis had become the primary wheat market of the world. Railroad lines radiating west from Minneapolis brought the wheat to the banks of the Mississippi River where the waterpower of St. Anthony Falls was used to grind it into flour. By 1900, the revolutionary development of the middlings purifier to remove the impurities in spring wheat and the roller mill to more efficiently reduce the wheat had increased Minneapolis's flour production to nearly 15 million barrels.[1]

Dominated by two giants, Pillsbury-Washburn Company and Washburn-Crosby Company, Minneapolis millers, under the leadership of Washburn-Crosby executive William Hood Dunwoody, organized a buying pool in 1876 that had a virtual monopoly over grain trading in Minnesota. A year later, Dunwoody traveled to England and convinced British bakers of the quality of Washburn-Crosby flour. By 1895, the Minneapolis company was shipping four million barrels of flour to European markets. Reorganizing as the Minneapolis Chamber of Commerce in 1881, the millers controlled hundreds of county elevators and had the power to set prices, control grades, and exclude non-members from the grain exchange. Controlling the flow of the Northwest's enormous wheat crop from the fields to their mills and on to the vast markets of Europe gave a few large corporations dominion over a rapidly growing empire.[2]

The prosperity and economic power of the Minneapolis millers, however, rested on a very shaky foundation. Although Pillsbury-Washburn had been managed for the decade of the 1890s by Charles A. Pillsbury, a majority of the company's stock was in the hands of foreign bankers and trust companies. Across the Mississippi, Dunwoody and James S. Bell were operating the Washburn-Crosby Company in mills leased from the eastern heirs of

Cadwallader C. Washburn. The city's third-largest milling company, North-western Consolidated, also operated in leased mills. In an economic era dominated by giant trusts such as Standard Oil and the Carnegie Steel Company, the entire milling capacity of Minneapolis's three leading flour-milling companies was owned by interests that were "indifferent to their ultimate fates or the fate of the industry itself so long as they could sell out at a satisfactory price," said one local trade publication.[3]

In December of 1898, New York flour dealer Thomas McIntyre unveiled a plan to combine his New York mills with the mills of Pillsbury-Washburn, Washburn-Crosby, Northwestern Consolidated, Minneapolis Flour Manufacturing Company, and nine mills in Milwaukee and Duluth. Capitalized at $40 million, McIntyre's U. S. Flour Milling Company would merge thirty-one mills with a combined capacity of close to 100,000 barrels of flour. The giant conglomerate would control 80 percent of the country's spring wheat milling and have a virtual monopoly of the industry. Control of the primary industry of Minneapolis and the Northwest would shift from Minneapolis to the East Coast.[4]

The leading industrial families of Minneapolis, however, were not ready to relinquish control of their empire. At Pillsbury-Washburn, the majority stockholders in England favored McIntyre's scheme. Alfred F. Pillsbury led a delegation to London to try to buy back enough stock to block the sale. By mid-February 1899, the Pillsburys and other Minneapolis interests owned a majority of both ordinary and preference shares. At Washburn-Crosby, Bell and Dunwoody immediately decided to attempt to secure absolute control of the mills. Dunwoody traveled to Philadelphia in early April 1899 and purchased 75 percent of the stock from Fidelity Trust and Deposit Company. The three Washburn-Crosby mills, with their 18,000-barrel capacity, were now beyond McIntyre's grasp. There would be no further negotiations with McIntyre.[5]

Despite these serious setbacks, McIntyre continued his attempt at consolidating the United States flour-milling industry. In July 1899, he finally succeeded in purchasing the Northwestern Consolidated Mills. A public outcry expressed the fear that McIntyre's trust would drive other Minneapolis mills out of business and end the city's domination of the industry. Without the enormous milling capacity of Pillsbury-Washburn and Washburn-Crosby, however, McIntyre's trust quickly floundered. By February 1900, the U. S. Flour Milling Company was in receivership. William C. Edgar, editor of the weekly *Northwestern Miller*, rejoiced that "there will be no flour trust in the U.S., and bread eaters may be certain that whatever other industries may be controlled by this monstrous power, the making of flour will continue to be done by free men." Control of the Northwest's flour-milling empire would continue to reside in Minneapolis in the capable hands of its ruling families—the Pillsburys, Washburns, Crosbys, Bells, and Dunwoody.[6]

While Minneapolis's industrial giants concentrated their attention on outside attacks, another threat was quietly growing inside their empire. Along with the revival of the American economy in the late 1890s came a mass advance of the labor movement. The American Federation of Labor's (AFL) membership increased from 278,000 in 1898 to more than 1,600,000 in 1904. It now had the power, according to a historian of the National Association of Manufacturers (NAM), "to inflict immense injury upon capital." Labor's growing power brought with it a period of widespread industrial unrest. In 1901, the nation's employers faced 2,218 union-ordered strikes, three-quarters of which were fought for increased wages, reduction in hours, recognition of unions, and similar issues. Even more disquieting, more than two-thirds of these union-ordered strikes were at least partially successful. Employers around the nation complained bitterly about the boycotts, strikes, and violence that labor unions used to force them to accept closed-shop contracts that would exclude all non-union workers from their factories. With unions in control of the factory floor, employers realized that they might lose the balance of power in their own factories.[7]

Although a printers' union had been organized in Minneapolis as early as 1859, Minnesota industry developed with very little interference from unions. In the twenty years preceding 1900, only 383 strikes involving 70,000 employees had been called in the state. In the same period, Minneapolis averaged fewer than three strikes per year. Although the formation of the Minneapolis Trades and Labor Assembly in 1883 and the Minnesota State Federation of Labor in 1890 gradually established a unified labor movement across the state, membership in local unions remained a closely guarded secret. Union membership usually meant dismissal from jobs and blacklisting. Strikes in Minneapolis from 1895 to 1899 remained at only five per year. At the turn of the century, there was little doubt about who controlled the workplace in Minneapolis.[8]

In 1901, however, with a booming economy, the Minneapolis business community faced its first serious labor challenge. Union membership in Minnesota nearly doubled between 1900 and 1902, reaching 28,338 in nearly 300 separate unions. With union strength rapidly growing, a record 142 strikes were won by Minnesota workers in 1900. The next year, unions were successful in 70 percent of their strikes. In Minneapolis, employers faced an onslaught of union activity that accelerated from eleven strikes in 1900 to twenty-four in 1902.[9]

The militant demands of the Minnesota State Federation of Labor deepened the severity of the threat. In its 1901 platform, the federation supported the eight-hour day; nationalization of telephones, railways, and mines; municipal ownership of local utilities; "the collective ownership by the people of all means of production and distribution when business monopoly became a menace to the best interests of the people"; and employer liability for all on-the-job injuries. A Minnesota chapter of the Eight Hour League was organized the same year to help push for the national eight-hour legislation being sponsored by the American Federation of Labor.[10]

In reaction, the business community attempted to convince union members that labor organization was "killing labor by its own device." Unions would "hinder them both in wage and individual advancement." *Commercial West*'s pleas to its business and financial subscribers failed to stem the advancing tide of Minneapolis's militant labor force. Without strong leadership and a unified business community, the unionization of Minneapolis industry appeared to be a definite possibility.[11]

In Minneapolis's sixty-two machine shops, employers faced a similar threat on both the national and local fronts. The increasingly complex machinery of the flour-milling industry had created a growing demand for highly skilled machinists. With only 3,139 machinists employed in the state's 175 foundry and machinery firms, a union threat in the metal trades was of critical importance to the entire business community. By 1901, the International Association of Machinists (IAM), founded in 1888, had grown to a national membership of more than 60,000. One of the largest and strongest unions in the important metal trades in 1900, the IAM authorized strikes in Chicago and Cleveland to force recognition of the union, the nine-hour day, limitations on apprentices, and the closed shop.[12]

While the IAM crystallized its demands, 150 Minneapolis machinists organized the Machinists' Union Local No. 91 in early 1900. The fledgling union joined the Trades and Labor Council of Minneapolis in February of that year. By the spring of 1901, it had organized the machinists of three Minneapolis foundries. The machine-shop owners, who had lost only one small strike in their history, now had to contend with an aggressive local union backed by the powerful IAM. From two of the many smaller shops that made up the industry in 1900 emerged two leaders, Owen Brooke Kinnard and Otis Pray Briggs, who not only effectively subdued the machinists' union, but ultimately became leaders of the Minneapolis business community for decades.[13]

Owen Kinnard was born on a farm in Pennsylvania in 1853. He moved to Minneapolis in 1878 as a representative of an Indiana engineering firm. Kinnard, however, wanted to run his own business. A trained machinist with an inventive mind, he organized the Kinnard and Haines Foundry and Machine Company in 1882. Relying on his experiences with farming and machinery, Kinnard developed a highly efficient gasoline-powered tractor. Expanding sales of the company's tractor into Canada as well as the United States established the firm as a market leader. Kinnard also promoted his industry on a national scale as one of the founders of the National Metal Trades Association (NMTA). He also served as a leader of Minneapolis's Calvary Baptist Church and was a loyal member of the Republican Party. It was as a leader and organizer of the local business community, however, that Kinnard would prove most influential.[14]

In 1877, William D. Washburn convinced his lifelong friend, Hiram W. Briggs, to move to Minneapolis from Maine. Briggs's twenty-one-year-old son, Otis P. Briggs, also came to Minneapolis and quickly found work in his uncle's iron works near St. Anthony Falls. After ten years at his uncle's shop and at Minnesota Iron Works, Briggs founded the Twin City Iron Works to produce engines and power-transmission machinery. In 1902, Briggs merged his company with Minneapolis Steel and Machinery Company, which eventually would occupy a twenty-eight-acre site and export its tractors around the world.[15]

Briggs, however, left his company within a year of its founding to devote himself to the national organization of the foundry industry. By 1901, he had already helped organize the National Founders' Association (NFA) and the National Metal Trades Association. Believing that a human being's greatest blessedness was "a work, a life long purpose," Briggs dedicated his life to an open shop labor policy that sought to eliminate all union members from the American workplace. By his death in 1928, he was known nationally and internationally as the dean of the open shop.[16]

Briggs and Kinnard, concerned about the growth of labor unions, took a deep interest in the formation of the National Founders' Association. The NFA was formed in 1898 to represent a few New York foundry owners in negotiations with local iron moulders. A year later, the NFA recognized the Iron Moulder's Union of North America and committed both management and labor to amicable negotiations and/or arbitration to settle all disputes. Briggs and Kinnard joined the NFA in 1899 and quickly rose to leadership positions. Serving first as commissioner and later as president, Briggs would dominate the NFA until World War I.[17]

In 1899, machine-shop employers in New York and Brooklyn faced a strike of the Pattern Makers' Union. An informal group of metal trades employers joined forces to fight the strike. Concerned about the growth of the IAM and the increasing frequency of labor disruptions in their industry, Briggs,

Kinnard, and their fellow NFA officers organized the fledgling New York group into the National Metal Trades Association. The NMTA modeled its constitution after the founders' association. The organizations shared officers and members and had joint committees and representatives. Once again, Minneapolis's two leading machine-shop employers assumed a prominent role. Kinnard chaired the committee on agreements while Briggs chaired the resolutions committee and sat on the three-member nominating committee. From his position on the administrative council and at the head of the NFA, Briggs was able to exercise a considerable influence over NMTA policies.[18]

Within a year, the NMTA, organized to end strikes and stabilize the industry, faced a major attack by the AFL, a machinists' strike authorized by the IAM. After initial negotiations between Chicago machinists and manufacturers failed in March of 1900, the NMTA, representing the employers, negotiated directly with IAM President James O'Connell. After the NMTA agreed to give up the blacklist and other anti-union practices, the two national associations agreed to institute the nine-hour day in one year, to limit apprentices to one for every five journeymen, and, most important, to submit all disputes to a committee of arbitration. Although the Murray Hill Agreement appeared to embrace mutual recognition and collective bargaining, the institution of the nine-hour day a year later would explode this temporary truce and have a profound effect on industrial relations nationally and in Minneapolis.[19]

On May 11, 1901, representatives of the NMTA and the IAM met to negotiate the implementation of the nine-hour day called for in the Murray Hill Agreement. O'Connell demanded a 12.5 percent wage increase, the nine-hour day, and national arbitration of disputes. The NMTA intended to maintain the same wages, which would mean a 10 percent pay cut with the shortened hours, and for all settlements to be negotiated locally. Although one-third of all employers nationally had already signed nine-hour day agreements, the NMTA refused to negotiate on what it saw as crucial issues. With the Murray Hill Agreement virtually defunct, O'Connell authorized a national strike. On May 21, 1901, nearly 50,000 machinists went out on strike across the nation.[20]

Several weeks earlier, on April 1, Minneapolis Machinists Local No. 91 had presented local employers with the IAM demands for a nine-hour day, a 12.5 percent wage raise, and time-and-a-half for overtime. Four weeks later, the union was informed that the proposed agreement was impractical; employers refused to concede on the issues. They contended that the machinists' demands would increase production costs 25 percent. A compromise might be possible on hours or wages, but not both. With negotiations hopelessly deadlocked, 365 union men struck on May 20, closing down every machine shop in the city. The employers publicly blamed the union for striking before they could consider IAM demands. In fact, the machine-shop employers had foreseen the conflict that winter and had made all their contracts contingent on strike conditions.[21]

Briggs and Kinnard had been organizing machine-shop employers nationally for two years and had neglected their own local industry. Largely as the result of heavy dues, Minneapolis's largest manufacturing firms had not even joined the NMTA. They faced Local 91's demands in disarray. One of the employers, Albert W. Strong, stated that he "had hardly heard of a labor union at that time." Realizing that the aggressive demands of Local 91 would bring closed-shop unionism to their shops and fearing that the unions would then control the shops, Briggs and Kinnard quickly brought the machine-shop employers together and organized the Twin City Association of Employers of Machinists. Thirty-three manufacturers representing a majority of Minneapolis and St. Paul shops met at the West Hotel in Minneapolis on the evening of May 20 to plan strike strategy. Kinnard was elected president of the association, which would include fifty firms a week later. While Kinnard and Briggs would represent the association in national negotiations between the NMTA and the IAM, a young, dedicated machine-shop proprietor, A.W. Strong, was elected secretary and would handle the association's battle with Local 91 in Minneapolis.[22]

Albert William Strong was graduated from Minneapolis Central High School in 1890 and attended the University of Minnesota before finding a job at the Hardwood Manufacturing Company. Like Kinnard and Briggs before him, Strong desperately wanted to be his own boss. In 1898, a wealthy friend loaned the eager young Strong $32,000 to capitalize the Strong and Northway Manufacturing Company. Reorganized as the Strong and Scott Company in 1906, it became one of North America's principal producers of mill and elevator machinery. With business success, Strong became an influential member of several Minneapolis clubs and a vestryman of St. Paul's Episcopal Church. Although he had not attained national stature by 1901, Strong quickly developed a dedication to the open shop, which he would advocate until his death in 1936.[23]

On the morning the strike began, the association hardened its position, announcing emphatically that it would not meet wage or hour demands and that it would not recognize the machinists' union. The union, now fighting for its existence, announced the next day that seven shops had already signed its agreement. Although these were small shops employing a total of only about twenty men and not members of the Association of Employers of Machinists, Strong took immediate action. To maintain the confidence of association members, he announced that "every machine shop is running, but of course with reduced forces. I should say that only about 25 percent of the regular forces are at work. As far as we know, they are all non-union men." On the same day, the association posted notices in every shop that all machinists who remained at work would retain their positions after the strike.[24]

Strong refused even to meet with the union until it changed its demands. The union waited, hoping that the potential loss of large Chicago contracts would force the employers to negotiate. Instead, the association brought in replacement workers and announced that strikers would be taken back only if they came back under the same conditions under which they had left. With the local situation stalemated, and the association insisting "that there will be no surrender," both sides looked to their national organizations for a solution.[25]

In Chicago, where 60 percent of the Chicago Association of Machinery Manufacturers belonged to the NMTA, the local employers and union agreed to let their national bodies arbitrate their differences. The NMTA and the IAM both acknowledged that this settlement would set the precedent for negotiations across the country. O. P. Briggs went to Chicago to represent the Minneapolis association in NMTA meetings. Briggs was immediately chosen by the NMTA administrative council to be one of the three employers on the crucial arbitration committee. Although the union lowered its wage raise demand to 10 percent, Briggs and his colleagues refused to raise their original 5 percent offer. With the failure of the Chicago arbitration, the Minneapolis strike was at a standstill. Kinnard announced in Minneapolis newspapers that the IAM had violated the year-old Murray Hill Agreement, and the employers would not arbitrate the strike.[26]

On May 29, with the strike in its second week, the NMTA's administrative council met in Chicago to decide its next strategy. In one day, the council dropped its policies of negotiation and recognition and adopted a set of belligerent anti-union principles. The council pronounced the Murray Hill Agreement null and void and announced a new set of policies that were officially adopted by the NMTA as its Declaration of Principles:

- We must, therefore, have full discretion to designate the men we consider competent to do the work and to determine the conditions under which our work shall be prosecuted.
- We will not admit of any interference with the management of our business.
- Disapproving absolutely of strikes and lockouts, the members of the Association will not arbitrate any question with men on strike.
- The number of apprentices, helpers, and handy men to be employed will be determined solely by the employer.

- We will not permit employees to place any restrictions on the management's methods, or production of our shops and will require a fair day's work for a fair day's pay.
- Employees will be paid by the hourly rate, by premium system, by piecework, or contract, as the employer sees fit.
- The above principles being absolutely essential to the successful conduct of our business they are not subject to arbitration.
- Hours and wages are to be arranged by the local association.

The NMTA would not accept the IAM demands; indeed, it would never recognize the union.[27]

The Twin Cities Association of Employers of Machinists met at the West Hotel on June 1 and endorsed the NMTA's action. A week later, the association, representing Minneapolis's largest machine shops, officially joined the NMTA. All agreements with the IAM were invalidated, and Minneapolis employers would under no conditions negotiate with the machinists as a union. Perhaps fearing an angry reaction from Minneapolis machinists, association President Kinnard announced, "We want it distinctly understood that we are not trying to antagonize our men. Reports to this effect have been spread, but they are not true. Nothing but the best social feeling exists between the manufacturers and employees. We feel that they have made a mistake and are not responsible for it." Two weeks later, Kinnard represented the association at the IAM's annual national convention in New York. "Every manufacturer was so hot" at the IAM's demand for a pay raise of 12.5 percent that they unanimously endorsed the council's Declaration of Principles as official NMTA policy. The short era of amicable relations between American business and labor was about to end.[28]

Although by mid-June the IAM claimed that two-thirds of the firms had signed union agreements, these were all small firms and not NMTA members. The NMTA quickly organized a strikebreaking service for its members and pooled the resources of its powerful constituents to ensure victory. By midsummer, the IAM had spent $154,128 in strike benefits and realized that its resources were no match for the NMTA. By the end of July, the IAM was forced to capitulate. The success of the NMTA's anti-union stance sent a clear message to the rest of the American business community: An organized, unified, and ruthless business community could destroy the American labor movement.[29]

The conflict in Minneapolis was even more lopsided and inevitably concluded with the same result. Although Minneapolis Machinists Local No. 91 initially paid six dollars per week in strike benefits and the Minneapolis Trades and Labor Council contributed $800, the IAM was unable to adequately support the Minneapolis local. On the other hand, the association had huge amounts of money from the East and offered the union up to twenty-five dollars for each man who returned to work. Machinists were brought into Minneapolis from other cities with the offer of permanent work. Anti-union letters were sent to union members stating that "there is nothing so infamously arbitrary as a labor union" and "the man who will slip up on another in the dark and stab him in the back is the soul of honor and chivalry and heroism compared with the boycotter, who seeks to deprive another of a chance to make a living."[30]

Despite the castigation of the union by the employers, no clashes with authorities occurred during the nine-week strike. Gradually the association's unity and its ability to induce smaller employers to hold out wore the union down. By July 1, strikers were breaking ranks and returning to work. By July 3, the association shops were short only thirty men and their advertisements were still running in local and outstate newspapers. When seven strikers returned to the Pillsbury Mills on July 20, the strike collapsed. The local union decided to return to work at their old conditions.[31]

In the short four months from the machinists' demands to the end of the strike, Briggs, Kinnard, and Strong had organized forty-two separate machine shops into an association that had, through their unified actions, completely defeated a strong, aggressive machinists' union. Although they had organized and established the open shop in only one industry, the importance of their victory was not lost on the business community. The entire manufacturing industry had been saved from employing union machinists. Although it would be two years before the rest of the Minneapolis business community endorsed the association's ideology, Briggs, Kinnard, and Strong had clearly shown that unions could be effectively crushed if business fought them with an aggressive united organization.[32]

Within two years, the leaders of the association would convince the rest of Minneapolis industry that their ideology and strategy were the only way to deal with unions. In 1903, Kinnard, Briggs, and Strong would unify the entire Minneapolis business community into the Citizens Alliance of Minneapolis to broaden and strengthen the war on unions. Over 200 of the city's leading industrialists, including owners of the major banks and flour mills, quickly joined the Citizens Alliance's drive to enforce the open (non-union) shop. Thirty-five years later, Citizens Alliance President Strong would remember that it was during the 1901 machinists' strike that "we won and established the principle of the open shop. And Minneapolis has remained an open shop town ever since, until the recent disturbances beginning in 1934." Just as significant was the development of a coherent open-shop philosophy by association leaders Briggs, Kinnard, and Strong. It was a philosophy that Briggs and Strong would continue to develop as leaders of the Citizens Alliance over the next four decades, and a philosophy that would play a vital role in the economic, political, and social life of Minneapolis and the state of Minnesota.

The NMTA's declaration of principles, which played an important role in spreading the anti-union, open-shop ideology through the Minneapolis business community for forty years, was obviously based on the self-interest of the machinist employers. Undoubtedly realizing this, Briggs and Strong publicly based their open-shop philosophy on the findings of the Anthracite Coal Strike Commission. President Theodore Roosevelt's commission had been created to arbitrate the 1902 United Mine Workers' strike that had threatened to create a "winter fuel famine." The commission report stated that "the right to remain at work where others have ceased to work, or to engage anew in work which others have abandoned, is part of the personal liberty of a citizen that can never be surrendered, and every infringement thereof merits, and should receive[,] the stern denouncement of the law." The report went on: "Common sense and common law alike denounce the conduct of those who interfere with this fundamental right of the citizen. The assertion of the right seems trite and commonplace, but that land is blessed where the maxims of liberty are commonplaces."[33]

The basic principle of the Citizens Alliance as expressed by the commission was individual liberty. To further validate his philosophy, Briggs equated the open shop with the Declaration of Independence and the Constitution of the United States: "All men, without regard to race, color, or previous condition are entitled to enjoy life, liberty and the pursuit of happiness, and . . . this should be exercised by each individual in a spirit of fairness and recognition of the rights of every other individual."[34]

Briggs's philosophy defines liberty in terms of the individual: The very organizational nature of unions violates the American spirit of liberty. The right of citizens to work when and on what terms they please cannot be denied. Unionism attempts to destroy this basic tenet of American life and is therefore evil. Unions deny workers the liberty to work. Thus, the open shop protects the liberty and independence of the employee.

The principle of liberty for the employee conveniently eliminated the legitimacy of closed-shop unionism. But, in Briggs's philosophy, the right to liberty must also extend to the employer. A. W. Strong's recollection of the 1901 machinist strike stressed that employers must have the freedom to be their own boss. The Coal Commission again supported this basic ideology: "The union must not undertake to assume, or to interfere with, the management of the business of the employer."[35]

The right of liberty for employers is the freedom to dispose of their possessions as they think fit. In one swift, philosophical twist, the right of property has been incorporated into the right of liberty. Briggs, Strong, and the other eventual members of the Citizens Alliance owned most of Minneapolis's factories and claimed the liberty to do whatever they wanted with their possessions. The combination of the right of liberty and property conveniently provided a philosophical justification for the open shop and the many anti-union policies established by the NMTA.

The 1901 machinists' strike forced Minneapolis employers to recognize that unions represented a collective association that created a power in counterbalance to the property rights of the employer. Realizing that "something had to be done to encourage all manufacturers to retain control of their shop," Briggs and Strong organized the Twin City Association of Employers of Machinists. Ideologically, the collective liberty of the unions would also seem to threaten the employers' liberty over their property. However, in Briggs's creed, the individual liberty of the employer superseded the collective liberty of union workers, because that collective liberty infringed on the personal liberty of workers who might want to work during a strike. While promoting individual liberty, the open shop also "protects the employee from the dictation and domination of third parties [unions]." The fact that the Citizens Alliance was an employers' association wielding the collective power of hundreds of companies was ignored, for obvious reasons.[36]

Although Briggs emphasized the worker's right to liberty, the open shop did not protect the employee from the economic inequalities that capitalism necessitates. In dealing with social justice, the Citizens Alliance's ideology diverges into a form of Social Darwinism. Inequality can be viewed as a necessary consequence of the economic incentives that are derived from liberty and essential to industrial capitalism. The *Citizens Alliance Bulletin* stated that the open shop "promotes individual initiative and ambition with greater reward for greater effort," and that "Every American boy is taught that he can be the President of the country, however humble his beginnings."[37]

Left unsaid was the corollary that such individual liberty also allows every boy and girl to work seventy hours a week for eighteen dollars. Inequality is simply the other side of equality of opportunity that liberty demands, according to Citizens Alliance philosophy. The alternative for society is unthinkable: The closed shop means strikes, disruption of commerce, fleeing businesses, radicals and reds, bombings and riots, and the destruction of law and order. The Citizens Alliance publicity claimed that the open shop in Minneapolis had created an economic environment where the workers were better fed, better clothed, better housed, and had a larger amount of money invested in banks and homes: "Every industry, every business, every citizen and the community as a whole are beneficiaries of this Association." The inequality inherent in a Social Darwinistic society must be accepted for the welfare of the total society.[38]

Inequality was also justified on moral grounds. The leaders of the Citizens Alliance believed emphatically in the work ethic and mentioned it frequently in their *Bulletin*. The January 1929 *Bulletin* stated that "The world today must come to the realization that work is a blessing, not a curse, to mankind, that there is no disgrace in manual labor; and that every child should be trained along occupational lines." President Briggs would often quote from Carlyle: "Know what thou canst work at and work at it like a Hercules," and "Blessed is he who has found his work; let him ask no other blessedness." In opposition to the five-day, forty-hour week the Citizens Alliance said, "It is not only bad economics, it is bad morals. It does not emphasize the importance of man's work, man's opportunity to serve." While labor unions promote unproductive laziness, the open shop promotes greater effort. The moral corollary in this ethical system is that the poor, the unemployed, or union members who strike are all evil and therefore deserve whatever treatment they get.[39]

The alliance's second purpose, once liberty was ensured, was to assist in maintaining law and order. This was a natural consequence of their basic principles. The alliance believed in the basic rights of property and liberty that are protected by laws in a capitalistic democracy. They therefore supported the laws that are promulgated under this system of government. The Citizens Alliance said: "To the opposers of individual freedom, the laws must and shall be obeyed and the rights of citizenship preserved."[40]

The power behind the laws, of course, was the government. The Citizens Alliance continually expressed a devout patriotism. The defense of property and liberty was synonymous with the defense of the nation. Unions, on the other hand, "try to enforce their mandates in defiance of the freedom guaranteed under the Constitution of our free country." Political or industrial radicals attempt to subvert or eradicate the very institutions that protect American society and its primary values. They must be stamped out.[41]

The basic expressed principle of the Citizens Alliance—in fact, of democratic capitalism—is the natural right to liberty. With the development of the social contract, this concept supports and finally becomes virtually indistinguishable from the right to property. The state exists to protect these two basic rights. The CA existed to protect the state and these basic rights. On an individual level, the manufacturers struggled to control their shops. On a community level, the Citizens Alliance fought to maintain absolute control over the economy of the city. On a societal level, the alliance fought to maintain an ethical and political system through which alliance members would gain virtual monopoly over the productive property of the Minneapolis economy—a monopoly that would enable them to wield immense power. The maintenance of this power was the alliance's primary mission—politically, economically, and ethically.

There is little doubt that 1901 was the pivotal year in the evolution of the Minneapolis business community's relationship to labor. The machinists' strike served as an incubator for the development of the leadership, ideology, and structure that became the Minneapolis Citizens Alliance. Briggs, Kinnard, and Strong emerged from the strike as local and national leaders in a vigorous new anti-union movement. They would lead the Citizens Alliance in its battle against labor unions for the next thirty-five years. The organization of the Twin Cities Association of Employers of Machinists and the unity created throughout the local industry guaranteed the failure of Local No. 91's strike and set an example for the community-wide organization of the Citizens Alliance.

The open-shop ideology developed by Briggs and Kinnard and their colleagues at the NMTA would justify the complex union-fighting apparatus that Briggs and Strong would employ in their long terms as presidents of the Citizens Alliance. The machinery industry organized in 1901, however, represented only a fraction of Minneapolis's growing wealth. Unless other industries were organized, and unless the powerful flour mill owners and bankers backed this organization, Minneapolis would remain fertile ground for unions.

2 Organizing Minneapolis Business for the Open Shop

THE BUSINESSMEN OF MINNEAPOLIS recognized the importance of organization even before Minnesota became a state when they formed the Union Board of Trade on July 1, 1855, to be "the faithful watchdog of the city's material interests." For the next forty-six years, the Board of Trade was Minneapolis's leading public body in the discussion of the financial, political, and social questions of Minneapolis and the Northwest.[1]

The Board of Trade's 200 members included many of the leading businessmen of the city, and the organization's presidents included John S. Pillsbury, president of Pillsbury-Washburn Flour Mill Company; Edmund J. Phelps, secretary and treasurer of Minnesota Loan and Trust Company; Judge Isaac Atwater; and Senator William D. Washburn. The board's sole purpose was to propose and encourage "public measures calculated to add to the growth of the city, enlarge the field of its trade, and enhance its general welfare."[2]

The board played an important role in saving St. Anthony Falls when it was threatened with disaster, in creating Minneapolis's system of public parks, in eliminating discriminatory railroad freight rates that hampered Minneapolis's expansion, in expanding the financial facilities needed to accommodate Minneapolis business, and in promoting the erection of buildings to house the wholesale houses the city needed to attract more jobbing enterprises. On the national level, the board represented Minneapolis in various commercial organizations, and promoted the development of navigation on the Upper Mississippi River.[3]

The cohesiveness of the Minneapolis business community was primarily a product of the area's unique resources and the people who migrated from the northeastern United States to exploit them. The lumbermen of Maine, particularly the Washburn family, utilized the state's vast white pine forests, the transportation network of the state's rivers, and the power of St. Anthony Falls to create an important lumber-milling center. Although flour milling would gradually surpass the lumber industry, the falls, controlled by a handful of New Englanders, would still provide the power to build the city of Minneapolis. In 1860, 79 percent of the city's population had migrated from the northeastern United States. It was these settlers "who laid the groundwork for the future state of Minnesota." They founded industries and established important institutions: "They were acutely aware of their role as builders of a civilization in the wilderness and confident that Minnesota would become the New England of the West." Many of these early entrepreneurs also shared a political philosophy based on individual sovereignty, freedom of enterprise, and the sanctity of private property. With a common background, shared ideological beliefs, and a singular interdependence woven around the power of St. Anthony Falls, the city's first businessmen were united by more than their shared desire for profit.[4]

Although successful in promoting the general interests of the Minneapolis business community, the Union Board of Trade was unable to focus on the specific needs of any particular trade. As a result, the flour millers and grain traders formed the Chamber of Commerce on October 19, 1881, to "facilitate the buying and selling of all products, to inculcate principles in justice and equity in trade, to facilitate speedy adjustments of business disputes, to acquire and disseminate valuable commercial information, and, generally, to secure to its members the benefits of cooperation in the furtherance of their legitimate business pursuits." The chamber primarily functioned as a trade organization, running the grain exchange and publishing grain-trading statistics. After its first year, the chamber had 534 members and dues had risen to $250 per member. Although the chamber refrained from taking a leading role in public affairs, many of its members were influential in the city's financial and commercial affairs.[5]

The prosperity of the Minneapolis business community in the 1880s depended on inexpensive and amicable laborers, much as it would fifty years later. To effectively promote economic prosperity, the Board of Trade and the Chamber of Commerce had to assure Minneapolis employers of stable and reasonable labor conditions. This role was challenged on April 11, 1889, when Thomas Lowry, president of the Minneapolis Street Railway Company, posted notices in the streetcar barns that said: "Owing to shrinkage in receipts and increased outlay we are compelled to reduce expenses in all departments." By dropping workers' wages by two cents to four cents per hour, Lowry hoped to save $25,000. Minneapolis newspapers suggested that Lowry needed eastern capital to expand cable lines and had lowered wages to prove that the streetcar company was profitable.[6] Motormen belonging to the Street Railway Employees Association went on strike immediately, and within two days Lowry's entire company was shut down. Lowry and his secretary were on hand at the Fourth Street car barns on April 12 when a large crowd of strikers turned back a streetcar loaded with a part of Lowry's squad of fifty special police. The special police quickly regrouped and managed to recapture the car and run it on the Fifth Street route. There was little doubt that Lowry intended to break the union.[7]

On the strike's third day, the unions met and promised to refrain from attacking company property if Lowry would agree to arbitration of their differences. Other Twin Cities' unions quickly offered moral and financial support. Lowry announced to the press, "I do not propose to arbitrate this matter in any form." Lowry's secretary, Calvin G. Goodrich, in a statement that preceded Albert W. Strong and Otis P. Briggs by twelve years, stated: "We have treated with them for two years and during that time they have run our business. Now, to change the order of things, we feel disposed to run our own business."[8]

Delegations from the unions petitioned the Chamber of Commerce to persuade Lowry to arbitrate. Although Lowry, a prominent member of the chamber, undoubtedly counted on its support, the Chamber of Commerce agreed to the union request. Lowry's answer to the strikers and to his own commercial organization was an adamant no. He immediately began hiring new men, who were required to sign a document that read: "I hereby agree that I will not, while in its [the streetcar company's] employ, join or belong to any labor union or organization. The violation of this agreement shall be sufficient cause for discharge." While the Chamber of Commerce supported the strikers' position, the Board of Trade maintained a stony silence.[9]

By April 13, abandoned by his natural allies, Lowry was losing control of his streetcars as violence erupted across the city. Large mobs of strikers and their supporters gathered outside the company's car barns and managed to stop any attempts at moving the streetcars. At the Fourth Avenue barn, Lowry's mounted police charged the crowd with drawn clubs. The crowd quickly barricaded the street and threw stones at the police. Terrified horses broke free from their cars and intensified the chaos.[10]

The union, with public sympathy on its side, asked the state legislature and the city council to take over the streetcar lines. Lowry was not intimidated: "If the city council tries to revoke our charter we will let them." With the public still walking on the strike's fifth day, Lowry finally received support from the mayor, E. C. Babb. Babb admonished the public not to interfere with the operation of the streetcar company and promised that public order would be maintained at any cost. With the endorsement of Mayor Babb, the Minneapolis Police Department gradually increased its presence on the streets and at the car barns. On April 17, the first cars were started on the Fourth Avenue and University Avenue lines. A car left every ten minutes with two to four policemen on board. A squad of forty-two patrolmen on Washington Avenue was given the authority to arrest anyone who disobeyed their orders.[11]

An aggressive police presence and a severe storm system combined to discourage union resistance. Lowry turned his attention to finding men to run his streetcars. Company agents were sent to Kansas City and Chicago with offers of four to five dollars per day for new men. On April 20, 108 "tough cowboys" arrived from Kansas City, Missouri, to help run the cars. Two days later, five lines were running regularly, with police guard. The crowds, perhaps intimidated by the many arrests and Minneapolis Municipal Court Judge George D. Emery's fines for interference with streetcars, had thinned out considerably. Confident of victory, Lowry announced on April 23 that the new men would not be displaced by any return of the old men. The same day, the police commissioner ordered his officers to arrest anyone who tried to dissuade a new employee from working. As the strike disintegrated, the Board of Trade belatedly sent a committee to meet with Mayor Babb to encourage the maintenance of law and order. The board's action had no effect on the outcome of the strike, which the streetcar company declared over on April 24. By the end of the week, all of Lowry's streetcars were running on their normal schedules.[12]

Despite Lowry's resounding defeat of the streetcar unions, the strike had revealed a disturbing defect in the organization of the Minneapolis business community. The city's two business organizations, the Board of Trade and the Chamber of Commerce, had failed to aid one of their most prominent members. This became particularly worrisome the next year when the Minnesota State Federation of Labor was formed. Over seventy-five unions from the State Farmers' Alliance, the State Eight Hour League, the St. Paul Trades and Labor Assembly, the Minneapolis Trades and Labor Assembly, and the District Assembly of the Knights of Labor met to join forces in St. Paul on July 7, 1890.[13]

The Federation of Labor's principles, particularly the eight-hour day, legislation to control railroads, use of union labels to aid the public in identifying and boycotting non-union merchandise, and weekly payment of wages were a potential threat to the profits of Minneapolis businesses. The Federation's establishment of a legislative committee to lobby for the state's labor agenda made this threat an immediate concern. Although the federation was still a relatively weak organization, its very existence, coupled with a statewide surge in union organization in the late 1880s, made the creation of stronger business organizations imperative.[14]

In 1890, Lowry and over 300 other Minneapolis businessmen moved to fill the vacuum that the streetcar strike had revealed. They organized the Minneapolis Business Union "for the express purpose of aiding the increase of Manufacturing and Jobbing interests" of Minneapolis. Lumber magnate Thomas B. Walker served as the group's first president. The Business Union's finance committee, which included banker Samuel A. Harris and miller Frank

H. Peavey, raised over $10,000 in dues each year and employed a secretary and two assistants to carry out its program. The board of directors met weekly and its committees actively investigated matters brought to their attention by the secretary. The committee represented the transportation, financial, iron and steel, and textile industries, and included Lowry, Briggs, and twenty-eight other businessmen who would lead the Citizens Alliance (CA) in the next decade.[15]

Business Union publications stressed the importance of its work, particularly the organizing of new manufacturing enterprises, increasing the capital stock of those already in existence, and inducing out-of-town businesses to relocate in Minneapolis. Secrecy was considered essential to the success of these activities. Although official Business Union publications do not mention a labor policy, this was undoubtedly an important concern in creating an attractive business environment in Minneapolis.[16]

Although it was one of the strongest and most effective organizations in Minneapolis, the Business Union operated for only five years and therefore was not involved directly in the formation of the Citizens Alliance. The operations of the Business Union, however, established a system of cooperative investments that financially bound many Minneapolis businessmen together. Business Union members pledged to invest a certain amount of money over a three-year period in selected manufacturers. To induce out-of-town businesses to move to Minneapolis, Business Union members paid for moving expenses and the loss of the buildings and other assets that they were leaving. Members would then buy stock to increase the company's capital and to gain influence over the new company's policies.[17]

In addition, the Business Union formed a land development company to make a "strong but discreet movement to build up industries" along Minneapolis's western border. The St. Louis Park Company also cleared off any pre-existing structures. The company bought a large tract of land close to the city with access to excellent railway facilities. Sections were then platted and cleared of existing structures and given to manufacturing companies for the construction of new or enlarged factories. The new concerns then received expert business advice and financial support from the land development company. The result of these investments was a remarkable network of financial ties between the various manufacturing and banking interests of Minneapolis—a network that enabled the Citizens Alliance to forge a cohesive business organization a decade later.[18]

Two years after the formation of the Business Union, in 1892, a larger group of prominent businessmen organized the Minneapolis Commercial and Athletic Club. The club, unlike the other civic groups, combined the social and literary culture of its members with the promotion of the welfare of the city of Minneapolis. By 1901, the social and gymnasium aspect of the club had been dropped and the organization became the Minneapolis Commercial Club. With over 1,000 members, the Commercial Club moved into larger quarters in the Andrus Building on Fifth and Nicollet.[19]

The Commercial Club again went through dramatic changes when the Board of Trade adjourned its activities in early 1901, leaving the Commercial Club as the only civic body looking after public work. In response, the Commercial Club appointed a Public Affairs Committee of fifteen members, each of which would chair one of thirteen subcommittees that would carry out the work of the committee in overseeing the development of Minneapolis. The thirteen subcommittees were composed of 150 of the city's younger businessmen under the direction of an advisory committee of older, more experienced business leaders. They considered a wide range of issues from public health and municipal affairs to publicity and manufacturing interests.[20]

The Public Affairs Committee activities encompassed most of the Commercial Club's important concerns and rapidly became a separate, semiautonomous organization. To carry out its plans, the Public Affairs Committee's finance committee solicited $100 subscriptions from Minneapolis businessmen with a goal of raising $10,000 by September 1, 1901. Perhaps invigorated by the threat of the 1901 machinists' strike, subscriptions had already reached $7,500 by July. The funds were to be used to provide suitable quarters for the committee's weekly meetings and to pay the salary of a secretary devoted full time to the committee's work.[21]

Although it was financially independent and had its own staff, the Public Affairs Committee and subcommittee members were all still members in good standing of the Commercial Club itself. In April of 1901, with local machinists demanding the nine-hour day and a strike looming, the committee decided to establish a subcommittee on arbitration and conciliation. The Commercial Club's board of directors, not yet perceiving a threat to the general health of the Minneapolis business community, rejected the committee's attempt to form a labor committee, allowing the strike to take its own course.[22]

Less than a year later, faced with "the exercise of the unjust and irresponsible power of the labor Organizations of our city," the Commercial Club was forced to reevaluate its position. Union membership in Minneapolis had mushroomed to over 13,000 members in 1902, and socialism, which the business community considered an "advanced step in the policy of trade unionism," was rapidly spreading through the union movement.[23]

A more immediate and dangerous development, however, was a truck drivers' strike that slowed Minneapolis commerce in May. The Minneapolis

Trades and Labor Council backed the strike and established a boycott against any business that employed non-union draymen. The Draymen's Protective Association, led by Boyd Transfer and Storage Company, warned the public that "the control by any union of all the truck-teamsters in the city would be a most serious menace, not only to our own business interests, but to those of our customers and patrons." The Draymen's Protective Association leaders realized that the truck drivers' union had "the power to tie up or to seriously damage or inconvenience nearly every line of business in the city, in order to enforce such demands as they might choose to make."[24]

With the help of a court injunction that prohibited the Trades and Labor Council from aiding the striking truck drivers, the Draymen's Protective Association defeated the strike and "saved the day" for Minneapolis business interests. The Commercial Club, now realizing that labor problems could present a citywide threat, finally allowed the Public Affairs Committee to establish an arbitration committee. Henry S. Gregg, president of the Minneapolis Iron Store Company and later a stalwart on the Citizens Alliance Board of Directors, chaired the committee's efforts to avoid the explosive labor problems that plagued businesses in other major cities.[25]

The 1901 machinists' strike and the 1902 truck drivers' strike had a more profound effect on Edmund J. Phelps and Judge Martin B. Koon, the most influential members of the Public Affairs Committee's advisory committee. Phelps and Judge Koon thought that the complete unionization of Minneapolis would threaten the life of the city's industry. Using their considerable influence, they began pushing for a Citizens Alliance to maintain the open shop throughout the Minneapolis business community.[26]

Phelps, president of the Belt Line Elevator Company and one of the founders of the Minnesota Loan and Trust Company, was the most prominent and experienced civic leader in the Minneapolis business community. He had served as president of the Board of Trade in 1884 and 1885, was a founder and president of the Business Union in 1892, and was president of the Commercial Club in 1898–99. Phelps also had considerable political influence, having served as the treasurer of the National Republican Convention in 1892. By 1903, in addition to his membership on the advisory committee, Phelps was treasurer of the Public Affairs Committee and sat on the important finance committee.[27]

Judge Koon had retired from his seat on the Fourth District Court in 1886 to practice business law. He served as a director at Minnesota Loan and Trust Company from its inception; as a director of Northwestern National Bank; as a director and general counsel of the Minneapolis, St. Paul and Sault St. Marie Railway; as a director and president of Minneapolis General Electric Company;

and as a director of the Twin City Rapid Transit Company. Judge Koon's unusual legal and business acumen established him as an influential and powerful advisor to Minneapolis's leading businessmen. Because of their status in
the business community, Phelps and Koon were able to convince their colleagues on the Public Affairs Committee of the gravity of the union threat and
galvanize them into organizing the Citizens Alliance.[28]

The important task of developing a constitution was assigned to Otis P.
Briggs, now the commissioner of the National Founders' Association (NFA). In
June of 1903, Briggs contacted the National Metal Trades Association (NMTA),
which served as a clearinghouse of information for employers organizing local
open-shop associations. The alliance's constitution and bylaws were written using the booklets of eleven established employers' associations as guides. In Article 2 of the constitution, the Citizens Alliance defined its objects and purposes:

1. To promote, on a fair and equitable basis, industrial peace and prosperity
   in the community, and the steady employment of labor.
2. To discourage strikes, lockouts, and unfair demands by either employer
   or employee.
3. To secure for employer and employee freedom of contract in the manner
   of employment.
4. To uphold the principle of the Open Shop.

The open-shop policy was based on the Anthracite Coal Strike Commission
findings of 1902 and reiterated the policies that Briggs and Owen B. Kinnard
had helped develop for the National Metal Trades Association during the 1901
machinists' strike.[29]

The membership and dues of the Citizens Alliance were defined in Article
3 of the constitution. Membership was restricted to persons or corporations
residing or engaging in business in Hennepin County, and applications were
approved by the executive committee. Individuals and professional people
(Class A members) paid annual dues of $10; small employers (Class B mem-
bers) paid $25; and large employers (Class C members) paid $50. Despite the
constitution's claim that there was no initiation fee, members paid $10 to join.
Every member of the CA was required to "support, foster and maintain the objectives and purposes for which it has been organized." If any member refused
to comply with the requirements of the various committees of the organization, they could be suspended by the executive committee. When labor troubles arose, any member could apply to the executive committee for the aid and
assistance of the alliance.[30]

With a constitution and bylaws established, Secretary Wallace G. Nye of
the Public Affairs Committee and Secretary George K. Belden of the Citizens

Alliance, kicked off the alliance's first membership drive in July, 1903. CA founders called meetings in their respective industries to explain the alliance and to solicit memberships. Fred R. Salisbury called a meeting of the furniture manufacturers on July 31, and managed to sign up five companies. A similar effort by founder Charles D. Velie netted eighteen agricultural implement manufacturers. Together with the machinery employers, this group included virtually the entire Twin Cities Association of Employers of Machinists and represented the largest single block of industrial members. The companies ranged in size from the Pioneer Fuel Company and the Old Tyme Bakerie, to the Miller-Davis Printing Company and the Cedar Lake Ice Company, to large firms like Dayton's Dry Goods and B. F. Nelson Lumber Company. The success of the 1903 membership drive was attributed by a Citizens Alliance founder to the "fact that there is an organization which is prepared to be of assistance to all employers of labor that are subject to unjust demands of employees either organized or unorganized." [31]

This perception was reinforced in October 1903, in the middle of the recruitment drive, when the Citizens Alliance backed up local electrical contractors and relieved them of a threatened labor problem. The "knowledge that they would not be compelled to carry all the burden themselves and stand all the loss" persuaded Minneapolis employers to join the CA and follow its principles. [32]

To run the alliance's operations, at each annual meeting the membership elected a board of directors consisting of fifty members selected to represent every branch of Minneapolis business. An executive committee, elected by the board, hired and fired employees, settled claims against the Citizens Alliance, and performed "all other duties that in its judgement are desirable to the welfare of the Alliance." E. J. Phelps, the grand old man of Minneapolis civic organizations, became the CA's first president. [33]

Although Phelps served only one year, the leadership of the alliance for the next thirty-two years was extremely stable. The three leaders of the Twin Cities Association of Employers of Machinists, Owen B. Kinnard, Otis P. Briggs, and Albert W. Strong, along with truck manufacturer John F. Wilcox, helped found the Citizens Alliance and would serve as its only leaders until 1936. Kinnard served as president from 1904 to 1907 and in 1915; Wilcox from 1908 to 1914; Briggs from 1918 to 1929; and Strong from 1916 to 1917 and from 1929 to 1936. The Citizens Alliance's staunch dedication to its open-shop philosophy and its unflinching defense of its economic position was undoubtedly due to the ideological stability of these four machine-shop proprietors. [34]

Although they held a dominant position in the leadership of the Citizens Alliance, the machine-shop employers represented a fraction of Minneapolis's industrial wealth. Without the backing of the Pillsbury-Washburn and Washburn-Crosby flour mills and their client banks, the Citizens Alliance would have been a weak, short-lived organization. The formation of the International Union of Flour and Cereal Mill Employees, in the fall of 1902, the first national labor organization based in Minneapolis, precipitated a sharp change in the labor-management relations in the flour mills. The flour-mill union, which was affiliated with the American Federation of Labor, quickly established a defense fund, published an *Official Monthly Journal*, and demanded eight-hour shifts without reduction in pay.[35]

James S. Bell, president of Washburn-Crosby Company, argued that "Minneapolis mills cannot pay for eight hours work higher wages than the mills in all other sections of the country pay for 12 hours work." The result would be "disastrous to the milling industry of Minneapolis." Despite Bell's warning, the mills granted the union demand for three eight-hour shifts to its skilled mill operatives within months of the union's demands. By 1903, this impressive victory had swelled the union ranks until virtually every worker in the Minneapolis mills was a union member.[36]

With union power growing, the flour loaders, who were still on a ten-hour day, went to the flour companies in May of 1903 and asked for an eight-hour day with a wage raise from $1.75 to $2.00 per day. The mill owners believed that if they granted this demand, there would be no end to the union's future wage demands under threat of strike. On Sept. 25, William H. Dunwoody, vice-president of Washburn-Crosby Company, wrote, "We have got to fight hard to defeat the plans of the union." At the precise time that the fledgling Citizens Alliance was organizing, the leading milling companies met and agreed that it was time to defy the union and to fight back, if necessary. The Citizens Alliance had gained the most important converts of its recruiting drive.[37]

The milling company executives, realizing that the union would strike in the fall when the new wheat crop was arriving in Minneapolis to be milled, began accumulating large stocks of flour at distribution points. The *Northwestern Miller* reported that "A shut down at this time will prove a most serious matter to both sides. The mills are entering on the most busy and favorable season of the year, and any interruption would prove a great sacrifice."[38]

On September 22, the day before the walkout, the mills posted notices stating that "all employees of this mill leaving their positions are discharged, and are no longer in the employ of this company." Ignoring this ultimatum, 1,800 workers walked out at midnight on Sept. 23, 1903, leaving fourteen of seventeen mills at Northwest Consolidated, Pillsbury-Washburn, and Washburn-Crosby Company paralyzed. The union's extraordinary organization and cohesiveness had removed virtually every packer and nailer, every loader and miller, from the mills. Nearly the entire production of Minneapolis's mills, over 70,000 barrels of flour per day, had been choked to a stop. Both sides claimed that they would fight to the bitter end. Dunwoody wrote: "We feel we must carry on the fight until the finish is satisfactory to us." The immediate fate of the flour unions and the viability of the Citizens Alliance hung in the balance as both sides dug in to outlast each other.[39]

Union leaders, perhaps aware of the gravity of their position, hesitated in their resolve within twelve hours of the walkout. While an unbroken chain of pickets surrounded the mills, union President John M. Finley appealed to Mayor James C. Haynes to appoint a committee of five citizens to arbitrate the controversy. Mayor Haynes presented the proposal to Bell at Washburn-Crosby Company, Henry L. Little, manager of the Pillsbury mills, and Albert. C. Loring at Northwestern Consolidated Milling Company. The three mill managers replied: "We prefer to shut down the mills if we cannot find men willing to work at the present scale of hours and wages." Arbitration meant a compromise with the union, and the mills were determined to block all union advances. While state and city officials pleaded for arbitration, the mills charged the unions with bad faith for not urging the extension of the eight-hour-day principle to competitive mills outside of Minneapolis.[40]

To win its war of attrition against the flour union, the milling companies needed to hire enough replacement workers to return the mills to full production. Following the successful example of the 1901 machinists' strike, the mills immediately began advertising in the University of Minnesota newspaper. The Minneapolis YMCA employment office helped sign up university students to work the night shift for twenty cents per hour. By the third day of the strike, seventy-five students were working in the Pillsbury "B" Mill.[41]

The mill owners also advertised outside Minnesota, offering recruits railroad fare, union wages, free board and lodging, and permanent work. They anticipated that the damage caused by these green recruits could be repaired by the millwrights who were not on strike. But the mills were still in desperate need of skilled millers. Inside the state, the owners successfully brought 150 men with milling experience up from New Ulm and Sleepy Eye. In addition, promotions and inducements were offered to the union men to get them to break ranks and return to work.[42]

By the fifth day of the strike, a trickle of millers had returned, and by October 7 three out of four Washburn-Crosby Company mills were running, several of them with full crews. Henry O. B. Harding, superintendent of the Washburn-Crosby Company mills, commented in the strike's second week, "We are really getting more men than we want to take on and have begun to pick and choose with more care." On October 9, Dunwoody wrote: "The strike now appears to be about over and we are running all our mills, largely with new help. I regret very much that we will be obliged to turn aside the old men as they come back." He added, "They have no one but themselves to blame."[43]

The most important factor in the mill owners' successful recruitment drive was their ability to guarantee replacement workers protection from the picketing strikers. Although the *Northwestern Miller* complained that the mayor and the police had not given employees adequate protection, the concentration of eleven mills on the west side canal below Sixth Avenue allowed the mills to erect a high board fence and create a stockade out of the mill district. With police protection along the railroad tracks, strikers were effectively shut out of the mills. Admission to the complex was by company pass only.[44]

Maintaining the security of replacement workers beyond the mill stockade, however, was difficult if not impossible. At first, the mills attempted to bring in meals, but local restaurants and hotels quickly refused to provide this service. The mill district was thickly picketed and replacement workers were frequently intercepted by union pickets and turned back. To counteract this threat, Pillsbury and Washburn-Crosby Company jointly refitted the empty Pillsbury oatmeal mill to lodge and feed replacement workers. The first floor was converted into a restaurant seating 250 workers at a time. Four cooks and thirteen waiters served up to 2,100 meals a day during the strike. During leisure times, the black cooks furnished entertaining music. The two upper floors of the oatmeal mill were fitted out with cots and blankets for sleeping quarters. With safe and comfortable eating and sleeping quarters available, the mills were able to rapidly recruit enough men to run the mills. The vacant cereal mill and a strong fence had turned Minneapolis's milling district into an impenetrable fortress.[45]

The successful stockade defense of the mill owners began to wear down the strikers' resolve within two weeks of the walkout. The union had exhausted its funds in a national organizing drive and could not survive a lengthy strike. By October 6, twelve of the seventeen mills were running, and production had grown to one quarter of capacity. One of the mill owners proclaimed: "The backbone of the strike is broken, and there will be nothing more doing in the way of strikes for some time." With only $3,000 of the $100,000 strike fund paid in and more union mill workers returning to work, union President Finley recommended ending the strike on October 9. The union membership, however, voted to continue the strike and threatened to boycott Minneapolis flour. With scattered violence and large gatherings of pickets outside the stockade fence, the Pillsbury "A" Mill still opened on October 12 and the Palisade Mill was up to two-thirds capacity. On October 16, John Washburn declared: "The strike is a thing of the past—all our mills are running, all the Pillsbury mills are running. . . . The old men are coming back almost as fast as we could ask them to come. We will get all of them we want."[46]

Despite a Minnesota State Federation of Labor boycott of Washburn-Crosby Company's Gold Medal Flour, the strike was essentially over by the last week of October. The eating and sleeping quarters in the Pillsbury oatmeal mill were abandoned as the mill district returned to normal conditions. Although many of the strikers regained their old positions on the mill owners' terms, the "orators, organizers, and agitators" were not rehired. The union was practically eliminated from the mills and would remain at low strength for decades.[47]

With the open shop firmly established in Minneapolis's leading flour mills, thirteen other grain companies and the city's major banks soon joined the Citizens Alliance. Two years later, the executives at Minneapolis Electric and Construction Company said: "The Citizens Alliance, representing, as it does, our foremost business and financial interests, has been and is one of the most potent factors in establishing the industrial peace which we now enjoy."[48]

The Citizens Alliance, which was organized for the "express purpose of directing its best efforts against that spirit of lawlessness which universally governs the efforts of the unions," now had the public influence and financial wealth of the Northwest's flour empire backing its campaign against closed-shop unionism. The ideological framework forged in the heat of the 1901 machinists' strike, the organizational drive of the Commercial Club's Public Affairs Committee, and the wealth of Minneapolis's flour mills had merged into a potent industrial force that would rule Minneapolis industry for the next three decades.[49]

3 *A Declaration of Class Warfare*

THE TRUE SPIRIT of the flour mill owners and the Citizens Alliance (CA) was revealed in late November of 1903 when David M. Parry, the militant president of the National Association of Manufacturers (NAM), spoke at a Commercial Club reception in Minneapolis. Parry, whose organization had aided the Pillsbury, Washburn-Crosby, and Northwest Consolidated flour mills in the recent strike, declared that closed-shop unionism "is a theory of government to which those who understand and appreciate American liberty and American civilization will never give their willing consent." He promised Minneapolis businessmen that the NAM's "educational campaign should forestall advances of socialism."[1]

Parry, a fervent proponent of the open shop, was willing to publicly state the true nature of the United States business community's drive against union labor: "I believe that we should endeavor to strike at the root of the matter, and that is to be found in the wide spread socialistic sentiment among certain classes of people." Commercial Club members were rallied to the cry that "Law and order must be enforced and that class domination over industry is not going to be tolerated." In a brief moment of candor, Parry had revealed the simple fact that the Citizens Alliance would attempt to conceal from the public for three decades: The open-shop movement was a war between the owners of American industry and the working class.

The National Association of Manufacturers was formed in 1895 and represented more than 5,000 of the country's leading manufacturers, which produced more than 75 percent of the total output of manufactured goods in the United States. One business historian called it "the most powerful body of businessmen which has ever been organized in any land, or any age." The NAM was a close and friendly ally of the other major anti-union national employers' associations. In fact, every member of the National Metal Trades Association (NMTA), including the Minneapolis machine shops of Citizens Alliance leaders Otis P. Briggs and Owen B. Kinnard, was also a member of the NAM.[2]

The legal counsel for the NAM joined forces with the NMTA and the National Founders' Association (NFA) to oppose pro-labor legislation in Washington.

Briggs, as president of the NFA, had a direct influence on NAM policies, and the CA could therefore undoubtedly count on assistance from the "mother" of all employment associations.[3]

The cohesive relationships between the various large national employers' associations and the smaller local associations like the Citizens Alliance grew from their common conviction that labor unions were evil and un-American. At the 1903 NAM convention, President Parry described trade unionism as "a system that coerces and impoverishes the worker, ruins the capitalist, terrorizes our politicians and destroys our trade—a system which seems to be hopelessly and irredeemably bad, a bar to all true progress, a danger to the state and a menace to civilization."[4]

The American Federation of Labor was viewed as the primary enemy. It was the "source whence proceeds such noxious emanations as the eight-hour day and anti-conspiracy bills" and "the fountainhead of inspiration which breeds boycotters, picketers and socialists." Parry felt that an employers' association must stand "for the right of its members to employ whom they please, for the right to hire as many apprentices as they deem necessary, and for the right to conduct their business untrammeled by the many exactions of unionism."

Parry's language and the Declaration of Principles adopted by the NAM in 1903 very clearly were derived from the principles developed by the NMTA during the 1901 machinists' strike. At Briggs's request, the NAM even based these principles on the 1902 Anthracite Coal Commission Report. With the denunciation of a common enemy and the adoption of the same principles as those set forth by the NMTA and the Coal Commission, Parry set the NAM to "the task of pulling up, root and branch, the un-American institution of trades unionism." For the next three decades, the NAM would fervently defend the open shop on a national scale and provide the Citizens Alliance with an important and powerful ally.[5]

While the NMTA and the NFA established elaborate strike-fighting forces to aid their members, the NAM defended the business community against legislation supported by national unions in Washington and attempted to educate the American public about the evils of trade unionism. The NAM was particularly vehement in its opposition to the proposed federal eight-hour law, which it felt was a "vicious, needless, and in every way preposterous proposition."[6]

Of greater long-term importance to the Citizens Alliance was the NAM's strenuous fight against even harmless anti-injunction bills. From its inception until World War II, the injunction would be one of the CA's primary weapons against labor unions. Even during its 1903 organizing drive, a decision by Hennepin County District Court Judge Willard R. Cray enjoined the Electrical Workers' Union from "interfering with the business of [the Minneapolis electrical contractors] by means of threats or intimidations of any kind or nature, directed against the customers or prospective customers." Cray's far-reaching order would eventually have meant the destruction of labor unions. Although the decision was modified by the Minnesota Supreme Court, Cray received lavish praise and promises of future support from alliance leaders Otis Briggs and Edmund J. Phelps.[7]

In Washington, D.C., the NAM's lobby was crucial in defending the business community's use of court injunctions to suppress unions. When the 1890 Sherman Anti-Trust Act's ban on business conspiracies in restraint of trade was extended to include labor unions, the NAM successfully fought for over a decade to defeat amendments that would have exempted unions from prosecution under the act. When the Clayton Anti-Trust Act finally legalized unions and appeared to ban anti-labor injunctions, union leaders hailed it as their Magna Carta. They soon discovered that NAM-sponsored amendments had diluted the statute just enough for pro-business judges to continue issuing injunctions that would halt union strike activities in their tracks.[8]

The NAM realized as early as 1902 that "public opinion is the guiding force in this nation today." If labor unions could sway the public to overwhelmingly support their legislation, the NAM's Washington lobbyists would be powerless to stop the erosion of business rights. To institute its propaganda or "educational campaign," the NAM began publishing the magazine *American Industries* on August 15, 1902. It quickly became the leading voice for the open-shop movement.[9]

American Industries, however, circulated primarily among government officials, members of Congress, and business groups, and therefore did not reach the mass of the people. To influence the mainstream press, the NAM brought immense financial power to bear on pro-labor publications. Major newspapers would only change to reflect the business viewpoints "as advertisers withdraw their support from newspapers . . . which seek circulation through means that are destructive of the real welfare of the people and especially damaging to the interests of those who support them with their advertising."

American Industries and other NAM publications supported the open shop and denounced labor unions, the closed shop, labor leaders, the boycott, and strikes. NAM propaganda also supported its legislative lobby. Labor legislation was shown to increase the cost of living and raise taxes. The NAM claimed that it fought this legislation for the good of the people. To affect working people, however, the NAM realized that it must demonstrate that it sincerely was working in their interests. Although the NAM's entire program revolved around defending the employer class, its public policy was "Let not the word class or classes pass our lips. We have no classes in our country."

Although the NAM was a powerful and effective organization, its influence was limited primarily to the country's manufacturers. At President Parry's request, the 1903 NAM convention passed the following resolution: "In order to meet in a collective, scientific and effectual manner the present industrial conditions arising from the organization of labor, it is necessary that there be a thorough organization among employers of labor in kindred crafts."[10]

On October 29, 1903, with the flour mill strike winding down in Minneapolis, representatives from 124 employers' organizations, including the Citizens Alliance, met in Chicago to form the Citizens Industrial Association (CIA). The new organization elected Parry as its first president and proclaimed: "The time has come when the employing interests and good citizenship of the country must take immediate and effective measures to reaffirm and enforce those fundamental principles of American government guaranteeing free competitive conditions."[11]

Emulating NAM policies, a Bureau of Education was formed to campaign against labor unions in the press and in public meetings. The CIA, however, through its member Citizens Alliances, was able to reach a much broader audience. The CIA executive committee, which included Citizens Alliance director James L. Record, realized that to be successful, the CIA must organize more local employers' associations to combat the growing threat of the American Federation of Labor (AFL). With the help of CIA promotion, citizens alliances and employers' associations quickly spread the open-shop drive through the cities of the West and Midwest. At the 1904 CIA convention, with membership expanded to 247 organizations, a Bureau of Organization was formed to coordinate the rapidly growing number of anti-union associations.[12]

At the 1906 CIA convention, President Charles W. Post commented: "Two years ago the press and pulpit were delivering platitudes about the oppression of the workingman. Now this has all been changed since it has been discovered that the enormous Labor Trust is the heaviest oppressor of the independent workingman as well as the common American Citizen." The "educational campaigns" of the NAM and the CIA had reversed public opinion and brought the growth of unionism to a dead stop. The national success of the alliance's allies would also have a dramatic impact on Minneapolis as the fortunes of organized labor ebbed.[13]

While the National Association of Manufacturers and the Citizens Industrial Association used their influence to defeat labor-backed legislation and turn public opinion against the AFL, other national associations would have to fight unions in the trenches when they struck local industries. The National Founders' Association, dominated by alliance leader Otis Briggs, was formed in 1898 under a policy of cooperation with unions. The next year, the NFA and the Iron Moulders' Union signed the New York Agreement pledging to recognize each other and to cooperate in negotiations.[14]

In 1904, under pressure from its many NMTA members, the NFA abrogated its agreement and adopted a labor policy virtually identical to the NMTA policy developed in 1901. NFA policy embraced the same open-shop principles that Briggs and Kinnard had developed in Minneapolis: No limitations on output or earning capacity; no union fines on workers; payment by hourly rate premium system, or piecework, as employers elect; freedom of employers to hire or fire anyone they want; no limit on apprentices; and no arbitration with workers on strike.[15]

Briggs considered the interests of the NFA, the NAM, and the NMTA to be identical and aimed to "cooperate with kindred employers' associations to the greatest extent possible." With his allies, Briggs pushed to have picketing outlawed, to halt anti-injunction bills, workers' compensation and minimum wage legislation, and to establish state constabularies.[16]

Fresh from his experiences fighting the machinists' and flour-milling strikes in Minneapolis, Briggs envisioned a more practical role for the NFA. In the next decade at the association, he would develop policies to defend the open shop, which he would later use in Minneapolis as president of the Citizens Alliance, from 1917 to his death in 1929. Employers fought unions on an individual basis in their own local communities. Briggs understood that, to be effective on a national scale, the NFA must help local founders prevent strikes or, when conflict arose, to crush union resistance.[17]

The best defense against strikes existed in the minds of the nation's foundry workers. To reach these minds, Briggs recommended "that the manufacturers of this country devote more money, more time, and more energy to the publication and dissemination of the proper kind of literature among the homes of the workingmen than has heretofore been the case." The NFA and the NMTA jointly published a monthly journal, *The Open Shop Review*, and mailed it free to more than 12,000 metal workers. The *Open Shop Review* argued the benefits of the open shop and castigated the closed shop. It portrayed the progress of open-shop cities, showed how workers advanced from wage earner to employer under an open-shop system, and branded union leaders as outside organizers and agitators. Briggs was convinced that the *Open Shop Review* was "having a tremendous effect upon the majority of these people." In 1919, as president of the Citizens Alliance, Briggs would put this conviction into practice in Minneapolis by publishing the *Citizens Alliance Bulletin*.[18]

The propaganda spread by the *Open Shop Review*, however, would be of little use if the foundry owners "apply [their] energy, instruction and money to poor stock [workers]." Briggs felt that with "a little extra effort, a little more care and thought on the subject we will find the very stock we are in need of." The employer should then make every effort to protect and advance the more honest and industrious workers.[19]

Briggs realized that only a thorough system of patriarchal benevolence would stay the influence of the unions. He wrote in the *Open Shop Review:*

> The carefully selected boy who is made to feel during his years as an apprentice that he is of some earthly good from his employers' standpoint; that his employer is interested in his welfare to the extent of his receiving a fair opportunity to learn his trade, who knows that his foreman has his interest at heart, can be safely counted on as maturing [into] an honest loyal journeyman, who will think twice before he joins the ranks of the strikers at the hand of the so called agitator.

Many of these "agitators" and the workers that they attempted to influence, of course, were recent immigrants to the United States. Briggs feared that the "ignorant foreign population" had been forced on the country too fast and that immigration should be stopped for ten or twenty years. Immigrants apparently fit Briggs's definition of "poor stock."

Preventing strikes also required that the NFA have the best possible intelligence about union agitation in the country's foundry shops. After the unsatisfactory use of private detective agencies, Briggs organized a secret service in 1904. Briggs's agents were employed, often as union members, within the shops of NFA members. They reported back on any "clandestine and insidious" agitation on the shop floor. Any undesirable workers could then be removed from the floor of the well-informed NFA member. If a union were planning a strike, the forewarned employer could stockpile products and advertise for replacements before the workers walked out. During a strike, the NFA could counter every union action before it took place. After the strike, criminal prosecutions could be based on evidence gathered by the secret service. Briggs felt that the secret service was "one of the very best investments the Association makes. Without it, I would hardly know how to direct the work of the Association. It seems to be an indispensable requisite to good results." Two decades later, Briggs used his valuable experience to develop a special service for the Citizens Alliance.[20]

As the newly elected president of the NFA, Briggs expressed in his 1905 acceptance speech the attitude that guided labor negotiations, on a national level at the NFA and on a local level in Minneapolis, for the next thirty years:

> I stand for tact, diplomacy, patience, conciliation and peaceful settlement of all difficulties between labor and capital. If, however, the inevitable happens, and peaceful settlements cannot be made, this organization is thrown into a fighting machine, and then I say, Let us fight to the finish.[21]

The basic negotiation policy under Briggs's leadership at the NFA and later in Minneapolis was very simple—fire all striking union members permanently and bring in replacement workers. The NFA backed up this policy with a complete defense system that helped its members eliminate unions. The NFA constitution guaranteed a struck member one of the following: Enough workers for 70 percent of its shop capacity; arrangements to do the work elsewhere at 70 percent production; or monetary compensation to hire workers up to 70 percent of the wage base.[22]

In practice, the NFA maintained a large body of well-trained independent moulders under a yearly or a sixty-day contract. A few of these men would be immediately dispatched to a struck plant to act as skilled trainers for the "green" men that the NFA supplied through its national system of labor bureaus. Bonus pay, new machines, and piecework were quickly implemented to boost production. Under this elaborate system, a member's foundry could be back in production within twenty-four hours of a strike.[23]

NFA assistance to local employers also anticipated the possibility of a strenuous and sometimes violent reaction to its policies by local unions. If violence erupted, the NFA would hire local guards to protect its replacement workers from angry union pickets. If local guards were unavailable, the NFA would import them. Pressure was also brought to bear on local police departments to maintain law and order. If these methods were unsuccessful, the NFA's labor bureau workers were fed and quartered in the struck plant. In the courts, the association's legal specialists would help local employers get injunctions limiting union actions. In return for the massive aid that Briggs's organization provided during strikes, NFA members agreed to operate their plants on an open-shop basis for at least one year after the strike.[24]

This thorough and successful system for establishing and defending the open shop, developed and implemented at the NFA by alliance leader Briggs, had a profound national impact on American industry for decades to follow and an immediate impact on Minneapolis industries. Local foundries could now count on the NFA to support their efforts to maintain the open shop. When Briggs stepped down as commissioner of the NFA to become its president in 1905, he also returned to Minneapolis to engage in business. The organizational system that the CA had created at the NFA would now provide him a framework with which he would personally lead the Citizens Alliance's fight against Minneapolis labor unions.[25]

Despite Briggs's effective leadership at the NFA and the NMTA, the national open-shop drive required a dedicated corps of businessmen working at the local level. Although the NFA was well designed to aid local employers, it was thinly represented in each city and represented only the foundry industry.

Briggs and Kinnard realized that an effective open-shop movement in Minneapolis must embrace the entire business community. While Briggs implemented their policies at the NFA, Kinnard led the Citizens Alliance's open-shop drive in Minneapolis from 1904 to 1907.[26]

To run the alliance's full-time operation, Kinnard hired James Ward as the organization's agent in its 1907 open-shop drive against the machinists and metal workers and in its drive against the building trades unions from 1908 to 1911. In industries where the open shop had been established, however, the CA's first priority was to prevent strikes. Employing the NFA's methods, the alliance placed informants in the Minneapolis Trades and Labor Assembly and in its various local unions. The alliance would then supply members with daily reports on discharged workers in an effort to eliminate them from all CA open shops.[27]

While Ward strove to keep CA shops union-free, alliance members gradually recruited more and more members. Kinnard fully realized that success depended on the widest possible business representation and employer unity — a unity that the Citizens Alliance would maintain with threats and force, if necessary. Effective strike prevention also required an active propaganda effort. Although the Citizens Alliance relied heavily on literature from the national employers' associations, which it distributed to convince employers and workers of the benefits of the open shop, it also ran its own anti-union campaign.[28]

When the Citizens Alliance convinced employers in a particular industry to declare for the open shop, however, lockouts or strikes by existing unions were expected and carefully prepared for. If unions struck for shorter hours or higher wages, the CA reaction was the same: Refuse to negotiate and hire replacement workers. If the alliance's own stock of strikebreakers was unable to meet the demand, Ward followed the pattern of the 1901 machinists' strike and the 1903 flour mill strike. He brought workers from Chicago and Milwaukee in 1907, and he advertised in country towns for carpenters in 1911. Employment agencies were used to tap transient laborers or recruit at country lumberyards. If the strike was in the foundry or machinist trades, additional strikebreakers were furnished by the NMTA or the NFA.[29]

When the safety of replacement workers was threatened during the 1907 machinists' strike, the employers appealed to Mayor James C. Haynes, who appointed special police to guard the machine shops. Agent Ward of the alliance provided the specials with badges, guns, and belts. Citizens Alliance members were still sometimes forced to feed and house their replacement workers inside their plants. With the experience gained from the flour mill's fortress defense in 1903, the alliance committed its resources to an all-out effort to keep struck plants operating.[30]

Behind the front lines of these early strikes, the alliance worked diligently to assure the defeat of Minneapolis's unions. Despite a very slight occurrence of violence on Minneapolis's picket lines, employers feared a loss of replacement workers and wanted to avoid the expense of housing workers on site. The Citizens Alliance, represented by lawyer Harlan P. Roberts, turned to the courts to limit union activities. Injunctions to restrict picketing were sought in most of the major open-shop drive strikes of the era.[31]

Of even greater strategic importance, however, was the ability of the Citizens Alliance to maintain the unity of its members when they were facing a loss of income and a possible loss of business as a direct result of a strike. To enforce unity during the stress of a strike, the Citizens Alliance employed a "carrot-and-stick" strategy. In the case of the 1907 machinists' strike, the "carrot" was financial support to struck employers from both the NMTA and the Citizens Alliance. To provide these funds, the alliance levied a special assessment of five dollars on each of its members to assist members "in their efforts to institute and maintain the 'open shop.'"[32]

If employers still wavered in their resolve to fight for the open shop, the Citizens Alliance, resorting to the "stick," threatened to put them out of business. During the building trades strike in 1911, the alliance threatened a materials boycott of any builder that signed with the unions. With CA members controlling lumber and other wholesale trades, these threats carried considerable force. Most employers were afraid to defy the alliance. By organizing across trade lines and including the entire business community, the Citizens Alliance was able to demand unity and, under threat, have their demands honored.[33]

The 1905 strike of compositors in Minneapolis's printing shops was fairly typical of the Citizens Alliance's early open-shop initiatives. Thirty-one of Minneapolis's print shops, including the larger shops of Harrison and Smith, Kimball and Storer, Miller-Davis Printing, and the Tribune Job Printing Company, had banded together to form an employers' association called the Minneapolis Typothetae. Each member agreed to give the Typothetae the final power over any contract changes, to operate on an open-shop basis, and not to steal customers from any member firm suffering from a strike. In addition, if any union struck a member, all members would lock out members of that union from its shops.[34]

The majority of Typothetae members, particularly the larger shops, were also members of the Citizens Alliance and proponents of the open shop. The printing employers' organization was considered one of the strongest in the United States and had complete control of Minneapolis's printing industry. Wages for the typographical workers had been held steady since November 21, 1903. Compositors who attempted to switch shops for better wages were blacklisted from all Typothetae shops. The printing employers were also backed up by the Citizens Alliance. Any Minneapolis printer who was not a Typothetae member was refused credit at alliance foundries.[35]

As early as 1901, the International Typographical Union had begun to agitate for an eight-hour workday. When this policy question was presented to the employers at the United Typothetae's 1904 convention, the eight-hour day was categorically rejected. The inevitable conflict erupted into a national strike in the fall of 1905. In Minneapolis, at a conference held before the strike, the Typothetae employers would agree only to meet with individuals and would under no circumstances recognize the union.[36]

On October 2, more than 100 union printers employed in thirty shops struck for the eight-hour day with no pay reduction and full union recognition. The employers were well-prepared: They had fired a number of union members the week before, worked ahead on orders, and had been scouring rural Minnesota, Iowa, and the Dakotas for three weeks, searching for printers to replace the strikers. The thirty-one members of the Typothetae, confident that a strike would be quickly crushed, posted a terse notice in their shops on October 2: "The undersigned employing printers of the city of Minneapolis will employ compositors without regard to union or non union affiliations. Wages and hours of work to remain as at present." The battle for the open shop in Minneapolis's printing industry had begun with Citizens Alliance printing shops leading the fight.[37]

The resolve of the Typothetae to force the open shop was clear from the first day of the strike when they began offering good workers guaranteed two-year contracts at union-scale wages. Combined with their pre-strike preparations, the affected shops were working at 50 percent capacity on the strike's first day. By the second day, Typothetae offices were crowded with out-of-town strikebreakers, who were arriving on every train into Minneapolis. Strikebreakers were recruited from the University of Minnesota and state prisons and reformatories.[38]

On the third day of the strike, the alliance mailed a circular to businesses throughout the city and the state announcing: "We heartily endorse the stand the employing printers have taken for the open shop in this struggle to rid themselves of union dictatorship and tyranny, and we pledge the master printers of Minneapolis our hearty cooperation and support and ask that all businessmen in the community be helpful and patient with the printing concerns that have been forced into this fight."[39]

Five days into the strike, the Typothetae's workforce was up to two-thirds of capacity and its members were training women to run their Linotype machines. The pickets, little more than an embarrassment for employers, were unable to slow the tide of replacement workers. At Kimball and Storer, where pickets were more effective, the new workers ate and slept under lock and key at the company building, often guarded by University of Minnesota football players. By October 10, there had been no Typothetae defections, and the printing employers needed only twenty-five more printers to be at full strength. The employers confidently proclaimed that the strike was practically broken already.[40]

The union, with 125 pickets out and the backing of the Trades and Labor Assembly, was completely satisfied with the strike's first week and felt confident of victory. The unions apparently did not comprehend the significance of the Citizens Alliance's intervention and continued to picket and predict imminent victory. The alliance strategy was to eliminate any financial damage that might force printers to sign with the union and to punish any printer that broke ranks with the Typothetae. To lessen the strike's impact on employers, the CA, in cooperation with the National Association of Manufacturers, gave direct financial support to the printers. They also successfully appealed to Minneapolis businesses to slow their printing orders to allow struck printers to fill all their contracts. In addition to these helpful measures, the alliance and the NAM put pressure on Typothetae members to continue their uncompromising open-shop stand. The threat of boycotts by Citizens Alliance newspapers and publishers urged on by the NAM was probably the most effective tool to enforce employer unity.[41]

By the strike's second week, there were no Typothetae defections, and, given the CA's intervention, the union's future appeared bleak. Even the union's ineffectual and non-violent picketing brought Citizens Alliance lawyers into court to unsuccessfully seek an injunction. In April, 1907, with the strike long over, the union claimed that the result of the Typothetae's replacement of strikers with non-union workers was a disorganized trade, reduced profits, and sloppy work.[42]

Whatever the accuracy of their claims, the printing shops of the Typothetae remained open shops. Despite this clear victory, the Citizens Alliance continued the offensive with a boycott campaign against the remaining small shops that had signed with the union. Stickers were sent out to businesses to attach to union-marked print jobs stating: "This is Returned because it bears the Union label, which is the trademark of the largest and most radical TRUST of the day. We are for liberty, and will not patronize those who are bound up with the combine, and use its mark."[43]

The cooperative efforts of the national employers' groups and the Citizens Alliance were even more important in the violent 1907 machinists' strike. Faced with union demands for a nine-hour day, the machine-shop employers refused to meet with union representatives and set out to firmly establish the open shop. The pattern of earlier Citizens Alliance victories, however, was rudely shattered in May when the Diamond Iron Works, one of the larger shops and a CA member, signed with the union. The Twin City Association of Employers of Machinists, the original organization of Briggs and Kinnard, with the aid of NMTA commissioner Robert Wuest, pressured Diamond to rescind its agreement. An NMTA representative was installed as the Diamond superintendent and, on May 18, the union was locked out without warning. The NMTA and the Citizens Alliance financed the employers and the NMTA provided strikebreakers from Chicago and Milwaukee.[44]

Because of unusually vigorous union resistance, Wuest had to feed and house these men inside the Diamond plant, guarded by special police who were armed by CA Agent Ward. With the added assistance of Minneapolis Mayor James C. Haynes, Police Chief Frank H. Corriston, and local courts, the alliance's bat-wielding guards were able to protect the NMTA's replacement workers. With these "open-shop heroes" willing to work indefinitely at half of union scale, the Citizens Alliance defense of the open shop was certain to succeed. The tenacious unity of machine-shop employers, enforced by the NMTA and the Citizens Alliance, reduced union resistance to an irrelevant irritation. Briggs's NFA strategy was gradually spreading the open shop to more and more industries.[45]

By the outbreak of World War I in 1914, the Citizens Alliance felt that the labor situation in Minneapolis was under control. The explosive growth of American labor that had characterized the first four years of the twentieth century had been slowed dramatically. In 1914, there were only four more unions in Minneapolis than in 1905. While union membership had grown by 20 percent, the population of Minneapolis had multiplied by 49 percent. The Citizens Alliance had successfully launched open-shop drives against printers, tailors, machinists, coopers, metal workers, bakers, moulders, and upholsterers, and had managed to partially breach labor's stronghold in the building trades.[46]

In addition to these practical gains, the flood of literature printed by national employers' organizations and distributed by the alliance had turned public opinion against unions. The *Minneapolis Labor Review* lamented: "Whenever there is employer union conflict the public sympathy is for employers." Fully confident that it had suppressed the labor threat, the Citizens Alliance scaled back its activities and turned the task of employer vigilance over to its parent, the Minneapolis Commercial Club, now reorganized as the Minneapolis Civic and Commerce Association.[47]

4 Controlling Public Affairs

FROM THEIR EARLIEST VICTORIES in the battle for the open shop, Citizens Alliance leaders realized that the defeat of union labor depended on the public policies of the city, state, and federal governments. Legislative or administrative changes at any level of government could alter the rules of class warfare and destroy the industrial and legal defenses that the Citizens Alliance had used in its first decade. The Citizens Alliance itself was ill equipped to face this challenge. It clearly represented the employer class of Minnesota's largest city and no one else. The larger civic role of its parent, the Minneapolis Commercial Club, had gradually waned since the turn of the century. By 1910, the business community's interests were represented primarily by the Public Affairs Committee of the Commercial Club, the Minneapolis Traffic Association, and the Minneapolis Publicity Club.[1]

The "advancement of Minneapolis's business interests" required one unified organization to represent all the commercial and civic interests of the city. Even a united city, however, would be unable to control events at the legislature in St. Paul. Businesses or even cities representing themselves before legislative committees would have insufficient influence to affect a legislature that had a heavily rural membership with quite different priorities. A permanent organization unifying employers from across the state was the only way to be effective in St. Paul.[2]

Fortunately, businesses across the country shared the Minneapolis business community's passion for the open shop and their fear of union labor. President Theodore Roosevelt's enforcement of the Sherman Anti-Trust Act, and the Progressive Era's public cry for increased business regulation had created a profound sense of insecurity in the nation's business community. In reaction, business organized a plethora of successful employers' associations such as the National Founders' Association (NFA), the National Metal Trades Association (NMTA), and the National Association of Manufacturers (NAM), fracturing any hope of a consensus of American business interests. Although these organizations lobbied the United States Congress zealously, they often worked at cross-purposes, confusing legislators in Washington, D.C., and contributing to the defeat of the very aims they sought to influence. If open-shop conditions were to be maintained, a nationwide organization was needed to direct the influence of all commercial interests of the nation. Only then would the federal government understand and support policies beneficial to American business.[3]

In 1907, the AFL officially assigned the task of seeking "state legislation favorable to labor" to the Minnesota State Federation of Labor. Realizing that a strong, well-organized labor lobby could threaten business's control over Minnesota industry, leading members of the CA joined their colleagues in St. Paul to organize a response. On December 14, 1908, at Carling's Restaurant on St. Paul's Robert Street, John F. Wilcox, president of the Minneapolis CA, met with ten businessmen from across the state to incorporate the Minnesota Employers' Association (MEA). George M. Gillette, president of Minneapolis Steel and Machinery Company, chaired the meeting and reviewed the work that the informal Employers' Association of Minnesota had done lobbying for legislation since 1904. Gillette, a prominent CA member, believed "that with a permanent organization more effective work could be done" at the state legislature.[4]

Gillette had previously retained the CA law firm of Belden, Jamison and Shearer to draft articles of incorporation. Article 1 stated that the MEA's purpose was:

> To inculcate just and equitable principles of trade and business among its members and their employees; to acquire, possess and disseminate useful business information; to adjust controversies and misunderstandings which may arise between individuals engaged in trade and business; and between employer and employee; to endeavor in all reasonable ways to prevent accidents to employees; to establish fair and equitable relations between employer and employee; and to promote the general welfare and interests of its members.

The eleven men had created a fledgling organization that would slowly become a major force in Minnesota politics, and, by the 1970s, grow to 2,800 companies. The MEA would also lead the CA's defense of the open shop at the state legislature.[5]

From its first year, the MEA fulfilled the goals that were required for it to be an effective weapon in the CA's open-shop war. The organization represented businessmen from throughout the state, including rural areas. It gave the business community one powerful voice at the legislature, and it was dominated by the CA. Although the fifty charter members represented only seven communities outside the Twin Cities, within weeks 116 firms from forty-nine outstate towns and cities had joined. By February 1909, with the mass sign-up of the membership of the Minnesota State Association of Builders' Exchanges, MEA membership leaped to over 800.[6]

President Gillette, realizing that the unity of the employers' association was crucial to its interests, made every effort to absorb or eliminate any competing business lobbies. With most of the state's large employers operating in concert, Gillette led a powerful and influential force. The CA's control over MEA policies was assured by its domination of the membership and finances of the organization. Over a third of the MEA membership were members of the CA. Dues from these firms accounted for 32 percent of the MEA budget. When combined with allied open-shop forces in St. Paul and Duluth, well over 60 percent of the MEA's membership openly supported CA labor policies. At annual meetings to elect MEA officers, where many outstate members were represented by CA proxies, open-shop support approached 80 percent. The organization that Gillette and CA President Wilcox had helped create in 1908 would continue to support open-shop policies throughout the life of the CA.[7]

The vital interest of the MEA in handling legislation before the 1911 Minnesota legislature was turned over to a special committee of three, which included CA leader Briggs and Herbert M. Gardner, a charter member of the CA. Under the committee's direction, James D. Shearer, a CA founder, was hired to lobby at the capital in St. Paul. A former Republican legislator, Shearer's effectiveness was enhanced by his position as president of the Minnesota State Bar Association.[8]

Well before each legislative session, George Gillette, Shearer, and Secretary Albert V. Williams started an exhaustive process of accumulating data on all legislative proposals that might affect MEA members. When the legislature finally considered critical legislation, the MEA would flood committee hearings with its members, usually led by Shearer or Briggs.[9]

Inside the legislature, the MEA exerted its influence through friendly conservative supporters, particularly CA lawyer Charles R. Fowler, who represented the state's largest labor district in Minneapolis. The MEA, however, exhorted its members that "the real pressure and influence must be brought to bear at home in the legislative districts of the members of the Legislature." Rural members, who were frequently associated with their legislators socially or in business, were considered crucial to the MEA 's efforts to defeat pro-labor legislation. A weekly bulletin listing and discussing important bills was published during each legislative session and sent to each commercial club, civic, or business association in the state to guide the business community in its efforts to influence legislation.[10]

Encouraged and informed by the MEA, the business community would then unleash a barrage of letters spelling out the impending disaster for the state if labor legislation prevailed. When a rare piece of labor legislation passed the 1911 legislature, the MEA wrote all employers in the state asking them to "deal with the members of the Legislature who voted for the Lundeen bill in such a manner as will make them sit up and take notice." Political retaliation, of course, was necessary only when the MEA's effort to "have proper men sent to the Legislature" failed and a few "extremely radical labor men" were elected. The Minnesota State Federation of Labor attributed the MEA with power that was so "great and far reaching that every really important measure save one [the Lundeen bill] of actual benefit to all laborers, failed of passage."[11]

While admitting that the MEA's legislative program was conservative and "sought only to protect the legitimate interests of employers," President Gillette added, "it has always opposed legislation which in its judgment, would not operate equally and to the best advantage of all persons." The MEA had never "advocated legislation unfair or unjust to any class."[12]

In reality, the MEA program closely resembled the National Association of Manufacturers' politics of class warfare. Gillette based his strident anti-labor activities on the threat that "the labor people are thoroughly organized and in the strife for political supremacy in this State, there is too great a tendency in the Legislature to propose legislation hostile to the industries of the State for the purpose of gaining political favor from the more radical." The radical element in organized labor was "hostile to the interests of the people as a whole, unfair to the general interest of the United States and . . . unpatriotic." Class warfare had been declared by the "socialistic" Minnesota State Federation of Labor (MSFL), and the MEA had responded in defense of the American public.[13]

Although the MEA tended and advanced a great deal of legislation affecting particular lines of trade or business—from specific measures relating to regulation of nursery stock, to the manufacture of ice cream, to the sale and distribution of obscene literature—its primary concern was stemming the advances of organized labor. The extensive lobby of the MEA opposed and succeeded in defeating all of the following types of labor legislation: limiting apprentices; setting a state eight-hour-day; establishing one day's rest in seven; prohibiting employment agencies; prohibiting retaining employees' money for relief associations; regulating conditions in foundries; regulating industrial camps; and regulating industrial safety.[14]

In 1911, for example, the MEA appealed for additional funds from its members to pay for the 26,750 letters that it had mailed during the four-month legislative session. Measures limiting the workday and establishing a minimum wage for women were passed despite MEA efforts, which were hampered by a lack of support by employers of women across the state. The executive committee, realizing that aggressive anti-labor measures were required, instructed Shearer to prepare legislation prohibiting boycotting and picketing, "which makes it impossible for an employer to enjoy his property, his personal rights and freedom on account of labor disturbances."[15]

Shearer also introduced legislation prohibiting unions from expelling members that joined the National Guard, a practice that the business community felt interfered with National Guard recruitment. While labor supporters advocated laws outlawing the importation of strikebreakers, the MEA supported outlawing the use of outstate labor agitators invited in by striking unions and supposedly the source of Minnesota's industrial disturbances. Despite Gillette's protestations, the MEA's program was to eliminate all government policies that might aid in the advancement of labor unions to the detriment of the membership of the MEA and the CA.[16]

The MEA also cooperated with the National Association of Manufacturers and other national employers' associations to combat labor legislation in Washington, D.C. A bill limiting the daily hours of laborers to eight, for all work done under contract to any agency of the United States government, was introduced in the United States House of Representatives on January 29, 1908. The NAM asked the MEA to organize and lead the opposition of Minnesota employers to the bill. Employers throughout the state were urged to write their congressmen and visit or write members of the labor committee to express their disapproval of House Bill 15651. Gillette warned that the bill "would drive hundreds of concerns out of government bidding; it might result in the establishment of government factories. It would be the irresistible entering wedge of new labor legislation; for the labor lobby would not stop there." The bill was an attempt "to legislate the hours of labor into the private enterprises (factories, mills and workshops), of the whole country by an act of congress."[17]

Two years later, Gillette and Eli S. Warner of St. Paul represented the MEA at a national conference in Chicago organized in 1910 to fight a national corporation tax law. Gillette had expressed the MEA's underlying mission in a 1908 circular:

> America has an enviable place among industrial nations, but it is no secure place unless those who have placed it in that position watch with unceasing vigilance that obstacles such as unwise laws are not enacted.[18]

The MEA's legislative program was primarily a defense against unions that was justified by its protection of basic American values. Ironically, however, it was the cost of employers' liability insurance that consumed most of President Gillette's energy during the MEA's first decade. Since 1903, Minnesota judges had awarded unusually liberal awards to injured industrial workers. By 1909, the Minnesota Supreme Court favored the injured worker in 73 percent of its decisions and casualty insurance companies were paying out 76 percent of their premiums. At a public hearing, Gillette complained that in Minnesota, "Industry bears as high a burden, I may conservatively say, as it does in any other state." Although the Minnesota Bureau of Labor accepted Gillette's contention, a 1908 study of 300 cases revealed that in 50 percent of fatal accidents, the family received no compensation, and only 11 percent received significant financial awards. In 1908, for example, Minneapolis Steel and Machinery paid only $6,785.32 in benefits and settlements for forty-three serious accidents and five fatalities.[19]

The state Bureau of Labor concluded that if Minnesota shows "employers' liability at its best the workmen of Minnesota may be glad that they do not work where it is at its worst." Gillette calculated that Minneapolis Steel and Machinery paid $18,000 for liability insurance in 1907, while its injured workers received only $3,000. The litigious and inefficient employers' liability system was rapidly becoming too expensive, particularly for Minnesota's smaller employers. The MEA, to protect the profits of its members, was forced to consider a workers' compensation law, despite "the sting of socialism from any system of this kind." The defense of the philosophical tenets of American society was in this case unprofitable.[20]

Following a demand coming from across the United States for changes in the way injured workers were compensated, Gillette joined William E. McEwen, secretary of the Minnesota State Federation of Labor, and Hugh V. Mercer, a prominent Minneapolis attorney who became president of the Minnesota Bar Association in 1913, on the Minnesota Employees Compensation Commission to study the complex issues and prepare legislation for the 1911 legislative session. Realizing that a thorough understanding of existing laws would strengthen the MEA's position, the association asked its members to contribute to a special fund to send Gillette and a statistician-linguist to Europe for a two-month fact-finding trip.[21]

Gillette returned from his tour convinced that workers' compensation would double or triple the cost of employers' liability insurance. To offset this expense, he demanded that workers should contribute 20 percent of the costs of their insurance and that employee benefits not exceed 50 percent of their wages. The MSFL, after unsuccessfully trying to negotiate these issues, concluded that the MEA was "not very enthusiastic about any kind of a workers' compensation act."[22]

When the commission rejected his demands, Gillette, who had commented that, "Except from a purely socialistic standpoint I have never heard any reason advanced why a workman should receive full compensation," wrote his own legislative code with input from the MEA board of directors to present to

the legislature. This code contained three provisions: a 50 percent basic benefit scale; employer discretion in paying medical expenses; and exclusion of occupational diseases.[23]

Without Gillette's support, the Compensation Commission's workers' compensation bill, which offered higher compensation for workers and required
employers to provide complete medical care for two weeks, was doomed. Representative Charles Fowler, a CA member, led the vigorous opposition on the
House floor, while Fowler's law partner, William A. Kerr, represented the insurance companies in their effort to forestall any change in the lucrative employers' liability system. Even the Minnesota State Bar Association, whose
president in 1911 was CA founder and MEA counsel James Shearer, refused to
back the bill.[24]

Gillette, who realized that his bill had little chance of passage, temporarily
resigned his position as president of the MEA. This allowed the MEA and its
membership to oppose all workers' compensation bills, including Gillette's,
while Gillette, aptly nicknamed the "Old Fox," was able to maintain a more reasonable image, positioning himself for future battles over workers' compensation. The commission bill died in 1911 before it reached the House floor, giving the MEA a two-year breathing space to maneuver toward a cheaper
solution. The MEA proudly reported to its members that all legislation detri-
mental to employers, with the exception of the Lundeen bill increasing the
amount recoverable for death by accident to $7,500, was defeated. Despite the
successful session, the employers feared that the new maximum compensation for death would become part of any bill that a special Senate Committee
would prepare for the 1913 legislature.[25]

With fifteen states already operating workers' compensation systems, the
MEA realized that the Senate Committee report to the 1913 legislature would
determine the course of Minnesota's industrial future. Gillette knew that it
was imperative for the MEA to prepare a bill for the Senate Committee before
the committee prepared its own bill, possibly with input from the MSFL. James
A. Emery, counsel for the NAM, was brought in to help an MEA committee investigate the laws of other states.[26]

After six months of study, the MEA executive committee authorized attorneys Shearer and George T. Simpson to prepare a bill modeled after the 1911
New Jersey law, which had the lowest benefit schedule of any state. To minimize
expense for MEA members, the 1913 MEA draft bill set maximum compensation
at ten dollars per week and a minimum rate of five dollars. The employer was
also allowed to deduct 20 percent of insurance costs from the workers' wages.[27]

Hoping to gain a valuable political ally in future battles over benefit increases, the MEA included farmers in its workers' compensation system. The

Senate Committee accepted almost all of the MEA bill, but couldn't stomach the politically unpalatable addition of farmers to the legislation. The committee also gave full compensation to alien dependents of deceased workers, and "released the employee from all negligence for accidents[,] thereby placing upon the employer full responsibility for all accidents."[28]

Gillette wrote an emphatic letter to MEA members asking them to protest measures that were "the most important on which we have ever asked your cooperation." A flood of letters vigorously protesting amendments or changes to the MEA draft bill poured into the legislature. When this campaign failed, rural businessmen were determined to defeat the final bill. CA leaders hurriedly met with the MEA executive committee to push for the MEA to make its support of the final bill, however flawed, clear to all members. On April 7, 1913, Gillette circulated an appeal to all MEA members to urge their legislators to pass the final version of Senate File 290.[29]

Despite the Minneapolis Trades and Labor Assembly's complaint that the bill was "vicious, unjust and unfair to the employee," Minnesota passed into law one of the most conservative workers' compensation statutes in the country. Although the MEA's demand for a 20 percent employee contribution had been eliminated, the compensation minimum of six dollars and maximum of ten dollars were very close to the original MEA bill. With the passage of Minnesota's first workers' compensation legislation in 1913, Minneapolis papers trumpeted the name of George M. Gillette as the "father" of Minnesota's workers' compensation law.[30]

Gillette also credited himself for the defeat of two bills providing for an amendment to the constitution of Minnesota, under which the state would insure all workers and compel all employers to contribute to a state insurance fund. Early in the session, MSFL President McEwen announced that "above all else we favor state insurance." By 1910, McEwen had concluded that the only way to lower premiums for Minnesota companies and raise the benefits for injured workers was to eliminate the casualty insurance companies. For McEwen, the solution was simple: Ban the insurance companies from writing workers' compensation policies and establish a compulsory, monopolistic state insurance system. Gillette argued that the state needed to operate under a compensation law for several years to gain the necessary information on industrial hazards before any decision could be made on state insurance. McEwen's constitutional amendment to authorize state insurance died in committee.[31]

Realizing that there was "very strong sentiment in favor of state insurance," Gillette warned the insurance companies to pay claims promptly and generously. If the new workers' compensation law was administered in an "exorbitant and unreasonable" manner, state insurance was inevitable. Although Gillette and the MEA had extinguished the specter of state insurance in 1913, he correctly predicted its reemergence after World War I, when the MEA would have to fight the same legislative battle again.[32]

With an effective lobby established at the state legislature by 1909, the Minneapolis business community could turn some of its attention to the erosion of the Minneapolis Commercial Club. In December of 1910, the business community formed a committee to work on a reorganization plan. Edward P. Wells, president of one of the leading investment houses in the Northwest and a Citizens Alliance member, chaired the committee for its yearlong study. CA founder Martin B. Koon and six other CA members also sat on the ten-member committee. Out of this reorganization emerged the Minneapolis Civic and Commerce Association (CCA). On December 7, 1911, the committee met to appoint the officers for the new association, which would embrace the memberships and activities of all the civic, commercial, and industrial groups of the city. Retail lumber magnate and CA member Arthur R. Rogers was chosen to lead the CCA.[33]

A week later, 650 of Minneapolis's most important and powerful men met in Donaldson's Tea Room to formally organize the CCA. Within the month, Wells and Rogers were sent to make a detailed study of the Chicago Association of Commerce, the Cleveland Chamber of Commerce, and the New York Merchants' Association, all recognized leaders in the civic and commercial fields. Following their report, in February of 1912, the Public Affairs Committee of the Commercial Club, the Publicity Club, and the Traffic Association merged into the Civic and Commerce Association. By April, the association had established a secretarial staff in its permanent headquarters in the Security Bank Building. With the formation of the CCA, Minneapolis had entered a new era of business unity.[34]

When asked by the *Minneapolis Tribune* to describe the purpose of the new association, President Rogers quoted Article 1 of the CCA's articles of incorporation:

> The purpose of the corporation and the nature of its business shall be to advance the civic and commercial interests of the City of Minneapolis and to promote the general welfare and prosperity of the city and tributary territory, [and to] give greater efficiency to the regulation and handling of matters of public or municipal concern.[35]

The organization was supposed to be non-political, democratic, and inclusive of all civic and corporate interests, including the Trades and Labor Assembly, the Minneapolis Building Trades Council, and other labor organizations. Ironically, the Citizens Alliance, fresh from the victories of its first decade, was at the same time temporarily turning its open-shop work over to its new parent, the CCA.[36]

Because the CCA intended to be a totally inclusive organization, it could presume to plan to systematize every detail of Minneapolis's public life, from private commerce and industry to governmental regulation to the infrastructure on which city life was based. As the *Minneapolis Tribune* so eloquently put it: "The entire city has been united under the banner of the new association for the carrying forward of its logical destiny."[37]

Despite the illusion of an inclusive and democratic organization, however, the CCA was controlled by a small, elite group of industrialists and bankers. Most of the powers of the CCA were concentrated in the thirty-nine-member board of directors. The board created departments, made all rules and regulations, elected officers, and appointed both the executive committee, which transacted routine business, and the membership committee, which recommended new members to the board.[38]

The first board, which was appointed by the incorporators of the CCA, had twenty-five CA members, including founders Koon and Fred R. Salisbury. Although the CCA proclaimed publicly that each member had one vote, sustaining members who donated at least $500 annually were allowed to nominate and elect five of the thirteen directors by themselves. Using rules that allowed cumulative voting, the sustaining members were also able to effectively influence the eight directors elected by the entire membership. The special privileges of the CCA's sustaining members and the board's control over future membership guaranteed that the CCA would be permanently controlled by Minneapolis's wealthiest industries—the flour mills, the major banks, and the railroads.[39]

Immediately after organizing, the CCA began an extensive membership drive with a goal of 5,000 members. Letters were mailed to 7,000 firms, corporations, and individuals that were thought to be logical candidates for membership. Thirty-five business and professional divisions were created, each with a chairman selected to recruit members in his industry. Lawyers were recruited by James D. Shearer, lumberyards by Benjamin F. Nelson, electrical supply firms by William I. Gray, and plumbing firms by George K. Belden—all CA founders.[40]

The membership campaign emphasized eighteen reasons for joining the CCA, systematizing the business community's public efforts, enlarging the city's market and influence, including directly serving members' interests and saving them time and money. Every possible facility would be provided "for maintenance of our manufacturing enterprises at their maximum efficiency."

The collective influence of the CCA would have a positive influence on legislation affecting the taxes and insurance rates of members. Specific details for ac-
complishing its widespread goals were missing from the CCA's campaign literature. To alleviate claims that its goals and methods would be based on narrow
self-interests, the CCA contended that it would be "thoroughly democratic and
that were be no politics in its platform."[41]

These pocketbook appeals had an immediate impact on the Minneapolis
business community. In its first year, nearly 2,500 businesses and individuals
joined the CCA, including the leading firms in every industry. The Radisson and
Nicollet hotels; the *Journal,* the *Tribune,* and the *Daily News* newspapers; Bovey-
Shute, W. I. Carpenter, and Harry B. Waite lumber companies; Dayton's, Don-
aldson's, and Powers department stores; Dean Webber and International
Harvester agricultural implement companies; First National and Northwest
banks; Pillsbury, Washburn-Crosby, and Cargill grain companies; the Great
Northern and Northern Pacific railroad companies; Gardner and Warner
Hardware companies; Minneapolis Steel and Machinery and Crown Iron
Works machine shop and foundries; and the Minneapolis Street Railway Company all quickly joined the CCA. The same powerful economic interests that
created and ran the Citizens Alliance would now also run its newly reorganized parent, the Civic and Commerce Association.[42]

One of the first and most important functions of the CCA was to take charge
of fostering and promoting the industries of Minneapolis. CA founder Fred R.
Salisbury, pioneer of the city's bed and mattress industry, chaired the Committee on Industrial Development as it moved aggressively to expand Minneapolis industry. The committee first organized the Minneapolis Industries
Association to buy land and organize freight facilities to lure new manufacturers to northeast Minneapolis. The CCA felt that this effort would assure "the
continued industrial supremacy of Minneapolis in the great Northwest." Unable to finance meritorious new manufacturing projects itself, the committee
endorsed the creation of a Minneapolis holding company to invest in the
stocks and bonds of new concerns. The committee also supported a "factory
incubator building" to provide low-cost heat, light, power, and railroad tracks
for new, smaller industries. By 1917, the industrial growth of Minneapolis had
expanded dramatically, with over $2,250,000 in new factory structures built
the previous year.[43]

The Committee on Industrial Development also handled labor problems for
the CCA. With Citizens Alliance leader Otis P. Briggs and two other CA founders
on the committee, the CCA had experienced open-shop campaigners to take
over the CA's work. An open-shop drive by CCA furniture manufacturers in
1914 followed the pattern of earlier alliance-led efforts. On January 9, 1914,

furniture employers, led by Levin Brothers and CA member McLeod and Smith, announced that their businesses would now be non-union shops. The States Detective Agency was hired to bring replacement workers from Wisconsin and Chicago to take the jobs of locked-out upholsterers. When violence broke out, the employers applied for injunctions in Hennepin County District Court and housed strikebreakers inside their factories. By March 1914, the employers, with the aid of the National Association of Manufacturers, were firmly in control of the now open-shop furniture industry. Minneapolis's open-shop CCA members had been able to conquer another industry, despite the temporary dormancy of the Citizens Alliance.[44]

By 1914, the CCA realized that the alliance's aggressive campaign to spread the open shop was only the first step in creating a union-free city. Wherever employees were mistreated and alienated from their employers, the evils of unionism would inevitably reappear, according to a CCA annual report. The CCA's Committee on Industrial Welfare spent 1914 preparing plans for profit sharing, stock purchasing by employees, insurance, pensions, and mutual benefit associations to address this problem.[45]

During 1915, the committee laid these plans before Minneapolis industries and offered interested companies assistance in installing the new, innovative programs. The committee stressed that if the programs were "kept free from the spirit of paternalism, benevolence or the suggestion of an ulterior end, [they would] undoubtedly have had a binding influence for good." Washburn-Crosby Company, for example, set up a health department in 1915, a group insurance plan in 1919, and a committee plan of employee representation during World War I. The flour-milling giant, using plans advocated by the CCA's Industrial Welfare Committee, was able to stave off union recognition until 1936, proving the committee contention that these programs "should make a marked impression upon the future development of Minneapolis industrially."[46]

During the winter of 1914, Minneapolis working men and women were faced with serious unemployment and the rapid growth of slum conditions in many areas of the city. An investigation by the CCA housing committee concluded that Minneapolis was becoming a city of bad tenement housing, which would become a major problem if not checked by vigorous and prompt action. The civic association pronounced that "every thrifty workingman" should be able "to bring up his family in an environment not antagonistic to the training of children to be good citizens morally, physically and mentally." A new housing code written by the CCA, which failed to pass the legislature, and a plan for the "best type of building adapted to the needs of the workingman" represented the CCA's best efforts to solve the housing problem.[47]

Following a conference with the mayor, the CCA's Committee on Unemployment, chaired by CA member William E. Satterlee, was appointed to alleviate the suffering caused by the local unemployment problem. The committee, which also included CA leader Briggs, mailed an urgent letter to employers requesting that they retain employees as long as possible to help with the acute unemployment conditions. Employers, householders, and churches were also asked to "Give the Unemployed a chance." The CCA, however, became alarmed when "zealots" made an attempt to issue $50,000 in municipal bonds for food, fuel, and an emergency work program. The committee recommended more study of the problem and cautioned against a "make-work" policy. The economic competition that the Citizens Alliance and the Civic and Commerce Association supported had little room for unions or interference from government relief programs.[48]

The industrial growth and prosperity of Minneapolis also depended on the efficient and economic operation of Minneapolis's city government. An efficient police force, public works department, and other public services would attract new businesses and customers and lower the drain of high taxes on the profits of CCA members. To effect the needed improvements in city government, the CCA opened a Bureau of Municipal Research during December of 1913. The bureau was "to endeavor through cooperation with public officials, to secure the adoption of scientific methods of accounting and administration and to collect, classify, analyze, correlate and interpret data with reference to the conduct of public affairs." The bureau was to promote better understanding and cooperation between the citizens of Minneapolis and their government.[49]

The Minneapolis City Council immediately accepted the bureau's offer of its services and instructed city department heads to cooperate fully. The bureau's first project was the complete reorganization of the records, forms, and procedures of the city's Civil Service. The bureau's work with the Health Department reached into such details as the physical arrangement of the offices, improvement of phone service, daily reporting systems, and a new stores and purchasing system.[50]

At the request of the comptroller, the bureau undertook a thorough study of the city's finances and assisted the comptroller in preparing budget requests to the City Council. By 1915, the bureau's work had extended into the police department, reorganizing the analysis and indexing of fingerprints, establishing a new system of detective records, and helping start a training school for police. Most of the bureau's work was done without formal reports or negative publicity. In this friendly, cooperative atmosphere, the bureau's experts were given access to every aspect of the city's business and were able to restructure the internal workings of the city's government without political repercussions. The CCA was to become, through its Bureau of Municipal Research, the unofficial "third arm" of Minneapolis's local government. While the CCA undoubtedly succeeded in its effort to promote efficiency and economy, it also created a quasi-business-political process that was organized and supervised by the CCA.[51]

Outside of Minneapolis, activity at the Minnesota state legislature could have a profound impact on all areas the CCA considered vital for the commercial well being of its members. Although the CCA declared itself non-partisan, it promised to "cooperate most heartily with officials of the city and state in furthering well considered legislation in the interest of the entire community and will be as vigorous in opposing those unworthy, ill advised or untimely."[52]

The bylaws created a committee on legislation, which lobbied both the Hennepin County delegation and other members of the legislature. In the 1914–15 legislative session, the committee concentrated its efforts, in conjunction with other civic, commercial, and business organizations, on killing a bill to repeal the merit system of Civil Service and opposing a bill to abolish the office of city purchasing agent. Other Civic and Commerce Association committees introduced legislation on a wide area of city concerns, from a new state housing code to the codification of Minnesota's child laws to better protect dependent, delinquent, defective, illegitimate, and neglected children.[53]

Achieving the legislative objectives of the MEA, CCA, and the CA depended on the ability of these organizations to influence the city government of Minneapolis and the state legislature. This would obviously be an easier task if conservative men sympathetic to Minneapolis business interests were elected to city and state offices. The Minneapolis business community's three organizations, all with overlapping membership, took an active role in political campaigns that could affect their dominant industrial position. When a number of candidates were running for congressional seats, the CA canvassed its members so as "to centralize our effort upon the man whom the majority prefer, and thereby be enabled to make an effort that will be effective."[54]

In the 1912 Minneapolis mayoral election, when a split conservative vote threatened to put socialist and unionist Thomas Van Lear into office, the CA and CCA brought the business community's influence to bear on Democrat city councilor Charles D. Gould, convincing him to withdraw from the race. They then formed a Citizens' Non-Partisan Committee to campaign for Wallace G. Nye. Newspaper ads and articles portrayed Van Lear as a threat to the development of Minneapolis. The *Sunday Journal* printed a committee statement on its front page proclaiming that Socialism's real program was to "overthrow the present organization of society, to destroy individualism, to abolish wages and the private employer, and to substitute the state as the sole employer."[55]

The CA and CCA campaign was rewarded by Mayor Nye's 2,421-vote victory—a victory that would have a significant impact on the huge 1916 Teamster's strike. The MEA, although primarily a lobbying organization in its early years, would later launch the largest campaign against radicalism in the CA's turbulent history. The threat of Minnesota's labor and radical political organizations had to be countered wherever possible if legislation important to the defense of the open shop was to be passed and labor legislation defeated.[56]

Even if successful in Minnesota, the MEA, the Civic and Commerce Association, and the Citizens Alliance realized that, alone, they would have very little impact on state or national legislation. To defeat its labor enemies, the business community had to ally itself with similar constituencies across the state and nation. In 1911, in reaction to these fears, a concerted effort was made to organize the business community in cities across the nation. Older and often multiple organizations were merged and revitalized or, in other cities, new groups were founded.[57]

In Minnesota, the Civic and Commerce Association and the St. Paul Association of Commerce (SPAC) were both incorporated on December 5, 1911. Four months later, 700 delegates from nearly every state and large city in the country met in Washington, D.C., and organized the Chamber of Commerce of the United States. The CCA and the St. Paul Association of Commerce both became charter members in the United States Chamber. In exchange for their cooperation in gathering, formulating, and disseminating business opinion and information, the chamber represented the interests of the CCA and the St. Paul Association of Commerce in Washington.[58]

To help expand the influence of the national organization, the CCA advised and financially assisted smaller Minnesota towns in their efforts to establish commercial clubs, which were then organized into the Minnesota Commercial and Civic Federation in 1915. By 1936, 122 towns had commercial organizations, from the Black Duck Community Club to the Caledonia Commercial Club, which were members of the United States Chamber of Commerce. With this widespread constituency acting as one entity, the United States business community hoped to have a serious impact on national affairs and policies.[59]

The national Chamber of Commerce's primary vehicle for assessing the concerns of its membership and turning these opinions into concrete policy statements of the entire nation's business community was the referendum. On issues of national importance, every member organization, including the CCA and SPAC, was polled to create the most comprehensive business opinion in United States history. The board of directors, which included CA member Lewis S. Gillette (brother of George Gillette), decided which issues should be submitted to referendum. In the chamber's first five years, referendums were overwhelmingly in favor of establishing "Vocational Schools of manufacture, commerce, agriculture and home economics throughout the land," limiting immigration to 5 percent of those already in the United States from any country to avoid "intolerable conditions, economic and political, as well as racial," and legislation to limit the rights of railroad workers to strike.[60]

The chamber's most vehement protest erupted when labor union supporters attempted to exclude unions from prosecution under the Sherman Anti-Trust Law. This kind of "class legislation" was "repugnant" to the fundamental principles of democracy, according to the chamber. These rather mild protective measures were radically expanded in the 1930s to include a full-blown defense of the open shop. The chamber established policies against labor boycotts, picketing, political contributions, and government strikes. The rights of the individual to negotiate and to work or not to work without union coercion were of paramount importance. After a quarter-century of evolution, the CA's open-shop philosophy had become the policy of the United States Chamber of Commerce.[61]

Each new chamber referendum was followed by a massive propaganda campaign to sway public opinion and force Congress to pass legislation supporting the chamber's policies. A monthly magazine, *The Nation's Business*, which argued in favor of chamber policies, was mailed to member organizations and the editorial desks of the nation's newspapers. The Resolutions and Referenda Department mailed a barrage of letters to members, government officials, and the press. A speakers' bureau prepared material, recruited effective speakers, and arranged speaking tours. Twenty-six thousand copies of *A Week's Work* described the chamber's activities to the nation while, during the Congressional sessions, a weekly bulletin reported on the progress of all legislation relevant to the business community.[62]

If these efforts failed to influence legislators, the chamber, through its members, organized pressure campaigns from legislators' home constituencies. Each bill was then monitored by the Promotion Division as it was studied through committee hearings. Whenever vital issues were before Congress, chamber experts lobbied legislators and testified before committees.[63]

With the political influence of the nation's entire commercial sector behind it, the chamber frequently arranged private conferences with pivotal legislators or the president. Although it was difficult for the chamber or its enemies to evaluate the effectiveness of this lobby, there is little doubt that the chamber, through its referenda and propaganda efforts, wielded considerable power over national legislation. The CCA, in alliance with similar organizations throughout the country, had magnified its power and influence until the CA's philosophy could have an effect on the legislative policies of the United States.[64]

The national Chamber of Commerce also realized that government administration must be made to conform to chamber policies. Like the CCA's Bureau of Municipal Research, the chamber attempted to mold the substance, structure, and personnel of the United States government. The business expertise of the chamber's membership and the needs of individual members to maximize their profits made the administration of American economic policy the chamber's first and primary target.[65]

The chamber's first referendum approved a policy supporting a national budget system. A persistent chamber lobby finally led to enactment of a budget law in 1921. During the early years of the United States Bureau of Foreign and Domestic Commerce, the appropriations, staff, and services were all organized in close consultation with the Chamber of Commerce. A decade later, close cooperation with the chamber was normal procedure for the federal bureau's eighteen industrial divisions. The Department of State, the Federal Reserve Board, the Federal Farm Loan Board, and the Budget Bureau also maintained close relations with the chamber. If government agencies ignored chamber policies, it lobbied publicly for an overhaul of both policies and personnel.

By 1914, the Minneapolis business community was defended in the halls of government in Minneapolis, St. Paul, and Washington, D.C., by a complex group of business organizations. The Minneapolis Civic and Commerce Association, the Minnesota Employers' Association, and the United States Chamber of Commerce not only maintained an effective anti-labor lobby in the city council chambers, the state legislature, and the halls of Congress, they had infiltrated and to some degree directed the development of government policies regulating business and labor.

5 An Industrial Institute for Open-shop Workers

THE SUCCESS OF THE OPEN-SHOP DRIVE in Minneapolis and across the nation deepened an already serious shortage of skilled workers. The production of United States manufacturers had almost doubled in the first decade of the twentieth century. In the first decade after the Citizens Alliance was established in 1903, the country's manufacturing work force expanded by nearly one-and-one-half million workers. At the same time, the nature of American industry and the work force that it required was rapidly changing. The specialization of modern industry had combined with rapid technological advances to increase the demand for highly trained workers. From 1900 to 1920, the United States' manufacturing industries needed two-and-one-half million new skilled workers. In the machinist trades, an area of vital importance to the Citizens Alliance (CA) and the National Founders' Association (NFA), the skilled work force expanded by 284 percent during this period.[1]

Unfortunately, CA leader Otis P. Briggs's local and national strike strategy of firing skilled union workers and hiring permanent replacements drastically reduced the available pool of workers to staff the complex machines of modern industry. As industrial education authority Charles A. Prosser noted in 1915: "The commercial prosperity and progress of the nation" rested on the ability of industry to solve the acute problem of supplying itself with the necessary trained workers.[2]

While the growth of American industry and the specialization of modern machinery steadily increased the demand for skilled labor, it also created a vast army of production workers who were needed to perform the simple and monotonous tasks required on the assembly line. Although these tasks were "socially and economically important" in their total impact on American industry, for the individual worker they were minute and simple operations that, when repeated endlessly, led to boredom and eventually alienation from the employer and the product of their labor.[3]

It was clear to industrial leaders and educators that social unrest among this great mass of uneducated laborers was a fertile ground for union organization and might threaten the stability of American society. The modern corporate employer wanted a worker who was loyal, dependable, punctual, cooperative, and a strict adherent to all company rules. The problem was a lack of what industrial educators termed "industrial intelligence." Industrial intelligence would allow workers to understand the total industrial process and appreciate the importance of their role. With proper training, the American laborer would realize the "dignity of work, the nobility of service," and labor agitation would fade away. The bottom line, as *Commercial West* pointed out, was that "The first command of Mother Nature is to hustle for your daily bread, and the first business of the public school should be to train the child for that service." The slogan, "education for life," in the early years of this century meant that "a boy or girl who is to be a manual worker should early learn the habit of work." The industrial order of American society depended on the education and acceptance of its values by the working class.[4]

As the demand for non-union skilled and unskilled workers grew, the lack of appropriate industrial training became apparent to the National Association of Manufacturers (NAM). The nation's public schools had failed to provide the vast number of trained workers needed, and union apprenticeship programs produced an inadequate supply of workers—workers who were hostile to open-shop employers. Following the 1872 example of R. Hoe and Company, a New York manufacturer of printing presses, many larger corporations established their own worker-training programs to meet their skilled manpower needs. Corporation schools usually involved on-the-job apprenticeship training combined with evening technical classes. These programs were designed to improve industrial production by increasing the efficiency of the work force.[5]

In addition, corporations hoped to weaken union disruptions by promoting industrial intelligence. Although the schools operated independently, they came together to organize the National Association of Corporation Schools in 1913, and in the next seven years increased their membership from thirty-seven to one hundred and forty-six schools. The combined efforts of the corporation schools were supplemented by the training programs of the national employer associations. By 1922, over twenty-five national employer groups, including the National Metal Trades Association (NMTA) and the National Founders' Association, were involved in employee training programs to support their open-shop members. While corporation schools developed a successful training model, the financial resources required restricted their development to the country's largest employers. The movement failed to provide the universal education that would maintain American industry.[6]

The growth of the corporation schools, however, was paralleled by the development of private, commercial, and philanthropic trade schools. The New

York Trade School, the country's first, formed in 1881, provided trade training with supplemental scientific instruction. Because the school was endowed by J. Pierpont Morgan and other wealthy benefactors, it could provide modern facilities and keep tuition low.[7]

Early trade schools usually required four years of training in a particular trade. The range of trades offered related to industrial demand, with the building and metal trades almost invariably part of a school's program. Although many of these full-time, long-term schools were extremely successful, they failed to meet the industrial needs of the American economy, primarily because they reached a very limited number of students and were excessively costly to establish and maintain.[8]

Beginning in Milwaukee in 1907, some of these private schools were taken over by local public school systems. Their programs gradually evolved into cooperative training that provided a combination of alternate weeks spent in school or in an industrial plant and in evening or part-time training. This allowed students to support themselves with full-time day jobs. Despite these adaptations, the private trade schools were graduating fewer than 5,000 students each year by 1921. Since the country needed over 100,000 skilled new workers each year, it was clear that the trade-school movement had failed. It would, however, provide a successful model for Minneapolis industry and the Citizens Alliance in 1914.[9]

With the realization that full-time trade schools were "not reaching millions and millions of children who become our mechanics," the NAM's education committee endorsed a system of basic public school education, industrial continuation school, and additional trade courses when necessary. To finance this system on a national scale, the NAM realized that state or federal aid would be required. With reluctance, the NAM joined industrial educators and the American Federation of Labor (AFL) in supporting the National Society for the Promotion of Industrial Education. This society believed that "The need for industrial education in the United States has become a social and industrial question of the first magnitude." NAM President James W. Van Cleave told the society that the nation must "give industrial education to all our American boys, beginning it in the lowest grades of our public primary schools, and making it free as the air and the sunlight." With committees in twenty-nine states, including Minnesota, and financial support from employer associations such as the National Metal Trades Association, the society waged a national educational campaign for publicly supported industrial education.[10]

In 1911, realizing that success lay in Washington, D.C., the Society for the Promotion of Industrial Education induced Dr. Charles A. Prosser, deputy commissioner of education of the state of Massachusetts, to become its secretary. Prosser traveled from state to state and to Washington promoting the society's principles. Industrial education historian Charles Bennett described Prosser's efforts as extremely influential because of his "legal knowledge, experience in Massachusetts, enthusiasm for vocational education, and exceptional ability as a public speaker."[11]

The rapid development of Minneapolis industry in the first decade of the twentieth century followed the pattern of the national economy. Even as the Citizens Alliance organized in the summer of 1903, CA publicist Herschel V. Jones called for an increase in manual training schools. He recognized that, for the open shop to be successful, "There is no knowledge, save the knowledge of right and wrong, that is more important to a community than a practical knowledge of mechanics."[12]

By 1908, with the open-shop battle raging in the machinist industry, Minneapolis machine shops needed 300 new machinists each year and would need an additional 800 machinists if all union machinists were to be replaced. The apprenticeship system in the remaining union shops was producing only forty machinists per year—and they were union machinists who were unacceptable to the CA. With scarcely any manual training schools in Minnesota and only three high schools offering machine-shop practice in their industrial education programs, the CA was forced to rely on machinists imported from other states to fill this gap. With the aid of the NFA and the NMTA, the CA could rely on an adequate supply of replacement workers for the short-term emergencies precipitated by strikes or lockouts that were part of its open-shop campaign. The national employer associations, however, faced the same shortage of skilled workers that confronted the CA locally. In the end, the CA realized that their open-shop workers would have to be trained in Minneapolis.[13]

The most obvious and practical solution was to have the public schools train the children of Minneapolis in the various trades. As early as 1905, *Commercial West* lobbied for an "ideal free school system, and the one this country must have if it remains in any full sense free, is a system where a boy is as free to learn bookbinding or plumbing or carpentry as he is to learn Latin or algebra." The CA's campaign for industrial training in the public schools included a passionate denunciation of the union apprenticeship system, which it called a "selfish, deliberate and inexcusable exclusion of our brightest youths from the trades . . . an unnatural and unjust condition of industry that must not be permitted to exist."[14]

This lobbying took a more concrete form in 1908, when the CA successfully pushed the Minneapolis School Board to ask the Minnesota legislature for the authority to issue $250,000 in bonds to establish a trade school. Although this effort failed, the CA lobbying did have some effect on Minnesota high schools. In the CA's first decade of existence, from 1903 to 1913, the percentage of Minnesota's high schools that had industrial education departments increased from 9.2 percent to 85.6 percent. Still, only six schools in the state in 1914 taught machine-shop practice. Without a vast expansion of these public school programs, the CA would continue to have trouble maintaining an adequate, trained, open-shop work force.[15]

Prospects for major advances in industrial education in Minnesota appeared bright in 1910 when the Minnesota State Federation of Labor (MSFL) followed the example of the AFL and endorsed the establishment of intermediate trade schools within the public schools and night schools with trade training in the various cities. Although the MSFL demanded that an "unbiased industrial history must be taught, which shall include an accurate account of the organization of the workers and the result there of," it was clear to the CA that the MSFL had endorsed the public training of its replacement workers for the CA members' businesses.[16]

The CA's trade school lobby, however, faced much stiffer opposition from Minneapolis unions, which were more intimately familiar with the CA's methods and objectives. The *Minneapolis Labor Review* said that the Stout trade school in Menomonie, Wisconsin, had provided "strikebreakers" in the bitterly fought machinists' and printers' strikes. Minneapolis unions could not agree with anyone who "advocates the erection of buildings and establishment of trade schools with public moneys, for we know, by indisputable evidence, that wherever such schools have been established, either under private or public control, they are breeders for strikebreakers."[17]

By 1912, with little success on the public front, *Commercial West* changed its tactics and endorsed a detailed plan by Professor Dexter D. Mayne, dean of the University of Minnesota Agricultural School, for a four million dollar vocational school at St. Anthony Park. The school would teach every possible trade to 8,000 students and be part of the state university system. *Commercial West* prophetically suggested: "Here is a field as yet untilled and where some man of large means could surely establish a monument for himself more enduring than granite and one that would be a tremendous benefit to the people of the state and nation for all future time." Having failed to excite the necessary public furor for industrial education, the CA now hoped desperately for an unnamed savior. *Commercial West* undoubtedly had a particular savior in mind in its 1912 editorial, for the Minneapolis business community had already been saved several times by William Hood Dunwoody.[18]

The CA, unlike its less-successful counterparts in other cities, received the solution to its work force problem as a gift from one of its richest and most influential members, William Hood Dunwoody. At eighteen, Dunwoody had entered his uncle's flour and grain business in Philadelphia. A few years later, he became a senior partner in the Philadelphia grain firm Dunwoody and Robertson and began a career that would take him to Minneapolis in 1869 and make him the leading member of the small, elite group of men who developed the great grain-milling industry of Minneapolis. Although Dunwoody was an officer and a major stockholder in ten Minnesota grain companies, his most important contributions were made at Washburn-Crosby Company. The preeminence of Minneapolis's mills grew to some degree from Dunwoody's leadership in 1876 in organizing a buying pool that created a virtual monopoly over grain trading in the Northwest.[19]

In 1877, Dunwoody went to Great Britain for Governor William D. Washburn and established direct connections to foreign markets, which would play a critical role in the growth of Minneapolis mills. Dunwoody's success propelled him into a leadership role as vice-president of Washburn-Crosby Company. The independence of the Washburn-Crosby mills and the future of milling in Minneapolis, however, were threatened in 1899 when eastern interests attempted to bring all the major flour mills of the United States into one huge corporation, which could then control the market. Dunwoody personally purchased the Washburn-Crosby mill from Governor Washburn's heirs, saving them from the takeover attempt.[20]

After stabilizing Minneapolis's flour industry with his private financial fortune, Dunwoody played a leadership role in the eradication of Washburn-Crosby's labor problem in the 1903 mill strike. It was from his position as president of Northwestern Bank that Dunwoody, during a 1907 financial panic, personally deposited one million dollars in Northwestern Bank to protect it against a run. As one of its most important members, Dunwoody would tackle the problem of creating an adequate supply of replacement workers for the CA.[21]

Dunwoody's fear of a shortage of skilled labor in the Washburn-Crosby mills inspired his interest in trade school education as early as the late 1890s. In the next decade, he would contact the Armour Institute in Chicago, the Tuskegee Institute in Alabama, and other notable trade schools, seeking specific information on operations and incorporation. Realizing the national importance of industrial training, Dunwoody quietly offered financial support to institutions in other cities.[22]

In 1911, Dunwoody's interest in industrial education began to take concrete form. Joseph W. Chapman, Dunwoody's vice-president at Northwestern Bank, led a campaign by the Minnesota Bankers' Association for educational reform of the state's public schools. Dunwoody, who had discussed his plans only with his close associates at Washburn-Crosby and Northwestern Bank, preferred to direct Chapman from the background. When Chapman was unable to make a fact-finding tour of Europe, in 1912, Dunwoody paid for and directed a committee of the Board of Education, led by CA member Horace N. Leighton, to make the trip. On its return from Europe, the committee reported directly to Dunwoody who, in conference with Chapman, was able to lay out a broad plan for an industrial institute. Dunwoody, however, died on February 8, 1914, before he could set his plan in motion.[23]

Fortunately for the CA, Dunwoody's 1913 will established the financial framework for a new private industrial institute that would provide the skilled workers needed to staff the city's open shops. Dunwoody stated in the thirty-ninth article of his Last Will and Testament:

> Believing that in the multiplied facilities for obtaining a liberal education by the youth of this state, enough attention has not been given to instruction in the industrial and mechanical arts, therefor, it is my purpose and desire to establish and endow a school to be called "The William Hood Dunwoody Industrial Institute," wherein shall be taught industrial and mechanical arts, giving as of special importance the art of milling and the construction of milling machinery, shall be given free to the youth of the city of Minneapolis and State of Minnesota without distinction on account of race, color or religious prejudice.[24]

After specific bequests were taken out of the Dunwoody estate, including one million dollars for the Minneapolis Society of Fine Arts (MSFA), nearly two million dollars remained for the endowment of Dunwoody's industrial school. Up to one-third of the fund was to be used to purchase a site and construct suitable buildings in Minneapolis, while 90 percent of the annual income from the remaining funds would be used to open and maintain the school. Dunwoody concluded that his purpose and aim was "to provide for all time a place where the youth of this city and state may, if they so desire, learn the different handicrafts and useful trades and thereby fit themselves for the better performance of life's duties." Dunwoody had also assured Washburn-Crosby and its CA brethren of an unending supply of skilled open-shop workers.[25]

Dunwoody's will also explicitly specified a twelve-person board of trustees to set up and direct his trade school. He believed strongly that a board should be a small group, primarily "businessmen, hard headed enough to look after the monetary affairs of the college [the institute] in a cool and practical way." Dunwoody's carefully selected board consisted of eight directors or executives of Washburn-Crosby Company, two executives of Northwestern Bank, and two executives of Minneapolis Trust Company—all of them close business associates and friends of Dunwoody's. The three companies with executives on the board represented three of the CA's five major financial backers. The will also gave the board the power to fill any vacancies caused by death or resignation "to the end that a continuity of purpose and the best interests of said school may be promoted and preserved."[26]

Dunwoody had created a trade school to be run exclusively and permanently by CA members acting in their own best interests. William H. Bovey, the general superintendent of Washburn-Crosby and a man with great scientific experience in the milling industry, was appointed president of the new board. Bovey immediately dispatched Joseph Chapman to Europe to further investigate the philosophy and operation of trade-school education. Chapman had been the closest confidant of Dunwoody's on the board and thus privy to Dunwoody's plans. He reported back to the board that the final aim of the undertaking should be: "The education of the citizen, *the education of the individual,* not only that he may take his place in the calling he has chosen, and that he may be able to stand *independent by virtue of his work,* but also that he shall contribute to the *well being of the body politic.*" Students at Dunwoody Institute would not only be prepared to fill the open shops of the CA, they would be taught to believe in the economic priorities of the Minneapolis business community. Dunwoody, through his will, had passed on his philosophy to the future of his city.[27]

William Hood Dunwoody Industrial Institute, occupying half of the old Central High School building at Fourth Avenue and Eleventh Street, opened its doors to seventy boys on December 14, 1914. Early advertisements addressed "To The Boys of Minnesota" asked: "What are you Going to Do For a Living?" and "Would You Like to Become a Skilled Workman?" Any boy in the state over fourteen years old was eligible for free instruction in ten trades.[28]

The institute was essentially masculine. Only a few girls and women attended classes in the printing or bakery shops. In addition to his chosen trade, each boy would be taught English, applied mathematics, drawing, industrial history, civics, elementary science, hygiene, and gymnastics. In its first year, students attended day school, full-time. By the second year, over 1,700 boys attended evening classes. While younger boys at Dunwoody generally spent half days in class and the other half in the shop, for an eighteen-month course, the more competent and industrious students were allowed to advance at their own pace unhampered by their slower classmates. Boys were encouraged to leave public school after eighth grade to seek the future employment advantages that a Dunwoody education promised. Once admitted to the institute, the board of trustees would determine whether or not a boy was able or willing to profit from the instruction.[29]

The trades considered appropriate for courses of instruction at Dunwoody Institute were chosen by the board of trustees, according to the demands of

Minneapolis business. Not surprisingly the first three courses offered—machine shop, printing, and carpentry—exactly matched the three industries in which the CA had launched concerted open-shop drives during its first decade. The machine shop at Dunwoody, which included a blacksmith shop, gas welding, and metallurgy, was instructing as many as 450 boys a week by 1917. The great demand for products, including the demand for war materials, and the stand taken for the open shop in the metal trades by the Twin City Employers of Machinists Association and the Citizens Alliance, had combined to make this Dunwoody's largest enrollment.[30]

The printing industry was Minneapolis's fourth-largest industry and had grown 22 percent between 1904 and 1909. Open shop since 1905, maintaining an adequate supply of printers was vital to the CA's control of Minneapolis's newspapers and magazines. In the building trades, Dunwoody offered a comprehensive program of day and evening classes, which included drafting and construction techniques. The expansion and development of Minneapolis's housing and commerce would, employers hoped, no longer be held hostage to union demands.[31]

Three years later, by 1917, the institute was supplying skilled workers for twenty-four different trades. Eventually, Dunwoody Institute would add departments in automobile, baking, electricity, painting, power, sheet metal, mechanical drafting, and highway construction. By 1927, over 35,000 students would have received training in sixty-five different trades covering the entire field of Minneapolis's commerce and industry.[32]

The demand of Minneapolis's expanding open-shop economy for skilled non-union workers was understood by the institute's board of trustees from the opening day at Central High School in 1914. Within a year of the start of the institute's first classes, the board used Dunwoody's endowment to purchase six city blocks across from the Parade Grounds on Wayzata Boulevard, near downtown Minneapolis. A month later, a committee toured the Boston School of Technology, the Carnegie Institute in Pittsburgh, and other eastern trade schools to gather information and ideas for the institute's architects. The contract for two football-field-sized buildings was awarded to Pike and Cook Company, one of the CA's original members, on August 23, 1916. An open design using only necessary supports for the second floors would give the school the flexibility to expand and change as industrial conditions demanded in the future. The two $750,000 buildings were occupied by the institute on Aug. 1, 1917. The final step outlined in Dunwoody's will had been executed.[33]

Despite Dunwoody Institute's large endowment and cohesive board of trustees, the school struggled through its first year without the benefit of an experienced educational leader. In his effort to establish business control over his school, Dunwoody had neglected to appoint a single vocational educator to his board. When Charles Allen Prosser, the secretary of the National Society for the Promotion of Industrial Education, visited Minneapolis in May 1915 to make an educational survey of the city, the board quickly moved to hire him as the director of the institute.[34]

Prosser, who had been a member of the important Douglas Commission in Massachusetts, superintendent of the New York Children's Aid Society, and assistant commissioner of education in Massachusetts, was considered a national authority on vocational education. More importantly for the board of trustees and the CA, Prosser understood the function of industrial education to weld the employer and the employee together. He quickly met with every employers' association and the employers of every industry in an effort to establish Dunwoody Institute as their first source of workers. Dunwoody Institute had "opened up, as it were, a funnel leading into industry."[35]

Prosser believed that "every fellow ought to have a chance to learn the thing he wants to learn," and that Dunwoody Institute would provide the boys of Minneapolis this opportunity. His motto for the school, "Opening the Way to Merit," was appropriate for the open shops that Dunwoody Institute students supplied. The CA had found in one man the experience and dedication to coordinate Minneapolis's open-shop industrial manpower needs, the training of skilled non-union workers, and the vocational guidance to bring these programs together.[36]

Prosser continued his lobbying efforts in Washington, D.C. The combined efforts of Prosser, the NAM, and the AFL led to the passage of the Smith-Hughes Act in 1917–18, which provided $1,700,000 to help establish vocational training in the public schools of each state. On August 15, 1917, Prosser, on leave from his permanent position as director of Dunwoody Institute in Minneapolis, was appointed director of the new federal Board of Vocational Education, which would guide and finance a new national system of industrial training. The NAM had achieved its goal of a federally financed system of industrial training. The uneasy truce between labor and business in the society would now become a battle for control of state training systems. The NAM, however, had Prosser, a close friend of the open shop, installed as the leader of American industrial education. By 1945, after thirty years as director of Dunwoody, Prosser would be a close friend of Minneapolis's industrial leaders and internationally noted as "the dean of vocational education."[37]

Prosser and the CA, however, had aims for Dunwoody Institute beyond teaching the skills of a trade and supplying trained graduates to Minneapolis industry. Dunwoody Institute's third aim was "to assist students in acquiring 'trade atmosphere' or a knowledge of the requisites of satisfactory service for

holding a position and obtaining advancement." Each student would be in-
doctrinated in "honesty, enthusiasm, determination, checking waste, preventing loafing on the job and inefficiency . . . remembering that the foreman
is boss," and "keeping in mind the interests of the concern for which he is
working." The tradesman must also be a good citizen, and "to be a good citizen a person must recognize superior authority and conform to rules of order which are enacted for the common good." Students were taught that:
"Your employer is your superior, and more entitled to your respect than you
are to his."[38]

In the Dunwoody Institute, ethical code and loyalty ranked next to obedience: "Loyalty to, and respect for, your employer, are as necessary as your duties in your work. Stand by him and with him, or leave him." Students were
warned that the primary evil in the industrial world was the ignorance that
led workers to "believe that the management is domineering, that its method
of manufacture are oppressive and wrong, and that the employer is making
enormous profits." The highly skilled workers produced in Dunwoody Institute's workshops would be of little use to the CA if they could be quickly recruited by union organizers. Instruction in "trade atmosphere" or "industrial
intelligence" was meant to forestall any union encroachment on the new
open-shop work force.[39]

Although Dunwoody Institute's primary role was supplying the "intelligent," skilled workers to maintain Minneapolis's open-shop economy over the
long term, Prosser's tight relationship with CA members enabled the institute
to adjust its programs on short notice when strikes created emergency manpower needs. When the automobile industries were hit by several strikes in
April 1920, Dunwoody Institute would play a crucial role in reestablishing the
open shop.[40]

Union members, starting in 1919, had quickly organized in the shops of a
number of Minneapolis vehicle manufacturers and garages. In early April,
union workers walked out on H. E. Wilcox Motor Car Company and thirty
other vehicle companies. Within a week, seven shops were shut down completely. Harry E. Wilcox, a member of the CA's executive committee, immediately called a meeting of the vehicle manufacturers from Minneapolis and St.
Paul. The thirty-seven firms formed the Twin City Vehicle Manufacturers' Association (TCVMA) and agreed unanimously to follow Wilcox's direction in
dealing with the labor crisis. Every member stated positively that there would
be no recognition of any labor organization and took a definite stand in favor
of the "open-shop basis of operation."[41]

Three weeks later, union automobile mechanics walked out of the city's
garages when employers refused their demands for ninety cents per hour and

a closed shop. The Minneapolis Garage Owners' Association joined with the Minneapolis Automobile Trade Association and the TCVMA to fight the union threat to their shared industry. The CA then directed the group's effort to eradicate any union presence in their shops. As a Boyd Transfer Company manager put it: "We are running an open shop, but it is closed against members of organized labor." All workers affiliated with organized labor were discharged. A blacklist was shared among automotive employers and CA members.[42]

The automobile industry's open-shop policy created an immediate and long-term shortage of skilled tradesmen. The termination of union employees shut down a number of shops, and the blacklist would keep these skilled workmen from returning. The Garage Owners' Association turned almost immediately to Dunwoody Institute in an attempt to keep their shops open. The institute supplied partially trained boys to the city's garages to help break the strike. The young workers were paid eight dollars to ten dollars per week to perform tasks for which they had not yet been trained. Despite efforts of the TCVMA to help supply a sufficient work force for the most seriously affected employers, the vehicle manufacturers realized "that the industrial future of the vehicle business is largely dependent on the establishment of a definite means for training men for such trades."[43]

On April 13, less than two weeks after the unions had walked out, the TCVMA contacted Dunwoody Institute to discuss the "establishment of a department for the special training of those who wish to become skilled in the various trades connected with the vehicle business." On April 19, Harry W. Kavel, assistant director of Dunwoody Institute, attended the TCVMA meetings to begin the organization of a training program for automobile woodworkers, blacksmiths, trimmers, and painters. Committees for these departments were appointed to confer with the institute and arrange a suitable program. The Minneapolis Garage Owners' Association followed suit and opened up its own negotiations to establish an institute program for the "better and more complete training of automobile mechanics." The automobile industry was determined that it would never again close its shops because of a lack of skilled workers.[44]

Prosser and Kavel suggested a full-time, one-year course in vehicle body building, followed by a two-year apprenticeship in the industry, combined with evening classes at the institute. The industry's open shops, however, were in a manpower crisis and couldn't wait a full year before they employed their new body builders. The TCVMA committee designed a three-year apprenticeship program that allowed the first-year student to work every other week in a TCVMA shop. For every two students, the employer would gain an immediate full-time employee who would gradually gain the necessary skills to keep the industry's open shops in business. The new apprentices would receive 50 percent of a journeyman's wage only for their shop time; the alternate week at the institute was unpaid. Wages were gradually increased to 95 percent of journeyman wages by the end of the third year. The three-year program would end with a Dunwoody Institute diploma and a full-time job in a TCVMA shop.[45]

The apprentice agreed in a signed contract to take any further part-time classes the TCVMA set up at Dunwoody Institute and to remain in the shop of his employer at least one year after graduation. The contract was intended to reduce labor turnover and the shifting of young learners from one employer to another. The TCVMA knew that the contract was legally meaningless: "It is in effect a gentleman's agreement, but it always results in a steadying employment because everyone dislikes to break a written promise."[46]

The contracts also formalized the close relationship between Dunwoody Institute and the TCVMA. Although the classes were taught at the institute, a committee of the TCVMA assisted the institute in formulating the courses to be taught, keeping them up-to-date, and securing competent teachers for the program. The committee would also loan Dunwoody Institute drawings, blueprints, models, and other materials for these classes. Individual members of the TCVMA would visit classes and make helpful suggestions.[47]

The TCVMA would also play a crucial role in recruiting students. Young men applying for employment in TCVMA shops were urged to first attend the Dunwoody Institute program. Advertising bulletins, pamphlets, or displays developed by the institute would be circulated among employees in TCVMA shops. Employees who attended Dunwoody evening classes would also be given preference in promotions within the TCVMA shops. The actual contracts that would seal the employer, the apprentice, and Dunwoody Institute into the three-year program were administered by Secretary Soderquist of the TCVMA. In effect, the vehicle body building training program at Dunwoody was created and operated as a joint venture between the school and the open-shop vehicle manufacturers, who were engaged in a battle to win a strike and eradicate unions from their shops. The CA could confidently lead the general open-shop charge, knowing that Dunwoody Institute would supply the working troops.[48]

The open-shop troops, however, had to move efficiently from Dunwoody Institute to their places in the front lines of the CA's industrial members. Although the institute had, from its inception, successfully trained young men in their respective trades and in an industrial attitude amenable to the CA's open-shop philosophy, the institute could flourish only if its graduates found gainful employment in Minneapolis industry. Despite the dominant role of CA members on the institute's board of trustees, hiring in Minneapolis industry was traditionally handled in a haphazard fashion by foremen or department heads and was unlikely to link up with the school.[49]

Realizing that there was no systematic way of selecting, training, hiring, and promoting workers, Prosser set out to meet with every employers' association and major employer in Minneapolis and establish their personnel and training needs. By 1917, Prosser had established relationships with twenty-four different industries. Employers in each trade agreed to take graduates from Dunwoody Institute, the Girls' Vocational High School, or Central High School as their first source of supply. Prosser had, indeed, opened up a "funnel" leading into the industries of the CA.[50]

In Dunwoody Institute's part-time, in-service training programs, the relationship with CA companies was closer and more financial in nature. Employers agreed to pay bricklayers half their wages during the slack season, for example, if they took classes at Dunwoody. The funds were held in escrow by the board of trustees to be paid to the students when they finished the two-month program. By 1917, Dunwoody was planning to expand the program to include painters, plasterers, and plumbers.[51]

In 1931, the Civic and Commerce Association recognized that the value of Dunwoody Institute to the city of Minneapolis and the state of Minnesota could "scarcely be overestimated." Of all the industrial trade schools in the world, Dunwoody Institute had the largest endowment, the largest enrollment, the largest investment in plant and equipment, and it taught the largest spread of trades. William H. Dunwoody's enormous financial bequest had eliminated the problems that restricted the national trade-school movement. With land and buildings paid for, a huge operating budget for staff, free tuition for students, and an open-shop city waiting to hire them, Dunwoody Institute was able to flourish.[52]

More than 50,000 students had acquired or sharpened their industrial skills at the institute by 1931. The CA, without any expenditure, had a guaranteed source of non-union labor. In the crucial machine-shop industry, Dunwoody Institute trained 85 percent of the new workers needed for the rapidly growing industry. This had a dramatic impact on the CA's ability to operate on an open-shop basis. *Commercial West* had accurately predicted the future in 1914, when it said: "In the years to come, when businessmen may go to such a school [Dunwoody] and obtain boys and girls trained in practical work for every line of business, they will daily remember with blessings the man who made this school possible."[53]

The struggle for the open shop in Minneapolis, however, was intertwined with the larger efforts of the national employer associations. The CA realized that success in Minneapolis would be difficult if the union movement succeeded across the United States. Playing its part in this national effort, Dunwoody Institute established cooperative arrangements with a number of national manufacturing and retailing associations. In many cases, the institute set up training programs directly for particular national companies. From 1928 to 1931, fifty-eight Dunwoody Institute students were sent to International Business Machine (IBM) Company of Endicott, New York. After an additional four-month course at the factory school, the boys were sent to various branches across the country, principally as service men. Dunwoody Institute's highly skilled and industrially "intelligent" students were in demand throughout the United States. This drain of Minneapolis's skilled trainees was compounded after World War I by an upsurge of union organization. Although Dunwoody would still supply the majority of Minneapolis's open-shop employers' skilled workers, it was not always enough.[54]

To bridge the training gap, the CA led Minneapolis industry in establishing and using trade schools directed by employers. During the 1920s, the CA would supplement Dunwoody Institute's classes with successful employer trade schools for metal trade workers, building trade workers, plumbers and steamfitters, electricians, printers and engravers, decorators, and bakers. A concerted union drive in the building trades beginning in 1920, combined with the CA's intensive educational efforts, created a flurry of trade-school activity.[55]

Open-shop contractors in Minneapolis and St. Paul quickly realized that "something must be done to start a new order of things" and formed the Minnesota Building Trades School, Inc. By March of 1921, over 350 students had enrolled in the school's bricklaying class. The school's six-month, ten-dollar tuition course was designed to eliminate union control over the supply of workers in the building trades. The growth of the Twin Cities would be under open-shop conditions. Smaller schools popped up when strikes or lockouts dramatically increased the demand for skilled workers in a given trade. During a 1921 printers' strike, the employers started a regular printers' school, "where boys can be taught the printer's trade without restrictions, limitations, or cost."[56]

The CA, in its *Special Weekly Bulletin*, advocated an employer school in every industry. Within three years, the printing industry was 90 percent open shop and the building industry 70 percent. While these schools helped extinguish union hot spots, it was Dunwoody Institute that formed the bedrock of the CA's battle for the open shop and was one of the primary reasons that Minneapolis was the United States' most open-shop city.[57]

6 The CA's Oligarchy and the Minneapolis Renaissance

THE SUCCESS OF THE CITIZENS ALLIANCE'S DRIVE to establish the open shop depended on the close cooperation of its diverse membership. This unity was constantly threatened by the intense competitive environment of Minneapolis's rapidly expanding economy. Cutthroat competition between CA members would bankrupt industries and destroy the corporate unity that had allowed the CA to so effectively suppress unions.

The common philosophy of anti-unionism held by Minneapolis's leading businesses, however, was not the only or even the most important cohesive force unifying the Citizens Alliance. The social and economic structure that had grown from common Yankee entrepreneurial roots had created an oligarchy to rule Minneapolis. The Minneapolis Business Union and the financial empires of Northwestern National Bank and First National Bank had helped create an economic interrelationship among most of the city's leading businessmen. The Minneapolis Civic and Commerce Association (CCA) and the Minneapolis Commercial Club had fostered shared civic responsibilities, and the Minneapolis Club and other social institutions had cemented the economic leaders into a social clique. Minneapolis leaders played golf at the Minikahda Club, and they sent their sons to The Blake School and their daughters to Northrop Collegiate School. In many cases, fostered by these close and long-term family associations, the children of these leaders married, creating even tighter family relationships among businesses.

Out of these social ties, a code of ethics developed that encompassed an understanding and sympathy that went beyond the mutual interest in destroying labor unions that had created the Citizens Alliance. The unity of the CA was held together by the many strands that bind an oligarchy together. Without the emergence of this ruling clique, it is doubtful that the CA would have maintained its single-purpose unity decade after decade.[1]

The social heart of Minneapolis's oligarchy began to beat in 1883 in the elegant rooms of the Minneapolis Club on the second floor of the Syndicate Building, where leading businessmen like Governor John S. Pillsbury, Charles

M. Loring, John Crosby, Alonzo C. Rand, and Martin B. Koon gathered to play cards and smoke cigars. The nine rooms were exquisitely furnished and decorated by John S. Bradstreet. The new, exclusively male club had grown out of the outdated social organization, the "Silver Grays," and was incorporated in 1885. Judge Koon, who would found the Citizens Alliance eighteen years later, chaired the first annual meeting and was president of the club in 1885 and 1887. He remained deeply interested in the club until his death in 1912. Despite its distinguished founders, the Minneapolis Club struggled for the next fifteen years under a large debt and a decline in membership. Only the dedicated efforts of Koon, Charles C. Bovey, Walter W. Heffelfinger, Charles M. Harrington, and Frederick C. Pillsbury kept the club alive and guaranteed the Citizens Alliance a spiritual home for the future.[2]

The close relationship between the Minneapolis Club and the Citizens Alliance went far beyond Judge Koon's involvement in creating both organizations. From 1903 through 1917, each of the club's fifteen presidents was a Citizens Alliance member. During the CA's expansion years, more than 150 members gathered at the club. This long list included many of the CA's most influential backers: John S. Pillsbury and Franklin Crosby of the flour milling industry, lumber magnates Arthur R. Rogers and Eugene J. Carpenter; and Edward W. Decker and Francis A. Chamberlain of the banking industry. Although Otis P. Briggs never joined the club, CA president Albert W. Strong was an active member and sang in the barbershop quartet in 1919.

The exclusiveness of this elite group was maintained by restrictive membership rules. Although applicants required the support of four members for nomination, most of these names gathered dust on the club's bulletin board. By 1926, more than eighty-two applicants languished on the nomination list. The solidarity of the club was also strengthened by rules that gave membership preference to sons and sons-in-law of current members. The club, through this rule, was able to reinforce the hereditary nature of Minneapolis's oligarchy. Franklin Crosby, club president in 1910, was followed by his son, George, in 1951; John S. Pillsbury, president in 1911, was followed by his son John S. Pillsbury, Jr., in 1960. The hereditary leadership of Minneapolis industries was shadowed closely by the social milieu at the city's elite club.

The real and symbolic leadership of the club was assumed in a stormy meeting on a hot summer night in 1905, when Judge Koon convinced the governing committee that a vastly enlarged and improved clubhouse was essential. A group of Citizens Alliance leaders was appointed to the building and advisory committee, which let the contract for the club's new citadel to Pike and Cook, an open-shop contractor and CA member. In eighteen months, while the

CA fought a bitter strike against machinists and metal workers, Frederick M. Crosby pushed through the construction of the new clubhouse, complete with its central turret.

The building committee reported: "The building, furnishings, and equipment are probably the most modern, complete, and elegant of any club west of New York." Like any self-respecting castle, the new home of Minneapolis's oligarchy was liberally decorated with a distinctive new coat of arms. The club's emblem featured a pine tree and a sheaf of wheat to "signify the original sources of the city's prosperity," the North Star, and the sign of St. Anthony of Padua, the patron saint of Father Hennepin, the first European to discover the Falls of St. Anthony.

Inside the new clubhouse, the city's business leaders relaxed in the luxury of rooms that were "the masterpieces of their designer, John S. Bradstreet." Art nouveau fixtures lit up the massive ceiling beams, the Spanish leather walls, and the cavernous fireplaces. For the pleasure and convenience of its members, the club provided a valet, a barbershop, a bar, a grill serving meals at all times, a massage room, a billiard room, bowling alleys, card tables, a swimming pool, and squash courts.

Membership and most of the club functions were men-only; women were allowed dining privileges but had to enter from the building's back door. Once inside, however, the dining was excellent. Club members and their guests sampled imported beluga caviar, lobster cocktails, New York oysters, saddle of lamb, roast ribs of beef au jus, new asparagus with Hollandaise, and a vast assortment of cheeses and desserts. After-dinner conversation was enjoyed with fine cigars—$53,975 worth per year.[3]

More importantly, as Minneapolis Club historian William C. Edgar writes, "Within its walls, the influence of its members, expressed and exercised informally, has actually been the determining factor in practically all of the important movements that have contributed to the city's welfare and progress since it was organized." From the arts to the education of the oligarchy's children, the club would serve as an incubator for change.[4]

On January 10, 1911, Judge Koon presided over a dinner at the club at which funds were subscribed to launch the Minneapolis Institute of Arts. Four years later, Northrop Collegiate School's board of trustees held its first meeting at the club to organize the school that would educate the daughters of club members. During World War I, club members created a businessmen's army, the Civilian Auxiliary, which was used to suppress the 1917 streetcar strike. When the peril of civil war threatened Minneapolis during the 1934 truck drivers' strike, it was a meeting between Governor Floyd B. Olson and Minneapolis employers at the club that precipitated Olson's deployment of the

National Guard to enforce martial law on the city. With only one meeting of the full Citizens Alliance board of directors each year, the unity and strategy of the CA relied on the secret, informal deliberations behind the red brick walls of the Minneapolis Club to facilitate their war on labor unions.[5]

Club members also met frequently on the fairways and greens of the Minikahda Club. In the fall of 1898, banker Clive T. Jaffray brought CA founder Judge Koon and two CA members, Northwest Bank President Joseph W. Raymond and grain merchant Charles M. Harrington, to an Excelsior hill. There he convinced them that this was the spot where Minneapolis's business elite should play golf. "Prominent men of the city" immediately pledged $50,000 to form the new golf club. William C. Edgar, who later would create the Minneapolis Club crest, proposed as the club name the Indian word for "by the side of water": *Minikahda*. The club emblem was the shield of "Swift Dog," an eminent Ojibwe chief.[6]

The next summer, on July 15, 1899, Judge Koon drove the first ball on the Minikahda course. The clubhouse was built by open-shop contractor Pike and Cook. The Minikahda, like the Minneapolis Club, was closely associated with the leaders and members of the Citizens Alliance. In the club's first twenty-five years, eleven prominent CA members served as president. CA founder Judge Koon served as club president from 1898–1900; CA President Albert W. Strong was club president in 1912–1913; and CA treasurer Charles B. Mills was president in 1922–23. Between these two exclusive clubs, Minneapolis's business elite were able to merge their business and leisure lives and create a social oligarchy.

Perpetuating this elite required the best possible education for the sons and grandsons of the leaders of the CA—an education that they felt could only be found in eastern schools such as Yale, Harvard, Dartmouth, and Princeton, where their sons would mingle with the sons of the country's most powerful industrialists. In November 1910, Washburn-Crosby executive Charles C. Bovey addressed the difficulty that Minneapolis boys were having in eastern schools. Minneapolis needed a permanent private school like the small academy started by William M. Blake in 1907.[7]

"The founding of such a school means a permanent asset in Minneapolis, not only to a man's sons but to his grandsons, to the city in general," said Bovey. Within two months, seventeen business leaders, including CA backers William H. Dunwoody, Charles S. Pillsbury, Elbert L. Carpenter, Charles D. Velie, and Thomas B. Janney each pledged $2,500 toward the school's operating budget and a new building. By October 30, 1912, Pike and Cook Company had constructed a large, brick Tudor-Gothic building that included a chapel, library, gymnasium, assembly hall, lockers, and plunge bath.[8]

The quartet of Washburn-Crosby executives brought in Charles B. Newton from an eastern preparatory school to run the new day school in Minneapolis. Newton brought four eastern teachers with him to set up a departmentalized system of instruction. Newton denied that Blake was a "school for rich men's sons," declaring that Blake's principles were efficiency and loyalty. The school would have fewer studies and more instructors than public schools to increase the thoroughness of each boy's education.[9]

With the new commitment of the business community, Blake quickly doubled its enrollment. In 1919, however, Newton resigned after revealing that the school's finances were on shaky ground. At an emergency meeting called by John S. Pillsbury and Charles Bovey, Pillsbury suggested that "Blake would have a more democratic effect on his sons than the public schools." Pillsbury contributed $10,000 to a fund drive that netted $88,000 in one evening. The future education of Minneapolis's hereditary oligarchy was assured. From 1913 to 1974, Blake would graduate 1,710 students representing several generations of Minneapolis's leading business families and send these sons on for training in East Coast colleges.

Now that they had established a boys' school, three of Blake's trustees, John Crosby, Frederick B. Wells, and Charles D. Velie turned their attention to the Graham Hall Girls School. On July 30, 1915, the first trustee meeting of the newly incorporated Northrop Collegiate School was held at the Minneapolis Club. The trustees moved quickly to purchase a large tract of land next to the armory facing Kenwood Parkway and the Parade Grounds not far from Lowry Hill. Hewitt and Brown, also the architects of Blake, designed a large, dignified building with an imposing central turret.[10]

The Northrop program would educate elite young women from kindergarten to the sophomore year of college, including studies in home economics, science, chemistry, physics, biology, nature study, and geography. Another area of the school was devoted to art and manual training and included a pottery room, kiln, sewing room, and art studio. An alumnae room was built to encourage the relationships begun at the school. Although the boardrooms of the CA and its members continued to be male-only bastions, the daughters of Minneapolis's business elite could now prepare for Vassar and Wellesley at Northrop Collegiate.[11]

The leaders of the Citizens Alliance looked to the East during the late nineteenth and early twentieth century for much more than the education of their children. The great accumulations of wealth by eastern industrialists and financiers like Carnegie, Morgan, and Vanderbilt had enabled these men to sponsor an American cultural renaissance. They may have been motivated by a simple desire to display their wealth and prestige, a patronizing need to educate the ignorant public, or a proud patriotism that had to glorify American civilization. Whatever the reasons, the grand public gestures of these men created the foundation of many of the country's major cultural institutions: libraries, museums, orchestras, and operas.[12]

Between 1907 and 1911, for example, the country's art museums, art societies, and art schools more than doubled to 944. These museums were intellectual and educational temples that collected and displayed European "masterpieces." The buildings that housed these institutions, like the homes of their rich patrons, were monumental edifices to the glory of capitalism. The castles and temples of Europe would now become part of the American architectural landscape. The elite and newly rich businessmen of Minneapolis watched these eastern expressions of wealth and quickly followed the cultural example of the nation's great capitalists.[13]

Lumber magnate and CA founder Thomas B. Walker assumed the role as leader and spokesman for the Minneapolis renaissance as early as the 1870s. Dubbed one of the country's ten wealthiest men by the *New York Times*, Walker was a confirmed capitalist who believed that the poor should use their strong arms to elevate themselves just as he had. Successful American businessmen, honoring a sense of noblesse oblige, had "contributed more to the upbuilding of the public institutions that are contributing so vastly to public welfare than has ever been known in any time or nation." The dissemination of intelligence to "the vulgar, ill bred would help build up the sound morality and healthy tone of public sentiment." The creation of public museums and libraries "would be most useful in this world of prejudice and hatred . . . in establishing better relations among the different classes."[14]

Walker, who had made a close study of socialism and understood its appeal, realized that his lumber empire and capitalism itself would flourish only if the public were trained into an appreciation of the American system. The creation of great public cultural institutions would also reflect on the prosperity and wealth of the city of Minneapolis. Walker and his fellow CA founders identified the image of Minneapolis closely with their own image. The establishment of an impressive art museum "would aid very greatly in making Minneapolis one of the finest and most attractive cities in the world." A great city would attract the most valuable and substantial citizens of the country to Minneapolis and help the city flourish. As Minneapolis's cultural importance increased, it would also increase the stature of its leaders among the tycoons of the East. Walker realized that as the economy and the image of Minneapolis rose, so would his own fortunes.[15]

Shortly after arriving in Minneapolis in 1862, Walker joined other businessmen in supporting the fledgling Minneapolis Athenaeum. Although the

Athenaeum gradually collected more than 15,000 books in its first two decades, these books remained inaccessible to the general public. Walker, believing that "a library will accomplish more towards civilizing, and improving the condition of the people than all the public schools we possess," led a revolution within the Athenaeum to liberalize its rules. Chairs and lights were brought in, reading room hours were extended, and the price of membership greatly reduced.[16]

In 1885, Walker, from his influential position at the Athenaeum, the Minneapolis Society of Fine Arts, and the Academy of Natural Sciences, helped establish an agreement with the City of Minneapolis to erect a library building to house the three groups and the Minneapolis Public Library. Walker, Thomas Lowry, William S. King, William D. Washburn, and the C. A. Pillsbury Company donated $5,000 each toward a private subscription of more than $60,000 to finance the construction of the first downtown library at Tenth Street and Hennepin Avenue.[17]

Walker, Lowry, and Judge Koon were all appointed to the new library board, where they quickly orchestrated an agreement for the Athenaeum to pool resources with the public library. Despite this impressive beginning, however, the growth of the city soon revealed the disadvantage of a single downtown library. Walker, president of the library board from its inception until his death in 1928, pushed continually for the expansion of the branch library system to give all citizens equal access to the library's collections. Minneapolis's wealthiest industrialists stepped in to establish new branch libraries. John S. Pillsbury donated land near the Pillsbury "A" Mill and built a suitably luxurious branch library of white marble furnished with mahogany. Charles C. Webber, a CA member and executive at Deere Webber Company, donated the second floor of a park building that he was financing for another branch.

In 1910, Walker argued that the city needed still more branches "to offset these temptations and demoralizing influences which to an ever-increasing extent afflict society." A year earlier, Walker had backed his conviction with the donation of land at Twenty-ninth and Hennepin for a branch library next to the new West High School. In 1912, Walker proudly asserted that Minneapolis had the highest per capita circulation of books of any major city in the country. The same year, Walker's national counterpart, the Carnegie Corporation, donated $125,000 for the establishment of four more branch libraries. By 1916, the main library and its sixteen branches were circulating more than a million and one-half books per year.[18]

Walker had begun collecting paintings and prints for his house on Eighth Street and Hennepin Avenue in 1874, "with the motive and intention of establishing a magnificent art and science collection for the benefit and use of the public." For the next forty years, he attended art sales on the East Coast and had dealers procure paintings, porcelains, pottery, jade, ancient glass, gemstones, and ancient Greek, Babylonian, Egyptian, Chinese, Persian, and Roman art collections from London and Paris.[19]

In 1879, Walker built a skylit gallery behind his residence, the first public art gallery in the Northwest, where visitors could view twenty paintings free. By 1916, his collection, which compared favorably with the leading private collections and public galleries of the country, filled fourteen rooms. Noted art historian Professor Eugen Neuhaus reported that the collection displayed a "comprehensiveness, variety of subjects and artistic quality" that revealed a "restrained note of aristocratic refinement."

Walker, however, was not alone in his appreciation and support for the arts. On January 31, 1883, the Minneapolis Society of Fine Arts (MSFA) was incorporated "To advance the knowledge and love of art through the exhibition of works of art, lectures upon subjects pertaining to art, the acquisition of books and papers for the formation of an art library." Unfortunately, the fledgling arts organization lacked the funds to operate a museum or start an art school. From his position as head of a campaign to raise money for a new public library building, Walker came to the rescue. In exchange for supporting the campaign, the society would receive quarters in the new building. Douglas Volk of New York directed the Minneapolis School of Art in a house on Hennepin Avenue in 1886.[20]

After three years in makeshift quarters, the school's building problem was finally solved in 1889 when it moved into the new library building, although raising operating funds remained a serious difficulty. In 1892, Thomas Lowry undertook a guaranty fund drive. CA leaders Walker, Judge Koon, Charles Pillsbury, James S. Bell, William H. Dunwoody, E. J. Phelps, and other businessmen donated funds to help hire teachers and keep the school functioning. With attendance supported by a scholarship fund donated by a CA member, more than 6,000 students would attend the art school over the next thirty-seven years.[21]

While the art school flourished, the goal of establishing a large permanent art exhibit languished in the expectation that Walker, with his own extraordinary collection as the foundation, would lead a movement to establish a major art museum in Minneapolis. At a meeting of prominent businessmen at the Minneapolis Club in 1907, a decision was made to push ahead without Walker. The next year, Dorilus Morrison privately agreed to donate the family's ten-acre estate in south Minneapolis if $500,000 could be raised for the construction of a museum building. When Dunwoody heard of Morrison's offer, he pledged $100,000 if the additional $400,000 could be raised.[22]

The society recruited CA lumberman Eugene J. Carpenter to lead the fund drive and Herschel V. Jones of the *Minneapolis Journal* to publicize the project. Dunwoody, John Van Derlip, Judge Koon, Carpenter, society president Edwin H. Hewitt, and E. C. Gale invited 200 prospective donors to dinner at the Minneapolis Club on January 10, 1911. The announcement of the Morrison and Dunwoody bequests galvanized the members of the Citizens Alliance to pledge a quarter of a million dollars in ninety minutes. The Citizens Alliance's three major financial backers, the Pillsburys, Twin City Rapid Transit, and the Washburn-Crosby Company, donated a combined total of $90,000. Within three weeks, Carpenter had raised $520,180 for the Minneapolis Institute of Arts.[23]

The problem of purchasing art to fill the proposed building was solved in 1914, when Dunwoody died. His will left a one-million-dollar trust fund and stipulated that the interest ($50,000 in 1916) could be used solely for purchasing art for the Minneapolis Art Institute. The "revolution of 1911" had brought new leadership to the art movement, created a great new museum, and left a legacy of art philanthropy that would endure through future generations of Minneapolis's oligarchy.[24]

Lumber magnate T. B. Walker, angry at the city for refusing to build a museum to exhibit his collection and at the business community for creating an art institute without him, refused to take part in the fund raising or to donate his art collection. After briefly flirting with San Francisco officials, Walker established the T. B. Walker Foundation in 1925 "to promote educational, artistic and scientific interests." Reflecting the architecture of the American renaissance, the new Walker Art Center on Lowry Hill featured Moorish terra cotta tiles, Romanesque colonnades on the façade, and a grand staircase inside. At the request of CA President Briggs, the contract and subcontracts were let to open-shop contractors.[25]

The American renaissance had also inspired a major expansion of the country's key orchestras in Boston, Philadelphia, Chicago, Cincinnati, and St. Louis. In 1903, Emil Oberhoffer, director of the Minneapolis Philharmonic Club, a local choral group, became frustrated with the difficulties of maintaining the quality of the group's orchestral accompaniment with amateur and temporary musicians. At Oberhoffer's suggestion, Elbert L. Carpenter, a wealthy CA lumberman and brother of E. J. Carpenter, held a luncheon meeting in the spring of 1903 to organize a guaranty fund drive to support a permanent symphony orchestra in Minneapolis.[26]

The CA's first president, Edmund J. Phelps, became one of the leading spirits of the campaign at the same time that he was organizing the CA. Within a couple of months, forty-four of Minneapolis's wealthiest industrialists had signed on to a fund of $30,000 to support the new orchestra for three years.

Almost all of them had also joined Phelps's new organization, the Citizens Alliance, pledging at the same time to support a symphony orchestra and the open shop.[27]

That summer, with the campaign gathering funds, Oberhoffer toured Europe, recruiting musicians for the new symphony orchestra. By September 1903, he had assembled fifty musicians and expanded the orchestra's inadequate music library. The next month, while Pillsbury and Washburn-Crosby built barricades around the milling district in their desperate war with union millers, the orchestra that the flour-milling executives had helped pay for was rehearsing three times a week.[28]

On November 5, 1903, with all the flour mills back into production, Minneapolis's business oligarchy fought its way through a raw, blustery wind to attend the first concert of the Minneapolis Symphony Orchestra at the old Exposition Building on Main Street on the riverfront. Oberhoffer, elegantly attired in top hat, silk cape, and gold-headed cane, led the finest orchestra concert in Minneapolis history. Despite a very thin string section, reviewers praised Oberhoffer as a marvelous, self-possessed director who had created, in a very short time, a surprisingly fine orchestra. "But would it last?" they asked. The orchestra needed a building to play in and the continued support of the business community.[29]

Within two years, W. F. Bechtel, president of Northwestern National Life Insurance Company, had built an auditorium at Eleventh Street and Nicollet Avenue in exchange for the sale of two million dollars in insurance policies. In March of 1905, the glamorous and wealthy of Minneapolis, bedecked in fineries and gems, strolled from their carriages to await the rise of the curtain, on which was painted the Acropolis. The four-day festival included a concert version of *Aida* with imported soloists.[30]

With the building issue settled, Carpenter and Phelps set out to solidify the orchestra's financial backing. In 1906, the guaranty fund was increased to $30,000 annually, and the next year the Orchestral Association of Minneapolis was incorporated, with Carpenter as president. Citizens Alliance leaders such as Dunwoody, Pillsbury, George Draper Dayton, Franklin M. Crosby, Sumner T. McKnight, and George H. Partridge joined the orchestra's board of directors and helped the guaranty fund rise to $125,000 per year by 1918. The increased financial support allowed the orchestra to expand to eighty-five full-time musicians and to have daily rehearsals. The profits of the open shop had created the nation's eighth major orchestra in its eighteenth largest city.[31]

The massive accumulation of the Minneapolis' oligarchy's wealth also fueled an architectural renaissance of the city's public, business, and residential buildings. To design the pride of Minneapolis's cultural development, the

Society of Fine Arts brought in the leading architectural firm of the American renaissance, McKim, Mead, and White of New York. To symbolize the values, permanence, and dignity of the Minneapolis Institute of Arts, the architects designed a central façade with many steps beneath six Ionic columns, which supported an unembellished entablature and pediment. The monumental stairs and extremely high ceilings of the interior also seem to be built for their symbolic status rather than for practical use. Despite the fact that only a part of the original grandiose plans was constructed, the Art Institute stood with the dignity of a Roman temple above Fair Oaks Park in South Minneapolis—a tribute to the wealth and importance that the Citizens Alliance had brought to the Minneapolis business community.[32]

Across the park from the Art Institute stood Fair Oaks, the most impressive domestic palace in Minneapolis. William D. Washburn had amassed a fortune by the 1880s in the lumber, railroad, and milling industries. The Washburn family dominated early Minneapolis waterpower, and its firm, Washburn-Crosby Company, would become one of the CA's most important backers. Washburn commissioned E. Townsend Mix of Milwaukee to design his nineteenth-century gothic mansion. Constructed on a massive scale of Kasota stone, the Fair Oaks tower stood ninety feet, dwarfing the surrounding trees.[33]

Inside, no expense was spared. The vestibule floor was mosaic, the walls were marble wainscoting, and the ceiling was frescoed. The twenty-two-feet by thirty-eight-feet Louis the Fourteenth-style drawing room was covered in tapestry silks and graced by a mantel of onyx and inlaid and gilt rosewood woodwork. The house's fourteen bedrooms were served by a $20,000 plumbing system. After dinner, the businessmen of the family would ride the elevator to the billiard room. Along with its ten-acre park, Fair Oaks was valued at $750,000 in the mid-1880s. Minneapolis clearly had its own Vanderbilt.[34]

Most of the houses of Minneapolis's oligarchy, however, were designed by local architecture firms closely associated with the CA or the CCA. After examining a number of plans, William H. Dunwoody selected William C. Whitney to design a mansion suitable for the president of Northwest Bank. Dunwoody, who had traveled extensively in England promoting the sale of Minneapolis flour, was intimately involved in the detailed planning of his $250,000 Elizabethan-Tudor home. "Overlook" was constructed in 1906 on the brow of Lowry hill overlooking the Parade Grounds and downtown Minneapolis. An elevator helped the family move around the forty-room, five-level house, which was set into the hill.[35]

A visitor entered Overlook under a stone-pillared portico, through a pair of massive wrought-iron doors and down a hallway paneled in Corsican walnut to the grand staircase. The huge library featured an intricately designed mosaic fireplace and a view of the new Basilica. A formal garden enclosed in a stone balustrade graced the five-acre grounds. A large millstone from one of the Washburn-Crosby Company mills, perhaps representing the source of Minneapolis's and Dunwoody's prosperity, was prominently displayed in the gardens.

In the case of prominent Minneapolis architect Leroy S. Buffington, "architecture for the elite" became an entire career. He gained a reputation for the "grandiose, but elegant" buildings that he designed for the Pillsbury family. During John S. Pillsbury's tenure as president of the board of regents of the University of Minnesota, Buffington designed Eddy Hall, Pillsbury Hall, Nicholson Hall, and, with Charles Sedgwick, Burton Hall. These massive and impressive buildings had a distinctive impact on the atmosphere of the state's major university.[36]

Buffington's most important commission from the Pillsburys, however, was for the design of the Pillsbury "A" Mill in 1881. With its construction, Minneapolis became the flour-milling center of the world. The wealth and power that backed the Citizens Alliance in its anti-union campaign rested on the milling capacity within Buffington's rock-faced limestone building. The massive façade of the mill is slightly curved and divided by arched windows in recessed vertical groupings that look down on the Mississippi River and St. Anthony Falls, the source of the mill's power and the Pillsburys' wealth.[37]

While most of the architecture of the Minneapolis renaissance was paid for and designed by the wealthy members of the CA, it was also built by open-shop contractors. The major contracting firms, C. F. Haglin and Sons, James Leck Company, Pike and Cook Company, and H. N. Leighton Company, joined the Citizens Alliance in its first years and faithfully built Minneapolis with open-shop workers. Subcontracts were also let to CA firms: electrical contractors W. I. Gray and Company and Minneapolis General Electric Company; heating contractors W. F. Porter and Company and Moore Heating Company; and plumbing contractors Black, Allen and Company and Kelly, Grant and Kelly Company.[38]

As the movement for the open shop incubated in 1900 through 1902, the nerve center of the grain industry, the Minneapolis Chamber of Commerce, hired CCA architect Frederick Kees and Colburn to construct a new headquarters on Fourth Avenue at Fourth Street. The elaborate terra cotta ornament of the building reflected Louis Sullivan's designs and was one of Minneapolis's more dignified commercial buildings. The construction contract was let to C. F. Haglin and Sons, one of the CA's staunchest supporters. Haglin and Sons was one of the first contractors in Minneapolis to use steel frame and Ferro concrete floors in constructing the Chamber of Commerce building.[39]

More important to the Minneapolis landscape, Haglin went to Europe in 1899 with Frank Heffelfinger to research concrete for use in grain storage. On his return, he constructed what is believed to be the first round, concrete grain-storage bin in America for the Peavey Company on the Beltline at Highway 7. Using open-shop labor and innovative construction techniques, Haglin would help shape the face of the rapidly growing city. The face of Minneapolis continued to change as the Citizens Alliance's grip on the building trades strengthened after World War I. CA businesses continued to hire open-shop architects and contractors to build the city's hotels, office buildings, banks, schools, stores, and hospitals. Most of the social and cultural institutions of the city, however, were in place by 1917.[40]

The open-shop oligarchy had created the clubs and schools where the close-knit society could flourish for generations. For the education of the public and the respect of eastern society, it had created the cultural institutions that would help shape the future of Minneapolis. The profits that were gained from the thorough and effective anti-union strategies of the Citizens Alliance were invested in the comfort, status, and image that would reflect the benevolence of the city's wealthy elite and conceal the less-than-benevolent activities of the Citizens Alliance that they had financed.

7 The Year of Emerging Threats

THE CITIZENS ALLIANCE ENTERED 1916 in a comfortable state of complacent dormancy. The Minneapolis Civic and Commerce Association (CCA) had united the commercial and civic forces of Minneapolis to reenergize the city's march of progress. The Minneapolis Employers' Association (MEA) had established a substantial influence at the state legislature. The establishment of Dunwoody Institute had, it was hoped, solved the problem of supplying the CA's open shops with skilled workers. And there were no union problems of "any great consequence." Describing this period with the wisdom of hindsight, CA leader Albert Strong remarked: "Dry rot is a great disintegrator. If you do not exercise your muscles, they do not keep strong."[1]

While the CA slept peacefully, the war in Europe increased the business activity and profits of its members. Partly as a result of the expanding economy, the American Federation of Labor's (AFL) membership gradually rose to 2,370,000. In Minnesota, union membership increased nearly 10 percent between 1914 and 1916. Although there were only three small strikes in Minneapolis in 1915, the electrical workers and the plasterers' unions both won wage concessions.[2]

Despite this industrial calm, however, there had been disquieting news on the political front. Minneapolis had been "threatened with the calamity of electing a Socialist Mayor" in 1912. Although the withdrawal of the Democratic Party candidate had saved the CA from the election of Thomas Van Lear, "a man confessedly at war with all business interests," as *Commercial West* put it, the dramatic growth of the Minneapolis Socialist Party, spearheaded by the local unions of the International Association of Machinists (IAM), should have warned the CA's leaders of an impending crisis.[3]

Ironically, the first challenge of 1916 came from inside the factory walls of Minneapolis Steel and Machinery (MSM) Company, where the industry's nemesis, Machinists' Local 91, was once again quietly organizing. Since defeating the machinists' union in 1901, Twin City Iron Works had merged with Minnesota Malleable Iron Company to form Minneapolis Steel and Machinery Company. Despite a half million capital investment and an impressive array of

buildings on Minnehaha Avenue, Minneapolis Steel and Machinery had struggled through its first decade while concentrating its production on structural
iron and steel work. The introduction of the popular Twin City 40 Power Tractor in 1910 and the development of a large market in Canada and the Western
United States successfully shifted the company's business into the expanding
agricultural machinery industry. By 1916, Minneapolis Steel and Machinery
was producing 2,600 Bull tractors and had more orders for Twin City tractors
than it could fill.[4]

In addition, Federal Reserve Agent John H. Rich, a Minneapolis Steel and
Machinery director, had helped the company land a two-million-dollar ammunition order from the Allied governments. To handle the rapidly expanding
business, Minneapolis Steel and Machinery quickly constructed another factory on land donated by the city. With 1916 profits reaching ten times those of
three years earlier, MSM had quickly become one of the largest industrial institutions in the state and one of the largest employers of labor. The small
machinists' union was attempting to organize the giant of its industry.[5]

Machinist Local 91 was also trying to organize the company that formed
the backbone of the CA. The *Minneapolis Labor Review* accurately portrayed
Minneapolis Steel and Machinery as "The biggest union hating concern in the
Northwest." A founding member of the CA, Minneapolis Steel and Machinery
was run by President James L. Record, a member of the CA's executive committee, and vice-president George M. Gillette, president of the MEA. Testifying
before the National War Labor Board in 1918, Record stated that Minneapolis Steel and Machinery had started out on the broad principle of the open
shop but, when union men assumed a dictatorial attitude in 1905, the company "decided that from that time on our shop should be a non-union shop."
The company made arrangements with Dunwoody Institute to train the
skilled workers necessary to run their machines without union workers. To appease their non-union workers Minneapolis Steel and Machinery followed the
CCA's strategy of promoting workers' welfare by establishing a medical department, a welfare department, and a mutual benefit association.[6]

These policies, however, could not offset the wages MSM paid—ten to eighteen cents less per hour than competing companies. With families unable to
support themselves on such substandard wages, the machinists' union was
able to build up inside the company despite the careful watch that the anti-
union management kept on the shop floor. During the first three months of
1916, Machinists' Local 91 recruited over forty new members each day, many
of them at Minneapolis Steel and Machinery. It was only a matter of time, according to the *Labor Review*, before "the bitterest and leading foe of organized
labor in the state" discovered the union presence and fought back.[7]

On March 23, seventy machinists at Minneapolis Steel and Machinery received layoff notices, supposedly because of a shortage of materials. On the same day, an advertisement appeared in the Waterloo, Iowa, newspaper: "Wanted—machinists—good wages—chances for advancement—permanent work and railroad fare. Minneapolis Steel and Machinery." Four days later, MSM President Record assembled the employees and announced that there would be absolutely no union men in the shop. Anyone wanting to work at Minneapolis Steel and Machinery would first have to surrender his union card.[8]

When seventy-five machinists refused to comply, the company locked them out. The machinists' union, led by socialists Van Lear and Lewis Harthill, voted unanimously to strike, demanding union recognition, better pay, and shorter hours. Record flatly rejected all demands, stating that "The company intends to run its own business instead of letting the men run it." Vice president Gillette had no doubt about the dangers posed by Local 91: "These radical elements or Socialists, opposed to every property right, seek to control industry and to divide up and re-distribute the property or wealth of the country." Drawn in these momentous terms, there was little hope for a peaceful resolution of the conflict.[9]

The machinists knew the futility of facing, as a single craft union, the overwhelming financial force of Minneapolis Steel and Machinery and its ally the CA. They immediately attempted to organize every worker at Minneapolis Steel and Machinery, whether munitions workers, packers, craters, sweepers, cleaners or oilers, into one industrial union. An organizational headquarters was set up several blocks from the plants, where meetings were held daily. Four picket captains were chosen to lead teams of twelve men in a tight, twenty-four-hour-a-day picket line. The *New Times*, a Minneapolis socialist newspaper, rashly predicted that prospects were bright for a speedy victory for the workers.[10]

Although the machinists' union was in good financial condition and was backed by the International Association of Machinists and the Minnesota State Federation of Labor (MSFL), it had little defense against a determined industrial giant like Minneapolis Steel and Machinery. If the company could bring in or train enough machinists to meet its production schedules, the union effort was doomed.[11]

Minneapolis Steel and Machinery, supported by the CA and the National Association of Manufacturers, had no intention of ever recognizing the union or rehiring the striking workers. With a shortage of local non-union machinists, Minneapolis Steel and Machinery advertised in outstate papers and put blind advertisements in the *Minneapolis Tribune*. Laborers were recruited through the Minneapolis Employment Company for twenty-two cents an hour. As quickly as possible, these men were placed on machines formerly operated by trained machinists. The Carling Detective Agency of St. Paul provided guards that were stationed on the roofs of the factory buildings as well as within the walls surrounding the entire Minneapolis Steel and Machinery compound. Union organizers were kept out of the factories by force if necessary. With the union watching from the streets outside, Minneapolis Steel and Machinery continued production at a record pace.[12]

Inside the plant, the company began publishing a newsletter, *An Enterprise to be Proud of*, extolling the virtues of Minneapolis Steel and Machinery. Prizes were offered for laborsaving ideas, and the men were urged to join the social and athletic club. While the battle took its inevitable course, the CA expanded its attack on the machinists' union. Other large manufacturers also began discharging union men, and a citywide blacklist of union machinists was set up. Although the *Minneapolis Labor Review* would continue its Minneapolis Steel and Machinery strike notice on the top of its front page until April 20, 1917, the machinists' strike was effectively defeated before the summer of 1916. The defeated socialists running Local 91, however, would pose a very different and more serious threat before the year was over.[13]

While Minneapolis Steel and Machinery dealt summarily with the machinists' union, on another front the CA faced "a crucial moment in the history" of Minneapolis. In March of 1914, a small band of Minneapolis Teamsters applied for a charter in the National Brotherhood of Teamsters. The Draymen's Association, following the precedent set in 1902, fired twenty-five union members the next day.[14]

The Teamsters spent the next two years secretly organizing, while the CA relaxed its vigilance. Protected by their anonymity and spurred on by wages of $13.50 for a ninety-six hour workweek, the Teamsters' union was able to thoroughly organize the Minneapolis transportation industry. When Twin City Taxicab and Transfer Company doubled its hotel baggage hauling rates on May 2, 1916, the union suddenly exercised its new strength and demanded a $1.50 raise. When the company refused to negotiate, the union immediately threatened a strike. Overnight, the CA was faced with a crisis. CA members realized that "When all transfer conveyances are unionized, then the union controls the delivery of everything—you cannot make a single exception." The threat that the Draymen's Association had defeated in 1902 had returned on a far greater scale.[15]

The immediate reaction at Twin City Taxicab and Transfer, a CA member recently recapitalized by George M. Gillette and other CA interests, was to lock out all union members. Non-union men, protected by Burns detectives, were then put on Twin City teams. Trunks began piling up at Minneapolis hotels picketed by Teamsters Local 23. Drivers for other transfer companies rapidly joined the hotel boycott and wore union buttons on the job. By early June, the city's larger transfer companies—CA members Cameron Transfer Company, Boyd Transfer, Murphy Transfer, Minneapolis Transfer and Storage, and Skellet Transfer Company—began discharging any employee wearing a union button. Within a week, the strike had exploded dramatically, encompassing 1,200 workers at 150 transfer firms. The transportation of goods in Minneapolis came to a halt. The Draymen's Association, backed and directed by the CA, moved in to organize what had become a battle for control of Minneapolis's commerce.[16]

Frank Mattison, manager of Twin City Taxicab and Transfer, took charge of the growing force of detectives and thugs supplied by local detective agencies and needed to guard the non-union wagon drivers. W. M. Babcock, secretary of the Draymen's Association and a CA representative, kept the transfer firms in line by threatening a boycott by the entire business community of Minneapolis. By June 11, a simple request for an increase of wages at one firm had mushroomed into the largest open-shop battle the CA had waged.[17]

In a desperate effort to reopen commerce and defeat the strike, Mayor Wallace G. Nye ordered one-quarter of the Minneapolis police force to ride aboard all wagons driven by non-union workers. There was little doubt which side Mayor Nye, a CCA member and one of the founders of the CA in 1903, was on in the 1916 strike. On June 11, however, the mayor, perhaps concerned about a City Council investigation of his use of the police, met with Thomas J. Skellet, a CA member representing the transfermen, and union representatives in an attempt to reach a negotiated settlement. Local 23 offered to return to work if its members could wear union buttons and if the companies would not discriminate against them. Despite the elimination of the wage issue, Skellet refused to back away from his insistence on maintaining the open shop.[18]

On June 13, the City Council voted unanimously to request the mayor to "remove all special and regular policemen from the wagons of the transfer companies." Acting in the interests of the CA, the mayor refused. The next day, the Efficiency and Economy Committee of the City Council held a conference between employers and the union in the mayor's reception room. Skellet and Babcock continued to insist that they would never hire any man who "shows any visible signs of belonging to a labor union." When Skellet agreed to form a committee of transfermen to negotiate with the union, W. I. Gray and Briggs, observing the meeting for the CA , interceded to end the conference. It was clear to both sides that the CA was dictating the policy of the transfermen and that there would be no compromise with the growing union force.[19]

The hardened attitude of employers also began to appear at the various transfer companies. At Excelsior Van and Storage, a detective whipped out his revolver, pointed it at a union man, and shouted, "When you talk to me, you talk to this!" At Cameron Transfer, a teamster was struck with the butt end of a revolver for standing near the Cameron barn. With the transfer companies hiring new men and union pickets being clubbed by detectives hired by the Draymen's Association, the Teamsters' only course was to escalate the strike. The Teamsters' Joint Council called for a general strike of all crafts "to show the Citizens Alliance that they cannot break the backbone of organized labor." On June 22, 1916, the Trades and Labor Assembly called out all teamsters and chauffeurs, reorganized their picketing, and drew up a manifesto for a mass meeting on June 26.[20]

The Minneapolis labor movement met at the Dewey Theater on Monday night and voted for a general strike. The union report on the meeting stated: "The Citizens Alliance had met with a foe to be reckoned with, and rightly so, for with a fighting machine like the rank and file Teamsters backed up by the entire labor movement, the odds must have been against the Citizens Alliance." Deliveries across the city slowed to a trickle as the strike force swelled. Printers, carpenters, machinists, plasterers, and cooks raised money or assisted the picketing Teamsters. Construction work slowed, grocers had difficulty keeping shelves stocked, even the hospitals had trouble maintaining supplies. Minneapolis unions felt that their day of deliverance from the CA had finally arrived.[21]

Instead, the threat of a general strike transformed the CA from a secret, underfunded, and semi-dormant group to a well-financed public crusade against unions. At noon on Tuesday, June 27, the CA called a meeting of 200 Minneapolis businessmen at the West Hotel to consider the Teamsters' strike. CA vice-president W. I. Gray chaired the discussion of the violence that was supposedly overwhelming the Minneapolis police force and intimidating the transfer companies. In fact, there had been only 24 arrests and most of the violence had been against the strikers. Transfer company executive Thomas Skellet complained about the cost of employing 150 guards but still maintained: "We're going to fight until we win because we must win or get out of business." It was clear to chairman Gray that the strike was "the opening wedge to tie up the city and force in union rule." [22]

After a full discussion, the businessmen unanimously agreed to give their moral and financial support to the CA's efforts to break the strike. Of equal importance, they signed a public statement decrying a "city anxious and willing to work, but who are deterred from doing so by threats and by fear of physical violence." The meeting affirmed "that every person has an absolute right to work regardless of his affiliation . . . to labor," and that every employer has "the right to carry on his legitimate business without interference and is entitled to sufficient protection." The meeting also resolved to support the city and mayor "in their efforts to protect life and property, maintain the public peace, and in enforcing the laws." With the publication of this resolution signed by 200 of Minneapolis's leading businessmen, the CA campaign for the open shop had finally come out of hiding.[23]

In addition to a public proclamation, the Teamsters' strike forced Minneapolis businessmen to confront the financial cost of maintaining an open-shop city. When asked for his views on the strike, Edward W. Decker, the president of Northwestern Bank, suggested that the CA appoint a committee to procure money. Decker declared that the "present situation was one which must be fought to a finish and at once." First and Security National Bank President F. A. Chamberlain also offered his support. CA leaders Gray and Strong called a Sunday meeting of eight business leaders to solicit funds. Within twenty minutes, the CA raised $20,000 for its first guaranty fund.[24]

Initially, the fund was earmarked to defray expenses of $1,500 per day for special policemen during the Teamsters' strike. As committees were organized to solicit funds by industry, however, the CA acknowledged that the guaranty fund was also "for the purpose of sustaining in the city of Minneapolis the vital principle of the 'open shop.'" A year later, in 1917, the fund total would be $50,000, enough to engage Otis P. Briggs to conduct the affairs of the CA. As Albert W. Strong remembers it: "Under his very energetic and able leadership, the strength of the organization rapidly developed." The guaranty fund and Briggs were put to more immediate use in fighting the Teamsters.[25]

Within days of the call for a general strike, it was clear to both Teamster strike chairman Jean Spielman and Draymen's Association attorney Babcock that their challenge to the CA was disintegrating on several fronts. The public declarations of the CA-led businessmen had finally moved Mayor Nye and Police Chief Martinson to take aggressive action against Teamster pickets. The strikers, desperately trying to fight off defeat, made a last attempt to stop truck traffic. A large group of strikers stopped an Upton Mill and Elevator truck on University Avenue and spilled its load of grain into the street. The police immediately arrested forty-three men. Across the river in south Minneapolis, twenty-five men were arrested for stopping teams on Twelfth Avenue. When the sixty-eight strikers appeared before Judge Winfield W. Bardwell a week later, they were released on the condition that they keep out of trouble until September 30, when the strike would be over.[26]

In one decisive action, the union's most aggressive pickets had been neutralized. Another critical struggle was taking place within the Teamsters' Joint Council. The Teamsters' international organizer, John L. Devering, had signed contracts for several locals without the knowledge of the strike committee. When the call for a general strike went out, Devering threatened all locals under contract with expulsion if they joined the strike. While chairman Spielman urged the strikers to hold out, Devering secretly issued permits allowing the union men to return to work. The Minneapolis Trades and Labor Assembly accused Devering of "breaking the backbone of the strike," and asked, "What was the object of the treacherous move?" With the Teamsters in turmoil, only the plasterers and the cement finishers honored the general strike call. The failure of the Minneapolis labor movement to decisively support the strike had doomed the Teamsters' efforts.[27]

On June 30, with the strike already weakening, the board of directors of the Civic and Commerce Association called a special meeting to draft a resolution regarding the Teamsters' strike. The CCA declared that "Minneapolis shall remain a city where life is safe, where property is secure, where every man, woman and child may enjoy liberty of conscience, freedom in thought and action and equality of opportunity." The CCA "condemns acts of violence, it asks obedience to the law, it demands enforcement of the law." The resolution also demanded "that the city authorities furnish such police protection as may be necessary to those willing to work, regardless of labor affiliations and we pledge the Mayor and city authorities our hearty support in their effort to preserve law and order." If the earlier CA meeting had left any doubts about the resolve of the Minneapolis business community, the CCA resolution put them to rest. The closely intertwined organizations would allow no interference with their member's control of Minneapolis's industry.[28]

Two days after the CCA resolution, the trickle of strikers returning to work became a steady stream of men desperately hoping to be rehired. Draymen's Association leader Babcock announced that "the backbone of the strike is broken." Employers would rehire only strikers who had not been involved in violence. Union activists would be blacklisted. Men who refused to return to work were threatened with vagrancy charges by Minneapolis police. Goods began moving through Minneapolis streets as union picketing decreased dramatically.[29]

By July 3, the CA and the Draymen's Association, supported by a growing guaranty fund, nervously replaced the Minneapolis police guard on their wagons with 200 special police. The city remained quiet as the big transfer companies reported their operations were back to normal with 400 to 500 strikers back at work. When the sixty-eight arrested strikers pleaded guilty in exchange for suspended sentences, employers, police, and some union leaders realized that the strike was over. The Teamsters' union was left an ineffective shambles with only 139 members.[30]

The reorganization and rejuvenation of the CA, however, would have a far greater influence on Minneapolis industry than the immediate impact of the Teamsters' devastating defeat. The business community's fear of the consequences of a union victory had tremendously intensified the activities of the CA. With the fate of the open shop at risk, Briggs, Gray, and Strong had been meeting every day to plot the course of the strike. It was clear that the CA needed a full-time paid staff. The guaranty fund, necessitated by the desperate need for guards, allowed the CA to hire Briggs as full-time president in 1916. With the financial might of the entire Minneapolis business community backing the CA, and an experienced national open-shop leader in command, it would be eighteen years before the Minneapolis union movement would mount another challenge to the CA. The Teamsters had lost a critical strike and in so doing had inadvertently created a business oligarchy to rule Minneapolis industry.[31]

While the general populace of Minnesota worried about the Kaiser's armies in France, and the CA eliminated the union threat in Minneapolis, the businessmen of the Civic and Commerce Association perceived a wider threat from the Industrial Workers of the World (IWW) and the Nonpartisan League (NPL). They were "facing a menace . . . the campaign being waged to throw control of the state, politically and industrially, into the hands of the Socialist-IWW-Nonpartisan combination." The Minneapolis labor movement completed the unholy quartet of traitorous organizations that expressed policies "that no loyal American can subscribe to." Although this conspiracy was exaggerated in business publications, the threat that these groups posed to the domination of Minneapolis industry by the CCA and the CA was real and immediate. If radical political groups gained control of rural Minnesota, they could exert an influence at the state legislature or even gain control of Minnesota state government. The Minneapolis business community realized that a disaster of this magnitude would undermine their domination of Minnesota industry.[32]

The first dramatic sign of trouble erupted on the Mesabi Iron Range during the Minneapolis Teamsters' strike. The unorganized miners, fed up with piecework contracts that often paid them $1.21 a day for ten hours of backbreaking work, walked out of the St. James Mine at Aurora. The IWW, a radical union that had been expecting and planning for the strike since February, immediately sent a corps of young organizers onto the range to take control of the strike.[33]

For over three months, between 7,000 and 15,000 miners, led by the IWW, severely restricted production on the Mesabi Range. From Local 490 headquarters in Virginia, the IWW made demands for the eight-hour day, a flat rate wage of up to $3.50 per day, and the abolition of private mine police. The union also distributed strike benefits and organized an 11,000-person strike rally at the Hibbing fairgrounds and a huge eight-mile march from Chisholm to Hibbing.[34]

The mining companies enlarged their police forces and barricaded the mine properties. Heavily armed police patrolled the mines and the Iron Range cities. The *Duluth News Tribune* hysterically reported: "What is faced on the ranges and threatened in Duluth is revolution, just that and nothing less." In Minneapolis, the IWW paper *Allarm* applauded "miners' threat to kill 3 police for every union death." Governor Joseph A. A. Burnquist telegrammed the St. Louis County sheriff, asking him to "use all your powers . . . for the preservation of life and property."[35]

By mid-July, most of the union leadership was locked in a Duluth jail awaiting trial for murder. Despite these setbacks and the continued brutality of company police, the IWW grimly held on until, in September, the resources of the striking miners were finally exhausted. Although the strike was successfully suppressed, it was clear that the IWW could quickly flourish where industrial conditions were extremely oppressive.[36]

Although Minneapolis businessmen were reassured by the suppression of the IWW on the Iron Range in 1916, poor working conditions in the mines and logging camps of Northern Minnesota would continue to encourage the radical organizing efforts of the IWW. The conditions in the logging camps of northern Minnesota the next winter were even more appalling than in the mines. Sixty men were stacked into twenty-eight by thirty-four-foot vermin-infested bunkhouses. With little ventilation and no bathing facilities whatsoever, the unevenly heated houses smelled of ripened racks of partially washed socks dripping over the single wood stove. For twelve-hour days, seven days a week, working in temperatures often 40 degrees or more below zero, the lumberjack received thirty to thirty-five dollars per month. A nonunion worker at the lumber mills in International Falls might earn as little as $1.75 for a twelve-hour day.[37]

The powder keg created by these harsh conditions finally reached flash point in late December at the huge Virginia and Rainy Lake Sawmill in Virginia. At dawn on December 28, several hundred strikers picketed the plant gates. With nearly 1,000 workers on strike, the operation of the plant's main sawmills was severely crippled. The IWW quickly sent squads of organizers out to the logging camps to inform the lumberjacks of strike plans and the IWW demands for a ten-dollar-a-month pay increase, a nine-hour day, and decent living conditions.[38]

By January 1, thousands of lumberjacks were leaving the camps, riding crowded trains into the Iron Range cities. In one week, the IWW had shut down the logging industry of northern Minnesota. After describing camp conditions, an IWW member commented, "Now is it any wonder this IWW is here? The IWW is a product of those conditions. . . . Whether the IWW . . . or any other organization were there, the strike would have taken place."[39]

The sheriffs of the northern counties quickly hired hundreds of deputies to stamp out what the state's newspapers called "a reign of terror." Although no witnesses ever came forward to substantiate these charges, the lumber companies launched a blitzkrieg offensive against the IWW. Members were rounded up in Iron Range towns and told to leave town or be arrested. By the middle of January, most of the IWW leaders were in jail and the members had fled to Duluth or Minneapolis. In two weeks, the lumber companies and sheriff's departments had destroyed the strike and eliminated the IWW from the forests of northern Minnesota. In Minneapolis, the *Tribune* applauded this vicious, unconstitutional treatment of IWW sympathizers. Although it was clear that radical and violent measures could effectively suppress radical organizations, the IWW had demonstrated that the abuses of unchecked capitalism could create an explosive and dangerous reaction from the state's underpaid workers.[40]

Although the major IWW strikes had been limited to the Iron Range, the CCA realized that the revolutionary union would also pose a threat to their industrial empire. The IWW wanted far more than "A fair day's wage for a fair day's work." The preamble of the IWW stated: "It is the historic mission of the working class to do away with capitalism. . . . The working class and the employing class have nothing in common. . . . Between these two classes a struggle must go on until the workers of the world organize as a class, take possession of the earth and the machinery of production, and abolish the wage system." While the advancement of Minneapolis unionism and the closed shop might diminish the CA's power over Minneapolis industry, the success of the IWW would abolish their right to own it at all.[41]

To combat the spread of the IWW's influence, it was imperative for the Citizens Alliance to develop intelligence that would identify the enemy. Fortunately for the CA, the Northern Information Bureau had already infiltrated the IWW before the 1916 strikes. Luther W. Boyce, who had formed his commercial detective agency in 1903, was able to obtain a practically complete membership list of IWW members in Minnesota, Iowa, and North and South Dakota from his two agents inside the IWW. Boyce's best source, E. C. Green, was appointed general secretary of the Minneapolis headquarters for the IWW throughout the Northwest. Realizing the potential value of his intelligence, Boyce approached the heads of several large corporations. Pillsbury Flour Mills, Washburn-Crosby Company, and other CA members agreed to pay from eight dollars to fifty dollars per month for reports on the IWW. The Northern Information Bureau was continually employed checking all employees of their clients for IWW members. By eliminating the members of the IWW from their plants, the CA undoubtedly hoped to avoid the large strikes that had afflicted the Iron Range.[42]

Reports back from the grain belt of the northwestern United States were disquieting. Farmers were facing a severe labor shortage, and the IWW was rapidly organizing the migrant field hands. Formed in 1915, the Agricultural Workers Organization (AWO) of the IWW demanded a minimum wage of three dollars per day, fifty cents overtime for every hour over a ten-hour-day, and adequate living quarters. From its headquarters on Hennepin Avenue in Minneapolis, the AWO aggressively and sometimes forcefully initiated thousands of harvest workers into the IWW. Armed with clubs, pick handles, and guns, organizers took over freight trains carrying workers to the harvest fields. Any rider that refused to join the IWW was forced off the trains. With a membership of more than 20,000, and rapidly growing, the AWO was able to control wages and working conditions on over one-half of the 1916 harvest.[43]

The effectiveness of the IWW's agricultural campaign presented a direct threat to the grain empire that had built Minneapolis and which to a large degree financed the operations of the CA. Without a cheap and malleable labor force, the banks and grain companies of Minneapolis might lose control of their industrial base. If the IWW succeeded dramatically in the grain belt, its revolutionary ideology would inevitably move into Minneapolis. The CA knew that "something, of course will have to be done to check the IWW."[44]

The CA also faced another growing threat on the western horizon in the summer of 1916. With the Teamsters' strike still raging in Minneapolis, the *Minneapolis Journal* warned that "the state of North Dakota is in the throes of another 'farmers' revolt.'" The Nonpartisan League was reported to be a "frankenstein whose very creators wonder at its numerical and financial strength." The league's socialistic program was a cause for deep concern in Minneapolis. The NPL proposed state control of industries for the benefit of the people of the state; state-built elevators, flour mills, warehouses, and packing plants; and a rural credits system financed by state funds. The program directly challenged the financial and marketing dominance of Minneapolis interests over the Northwest's grain belt. With over 30,000 members and $50,000 a week flowing into its campaign, the league was expected to win the Republican primaries across the state of North Dakota. The *Jour-*

nal described the league as intending to "plunge North Dakota hell bent" into state socialism.[45]

On November 7, league candidate Lynn Frazier won the North Dakota governor's race by more than four to one, while league candidates took eighty-one of one-hundred and thirteen house seats. The *Journal*'s dire predictions had become a real threat. The 1917 North Dakota legislature opened to a flurry of controversy as league legislators attempted to rewrite the state's constitution to facilitate their radical social plans. At the same time, the league moved its national headquarters from Fargo to St. Paul and intensified its infiltration of both the Democratic and Republican parties in Minnesota. Although the most radical elements of the league program failed in the 1917 legislature, Minneapolis businessmen feared that "League progress in Northern Minnesota had brought peril within range of the Twin Cities." Minnesota farmers had already contributed an estimated $50,000 to the league, which was planning to cover Minnesota with over 300 automobile-driving solicitors that spring. CCA leader Fred B. Snyder felt that "Unless something is done to counteract this movement . . . I fear that our State offices and the control of the Legislature will pass into the hands of that [NPL] organization." In comparing the threat of the IWW and the NPL, CCA leader Judge John McGee stated that while the IWW is "dangerous, they do not begin to be as dangerous as the Nonpartisan League." Apparently a real political threat was more dangerous than a potential revolutionary threat. The CCA and the CA took both very seriously.[46]

On the local political front, the CA faced a more immediate challenge. Socialist Thomas Van Lear was mounting a third campaign for mayor in 1916. With the Teamsters' strike still being fought on the streets of Minneapolis, the working people of the city voted overwhelmingly for Van Lear in the June primary election. Mayor Nye, suffering the political results of his use of the police as strikebreakers, finished a dismal third. Van Lear's campaign proudly trumpeted the platform of the Socialist Party of Minneapolis, which condemned the "present organization of industry," under which "the Capitalist Class will monopolize the machinery of production and will appropriate, through the wage system, the wealth created by the working class." With full Marxist fervor, the party platform called for the workers to "overthrow the power of capitalism, abolish industrial classes in society, terminate forever the class struggle by securing the Collective ownership and Democratic management of the means of production and distribution." The CA open-shop philosophy, based on the sanctity of private property, would be under immediate attack if Van Lear were elected.[47]

On a more practical level, the Socialist Party's "Working Program" called for no police interference during strikes, a shorter work week, union wages on public employment, the right of the city to own and operate all public utilities, a public defender to represent workers, a public welfare system for indigent children, and a municipal safety inspection of all factories. If Van Lear ever established this program, the CA and its members would face not only higher costs in wages and plant improvements but also unimpeded and well-defended strikers. Twin City Rapid Transit and other public utilities, all CA supporters, would face the catastrophic appropriation of their businesses. Fortunately for the CA, however, without a socialist city council, Van Lear would be incapable of putting most of the program into effect.[48]

With Mayor Nye out of the race, the CA threw its support behind Sheriff Otto Langum. A "Citizen's Mayoralty Committee" of CA members was formed to lead "the most important mayoralty campaign that the city has ever had." The campaign, heavily funded by the CA and CCA, set up an independent headquarters to be run by CA lawyer Charles R. Fowler. The campaign issue was socialism. Fowler announced to the Minneapolis press that socialism meant the destruction of all social relations, the confiscation of property, and the establishment of a socialistic, cooperative commonwealth conceived in ignorant idealism and incompetency." Van Lear would be a puppet of the dangerous Socialist Party.[49]

Committee funds and a friendly press allowed Fowler's negative campaign to get a thorough hearing among Minneapolis voters. Langum was portrayed as a man "who believes in the rights of individuals, conservation and protection of property and in the constant betterment of human existence by education and evolution." Perhaps fearful of the political repercussions of the Teamsters' strike, Langum declared himself in favor of labor organizations.[50]

At the same time, however, the CA was donating $15,000 to employ tailors to lock out union tailors and carry their fight for the open shop to the finish. With the Trades and Labor Assembly and the Building Trades Council backing Van Lear's socialist candidacy, and the *Minneapolis Labor Review* reporting on CA activities, there was little doubt that Minneapolis's working class citizens would vote for Van Lear.[51]

On November 7, 1916, over 33,000 Minneapolis citizens voted Thomas Van Lear, Minneapolis's first and only socialist mayor, into office. Van Lear declared: "The victory belongs to the common people of this city. The contest between special privilege, seeking control of all city affairs, and the common people who want justice and demand that the people and not the financially powerful should rule." The CA had suffered a traumatic defeat, but one which even the socialists realized would have little immediate impact on the outcome of class warfare in Minneapolis. Minneapolis's weak-mayor system and a non-socialist city council would neutralize Van Lear's power.[52]

The new mayor's appointment of socialist Lewis Harthill as chief of police in December of 1916 was a different matter. Chief Harthill was determined that the Minneapolis police would never be allowed to shift the balance of power to the employers during a strike. The CA, however, could still count on Sheriff Langum to deputize the forces necessary to control a strike. Despite these drawbacks to Van Lear's election, Minneapolis socialists now had a legitimate platform from which they could effectively popularize their programs. Even more threatening for the CA, Minneapolis's working class "had learned for the first time to stand together in support of their own interests and vote solidly for a working class candidate, endorsed and put into the field by the Party of the working class, the Socialist Party." The awakening and organization of Minneapolis's working class, joined with the outstate growth of the IWW and the NPL, created a threat to the CA that would test its resources for the next two decades. Fortunately for the CA, however, the first battles would be fought during World War I, when the cloak of patriotism would become its staunchest ally.[53]

8 The Minnesota Coup

THE ENTRY OF THE UNITED STATES into World War I quickly created labor shortages that strengthened the position of the country's labor unions. The war, however, also unleashed an enormous surge of patriotic fervor across the country. In a climate of pro-war hysteria, the suppression of any group expressing anti-war sentiment became inevitable. The Minnesota Republican Party and the CCA ruthlessly used this patriotic explosion to construct an institutional system that would severely damage the Nonpartisan League (NPL), the Industrial Workers of the World (IWW), Minneapolis socialism, and the growing labor movement in Minneapolis.

The Minnesota Commission of Public Safety (MCPS) was created by an act of the state legislature on April 16, 1917, only days after the United States declared war. One million dollars was appropriated for its creation and use. The MCPS was empowered

> to do all acts and things non-inconsistent with the constitution or laws of Minnesota or of the United States which, in the event of war existing between the United States and any foreign nation, are necessary or proper for the protection of life and public property or private property of a character as in the judgment of the commission requires protection, and shall do and perform all acts and things necessary or proper so that the military, civil and industrial resources of the state may be most efficiently applied toward maintenance of the defense of the State and Nation.

For the duration of the war, Minnesota was governed by this dictatorial group.[1]

The MCPS stated from its inception that its purpose was to maximize the prosecution of the war on the home front. The United States was "in the midst of the greatest war of which human history contains a record." In peacetime, the industrial machine could be left to itself,

> but when the country's life was at stake, the situation was different. If our soldiers need food and munitions, the man who will not help to their supplying according to his ability, or whom by his conduct, interferes with others producing,

is as much an enemy of the country as those in arms against it. . . . It goes without saying that a state which has the right to use its strength to crush its foreign enemies can also protect itself against those at home whose behavior tends to weaken its war capacity.

The legitimate activities of the Nonpartisan League, the IWW, socialists, and labor agitators might disrupt war production and they were therefore enemies of the state. The MCPS considered it a logical and patriotic duty to suppress these groups.[2]

It was not a coincidence that the fears and goals of the MCPS and the CCA were identical. The idea for the MCPS supposedly originated in the St. Paul Patriotic League, an organization formed by an elite group of St. Paul business and civic leaders to campaign for patriotism in the Capital City. Its establishment was drafted into a bill by Ambrose Tighe, a lawyer for Twin City Rapid Transit Company and a prominent CCA member. Several important association members, in addition to the Patriotic League members, lobbied for the bill while it was still in a legislative committee.[3]

At the same time, the *Minneapolis Journal* editorialized: "Minnesota will never have a responsible and efficient State Government until responsibility is focused in central control." *Commercial West*, for years an admirer of Germany's autocratic government, stated that: "When stress of war comes such government mechanism must of necessity become more or less autocratic." Both the *Journal* and *Commercial West* were closely associated with the CCA and were undoubtedly working in its interests. People in the "banking, grain and milling circles" in Minneapolis lobbied for the appointment of prominent CCA member Judge John F. McGee to the MCPS. Historian Carl H. Chrislock points out that: "Although McGee was not a member of the legislature, his influence apparently shaped the Safety Commission Bill and contributed to its passage."[4]

McGee vividly expressed his intentions for the MCPS a week before the bill was signed by Governor Joseph A. A. Burnquist: "If the Governor appoints men who have backbone, treason will not be talked on the streets of this city and the street corner orators, who denounce the government, advocate revolution, denounce the army and advise against enlistments, will be looking through the barred fences of an internment camp out on the prairie somewhere."[5]

Tighe's suggestion that Charles W. Farnham of the St. Paul Patriotic League be appointed to the commission was ignored in favor of McGee, but Tighe himself was appointed as counsel. In fact, before being named to the commission, McGee had confidently stated that: "If I would say to the Governor that I would go on [the commission] and that I wanted to go on, he would appoint me." Once on the commission, McGee, "a violent tempered and strong

willed and intolerant person," quickly became the commanding figure. The
state of Minnesota, as represented by the commission, was ready to defend the
business interests of the CCA.[6]

The influence of the CCA became apparent from the Public Safety Commission's first meetings when a delegation from the Civic and Commerce Association offered its entire resources—funds, facilities, and staff—to the cause. In
response, the commission appointed Fred B. Snyder, a member of the CCA
board of directors, to be the director of the Hennepin County MCPS. The CCA
then appointed Snyder to be its war commissioner, thus strengthening its position as the local arm of the Public Safety Commission. McGee's appointment
to head the Military Affairs Committee was an even greater triumph for the
CCA. From this position, he created a system that proved vital in defending Minneapolis against the labor radicals that were shielded by a socialist mayor. Fellow commissioner John Lind attributed McGee's successful manipulation of
the commission to his "dominating spirit—poor Burnquist who I think is a
good man at heart is weak and was absolutely under McGee's thumb."

On April 25, 1917, McGee was assigned the job of planning the creation of
the Minnesota Home Guard to replace the National Guard, which had been
pressed into wartime service. Three days later, the commission issued Order
No. 3, in which Governor Burnquist was named commander of the force of
eleven battalions, totaling about 4,400 men, and given the responsibility for
appointing all officers during the winter of 1917–18. The enlisted men were
volunteers who had to furnish their own uniforms and were not reimbursed
unless they served more than five days consecutively.[7]

The volunteer system, which was used extensively during the war, effectively limited membership to people of means—employers or employees who
could take a leave of absence. With the governor under McGee's influence and
local units staffed by officers and enlisted men from the business community,
the Home Guard became an effective force for minimizing labor disturbances
on the Iron Range, intimidating strikers in Minneapolis, and suppressing riots
in St. Paul. The commission hoped that the effective use of the guard might
"open the way for the later development of a permanent constabulary force"—
a prospect that would long be a top priority for the CA.[8]

The Home Guard, however, was slow to muster full strength and was primarily designed to deal with large disturbances. In order to guard property
and deter "evil-minded persons plotting crime or destruction of property," the
commission ordered the appointment of peace officers. Eventually, 609 men
were given constabulary authority, enabling them to carry guns, make war-
rantless arrests, and break into private dwellings. Approximately one-third of
these officers were appointed in Minneapolis, and 175 of them belonged to

either the Minneapolis division of the American Protective League (APL), a national organization devoted to suppressing anti-war activities, or the Hennepin County Public Safety Commission, which was created to enforce MCPS orders locally. Both organizations were financed, organized, and staffed by the Civic and Commerce Association. Corporate members of the CCA, such as Northwestern Telephone Exchange Company, were also able to request peace officers to guard property. With the state's gold "Star of the North" as a seal, the commission bequeathed legal status and authority to members of quasi-official volunteer organizations, groups that were indistinguishable from the CCA and that were used to combat its enemies.[9]

The IWW would become the MCPS's first and primary target for suppression. To facilitate the attack, ex-Governor John Lind was appointed to the MCPS and charged with suppressing labor disturbances throughout the state. Lind, also a member of the CCA, was immediately assigned field agents to watch over the IWW. In addition, on April 10 the 1917 legislature had passed a Criminal Syndicalism statute, which virtually outlawed all activities of the IWW. The far-reaching law forbade "any person who by word of mouth or writing, advocates or teaches the duty, necessity or propriety of crime, sabotage, violence or other unlawful methods of terrorism." To encourage the enforcement of the syndicalism statute, the MCPS, the CCA, and the CA distributed copies of the act throughout the state. The method for eliminating the IWW was clear from the earliest days of the MCPS: investigate the IWW, collect evidence of its violation of syndicalism and federal espionage statutes, and prosecute. With McGee and Lind controlling the state military and labor policy, the CCA was ready to begin its campaign of eradication.[10]

The MCPS took immediate action against the IWW without waiting for the results of its intelligence operations to pour in. On April 24, McGee motioned and Lind seconded the MCPS's first order, which banned the sale of liquor and the operation of pool halls, theaters, and other places of amusement in Minneapolis's Bridge Square district. The order wiped out the "menacing" hotbed of IWW organizers and loafers in the elevator and mill district. Elizabeth Gurley Flynn and other IWW speakers planned to address a May Day rally on the Iron Range but were arrested as vagrants and released only when they agreed to leave the state.[11]

On June 5, the MCPS's Order No. 8 restricted the sale of liquor in the proximity of mines and timber lands of the Mesabi Range after it was revealed that "blind pigs" were a "danger to continuous operation of the mines, essential to the country's production of war materials." Representatives of nineteen Iron Range communities were requested to attend a special meeting with the MCPS on June 20, where Commissioner Lind outlined the IWW threat. After discussing the difficulties caused by the "agitation of unpatriotic elements" and the danger of "blind pigs," the MCPS went into executive session and decided that the syndicalism and sedition acts had to be translated into Finnish, Croatian, Slovene, Bulgarian, and Italian and distributed on the Iron Range to inhibit IWW activities. Representatives of the Iron Range communities pledged their loyal cooperation in preserving order.[12]

The MCPS also announced at the June 20 meeting that an ordinance was being prepared to provide municipalities with a method for restraining anyone who hindered the conduct of the war. The vagrancy ordinance was originally Lind's creation, but MCPS lawyer Tighe altered it to include "those who are engaged in whole or in part in the occupation, whether for gain or gratuitous, of advocating, advising or teaching the inhibited doctrines." The ordinance was eventually passed by 154 communities and, according to Tighe, was one of the MCPS's "most ingenious and effective measures." The primary target of the vagrancy ordinance was, of course, the IWW.[13]

While Commissioner Lind provided local authorities with the legal means to suppress the IWW, the CCA also exerted direct pressure on communities through its financial influence. When a Bemidji lumber mill burned down in July 1917, local businessmen blamed the IWW despite the lack of any evidence. The Shevlin-Carpenter Lumber Company, a CCA member, announced to members of the Bemidji Commercial Club that it would not consider rebuilding the mill until "the IWW was driven from Bemidji." The next day, over 150 Bemidji citizens, led by the mayor and chief of police, marched on IWW headquarters. All literature, fixtures, and property were confiscated and twenty-five IWW members were marched to the railroad station and shipped out of town. Although the IWW complained bitterly about the illegal deportation, the MCPS fully supported the "clean up." A score of extra police were quickly deputized to guard the city from any return of the deported IWW members. Bemidji friends of the IWW were warned to change their attitudes or face a similar banishment.[14]

The Home Guard under McGee's command, of course, would function effectively only if the MCPS could pinpoint the hotspots of IWW agitation quickly and accurately. Shortly after the MCPS was formed, Lind appointed two agents to investigate the extent of IWW agitation on the Iron Range. Reports from agents Joseph A. Salo and Anthony Pleva were "very satisfactory." As early as May 16, Lind reported that "the Slavs are not disposed to take up with the IWW as readily this season as they did last. The Finns are still a little turbulent, but nothing serious yet."[15]

Despite these detailed early reports indicating that the IWW on the Iron Range was quiet, Judge McGee moved at the MCPS May 22 meeting that a secret service system be established. To meet the perceived urgency of radical agitation before a secret service could be organized, the MCPS hired O. R. Hatfield, superintendent of the St. Paul Pinkerton's Detective Agency, to begin immediate statewide investigations. Although Hatfield's men were given a wide-open order to watch suspected German sympathizers, socialists, and Nonpartisan Leaguers, the IWW was the primary target. Pinkerton agents reported to Hatfield on Iron Range conditions on a daily basis. Hatfield then passed the information on to McGee or Governor Burnquist. After two months of undercover work, Hatfield's agents confirmed the reports of Salo and Pleva: The "IWW was as good as out of existence on the [Cayuna] range."[16]

When the *St. Paul Daily News* revealed large payments of public funds to private detective agencies, however, the agencies quickly became a political liability. Commissioner Charles W. Ames publicly claimed that "it is legitimate and necessary for the safety commission to obtain first hand information along many lines." On June 30, the MCPS appointed CCA member Thomas G. Winter to head a new intelligence bureau, the Minnesota Secret Service (SS). Although the MCPS claimed publicly that the SS had replaced the Pinkertons, the same detectives remained in the field. The same agents reported to Pinkerton Superintendent Hatfield who in turn reported to Winter. Although Winter acted as chief of the SS, he received orders and authorizations from both McGee and Lind. Payments to the SS agents were funneled through Winter's assistant, Minneapolis attorney Clyde R. White, to avoid public scrutiny. The new agency put control over the statewide intelligence activities into the hands of the trio of CCA members—Winter, McGee, and Lind—with the authority of the state behind them.[17]

Before Winter even assumed his new duties, he discussed with Hatfield the "possible removal of the IWW organization from Minneapolis." Hatfield suggested that "steps should be taken to eliminate the IWW situation in the state." While Winter carefully cataloged the mass of information already collected by the Pinkertons on 200 suspects, Hatfield's agents actively sought new intelligence in northern Minnesota. Agent number 45, for example, questioned miners in Eveleth and Elba on August 14, hung around Duluth IWW headquarters in work clothes on August 17, and met with an informant in the inner circle of the Bemidji IWW on August 19. Agent 45's reports indicated no labor trouble on the docks or in the mines or lumberyards. Other agents sifted through confiscated IWW literature and records, collecting evidence that might be useful in future prosecutions. All reports and significant evidence were shipped to Hatfield or Winter in St. Paul.[18]

The Secret Service reserved its greatest efforts in time and staff for Carl E. Ahlteen, editor for the IWW paper *Allarm*, a Swedish-language newspaper which was published in Minneapolis. Winter and Hatfield both felt that Ahlteen and his anti-war paper had to be "promptly stopped," because "Every day that he is allowed to run means the stirring up of more trouble." Hatfield believed that the *Allarm* should not be distributed in Minnesota during a state of war. Ahlteen editorials pronounced that "the damnation of generations is over the heads of those who have been too cowardly to refuse to go out and murder innocent people and destroy the blooming lands and innocent inhabitants."[19]

In early July, the ss instituted an intensive surveillance of Ahlteen. Three agents, based in a hotel room rented across the street from iww headquarters, shadowed Ahlteen night and day. A fourth agent investigated leads from their reports. On July 15, for example, agent "D. J. G." questioned the inhabitants of three buildings that Ahlteen had visited the day before. Winter was infuriated when this painstaking effort was temporarily ruined by federal authorities who prematurely arrested Ahlteen without obtaining evidence that the ss had already located. Winter was forced to bide his time as reports of the released Ahlteen's "dangerous" activities continued to pour in.[20]

In addition to the Pinkerton detectives, intelligence on the iww flowed to Winter's ss from a wide range of sources. The Minnesota Game and Fish Department, the State Fire Marshal, and other state agencies were asked to forward any information on the iww to Winter. Private organizations associated with the cca or the ca also reported to Winter. Suspicious letters to the editor were forwarded from the *Minneapolis Journal* to the ss. While Pinkertons supplied the basic manpower for the ss, other detective agencies were asked to send any information on the iww to Winter. To facilitate arrests and prosecutions based on ss intelligence, Winter shared information with local sheriffs, Thomas E. Campbell of the United States Department of Justice, the United States Secret Service, United States District Attorney Alfred Jacques, and innumerable other law enforcement authorities.[21]

The closest cooperation between intelligence agencies centered on Winter's ss attorney, Clyde R. White. White, who was also a United States Military Intelligence agent, passed raw agent reports to the Department of Justice and Military Intelligence. The federal government could therefore supplement the work of its own informants, who were deeply embedded in the iww structure. This informal network of agents worked for the cca, the mcps, and the United States Military Intelligence.[22]

In July 1917, Winter began gradually to reduce the number of Pinkerton agents employed by the ss. They were replaced by agents of the Minneapolis branch of the American Protective League, a volunteer organization whose mission was to maintain constant vigilance in an effort to discover plotters and evaders engaged in undermining the morale of the nation. The Minneapolis

APL was organized by the CCA, and its 400 agents were virtually all CCA members. The APL, nominally operating under the direction of the Bureau of Investigation (later renamed the FBI), set up headquarters in room 306 of the Federal Building with equipment and staff paid for by the CCA. With the cooperation of the MCPS, the chosen men were sworn in as peace officers and authorized to make arrests and carry guns. The SS, which had from its inception been controlled by CCA members, was now functioning completely as the CCA's private intelligence service.[23]

After two months of concentrated intelligence operations reports convinced Winter and Lind that the IWW was no longer a threat to the prosecution of the war. On July 9 and again on August 16, Winter reported to the MCPS that the IWW had "practically gone to pieces in Northern Minnesota." By August 27, the IWW's collapsed state "hardly need claim our interest," according to Winter. Lind bragged to Secretary of Labor William B. Wilson that the MCPS had "better control of the IWW than IWW leader 'Big Bill'(William D.) Haywood," its most active organizer. Occasional reports noted rumors of general strikes, but the actions never materialized.[24]

In agricultural regions where farmers frequently were sympathetic to the Nonpartisan League, labor shortages were a more significant problem than the IWW. Rumors that the IWW planned to burn crops were often started by intelligence agents attempting to induce radicals to reveal their plans. In any case, the suspected sabotage never took place. The MCPS confidently predicted that fifteen or twenty men armed with clubs could turn aside any IWW activity in the agricultural region.[25]

In the lumber mills, where a shortage of labor was again the primary problem, the SS intercepted an IWW communication that actually advised against violence and warned IWW members against advocating violence. It was clear by mid-summer that the MCPS and local authorities had extinguished any threat the IWW posed to the war effort. Despite these reports, the MCPS gathered seventy-five of the state's county sheriffs together to explain in great detail the many state and federal laws which they were encouraged to use to suppress the IWW and other seditious groups.[26]

The vagrancy ordinance, the Home Guard, and even Lind's radical suggestion that the IWW be put in special indoctrination camps, however, would suppress the IWW only for the duration of the war, and only in Minnesota. The CCA had a longer-range mission—maintaining the open shop after the war. With the CCA enjoying unprecedented influence over state government, the time was ripe to eliminate the IWW completely. As the MCPS explained later: "To successfully handle the problem, there was needed concerted action through the Federal Department of Justice, having jurisdiction in every state, and this action must take the shape of eradicating the organization's motive power by the arrest and conviction of Haywood and his associates."[27]

Chief Winter first wrote to Charles D. Frey of the Chicago Division of the APL in early July 1917, suggesting that the evidence his agents had collected on the IWW be pooled with that of Frey's Chicago agents and used for federal prosecution. Frey forwarded Winter's letter to Hinton G. Clabaugh, superintendent of the Chicago division of the Department of Justice, who agreed enthusiastically to Winter's request. Within two weeks, Lind and the MCPS would endorse Winter's strategy to destroy the IWW, despite the thorough intelligence that the IWW was completely under control. On July 26, Commissioner Lind met with Clabaugh, Campbell of the Minneapolis Department of Justice office, and MCPS attorney Tighe. The conference participants concluded that they had "sufficient data to proceed effectively against the head [main IWW] organization at Chicago, the agricultural organization here and to extend the drive as much further as is deemed expedient." Lind telegrammed and wrote United States Attorney General Thomas W. Gregory the same day explaining the urgent need for "prompt" federal action.[28]

Despite intelligence to the contrary, Lind indicated that, without immediate action, "Our crops will be wasted and lost. The lumber industry in this state will be paralyzed." Lind suggested that the IWW be "proceeded against under the conspiracy statute for conspiring to commit offenses created by the acts of Congress and for defrauding the Government by hindering its efficient prosecution of the war." Lind also suggested that the Labor Department deport IWW members as criminal aliens and that the Postal Service take action against IWW publications.[29]

When the federal government ignored Lind's suggestions, the MCPS sent Tighe to Washington where Assistant Attorney General Warren assured him that the Department of Justice had considered the problem and concluded that no federal statute was applicable. Warren had no sympathy for a "scheme of anticipatory action"; federal criminal proceedings were out of the question. Warren did agree, however, to call in one of his criminal law experts, O. E. Pagan, who agreed with Tighe's suggestion "that the important thing was not ultimate conviction but the immediate paralyzing of the movement by summary arrests of the leaders over a wide territory." Lind, however, believed that the prosecutions would be successful in the wartime hysteria. On August 5, Lind met in Chicago with Pagan, Clabaugh, and a Mr. Schluetter, Chicago chief of police, where Pagan finally committed the federal government to a plan of simultaneous raids on IWW headquarters throughout the country.[30]

On September 5, the plan that the CCA trio, Winter, McGee, and Lind, had hatched for controlling Minnesota's state government, finally went into action as federal authorities led the raids on IWW headquarters across the country. In Chicago alone, more than five tons of IWW literature were confiscated. In Minneapolis, three United States marshals and Department of Justice agents searched the offices of the IWW newspaper, *Allarm*, at Eleven and One-Half Western Avenue, the main office of the Agricultural Workers of the World branch of the IWW in the Kasota Building, and local agricultural branch Number 400 offices at Fourteen First Street South. Working late into the night, the teams removed "quite a quantity of letters, mailing lists, copies of various pamphlets and IWW literature and membership records to the Bureau of Investigation office." The MCPS report on its participation in the IWW raid indicated that "its work ended when it induced the prosecutions." The report neglected to mention that an agent of the CCA's American Protective League was on the raiding team.[31]

Winter's policy of concentrating his efforts on *Allarm* editor Carl Ahlteen continued on September 5, when Ahlteen's rooms were searched and his letters, documents, liquids and acids of various kinds, and IWW and socialist literature were all confiscated. To circumvent any possibility of Ahlteen fleeing prosecution, he was arrested the same day on an indictment returned by a Hennepin County grand jury, charging him with interfering with enlistments through the printing of seditious literature. The case against Ahlteen had been investigated and presented to the grand jury by Winter's SS. Later that month, the Postal Service withdrew second-class mailing privileges from *Allarm*. Ahlteen eventually served a five-year sentence on his federal convictions before he was deported to Sweden in 1923. The CCA had successfully suppressed the opposition press.[32]

Although the MCPS claimed that they "did not participate in the actual trial of the offenders," Winter's entire Secret Service files on the IWW were sent to Clabaugh in Chicago to be used in the federal prosecution. Department of Justice agent Campbell culled through the evidence taken in the raid and mailed it to Clabaugh to supplement the Minnesota SS evidence in Clabaugh's presentation to the Chicago grand jury. When difficulties with Minneapolis arose, one of the detective agencies that worked for the SS provided assistance in identifying Carl Ahlteen's handwriting. From conception to conviction, the MCPS and the CCA were intimately involved in the operation to destroy the IWW.[33]

The IWW had been beheaded, but a large and active body remained. Two years later, Luther W. Boyce of the Northern Information Bureau estimated that Agricultural Workers' branch number 400 still had 30,000 members. Although these were men who worked in the harvest fields and mining and lumber camps, IWW headquarters were in Minneapolis and they manned the industries on which the CCA's financial and industrial empire was based.[34]

Although the CCA's enmity for the Socialist Party was probably as great as or greater than its hatred of the IWW, the election of Thomas Van Lear as Minneapolis's mayor in 1916 had given the radical party a political legitimacy that the IWW could not claim. Fortunately for the business community, the Socialist Party's anti-war stance left it vulnerable to wartime suppression. McGee, however, was not satisfied with his small success in thwarting Van Lear. Van Lear's election in 1916 had made McGee "sick." When McGee was appointed to his powerful position on the MCPS, he was determined to drive Van Lear from office—or at least to undermine his administration. For McGee, 33,000 American citizens in Minneapolis voting to turn the city government over to the socialists was "the last straw."[35]

After the United States declared war in April 1917, Van Lear, as Minneapolis's mayor, appointed thirty-nine men to the local draft boards. McGee, convinced that these men were all socialists and pro-Germans, investigated each appointment and managed to eliminate eighteen of them. After a conference with Van Lear's police chief, McGee misquoted Chief Harthill to accuse his police officers of consorting with and condoning prostitution.[36]

The next step was to gather intelligence on subversive socialist activities. By early June of 1917, Winter's Secret Service agents were carefully scrutinizing the activities of known Socialist Party members. They concentrated their efforts on the editor of the *New Times*, Alexis E. Georgian. The *New Times*, the voice of Minneapolis's Socialist Party, had played a vital role in Van Lear's election. If the *New Times* met the same fate as the IWW's newspaper, *Allarm*, Minneapolis's radical press would be extinguished.[37]

Secret Service agent "C. H." visited the *New Times* bookstore, "the home of radical publications," on June 6, 1917, to buy copies of Socialist and IWW papers. He learned that Georgian was the editor of the *New Times* and the owner of the bookstore. The next day, using Minneapolis directories for a starting place, C. H. began a detailed investigation of Georgian's character and activities. Interviews of Georgian's neighbors and the local grocer revealed a respectable homeowner and family man who had emigrated from Russia fifteen years earlier. Although the Georgians were generally considered to be very fine people, "the neighbors do not associate with them on account of their being radical Socialists." C. H.'s investigation at four previous Georgian neighborhoods dating back to 1911 brought similar results. Although his credit was somewhat suspect, the Secret Service had not found any evidence on which it could prosecute Georgian.[38]

While Winter waited patiently for his opportunity to legally squash the Socialist paper, United States Army officers stationed in Minneapolis to recruit soldiers took direct and immediate action. In early June, they began making a sweep of Minneapolis newsstands to confiscate all copies of the *New Times*. At the Century News Store, purchased copies were even snatched from the hands of patrons. Newsboys on the street were threatened with jail if they were found selling the Socialist paper. The *New Times*, with its circulation badly curtailed, appealed to its subscribers to help distribute each issue. Georgian personally handed out the paper at outstate Socialist gatherings.[39]

Within a week, on June 16, 1917, Congress passed the Espionage Act, which "hereby declared to be unmailable" any publication "containing any matter which is intended to obstruct the recruiting or enlisted service of the United States." In Chicago, the postmaster quickly used the new remedy to suppress the *American Socialist* paper. Georgian realized that the *New Times* had been doomed by its anti-war message.[40]

At the same time, Governor J. A. A. Burnquist reminded the state's sheriffs that they had the authority to disband any meeting where seditious statements were being made and to arrest the disloyal speakers. With open season declared, county officials across the state took action against Socialist Party gatherings. When Andrew Hanson attempted to hold a meeting in Greeley, he was quickly apprehended by the local sheriff and run out of town. In Dale, a company of Home Guards from Hinckley and sheriffs from Pine, Isanti, and Chisago counties raided a large Socialist picnic. Socialist signs and pennants were thrown onto a bonfire along with a thousand copies of the *New Times*.[41]

The speakers at these meetings, usually Socialist Party leaders, were arrested and prosecuted by local and federal authorities. Abe L. Sugarman, secretary of the state organization, was arrested for "attempting to cause insubordination, disloyalty, mutiny and refusal of duty in the military forces of the United States." Jacob O. Bentall, Socialist candidate for governor in 1916, was convicted of obstructing the draft, while St. Paul leader Otto Wangerin was arrested for failing to register. Another prominent St. Paul Socialist, Allen S. Broms, was arrested for making seditious utterances in Litchfield. He had vaguely suggested that the draft law was unconstitutional. It was clear that the Socialist Party's anti-war message was not going to be tolerated in Minnesota. The socialist advances that had elected Van Lear mayor of Minneapolis were under direct assault. The CCA, through its influence over Governor Burnquist, the MCPS, and the Secret Service, was gradually destroying Van Lear's base of support in Minneapolis and across the state.[42]

In August of 1917, however, Van Lear's position as mayor and his control of the Minneapolis police force threatened to embarrass the city across the nation. The People's Council of America for Democracy and Peace, a national anti-war group formed in New York three months earlier, planned its first national convention to be held in Minneapolis in early September. It undoubtedly expected a friendly reception from Minneapolis's socialist mayor. Two special trains were to transport hundreds of anti-war delegates, representing hundreds of labor, agricultural, educational, women's, and socialist organizations, to Minneapolis from the East and West coasts.[43]

Van Lear welcomed the council and promised it the full protection of the Minneapolis police force. The CCA was appalled and determined to prevent the disloyal spectacle. Under pressure from Minneapolis's business leaders, the city's large meeting halls quickly became unavailable. The Peace Council rented a picnic grounds on Minnehaha creek and arranged to bring in two large tents. Stymied in their efforts to derail the convention, the *Minneapolis Journal* and the *Tribune* tried to arouse the patriotic indignation of the public by denouncing the "mistaken zealots" and "pro-German marplots" as anti-American traitors.[44]

On August 24, Mayor Van Lear eloquently defended the right of the Peace Council to meet: "While I am Mayor of this city, I do not propose that these hard-won testaments [the Bill of Rights] of our liberties shall in Minneapolis be treated as mere scraps of paper. . . . I assume that a constitutional democracy is still the form of government within the United States and that the people may with all propriety peaceably discuss subjects of vital interest to themselves." He was quickly to find that his assumption was mistaken.[45]

On August 27, Governor Burnquist, succumbing to public pressure, telegrammed an order to Hennepin County Sheriff Otto Langum to prevent the holding of the meeting if it would "in any way tend to injure the Government in the prosecution of the war or disturb the peace within the city of Minneapolis." Burnquist added his opinion that "intentional or unintentional arousing of anti-American sentiment or the dividing of our forces through ill advice and futile peace talk at this time will only aid and abet the enemy." Langum was authorized to use whatever forces were necessary, including the Minneapolis Civilian Auxiliary, a paramilitary militia organized that summer by the CCA. Given Van Lear's apparent determination to use Minneapolis police to protect the rally, the potential had been created for an explosive civil conflict between the police force and Langum's auxiliary. CCA President Albert M. Sheldon led a committee of five CCA directors to St. Paul to appeal to the Public Safety Commission for state intervention. They presented a unanimous resolution of the CCA board of directors that exhorted "His excellency, the Governor" to forbid the Peace Council meeting because it would "weaken the hands of government and encourage direct and treasonable resistance to the Selective Conscription Act of Congress" and "endanger the lives of the people of this city."[46]

After a lengthy conference between Langum, the CCA, and the MCPS, the Public Safety Commission passed a resolution introduced by Commissioner

McGee banning the Peace Council meeting. Governor Burnquist immediately issued a proclamation banning the Peace Council from the entire state because it could "have no other effect than that of aiding and abetting the enemies of this country." Accepting the reality of the governor's plan, the People's Council leaders canceled their meeting. The CCA, with the aid of its allies in St. Paul, had clearly shown the Socialist Party that they, and not Mayor Van Lear, were in charge of the city.[47]

Although McGee's actions against the Peace Council and draft boards may have restricted the scope of Van Lear's administration, by December 1, 1917, he was still the socialist mayor of Minneapolis—an untenable situation for both McGee and the CCA. Perhaps emboldened by the MCPS suspension of the mayor of New Ulm on August 22, McGee sought a simple but effective solution. On December 5, McGee suggested that the MCPS remove Van Lear and Harthill from office. From McGee's perspective there was ample evidence of their anti-war sentiments to justify his action. McGee's plan, however, was blocked by Commissioner Lind, who felt that "such action would have been in violation of the law and might have provoked 'civil war' in Minneapolis." Just three weeks after McGee's aborted attempt to remove him, Van Lear, obviously not intimidated, vetoed a proposed City Council ordinance recommended by the MCPS banning the "criminal syndicalism" of the IWW. With McGee stalemated and Van Lear unrepentant, the CCA would have to wait until the 1918 election to unseat Minneapolis's first and only socialist mayor.[48]

To defeat Van Lear at the polls, the CCA had to shut down the Socialist's Party's newspaper the *New Times*, which had continued to publish its weekly paper despite military harassment. For three years, the *New Times* had been printed by the Standard Press. On December 15, 1917, the printer suddenly demanded that the *New Times* pay all its outstanding debts before it would release the latest issue of the paper. While the dispute worked its way through the courts, Standard Press printed and then held back another *New Times* issue. At the same time, the Minneapolis Typothetae, an employers' association of printers and a close ally of the CA, stepped into the controversy. Typothetae lawyer Mr. Palmer informed the *New Times* that no printer in Minneapolis would print the Socialist paper. Immediately realizing the gravity of the threat, the *New Times* appealed to its readers for $800 to establish its own printing plant.[49]

As money slowly dribbled in, the United States government struck another financial blow against the CCA's radical enemy. United States Postmaster Burleson informed the *New Times* that a hearing would be held on April 19, 1918, at which the newspaper would be given the opportunity "to show cause why the authorization of admission of 'The *New Times*' to the second class of mail matter should not be revoked upon the following ground: This publication being in conflict with the Act of June 15, 1917 [Espionage Act]." No specific charges accompanied the request. The *New Times* realized that it would be impossible to bear the additional cost of first-class postage, one cent per paper. On its April 6, 1918, front page, the newspaper charged: "The powers that be want to deprive the socialists of Minneapolis of the Socialist paper for use in the coming important political campaign. The *New Times* has been so advantageously used in previous campaigns, notably in the Twelfth Ward, that the capitalists are determined to suppress it." The various efforts to undermine the Socialist newspaper had a devastating effect. By the time the November 1918 election approached, the *New Times* was an abbreviated monthly shadow of its former vigorous weekly self. Without the support of the *New Times*, Van Lear lost his bid for reelection by a small margin.[50]

The suppression of the Nonpartisan League was a much more difficult task. Despite its radical program, the league was an established political party that controlled the neighboring state of North Dakota. More important to the anti-league strategists, the NPL officially backed the war and, as the war progressed, became a firm supporter of President Wilson's policies. In response, the national government "at all times cooperated with the league, considering it an important spokesman for the northwest farmer." George Creel, head of the National Committee on Public Information, stated: "The federal government is not concerned with the political, economic, or industrial beliefs of any organization at a time like this, insisting only that every individual stand behind this war, believing absolutely in the justice of America's position. The Nonpartisan League, by resolution and by organized effort, has given this pledge of loyalty." The United States government, an effective ally in the suppression of the IWW and the Socialist Party, would observe the battle against the NPL from the sidelines. Without federal backing, all-out legal and military suppression of the league became impossible. The CCA and the MCPS, however, had sufficient intelligence and propaganda resources to mount a vicious political campaign against a formidable political enemy.[51]

Winter's Secret Service agents had begun watching NPL meetings during the summer of 1917. On July 13, agent "G. W. S." called Pinkerton Superintendent Hatfield to inform him that NPL leader Arthur C. Townley might be speaking in Boyd that evening. G. W. S. was instructed to make a detailed report on the possibly seditious meeting. Although Townley did not speak, G. W. S.'s report quoted a Mr. Titeen as telling local farmers that they were being asked "to give your sons as cannon fodder and give what little money you have ever received for your products to the purchase of liberty bonds." G. W. S. had to intercede when a gang of young men broke up the meeting and forced Titeen to kiss an American flag.[52]

The violent local reaction to NPL meetings in counties across the state quickly rendered the Secret Service vigilance irrelevant. When the meetings were not banned outright, local authorities were instructed to report any seditious remarks directly to the MCPS. Relieved of what might have been an extensive responsibility, the Secret Service concentrated its surveillance activities on the Socialist Party and the IWW.[53]

The MCPS had to reevaluate its position in September, however, when Progressive Wisconsin Senator Robert M. LaFollette, the most dedicated opponent of American entry into the war in Congress, appeared before the NPL convention and allegedly made a speech that the *Minneapolis Journal* described as "more disloyal, more treasonable, than the utterances that have landed lesser pro-Germans in prison." League leader A. C. Townley was summoned before the MCPS to explain the aims and methods of the NPL. The commission quickly appointed Charles W. Ames, T. G. Winter's brother-in-law and one of St. Paul's leading open-shop employers, to investigate "their method of operation, their financial methods, their purposes, their various activities, and the effect there of."[54]

From the beginning of his investigation, Ames was convinced that in "war time we cannot look tolerantly on any movement which seeks to crystallize discontent and to establish class distinctions." Despite Townley's rousing speeches for the liberty loan drives, Ames was convinced that he was a dangerous man. The NPL was particularly damned by its association with the IWW. The CCA had an able and dedicated ally working to undermine the league.[55]

To support this hysterical upswelling of patriotism, the MCPS appointed a director of public safety in each county. By the end of May 1917, every county had its own Public Safety Commission working under the guidance of the state body. On June 13, 1917, all these directors met in St. Paul to plan a cooperative effort of the entire state's defense organization. The county commissions, often acting in concert with local sheriffs, were particularly effective in suppressing the NPL, calling out the Home Guard units when force was necessary. In Swift County, for example, the director of Public Safety issued an order on February 16, 1918, forbidding seditious meetings. The order explained that meetings of the NPL "have in many instances been actually seditious and unpatriotic, and have given assistance, aid and encouragement to the common enemy." Following the inexorable logic of the MCPS, the league was seditious and therefore "all public meetings" of "the NPL or any like organizations, are hereby forbidden."[56]

Twenty other counties followed suit, severely hampering the ability of the NPL to run a statewide political campaign. Although the MCPS claimed that it "never at any time prohibited the NPL from holding meetings," its instructions to county officials encouraged local suppression. A printed opinion of the attorney general that each sheriff received made the MCPS's position quite clear: "I may add that any meeting, the tendency of which is to create or promote disloyalty to the United States in time of war, should not be tolerated," it instructed, "Any illegal and disloyal meeting must be prohibited." The MCPS tried to dodge responsibility by officially assigning the final decision in each case to local officials. Unofficially, the local suppression of NPL meetings was heartily encouraged.[57]

Governor Burnquist's loyalty campaign was supported by the separate efforts of the state's conservative business community. On October 7, 1917, twenty-six "Representative Americans" from across the state met at the St. Paul Hotel "for the purpose of opening a campaign to combat the traitorous and seditious influences in this state which have centered very largely in the NPL." W. Frisbie, a Minneapolis newspaperman and one of five CCA members present, suggested that a direct attack on the NPL might be imprudent. Instead, "we should make patriotism so popular that anything to the contrary could not live." Ambrose Tighe, representing the MCPS, asked the many newspaper people present if public opinion would approve of the suppression of NPL meetings. A consensus advised Tighe that the MCPS should concentrate its efforts on eliminating Townley. The newspapers of the state would "cooperate to the limit in every way possible."[58]

Several committees were appointed to organize immense loyalty meetings on November 16 and 17 in Minneapolis and St. Paul to "unite the people in support of the Government in its gigantic task of winning the war, and to make Americanism the paramount issue of the present." The *Duluth Tribune* announced from St. Paul that "every loyal man and woman in Minnesota will want to attend the convention and to make it so effective that it will stand as a final, crushing, cleansing answer to the polluting NPL gathering in this city." The arrangements committee outlined organizational plans for a patriotic association representing every county of the state to be formed at the Northwest Loyalty Meetings. On November 16, 1917, over 10,000 delegates jammed into the St. Paul Auditorium and founded the America First Association (AFA). The method and the organization to fight the NPL were ready even before Burnquist's campaign for reelection had been launched. Under the cloak of Americanism, Minnesota businesspeople hoped to destroy the NPL.[59]

At the first meeting of officers, President Frank W. Murphy explained that "it was the task of the America First Association to arouse the soul of America and to carry the meaning of the war to every individual citizen." Beginning on December 10, an America First loyalty meeting would be held in every township of the state over a two-week period. In cooperation with county committees, a central speakers' bureau was formed to coordinate the patriotic message of this enormous campaign. Within three months, over 100,000 Minnesotans joined the AFA. At fifty cents per member, a war chest of $50,000 was created. It was agreed that the AFA would absorb or guide other patriotic organizations. Pamphlets would be published to augment the patriotic effect of the loyalty meetings.[60]

Loyalty, of course, could also be enhanced by the creation of a fear and loathing of all things un-American. In one AFA pamphlet, *Americans Do Your Duty*, President Murphy branded the socialists and Russian Bolsheviks as the ultimate enemy of everything American. When the socialists (meaning the NPL) take over, "Law and Order are unknown. Chaos reigns. Men rule for a day by virtue of force and terror. Neither the rights of property or person are respected or safe."[61]

The loyalty campaign in Minneapolis was to be run by the Hennepin County AFA committee led by CCA leader Fred B. Snyder, who was also Hennepin County Public Safety Director. The CCA was also influential on the state level, where six members sat on the AFA executive board, including CCA President Cavour Langdon. To coordinate the CCA's loyalty activities, a Campaigns and Financial Appeals Committee was formed in October 1917. The chairman of the committee, Russell M. Bennett, a mineral lands dealer and vice president of the Minneapolis Society of Fine Arts, joined and played a leadership role in AFA and other loyalty campaigns.[62]

Loyalty meetings, unfortunately, were primarily attended by the already converted patriots of the state. The CCA realized that more active and direct means of spreading its message were necessary. At a later AFA meeting, CCA member architect Leroy S. Buffington moved that the executive officers of the AFA "be fully and completely empowered and authorized to do anything necessary to fight Bolshevikism or anything else that is un-American and take any steps that are necessary to reinstate Americanism."[63]

The CCA moved quickly to mail the message of Americanism directly to the farms of rural Minnesota. Bennett and Eli S. Warner, chairman of the Ramsey County AFA, were appointed to represent Minneapolis and St. Paul on a three-member committee to run another anti-NPL educational campaign, particularly in rural Minnesota. Charles S. Patterson, a St. Paul open-shop employer, was brought in to direct the operation in early October 1917. Patterson immediately hired the Van Hoesen and Collins advertising company from Chicago to develop an illustrated letter to inform 10,000 Minnesota merchants of the dangers of the NPL. Traveling salesmen employed by business members of the CCA and the St. Paul Association would then lobby the same merchants to reinforce the message.[64]

By January 1, 1918, the plan had expanded dramatically. Bennett, Warner, and Patterson signed a contract with On The Square Publishing Company, which Van Hoesen had created in St. Paul just to produce a high quality, anti-NPL magazine. Each monthly issue of 200,000 would be mailed free to a special list of farmers with a separate cover for each county. The cost of developing the mailing list, producing the first two issues, and mailing would be borne by the business members of the CCA and the St. Paul Association that Bennett and Warner represented. The funds were funneled through CA members First and Security and Northwestern Banks of Minneapolis and First National and Merchants National Banks of St. Paul. Although Van Hoesen expected his new company to be $30,000 in debt after two issues, he was confident that subscriptions and advertisements would soon turn a profit. The CCA's educational campaign was going to rely on the skills of a professional propagandist.[65]

Patterson and his CCA backers realized that to turn the farmers of the state against the NPL, On The Square would need an explosive exposé of corruption or sedition. Van Hoesen promised to develop files, handle the details of follow-up work, and write and edit the magazine. Patterson had the intelligence connections necessary to uncover any hidden skeletons in the NPL closet. Investigator Ames from the Committee on Public Safety and Minneapolis detective Luther W. Boyce of the Northern Information Bureau failed, however, to develop the explosive material that was needed.[66]

With the NPL still showing strength in Minnesota after the December loyalty meetings, prominent CCA leaders took the initiative in developing intelligence on the league. CCA attorney Rome G. Brown approached allegedly disaffected league organizer Walter E. Quigley. Quigley traveled from Lincoln, Nebraska, to meet with Brown; F. H. Carpenter, a millionaire CCA lumberman and prominent Republican; Republican political boss Ed Smith; and Harry W. Hunter, editor of the *Minneapolis Tribune*. The group claimed to represent other Republican leaders and "other persons and interests opposed to the league." Quigley was offered $200 per month plus expenses to find the proof necessary to expose the league as pro-German and socialistic. Unfortunately for the enemies of the league, Quigley reported the entire plot back to the NPL. On January 21, 1918, the *Nonpartisan Leader* published the entire sordid effort. *On The Square* would have to rely on more conventional sources.[67]

The first issue of *On The Square* appeared on the streets and doorsteps of the state in early May of 1918, in time for the June primary election. Its "educational campaign" included a long article, "Come Clean: Do Away with Pretense," which connected A. C. Townley with the Socialist Party and the IWW. An editorial, "Obey the Law," proclaimed that "the loyal men and women of Minnesota have come into their own—the fear of the law has [been] put into the heart of every Shadow Hun and disloyalist." A full-page advertisement pushing *On The Square* subscriptions warned that "Never before in the history of the world were conditions as they are today—Never were times more favorable for disloyal—seditious—backbiting—pro-German propaganda that is abroad in our land—vindictively flaying—endeavoring to ruin—your business and ours—a menace to our Government—our freedom—our liberty and our homes—our loved ones—everything we hold dear." For one dollar a year, "true—loyal—patriotic Americans could pay for this educational campaign, the like of which you have never seen." The June issue featured a lengthy article praising the Minnesota Commission of Public Safety, whose support for the farmers of the state was "best shown in its almost complete banishment from the state of the despicable IWW and kindred organizations." A full-page AFA ad insisted that "Loyalty vs. Disloyalty" was the only issue of the campaign. The June 17 primary was Minnesota's chance to "aid for once and all in ridding from our state the grave menace of socialism." [68]

By the time the second issue of *On The Square* hit the streets in June, Van Hoesen was having financial problems and seriously thinking about selling out. The anticipated landslide of subscriptions and advertisements had not occurred. *On The Square* folded ignominiously after two issues, nearly $40,000 in debt. The CCA and its St. Paul allies, perhaps feeling that the paper had already served its purpose, made no effort to resuscitate it.[69]

While reports of supposed NPL disloyalty poured in from across the state, Ames concentrated on the actions and utterances of league leaders. On February 25, 1918, Ames reported to Governor Burnquist that "the loyalty of the league is a sham and . . . the war sympathies are rather with Germany than with America and allies. The evidence of disloyal purposes on the part of Townley and his associates are, to my mind, overwhelming." Ames's report, however, contained very little new evidence against the NPL. Convinced that he had a first-class case, Ames began a long campaign to convince the federal government to prosecute NPL leaders. If successful, the NPL could be destroyed in its North Dakota base as well as in Minnesota. In early February, Ames traveled to Washington, D.C., to present a great quantity of data, briefs, and complaints against Townley and his associates. Ames was quietly ignored. The Department of Justice felt that "Mr. Ames and his associates had a wrong conception of the Espionage Act," and concluded that all of Ames's evidence was merely "the expression of views on economic and political subjects."[70]

Desperate to suppress the "revolutionary" league, Ames continued his investigation for several years, hiring his own agents after the MCPS folded. With the aid of Minnesota Congressman Clarence B. Miller, he lobbied the halls of Congress and corresponded frequently with military intelligence officials—to no avail. The Wilson administration would never agree to prosecute the NPL leadership. The MCPS and the CCA would have to defeat the league without federal assistance. The wartime showdown would take place in the voting booths in the 1918 election.[71]

As the election campaign of 1918 heated up, the NPL was "isolated as the prime target of the Public Safety Commission." Judge McGee, with his usual candor, suggested that "now we should get busy and have that firing squad working overtime." Instead, Governor Burnquist ingeniously announced that he would not be campaigning for reelection because he did not "believe this is a time to go into politics." In fact, Burnquist combed the state giving "loyalty speeches" at loyalty meetings that his campaign workers tirelessly encouraged.[72]

At the same time, masses of virulent propaganda poured from the MCPS presses. The pamphlet *Aiding the Enemies of Our Nation!* warned the state of the dangers of electing NPL candidates. In the pamphlet, Burnquist stated that "such arraying of class against class would be welcomed by the enemies of our republic for such a course will tend to defeat our nation in this war and eventually will mean the dissolution of our form of government and the undermining of the economic and political freedom of our people." Burnquist continued: "Any individual who will do so when our nation is in a life and death struggle is knowingly or unknowingly a traitor to his state and to his country."[73]

For Burnquist, the 1918 election was a fight between "two parties—one composed of loyalists and the other of the disloyalists." Burnquist and the MCPS, however, undoubtedly realized that their simplistic message would be more effective if the voters of the state were not allowed to hear the NPL's competing message. The MCPS's statement on citizenship urged that: "Citizens who uphold the government must not permit dissent to run away with public opinion. Loyalty meetings must smother assemblies of discontent."[74]

Burnquist's inflammatory remarks created a maelstrom of violence against the NPL. Across the state, townspeople, often leading citizens, ran league speakers out of town. In Rock Creek, farmer and league organizer Nels Hokstad was beaten and later tarred and feathered. In Le Sueur County, a league member was painted yellow by a mob, which then painted obscene pictures on his barn. On April 30, 1918, the chief witness for the defense of an NPL organizer was driven out of Red Wing before he could testify. Seventy-two NPL candidates, desperate for the end of the "Minnesota reign of terror, intended to prevent farmers from participating in self government," finally appealed to Governor Burnquist. The governor ignored the request. The week before the primary election, NPL gubernatorial candidate Charles A. Lindbergh, Sr., was arrested and thrown in jail in Martin County for attempting to hold a meeting. Across the state, forty of two-hundred-and-fifty scheduled NPL meetings had to be abandoned. Violence against the league was reported in twenty-seven counties.[75]

When the June primary votes were finally counted, Burnquist defeated Lindbergh by close to 50,000 votes. Lindbergh, however, had received over 150,000 votes despite the wave of patriotic hysteria that suppressed his campaign. NPL historian Robert Morlan concluded: "The league and its candidate had put up a valiant fight against tremendous difficulties, but the odds proved too great"—odds that were stacked by the MCPS and the CCA. The onslaught of anti-NPL propaganda and patriotic hysteria orchestrated by the CCA had panicked enough Minnesotans into voting for Burnquist to turn the tide against Lindbergh and the league. Although the league was also defeated in the November election, it had made astounding inroads on the Minnesota political landscape. The CCA, aware of this threat and the limitations of its 1918 educational campaign, began planning for another showdown in 1920.[76]

9 The CA's Private Army and the 1917 Streetcar Strike

DESPITE THE REASSURING EXISTENCE of a friendly and powerful dictatorship in the capital, the Civic and Commerce Association realized that state interests might respond slowly to a disturbance that was purely local or that might be politically sensitive. Governor Burnquist was wary of alienating labor totally and might ignore Public Safety Commissioner McGee's advice regarding a local strike. The CCA planned accordingly and built its own system of defense.

Immediately following the United States' declaration of war in April 1917, the association formed the Civilian Auxiliary. This "army of citizens" was purported to be engaged merely in military training for the "intelligent" backing up of the boys at the front. Most of the men recruited, however, were businessmen affiliated with the association and were well beyond the age of active military service. Their only conceivable use was in the defense of the home front.[1]

Colonel Perry G. Harrison, an association member and a former lieutenant colonel in the National Guard, was placed in command. Over 300 Minneapolis men attended the first drill sessions at the College of St. Thomas in St. Paul on April 11, 1917. Archbishop John Ireland made the staff and facilities available to train the auxiliary and a similar group organized by the St. Paul Association. This force rapidly grew to over 1,000 businessmen, divided into eight companies. The drills were then moved to the University of Minnesota, which provided Springfield rifles. According to the CCA, an "esprit de corps and discipline developed which made possible the most effective use of the auxiliary in important community service."[2]

During the summer of 1917, the auxiliary's lack of usefulness led to a gradual decline in both numbers and enthusiasm. A great demonstration with marches and sham battles at the State Fairgrounds in late May and running the Red Cross War Fund campaign in June were briefly exciting, but with the summer heat and vacation season, the auxiliary rapidly dwindled. In August, morale reached its lowest ebb, and officers were considering a vote on whether or not to disband. Developments on the Minneapolis labor front were responsible for saving and reinvigorating the force.[3]

Angered by low wages and poor working conditions, the employees of the Minneapolis and St. Paul railway lines, the Twin City Rapid Transit Company (TCRTC), selected representatives from each car barn during the second week of September. The committee of workers, which had no union affiliation, visited the offices of the streetcar company and asked for a three cents-per-hour wage increase and improved working conditions. The men claimed that it was impossible "to give our wives and children a somewhat decent existence" on the wages paid and complained that a ten-hour day often lasted up to eighteen hours with no pay for the extra hours.[4]

When TCRTC President Horace B. Lowry refused their request, the men called a meeting for Sunday, September 23, and invited the Minneapolis Trades and Labor Assembly to send an organizer. Within two days, Lowry had learned, either from his company or the CA's intelligence operatives, the names of twenty of the thirty-two men involved. They were immediately discharged. Lowry's action galvanized the employees into seeking help from the International Amalgamated Association of Street and Electric Railway Employees. On the next Monday, over 400 employees attended a meeting at the Trades and Labor Assembly hall. Suddenly the union movement had a firm and growing foothold in one of the CA's most important members. The keystone for the maintenance of the open shop, the transportation industry, was once again threatened.

Lowry and CA leaders, with fourteen years of union-crushing experience behind them, knew what to do: Refuse to negotiate, clean out union agitators, offer better wages and conditions, accuse radicals of fomenting the union upswelling, and prepare to overwhelm strikers with superior military or police force. In an effort to check the mushrooming union, Lowry immediately offered his men the 10 percent raise and improved working conditions that they had requested. At the same time, he fired another thirty-seven employees involved in the rebellion. The union organization was quickly blamed on Lynn Thompson, a socialist member of the Minneapolis School Board and a pacifist.[5]

Fortunately for the CA, the military force had already been organized. In preparation for the battle to come, officers of the Civilian Auxiliary met at the Minneapolis Athletic Club on September 6 and decided to reorganize into four companies of 150 men each. A letter to members stated: "The auxiliary should have a more definite object and duty." To accomplish this, they would all enroll as deputies to the Hennepin County sheriff.[6]

On Thursday night, September 13, Sheriff Langum swore in the members of the Civilian Auxiliary. This step increased membership and morale, finally gave the CCA's essentially illegal private army an official status, and created a nominal governmental authority, which the association could still control. On September 25, Sheriff Langum sent out special instructions to the Civilian Auxiliary, giving its members the same police powers he held, which included bearing arms and making arrests. Colonel Harrison would be in command in the field, but he would receive orders from Langum. Langum also told the organization "to perfect its system of mobilization at once, in order to enable it to promptly respond when called."[7]

With any hope of negotiations gone, the Minneapolis Street and Electric Railway Employees union struck at 1:00 A.M., Monday, October 6. Word of the strike was rushed to Sheriff Langum, who immediately ordered the mobilization of the Civilian Auxiliary to protect the property and employees of the streetcar company. Colonel Harrison and Major Henry A. Bellows orchestrated the meticulously planned maneuvers from their headquarters in room four of the Minneapolis courthouse. In anticipation of the strike, a "war map" of the city had been drawn, and duties of notification and assignments of posts had been clearly defined for the 600 members of the force. Headquarters called Captain L. Merle Wilson of Company B, who then notified lieutenants Henry C. Mackall, Walter H. Newton, and Sergeant Paul H. Struck. For several hours, the city telephone operators busily completed the chain for each of the four companies. The Civilian Auxiliary, armed and uniformed, rushed to protect the city's transportation system.[8]

At 1610 West Franklin Avenue, Sergeant Edward B. Karow of Company B received a telephone call from Lieutenant Newton. Karow, an assistant to streetcar company President Lowry, notified the other men assigned to car no. 10: Arthur C. Asleson, president of Minneapolis Equipment Company; Edwin C. Brown, a Minneapolis lawyer; Paul M. Marshall, assistant manager of Shane Brothers and Wilson Company; and Edwin S. Pattee, an inspector at Minneapolis Steel and Machinery Company. As soon as they were joined by a half-dozen other cars at the Parade Grounds, their preliminary mobilization point, they proceeded to Company B headquarters at the streetcar firm's Northside car barn at Twenty-fourth Street and Washington Avenue North. By 5:00 A.M., all twenty-seven cars had arrived, and the patrols were sent out to their assigned posts. A little over four hours after the strike was called, Sergeant Karow arrived with three of his men at the intersection of North Plymouth and Sheridan Avenues, armed and ready to defend the property of the streetcar company.[9]

Patrols found little to do in the early morning hours of October 6, except chase a gang that had stolen a switch tongue. Later in the day, a crowd of 150 union sympathizers gathered outside the Northside barn. The crowd tried to dissuade carmen from going on their routes and occasionally threw rocks through the windows of departing streetcars. Despite these minor incidents, service continued on a normal schedule. The threat increased that evening when over a hundred union sympathizers, men and women, marched toward the barn armed with clubs, bricks, and stones. Sheriff Langum had said: "Just let somebody start something." Despite the ominous gathering, he had reason to be confident. Company B boasted an armory of 66 Krag-Jorgensen rifles and 115 Springfields, 40 of which were in use guarding each carbarn. The crowd was dispersed, and one of the leaders was charged with attempting to incite a riot. The only significant resistance during the Minneapolis strike was crushed.[10]

The Civilian Auxiliary remained on duty for the duration of the four-day strike, patrolling the streets while the cars ran and sleeping in the barns at night. The streetcar company furnished cots and blankets, meals and smokes. The only displays of opposition were sporadic incidents of rock throwing. The highly organized and heavily armed force maintained order in what was potentially a highly volatile situation.[11]

The St. Paul scene, however, was markedly different. The *Pioneer Press* reported: "Wild rioting in which the police were unable to control mobs numbering in the thousands marked the end of the first day of the street car strike." For four hours, the mobs roamed downtown St. Paul streets, breaking windows and attacking whichever streetcars were attempting to move. Without a call-up of the lightly armed St. Paul Auxiliary, the railway company was forced to shut down.[12]

To forestall an invasion of Minneapolis by St. Paul strikers, Sheriff Langum posted heavy guards on all the bridges between the two cities. On Sunday, at the request of Governor Burnquist, over 500 federal soldiers from the First, Thirty-sixth, and Forty-first Minnesota Infantry units under Fort Snelling Commander Colonel Parmeter were ordered to patrol the streets of St. Paul with bayonets and rifles. This show of military strength intimidated the rioters of the previous day and allowed Lowry to return his streetcars to a normal schedule. While an argument raged between Governor Burnquist, Adjutant General Walter F. Rhinow, and St. Paul businessmen on whether to call out the Home Guard or more federal troops, Sheriff Langum announced that he was opposed to any call-ups for Minneapolis. The Civilian Auxiliary had already proven itself capable of maintaining order and would continue to do so.[13]

After four days, the Commission of Public Safety, concerned about the violence and loss of service in St. Paul, decided to intercede. On October 9, Lowry, Briggs, George Lawson, secretary of the State Federation of Labor, and other representatives of the company and the union were questioned by the commission. The MCPS then ordered the strike to cease and all strikers to be reinstated. The MCPS would investigate the status of the fifty-seven fired men and rule on each case. The strike was over.[14]

Lowry thanked Colonel Harrison profusely for the actions of the Civilian Auxiliary in Minneapolis and quietly agreed to abide by the MCPS order. By October 12, all but thirteen of the men were back at work. The unions claimed a victory—they had received a 10 percent pay raise, better working conditions, and the reinstatement of their men. They had also demonstrated their power to shut down public transportation in St. Paul. The upheavals in St. Paul might have eventually forced Lowry and the CA to capitulate, thereafter swinging the balance of industrial power to the unions. The commission, by its action, had saved Lowry and the CCA from what might have been a bitter defeat. But the war was far from over.[15]

The Twin City Rapid Transit Company reacted quickly to the growing union threat and organized the Trainmen's Cooperative and Protective Association for its workers. Lowry was the constitutionally decreed president of this company union, with final arbitration power over its various worker committees. The membership card pronounced the ability of carmen "to manage their own affairs and represent and look after their own interests without interference by or affiliation with any other individual or organization." Each member was given a button to wear on his lapel or cap.[16]

The campaign backfired. The Minneapolis local of the Amalgamated Association of Street and Electric Railway Employees issued its own buttons to its members and stepped up recruitment. One hundred-and-sixty men from the Eastside barn abandoned the transparent Protective Association and swelled the union's ranks. The buttons readily identified the two camps as tension rapidly increased. Company foremen intensified a campaign of insult and intimidation against union members: Verbal abuse, beatings, and work harassment became daily events. The company and the Protective Association made a determined effort to force the Amalgamated Association into retreat, but instead, on November 1, the union once again appealed to the Commission of Public Safety.[17]

The commission declared that all agitation should cease, and named Samuel F. Kerfoot, president of Hamline University; Robert Jamison, a Minneapolis lawyer; and Norman Fetter, a St. Paul businessman, to a special committee to investigate the allegations of both sides. The biased nature of these appointments became apparent three days later when Jamison resigned because he owned Twin City Rapid Transit stock. He was replaced by CCA member Waldron M. Jerome. Although rumors were denied that Fetter also owned stock and that Hamline had been endowed by Thomas Lowry (Horace's father and the first president of the transit company), the fact that the president of

Hamline's board of trustees was also a director of the Citizens Alliance and a cca member suggests a likely bias on Kerfoot's part. The special committee's final report confirmed these suspicions, stating that it "felt it necessary in discretionary cases where the evidence was evenly balanced to resolve doubts in favor of the company." The union's fate had already been decided when the hearings began on November 7.[18]

While the special committee deliberated, the ca and streetcar company prepared for the next battle. Edward Karow, now a staff lieutenant and ordnance officer, was dispatched to St. Paul to train the St. Paul Civilian Auxiliary. Although newspapers proclaimed that the St. Paul unit was fully equipped and armed, Karow's effort was frustrated by the interference of commission member Charles W. Ames. He and Ramsey County Sheriff John Wagener assured the business community that all was being taken care of—when in fact nothing was actually being done. Karow returned to Minneapolis to write a manual for the use of the Civilian Auxiliary's 600 new riot sticks. The organization's general service manual stated that while the stick was to be the primary weapon for riot control, each company would also have ten men with loaded, high-powered magazine rifles in case the commanding officer decided to shoot the leaders of a mob. The unions complained to Governor Burnquist that the Civilian Auxiliary was essentially a private army for employers and that wearing army uniforms and carrying rifles were illegal. They wanted the auxiliary disbanded. The only response was the issuance of new steel-gray uniforms that could not be mistaken for United States Army khaki.[19]

On November 19, the special committee recommended "total disuse and abandonment of buttons or other insignia symbolizing the Union or the Nonunion organizations." It further stated that both sides had agreed to this stipulation. However, the committee also recommended that all union solicitation and propaganda "shall cease on the company's property, in and above stations, and upon the cars." The streetcar company was to enforce these rulings. [20]

The next day, the mcps adopted these recommendations in full, and Lowry immediately posted the following order:

Effective Immediately

In compliance with the above, employees shall be governed strictly by the following rules:

1. No employe shall wear any button indicating Union or Non-Union affiliation.
2. No employe shall discuss on Company property, in or about Stations or on the cars, the subject of Unionism or Non-Unionism and all agitation of this subject shall cease.

**3. It is the patriotic duty of all of us to abide by the orders or rec-
ommendations of the MN. Commission on Public Safety.**

**In the interests of public service we feel sure that all of our employ-
ees will cheerfully comply with the above and cooperate in the interest of harmony.**

Nov. 21, 1917   Horace Lowry, President

Most of the union men, who had not yet voted on the agreement, refused
to comply. After discussions with the commission, the union agreed to vote on
November 26, but word was leaked to the company on the 24th. On November 25, Lowry issued an ultimatum that any men wearing buttons or agitat-
ing on company property would be fired. The amalgamated saw this as an attempt to destroy its organization; approximately 800 men considered
themselves locked out. The union contended that the commission's recommendation was unenforceable and gave Lowry no authority of dismissal.[21]

The MCPS firmly backed the company and issued Order No. 16 on November 27, giving its recommendations the force of law. In hopes of averting a
crisis, the order also allowed for reinstatement of the 800 men. The union
adamantly refused to comply, playing into Lowry's hands. Instead of merely
striking the company, the workers were now in direct opposition to an order
of the commission. The dispute would move to the streets and the transit
company and the CA would be backed by all the force of the state of
Minnesota.[22]

While CA leader Otis P. Briggs directed the streetcar company's battle with
the unions, he also quietly lobbied for a "status quo" ruling. In early May,
United States Secretary of Labor William B. Wilson had stated: "This is no time
to take advantage of emergencies to force recognition of the union. It is the
height of disloyalty to force or bring about a stoppage of our industries in order to force the establishment of standards they have not been able to force
during normal conditions." The Citizens Alliance interpreted this to mean
"that there shall be no attempt of Organized Labor to further unionize the
country." Although the status quo would also apply to employers, this was not
a disadvantage for the alliance because Minneapolis was already 95 percent
non-union. There were to be no strikes or lockouts; the open shop would be
preserved for the duration of the war.[23]

Briggs lobbied the MCPS tirelessly for his principles while he secretly represented the employers in strike discussions with the commission. On November
20, in the middle of the controversy, McGee moved that the commission adopt
a status-quo resolution. The passage of this resolution, which ordered that no
"individual or combination of individuals begin to unionize or undertake dur-

ing the like period, to further unionize or close an open or non-union shop or industries," probably precipitated the union's non-compliance with the button order. While Order No. 16 would halt organization of the streetcar work-ers, McGee's resolution attempted to stop all such activity statewide. The unions could not accept measures that outlawed their activities on this scale.[24]

While association members sent a flurry of telegrams to Governor Burnquist congratulating him on his wisdom and integrity in handling the controversy, the unions appealed to the federal government. Fearing an outbreak of violence, officials in Washington appointed federal conciliator Robert S. Coleman to arbitrate. The unions agreed immediately. Lowry and Briggs refused. Acting Secretary of Labor Louis F. Post urged Lowry to submit the point in dispute to fair arbitration. Lowry telegraphed: "You surely do not intend to suggest arbitration whether the company shall obey or disobey an order made after full hearings by the Minnesota Commission of Public Safety."[25]

The commission order had effectively locked the union out; now Lowry, Briggs, McGee, and the CCA could concentrate on defending the authority of the state. Burnquist had to join them. On December 1, he wired Post, "Interference at this time will simply result in an attempt to defy a duly constituted authority of Minnesota.... I shall use every power at my command to uphold the dignity of the State."[26]

On Sunday, December 2, the tense situation finally exploded on the streets of St. Paul. As the crowd dispersed from a labor rally in Rice Park, angry mobs began attacking streetcars. Fifty non-union car operators were injured, and evening service was completely halted. With Sheriff Wagener refusing to call out the auxiliary, the police department was unable to control the situation. The St. Paul Home Guard was finally called out at 1:00 P.M., and in two hours it had cleared the downtown area and established barricades around what was called a restricted area. The next day, Governor Burnquist, angry over his hesitation, removed Sheriff Wagener from office for dereliction of duty.[27]

On December 4, Adjutant General Rhinow sent out an emergency order to Home Guard units across the state. The men of Company C, Seventh Battalion of Austin, hurriedly left their stores and offices, hopped a special train, and three hours later were the first troops on the ground to fight "The War of St. Paul." They were quickly joined by 3,200 armed men from Red Wing, Mankato, Winona, and Duluth. The Home Guard troops slept on the floors of the Capitol and were provisioned by the St. Paul Auxiliary. Like the Minneapolis Civilian Auxiliary, many of these St. Paul units were staffed by the merchants and businessmen of their communities. Although the approach of the holiday season worked a hardship on these volunteers, their first "taste of blood" raised the enthusiasm of the state's newly created troops.[28]

In Minneapolis, the situation was markedly different: Sheriff Langum called out the Civilian Auxiliary immediately after the St. Paul riots began. The heavily armed patrols of the auxiliary's four companies rushed to protect the transit line's property. Downtown streets were swept clean of any potential troublemakers by columns of riot-stick-toting men. Scattered fights broke out as auxiliary members prodded people coming out of downtown union meetings, but these aggressive tactics prevented any large crowds from forming. In their recently issued moleskin uniforms and sheepskin-lined overcoats, the businessmen easily withstood the 25-degree-below-zero temperatures. With increasing violence threatened, Northwestern National Bank donated sixty-six additional .30 caliber rifles with bayonets. The CCA had thoroughly prepared its army and once again controlled the streets of Minneapolis.[29]

Although the Civilian Auxiliary and the Minnesota Home Guard had temporarily quelled the rioting in St. Paul, a massive labor convention of representatives from Minneapolis and St. Paul unions and the Minnesota State Federation of Labor was scheduled for December 5, and the possibility of a general strike was threatened. In Washington, Secretary of War Newton D. Baker entered the controversy. A general strike would halt Twin Cities' war production and tie up vital rail traffic. Baker wired Governor Burnquist: "The serious situation which would exist if widespread sympathetic resistance to these orders occurs" must be avoided. Baker suggested that MCPS Order No. 16, which severely curtailed any union activity, be suspended and the entire situation reopened. The federal government would then assist the commission in adjusting grievances.[30]

McGee and the streetcar company were appalled. Federal intervention could be disastrous to the CCA's position. McGee immediately wired Baker, Secretary of the Treasury William G. McAdoo, and Senator Knute Nelson that the trouble was practically over and interference from Washington would only revive it. The matter could not be reopened "without impeaching the integrity, intelligence and competency of the Public Safety Commission." Once again, Burnquist was forced to defend both himself and the business interests. He told Baker: "Reopening of the decision as matters now stand would be a surrender of government by reason of riots and agitation and would be an incentive to further riots and agitation." The federal government wavered and waited for further developments.[31]

On Wednesday morning, in zero-degree weather, 15,000 unionists stopped work and gathered at the St. Paul Auditorium. All pledged support for the streetcar unions and demanded that Ames and McGee be fired. The public, offended by the Public Safety Commission's attack on the liberties of the union men, generally supported the strikers. Minneapolis Mayor Van Lear vehemently denounced the CCA and the MCPS and declared labor in accordance with the principles of President Wilson. The convention decided to wait for federal intervention until December 11, at which time it would reconvene and vote on a general strike.[32]

Burnquist, in a public attempt to convince Washington that he was not anti-labor, fired Ames. In fact, Ames had been in Washington counseling with Baker on federal intervention and therefore had infuriated McGee and Burnquist. McGee, of course, maintained his position on the commission. While the Civilian Auxiliary continued to patrol Minneapolis streets, both sides waited for a decision from Washington, where Post, Baker, and President Wilson vacillated between the necessity for intervention and the inevitable problems that it would create for the state of Minnesota.[33]

During the lull, the CCA's private intelligence service continued its investigations of all suspected disloyalty. On December 7, following up on a tip, agents investigated a suspected headquarters for anti-government propaganda in the Upham Building at University and Raymond avenues in St. Paul. The site turned out to be the office for a faction of the machinists' union. Agents listening in on conversations from adjoining rooms learned that the machinists were making plans for a statewide general strike in the event that union leaders failed to defeat the streetcar company. American Protective League Chief Charles Davis then wrote to Commissioner Henry W. Libby, who had replaced Ames, to report on the incident and ask for further instructions. The league would be glad to assist Libby in any way, Davis assured him, and it would be easy to watch the union office secretly to obtain additional information.[34]

A sympathy strike of all union members in the Twin Cities was finally called for 10:00 A.M., December 13. Adjutant General Rhinow announced that martial law might have to be declared to handle the 30,000 people that the union estimated would stop work. Burnquist ordered all liquor stores closed and instructed Sheriff Langum and Acting Sheriff Earnest H. Davidson of Ramsey County to maintain order. More than 10,000 workers had left their jobs by noon, when Washington finally decided to act. Secretary of War Baker, on President Wilson's authority, telegraphed William B. Wilson, chairman of the President's Mediation Commission, that because of "federal interests" the commission should stop in the Twin Cities and look into the controversy.[35]

As a result, State Federation of Labor President E. G. Hall called off the strike at 1:30 P.M. It had lasted less than four hours with no reports of violence. Governor Burnquist, however, accused the President's Commission of "creating an opportunity for further agitation" and of undermining "a wholesome respect for law and order and for state and national government."

Although the governor agreed to meet with the Mediation Commission, he insisted: "The matters in dispute . . . have been decided, and the decision can not now be reopened."[36]

The President's Mediation Commission heard testimony at the Radisson Hotel in Minneapolis from union representatives, from Lowry and Edward W. Decker of the streetcar company, from a delegation from the Civic and Commerce Association, and from members of the Public Safety Commission. Then the commission obtained a written agreement from the unions not to strike, and returned to Washington.[37]

Whether they feared losing a strike or simply misunderstood the issues that were now paramount is unclear, but, for whatever reason, the unions had signed away their last chance. The MCPS continued to insist that the issue was closed, and, given its record, there was certainly no reason to doubt its convictions. Lowry felt that the issue was "so serious that no matter who signs the communication from Washington, it will be necessary for us to refuse to comply." Governor Burnquist remained just as adamant. The unions refused to believe the obvious: Lowry, the CA, and the MCPS fully intended to ignore any federal intervention.[38]

While the workers waited through January for the findings of the Mediation Commission, the streetcar company began advertising in the smaller agricultural towns of the state in order to recruit a new labor force that had no connection with Twin Cities' unions. Lieutenant Karow placed ads in rural papers offering "healthy, outdoor, interesting work." The CCA was also instrumental in setting up the State Employment Bureau in Minneapolis, which was active in finding clients railway jobs. The new employees were assured that their positions were permanent. Lowry had no intention of ever rehiring union men.[39]

On February 14, 1918, the President's Mediation Commission recommended that the streetcar company re-employ union men at their pre-strike wages and status and not discriminate against members of trade unions. Secretary of War Baker requested that the MCPS urge the company to comply. The CA concluded that "the so called Federal Mediation Commission was merely a strongly pro-union body clothed with a large degree of authority by the Federal Government, which was making a business of forcing the closed shop on to every business institution, where labor troubles occurred."[40]

Lowry replied that compliance "would be imposing a gross injustice" upon the men who had remained loyal and operated the public service throughout the controversy. The MCPS continued to consider the issue closed and claimed that the federal government had no power to force compliance. The CA now had the backing of the MCPS "in resisting the subversive policy of the Federal Administration." Policies with respect to labor unions "constituted a grave menace to the industrial and social life of the nation and it is high time that effective action should be taken to check the Bolsheviki tendencies of the Democratic Administration, which seeks to build up the power of irresponsible labor agitators to a point where they would have dictatorial powers with respect to industrial and economic matters," according to Harlow H. Chamberlain.[41]

J. H. Walker of the President's Commission wrote in frustration to the unions that, despite the approval of the National Council of Defense, "The company has positively refused to agree to the findings of the commission. . . . They have thus put themselves squarely on record in opposition to the war policies of our government at this time." The Mediation Commission worried that the attitude and policies of the MCPS and the CA were alienating a growing number of Minnesota's citizens from the federal government at a crucial moment in United States history. Briggs of the Citizens Alliance, echoing the CCA's opinion, concluded that Walker was just as much a socialist as Mayor Van Lear. Commissioner McGee accused the President's Commission of being "union labor men and socialists." He added: "There is no power on earth that can budge me one inch from following the path of duty as I see it." McGee's vision, of course, was dramatically opposed to the policies of the federal government.[42]

The anti-government stand taken by Lowry, the CA, and Burnquist was a publicity bonanza for the unions, which accused the company of aiding and abetting the enemy. The *Minneapolis Labor Review* said that Lowry "still stands, as does the Kaiser of Germany, opposed to the wishes of the Government." This campaign, however, failed to modify the MCPS's stance. Lowry and the CA, backed by the MCPS, remained defiant and triumphant.[43]

The winds of change, however, were beginning to blow from the nerve center of the nation's war effort. In January, disturbed by the effects of industrial disputes on war production, the secretary of labor appointed a War Labor Conference Board to develop a new federal labor policy. On March 29, 1918, the Conference Board recommended the creation of a National War Labor Board (NWLB) to mediate controversies between employers and employees that might "affect detrimentally" war production. On April 8, President Wilson issued a proclamation establishing the new NWLB and basing its policies on the principles developed by the conference board.[44]

The new federal labor policies outlined by President Wilson spelled disaster for the CA: The right of workers to organize in trade unions and to bargain collectively was recognized and affirmed: "This right shall not be denied, abridged, or interfered with by the employers in any manner what so ever. . . .

Employers should not discharge workers for membership in trade-unions, nor for legitimate trade union activities." The policies established a status quo for union shops and open shops that included union and non-union workers, but ignored the non-union shop that the Minnesota Commission of Public Safety had included in its November 20, 1917, resolution. The federal government made quite clear that the status quo could not be used in any way to impede the formation of labor unions or the right of workers to belong to a union.[45]

If these principles were fully enforced, they would have a revolutionary effect on Minneapolis industry. The city's major industrial shops would have to allow their employees to unionize. At Minneapolis Steel and Machinery and other CA plants, where the "open shop" had in reality been the non-union shop for many years, the machinists' union would now have the opportunity to organize and grow. The industrial power gained through the CA's impressive victories in the 1916 Teamsters' strike and the 1917 streetcar strike was now threatened by federal intervention.

Briggs and George Gillette and their friends on the MCPS realized that the state had to create its own arbitration procedures before the NWLB established itself as the arbitrator of Minnesota's labor relations. The day after the Federal Conference Board issued its startling recommendation, Governor Burnquist, who was constantly advised on labor matters by the CA's Briggs, issued his own proclamation. In it, he requested the moribund State Board of Arbitration "to confer at the earliest possible opportunity with labor organizations and with employers' associations in order that an understanding may at this time be reached whereby disputes involving unionism or non-unionism or other controversies resulting in strikes or lockouts shall be eliminated during the war." As president of the Minnesota Employers' Association, Gillette would represent the CA's interests in meetings with representatives of the Minnesota State Federation of Labor.[46]

Labor leaders supported an agreement that roughly paralleled federal policies. Employers would not attempt to break up existing unions, and employees would not seek the recognition of new unions. The initial draft also guaranteed the right to join a labor union without fear of discrimination. Gillette, who was also vice president of Minneapolis Steel and Machinery, a non-union shop, managed to rewrite the petition at the last stage of negotiations, inserting "that employers and employees agree in good faith to maintain the existing status, in every place of employment, of a union, non-union or open shop."[47]

Briggs, realizing that the MSFL would object to any protection of the non-union shop, suggested that the governor offer to settle the streetcar strike if the MSFL would agree to Gillette's labor policy. Foolishly, MSFL Secretary George Lawson signed a copy of the revised petition on the condition that his approval was tentative and would be finalized only after the settlement of the streetcar strike. Governor Burnquist, with Lawson's signature as proof of the MSFL's acquiescence, immediately issued Arbitration Order No. 30, which now gave McGee's status-quo resolution of the preceding November "the force and effect of orders of this Commission during the war." The policies of the CA were now the orders of the Minnesota Commission of Public Safety. [48]

Three weeks later, the Electric Railway Employees Union, undoubtedly expecting the TCRTC to honor the promises of the MEA, submitted its grievances to the State Board of Arbitration. The employees demanded the reinstatement of all union men, one-half pay from November 24, and the right to belong to a union without discrimination. Briggs and Lowry, of course, were not about to agree to a stipulation that would nullify the non-union shop that was legitimatized by Order No. 30. In fact, with Order No. 30 now an established state policy, there was no longer any reason to honor the promise to settle the streetcar strike. Lowry flatly refused to submit to the board, claiming that Order No. 30 did not apply to the streetcar strike. He added: "It must be clearly understood that we have always maintained a positively Non-Union place of employment." [49]

On June 12, without even hearing from the company, the Arbitration Board awarded the union a partial victory, ordering the company to re-employ desirable men at their old seniority and wage rate. The board, operating under the rules of Order No. 30, did not address the issue of union membership. Lowry had no intention of ever rehiring the dismissed union employees. He simply refused to honor the award. The MCPS, no longer in need of union cooperation, ignored Lowry's defiance of the Arbitration Board. It was now clear to the Minneapolis labor movement that they would never receive fair arbitration from the state. The only option for the streetcar men was to appeal to the National War Labor Board. [50]

While the CA waited anxiously for a response from the NWLB, Local 91 of the Machinists' Union began an organizing campaign at Minneapolis Steel and Machinery (MSM). Low wages, a poor safety record, and a management that was hostile towards its laborers made MSM an easy target for union organizers. Without the knowledge of the CA, the union quickly signed up over 600 men. On July 28, 1918, a mass meeting of employees elected a committee of twenty-seven employees, thirteen non-union and fourteen union, to represent the entire workforce in negotiations with management. Three members of the committee attempted to meet with MSM President Record to ask for a large increase in the wage scale. Record refused to meet the committee because it was selected at a meeting held under union auspices. Minneapolis Steel and Machinery was a non-union plant and would remain so. [51]

The machinists' union joined the streetcar men in their appeal to the NWLB. Their complaint alleged that "MSM, with the assistance and active cooperation of the MCPS and the CA, has endeavored to maintain a non-union shop" and has "conspired together for the purpose of preventing the workers of the said MSM from organizing under the terms and conditions laid down by the NWLB." The federal government would now have the opportunity to change the industrial policies of two of the CA's most influential members.[52]

The NWLB dispatched two examiners, Raymond Swing and Herbert R. Brougham, to investigate the union allegations at MSM. Gillette told the examiners that he ran a non-union plant and would invoke Order No. 30 to maintain this status if labor difficulties arose. He insisted that there were no current difficulties at MSM and refused to let Swing and Brougham have free access to his plant. Gillette insisted that the NWLB "should in conformity with its announced policy exhaust the powers of the State before exerting its own powers." Even when the examiners pointed out that Order No. 30 was in conflict with federal policy and had been issued after it, Gillette and Record insisted that Order No. 30 should take precedence. In addition, Gillette suggested that the NWLB principles about the right to organize were a mistake. Unions were after all "hostile to the interests of the people" while the United States was fighting a world war. Recognition of union rights would turn an important war production facility over to the "pro-German socialists" in control of the local machinists' union.[53]

Swing and Brougham quickly realized that Gillette had written the parts of Order No. 30 in conflict with federal policy and that the Minnesota State Federation of Labor had been deceived into accepting the non-union clause. In effect, they concluded, there was no agreement between capital and labor in Minnesota. Order No. 30 was clearly an attempt to evade federal labor policy. The examiners, concerned about the militant attitude of MSM, questioned the Public Safety Commission about the discrepancies between federal and state policy. Although unwilling to admit that any difference existed, commission members reluctantly agreed to accept federal precedent if the NWLB intervened. Confident that the defiance of the President's Mediation Commission would not be repeated, the board decided to hold hearings in Minneapolis to determine if the NWLB had jurisdiction over the Minneapolis Steel and streetcar cases.[54]

In an attempt to stave off catastrophe, Gillette and a delegation of Minneapolis civic leaders descended on Washington, D.C., to lobby against the NWLB hearings. Their pleas were ignored. On October 8, Briggs and Gillette sat in a packed hearing room and listened to corporate lawyer Pierce Butler argue their case before ex-President William H. Taft and Frank P. Walsh. The primary

strategy was to fight the NWLB's jurisdiction over the Minneapolis cases. Butler, arguing the case for MSM, contended that there was no controversy for the
federal board to mediate. The complaint had been filed by a union that did not
represent the employees. Any negotiations between the company and a union
would violate its pre-war non-union shop policy. Taft and Walsh summarily
dismissed these arguments as not relating to the issue of jurisdiction.[55]

The most serious issue at stake was whether the Minnesota State Board of
Arbitration or the NWLB should have jurisdiction over Minnesota labor disputes. Briggs, Gillette, and Butler argued that the agreement of the Minnesota
Employers Association and Minnesota State Federation of Labor, embodied in
Order No. 30, effectively blocked federal action. The state of Minnesota had a
perfectly adequate system for settling labor disputes and the federal government should allow it to do so. In addition, the production of war materials in
Minnesota was at peak efficiency and therefore there was no cause for federal
intervention. Butler argued that each case should first be arbitrated by its company union. If this failed, the state would intercede. When Taft and Walsh
seemed unimpressed with his arguments, Butler finally pleaded that "our
money is at Stake." The MEA quickly passed a resolution, hoping that its influential voice would back up Butler's arguments. Both efforts failed.[56]

In the case of the Minneapolis streetcar company, Taft and Walsh ruled
that the controversy was already being heard by the Public Safety Commission
and therefore should remain in the jurisdiction of the state. A union appeal
was also rejected. Lowry and the CA had finally won an important victory, the
1917 streetcar strike. The Minneapolis Steel and Machinery case, however, had
not yet come under the state's review. The hearing board held that com-
plainants had an equal right to seek redress before the state or federal board.
In this case, the union had complained to the NWLB, which therefore could assume jurisdiction.[57]

Although Taft and Walsh acknowledged the conflict between state and federal policies they avoided ruling on the legitimacy of Minnesota's non-union
status quo, leaving Order No. 30 intact. In reality, however, Minnesota's
unions could now appeal to the federal board whenever possible. Workers at
other important CA companies—Washburn-Crosby, Pillsbury Flour Mills,
Northwestern Consolidated Milling, Russell-Miller Milling Company, and Minneapolis Gas Light Company—would also complain before the NWLB. The final
ruling on the wage and organizing issues in these cases would spread across
Minneapolis's most important industries.[58]

While the CA and the Minneapolis union movement waited for the NWLB
to decide their fate, the State Arbitration Board continued to handle
Minnesota's labor disputes under the policies of Order No. 30. Despite the

inability of the board to settle the streetcar strike, employees submitted twenty-four disputes in the next fourteen months. According to the board, it managed to settle 85 percent of these minor disputes to the satisfaction of both sides. Lowry's streetcar company was the only significant case of defiance. Although twenty-seven strikes took place, only two or three lasted more than several hours. The board reported that it had checked threatened "strikes in their incipient stages, preventing serious conflict involving thousands of men and the imminent danger of such disturbances affecting the entire industrial activities of the State." The board, operating under the mandate of Order No. 30, also issued orders in its settlements that the status quo was to be maintained. Gillette's carefully crafted labor policy was being methodically enforced by the state of Minnesota.[59]

On April 18, 1919, the *Minneapolis Labor Review* pronounced the NWLB award a "Grand Triumph for Workers." In the Minneapolis Steel and Machinery case, the NWLB findings were a bitter pill for Gillette and the CA. The wages of first-class machinists were raised to seventy-two cents per hour. The raised wages for all workers were effective retroactively to October 1, 1918. This severe financial blow for MSM was compounded by the NWLB order for time-and-a-half for overtime and equal pay for women. More importantly, the board affirmed the right of MSM employees to organize in trade unions. The company was enjoined from spying on or interrogating employees and was prohibited from discharging union members. Those already discharged were to be reinstated with back pay. The board indicated that any "actions the intent of which is to discourage or prevent men from exercising this right of organization, must be deemed interference" with workers' rights protected by federal law. While the NWLB's decision, which in essence prohibited most of the activities of the CA, was a disaster for its members, Briggs and Gillette found one glaring beacon of hope among the lengthy enumeration of union rights: Section seven stated: "This award shall be effective for the duration of the war." Their only hope for escaping this far-reaching decision was a strategy of delaying its implementation.[60]

Time, however, was on the side of Gillette and Briggs. Hostilities were over in Europe in November 1918. At the same time, an escalating "Red scare" cast suspicion on labor unions and their possible link with radicals, and a Republican Congress was elected. Pressure for the Wilson administration to defend the rights of labor unions quickly faded. MSM and other CA firms simply ignored the NWLB's assertion of union rights and continued to operate open shops. When federal auditors arrived in Minneapolis to inspect MSM books and assess the amount of the back-pay award, they found a payment and job classification system that was indecipherable. The records were so poorly kept that they were unable to determine how much to pay, or even to whom to pay it. Union attorney Arthur LeSueur, realizing that "it will be a very bad black eye for the unions in this section of the country" if the award was not honored, in 1920 asked the American Federation of Labor to put pressure on the federal government. LeSueur's efforts produced no result. Four years later, he was still involved in a court battle to force payment of the award.[61]

By 1925, Minnesota congressman August H. Andreson introduced a bill to authorize a special payment. MSM President Record explained: "There are no records available whereby such payments can be straightened out." Without federal enforcement, the NWLB award was worthless. The efforts of the CA, the CCA, and its ally the MCPS, had defeated the streetcar strike and stymied the federal government in its attempt to support unionized labor. As World War I ended, Minneapolis remained an open-shop city.[62]

In the face of labor shortages and the growing radical movements of the World War I era, the CCA had organized an effective military defense on both the local and state levels. In the brief span of twenty-one months, the CCA, the CA, and the MCPS managed to neutralize the IWW, the Nonpartisan League, Minneapolis socialists, and the Twin Cities' labor movement. The combined efforts of the Minnesota Commission of Public Safety and the Minneapolis business community also revealed a dark side of American culture: In the face of imagined threats, the basic rights of American citizens were trampled at will. An unconstitutional dictatorship governed Minnesota, while a private army patrolled the streets of Minneapolis. The interests of business became the interests of the state. Fortunately, the extraordinary circumstances that created these unusual institutions died with the end of World War I.

The end of the war brought a dramatic change to this elaborate and effective system. The MCPS, created as an emergency wartime measure, met only three times in 1919, primarily to close itself down. On January 14, 1919, the MCPS declared that all of its orders now in force would be inoperative as of February 5, 1919. The state of Minnesota would now return to democratic and constitutional government. Governor Burnquist, the state legislature, and the state and federal courts would determine the rules of conflict between the Minneapolis business community and union labor.

The CCA and the CA were now faced with the serious challenge of electing friendly legislators, judges, and governors. They would also have to reorganize their defense of the open shop. The Civilian Auxiliary and the state Home Guard were emergency wartime organizations. The business community would have to move quickly to maintain its influence over the state military as wartime units were reconstituted into the Minnesota National Guard. Even more important, a new private intelligence system would have to be developed to replace the state Secret Service and the semi-official American Protective League. Although these were serious problems, the CCA and the CA had the money and the experienced military commanders and intelligence operatives to do the job. While the structure of a business dictatorship disintegrated, its various functions would continue in a new form.

10 *Saving Minnesota from Radicals*

ALTHOUGH THE CIVIC AND COMMERCE ASSOCIATION (CCA) and its allies had defeated both Charles Lindbergh for governor and Thomas Van Lear for mayor of Minneapolis in the 1918 election, they had not extinguished radical political sentiments across the state. In Minneapolis, Van Lear's narrow loss and the disintegration of the local Socialist Party had merely redirected the radical effort. In February 1918, the Minneapolis Trades and Labor Assembly created the Municipal Nonpartisan League to function as the permanent political arm of the local labor movement. Van Lear, who had been kicked out of the Socialist Party in 1918, and other ex-socialists quickly assumed the leadership of the new party. Avoiding the mistakes of the Socialist Party, the Municipal NPL declared "Minneapolis for a hundred percent 'Americanism,'" and followed the NPL strategy of endorsing President Wilson's policies.[1]

The rest of the platform, which called for "municipal ownership of street railways, telephone, gas, and electric plants, for public distribution of power, heat and light," was very similar to the socialist principles that Van Lear popularized during his successful 1916 campaign. The Municipal NPL platform also called for "equal rights to all, special privileges to none." By the spring of 1919, it was clear that the radical threat was still very much alive and growing on the Civic and Commerce Association's doorstep.[2]

In response, the Minneapolis business community formed the American Committee of Minneapolis (ACM) and issued "A CALL TO CITIZENS." The ACM Declaration of Principles said: "It is well known that sinister influences are at work in Minneapolis and in many other cities throughout the land to undermine the confidence of our people in their form of government. . . . The time has come when these influences must be squarely faced and challenged." The ACM, "composed of citizens from all walks of life[,] is about to institute an educational campaign against these pernicious and subversive doctrines." The ACM planned to circulate instructive literature and conduct a speaking campaign "in order to bring home the principles of Americanism to every citizen" in the city. More specifically, they were "planning cooperation with the conservative elements in the labor unions. It will be our aim to help them rid themselves of the radicals who, in many cases, have usurped their control."[3]

Echoing the successful propaganda of the Minnesota Public Safety Commission, the ACM called for an "aggressive, assertive Americanism" that would include public speeches in halls, theaters, and on street corners; debates; advertisements; editorials; and pamphlets. The men and women of Minneapolis must abandon their aloof attitude "and become ardent propagandists of Americanism if the issue is to be met." ACM's Declaration of Principles clearly stated its opposition to "socialism in every shape and under all disguises." The allegiance of Minneapolis's workers to Thomas Van Lear and the Municipal NPL would now be contested at every turn.[4]

The ACM claimed publicly that it had no political affiliations and was "committed to no fixed social or economic order beyond that involved in the maintenance of the fundamental principles of the Constitution." ACM President James H. Ellison and Treasurer Francis A. Chamberlain were both closely associated with First National Bank, a prominent Citizens Alliance (CA) firm. Ellison was a senior vice president of the CCA, and Chamberlain served on the CA's board of directors. ACM Secretary James F. Gould served simultaneously as secretary of the Republican State Central Committee and as an intelligence officer for the Minnesota National Guard, while working as the manager of the state land department. Guiding the ACM from their positions on the executive board were CA President Briggs and Fred L. Gray, a national leader in the insurance industry and a director and vice-president of the CCA; George D. Dayton, director of the CCA and an original member of the CA; and J. S. Pomeroy, vice-president of First National Bank and a CA member.[5]

The *Minneapolis Labor Review* reported that the ACM was run by "a clique of exploiting employers who seek to dominate the city and state for the protection of their profits." The Minnesota State Federation of Labor adopted a resolution at its 1919 convention declaring the ACM unfriendly to organized labor. The labor movement had quickly recognized that a pseudo-patriotic propaganda organization run by officials of the CA, the CCA, and the state Republican Party was very unlikely to benefit the working men and women of the state.[6]

The educational campaign of the ACM was to be financed by a one-dollar annual membership fee from a massive membership of all the truly American men and women of Minneapolis. Letters with application blanks were mailed out by ACM Secretary Gould, warning that "the black and dismal pit of national chaos is yawning ahead. Revolution is in the air. The mob spirit is rampant in the land." ACM Treasurer Chamberlain, also a member of the CCA's radical-fighting Campaigns and Financial Appeals Committee, quickly col-

lected large donations from the city's major businesses. The powerful banks of
the Minneapolis Clearing House—all Citizens Alliance members—apportioned
a donation of $20,000 among the members. E. J. Longyear Company, a CCA
member, subscribed $1,000. Once again facing a determined radical threat,
the business community raised $200,000 in less than two months. While the
educational campaign would try to convince Minneapolis voters to save the
city from socialism, their one-dollar donations were not really needed. The CA
and the CCA had provided the ACM with a war chest to finance its campaign.[7]

Before the organization was formed, the primary voice of the ACM was already preaching the gospel of Americanism from the pulpit of The Church of
the Redeemer in Minneapolis. Dr. Marion D. Shutter had moved to Minneapolis in 1881 and five years later assumed the "burden of the pastorate" of the
First Universalist Church, a position he would hold for fifty years. Dr. Shutter's
interest in his community and his efforts to better the lives of Minneapolis citizens gradually elevated him to a position of moral leadership in the community. Having organized the city's first Kindergarten Association and founded
the Unity House Social Settlement in 1897, Shutter was appointed chairman
of the city's Vice Commission in 1911. He would later serve as chairman of
the Morals Commission, which was established on his recommendation.[8]

Shutter also had a deep interest in and fear of the Bolshevik government in
Russia. "Russia," he preached in a March 1919 speech, "was the greatest object lesson that the hand of Revolutionary Socialism has ever painted, with the
torch of the incendiary and the dripping dagger of the assassin, upon the can-
vas of history!" And, he warned, "The road from Constitution to Chaos, so
rapidly run in Russia, may also be run in our own country." Said Shutter, "The
Duty of Americans" was to "work and vote against any party that allies itself
with the elements of lawlessness and violence, as the Socialist party in this
country has done and is doing"; to shut the gates of America and "SAVE THE
NATIONAL TYPE"; and to "cultivate patriotism at home." Shutter suggested
that all other political issues be dropped. "Let it be a square fight between
Americanism and Revolutionary Socialism . . . ! If the test must come, let it
come now! Let it come before the rills and rivulets of treason have swelled into
a mighty flood that may sweep away our foundations." The ACM had found its
champion.[9]

With a $200,000 budget, the ACM published a series of pamphlets based
on the speeches of Dr. Shutter. The pamphlets were distributed through CCA
members to the workers of Minneapolis and by paid agents in the city's ethnic
communities. Shutter's mission was to extol the virtues of the American way
of life and warn of the "Menace of Socialism," which threatened to destroy the
country. The basic underpinnings of America were "the Institution of the

Family, the Establishment of Private Property, the Rise of Capital, and Religion." While Shutter admitted that "selfishness may attach to the family, avarice to poverty, oppression to capital and superstition to religion," if they were taken away we would be "back in the cave and the jungle."[10]

Organized socialism sought to overthrow the "present political, social, and industrial order" and establish the Cooperative Commonwealth, said Shutter's pamphlets, "in which land and all means of producing and distributing wealth, shall be owned and administered by manual labor." After socialism transformed the ownership of property, the bourgeois system of family and marriage would vanish with the disappearance of capital. The Christian doctrines of the sanctity of marriage, the sacredness of motherhood, and the recognition of virtues such as meekness, gentleness, patience, and sacrifice would also vanish. The resulting nationalization of women would rob them of their family life and steal their spiritual ideals. Under socialism, free love, polygamy, and prostitution would replace the American family.[11]

Shutter concluded: "We must meet it and conquer it or be destroyed by it." The first force of the attack today is against private property. Echoing the ideals of the open-shop movement, Shutter recognized private property as the most important principle of America: "We surrender the principle itself at our peril. . . . It must be kept and safe guarded." Without private property, capital, marriage, family, and religion would all be at risk. The ACM's philosophy mirrored the ideals of the CA.[12]

As a member of the Civic and Commerce Association, however, Dr. Shutter had little credibility with the city's union workers. To appeal to the working-class citizens, the ACM brought in Peter W. Collins, a nationally known anti-socialist lecturer. Collins had been secretary of the International Brotherhood of Electrical Workers and a delegate to numerous American Federation of Labor conventions. In an ACM pamphlet, Collins explained *Why Socialism Is Opposed to the Labor Movement*. The socialists were out to "capture the economic organizations (trade unions) and revolutionize (destroy) them." Although socialists worked within the trade unions they used their position to fight trade agreements and agitate for hopeless strikes because discontent "is the seed of Socialism." The antiquated ideology and static mental state of the AFL had to give way to a more revolutionary view.[13]

Collins quoted the Central Committee of the Socialist Party: "We have the helpless scab, that pitiful specimen, who, through economic necessity, the pressure of want, the appeals of starving wife and children is forced to desert the ranks of the strikers. This class of men we cannot expel from our party, without expelling a considerable part of our membership." Collins claimed that harboring scabs was the official policy of the Socialist Party. The ACM hoped to use the wedge of Collins's socialist scabs to drive apart the radical and union movements. The CA undoubtedly approved of this divisive strategy.[14]

The ACM also pursued other methods of opposing the growth of radicalism in Minneapolis. Secretary Gould, satisfying the requirements of his many political, intelligence, and patriotic roles, took on the enormous task of coordinating anti-radical intelligence activities in Minneapolis. His primary source of information was L. W. Boyce, whose agents at the Northern Information Bureau (NIB) continued their wartime surveillance of the IWW, NPL, and radical unionists. In addition to the regular reports of the NIB, Gould received personal, confidential evaluations of radical groups and reports on individual radicals and rumors of possible retaliatory investigations of the ACM itself.[15]

Gould, acting on intelligence from other sources, frequently instructed Boyce to conduct surveillance on communists, union activists, and outstate IWWs. In his position as ACM secretary, Gould cooperated with and coordinated the intelligence activities of the Minneapolis Police Department, the United States Department of Justice, members of Congress, formal and informal groups such as the New Nebraska Federation of Omaha, "our Winnipeg friends," local Minneapolis businesses, union informants, and other loyalty organizations such as the Loyal American League, and even, in one case, the British Secret Service. The lengthy and detailed correspondence between Boyce and Gould, of course, was "extremely confidential." Boyce warned Gould of the dangers if any of their intelligence activities were to "get into the hands of the 'enemy.'"[16]

Despite the decimation of the IWW's leadership in 1917, Secretary Gould used the NIB to keep a close watch on their activities. Boyce reported that, although the IWW was afraid to hold large meetings because of possible federal raids, the membership of the Agricultural Worker branch No. 400 was still nearly 30,000. While most of these radicals spent their time in the harvest fields and in the mining and lumber camps, their headquarters were still in Minneapolis. The IWW's Construction Worker, Metal Machinery Worker, Railroadmen, and Public Service Worker branches, although much smaller, were considered to have a "greater possibility for positive and definite injuries to industries and the community at large."[17]

Particularly worrisome was the IWW strategy of joining "decent labor organizations who are known to be believers in American ideals, and when once in the union they can spread their IWW propaganda" and attempt to influence the union's policies. In the fall of 1919, one organizer claimed to have lined up 25 percent of the Carpenters' Union membership and promised to bring the entire organization into the Construction Workers' branch of the IWW. In order for Gould to keep track of all IWW members, Boyce, who had agents inside IWW headquarters, had all membership lists brought to his NIB office, copied, and forwarded to Gould. When a large IWW meeting appeared imminent in September 1919, Boyce and Gould planned to mobilize several hundred ex-soldiers of the Loyal American League to disrupt the rally and "take some of the 'pep' out of the IWW."[18]

When Boyce or Gould's intelligence sources uncovered the radical element trying to extend its influence, the ACM was quick to exert an opposing pressure. They were particularly sensitive to the infiltration of the police force and the school system, two bastions of the American way. In the fall of 1919, Boyce's agents reported that Lynn Thompson, a socialist organizer and school board member, was "busily engaged in trying to stir up a strike among the police and the firemen of this city." While Boyce attempted to further reveal Thompson's activities in the police union, the ACM used its considerable influence to push the police department into a more active role in suppressing radical meetings and propaganda.[19]

Several months later, the ACM made public accusations that a Minneapolis schoolteacher, William R. Ball, was criticizing the draft, discussing socialism, and planning to bring in a Bolshevist speaker to address his Americanization classes. A committee of three led by CA school board member Horace N. Leighton investigated the charges and admitted that they had no reason to "doubt Mr. Ball's character, devotion, sincerity and loyalty as a citizen" but that it was nevertheless unwise for Mr. Ball to continue with Americanization work. Ball's real crime was suggesting in his classes that "Americanism recognizes only one class of people, we the workers" and voicing his hope that Minneapolis teachers would soon be unionized. Although Gould and Boyce spent a great deal of time and resources watching the IWW, they reacted with greater alarm when radicals attempted to unionize the city's police and teachers.[20]

While the ACM was keeping a close watch on radical unions, the Citizens Alliance was facing a much greater threat on the political front. The leaders of the Municipal NPL in Minneapolis were joining forces with St. Paul union activists to spread their program throughout the state. On July 20, 1919, the Minnesota State Federation of Labor formed the Working People's NPL (WPNPL) to act as its political arm and to work with the farmers' NPL. Undoubtedly referring to the CA and the ACM, the WPNPL's Declaration of Principles stated: "The industrial autocrats have extended their evil influence into the realm of government, and have corrupted and dominated our political institutions, and have employed the press and other agencies of information and education to misguide the people."[21]

The WPNPL program called for an eight-hour day, the unqualified right to organize, "public ownership and operation of railways, steamships, banking business, stockyards, packing plants, grain elevators . . . and all other public utilities and the nationalization and development of basic natural resources. . . . The autocratic domination of the forces of wealth production and distribution . . . shall be superseded by a process of government supervision . . . for the benefit of all the people."[22]

The Working People's NPL intended to organize the state to elect public officials who would enact its program. The NPL, which already controlled the legislative and executive branches of government in North Dakota and had a powerful organization in Minnesota, now was closely aligned with Minnesota's growing labor movement. It was clear to Secretary Gould that the industrial order carefully cultivated by the CA for sixteen years would be eradicated if the NPL and the WPNPL gained control of Minnesota's state government. To effectively combat the WPNPL, it was imperative that the Minneapolis business community be informed in detail as the 1920 election approached. Boyce's agents, who had already infiltrated the NPL, were now placed in the WPNPL. Boyce reported to Gould that the NPL had already collected a million-dollar war chest and was in close touch with forty-five friendly newspapers in Minnesota. On November 3, Boyce reported that the NPL was devoting a great deal of attention to organizing the WPNPL.[23]

From the Security Building in Minneapolis, the WPNPL's chief organizer, a man named Pflagman, a former business agent of the Minneapolis Teamsters' Union—whom Boyce characterized as a drunkard and a gambler—and seven organizers fanned out across the state. They canvassed the farm country, attempting to arouse interest and then calling meetings in the nearest towns. Boyce warned Gould that the WPNPL organizer seemed to be meeting with "considerable success so far." A month later WPNPL Secretary Thomas Van Lear told an NIB agent that he was extremely excited by the prospects of the new WPNPL newspaper, the *Daily Star*. In the last few days, Van Lear had stolen six of the best newspapermen on the *Minneapolis Journal* and *Minneapolis Tribune* staffs. He predicted that the *Daily Star* would disrupt the "old time machine effort which has always been made by the *Tribune* and *Journal*," and indicated that he had no doubt that he would be the next Mayor of Minneapolis.[24]

The potential threat to the CA detailed in Boyce's reports to the ACM soon became a stark reality. On March 24 and 25, 1920, the Minnesota NPL and the WPNPL met in adjoining halls to pick a candidate to run for governor in the state Republican primary. After seriously considering St. Paul labor leader James Manahan, 1918 candidate Charles Lindbergh, Sr., and Thomas Van

Lear, the conference committee of the two organizations unanimously nominated Henrik Shipstead. A master plan for organizing local bodies and raising campaign funds was unveiled by Van Lear and quickly endorsed. Shipstead's campaign would be backed by the WPNPL's 45,000 members and the establishment of a new major metropolitan newspaper, the *Minnesota Daily Star*. Despite prolonged financial difficulties caused by the business community's advertising boycott of the paper, the *Daily Star*'s eight-page paper reached 35,000 metropolitan residents, a little over one-third of the *Journal's* circulation. Echoing Van Lear's predictions, the *Daily Star* supported the Shipstead ticket and ignored the "steel trust candidate" of the Republican Party. The election was a case of the "steel trust vs. Progress" and a last chance to "Oust Gangsters."[25]

Republican Party leaders realized that farmers across the state were flocking into the NPL and that Van Lear was attracting a labor following even outside of the Twin Cities. To defeat the NPL, they had to "convince the middle class that it has even more to fear from the bottom of society than from the top; that proletarian domination is more unreasoning than domination by the upper class; and that the program of the proletariat strikes at that which is the basic characteristic of the middle class . . . the possession of property."[26]

As the election primary approached, Republican leaders, fearing that a split vote would doom their own candidates, called an unofficial convention in May and chose state auditor J. A. O. Preus as gubernatorial candidate to lead the battle of "Americanism against socialism." Preus declared adamantly: "Socialism is the issue of the coming campaign. Before Socialism or communism can commence, property rights, Christianity and marriage must be destroyed." Preus's entire campaign centered on the danger posed by the socialists who controlled the NPL and WPNPL: "It was up to the honest, God-fearing electorate of the State of Minnesota to prevent the government and the resources of this State from being exploited by professional Socialist agitators." A Preus biographer commented after the election that those familiar with conditions in Minnesota at the time assert that "any other candidate, without Preus's personality, courage and vigor, would have succumbed to the League's campaign."[27]

Preus's campaign to defeat socialism would, of course, have the enthusiastic support of the *Minneapolis Journal* and the *Minneapolis Tribune*. Although the publishers of both papers were members of the CA, Herschel V. Jones, owner of the *Journal*, had a particularly close relationship. Jones's close ties with the business community began in 1901, when he established *Commercial West* to report on financial news in the Twin Cities. As chairman of the Real Estate and Investments Subcommittee of the Commercial Club's Public

Affairs Committee in 1902, Jones had access to the council of Minneapolis's leading businessmen.[28]

The next year, when the Public Affairs Committee was organizing the Citizens Alliance, Jones took on the important task of publicity chairman. The CA, however, had bigger plans for the faithful newspaperman. When the *Journal* came up for sale in 1908, the business community took action to ensure that the paper continued to support the CA. Minneapolis business interests financed the $1,200,000 purchase price of the *Journal* for the then-bankrupt Jones. A CA member was now the director and controller of Minneapolis's largest newspaper. The continued anti-labor slant of the *Journal* was assured, at least until Jones's death in 1928.[29]

Jones's message to Minneapolis during the 1920 election campaign was clear and forceful: The *Journal* warned that "practically every leader in the League from Townley down is an avowed Socialist. The organization is run not by farmers but professional agitators." By means of the unnatural alliance of farmers and laborers, "whose real interests are in opposition, the Socialist plotters hope to be able to seize control of Minnesota and other State governments."[30]

Jones revealed that the socialists had abandoned an open political movement for a plan of "boring from within." In order to prove his contention that the NPL was dominated by Socialists, the *Journal* ran a series of reprinted NPL documents from a booklet of Representative Asher Howard. Socialist NPL leaders defended violations of the espionage act, believed in the dictatorship of the proletariat, would nationalize all farm land, and had even infiltrated public schools to "instill socialist principles into children," according to the booklet. The *Journal* left little doubt that the NPL and the labor radicals of the cities were "aiming at taking over the government of the state of Minnesota." However, "Minneapolis with the help of the sane and loyal vote of the rest of the State can block the schemes of Townley and his Socialist lieutenants, but it will take hustling and cooperation all around."[31]

The editorials of *Commercial West* contained an even more detailed and damning portrait of the NPL and the WPNPL. The business community's magazine complained of the socialist NPL's plan to heavily tax larger incomes, have the state administer workers' compensation, take over all basic industries, acquire all banks, take over all insurance businesses, cancel American war debts, and recognize the Russian Soviet government and the independence of Ireland. These plans were all part of a socialist scheme of world domination.[32]

Commercial West cited the horrific example of North Dakota where "Townleyism has seized the state government and made it most difficult for democracy to function." Townley's schemes to "enthrone autocracy" have failed to accomplish "complete slavery" only because some of his trusted lieutenants had revolted and defied his rule. Echoing the *Minneapolis Journal*, *Commercial West* stressed: "The public should be thoroughly aroused to the importance of strenuously and efficiently combating" the socialist NPL. Unfortunately, the hard-line, anti-socialist propaganda of the ACM, the *Minneapolis Journal*, and *Commercial West* primarily reached metropolitan and business audiences. The outstate vote could still produce an NPL governor as it had done in North Dakota.[33]

Two determined voices had long been calling out for the Citizens Alliance to expand the campaign of the ACM to cover the entire state. Although the dissolution of the Public Safety Commission had cancelled Charles Ames's official investigation of the NPL, he had continued to privately campaign for its suppression. On July 8, 1919, Ames wrote John Crosby that "private reports keep coming to me [which] show conclusively that a political revolution in this state can be averted only by the united and organized efforts of the conservative forces." Ames placed the failure to form any effective statewide organization on the shoulders of Minneapolis business people and appealed to Crosby to help organize the state immediately. Crosby felt that it was "impossible that people here be pulled into line at present to fight 'revolutionary forces' across the state."[34]

Ames, however, had a well-informed and effective ally working in North Dakota. Harry Curran Wilbur had been intensively studying the socialist movement since 1907. In speech after speech across the state, Wilbur warned that the socialists were concentrating their forces on Minnesota and operating through the NPL and the WPNPL, and he presented a mass of intricate facts to back up his contention. Wilbur urged: "There should be placed in the field an organization absolutely non-political in character, barring no one because of race, creed or partisan affiliation, that, with truth for its shield and buckler, could take all the facts to all the people of Minnesota and carry on an educational campaign in the interest of fundamental Americanism and constitutional government."[35]

As early as May 29, 1919, the executive committee of the Minnesota Employers' Association, which was dominated by the Minneapolis, St. Paul, and Duluth Citizens Alliances, had taken up the problem of "securing the services of some men whose duty it would be to direct that work and to cooperate in the movement to cope with the radical movement, which is rapidly spreading over the northwest, under the guise of the NPL." A committee made up of CA vice president Strong and St. Paul association leaders Eli S. Warner and Will O. Washburn was given the task of finding a suitable person to take charge of the movement and to run the coming election campaign effort. By mid-August, the committee, despite the urgings of Ames and Wilbur, reported to a special meeting of Minneapolis business people that "further time was necessary, that the selection of a suitable party was a matter of very great importance." In the meantime, the MEA would support the statewide work of the America First Association. On November 1, the special campaign committee, at the urging of CA President Briggs, hired Wilbur to act as general manager of the MEA and to create a statewide educational campaign that would defeat socialism and elect the Republican Party candidate.[36]

To generate statewide support, Wilbur realized that the campaign must at least have the appearance of a massive grass-roots movement. The MEA hastily assembled a meeting in Rochester of representatives from the southern counties. Wilbur presented facts showing "an organized effort to overturn the fundamentals of our government in Minnesota and to strike at our homes, churches, and schools." A committee led by Blue Earth lawyer Frank E. Putnam was formed to arrange a statewide conference to be held at the Schubert Theater in Minneapolis on January 30, 1920. Prominent citizens across the state who could be relied on "to rally for God and home and Country" were urged to attend.[37]

Business people from across the state attended the MEA's meeting and created the Minnesota Sound Government Association (MSGA). In his opening address, Chairman Putnam, soon elected secretary, beseeched the 350 business people in attendance: "We must save the state from the control of the Socialist Nonpartisan League." The MSGA's Declaration of Principles expressed a belief in the American system of government and opposition to all socialist theories, which would destroy "the initiative of the individual be he laborer, farmer, merchant, mechanic, wage earner, business or professional man." The MSGA stood for property rights and would "assist in the dissemination of knowledge of our present theory of government." Cyrus Northrop, the highly respected president of the University of Minnesota, was elected to head the Minnesota Sound Government Association. All Minnesotans were invited to join. The five-dollar fee that thousands of loyal Americans would pay when they joined the MSGA would finance the educational campaign. This was the public image of the MSGA. The CA's and the MEA's role in this work was kept a closely guarded secret. In reality, Northrop was a powerless figurehead, and fewer than 1,200 Minnesotans joined the organization.[38]

The MEA, following Wilbur's plan, organized a secret parallel organization, which was to work in harmony with the Northrop group and "do the real work." A special MEA committee of Albert Strong, W. O. Washburn, and E. S. Warner was appointed to direct and control the campaign that Wilbur would manage. An elaborate and secret fund-raising drive was conducted by members of the Minneapolis, St. Paul, and Duluth Citizens Alliances. Special meetings were held in late 1919 at the Minneapolis Club, the Minnesota Club in St. Paul, and the Kitcha Gami Club in Duluth. In Minneapolis $130,000 was funneled through Francis A. Chamberlain at First National Bank and Vice-President Strong, who then turned it over to St. Paul banker Frederick G. Ingersoll, the treasurer of the secret MSGA. In Duluth, CA treasurer David Williams of First National Bank of Duluth collected nearly $70,000 from 100 businessmen. St. Paul treasurer John R. Mitchell collected $180,000, almost all from St. Paul. MEA secretary Wilbur would pay MSGA accounts after the expenditures were approved by the committee of three. All expenditures of the $375,095 fund were then carefully monitored by Brigadier General Harrison, an influential CA leader. With a public figurehead, a secret organization, and a huge war chest, Wilbur was ready to attack socialism.[39]

To counteract the influence of NPL speakers throughout rural Minnesota, Wilbur quickly used influential MEA and Republican supporters to set up Sound Government organizations in each county. In Otter Tail County, for example, a committee of three men was recruited by Republican representative and publisher of the *Fergus Falls Journal*, E. Elmer Adams. The committee was to serve as the MSGA's eyes and ears on the ground and report back to Wilbur. With advance warning the MSGA could follow up socialist or NPL speakers with patriotic speakers provided by Wilbur. James Gould, who was already handling a volunteer speakers' bureau for the American Committee of Minneapolis, was enlisted to help recruit the corps of experienced speakers. The speakers were brought to St. Paul for two or three days of instruction and then paid fifty dollars per week plus expenses. The anti-NPL speeches were frequently given in movie theaters across the state in conjunction with a special film developed by the MSGA.[40]

One of the most accomplished of Gould's recruits also wrote anti-NPL pamphlets for the Minnesota Sound Government Association. Noel G. Sargent was a twenty-five-year old professor of economics at St. Thomas College and the acting editor of the *American Economist* in 1919. In 1920, he would leave Minneapolis to organize and direct the Industrial Relations Department at the National Association of Manufacturers. Sargent's MSGA pamphlets attacked the socialist and IWW underpinnings of the NPL. He presented facts that were "absolutely and beyond the possibility of successful contradiction," stating that "the NPL is controlled and dominated by Socialists. . . . Socialism in its complete form means abolition of private land-ownership," he went on, "and the IWW are an offshoot of Socialism—they destroy property—and also want to take over all the farms for themselves." Nearly $82,000 of the MSGA's budget was allocated to printing and mailing Sargent's pamphlets and to the speaker's bureau. The Citizens Alliance had found a champion to defend the property rights of its members—a voice, financed by the MSGA and the ACM, that would be heard across the state before Sargent vaulted onto the national open-shop stage.[41]

Wilbur was concerned, however, that lectures and pamphlets would not turn the tide against the flood of radical propaganda inundating the state. In addition to the *Minnesota Leader*, the NPL controlled forty-two local newspapers in thirty-five counties. To meet the NPL threat, the MSGA created its own bi-monthly publicity "newspaper," *Minnesota Issues*, which it mailed free to every farmer in the state at a total cost of $143,500. The MSGA message was carried through nineteen issues, which featured such lurid headlines as: "LET US SAVE Minnesota," and "WHO WOULD DESTROY OUR GOVERNMENT?" and "RADICAL FORCES ARE AT WORK" and are "reaching out to wreck and tear down in class hatred."[42]

The IWW, Bolshevism, and socialism, all of which were allied with the NPL, wanted to repudiate democracy and establish a dictatorship, confiscate all land, factories, and even churches, establish compulsory labor, legalize prostitution, and abolish Sunday School, according to *Minnesota Issues*. The second issue announced the formation of the MSGA to "Save the State of Minnesota from Radicalism." The third issue, preparing the ground for the June Republican primary, explained in great detail the socialist connection of the NPL and the WPNPL. The Preus campaign received a rejuvenating boost as *Minnesota Issues* reverberated across the rural landscape of the state with its anti-radical message.[43]

Wilbur carefully tailored the MSGA message to the new political reality of the 1920 election. On Tuesday, November 2, 1920, the women of Minnesota would vote in the general election for the first time. *Minnesota Issues* of October 10 featured "A Message to Minnesota Womanhood," written by Minnie J. Nielson, the state superintendent of schools of North Dakota, who was fighting to defend the children of her state against the NPL "who sought to spread through the schools and libraries the doctrines of Socialism, Bolshevism and free love." Nielson warned Minnesota women: "The plan of the NPL leaders is to get complete control of the entire educational system of the state. They well know that as the children [are] taught so will the next generation think and act. There could be no better agency for inoculating and spreading Socialistic propaganda than the schools." She ended her message by advising "everyone who believes that the home, the school, the church and the state are the foundation of Christian civilization to open their eyes to the true situation in this fight and take a stand." The MSGA reprinted "A Message to Minnesota Womanhood" as a pamphlet for further distribution across the state.[44]

Despite the Minnesota State Federation of Labor's support for the WPNPL, Minneapolis's open-shop forces also tried to reach the union movement with its anti-radical message. In November 1906, Elbert E. Stevens, the editor of *The Union*, had denounced the moulders' union for a strike supposedly inspired by radical forces. Within two years, Stevens had transformed *The Union* into *The Labor Digest*, which stood opposed to strikes, boycotts, and lawlessness. For the next two decades, Stevens, a close friend of Otis P. Briggs, spread the gospel of the open shop with the active support of the CA.[45]

As the 1920 election approached, *The Labor Digest* warned that the "NPL Plague had marked Minnesota for Looting and Slaughter." It exhorted: "If the ownership of property is to become a crime, if education shall be banished, if religion shall be dethroned, if the home shall be broken up, then the future of the worker will be dark indeed." Women were warned that "their homes are to be destroyed, their families broken up, their babies turned over to the care of the state, their daughters made the creatures of whatever lustful beast may care to choose them for a time." *The Labor Digest* pressed the point: "Our most dangerous enemy is not some foreign land. He is now within our gates. . . . Radicalism, in Whatever Guise it May Assume, Must be Crushed if Our Beloved Country is to Continue to Exist."[46]

Another weekly paper, *The Northwestern Appeal*, was set up in February 1919 to sway the votes of Minnesota's 100,000 veterans. F. G. R. Gordon, whom Briggs had recruited from Massachusetts to write for the America Committee and the MSGA, was engaged in September of 1920 by *The Northwestern Appeal* to run its "Anti-Socialist Department." Gordon, who was secretary of the American Anti-Socialist League, had been in charge of anti-socialist campaigns in several eastern cities and had written thousands of anti-socialist newspaper and magazine articles. A Massachusetts congressman had stated that "no man in America is so feared by the Socialists as F. G. R. Gordon."[47]

Briggs, realizing the potential of Gordon's work, channeled funds from CA members into *The Northwestern Appeal*. The small servicemen's newspaper quickly changed its mission to confront the menace of the "worldwide socialist movement." Noel Sargent, the Reverend Shutter, and other ACM and MSGA propagandists were brought in to beef up *The Northwestern Appeal*'s editorial staff. *The Appeal*, which would brook "No Compromise with Socialism," now claimed to be the only newspaper of its kind in the United States. *The Appeal*, of course, also helped spread the CA's open-shop message. T. B. Walker, one of the main financial backers of both the CA and *The Northwestern Appeal*, concluded a year later that Gordon's newspaper had had a "very material influence in the last general elections against Socialism and Anarchy" and had been very effective in helping secure the election of Republican candidates.[48]

The headlines of *The Northwestern Appeal* after the June 21, 1920, primary election proclaimed: "SERVICE MEN LEAD Minnesota TO VICTORY FOR AMERICANISM," while warning, "The Menace of Socialism Still Remains." When the primary votes were tallied, Preus had barely defeated Shipstead by slightly fewer than 8,000 votes and had actually lost in fifty-four counties. The Minnesota Sound Government Association rejoiced in *Minnesota Issues:* "The forces of sound government have won a notable victory at a time when it seemed to appear that the advocates of Socialism were about to overrun the state." The Citizens Alliance had played a critical role in this narrow defeat of the NPL and saved the rule of the Republican Party over Minnesota for another decade.[49]

By November, the anti-radical campaign marshaled by the Citizens Alliance had had a far greater impact on the voters of the state as Preus defeated Shipstead by a resounding 451,805 to 281,402 margin in the general election. The MSGA pronounced it a "Great Victory over Radicalism . . . which was the result of a continuous, consistent campaign of education extending over a considerable period of time." *The Northwestern Appeal* claimed that the "United Vote of Minnesota Yanks Hurl Reds Back" to "Save State From Townleyism."[50]

Despite the impressive victory, the MSGA continued to publish *Minnesota Issues* through the 1921 legislative session. The continued fear of "Anarchy, revolution, communism and socialism" would help in implementing the MSGA's seventh principle, "to correct by established constitutional methods any defects in the administration of our laws." Briggs also fostered the emerging need for anti-radical legislation by reporting a "communist scheme of revolution in this country, outcroppings of which have been noted in this city for a long time" to Governor Preus and Adjutant General Rhinow. Briggs referred in particular to an American Protective League (APL) intelligence report on communist bookstore owner Alexis Georgian, who was accused of advocating anarchy and overthrowing the government by force and who had bought no liberty bonds during the war.[51]

To meet this supposedly serious threat of "revolution," the National Guard would have 700 soldiers at the ready on May Day to move on the radicals gathered at the Parade Grounds. The reality of this threat was less important than its impact on a Republican-controlled legislature that had narrowly escaped disaster in the 1920 primary. In response, the 1921 legislature removed the NPL threat by passing a new primary law that barred potential office seekers from filing for a primary election if they had opposed the regularly nominated candidate of the party in the last election. This bill effectively forestalled Shipstead or any other NPL leader from running in the 1922 Republican primary.[52]

The continuation of the anti-socialist campaign into 1921 was also necessary to counter the final WPNPL threat, Thomas Van Lear's bid for reelection as

Minneapolis's mayor. The Minneapolis Republican Party, chaired by CCA member Fred Carpenter, held its convention at the Minneapolis Auditorium and chose Colonel George Leach, returning war hero and commander of the 151st Artillery of the Minnesota National Guard, to run against the popular socialist ex-mayor. When Leach refused the nomination, Horace Lowry, president of the Twin City Rapid Transit Company and a prominent CA member, visited him at 1:00 A.M. and convinced Leach to discuss the election with his boss, Fred W. Van Dusen, also a CCA member. When Van Dusen agreed to pay Leach his insurance company salary while he was mayor, Leach finally acquiesced. Carpenter became Leach's campaign manager and the "influential men in town" quickly raised $50,000.[53]

After being outpolled by Van Lear in the primary, Leach vilified Van Lear as disloyal and un-American and on June 13 won the general election by 15,000 votes. The CA considered this the final knockout for socialism and the NPL. The voters had turned back "radicalism tainted with disloyalty." The CA could now dismantle the American Committee and the Minnesota Sound Government Association and turn its attention to suppressing labor unions and maintaining the open shop.[54]

11 The Establishment of the American Plan

DESPITE THE CIVIC AND COMMERCE ASSOCIATION'S impressive wartime victories over its radical and labor enemies and the enormous growth of Minnesota's economy, the Minneapolis business community viewed its peacetime future with an uneasy concern. Stimulated by a shortage of labor and a national industrial boom, the American Federation of Labor's membership soared to over 4 million workers in 1920. With millions of dollars pouring into the war chests of the international unions, American trade unionism launched the largest organizing drive in its history. Strikes across the country continued at a record pace. In 1919, over a million workers walked out in outlaw strikes alone. Employers across the nation now negotiated with local unions backed by immense national labor organizations.[1]

In postwar Minnesota, trade unions, stimulated also by the annual convention of the AFL in St. Paul in June 1918, quickly made unprecedented gains. From 1918 to 1920, union membership grew 70 percent, to nearly 90,000 members. Of the 670 Minnesota unions, over 80 percent had received wage increases. In St. Paul, labor had established the closed shop in the building trades and was swiftly expanding. In Duluth, a rapidly growing union force struck for higher wages in several industries. Even more disturbing to the business community, membership in the 116 Minneapolis unions had passed the 30,000 mark. The Minneapolis Trades and Labor Assembly, supported by the AFL, concentrated its attack on one industry after another. By 1919, Minneapolis building construction was very largely unionized. The CCA and the CA were faced with another serious challenge to their dominance of Minneapolis industry.[2]

The national employers' associations that had successfully combated the AFL in the first decade of the century had failed to keep pace with the unions' organizational drive. Organizations such as the National Founders' Association (NFA) or the National Metal Trades Association (NMTA) still represented a single industry. They were ill equipped to deal with a general strike that crossed the boundaries between the various trades. Despite these failings, however, they had kept the ideology of the open shop alive. The National Association of Manufacturers (NAM) realized that "public opinion is the guiding force in this

159

nation today." Its extensive propaganda efforts advocated the open shop, a leading principle for fifteen years. The NFA, led by Otis P. Briggs until he retired to lead the CA in 1916, published the *Open Shop Review* each month throughout the war decade. A flood of pamphlets labeling wartime strikers as traitors and unionists as Bolshevists was mailed to teachers, editors, and social leaders. The NFA tried to educate the nation's leaders to the necessity of the open shop.[3]

Local employer groups such as the CA received *The Open Shop Primer* and other instructional literature. The NMTA mailed the *Open Shop Review* into 17,000 homes and spent $10,000 yearly on anti-union publicity. The Employers' Association of Washington and other local associations also published literature and distributed it nationally to encourage the open shop. Despite the lack of a national federation, local employers were well informed and primed for an open-shop drive.[4]

Local employers and their local associations also received more practical support in their struggle with labor during the century's second decade. The NAM cooperated with other associations in breaking strikes, particularly on the West Coast. In Minneapolis, for example, the NAM backed the major furniture manufacturers in a 1914 effort to eliminate the upholsterers' union. The NFA operated its strikebreaking forces continuously from 1904 through World War I. In 1918, it assisted thirteen members in nine different cities. The next year, the NFA combated sixty-seven strikes in thirty-five cities. Each member company receiving assistance was required to pledge that it would "be operated hereafter strictly as an 'Open Shop.'"[5]

In addition, the NFA and the NMTA both cooperated with state and local associations, particularly through their local branches. Backed by their national associations, a solid core of open-shop employers across the country fought off the steady gains of the AFL. Armed with the open-shop propaganda and their own successes, they were well positioned to spread the gospel of the open shop in their own communities. In Minneapolis, Detroit, and Indianapolis, strong open-shop associations that had been established during the first open-shop drive had been maintained for over fifteen years.[6]

Creating a national federation of local open-shop associations to more effectively combat the AFL still remained a problem by 1919. The NMTA had agitated unsuccessfully for an American Federation of Employers in 1913 without result. Three years later, the NAM invited leaders of state and local associations to its national convention in an effort to federate employers' associations. Local associations representing every industry in their community were reluctant to affiliate through the auspices of a national group that represented a single industry.[7]

Many of the resulting organizational problems were solved by the ascendancy of a local association with national aspirations. The Associated Employers of Indianapolis (AEI) had a history and ideology very similar to the CA. "It was unalterably opposed to the principle of the closed shop" and used the same methods to combat unions that Briggs had brought to Minneapolis. The AEI proudly repeated the union description of Indianapolis as "the graveyard of union aspirations, the scabbiest hellhole in the U.S.!" The AEI was convinced that the AFL "seeks absolute control over Government, industry, business, and labor, through the instrumentality of the closed union shop." The closed-shop system advocated by the AFL must be supplanted by the open shop throughout the United States, according to the Indianapolis group.[8]

Under the aggressive leadership of Andrew J. Allen, the AEI distributed 1.5 million pieces of open-shop literature across the country in 1919. As secretary for the local branches of the NFA, the NMTA, and the AEI, Allen was perfectly situated to extend his mission from Indianapolis to the rest of the nation. The AEI served as a clearinghouse for open-shop information, collecting newspaper advertisements, resolutions, and pamphlets from cities across the country and then reprinting and distributing them to other associations. Keeping in close touch with a thousand local, state, and national associations, Allen had daily communications with all parts of the country. In his work promoting the open shop, Allen frequently attended meetings of other associations where he encouraged cooperation on a national scale. More important for the spread of the open shop, Allen was frequently called upon to aid in the organizational work in other cities. While the national open-shop movement of 1920 appeared to be disorganized and leaderless, AEI, through its vast network of local employers and associations, had been instrumental in launching the anti-union offensive.[9]

The Citizens Alliance in Minneapolis, one of the most prominent local associations, received a steady stream of open-shop literature generated by AEI and the national associations. At its March 18, 1919, convention, the CA, in support of the budding national movement, voted unanimously to reaffirm its present policy and convictions upholding "the principle of the Open Shop." For the leaders of the CA, of course, the open shop really meant a closed non-union shop. George M. Gillette of Minneapolis Steel and Machinery commented at a national conference of manufacturers' associations that it was hypocritical to support the open shop when everyone knew that union and non-union workers "don't mix any more than water and oil."[10]

The open shop was simply the application of the ideals of the Declaration of Independence and the Constitution of the United States to the management of a shop, factory, or store, according to the CA. It expressed "its disapproval of any system [closed-shop unionism] which does not guarantee to every man and woman equal rights and opportunities and which imposes limitations upon his or her efforts to attain success." The Civic and Commerce Association, having vigorously defended the Minneapolis business community during World War I, now wanted to transform its image and turn its attention to civic improvement. The parent of the CA openly endorsed the open shop, and then turned the campaign over to its organizational offspring. [11]

With Otis P. Briggs of the NFA running its program, the CA had little need for the advice or assistance of the AEI. Briggs had recognized the need for an educational campaign in Minneapolis during the 1916 Teamsters' strike. He felt that the workers and the public were flooded with radical union and communistic propaganda while receiving almost no information from the employer's perspective. In December 1916, the CA began publishing a *Monthly Bulletin* to overcome this lack of information. Up to 7,000 copies of the *Bulletin* were mailed each month to workers, clergy, teachers, and newspaper editors throughout the state. Like the literature of the AEI, the primary purpose of the CA *Bulletin* was to spread the gospel of the open shop. In addition to reprinting open-shop material from across the country and England, the *Bulletin* frequently debated the merits of the open shop, which provided for freedom of employment and increased production, versus the closed shop, which meant union monopoly and decreased production. The AFL received frequent and vicious condemnation in the four-page *Bulletin*. The CA was fully convinced that the *Bulletin*'s message was a major contribution to its maintenance of open-shop conditions in Minneapolis. [12]

The real business of the CA, of course, was the elimination of union interference with the open shop. For the 686 member firms of the CA to fight as a united force, the CA needed a more direct, practical, and secretive method of communication. On a Saturday morning in mid-December 1918, the first of a series of more than 900 *Special Weekly Bulletins* arrived on the desks of CA members only. The *Weekly Bulletin* informed members of the current union threats posed by the AFL, the Trades and Labor Assembly, or more radical elements. When strikes erupted, the *Weekly Bulletin* kept members informed on the conflict, the actions the CA had taken, and what other members could do to help. Schools to train replacement workers for struck members were advertised and lists of open-shop firms were published with an admonition for all members to buy open-shop products and services and to boycott closed-shop firms. The successes of the CA's open-shop campaign were featured, both to buoy member confidence and to increase open-shop solidarity. Yearly reports and pamphlets were also published to spread the news of the CA's victories. It was the *Weekly Bulletin*, however, that functioned as the vital link between the CA and its members during the open-shop struggle.[13]

One of the most important functions of the national associations in the first open-shop drive, beginning in 1903, had been to provide workers to replace union strikers. Although CA members had been instrumental in establishing Dunwoody Institute and other smaller trade schools, by 1919 there was still no regular system for supplying workers for the open shops of the CA. Before the war, however, one of the CA's founders, Fred R. Salisbury, became acutely aware of the problem. Salisbury, the president of Salisbury and Satterlee Mattress Company, had organized the furniture employers for the CA in 1903. He realized that controlling the flow of workers in and out of CA shops was critical for the maintenance of the open shop. He proposed creation of a CA employment office that would be completely free of charge for both employee and employer, "where they could meet on common ground" and "where the job and the man could be brought together." Although World War I delayed the realization of Salisbury's idea until after his death in 1918, Briggs directed the establishment of the CA Free Employment Bureau on May 1, 1919.[14]

The CA claimed that the bureau helped establish "economic and employment stability of the individual" Minneapolis worker and therefore influenced the moral character of the community. The bureau's pamphlets glorified the benefits of work: "Work opens the only road to both success and happiness. . . . What a priceless boon—the Right to Work!" Briggs felt that "what the self respecting man wants is work—an opportunity to earn a living, and this is what the CA Free Employment Bureau affords him at no cost to himself." Although the CA officially welcomed union and non-union workers, it clearly was not interested in encouraging the placement of union members in the shops of its members.[15]

In the practical task of placing workers in the city's open shops, the bureau was an immediate success. In the first five months of operation, 4,500 skilled mechanics, common laborers, bookkeepers, typists, stenographers, and housemaids were placed. During the 1921–22 depression, the bureau placed more workers than all the other free employment bureaus in the city, including the state bureau. The doors of the bureau opened at 7:00 A.M. every working day of the year and often placed fifty to seventy-five workers before 8:30 A.M. Over 300 workers were given permanent placements each year, while the total number of placements per year rose to 36,372 in 1929. The bureau furnished employment for skilled and semi-skilled trades people in 177 job classifications, including many that were essential to maintain the open shop in Minneapolis. Truck drivers, teamsters, machinists, printers, and building trades workers—all types of skilled workers who would be important in the

CA's battle with union labor—obtained jobs through the bureau in large numbers. Detectives, guards, and sheriffs who would work directly with the CA in its anti-union activities were also placed. The CA considered the bureau "to be one of the most beneficial lines of endeavor undertaken by any organization." The service rendered by the bureau, which was of "inestimable value," cost the CA $10,000 per year.[16]

In organizing the flow of workers through CA shops, the bureau maintained meticulous records concerning local employment trends. During its first decade, the bureau gradually built up personnel files and employment indexes. Whenever a CA member required an immediate influx of new workers, for a strike or a production peak, the bureau was ready. The personnel files allowed the bureau to follow an employee from plant to plant and retain a record of his or her work. Undesirable union activists or radicals who might have moved from company to company without being traced could now be identified. A citywide blacklist could be effectively maintained. These records were particularly useful in the building trades, where employment was often temporary. Because the bureau kept detailed records of every building construction job over $30,000, they were able to accurately claim that building construction in Minneapolis was 88 percent open shop. With workers moving in and out of most of the city's major employers, the bureau also presented a unique intelligence opportunity for the CA to exploit.[17]

Providing the jobs for the bureau's placements required a network of contacts between the Free Employment Bureau and Minneapolis employers. The *Bulletin* advertised that the U.S. Department of Labor considered the bureau the "most efficient employment office they ever visited." CA members were asked to "not fail to patronize your own employment office." The *Monthly Bulletin* urged Minneapolis employers to "cooperate and place their orders with the Bureau." A field representative contacted individual employers and thirty-one employers' trade groups.[18]

The bureau also actively cooperated with various educational and poverty agencies to supply employment for their clients. Its relationship with Dunwoody Institute was particularly important. Training a new labor force for the CA's open shops would fail dismally if the trade-school graduates sought union employment. To assure a steady supply of skilled workers, the bureau cooperated with Dunwoody's apprenticeship programs and helped place them in open shops. The bureau also cooperated with the Minnesota Builders Employers' Association in establishing wage scales in the building trades that had been rejected by the various unions.[19]

Briggs quickly realized that the close working relationship between the various employer groups fostered by the Free Employment Bureau could serve another, more important purpose in the coming open-shop fight. The CA, although it represented the entire spectrum of the business community, was perceived by the public as a single, anti-union organization. If all of the various civic and trade associations could be forged into one umbrella organization standing for the open shop, the CA's message would have a far greater impact on the public and on employers who were willing to negotiate with labor unions.

In September 1919, Briggs called for a general conference of delegates from all the various organizations whose members employed labor in Minneapolis. He laid out plans for a federation of these organizations that would be able to function together quickly and effectively on city, state, and other matters of common interest. The primary purpose, of course, was the expansion and maintenance of the open shop. By February 10, 1920, ten of the city's business organizations had agreed to form Associated Business Organizations (ABO) of Minneapolis and accepted a constitution which called for united actions on all matters "affecting the business interests and common welfare of Minneapolis." Each organization that joined the ABO was represented by three delegates, one of whom would sit on the governing body, the executive committee. For the next two months, the fledgling organization concentrated on recruiting a wider network of employers. This drive was facilitated by the members of the CA, who in most cases also belonged to one or more of the trade associations.[20]

In August 1919, the Minneapolis Retailers' Association (MRA) had appointed a labor committee, which included three CA members, to represent the association in dealing with labor problems. Leon C. Warner, president of Warner Hardware and a longtime CA member, realized from the first meeting that Briggs intended to create a huge open-shop organization. The Retailers' Association had had a close relationship with the Civic and Commerce Association since 1912, and many of its most prominent members had supported the CA's open-shop efforts in 1903 and 1916. Despite this history, the retailers hesitated to join in the coming public battle. They wanted "to know what support will be accorded our membership by the other interests involved, and especially by the bankers." Without the financial support of the large banks, the other industries would have to expand their financial commitment or scale back the activities of the ABO. On February 25, 1920, the Minneapolis Clearing House voted not to join the ABO. The bankers, of course, were still members and heavy financial supporters of the CA itself. Their substantial contributions would still support the ABO. Possibly reassured by their inside knowledge of the CA, the retailers joined the ABO in late February. By March 2, the Retailers' Association agreed to publicly endorse the coming ABO open-shop campaign.[21]

In industries where no employer association existed, the CA rushed in to organize. When the auto mechanics and other vehicle-manufacturing unions struck in April 1920, the employers were unorganized and defenseless. The auto mechanics' union brazenly demanded a 45 percent wage increase and a closed shop. Within days, Harry E. Wilcox, president of the H. E. Wilcox Motor Car Company and a member of the CA's executive committee, had gathered together thirty-one Minneapolis and seventeen St. Paul firms to form the Twin City Vehicle Manufacturing Association (TCVMA). The membership unanimously agreed with Wilcox's plans for combating the strike: "There would be no recognition of any labor organization and [the members] took a definite stand in favor of the 'open shop' basis of operation." Striking union members were told that they no longer had a job. Members of the TCVMA all reopened within three weeks on an open-shop basis. The first shops to reopen loaned non-union employees to shops experiencing difficulties. Negotiations were started immediately with Dunwoody Institute to train new open-shop workers for the industry. A blacklist was established to maintain the security of the open shop.[22]

Wilcox's suggestion that the new group join the ABO was also agreed to at the TCVMA's first meeting. Within a week of its formation, Wilcox's organization had established a guaranty fund to fight the labor crisis and had been accepted as a member of the ABO. The CA, in the short span of two weeks, had helped suppress a union uprising in the motor-vehicle industry and had created a new industrial association to buttress the ABO's growing force. By mid-May, twenty other associations, including the Builders Exchange, the Manufacturers' Club, and the Rotary Club, had joined the CA on the ABO's membership list.[23]

Although the Citizens Alliance remained the Civic and Commerce Association's primary union-fighting force, the Association of Business Owners took over many of the political and publicity functions. In May of 1920, the ABO's executive committee began a campaign to pressure the City Council to increase the size of the Minneapolis police force. With the defeat of Thomas Van Lear as mayor, the police department, headed by Chief John F. Walker, was now considered to be in friendly hands, an ally whose greater strength might be needed in case of a labor crisis. The ABO also attempted to arouse all of its members when the Trades and Labor Assembly tried to intimidate the City Council into establishing a four-tickets-for-a-quarter fare on the street railway system. The business interests of the city were backing a proposed increase in fares.[24]

The success of the ABO's political activities, of course, depended on the election of sympathetic council members and representatives. Prior to the June

1920 primary, the owners' group established a committee to recommend candidates. The secretary of each member organization was responsible for distributing circulars to each company. The ABO also confronted a skilled-labor crisis that developed in the spring of 1920, when companies from Michigan, Wisconsin, and Illinois lured thousands of workers away from Minneapolis. Members of the ABO were urged to lobby the *Minneapolis Tribune*, the *Journal*, and the *Daily News* to refuse out-of-state employment want ads, "which can have only one result, and that is to disrupt the organizations of the employers of Minneapolis." The CA, through the development of Dunwoody and other trade schools and the Free Employment Bureau, had created an ample supply of skilled labor for its open shops, a supply that was now vulnerable to poaching from other states. The ABO's executive committee quickly came to an agreement with the sympathetic newspapers to eliminate all want ads that came from outside of Minnesota, the Dakotas, and Montana.[25]

In the first months of the ABO's existence, the officers of the member associations were frequently quoted in the press on the current labor situation, such as wages paid, hours of work, and their relations with unions. These often-misleading and contradictory statements defeated the purpose of the ABO—to control the labor situation through the unified efforts of all of the city's employers. On April 14, 1920, the ABO asked the boards of directors of each association to direct its officers "to decline to furnish such information with reference to the labor situation for publication in the daily press unless . . . first approved by the executive committee of the ABO." Controlling the press release of its members was important to make sure nothing detracted from the ABO's primary role in the open-shop drive—a massive advertising campaign for the open shop.[26]

A series of full-page newspaper ads extolling the virtues of the open shop appeared in the *Tribune* and the *Journal* in the spring of 1920. The top of each ad featured a drawing of an arched stone factory doorway with the legend "OPEN SHOP" printed in large letters across the arch welcoming a packed crowd of well-dressed workers. All the organizations that composed the ABO were prominently listed at the bottom, starting with the CA, "Composed of the People who are interested in the welfare of Minneapolis." The ads stressed the magnificent prosperity that the open shop had brought to Minneapolis: "Minneapolis is the most healthful city in the country" because of its "citizens and employers who always have been and are determined to maintain The Open Shop Principle."[27]

One advertisement, surrounded in the margins by the repeated legend "OPEN SHOP," announced: "Workmen in every line are earning more money today than they ever dreamed they would be able to earn. . . .Why not, with your present good wages, add to the comfort and happiness of your own family?" Although very little anti-union material appeared in the ads, one admonished, "Labor strife is expensive to everybody," while another criticized the closed shop for limiting production needed to "save the world from hunger." One advertisement read: "The Open Shop Applied in Industry or Commerce, Means a Square Deal for the Employee, the Employer, and the Public." The open shop stood for "A fair day's wage for a fair day's work." The basic fairness of the open shop, according to the ABO, also embodied the great American ideals of freedom, the pursuit of happiness, peace and harmony, and giving workers due credit and encouragement for their efforts. The ABO claimed, with a flourish of exaggeration, that the philosophic wellspring of the open shop was responsible for every positive aspect of the Minneapolis community.[28]

With the establishment of the Free Employment Bureau, the monthly and weekly bulletins, and the ABO's open-shop campaign, the CA was ready to maintain the open shop in Minneapolis. O. P. Briggs, however, like A. E. Allen in Indianapolis, realized that conditions across the state could seriously affect the battle in Minneapolis. If the closed shop provided better wages and working conditions in St. Paul and Duluth, skilled workers would leave Minneapolis's open shops in droves. The CA would have an increasingly hard time holding the open-shop line when its members had to compete on the open labor market with AFL shops across the state. In 1919, with the national drive still in its infancy, Briggs set out to organize the businessmen of Duluth and St. Paul and commit both cities to the open shop.

The businessmen of the Duluth Commercial Club responded almost immediately to Briggs's entreaties to join Minneapolis in establishing the open shop. The dominant business interests in Duluth had formed a "Committee of One Hundred" in 1907 to combat unions in the building trades, and they still harbored a strong open-shop sentiment. On October 3, 1919, the *Duluth Herald* announced the formation of the Duluth Citizens Alliance (CA). Newly elected President Luther C. Harris claimed that the organization "is for the purpose of bringing about industrial peace and harmony to the end that industry may be kept at the highest point of efficiency in producing the necessities of Life." The policies and principles of the Duluth CA were copied word for word from the CA's constitution, including number four: "To uphold the principle of the open shop." Harris, following the example of the CA in 1903, based this open-shop policy on the findings and award of the Anthracite Coal Strike Commission, which found that the "closed shop is not only uneconomic, but is undemocratic and unfair." In close contact and cooperation with Briggs, the Duluth CA had copied the CA in every detail of its philosophy and operation.[29]

Harris realized that, to follow the CA's example, the Duluth CA must "induce every substantial business man or concern, to join and support it, financially and morally." The Duluth CA board of directors represented the banking, wholesaling, manufacturing, and mining interests that formed an interlocking directorate of Duluth's business life. The initial membership included nearly 600 of the foremost business and professional men of the city. The support of representatives of Duluth's major banks was vital, both for the pressure and control of business credit and the substantial financial resources that would help underwrite the Duluth CA's guaranty fund.[30]

For the Duluth CA to succeed, however, the membership must be unified and completely committed to the open shop. Harris explained to members that "the Minneapolis CA does not confine its efforts to the building trades, but it constantly and in almost every letter it issues to its members urges them to support and give their trade, in all lines, to those who are members of the alliance and who are aiding in bringing about open shop conditions in the community. . . . The friends of the open shop must, therefore, cooperate with each other and aid and support each other, and, if they do not, the open shop organization will go down to defeat." This program also, of course, meant "withholding patronage from firms which do business under the union shop."[31]

The task of breaking union-sponsored strikes presented the same difficulties in Duluth as those faced by the CA in Minneapolis. However tight the boycott-enforced unity of employers might be, they needed skilled workers to replace the striking union men. The Duluth CA, coached by Briggs, stepped in to supply the means and facilities for bringing in outside workers. A Builders' Employer Council was formed "to centralize and coordinate employment problems of the 'open-shop' employers in the building industry."[32]

Edward H. Whalen, labor agent for the Duluth CA, was put in charge of supplying Duluth's contractors with non-union workers, many of whom were shipped in from out of state. To protect themselves against the expenses incurred in a strike, Duluth employers purchased a full year's insurance through an employer's insurance program. When strikes were finally won and the open shop established, a blacklist of union members was maintained to avoid future union growth. Although the Duluth CA strike-fighting machine was rudimentary when compared to its ally in Minneapolis, with the guidance of Briggs a surprisingly cohesive open-shop program had been established in a very short time.[33]

To win the open-shop battle, the Duluth CA needed to convince both its members and the general public that the open shop was the morally correct and American way to do business. Following the Minneapolis Citizens Alliance example, the Duluth CA published a monthly bulletin and occasional special bulletins. The Duluth *Citizens Alliance Bulletin* reported on the development of the open-shop battle across the state and the marvelous cooperation of Duluth, St. Paul, and Minneapolis in inaugurating this drive. The importance of the open shop for the prosperity of Duluth and the essential need for unity to obtain this goal were featured in both of the bulletins. Material from the *Citizens Alliance Bulletins* of St. Paul and Minneapolis were frequently used as examples and lessons for the Duluth CA's members.[34]

In addition to this general propaganda, the special bulletin "To Our Members" was used to direct the defense of the open shop during strikes. It gave specific instructions and helpful information for the members under attack and appealed for aid from other industries. A newspaper ad campaign similar to the ABO's was used to convince the general public of the virtues of the Duluth CA's principles. One large ad announced that the Duluth CA was "organized to bring about such conditions that industrial peace and prosperity may prevail in the community as a whole. It [the CA] was not formed to advance the personal interests of its members, either at the expense of their employees, or of the public." The ad continued: "This would be accomplished, of course, through the OPEN SHOP, [which] rests upon the fundamental principles of Democracy—freedom of action, independence in thought, self-reliance and self-development."[35]

In addition to the "hearty cooperation" between the Citizens Alliances of the state's three major cities, the Duluth CA had close ties to other open-shop interests on the Iron Range and in Duluth itself. Organizations such as the Duluth Builders Exchange and the Employing Printers' Association of Duluth represented the various industries of the city. With overlapping memberships and the common goal of the open shop, the statements and actions of these groups were often indistinguishable from those of the Duluth CA. The Building Employers' Council of Duluth, for example, was essentially a creature of the Builders Exchange and the Duluth CA.[36]

As the ABO had demonstrated in Minneapolis, this type of unity was crucial for the success of all employers involved in the open-shop campaign. The Duluth CA and its business allies also helped the CA in its efforts to spread the open-shop fight to the entire state. Duluth building contractors helped spread the open shop in their construction work on the Iron Range, while Fred Armstrong, secretary of the Duluth Builders Exchange, was instrumental in forming the Citizens Alliance in Bemidji.[37]

Despite a long history of cooperation between the St. Paul Association and the Citizens Alliance that stretched back to the CA's first months in 1903, many of St. Paul's leading businessmen were bitterly opposed to a public campaign for the open shop in their city. A small group within the association, however, led by Earnest Davidson, Ramsey County sheriff and vice president of the Industrial Affairs Committee, felt that it was time to attack the city's now-powerful unions. Five members of the CA were invited to a luncheon at the Minnesota Club in St. Paul on January 3, 1918, to assist in starting a Citizens Alliance in St. Paul. Almost two years later, the cumbersome and reluctant machinery of the St. Paul Association was still inching secretly and very slowly forward.[38]

In February 1920, however, a Teamsters' strike erupted in St. Paul. The Teamster threat to refuse to haul "unfair" goods brought the "closed shop to our very doors," according to the CA newsletter. The businessmen of the St. Paul Association realized "that through control of the teaming industry of a city it is possible to enforce the closed shop domination in practically every industry in a community." This affront to the business community was soon followed by an entire slate of "radical" organized labor candidates in the 1920 city elections. St. Paul businessmen were faced with an extremely difficult situation.[39]

On March 19, Charles Patterson chaired a meeting of about 100 businessmen who formed the Citizens Alliance of Ramsey and Dakota counties as "a defensive organization for the protection of the city's interests." The fast action of the strong and unified new employers' alliance quickly squashed the Teamsters' strike.[41] After a thorough study of the Minneapolis organization, the founding members of the CA of Ramsey and Dakota Counties adopted a set of principles and bylaws that exactly copied the "objects and purposes" from the 1903 constitution of the CA. Its principles of discouraging strikes and lockouts and ensuring freedom of contract and the open shop were again based on the award of the 1903 Coal Strike Commission. [40]

The same week, the St. Paul Association also announced its intention "to maintain St. Paul as an open shop city by preventing the "extension of unionism to trades not now organized." The CA of Ramsey and Dakota Counties claimed that it was "organized primarily as a defense organization to preserve and perpetuate individual freedom." Employer associations such as the CA of Ramsey and Dakota Counties must uproot the "tree of class consciousness" planted by the unions if freedom and industrial progress were to be preserved. The CA's seventeen-year-war on labor unions was now a Minnesota campaign.[41]

CA of Ramsey and Dakota Counties President E. H. Davidson, a St. Paul real estate magnate, understood that two things were "absolutely essential to the success of the Open Shop Movement. One is influence and the other is money and both are based on a large membership." Months after its formation, Davidson implored members to spread the word of the CA of Ramsey and Dakota

Counties throughout the city's business community because it was "of the utmost importance that the membership of the CA be made as large as possible immediately."[42]

Although Davidson's goal of signing up every business concern in St. Paul was never reached, the CA of Ramsey and Dakota Counties' board of directors included many of the city's most prestigious firms, representing the financial, construction, manufacturing, transportation, real estate, and other industries. The board of directors included such leading businessmen as Charles W. Ames of the Public Safety Commission; Eli S. Warner, one of the founders of the Minnesota Employers' Association; M. W. Waldorf of Waldorf Paper Products Company; W. O. Washburn of American Hoist and Derrick Company; C. G. Roth of the St. Paul Hotel; J. G. Ordway of Crane Company of Minnesota; Frederick R. Bigelow of St. Paul Fire and Marine Insurance; and Leslie Gedney of Gedney Pickles.[43]

More important for paying Davidson's $12,000 salary and the $100,000 annual funding for the CA of Ramsey and Dakota Counties' propaganda and employment operations were the board memberships of Cyrus P. Brown, president of First National Bank, William P. Kenny of Great Northern Railway, as well as the financial contribution of Northern Pacific Railway Company. To increase membership and strengthen the open shop, the CA of Ramsey and Dakota Counties encouraged its members, who were required to employ more than 50 percent non-union workers, to do business only with other open-shop businesses. By 1922, it would be clear that Davidson had recruited enough influence and money for the CA of Ramsey and Dakota Counties to successfully combat labor unions.[44]

The establishment of the open shop in St. Paul, particularly in the building trades, required skilled workers, who were simply not available in 1920 and 1921. Union limitation of apprentices and the postwar building boom had created an acute shortage of bricklayers. In response, the CAs of the Twin Cities joined forces to create the Minnesota Building Trades School. Over 350 students entered the four-to-six-month course held in the Midway district. When they reached a high enough level of competency, they were employed by open-shop contractors in Minneapolis and St. Paul. When a 40 percent shortage of plasterers began slowing open-shop construction work in St. Paul, the CA of Ramsey and Dakota Counties created the St. Paul Building Trades School. A free six-week course in plastering was opened on Jackson Street in downtown St. Paul. When students had learned the rudiments of the trade, they were quickly employed by open-shop contractors for fifty cents an hour. When a serious shortage of skilled metal lathers and plumbers threatened to curtail the building boom in St. Paul, the CA again created schools to train new open-shop mechanics. The success of these industry-supported trades schools in helping the Twin Cities maintain the open shop was noted and quickly copied across the country.[45]

To handle the vital job of placing the newly trained open-shop workers, the CA of Ramsey and Dakota Counties opened the Free Employment Bureau in the Endicott Building on June 15, 1920. By September 1920, over a thousand workers were being placed each month. The CA of Ramsey and Dakota Counties, however, conceived of the bureau as more than a placement service. It was operated with a definite program of promoting an industrial relations policy that would lead to stable labor conditions and efficient production. The Free Employment Bureau's manager attended the meetings of the St. Paul Building Employers' Council to encourage their use of open-shop workers and to keep track of job opportunities. He also frequently visited the various construction projects across the city to check job progress and worker requirements and to maintain close personal contact with the workers.[46]

"By showing the personal interest in the welfare of the men who patronize the bureau, a spirit of appreciation and loyalty to the Employment Department is created that has a decided beneficial effect when labor difficulties are imminent," according to a department pamphlet. A small magazine, the *Saint Paul Builder*, listing every construction project over $10,000, was published and distributed to open-shop workers to inform them of current and future job opportunities. The *Saint Paul Builder* also served "as a splendid medium to give the men a few 'hot shots' on the open shop." When construction slackened, the bureau would try to temporarily place its workers in nearby communities to maintain a solid base of available open-shop workers.[47]

To keep the allegiance of these workers, the bureau had to frequently defend them against unfair employers. Because it dominated the open-shop labor market, the CA of Ramsey and Dakota Counties used the bureau to enforce specific wage rates. Unusually low wages by any employer quickly brought the condemnation of the CA of Ramsey and Dakota Counties, backed by the influence and money of St. Paul's major banks. The CA of Ramsey and Dakota Counties considered its Employment Department to be a "factor of tremendous importance in the maintenance of open-shop conditions in the building trades."[48]

Although the CA of Ramsey and Dakota Counties structured its propaganda campaign after its Minneapolis ally, the tone and context of its message had to meet very different circumstances. Unlike Minneapolis, the CA of Ramsey and Dakota Counties faced an entrenched and popular union movement. Its newspaper ads, instead of glorifying the open shop, concentrated a scathing attack on closed-shop unionism. The ads repeatedly stressed that the public sympathy for union labor was quickly waning, "because the public knows that, in spite of high wages, labor has not delivered a fair day's work, even for a greatly increased wage. . . . Radical labor Agitators . . . have misled labor into a position that had forfeited public sympathy. The limitation of production in opposition to economic laws and common sense is dangerous to the public welfare." [49]

The CA of Ramsey and Dakota Counties deplored the violence practiced by unions "attempting to prevent others from working." Although the CA of Ramsey and Dakota Counties did not form an organization similar to Associated Business Organizations of Minneapolis, it did solicit twenty-three other civic organizations to endorse its ad campaign. An open-shop endorsement by the St. Paul Association, the Rotary, Kiwanis and Lions clubs, the St. Paul Real Estate Board, the Builders Exchange, and the St. Paul Chapter of the American Banking Institute, all appeared below the legend "THE CITIZENS ALLIANCE" at the bottom of newspaper ads. [50]

The CA of Ramsey and Dakota Counties' monthly bulletin, *The American Plan*, which primarily targeted St. Paul employers, extolled the virtues of the open shop. Without the open shop, a city "cannot hope to compete with its more successful and enterprising rivals. The three large cities in the U.S. that have had the greatest percentage of growth in the last decade [Akron, Detroit, and Los Angeles] are militant 'open shop cities.'" News of specific strikes and actions taken or planned by the CA of Ramsey and Dakota Counties were communicated to members through the bulletin. In its first issue, on May 14, 1920, members were requested to "refrain from using the Union Label in any manner whatsoever, as this is the symbol of the closed shop." With the counsel and guidance of O. P. Briggs, the CA of Ramsey and Dakota Counties had established the basic structure and functions of an effective open-shop association. With the state's major cities organized, the Minneapolis CA could now lead a cohesive force against the state's labor unions. [51]

The first target for the three CAs would be the building trades, which were mainly conducted on a closed-shop union basis. Even in open-shop Minneapolis, the difficulty of suppressing unions in the complex, constantly shifting construction industry had allowed unions to gain a foothold. Following the Minneapolis CA's plan, the CAs of Minnesota's three major cities worked with the Builders Exchanges for over a year to organize the building contractors of the entire state into the Minnesota Building Employers' Association (MBEA). One-hundred-and-twenty-five representatives from across the state met at the Builders Exchange in St. Paul on February 11, 1921, to develop a cohesive anti-union program. The new organization agreed that construction across the state would all be let to subcontractors who worked on an open-shop basis.

There would be no negotiations with unions on wages or working conditions. Two days later, the MBEA unilaterally announced a 20 percent wage reduction, to be implemented across the state in ten days, unless contracts were in force. The building trades' unions had no choice but to reject an offer that was obviously meant to destroy them.[52]

In Minneapolis, the Building Trades Council called for a strike despite the fact that the major building contractors were long-time CA members and supporters of the open shop. The Electrical Workers' Union No. 292 appealed to the city's contractors not to abide by the MBEA's wage policy. The union workers were already living below the government-specified minimum wages for families. A 20 percent reduction would make their wages "insufficient to enable [them] to decently live, unhampered by fear of unemployment and want in old age." They asked the contractors for "fundamental justice."[53]

The CA contended that Minneapolis workers were as "happy and contented, as well paid, well housed and thrifty as the working people in any community in the U.S." This prosperity, of course, was due to the open shop. A CA survey showed that only 150 union workers went out on strike and were quickly replaced by men from the CA Free Employment Bureau. Because of the actions of the MBEA and the CA, Minneapolis landmarks such as the University of Minnesota stadium, the Nicollet Hotel, the Walker Art Center, L. S. Donaldson Company, the Ritz Hotel, and the Lincoln Bank Building would all be built by open-shop firms.[54]

In Duluth, the local Builders Exchange pressed the city's contractors into following the MBEA's recommendation of an across-the-board 20 percent wage cut. By February 26, 1921, every union bricklayer, tile layer, sheet metal worker, and electrical worker had walked off the job. Duluth CA members were asked to morally and financially support the building contractors. Every contractor "has let his entire force of workmen walk out. He has temporarily wrecked his business, he is taking voluntarily, big losses every day, and largely, that you and the city might profit," according to the CA. The unity necessary to win a war of endurance was enforced by a Duluth CA-backed threat of a business boycott of any contractor that dealt with the unions.[55]

Without a ready reserve of open-shop workers available, the CA was forced to raise a guaranty fund to pay for importing skilled workers from Chicago. Building tradesmen were also supplied by the Minneapolis CA. To gain public support as the strike ground on, the Duluth CA placed large ads in the *Duluth Herald* accusing the unions "of refusing to work at fair wages; if their action should result in preventing the growth of the city and the expansion of business; if it should result in the continuance of high rentals and in unemployment for themselves and fellow workmen, then the responsibility must rest

squarely on their shoulders." In all discussions with the various trades, the Duluth CA made it quite clear that Duluth's workers would work in open shops or
they would not work at all. Two years later, in 1922, with construction in the
city doubling, the Duluth CA proclaimed its open-shop campaign an unqualified success.[56]

The contractors of the St. Paul Builders Exchange formed the St. Paul
Building Employers' Council to cooperate with the CA of Ramsey and Dakota
Counties in implementing the open-shop policies and wage cut of the MBEA.
On February 21, the Building Employers' Council alleged that several of the
trades unions had violated their contracts and were now to work under the
proposed MBEA policies. The council established a fifty-fifty rule whereby at
least 50 percent of the workers on any job had to be non-union.[57]

Union leaders realized that to win they would have to shut down St. Paul
construction and wait for local contractors to crumble. The Building Trades
Council announced that it had been locked out and withdrew union men from
St. Paul construction projects. Replacement workers were brought into the
city by the contractors and the CA of Ramsey and Dakota Counties and, if necessary, trained in local trade schools. To justify their actions, the Building Employers' Council placed ads in the *St. Paul Pioneer Press* arguing that local unemployment had been caused by the union wages that were depressing the
building industry. The 20 percent wage cut would restore vigor to St. Paul's
greatest industry, and this could only be done if the open shop replaced the
domination of St. Paul's trade unions over local building construction.[58]

While the propaganda war was waged in the newspapers, the open-shop
contractors continued to bid and work on St. Paul projects. In the first season
of open-shop building, St. Paul had the second-largest building year in its history. Two-thirds of this construction was 100 percent open shop. Only the
bricklayers and plasterers managed to briefly maintain closed shops. By 1922,
the building trades of St. Paul joined Duluth and Minneapolis in the open-shop
camp. The Minneapolis CA's campaign to organize Minnesota's other major
cities had succeeded in routing the state's strong building trades unions. The
printing industry was the only major industry still "seriously hampered in its
progress by the domination of the closed shop."[59]

While the CA efficiently created open-shop organizations in Duluth and St.
Paul, the "American plan of employment" exploded across the country. By the
fall of 1920, there were nearly 500 local open-shop associations in 240 cities
in 44 states. This included the major East Coast cities of Boston, New York,
Philadelphia, and Washington, D.C.; the Midwestern cities of Detroit, Kansas
City, St. Louis, and Chicago; the Southern cities of Dallas, Fort Worth, New Or-
leans, and Miami; and the West Coast cities of Los Angeles, San Francisco,

Portland, and Seattle. More important for the labor situation facing the CA in Minnesota, the border-state cities of Grand Forks, Sioux Falls, Des Moines, Madison, Milwaukee, Superior, and La Crosse also established open-shop associations.[60]

The open-shop philosophy had become so pervasive in the nation's business community by the fall of 1920 that a United States Chamber of Commerce referendum on the open shop passed 1,665 votes to 4 in the largest vote ever cast. The long-term survival of the open shop would depend on the country's politicians and courts, which were ultimately responsible to the American people. Creating acceptance of the open shop among the general public, however, was a much more difficult challenge. By the summer of 1920, the National Association of Manufacturers realized that it was necessary to "in a special and systematic manner undertake the defense and promotion of the open shop."[61]

In October, the NAM formed an Open Shop Department for "the collection, compilation and dissemination of information" on the open shop "and its essential relation to our national ideals and institutions and to industrial stability, productivity and national progress." The department was also to initiate and encourage local movements for the maintenance or extension of open shop operations or the spread of open shop principles. With the emergence of the NAM as a national open-shop leader, the Associated Employers of Indianapolis dropped its plan for a federation of local open-shop associations and urged them to cooperate. [62]

The unity of American industry in its drive for the open shop in 1920 and 1921, however, did not initially extend to the printing industry. The United Typothetae of America was evenly divided between a Closed Shop and Open Shop Division. Conflict between these independent groups flared when, on May 1, 1921, the Closed Shop Division reached an agreement with the printing trade unions to shorten the workweek from forty-eight to forty-four hours. Printing unions across the country were mistakenly informed that the forty-four-hour-week should become the law of the trade. The Minneapolis Typothetae had finally found a reason to break its closed-shop contracts. As early as December 1920, the CA began efforts to line up support for the open shop among Minneapolis printers. In January 1921, employing printers of over 90 percent of the printing business in Minneapolis agreed to delegate full power to act on labor matters to the Minneapolis Typothetae. In preparation for an expected strike, the Typothetae encouraged and then handled the purchase of strike insurance by its members.[63]

By mid-March, it was clear that any new contract would be controlled by the Minneapolis Typothetae and would not include the forty-four-hour-week.

Two delegates from Minneapolis were sent to Cincinnati, where they helped form the National Forty-eight Hour League, representing over 5,000 printers employing 150,760 workers in 39 states. Local Forty-eight-Hour chapters in Minneapolis and St. Paul would coordinate the coming battle. On March 27, the Minneapolis Typothetae invited E. H. Davidson and O. P. Briggs to a special board meeting to help decide their course of action. The leaders of the Twin Cities' CAs advised the Typothetae "to remain firm in their position." The Typothetae immediately voted to end its contract with the union as of June 1, 1921. The CA had helped draw the last lines of battle in its open-shop campaign.[64]

As the June 1 deadline approached, the Minneapolis Typothetae stepped up its preparations for battle. A joint committee of the Minneapolis and St. Paul printers met with Twin City printers' supply houses to negotiate regulations that would restrict the sale of new printing plants. A cash-down price of $1,000 for small presses and $2,500 for presses worth over $5,000 was agreed upon to discourage the union from setting up competing closed-shop presses. The Typothetae office was to handle the registration of new employees recruited from across the country or through ads rotating between the *Tribune*, the *Journal*, and the *Daily News*. Advertising to maintain the business of struck plants was handled by the CA and the Typothetae. The *Citizens Alliance Bulletin* for April 15 told its members, many of whom were also Typothetae members, that "the whole-hearted cooperation of the principal buyers of printing will encourage and enable employing printers to change [conditions] by declaring for the open shop."[65]

The Typothetae distributed folders complaining that unwarranted union demands raise printing costs from 15 to 35 percent. They asked the business community "to purchase all . . . printing and stationery from any of the firms listed on the back page who are loyally trying to help in the revival of trade, industry and prosperity of Minneapolis by operating on the Forty-eight hour basis." The folders claimed that the seventy-four listed firms represented at least 90 percent of the printing production in Minneapolis. The Forty-eight-Hour League of Minneapolis also mailed out *Bulletins* that detailed the national status of the struggle and asked everyone to buy from Forty-eight-Hour shops.[66]

On June 1, as expected, nearly 550 typesetters, pressmen, press feeders, and bookbinders went on strike at sixty of the sixty-five job printing shops that were members of the Forty-eight-Hour League. Typothetae and Forty-eight Hour League President William K. Jeffrey announced that "the employing printers have no idea of granting the 44 hour a week demand at this time." The Typothetae and league met that afternoon to discuss the question of the open or closed shop. After listening to Briggs describe the virtues of the open shop, the sixty printers present voted unanimously to insist on the open shop. The CA implored its members not to send their work out of town: "It can be handled satisfactorily here in Minneapolis by printers who have declared for the open shop."[67]

Within a week, the Typothetae had authorized an open-shop label to help its customers distinguish between closed- and open-shop printers. In the CA's *Weekly Bulletin*, Briggs explained the significance of the struggle: "A clean-cut victory for the employing printers in this controversy will practically clean the slate and make Minneapolis mighty near 100 percent open shop. . . . This action of the union men striking these shops has been a God-send to the employers. The union itself has opened these shops up on a strictly open-shop basis, the greatest opportunity that could be given the proprietors to change from a closed to an open shop."[68]

The Minneapolis Typographical Union Local 42 claimed from the beginning that the printers had violated their contract and then locked them out. Realizing that they were fighting for the union's very existence, and backed by the International Typographical Union and a 6 million dollar strike fund, Local 42 fought back vigorously. All Forty-eight Hour print shops were picketed, and union supporters were encouraged to frequent only businesses using union label printing. A small printing shop was started up almost immediately while the union planned a huge cooperative printing plant, the Printing Service Bureau, in the Midway district. The CA appealed to its members to boycott the new plant and reported "that prospects for another clean-cut victory for the open shop are mighty good."[69]

By late June, with eighty-two firms still resolved for the open shop, violence broke out on picket lines across the city. Four motorcycle pickets were arrested and convicted of harassing employees at Mullowny Brothers on June 27. With its forces stretched thinly across the city, the union concentrated its attack on the Bureau of Engraving. Sixty to one hundred pickets gathered outside the bureau each day and called the remaining workers "scabs, dirty rats, bastards and God damn son of a bitches." The remaining workers and replacements for the strikers were threatened and harassed from the time they left the plant until they reached their homes. On a company picnic at Lake Rebecca, a large group of pickets were alleged to have viciously assaulted Bureau of Engraving employees.[70]

In order to keep its employees, the bureau was forced on June 4 to bed and board them inside the plant. The CA dispatched its veteran union-fighting lawyers, Nathan Chase and Sam J. Levy, to apply for an injunction in Hennepin County District Court. On July 6, Judge Edward A. Waite issued a temporary restraining order prohibiting the assembly of crowds around the bureau and the use of intimidation to compel the bureau's employees to quit work or join the union.[71]

The Minneapolis and St. Paul Typographical unions, stymied by the court and, in St. Paul, by the CA of Ramsey and Dakota Counties' request for extra sheriff's deputies, sent a delegation to Governor Jacob A. A. Preus to complain about the unjust treatment they were receiving. The governor instructed J. D. Williams, commissioner of the Industrial Commission, to investigate the strike. On July 11, at a hearing at the State Capitol, Williams asked both sides in the controversy if they would accept arbitration. Although the Industrial Commission's report eventually concluded that industrial peace and the welfare of society depended on worker organization and collective bargaining, both the Minneapolis and St. Paul Typothetae refused to submit to arbitration.[72]

By early August, with striking pressmen applying for their old jobs back, the Typothetae ratified its bylaws to require all member firms to make "the maintenance of the Non-Union shop" their labor policy. Following a recommendation of Briggs, the Typothetae established a permanent printers' school to train non-union apprentices in the trade without union-imposed restrictions.[73]

By August 4, the court injunction was still in place, and ninety-one firms were holding out for the open shop. The CA declared the "Printers' Strike is a thing of the past." Although the International Typographical Union would continue to pay strike benefits until July 1924, the Minneapolis Typothetae, thanks to the support and guidance of the CA, had successfully embraced the open shop. The CA's postwar campaign for the open shop had claimed its final victory.[74]

12 *Shaping the Hand of Justice*

WITH THE ESTABLISHMENT OF THE OPEN SHOP in labor's last major stronghold, the printing industry, the Citizens Alliance had achieved effective control over Minneapolis's commercial and industrial workforce. The strategic task of the next decade was to maintain "law and order" and "the open shop." The CA's aggressive and uncompromising policies toward unions would, of course, inevitably create the seeds of resistance and conflict. It was imperative that the business community develop an elaborate defense system. The primary weapon was the labor injunction. Under prevailing law, employers could obtain restraining orders from sympathetic judges that stopped strikes, boycotts, and picketing in their tracks.[1]

The labor injunction, of course, was effective only if it was strictly enforced, by physical force if necessary. Control of local law enforcement agencies was essential. If that failed, the establishment of a state constabulary became an absolute necessity. A secret service, which Otis P. Briggs felt was "an indispensable requisite to good results," would inform and direct the constabulary. The policies that Briggs developed at the National Founder's Association would shape the character of the CA's struggle with labor until the onset of the Great Depression.[2]

Since its establishment in the late 1880s, the labor injunction had become a devastating weapon in suppressing organized labor's bargaining and organizing programs. From sympathetic judges employers could obtain restraining orders that prohibited boycotts and picketing. Preliminary injunctions were often based on little more than employer affidavits and were frequently drawn up by the employer's lawyers. If unions defied these orders, their leaders were jailed for contempt of court with no right of trial by jury. Even if the unions could win in a court appeal, their strike or boycott had usually long since been broken.[3]

Employers' organizations successfully defended their right to this deadly weapon until the passage of the Clayton Anti-Trust Act of 1914, which AFL President Samuel Gompers hailed as labor's Magna Carta. Gompers had incorrectly assumed that the Clayton Act outlawed the labor injunction.

Although this was clearly what the act intended, the NFA, the League for Industrial Rights, and other business groups had cooperated in an intense lobbying effort to emasculate the sections of the act pertaining to labor. The general counsel for the League for Industrial Rights, Daniel Davenport, had managed to insert the "lawful" clause in every area granting new freedoms of action to labor unions. It was this crucial word that would later allow the anti-labor Supreme Court of the 1920s to ignore the Clayton Act and allow employers to continue to use the injunction at will.[4]

In Minneapolis, the business community used the labor injunction as early as the 1902 Draymen's strike that precipitated the organization of the CA. With the teamsters threatening to shut down the city's commerce, the Draymen's Association obtained an injunction that prohibited the union "from doing anything but breathe." The legal scope of this weapon was determined the next summer when Minneapolis's electrical contractors asked Judge Willard R. Cray, a Commercial Club member, for an injunction against the Electrical Workers' Union and the Building Trades Council.[5]

Not surprisingly, Judge Cray gave the newly formed CA precisely the legal weapon that it needed in 1903. In a decision that became an important legal precedent in Minnesota, Cray enjoined the union "from further combining and conspiring to interfere with, injure and cripple the business" of the electrical contractors; "from interfering with their business by means of threats or intimidations of any kind or nature, directed against [their] customers or prospective customers"; from notifying anyone that the contractors were "unfair"; or from trying to persuade allied unions to stop working for these contractors.[6]

Briggs and CA President Edmund J. Phelps congratulated the judge on his "manly, and fearless way," assured him of a lucrative law practice if labor radicals voted him out of office, and advised him on the status of injunction law in other jurisdictions. The Minnesota State Federation of Labor (MSFL), realizing that the injunction would "prove a death blow to organized labor throughout the state," hired lawyers to appeal the case to the Minnesota Supreme Court. To the dismay of the CA, the court recognized that "labor may organize as capital does for its own protection and to further the interests of the laboring classes. They may strike and induce others to join them." However, it also stated that when unions "resort to unlawful means to cause injury to others with whom they have no relation, contractual or otherwise, the limit permitted by the law is passed and they may be restrained." Although the severity of Judge Cray's order had been modified, his broad definition of union threats and intimidation as an illegal secondary boycott would stand for decades as a precedent on which judges friendly to the CA would base their anti-labor rulings.[7]

The CA quickly learned that its use of the labor injunction depended on anti-union interpretations of the law administered by judges sympathetic to the business community. During the 1905 printing strike, Judge John Day Smith denied the employers' application for an injunction, stating: "Persons upon the streets of this city, who were not intimately acquainted with the printer's business, would not know that a strike was on if they had not read it in the newspapers." Realizing the importance of the labor injunction, the CA intensified its efforts for the appointment and election of pro-business judges. CA leaders lobbied the governor's office for the appointment of both municipal and district court judges. These efforts were rewarded by Governor Adolph O. Eberhardt, who appointed the first wave of pro-injunction judges to the Hennepin County District Court.[8]

For the second wave of judges and the second terms of Governor Eberhardt's appointments, the CA would have to convince the voters of Minneapolis that their welfare depended on a conservative judiciary. The CA's two injunction lawyers, Nathan Chase and Samuel Levy, both played prominent roles in these elections. Chase solicited funds from the city's lawyers while Levy canvassed the business community, arguing that if the CA's conservative judicial candidates were defeated, labor unions would win complete control of the city. Levy, who had recently been a law partner with one of the new judges, ran another judge's campaign. By 1922, the CA's efforts had produced a conservative, Republican, and anti-union court that would take an active judicial role in the maintenance of the open shop.[9]

The importance of the court was magnified when the 1917 legislature passed the "Magna Carta" of organized labor, a state act modeled after the federal Clayton Act. Section four of the act stated that the "labor of a human being is not a commodity or article of commerce," and therefore removed unions from the conspiracy provisions of the anti-trust laws. The right of unions to organize in Minnesota was now clearly protected. The courts were prohibited from enjoining unions from striking or peacefully assembling in a lawful manner for a lawful purpose. While this appeared on the surface to be a severe blow to the CA's use of labor injunctions, the act allowed injunctions in cases where it was necessary to prevent irreparable injury to property or to a property right of the person applying for an injunction. The legislature had left the door ajar for the pro-business judiciary of Hennepin County.[10]

The legal battle that would determine the fate of the labor injunction started innocuously in a small movie theater at 27 South Washington Avenue in downtown Minneapolis, months before the United States entered World War I. John J. Campbell, owner of the Wonderland Theater, was losing money due to falling attendance. He decided to lay off his motion picture operators and save money by operating the machines himself. Campbell gave his employees, both members of the Motion Picture Machine Operators of Minneapolis, Local 219, two weeks' notice on February 10, 1917. Operators Edmund B. Dixon and Roy Bradford sought assistance from Local 219, which immediately met with Campbell. Campbell offered to join the union himself and hire one part-time operator, but the union refused to accept the loss of the two positions. Union representative Howard Sloan warned Campbell that if he went ahead and discharged the two men, his theater would be bannered and picketed. Campbell, after consulting with his financial backer, disregarded the warning and discharged the operators on February 24. At 10:00 the next morning, the picketing of the Wonderland Theater began.[11]

One picket walked back and forth in the street in front of the Wonderland carrying a banner with the words "This Theater is Unfair to Organized Labor" printed in large letters. Except for one brief two-week period when Local 219 business agent Louis G. attempted to negotiate with Campbell, the picketing would continue from 10:00 A.M. opening to 11:00 P.M. closing for three-and-one-half years. For the first three to four months, small crowds occasionally gathered to argue about the merits of the banner, unionism, and other subjects. Although the arguments intensified when Campbell put his own picket out with a larger, opposing banner and the police were called several times, the only arrest made was when one of Campbell's non-union employees, Emmett T. Dillon, slugged a man in the crowd. The only other act of violence on the site occurred when Campbell hit a man who had unknowingly insulted him. Considering the transients that frequented the many neighborhood saloons and the duration of the picketing, this was an amazing record.[12]

While the picketing continued, Local 219 also sought assistance from the Minneapolis Trades and Labor Assembly. The assembly immediately passed an "unfair" resolution putting the Wonderland Theater on its "We Do Not Patronize List," which was then printed in bold letters across the top of the front page of the Trades and Labor Assembly newspaper, the *Minneapolis Labor Review*. The effect of these efforts on Campbell's business, an important factor in later court action, was more controversial. At the 1919 trial, Campbell and his employees claimed that customers would approach the ticket counter and then leave when they saw the banner. At the time of the picketing, however, Campbell told Cowan to go ahead and keep his pickets out because they were helping his business. After three months of picketing, Campbell had also been doing well enough to hire non-union operators to run the machines for him.[13]

These facts and other perjured Campbell testimony cast doubt on what was to be a crucial issue in the legal battle that would be fought over the Wonderland Theater. With the business of a member threatened by boycott, the CA

moved in to financially support Campbell, both in the operation of his theater
and in the legal battle that would continue for five years. The financial viability of the Wonderland Theater, however, was of minor importance: The CA was
interested in establishing the open shop. Local 219's use of picketing and the
Trades and Labor Assembly use of the boycott as a weapon, were serious
threats that had to be eliminated. On behalf of Campbell, CA lawyer Chase
petitioned Hennepin County District Court for a temporary injunction. When
the court declined to grant it, Chase appealed to the Minnesota Supreme
Court, which sustained the lower court. The CA would have to wait for the
court to hear evidence and reach a decision on a permanent injunction.[14]

In December 1919, the Wonderland Theater case was finally tried before
Judge Winfield W. Bardwell in Hennepin County District Court. Although the
long wait for the trial had allowed Local 219 and the Trades and Labor
Assembly to continue their activities, the CA and Nathan Chase must have
approached the trial with extreme confidence. Judge Bardwell had a long and
close association with the CA. After leaving law school, Bardwell practiced
in the office of Harlan P. Roberts, a CA member. In 1903, he represented
William I. Gray and George K. Belden, two of the CA's founding members, in a
similar action against the Building Trades Council. In 1907, Bardwell formed
a partnership with Samuel Levy that lasted until he was appointed to the municipal court by Governor Eberhardt in 1921. Levy then joined forces with
Nathan Chase and later would become the CA's lawyer.[15]

More important for the current case, Judge Bardwell was a member of the
Civic and Commerce Association with a long association with the Citizens Alliance. Finding a friend of business on the bench was not a lucky coincidence.
Even while the Wonderland case languished in the courts, CA attorney Chase
and his partner Samuel J. Levy lobbied strenuously for the election of other
pro-business judges. Chase raised money from Minneapolis lawyers while Levy
solicited funds from the business community and ran Judge Edmund A. Montgomery's campaign. O. P. Briggs would leave nothing to chance.[16]

Judge Bardwell did not disappoint the business community. On July 7,
1920, he issued a sweeping injunction banning all the activities that Local 219
and the Trades and Labor Assembly were using in their confrontation with
Wonderland owner Campbell. Officials of the local, the Trades and Labor Assembly, and the *Minneapolis Labor Review* were "permanently and perpetually
enjoined and restrained . . . from in any manner . . . conspiring together . . . to
utter or convey, by means of any picket, banner, sign, transparency, writing,
printing, dodger, card, notice or otherwise, any threat, intimidation, or statement of any character . . . which would interfere with the goodwill, trade, conduct, or patronage of plaintiff's said theater business." The picketing of the

theater and the "Unfair List" publications of the *Minneapolis Labor Review* had been banned.[17]

Judge Bardwell based his decision on Section 8973 of the 1913 *General Statutes of Minnesota*, the Minnesota version of the federal Sherman Anti-Trust Act. Section 8973 declared that no person or association of persons shall enter into any pool, trust agreement, combination, or understanding whatsoever with any person or association, corporate or otherwise, in restraint of trade within this state. The unions had attempted to discourage Campbell's potential customers and therefore in Judge Bardwell's view had conspired to damage his trade. In effect, the judge's order would prohibit any aggressive or defensive activity by unions, including most strikes.

Although Judge Bardwell's interpretation of the Sherman Anti-Trust Act was based on federal precedent, it totally ignored more recent Minnesota law, which prohibited any injunction from restraining "any person or persons, whether singly or in concert, . . . from ceasing to patronize any party to such dispute; or from recommending, advising, or persuading others by peaceful and lawful means so to do." There was as yet no federal precedent for Bardwell's dismissal of Minnesota's version of the Clayton Act. The judge had on his own volition interpreted Minnesota law to benefit the business community.[18]

For organized labor in Minneapolis, already suffering low wages imposed by open shop employers, the Bardwell injunction was a disaster. The *Minneapolis Labor Review* warned that the injunction could "drain the treasury of every union, disrupt all organizations and enslave every worker." Local 219, whose treasury of $6,000 had already been drained for legal fees, picketing, and other expenses, withdrew its picket from the Wonderland Theater. Union activists bitterly assailed the injunction as "one man rule, government by injunction, where a judge is prosecuting attorney, jury and judge. The workers must never cease until they have made forever impossible the power of the courts to set aside the constitution of the U. S." Minneapolis unionists rallied around this "unwarranted attack of Free Speech and Free Press" by injunction.[19]

Following the policy adopted at the 1917 AFL convention, the Trades and Labor Assembly ignored Bardwell's order and continued to publish its "Unfair Notice" on the Wonderland Theater. Chase quickly took his case, the July 16, 23, 30, and August 6 issues of the *Minneapolis Labor Review*, back to Judge Bardwell's courtroom on August 11. Nearly a thousand railroad workers, building tradesmen, and others quit work to fill the courtroom and the corridors, practically paralyzing the business of the courthouse while Sheriff Brown's men watched. Judge Bardwell, perhaps temporarily intimidated by the crowd, delayed his ruling until August 13 and then found the labor leaders guilty of contempt and sentenced them to a $125 fine each or six months in Hennepin County Jail. The *Labor Review* announced in its next issue that the four defendants would refuse to pay fines "that would go into the bloody hands of the Minneapolis frameup gang which dubs itself the CA" and would serve their full sentences.[20]

The *Labor Review*'s public defiance of a court order immediately bolstered the CA campaign for law and order. The Citizens Alliance *Bulletin* appealed to the insecurities of the community when it proclaimed that "the courts are the very foundation of our country. What will become of the Nation, the State, the City, our homes, if any individual or group of individuals is permitted to get away with the policy set up by leaders of the Minneapolis Trades & Labor Assembly?" The decision of Judge Bardwell "stands as the law and must be obeyed."[21]

To try to undermine the financial support of the *Labor Review*, "which we've got to put out of business," CA President Briggs also took advantage of the "attempted intimidation of the court in the Campbell Theatre case by the act of from 1,500 to 2,500 radical sympathizers leaving their jobs and appearing in the courthouse." Briggs wrote local businesses an anti-labor letter urging that all advertising dollars be withdrawn from the *Labor Review*: "Do you know that every dollar contributed to these papers is used to force the Closed Shop in opposition to the Open Shop?" Unfortunately for Briggs, the *Labor Review* obtained a copy of the letter and publicly pointed out that, while the CA had "gone into court and secured an injunction to prevent the workers from withdrawing their patronage from the unfair Wonderland theater," it had also "circulate[d] a boycott letter against the *Labor Review*."[22]

The four convicted and sentenced labor leaders responded on Saturday, August 28, by leading a massive parade of protesting unionists from Parade Stadium to the courthouse. They were followed by a union marching band, a detachment of World War I veterans in uniform, and thousands of labor supporters, many of whom carried "The Wonderland Theater still Unfair to Labor" signs in open defiance of Judge Bardwell's order. After giving speeches from the courthouse steps, the four men turned themselves in to Sheriff Brown, who, claiming that he didn't have the appropriate paperwork, refused to accept them. The *Labor Review* suggested that the sheriff had been intimidated by the crowd. The four labor leaders finally went to jail in September with the ringing words, "Tell the world that the Wonderland Theater is still unfair and we will continue to defy Judge Bardwell's injunction."[23]

From his jail cell, editor Robley D. Cramer continued to edit the defiant *Labor Review*, which now included his column on the evils of capitalist jails. Of greater significance to the CA, the Trades and Labor Assembly formed a

Defense Committee, which organized a rigid union boycott of the downtown business area of Minneapolis. The committee also intensified its union organizational drive and urged all unionists to withdraw money from local banks. Whatever the effectiveness of these tactics might have been, they failed to nullify Judge Bardwell's order.[24]

The CA fought back with contempt proceedings against six more unionists, several of whom were also public officials. Union attorney George B. Leonard appealed the contempt charges and the boycott decision. Leonard's argument that the state anti-trust law was not applicable to labor cases was rejected by Judge Bardwell. Judge William E. Hale, however, delayed deciding the fate of the second group charged with contempt until the Minnesota Supreme Court decided the fate of the Trades and Labor Assembly leaders. After Leonard appealed to the Supreme Court, Judge Bardwell was forced to sign release papers for the four jailed union leaders. The various Wonderland cases and the legality of two of the labor movement's most important weapons, the unfair list and picketing, would have to wait until 1922 for the Supreme Court's decision. The CA would again put this battle in the capable hands of Nathan Chase.[25]

After labor appealed Judge Bardwell's decision, the Wonderland Theater case finally came before the Minnesota Supreme Court, on October 11, 1921. Chief Justice Calvin L. Brown and Associate Justices Oscar Hallam, Homer B. Dibbell, and Andrew D. Holt listened to labor attorney Leonard argue that a theater does not deal in any article of trade and therefore is not covered by the anti-trust statute, and, in any case, an injunction cannot be granted in the complaint of a private person. Because the main action was void, Leonard argued that the contempt charges were invalidated. CA counsel Chase argued in defense of the sanctity of the courts and the integrity of private property. "What we want to know is whether or not an employer can operate his business as an open shop without interference?" Chase asked the court. He suggested that "where the radical element is avowedly pursuing a rule or ruin policy it is highly imperative that . . . property rights be defined by the court."[26]

The strident arguments of Chase and labor attorney Leonard, however, were unable to sway the court. When the court voted three to two on January 27, 1922, to uphold Judge Bardwell's injunction, it was the vote of the Justice James H. Quinn, who had missed the arguments of Chase and Leonard, and three recent decisions of the United States Supreme Court that turned the tide for the CA. Even at the Minnesota Supreme Court level, it appears likely that the CA was able to influence the court's decision. Justice Quinn, a Fairmont Republican, had been narrowly elected in 1916 and was facing reelection in 1922. In 1916, his campaign had received substantial aid from the Shevlin-Carpenter Lumber Company, First National Bank Vice President Archie

Cramer, Judge David Simpson, and Minneapolis lawyer Charlie Fowler, all of whom were members of the CCA or the CA. A committee of Minneapolis businessmen had also raised $75,000 for publicity during Quinn's campaign. Justice Quinn's election in 1916 and his reelection in 1922 relied in large part on the support of the CA. It is not surprising that the *Labor Review* accused him of using his position to support the CA in the Wonderland decision.[27]

Writing the majority opinion, Commissioner Edward Lees stressed the preeminence of the principle that the "law controlling the conduct and rights of employer and employee be definite, clear, and administered in harmony with a single standard in all the courts of the country." Because the issue was before the state court for the first time, the court felt compelled to adopt a construction of Minnesota statute "in harmony with that given by the Federal Supreme Court to the Sherman Anti-Trust Act." While this opinion followed Judge Bardwell's lead in ignoring the Minnesota version of the Clayton Act, which declared that labor is not a commodity or article of commerce, it was bolstered by three recent U.S. Supreme Court decisions that rendered the Clayton Act useless as a defense against labor injunctions. Ironically, Lees at the same time used other sections of the Minnesota version of the Clayton Act as his authority for the right of private parties to sue under the anti-trust statute.[28]

Lees also concluded that "the right of free speech is abused when words become verbal acts and are then as much subject to injunction as the use of any other force whereby property is wrongfully injured." By printing that the Wonderland Theater was unfair to union labor, the *Labor Review* had conspired to injure Campbell's business and therefore the injunction was legal. To explain this decision to all of the Minneapolis business community, the CA devoted its March 1922 *Bulletin* to a reprint of the court's decision. Counsel Chase had won an extraordinary legal victory that would sharply curtail aggressive union activities.[29]

The importance of the Wonderland case became apparent a year later when a strike erupted at the Lincoln Manufacturing Company. In early February, seven employees at Lincoln contacted the Amalgamated Clothing Workers' Union to complain that they often worked seventy to ninety hours per week for a maximum of twelve dollars a week. The atrocious working conditions enabled the union to organize Lincoln's employees in less than two months. On March 15, employees met with plant management and demanded that the company's officers meet with a union committee. When Lincoln, an open-shop CA member, flatly refused, all but five employees walked out.[30]

Starting on March 19, from twelve to forty union members and sympathizers gathered on the sidewalk and street outside the plant every day. Company officers and new employees alleged that they were harassed and followed when they entered or left the plant and were called "scabs," "dirty scabs," and other indecent and vile names by persons in the crowd. Lincoln's treasurer claimed that the union representatives threatened to beat up new employees. One of the female Lincoln strikebreakers was alleged to have been physically assaulted by the strikers. The company elected to send female employees home in taxicabs to avoid any confrontation. With Lincoln Manufacturing facing the increasingly difficult task of running its factory with frightened replacement workers, the CA stepped into the fray.[31]

The CA dispatched its lawyers, Nathan Chase and Samuel Levy, to Lincoln to collect affidavits attesting to union violence and intimidation. Working quickly, the CA lawyers submitted the detailed affidavits and a twelve-page complaint to Judge Bardwell on March 29. They asked Bardwell to permanently restrain the union from assembling near the plant with intent to threaten employees, to induce the employees to quit working, to utter any insulting language, to make the Lincoln Manufacturing Company employees subject to hatred, scorn, disgrace, or annoyance, or to attempt to intimidate or threaten employees into joining the union. They suggested that the union be allowed one picket, who could only inform passersby that the company was working on an open-shop basis.[32]

Judge Bardwell immediately issued a restraining order granting the CA requests virtually word for word. After an April 12 hearing and the submission of union affidavits denying most of the CA's contentions, Judge Edward F. Waite granted a temporary injunction in the same precise language. The CA reported these important developments to all of its members in its April *Special Weekly Bulletins.* Although both injunctions had been honored by the union, Judge Joseph W. Molyneaux made the CA's request a permanent injunction on June 27. The union, limited to one picket and restrained from recruiting new members at the plant, had been stopped in its tracks by Chase, Levy, and three friendly judges whom they had helped elect. The labor injunction had played a vital role in the CA's defense of the open shop.[33]

CA President Briggs printed the entire text of Judge Molyneaux's decision in the July 1923 CA *Bulletin.* Briggs wrote: "The great trouble with picketing is the gathering of mobs." The essence of Molyneaux's decision limits "the number of pickets to one to an entrance, this one picket not to interfere or converse with the employees of the company without their consent, thus precluding the gathering of dangerous mobs. . . . This decision, in conjunction with many others being rendered all over the country at this time with relation to lawful picketing, is having a very salutary effect." The decision also established "a sane method of picketing conducive to the observance of law and order. This method is most practicable and fair alike to employees, employers, producers and the public. It does not prohibit picketing but finds a way to confine it to lawful practice." Briggs did not need to mention that the decision was a significant victory for the CA strategy for maintaining the open shop.[34]

In 1926, at the cap manufacturing plant of T. W. Stevenson Company, the union response to the actions of the courts was to limit picketing to a few union members only and tightly control their actions to avoid any suggestion of threat or intimidation that might serve as the basis for an injunction. After T. W. Stevenson combined with a St. Paul firm, all manufacturing moved to Minneapolis. The union workers at the St. Paul plant struck when they were eliminated. Their jobs were taken by open-shop workers in Minneapolis.[35]

CA Field Agent Lloyd M. MacAloon and Secretary Jack W. Schroeder watched from the factory entryway for five days while three pickets with a banner declaring "T. W. Stevenson Unfair to Cap Manufacturers Union" peacefully stood on the sidewalk. In frustration, MacAloon berated and threatened the pickets and brandished his Minneapolis police badge. When the pickets remained calm, a company foreman offered a former employee fifty dollars and a job to create a disturbance. On the fifth day of picketing, Lawrence Horowitz slugged two willing victims employed by the plant and then escaped while the poised and waiting agents of the CA quickly removed the victims and presented them to the police to sign a complaint.[36]

Early the next week, Chase and Levy applied to Hennepin County District Court for an injunction to stop the physical assaults on T. W. Stevenson employees. On November 26, Judge Waite issued a temporary restraining order that was an exact copy of Chase and Levy's request. All bannering, picketing, violence, and intimidation were prohibited. The CA reported to its members that the union had obeyed the court order and stopped all their activities. Law and order had prevailed.[37]

In the permanent injunction issued several months later, the court agreed with the CA that there was never any strike or lockout or any dissatisfaction or complaint by the T. W. Stevenson employees over wages, hours of employment, or working conditions. By simply transferring production from a union to a non-union plant, all union jobs and rights were effectively eliminated. The court had created a powerful new strategy for the CA.[38]

A long, bitter strike at the Brooks Brothers Parlor Furniture Company the next year would have a far greater effect on the struggle between the CA and organized labor. When 131 members of Upholsterers' Local Union 61 walked out on August 19, 1927, Briggs's assistants, Schroeder and MacAloon, moved into an office in the Brooks plant to take charge of the fight. Following the pattern that it had used since the Wonderland court case, the company refused to rehire the workers; meanwhile, CA lawyer Chase sought an injunction in

Hennepin County District Court. Judge Montgomery granted an immediate restraining order, without hearing any evidence from the defendants, that prohibited loitering and intimidation and limited the union to two pickets at each
factory gate. After the hearings, Judge Horace D. Dickinson granted a temporary injunction that upheld the first order and expanded the prohibited behavior to annoying, harassing, and ridiculing replacement employees. A federal Department of Labor conciliator investigated the plant and reported, "The
plant is being picketed but the present employees go and come without
molestations," suggesting that the CA witnesses had perjured themselves.[39]

In January, still unable to break the strike, Chase went back to court and obtained from Judge Mathias Baldwin a temporary restraining order that forbade
all picketing. In response, the Central Labor Union of Minneapolis called a
mass meeting on October 21, 1927, "the most important ever called by organized labor," to "open the anti-injunction campaign in Minneapolis." The *Labor Review* protested the tyrannical exercise of the injunction, which was
"used by unscrupulous employers to deny the right to strike, to prevent picketing and abridge free speech." The *Review* went on: "Either the Labor injunction or trade unions must go." The Wonderland case, which had dominated
the Minneapolis labor battle for six years, was now to be challenged.[40]

The CA had nothing to fear from the judicial system, but on the political
front the Minnesota Farmer-Labor coalition had had their one startling success in the 1920s, the election of Henrik Shipstead to the United States Senate
in 1922. It was Shipstead who led the battle against the labor injunction. In
1927, Shipstead introduced a one-paragraph amendment to the laws relating
to the judiciary, which would allow equity courts to protect only property that
was "tangible and transferable." Shipstead stated, "The extension to which equity jurisdiction has gone robs the average working man . . . of his right to be
governed by law as distinct from being governed by judicial discretion, which
is another name for the absolutism of kings by divine right." CA lawyer Chase
responded that "the real purpose of this proposed legislation is to give the lawless and irresponsible element of organized labor . . . full sway in labor disturbances; including mass picketing, the use of the primary boycott, and assaults
upon and intimidation of those desiring to work."[41]

In Washington, the Senate Judiciary Committee sought the complete court
record of the Wonderland case as an example of the unwarranted use of the
injunction. The CA was represented in Washington by James A. Emery of the
NAM, who argued that the act would somehow give labor organizations "the
right to issue injunctions of their own." When the bill failed to pass, Shipstead
introduced (in the 71st Congress in 1930) a similar measure that was restricted to injunctions that "grow out of a labor dispute."[42]

The CA adopted a resolution opposing the bill and urged all members to contact Minnesota's senators. The Shipstead Act, members were informed, would curb the power of the courts to issue injunctions and invalidate the use of individual employment contracts. Emery insisted to the Senate Judiciary Committee that the bill was "arbitrarily contrary to the facts of our social and industrial life, insidiously and gratuitously discriminating and in violent conflict with the public policy of the people of the U.S., declared in the constitution." The committee majority killed the legislation in July 1930, reporting that the bill "would be as well as a denial of constitutional liberty and property without due process." The CA's most vital weapon, the labor injunction, was temporarily safe.[43]

In Minnesota, St. Paul union business agent Joseph A. Kozlak introduced a diluted anti-injunction bill in the 1929 session of the Minnesota House. House File 994 sought only to limit the practice of restraining orders being issued pending future hearings. The Minnesota Employers' Association called a conference of the counsels of the state's three major CAS to plot a strategy for opposing the bill.[44]

When the bill came before the labor committee, the representatives of the CAS of Duluth, St. Paul, and Minneapolis, the Mankato Builders' Exchange, the Minnesota Building Employers' Association, and the MEA all lobbied for pro-business amendments. The MEA stated in a flier that the bill would allow damage to property to be "done and consummated before notice could be given and a hearing held" and suggested that it was "part of a nationwide plan of organized labor." CA lawyer Chase argued before a senate committee that "the sole object of this bill is to permit force, violation and intimidation to continue until an injunction application is heard." The bill passed both houses unanimously after it was amended to allow restraining orders without hearings "upon a proper showing of violence." Although the anti-injunction bill was signed into law by Governor Theodore Christianson, the business community had rendered the bill totally ineffective.[45]

The CA's successful defense of the labor injunction and the NAM's work in Washington received a potentially devastating blow three years later when the Norris-LaGuardia Anti-Injunction Bill (a later version of the Shipstead bill) became federal law. A Mankato paper commented: "For a long fight for this law, Senator Shipstead has made a name for himself that will live on long after he is gone. His work will be a tangible factor for the common good in the age-old struggle against special privilege."[46]

The bill forbade all United States courts from issuing injunctions that prohibited "giving publicity to the existence of, or the facts involved in, any labor dispute, whether by advertising, speaking, patrolling or by any other method not involving fraud or violence" or "assembling peaceably to act or to organize to act in promotion of their interests in a labor dispute." The landmark Wonderland Theater case that had enabled the CA to suppress union picketing and the unfair list now appeared to be in serious danger.[47]

On March 1, 1933, State Representative Roy Wier of the Central Labor Union of Minneapolis and three other legislators introduced House File 1255, an almost literal copy of the Norris-LaGuardia Act. Two years earlier, the MEA had worked with the legal departments of the NAM, the League for Industrial Rights, and the Citizens Alliances of Minneapolis, Duluth, and St. Paul to defeat similar legislation. In 1933, however, faced with enactment of the federal anti-injunction statute, the MEA exerted its influence on the legislature to amend the following, more obnoxious, provisions of the Minnesota act.

Although the federal statute allowed temporary restraining orders without a hearing for five days, the Minnesota act was amended to allow ten days before a hearing was held, which might stretch to two weeks before a decision was handed down. The section of the Norris-LaGuardia Act that allowed injunctions only if employers exhausted negotiations and governmental arbitration was stricken from the Minnesota act. A provision that might have forced the CA to bargain collectively with labor unions was eliminated. An amendment was tacked on to the federal statute that the act would not apply to policemen or firemen.

With the Farmer-Labor Party in power, the changes gave the CA a legal weapon to force local police to protect the interests of employers. The MEA had managed to amend the Minnesota act to conform to the anti-labor union strategies of the CA.[48]

The *Minneapolis Labor Review* considered the 1933 Labor Disputes Injunction Act an "outstanding labor measure" and no doubt expected it to curtail the use of the labor injunction. The MEA, more realistic in its assessment of Minnesota's judiciary, also endorsed the amended act, which was passed by the conservative senate by fifty-two votes to one. The act did establish that employees "shall be free from the interference, restraint, or coercion of employers of labor" when organizing or bargaining collectively, and it outlawed the "yellow dog contracts" that forbid participation in labor unions.[49]

The rest of the Labor Disputes Injunction Act, however, would have little impact on the anti-union strategies of the CA. Boycotts, as defined in the 1903 Gray case, were still illegal. Although peaceful picketing and other legal union activities were placed beyond the reach of the injunction, any violent or intimidating acts, even for legitimate union purposes, could still be enjoined. As long as friendly judges sat on the Hennepin County District Court, the CA could count on restraining orders, which were still available without a hearing if the employer could show "that substantial and irreparable injury to property" would follow. With union violence and intimidation hampered, the CA could continue to fire all striking union members and hire permanent replacements without fear of retaliation.[50]

Labor's hopes for the Labor Disputes Injunction Act were quickly dashed when a strike was called at the Robitshek-Schneider clothing manufacturing company on July 4, 1933. Working under individual "yellow dog" contracts since 1931, the employees, encouraged by their new-found rights to bargain collectively under Section 7A of the National Industrial Recovery Act (NIRA), began to rejoin the Amalgamated Clothing Workers' Union. The plant manager quickly called a meeting of all employees and threatened to close the factory if employees joined the union.[51]

The CA, realizing that this was the first of a probable avalanche of union activity in the wake of the new federal legislation, stepped in to handle Robitshek-Schneider's union difficulty. Under the threat of a plant closing, the employees were forced to sign up with the American Plan Garment Worker's Association, a company union created and fostered by the CA. Aware of the CA's role, the cutters insisted on their right to join the Amalgamated Clothing Workers and went out on strike. A picket line of twenty to thirty union members was set up in front of the factory on the morning of July 24 and instructed by union leader Sander Genis to patrol with a union banner and "to conduct themselves at all times in an orderly and lawful manner."[52]

As the strike dragged on into August, the size and ferocity of the picket line and the crowd of onlookers gradually grew. Newly hired employees had to run a gauntlet of jostling and a chorus of "scab," "rat," "yellow belly," and "skunk" to reach the factory. As access to the factory became more difficult, CA field agent MacAloon once again appeared in front of the factory. When one of the strikebreakers charged into the crowd on August 21, MacAloon just happened to be there with a photographer to get pictures of the resulting melee. With proof of an act of violence, the CA was ready to test the Labor Disputes Injunction Act in the friendly confines of Hennepin County District Court.[53]

Within four days of the incident, CA attorney Levy had appeared in District Court to apply for an injunction on behalf of the employees of Robitshek-Schneider who were still working. Judge Levi M. Hall found that "great and irreparable injury to plaintiff's property and rights" were threatened and issued a restraining order that forbade any "assembling or loitering" in front of the factory to "threaten, molest, injure or insult the employees." The ruling was a curious defense, as Judge Hall did not explain what property of the employees was threatened and their rights were not a part of the 1933 act which was based on equity law.[54]

The restraining order remained in effect until Judge Waite issued a permanent injunction on October 9. The ten-day limit that was mandated in the

1933 act clearly had little practical effect on the practice of the court. In the hearings before Judge Waite, Levy claimed that the Anti-Injunction Act was unconstitutional, while defense counsel Arthur LeSueur argued that there was no evidence that the union authorized the supposed violent acts.[55]

Judge Waite confounded both sides. He ruled that the act was constitutional, but only if the union were held responsible for any violence that occurred on or near the picket line, despite clear language in the act that demanded direct evidence of union participation in or authorization of any violence that was to be enjoined. The judge rectified Judge Hall's faulty interpretation of the 1933 act, explaining that an injunction was justified because the replacement workers' "right to do lawful work where they choose is their 'property,'" and injury to this "property" would be "substantial and irreparable."[56]

Why these same jobs were not the "property" of the strikers was not discussed. The permanent injunction ordered the union to refrain from gathering to obstruct free entrance to the plant, from placing the employees in reasonable fear of bodily harm, or from using insulting epithets like "scab." Although all disruptive acts were banned, Judge Waite acknowledged that the new act did say that "picketing" or "patrolling" was still permitted as long as it did not involve "fraud or violence." While the *Labor Review* celebrated this hollow victory, it was clear that the 1933 act was going to have very little effect on the balance of power in Minneapolis. Two or three peaceful pickets stood no chance against the powerful juggernaut of the CA.[57]

A month later, Levy brought to Judge Baldwin's courtroom affidavits that accused striking upholstery workers at the Grau-Curtis Company of "mass and mob picketing" that endangered the lives of employees and restricted their safe ingress and egress to the plant. Judge Baldwin, following over a decade of injunction tradition and ignoring the 1933 Labor Disputes Injunction Act, issued a restraining order that once again gave Levy and the CA exactly what they had requested. On November 14, 1933, the union was restrained from gathering to obstruct access, physically intimidate, or verbally abuse the plant's employees.[58]

Eight days later, the order was amended to restrict the union to "ten pickets, who shall at all times conduct themselves in an orderly manner," and to prohibit them from following the employees when they left work. After the legally mandated ten-day period had passed, union attorneys challenged the court's jurisdiction. Judge Lars M. Rue heard lengthy arguments from Levy and union attorneys and ruled that the question of jurisdiction was not before him. With the restraining order still in force, the *Minneapolis Labor Review* belatedly concluded that "Justice For Workers Appears To Be Impossible In Present Courts."[59]

13 *Guarding an Empire*

O. P. BRIGGS KNEW that the labor injunction was an effective weapon only if the power of the courts rested on the bedrock of physical force supplied by the police and military forces of the city, county, and state. Following World War I, the Citizens Alliance board of directors stated that an "efficient (and friendly) National Guard is of the utmost importance in preserving 'law and order' throughout the state." The Civilian Auxiliary had proven extraordinarily successful in suppressing labor disturbances during the 1917 streetcar strike. But when the European conflagration ended, the CA's private army would have to disband, to be replaced by a reorganized Minnesota National Guard. The CA considered it imperative that the Minneapolis National Guard units return to their renowned pre-war status, manned and commanded by reliable Minneapolis businessmen.[1]

The Minneapolis Light Infantry was organized in 1879. Required to uniform and arm themselves, the infantry was primarily composed of young men of means and social status. When the state militia was organized three years later, the Light Infantry was honored as Company A of the First Minnesota Regiment. Despite its new status as part of the state militia, the city's first armory, completed in 1883, was built from private funds by Light Infantry members.[2]

Minneapolis businessmen, who would later become prominent CA members, quickly assumed command of the city's militia. Civilian Auxiliary commander Perry G. Harrison, one of the Light Infantry's founding members, later commanded the militia unit during the 1880s. Twenty years later, CA Secretary George K. Belden gained first-hand military experience as second in command. In 1910, George E. Leach, who eleven years later would be a close political ally of the CA, assumed command of the Light Infantry. Throughout its forty-year history, the leaders of the Minneapolis Light Infantry became acutely aware of the militia's potential practical role as the defender of the Minneapolis business community.[3]

Captain Harrison and the troops of the Minneapolis Light Infantry were mobilized to quell local disturbances four times in the unit's first fifteen years.

197

When the Stillwater penitentiary caught fire in the winter of 1883–84, Company A was summoned to guard the most hardened criminals for three weeks until temporary quarters were constructed. Four years later, Company A was called out to disperse a large lynch mob at the Hennepin County courthouse.[4]

Although neither of these engagements affected the labor situation in Minneapolis, they gave the infantry experience and confidence under arms. When violence erupted during the 1889 streetcar strike, the local militia was again armed and assembled at the Armory awaiting commands to restore order. Although the order was never issued, the mobilization undoubtedly reinforced the intransigence of the streetcar company. In 1893, word reached Mayor William H. Eustis that "Coxey's Army" of the unemployed was about to march into Minneapolis. Ordered out by the mayor, the infantry camped under full arms in the old City Market to wait for Coxey, who then detoured around the city. The Minneapolis business community was slowly learning valuable military lessons for their war on labor unions.[5]

The ultimate value of the Minnesota National Guard became evident when strikes erupted on the Iron Range in 1892 and 1894. More than 600 men struck the Minnesota Iron Company at Soudan during the summer of 1892 when the company laid off 315 workers. After the strikers captured several engine houses and shut down the pumps to flood the mines, the outnumbered sheriff requested that the National Guard be called. On Governor William R. Merriam's orders, three Duluth companies of the National Guard arrived via a special train to restore order. Under the direction of the mine superintendent, the streets were cleared, mine property was restored to the company, and the strike leaders were arrested. In its report on the incident, the National Guard "regretted that so few of our good people realize the full value and importance of a well organized and thoroughly disciplined military force, ready at all times to respond to the call of the Commander-in-Chief." The National Guard had proved its unparalleled ability to quickly and efficiently break a strike.[6]

Two years later, 500 men struck the Franklin mine near Virginia on the Mesabi Range. Within two days, the strike had spread across the Iron Range and to workers outside the mines. Local papers reluctantly admitted that public sympathy favored the strikers, who were not being paid a living wage. Despite a lack of violence, the sheriff asked Governor Knute Nelson to call out the National Guard. Two Duluth National Guard companies were quickly dispatched to restore "order" and eliminate any threat that the strikers might pose to the mining companies. The presence of armed troops and a wage raise at the Franklin mine quickly ended the disturbance. The National Guard reported to the governor that "the recent strikes and labor troubles which have agitated the public mind to so great a degree, have demonstrated that a military force is essential to the preservation of society from disintegration." Thirty years later, the CA would appreciate this lesson and maneuver its powerful influence to gain control of the National Guard.[7]

The first step in reestablishing the National Guard was to transfer, at the invitation of Adjutant General Rhinow, the Civilian Auxiliary *en masse* into the state Home Guard. The plan, approved by Civilian Auxiliary commanders Colonel Perry Harrison and Major Henry A. Bellows, allowed the Civilian Auxiliary, now the Thirteenth Battalion of the Home Guard, to be called out by Governor Burnquist in the event of a state crisis or by Hennepin County Sheriff Otto Langum to deal with local disturbances. The transfer allowed federal rifles and ammunition to be used to rearm the battalion at no cost to the Civic and Commerce Association. More importantly, Colonel Harrison was promoted to a powerful position on the adjutant general's staff, and the employers' army, under the command of Major Bellows, was given legitimate status as part of the state militia.[8]

The Home Guard, however, had been created by the Minnesota Commission of Public Safety for protecting the state during the absence of National Guard units fighting in Europe and would be disbanded after the war ended. On May 4, 1918, the War Department in Washington authorized the adjutant generals of every state to organize a new National Guard force to "suppress insurrection, repel invasion and execute the laws of the union." The new units would receive federal recognition, aid, and guidance only if they had suitable armories, personnel grouped by locality, and probable permanency.[9]

The federal government authorized three new regiments of Minnesota National Guard, which would be organized from the state's most efficient Home Guard units. The Thirteenth Battalion "already had the best record of public service performed of any unit in the state and . . . was the largest, the oldest, and the most fully equipped military organization in the state." The Thirteenth Battalion was joined with the Second Battalion and the Fourth Minnesota Infantry to form the First Minnesota Infantry. Lieutenant Colonel Bellows was promoted to second in command of the regiment, and Major Edward B. Karow led the Thirteenth Battalion, which was transferred *en masse* with its officers and roster intact. By July of 1918, the Civilian Auxiliary and its commanders had become the Minneapolis unit of the National Guard. With Rhinow, Harrison, Bellows, and Karow in command positions, the CCA was assured of a friendly state militia.[10]

The National Guard, however, was not a satisfactory replacement for a state constabulary. Basically a military unit, the guard was undertrained and available only for emergency call-up by the governor. Realizing these difficulties, the CA turned its attention to the recently formed Motor Corps. In 1917, the Minneapolis Automobile Trade Association had initiated a statewide organization, the Minnesota Motor Reserve, which was to be "a decisive factor in the protection of the rural districts from the depredations of lawless actions." The squads, made up of twenty-seven cars each, were commanded by the county sheriffs and the county public safety directors.[11]

A year later, Winfield R. Stephens, an employee of Pence Auto in Minneapolis, conceived a plan to militarize the moribund reserve. With the authorization of the adjutant general and the help of his employer, Harry E. Pence, Stephens quickly organized a motor corps "composed entirely of business and professional men who own automobiles of five passenger capacity." Within three months, the automobile dealers of the state had enlisted enough members to fill five full battalions. "The Marines of Minnesota" were completely outfitted and equipped at their own expense and ready for action.[12]

Commanded by Stephens, the Motor Corps was the only military organization of its kind functioning during the war and it quickly reached a strength of 1,200 men. When Sheriff Langum banned a demonstration of the Socialist Party on November 25, 1918, the Motor Corps quickly proved its usefulness. One-hundred-and-eighty cars strong and able to mobilize in less than forty minutes, the Minneapolis battalion of the Motor Corps responded to Governor Burnquist's call to establish martial control of downtown Minneapolis. Adjutant General Rhinow and Brigadier General Harrison commanded the troops of the infantry and the Motor Corps as they swept through downtown streets with machine guns and bayonets. Motor Corps members ferried arrested demonstrators to jail and helped keep a close watch on the Trades and Labor Assembly Hall. Following the Armistice, the Motor Corps moved into the National Guard Armory in Minneapolis and sought federal recognition.[13]

While waiting for a reaction from Washington, State Senator Charles R. Fowler, a lawyer and CA member, introduced a bill in the state legislature to create a military unit to be known as the Minnesota State Motor Corps. The organization, armament, and discipline of the new Motor Corps were to be the same as those already existing. In addition to functioning as a militia at the call of the governor, the adjutant general was "authorized to appoint patrol men as he may deem advisable for the . . . protection of life and property," to be financed by the yearly appropriation of $150,000. With Rhinow in command, this force would undoubtedly deal effectively with lawless unions.[14]

Twin Cities' labor unions, which had opposed state constabulary measures before the war, quickly recognized the CA's intent for the Motor Corps. Thousands of "wild eyed" railway shopmen swarmed into the Capitol to protest the Motor Corps bill, until the doors were locked against them. Union leader A. E. Smith stated that they were "opposed to the bill as it now stands

because it makes the corps a state constabulary, for which there is no need."
The *Minneapolis Tribune* asked, "Why should anybody who intends to behave
himself and obey the law object to the passage of the Motor Corps bill?" The
measure never reached the floor of either house for a vote.[15]

The Minnesota Senate Military Affairs Committee was asked to insert the
Motor Corps in an amendment to the 1917 National Guard Code, but Chairman S. A. Rask declared the effort useless because federal law made no provision for a motor corps. The Motor Corps, having no legal basis, was forced
to disband, but the CA's postwar campaign for a state constabulary had just
begun. As *Commercial West* pointed out, unless vigorous action was taken
against "Reds," the "American Legion boys may be forced to organize another
Ku Klux Klan."[16]

While CA Vice President Strong led a recruitment campaign to strengthen
the Minneapolis National Guard, the final challenge to the CCA's domination
of the guard was quietly returning from the battlegrounds of Europe. The
commanders of Minnesota's infantry units in France requested that the current National Guard units be broken up and reorganized with the inclusion of
the World War I veterans. Governor Burnquist turned the controversy over to
the state Military Board, which was composed of Colonel Bellows, Brigadier
General Harrison, and the commanders of the other infantry units already operating in Minnesota, all of whom had a vested interest in maintaining the
integrity of the peacetime battalions. Harrison quickly announced that the reorganization would temporarily leave the state unprotected and was therefore
impossible. The Minneapolis Civilian Auxiliary with Colonel Leach now in
command finally became the 151st Field Artillery. CA members believed Leach,
a returning war hero, was trustworthy. Karow was promoted to lieutenant,
second in command to Leach. The transition to a peacetime military had been
completed with the Civilian Auxiliary still intact and with officers friendly to
the CCA and the CA in command.[17]

The defeat of the Motor Corps bill now made the National Guard the only
large statewide force that could be used to maintain law and order. Leach,
Karow, and Bellows felt that an efficient state constabulary could maintain order better than the undertrained volunteers of the National Guard could. They
proposed to amend federal laws to create a National Guard constabulary. The
full-time paid force would maintain order and allow the volunteer units to fulfill the more appropriate function of a reserve army. The plan was never
adopted.[18]

St. Paul Association leader William H. MacMahon argued that the National Guard was "also a warning to any lawless forces which may exist that
violence and disorder and destruction of property will never be tolerated. In

time of riot or insurrection it might conceivably be the one and only force in our community to protect you and your property against the irresponsible forces of mob rule." The response of Minnesotans to these fears was clear and enthusiastic. By the fall of 1919, the state had recruited 4,263 men into the reorganized National Guard, one of only two states in the country to recruit more than their authorized strength.[19]

In a special message to the 1921 legislature, Governor Preus opened the CA's campaign for a state constabulary. A "terrific" wave of crime was sweeping across the nation, and a state constabulary was the only way to effectively deal with it. Preus asserted that because of the growth of the highway system, local police forces could no longer deal with a highly mobile criminal class. CA publications supported Preus's efforts to stomp out the new wave of youthful criminals, which the CA contended was caused by movies, pool halls, and war experience. Preus supported a bill to create a Department of State Police of 100 men to act as peace officers throughout the state.[20]

Despite a clause that the force "shall not be employed in strikes arising out of labor controversies between employers and employees," the legislature, probably realizing that labor opposition would doom the bill, ignored Preus's effort. Instead, William I. Nolan and George Wicker introduced a bill to create a state Public Safety Commission to coordinate the activities of all public peace and prosecuting officers of the state. The CA immediately supported the Wicker-Nolan bill as a first step toward a state constabulary. On March 30, the bill passed the Senate by a forty-one to twenty-two vote.[21]

The *Minneapolis Labor Review*, warned by the support of the Motor Corps and rumors that anti-labor Minneapolis police chief John F. Walker would become the commissioner, realized that the bill provided that the commissioner could "direct the activities of all public peace officers of this state" and "could remove any such official who shall willfully refuse to perform any official duty imposed" by the bill. The *Labor Review* feared that the bill would "give one man complete control over all the police forces of Minneapolis and other cities." The labor community was mobilized in a petition drive against the bill. Despite continued support by the business community, the bill was defeated in the House by a close 61 to 53 vote. This was the closest the CA was ever to come to their goal of establishing a state-controlled police force of the constabulary type.[22]

While the CA campaigned for a state constabulary, the meatpackers' union went out on strike in South St. Paul. Although there were few reports of violence, Governor Preus, under pressure from the St. Paul Association, called out the National Guard. The state military troops cleared all strikers from the streets with bayonets drawn and restricted picketing to a few strikers at each gate. From his temporary headquarters in the general offices of one of the packinghouse companies, Adjutant General Rhinow also sent his troops into Ramsey County to patrol for union activity. Rhinow had reportedly told his troops, "Don't shoot unless necessary, but if you do shoot, shoot to kill!" *Commercial West* congratulated Governor Preus on breaking the strikers' "Soviet control of the packing industry at South St. Paul." When the packing companies used this protection to bring in replacement workers, the state was placed in the "untenable position of taking sides where it professes to be merely maintaining law and order."[23]

Although use of the National Guard to win the South St. Paul strike was precisely the reason the CA had supported the National Guard and Governor Preus, it created an unforeseen backlash. The labor bloc on the Minneapolis City Council voted down appropriations for the operation of the Minneapolis Armory. Its members argued adamantly that "when workers go on strike for the improvement of their living conditions then the guard is used against them," as when "Governor Preus sent troops into South St. Paul without any cause except to break the strike of the butcher workers." Without the appropriation, the Armory would have to close, leaving Minneapolis without a base for its National Guard. Generals Rhinow and Harrison and Mayor Leach went to the CA's board of directors with an emergency proposition. The CA, recognizing "the danger to this community if it were left without military protection in case of need," raised $4,000 within three weeks, which it paid into the mayor's contingency fund, thereby saving the city from the council's "communist conspiracy."[24]

The Minnesota State Federation of Labor argued that the National Guard "entails a heavy expense on the state which the taxpayers must meet." Two years later, O. P. Briggs agreed, arguing that a state constabulary would be the "cheaper way to protect the state." Briggs stated: "The reason labor unions oppose it is apparent. Labor does not want to obey any laws during periods of strikes. The strike of a few years ago in the South St. Paul packing industries tended to prove this fact. The cost to the state in calling out the militia to patrol the district of the strikers showed the need of adopting a state constabulary in Minnesota."[25]

Governor Preus also continued to press for a state police. In the summer of 1922, he appointed a Crime Commission to "ascertain the need of the state for better methods of bringing criminals to justice" and to make recommendations to the 1923 legislature. In his opening remarks, the governor stated: "We must have some central bureau of identification as well as a state police system." The commission recommended both the establishment of a state constabulary and a Bureau of Criminal Records and Criminal Investigation. *Commercial West* rallied to support the measures needed to check the "bandit warfare, which is more or less rampant in the larger business centers. . . . The state of Minnesota has no more important business on hand today than to establish a state constabulary." Despite these intensive efforts, the 1923 legislation never reached a vote in either the Senate or the House. Labor opposition to a state police had again triumphed.[26]

How to overcome labor opposition to a state police was the critical problem for the CA. In reality it was highly unlikely that any argument or subterfuge would sway labor concerns that "state constabularies are a menace wherever they are." Labor felt that they "disregard and sometimes destroy human liberty, and leave only hate and malice in its place." CA arguments against crime were considered "a cloak to cover the real purpose and use of a state police." Recognizing this political reality, state police advocates changed their strategy and backed a bill in the 1925 legislature submitted by Highway Commissioner Charles M. Babcock to create a state highway patrol whose powers would be restricted to enforcement of traffic laws.[27]

"But organized labor fears," *Commercial West* pointed out, "and probably with reason, that a highway police would be the first step toward a state constabulary with much fuller powers. And it ought to be." The Minnesota Federation of Labor recognized that "sooner or later . . . some police power [would] be given to our highway department" and that the Babcock bill "would take away a lot of propaganda of those interested in a state constabulary." Despite fears that conservatives would later try to expand the powers of the highway police, the federation finally decided to support the bill. Labor senators, however, ignored the federation and defeated the bill by one vote.[28]

Pressure for a state constabulary in the 1927 legislature began shortly after the 1925 legislature failed to pass the Highway Patrol bill when the Minnesota Bankers' Association organized the Minnesota County Rangers. An armed and mobile force of 4,000 handpicked former servicemen was deputized by the counties and instructed to "shoot to kill." The CA used this makeshift vigilante force as a major argument in favor of a state police. The County Rangers "can never prove as effective in preventing crime and trailing down criminals as a well trained state police body," according to *Commercial West*.[29]

Two companion bills were introduced to organize a Minnesota state police, which "shall have power of peace officers throughout the state." In an effort to placate labor, both bills stated that the police "shall not enter upon duty for the purpose of policing a strike, except by the order of the Governor, or upon request of the Mayor of a city or the Sheriff of a county, approved by the Governor." Even with the original force of 350 patrolmen reduced to 50, labor opponents invaded the hearings set for the bill's supporters to protest the creation of a "cossack ridden state." The CA's campaign for a state constabulary finally seemed doomed for the foreseeable future.[30]

But the 1927 legislature could not totally ignore Governor Christianson when he dramatically stated: "During the last decade a crime wave increasing in volume and seriousness has been sweeping over the world. Minnesota, in common with other states, has a serious crime problem." In the press furor, primarily created by CA publisher of the *Minneapolis Journal* Herschel V. Jones, that followed the murder of a Minneapolis policeman by a paroled criminal, the governor had created another crime commission. The commission recommended the creation of a Central Bureau of Law Enforcement that did "not in any manner involve the creation of a State Constabulary."[31]

House File 1158, to create a Bureau of Criminal Apprehension, was passed overwhelmingly by both houses in April of 1927. The bureau was to coordinate the work of peace officers and promote greater efficiency in detecting and apprehending criminals and was limited to twelve employees. The law was undoubtedly passed because it obviously was not an immediate threat to labor. The appointment of longtime CA friend Adjutant General Rhinow as superintendent and the very existence of a state law-enforcement body ensured a foothold from which the CA could launch future campaigns.[32]

While the 1927 legislature was still in session, a Hennepin County grand jury was ordered to investigate a series of eight "bombing outrages" that had taken place at the home or property of employers of labor during controversies with various labor unions. The controversy, as it expanded in 1925 and 1926, once again was centered on the city's movie theaters. On May 18, 1926, a midnight explosion at the Main Theater at Main Street Northeast and Broadway "tore the front of the building out, scattering broken bits of wood and glass for a block around . . . and brought 1,000 persons, many of them dressed in night clothes, to the scene." This was the fourth theater bombing in less than a year and each, the CA pointed out in a weekly bulletin, was on the "unfair" list of the Motion Picture Machine Operators Union. Two of the bombing attempts had been at the Wonderland Theater, "against which such vicious tactics were employed in 1917."[33]

The CA demanded that the responsible parties be apprehended and properly punished immediately. The *Minneapolis Labor Review* suggested that the circumstances surrounding the bombs that were found before they could explode at the Wonderland were highly suspicious and that the bombings were clearly a CA frame-up. The grand jury, empowered by CCA Judge Bardwell, run by foreman Albert M. Slocum, a CCA member, and dominated by CCA members, believed implicitly in the CA version of the story. This was not a coincidence. Grand jury members were selected at random from a short list of fewer than

200 people who were personally picked by the district court judges. The 1920s grand juries were predominately CCA members or their wives. When labor complained about less than 5 percent representation, Judge Dickinson commented: "We put men of affairs on the grand juries." The CA's expensive campaign efforts for friendly judges and the conservative nature of the judiciary of the period were largely responsible. Hennepin County grand juries of the era were essentially creatures of the CA.[34]

Although the grand jury was unable to prove that unions were responsible for the bombings, they did discover "that almost the entire police department in Minneapolis is an organized labor union, being affiliated with or a branch of the AFL." The CA had been aware of the police union for years but, satisfied with the performance of the Sheriff's Department and the National Guard, had ignored the potentially dangerous situation. The bombings, however, presented the perfect opportunity for eliminating the threat. The grand jury suggested that "the police department should be unhampered by alliances with any special interests or organization." The CA pointed out that the oath taken by AFL members, "that I will obey the rules and regulations of this Central Labor Union," was "in direct conflict with the oath which a policeman takes as a peace officer." In a special pamphlet, the CA accused the police of being under the Central Labor Union's control and demanded that "our public servants be deunionized." Bombings, strikes, violence, and intimidation were all laid at the doorstep of this un-American alliance. The CA tried to rekindle the issue in its May-June 1927 *Bulletin*, but the uproar died down without action.[35]

In September of 1927, 150 Minneapolis and St. Paul theater stagehands walked out when the Northwest Theater Owners' Association accused them of being communists and refused to grant their last demand, one day's rest in seven. When the motion picture operators and other theater unions walked out in sympathy, more than seventy-two Minneapolis theaters were shut down. All the theaters quickly reopened with non-union stage operators. During the short strike, there were dynamite bombings at the Paramount Film Exchange and the New Logan Theater and a series of stench bombings at other theaters. The CA had ammunition to reopen the police union controversy. A new Hennepin County Grand Jury, empowered by CA judge Mathias Baldwin and run by CCA member J. J. Fehr, denounced the police union. In its November 7, 1927, report, the grand jury urgently recommended "that those in authority forthwith take such measures as will abolish, and in the near future prohibit, membership of any member of the police force in any union."[36]

The CA publicized the report in a double-length issue of its *Bulletin* which included such leads as "How can a Policeman serve two masters?" and "Lawlessness and Disorder Here Alarming." It concluded: "It is up to you, the people! What are you going to do?" The *Minneapolis Journal* and *Commercial West* also demanded that the police abandon their union. O. P. Briggs informed Governor Christianson of the problem and orchestrated a flood of delegations, petitions, and letters to Mayor Leach. Leach, bowing to pressure, asked the city attorney for a legal opinion. City attorney Neil Cronin stated that "Insofar as legality is concerned I see nothing objectionable in the constitution and bylaws of the police officers federation."[37]

Despite this opinion and the well-publicized fact that the police union's constitution stated that under no consideration shall the members of the police force go on strike, Mayor Leach requested a full explanation of the relationship between the police and the Minneapolis Central Labor Union. Union president David Broderick, trying to assess his support before replying, took a straw poll in which policemen voted 301 to 41 in favor of retaining their union affiliation. The *Minneapolis Journal* pointed out that the mayor was in charge of the police department. Briggs lamented the "sad state of affairs" at a Commonwealth Club luncheon where he debated Robley D. Cramer, editor of the *Labor Review*, and once again demanded that the police disband its union.[38]

Desperately trying to stem the tide of public opinion, Broderick wrote a lengthy reply to the mayor laying out the many strike-related actions taken by the police and stating quite simply that "the police oath is our only oath." The public furor continued unabated until the police officers' union finally caved in on December 17, 1927, and severed its connection with the labor movement. After months of vilifying the police, the CA was now very gratified that this "splendid body of men—none finer" had de-unionized themselves.[39]

A year and a half later, the 1929 Minnesota legislature marked the first establishment of a statewide law enforcement body. After a decade of lobbying by the CA, Governor Christianson approved House File 447 on April 26, creating the Minnesota Highway Patrol. To get it through the House on a close sixty-nine-to-sixty vote, however, the bill limited the force to thirty-five men and allowed them to enforce only "laws relating to use and operation of motor vehicles on the trunk highways. The patrol had the power of peace officers for this purpose only."[40]

Although this compromise destroyed the impact of the patrol, the CA considered it a first step towards a state constabulary and was overjoyed at the appointment of Hennepin County Sheriff Earle Brown as chief of the new Highway Patrol. Chief Brown, a CCA member and former state inspector of the American Protective League, carefully selected candidates for the patrol, which would be trained on his farm. The essentially private training school was paid for and organized by Brown, who donated farm buildings for a dining hall, sleeping quarters, and classrooms. Captain J. Glenn Dahl, former

Hennepin County Deputy Sheriff under Brown, was in charge of instruction at the school. The men were trained in traffic laws, geography, first aid, pistol shooting, and jujitsu. The patrol cruised the highways on twin-cylinder motorcycles equipped with sirens and first-aid kits and were armed with .38-caliber pistols.[41]

The patrol immediately captured the imagination of the state when, on August 9, 1929, Chief Brown and Patrolman Mike Austos captured three bank robbers: "Mr. Brown wounded one of the gunmen in a thrilling 70-mile-an-hour gunfight in which one bullet blew out the front tire of Brown's car." Local newspapers throughout the state praised the patrol chief and called for a state constabulary headed by Brown. H. V. Jones of the *Minneapolis Journal* wrote: "This outstanding deed was the one thing needed to sell the people of Minnesota the plan for a State police force." The legislature had created an ineffectual Bureau of Criminal Apprehension and Highway Patrol, and now "the only logical thing is to expand that bureau and combine it with the patrol in a genuine State police department." A Minnesota state constabulary finally appeared within easy reach of the CA.[42]

In 1931, Governor Christianson supported the idea of enlarged and combined law enforcement agencies under his control and created a state Crime Commission to develop recommendations for the 1931 legislature. E. George Hall, labor's representative on the commission, opposed the state constabulary idea and was joined by the now-famous Highway Patrol Chief Earle Brown, who apparently feared losing control of his privately trained force. The commission recommended enlarging the Bureau of Criminal Apprehension to at least fifty men with statewide powers and enlarging the Highway Patrol to one hundred men and expanding their authority to all felonies. Both agencies would be prohibited from any interference in strikes and lockouts arising from labor disputes. When these recommendations finally became law, the CA's long struggle for a state constabulary was frustrated, and, ironically, it was the arguments of its own law enforcement leader, Chief Brown, that doomed its efforts.[43]

Despite these setbacks, however, the Highway Patrol proved in 1932 that it was more than a traffic police force. On Sept. 8, 1932, the National Farm Holiday Association, a militant farmer's organization with a strong Minnesota chapter, called for a campaign to withhold grain and livestock from the market in an effort to raise the disastrously low prices. Eleven days later, 400 farmers, armed with clubs and spiked machinery belts, blocked the highways near Worthington, Minnesota. The strike spread and strengthened, and the rural towns of Austin and Sioux Falls were completely blockaded.[44]

As the strike escalated in October, Minnesota Farm Holiday strikers began picketing the highways into the Twin Cities. On October 12, a riot broke out when 500 strikers stormed the stockyards in Howard Lake in an attempt to shut off the movement of livestock into the Twin Cities by railroad. As a result, the Anoka and Hennepin county sheriffs joined forces and threatened to break up any picketing with tear gas bombs if necessary. Despite Sheriff Wall's warnings, his small department was vastly outnumbered and could handle only a highway or two at a time. By October 16, the Twin Cities were effectively blockaded on three sides and the noose was tightening. When county authorities asked Governor Olson for the militia, he refused to intervene. The grain shipments that fed the great flour mills of Pillsbury and General Mills were in danger of being cut off.[45]

When the Republican State highway commissioner requested a definition of the highway patrol's powers, Attorney General Henry W. Benson ruled that it was the patrol's duty to keep the highways open. Benson's interpretation ignored the Minnesota Statute adopted when the highway patrol was created that prohibited the patrol from rendering "public service in connection with strikes and other industrial disputes." Almost immediately, 409 highway patrolmen descended on a farm strike meeting at Forest Lake where Captain George J. Kuch announced that the "highway patrol is going to stop all violence on the highways. There will be no more using of nail-studded planks and belts." Kuch added that if the strikers "want to go in for violence we will show you some hard boiled action."[46]

The highway patrol followed Kuch's warning with raids on farm strike picket camps in Anoka and Washington counties, where they collected and burned all nail-studded boards and belts. Pickets were allowed to stop and talk to truck drivers, but the Highway Patrol escorted produce and grain trucks into the Twin Cities. Within two days, virtually all picketing had ceased and the blockade was abandoned. Although Earle Brown had resigned from the patrol to run for governor, his highway patrol had quickly and effectively crushed the farm strike while the Minnesota National Guard, ultimately under the command of a Farmer-Labor governor, stood by and watched. This inaction must have been a cause for deep concern in the inner circle of the CA. When Governor Olson did call out the National Guard during the 1934 Teamsters' strike and the 1935 Strutwear strike, he refused to use them to crush the strikes for the CA. It was clear that, until the CA could elect a friend of business to the state's highest office, it would have to rely on the local forces of law and order.[47]

The Minneapolis Police Department, however, was controlled by Farmer-Labor Mayor Thomas E. Latimer by the mid-thirties. The CA realized that an independent police force removed from the volatility of the local political climate and controlled by the business community would permanently solve their local law enforcement problem. As part of a general plan to defeat the radical unionization of Minneapolis, the CA and its allies proposed a charter amendment that would drastically alter the Minneapolis police force. Under Police Amendment 9, the Civil Service Commission would pick two candidates for chief and then the City Council would select one of them. Unless the three-person commission unanimously voted to end the chief's term, he would serve for life.[48]

The new chief would "have the power, in case of riot, large public gatherings or other unusual occasions . . . to appoint temporary police as may be needed." The temporary police would have all the powers of constables. The police chief could also appoint special police officers to serve as guards for any local firm. The *Minneapolis Labor Review* argued that Amendment 9 was "conceived with the idea of slaughter and the purpose of smashing trade unions." The labor weekly reported on May 14, 1937, that the "workers of Minneapolis knocked vicious Fascist Amendment No. 9 cold at the primary election Tuesday." Although Amendment 9's defeat destroyed the CA's attempt to permanently control the police department, Republican Mayor George Leach, supported by the CA, was elected as mayor once more, and a friend was again in charge of the Minneapolis police department.[49]

Despite the negative impact of Governor Olson's role as commander of the state troops, the CA found other ways of using the National Guard. CA vice president and field agent MacAloon realized that the Minneapolis Guard, dominated by the CA, could be used to break strikes without being called up by the governor. MacAloon's methods were revealed when Governor Benson requested an investigation of the National Guard's role in a 1938 strike at J. R. Clark Woodenware Manufacturing Company in Minneapolis.[50]

Clark, a close friend of Mayor Leach, had been a member of the CA since its organization in 1903. When Furniture Workers Local 1859 demanded a five-cent wage increase and plant seniority rights, Clark refused to negotiate. On February 7, 1938, Local 1859 voted unanimously to strike. Two days later, negotiations were briefly resumed with CA field agent Lloyd MacAloon representing the company. When the workers walked out again the next Monday, Clark boasted that Mayor Leach would provide police to operate the plant. The same day, Sergeant Lucien Houle of the 151st Field Artillery of the Minnesota National Guard scoured the city recruiting unemployed national guardsmen to break the Clark strike. The men were instructed to report to the armory and were later taken to the West Hotel. The next day, representatives of the union called on Governor Benson and asked him to initiate an investigation.[51]

Testimony before a board of inquiry revealed a startling misuse of military authority. Captain George Sylvester, superintendent of the Clark plant, had, with the approval of his superior Major Clark, assigned his sergeant, also a plant employee, to obtain national guardsmen to work in and guard the plant. The board of inquiry established that Captain Sylvester and Sergeant Houle used the National Guard records and facilities to hire thirty men from the Minneapolis garrison to work at the Clark plant. Military-issue cots and blankets from the armory were used to keep men in the plant for two nights. Records were falsified so that several of the guards were paid for National Guard drill that they missed while in the plant. The other men were met at the West Hotel Bar by two of Sylvester's lieutenants and paid five dollars for each night. According to the testimony of W. W. Haldeman, the employment of guardsmen by their superior officers was a common practice. In fact, both Houle and Sylvester had worked with the CA's Lloyd MacAloon to break a strike in February 1938 at the Northwestern Casket Company, where the funds were actually paid out of a National Guard sinking fund.[52]

Despite the efforts of Major Clark and Captain Sylvester to conceal their activities, the board of inquiry found that the two officers, by using the National Guard in an attempt to break the strike, had engaged in "conduct to the prejudice of good order and of a nature to bring discredit to the National Guard." Under pressure of the board of inquiry and the resulting publicity, Clark had given in to the initial union demands for a wage raise and seniority rights and had also recognized the union as the only bargaining agent for the employees. The final blow came on March 10 when Governor Benson directed Adjutant General Ellard A. Walsh to court martial both Clark and Sylvester. More importantly, the investigation had revealed and destroyed an important weapon in the battle between Minneapolis's open-shop employers and the city's labor unions. MacAloon's use of the National Guard to break strikes was now public knowledge and National Guardsmen would cooperate with him at the risk of a court martial. Once again, a Farmer-Labor governor had thwarted the CA's plans for maintaining the open shop.[53]

CA President Frank E. McNally and Jack Schroeder both felt that if the Farmer-Labor Party was defeated and a Republican administration took control of the state, the police, the courts, and the National Guard would properly enforce law and order and the CA could return to the dominance it enjoyed during the 1920s. Their political hopes were realized in November of 1938, when Republican Harold Stassen was elected governor. Immediately after his election a confident delegation from the CA met with Stassen and assured him that "Now that the guns [the National Guard] are on our side we'll take over and make some changes." Local 544 (formerly 574) would not dare challenge the National Guard in the streets if they knew that the commander-in-chief would order the guard to open fire and the guard, frustrated for years by

Governor Olson, would relish the opportunity to destroy the Communist leaders of the union movement. Unfortunately for the CA, Stassen replied that "the guns are on neither side now, hereafter they belong to the state." Although Stassen had finally crushed the CA's fantasy of victory by violent military force, he would later cooperate with them in redefining the relationship of business, labor, and the state in Minnesota.[54]

14 A Network of Spies

TO EFFECTIVELY CHECK THE PROGRESS of radical union-
ism and Bolshevism using the military and police forces under its influence,
the CA needed a thorough and far-ranging intelligence service. The development of the American Protective League (APL) during World War I had provided the perfect training ground for watching the spread of Bolshevism
among the "evil foreign element colonizing" Minneapolis. Under the direction
of Chief Charles G. Davis, the Civic and Commercial Association's wartime intelligence agency had established an elaborate command structure, compiled
detailed files on suspected traitors, recruited 491 agents, and created an auxiliary legal department.[1]

In over 15,000 cases, 326 agents had gained extensive experience conducting night patrols, massive raids, and thorough investigations. In over sixty
instructional sessions, APL operatives had trained teams to tail suspects, inter-
rogators to interview suspects, operatives to examine business records, and
agents to install dictographs, tap telephone wires, and open mail. As the result
of the APL's elaborate security procedures, the identities of both the operatives
and their many informants remained a well-guarded secret.[2]

When the APL disbanded on January 31, 1919, it left behind a well-
organized and trained corps of secret intelligence agents, which many people
felt was "largely responsible for preventive measures which protected the community against the development of any alarming disloyalty," as one operative
report stated. The highly effective intelligence agency that the CCA had developed to aid the United States Department of Justice could now turn its eyes and
ears to the defense of the CA and its members.[3]

The CCA realized, however, that, without the wartime emergency and the
authority provided by the Department of Justice, it would have to seek legitimacy through the support of local public officials. CCA leaders arranged for
Mayor J. Edward Meyers to call a meeting on January 22, 1919, at the Minneapolis Athletic Club to discuss the formation of a committee to reduce vice
and crime in the city. Earle Brown, state inspector of the APL; Herbert M. Gardner, the CCA's war director; CCA leaders Charles C. Bovey and William A. Durst;

Dr. H. G. Irvine, director of the state Board of Health's Venereal Division; and Mrs. Robbins Gilman of the Women's Cooperative Alliance were assigned the task of organizing the Committee of Thirteen. With a budget of $25,000, Executive Secretary Charles G. Davis was the perfect man to direct the work of paid operatives in the Committee of Thirteen's "crusade against commercialized vice, robbery and unrest."[4]

The official purpose of the new organization was "to promote a thorough understanding of and sympathetic attitude toward American laws and institutions . . . to instruct citizens of foreign birth . . . in the duties of citizenship, to encourage respect for and to sustain public officials in the enforcement of law." The Committee of Thirteen's plan of operation was to "discover disrespect for and disobedience of law" through its agents; to bring facts before public officials; and generally to foster wholesome public spirit. By February 15, 1919, the APL was ready to operate under the guise of its new anti-vice camouflage.[5]

The expansion of the CCA's intelligence agency into the fields of prosecution and propaganda, however, created security problems for Davis's agents. Although the composition of the Committee of Thirteen's board remained a closely guarded secret, the usefulness of sixty-nine of Davis's operatives was destroyed in the first year when their identities were revealed. In an attempt to maintain security, APL agents were asked to join a new organization in early February, the A-P-L. This postwar version was still run by Chief Davis under the direction of H. M. Gardner at the CCA. The A-P-L operated as an auxiliary to the Committee of Thirteen and both were directed by Davis. A-P-L agents were to watch for bootlegging, sedition, and, more importantly, "The Red Radicals of Minneapolis." The CCA depended on these agents "to report the striking of the match that might start the bonfire of revolution."[6]

For the next three years, Chief Davis had the complete files of the American Protective League, which were said to contain information on every person of consequence in Minneapolis. He also had secret, private funding from the leading banks and businesses of the city and over 400 trained agents to work with. The CCA sought legal authority for Davis's agents through cooperation with federal and local law enforcement agencies. Davis, although no longer officially affiliated with the Department of Justice, was still in close communication with T. E. Campbell, special agent in charge of the Minneapolis office of the Bureau of Investigation. Under the friendly guidance of Mayor Meyers, Police Chief Walker conferred legitimate governmental authority on nearly 400 agents by appointing them to a special police brigade headed by Chief Davis. The brigade functioned as an "undercover" auxiliary to the police department.[7]

Cooperation with the Hennepin County Sheriff's Department was facilitated in May of 1920, when a Committee of Thirteen investigation of a Prohibition-era whisky conspiracy led to the federal indictment and conviction of the incumbent sheriff, Oscar B. Martinson. In addition to the sheriff, the county attorney, two of his inspectors, and four deputy sheriffs were either removed from office or convicted of liquor-related crimes. The CA, using its considerable influence on the county commissioners, managed to have Earle Brown, millionaire state inspector of the APL and chairman of the Committee of Thirteen finance and membership committee, appointed sheriff. By 1920, the CCA's intelligence network, completely reorganized, and fully staffed and financed, had governmental authority and was well-connected with all other law enforcement agencies.[8]

In its first two years of operation, the Committee of Thirteen brought 110 major cases to court. One case involved the arrest of 317 men, all of whom were convicted. To aid in the investigative workload, a crime bureau was installed to track and record every crime committed in Hennepin County.[9]

Although the committee claimed to be neutral in controversies between labor and capital, it concentrated much of its investigative work on Minneapolis radicals, including the leaders of the Trades and Labor Assembly. Committee operatives reported optimistically that William Z. Foster, the Communist head of the Trade Union Educational League, who was financed by the Russian government, was creating dissension in the labor movement that might wreck the AFL. Evidence obtained by Chief Davis's agents led directly to the deportation of over a dozen foreign undesirables who advocated the overthrow of the Unites States government. In addition to surveillance of radicals, committee agents took to the streets on May Day to help Minneapolis police protect the citizens from "Minneapolis Reds." Ridding Minneapolis of radicals, of course, would be ineffective if they merely relocated in St. Paul or other communities. Recognizing this difficulty, Chief Davis offered the services of his agents to other cities. A fee would be charged, which would then help offset the financial burden of the entire organization.[10]

The committee's pro-business activities quickly destroyed any illusion that it was an impartial organization. To avoid the supposed "confusion and misunderstanding prevalent among the general public," the Committee of Thirteen changed its name to the Law Enforcement Association (LEA) of Hennepin County during the fall of 1921. Chief Davis publicly insisted that the association's goals remained the "strict and impartial" enforcement of all laws. The broad coalition put together to camouflage the committee's real constituency also began to fray. Mrs. Robbins Gilman of the Women's Cooperative Alliance apparently finally recognized the true purpose of the LEA and resigned from the executive committee and the board of managers.[11]

A more serious setback struck Chief Davis's organization in 1923. Mayor Leach had shocked the CA by suddenly favoring collective bargaining and fighting for municipal control and development of the high dam power project (the Ford Dam) at Forty-sixth Street on the Mississippi River. In an attempt to discredit the Leach administration, Davis, as intelligence chief, instigated an investigation which led to a grand jury indictment of Police Chief Anton C. Jensen for willful neglect of official duty. The LEA's attack quickly proved to be a costly mistake. Mayor Leach immediately removed Davis's legal authority as a special police officer. When forty-six of Davis's agents turned in their badges in protest, the mayor gladly accepted the resignations and claimed, sarcastically, that "Minneapolis need have no fear" at the loss of these police officers. Although Davis continued to run the LEA for the rest of the decade, the CCA's intelligence arm was now without legal authority.[12]

The CA and many of its most prominent members, however, already had other sources of intelligence on Minneapolis radicals and labor unionists. Two of the CA's largest financial backers, Pillsbury Flour Mills and Washburn-Crosby Company, had both signed contracts with the Marshall Service of Kansas City in July of 1920. The Marshall Service was "to obtain information regarding any actual, or threatened labor troubles, or agitation and try to protect the mills from robbery, theft, arson, labor troubles, strikes or mob violence." A Marshall Service operative was quickly placed on the job in each of its client's mills. The names of union agitators were reported back to the companies with a recommendation that they be discharged. To maintain security, orders and reports were sent by coded telegrams. The operatives paid special attention to Jean Spielman, a leader of the International Union of Flour and Cereal Mill Workers Local 92, the resurgence of the IWW in the mills, and the supposedly Communist-inspired organization of One Big Union, which would soon demand the closed shop and a dollar-a-day wage hike. The Kansas City-based agents were also used to spread anti-union propaganda inside the mills in an attempt to disrupt union organizers.[13]

While the Marshall Service provided intelligence from inside the mills, Pillsbury and Washburn-Crosby turned to the Northern Information Bureau (NIB) for industrial counter-espionage within the organizations of Minneapolis's radical community. Continuing their wartime work, NIB employed six men full-time within the ranks of the IWW, NPL, Socialist Party, and Communist Party. The NIB agents were "recognized as being active and capable in the 'red' ranks and considered by the rank and file of the 'reds' as being men of consequence."[14]

The NIB's $1,000-per-month budget was underwritten by most of Minneapolis's major corporations, including important CA company members Northwestern Bank; First National Bank; Janney, Semple, Hill and Company; Minneapolis Gas and Light Company; Minneapolis General Electric Company; Minneapolis Street Railway Company; and by the Minneapolis Chamber of Commerce and T. B. Walker. Major Twin Cities' newspapers such as the *Minneapolis Journal* and the *St. Paul Dispatch* also subscribed to the NIB's reports. Sheriff Earle Brown, Minneapolis Police Chiefs Walker and later Frank W. Brunskill, and the United States Department of Justice depended on the NIB for "red" information. Luther W. Boyce continued to claim after the war that the NIB was "furnishing more accurate and complete information regarding radical organizations than any organization in the Northwest." Without any expenditure of effort or funds, the CA received through its members a thorough intelligence briefing on radical activities.[15]

Although the NIB's intelligence activities concentrated on radical organizations, Boyce must have realized that his clients were also vitally interested in the strength and strategy of Minneapolis union locals and the Trades and Labor Assembly. Moving into direct competition with the Marshall Service and other local detective agencies, Boyce placed an agent in the Butcher Workers' Union. During 1919, Boyce was able to inform employers of the union's wage demands and picketing schedule for recalcitrant businesses. Details of the union's fund-raising and use of the unfair-to-organized-labor list in support of the Butcher Workers' boycott were also sent out in frequent reports. A year later, when the CA launched its open-shop drive, Boyce reported on the Trades and Labor Assembly's plans to boycott the "loop" district (downtown). The September 14 NIB report described the union's fund-raising efforts to support its fight against the open shop and its organizing drive to unionize 100 percent of Minneapolis butcher workers.[16]

The NIB intelligence work in the union field brought it into direct competition with the CA. Boyce frankly informed his clients, mostly CA members: "We do not believe the CA or any other agency in the city would have found it possible to furnish this advance information. . . . Such information can only be gained by close and constant application and by using operators who devote every moment of their time to the matter under investigation." Boyce also questioned the overall strategy of the CA's open-shop fight. NIB interviews with conservative union leaders suggested that the CA's "methods of agitation and oppression" were "very rapidly converting conservatives into becoming radicals of the fighting type." Boyce undoubtedly launched his anti-CA propaganda in response to the CA's aggressive move into the intelligence arena.[17]

On May 5, 1919, the CA opened its Free Employment Bureau, ostensibly to facilitate and stabilize the employment and movement of open-shop workers among CA firms. With over 24,000 skilled and unskilled workers placed in open-shop firms in 1922, the Free Employment Bureau (FEB) was the perfect conduit for information on labor union activities on the shop floors of CA members. The butchers, printers, teamsters, truck drivers, and street railway motormen of the city were all placed and tracked by the CA. Although the CA claimed that the FEB placed union and non-union workers without discrimination and promoted "harmonious industrial relations," it was actually an efficient intelligence operation used to identify and eliminate any radical or union threat. The best opportunity for workers who wanted a job in Minneapolis's open-shop industries was through the FEB. There they would be cross-examined by Captain Fiske, who determined which workers were likely candidates. They would be offered jobs only if they agreed to inform Fiske on the conditions in the industry in which they were to work. With 24,000 potential informants, the CA obtained a steady stream of intelligence from the shop floors of Minneapolis's various industries. This vast intelligence network functioned at little or no cost to the CA. As Boyce had pointed out in his NIB reports, however, these informants were part-time amateurs with no training or special espionage skills.[18]

To back up this system, the CA employed six full-time experienced agents. When informants identified a radical or union hot spot, the CA's intelligence operatives could then infiltrate onto the shop floor through the FEB to more fully investigate the threat. Under the camouflage of an employment agency, the CA was able to fulfill its promise to keep its members informed "on the activities of subversive movements which threaten the industrial peace and tranquility of the community."[19]

The state and federal governments provided the final cogs in the CA's intelligence network. In addition to breaking the picket lines in the 1922 South St. Paul strike, National Guard intelligence officers were on duty in South St. Paul. When 7,000 railroad workers quit work to support a nationwide strike in July 1922, Governor Preus issued a proclamation urging "all county and municipal officers to aid in the preservation of law and order and to take steps to prevent any unlawful acts." Adjutant General Rhinow dispatched seven to ten intelligence agents to watch picketers and determine if strikers were turning violent. Their reports were forwarded to the governor. With the command structure of the National Guard in friendly hands and A-P-L agent Robert G. Watts serving as one of Rhinow's intelligence operatives, it is quite likely that the CA was also informed. The Minneapolis Police Department, Hennepin County Sheriff Brown, and the National Guard would all have adequate warning if they were needed to maintain law and order.[20]

In Washington, D.C., the primary mission of the United States Military Intelligence (USMI) was "the surveillance of all organizations or elements hostile or potentially hostile to the government of this country, or who seek to overthrow the government by violence." USMI asked for the cooperation of local law enforcement agencies in collecting intelligence on the IWW, Communists, One Big Union, Anarchists, Socialists, the NPL, and the AFL. The active surveillance of Minneapolis radicals by USMI, however, was turned over to the Department of Justice after World War I. Its agreements with L. W. Boyce to use NIB agents were cancelled. CA agents now served as informants for the Department of Justice. These reports were then forwarded to USMI. The extensive files of the general manager's department of the Minnesota Employers' Association (MEA) were also forwarded to the different divisions of the War Department. After USMI collected intelligence from a vast array of sources, it used the information to help local agencies and organizations disrupt the activities of local radical groups.[21]

From the defeat of the Nonpartisan League in the 1920 election to the mid-1920s, a steady stream of intelligence reports raised serious concerns for the CA, the CCA, and the MEA. It was clear to CA leaders that the radical threat had not been extinguished. USMI estimated that there were over 75,000 members of radical groups in Minnesota in 1921. Five years later, L. W. Boyce estimated the strength of radicals in the United States at a staggering 3 million—1 million of whom were allied with, identified as, and devoted to certain radical organizations.[22]

Although the number of radicals grew, the Citizens Alliance could report to its members on January 1, 1925, that "the open shop is more firmly established in private industry than at any time in the history of the city." Only one small strike of union asbestos pipe coverers disrupted the CA's total dominance over Minneapolis industry. But even in the CA's stronghold, there were disquieting signs. The city and courthouse workers were controlled by Public Service Union 16514. The Trades and Labor Assembly had reorganized to eliminate internal difficulties and was determined to unionize and break the open shop. Many of the unions the CA had defeated were becoming radicalized. Boyce guessed that "at least 50 percent of the members of any craft union that I have come in contact with or know anything about, are radical and very radical." He warned that the carpenters' union, the largest in Minneapolis, was dominated by radicals. The CA was clearly paying a price for its success.[23]

Despite the decimation of the IWW leadership during World War I, the radical labor organization still had over 20,000 members in Minnesota in January of 1921. By 1924, NIB agents, still working inside the Minneapolis IWW, reported the best attendance in several years at IWW meetings and the

application for a charter of a railroad workers' branch. The NIB warned of an
IWW plot to attack the newspaper industry, "the bulwark of American Capitalism," by shutting down eastern mills. Boyce's agents also reported massive
and elaborate plans for the fall harvest field campaign in western Minnesota
and North and South Dakota. IWW field delegates would attempt to establish
IWW halls in the larger towns in each harvest district. One NIB agent attended
the Working People's College in Duluth to report on the training of IWW agitators. CA members were informed by NIB reports that the radical college was
financed by the national IWW branches and Finnish organizations outside the
IWW and that there were plans to move the school to the Twin Cities.[24]

By the winter of 1924, however, the NIB reported: "The IWW and their
efforts are now secondary in consequence as the Communists have eclipsed
them in every direction and the Communist Party is now actively engaged in
breaking up the IWW and absorbing it into their own organization." William Z.
Foster wrote Alexis Georgian in Minneapolis—a letter that the NIB intercepted—that the union of the IWW and the Workers' Party would complete the
radical organization of the United States and facilitate the actions of the Communist Internationale. NIB agents attended as many Communist Party meetings as possible to determine exactly what radical strategy was planned and to
obtain lists of the officers and members of Workers' Party District 9 (Minneapolis), the Young Workers' League, and the Communist Sunday School. By
the summer of 1925, the encroachment of Communism had caused a split in
the IWW, which Boyce predicted would eventually eliminate the IWW. In the
same report, Boyce warned that the recent election in the Trades and Labor
Assembly had given the Communist Party complete control of the Minneapolis union movement and that they were "now in a position to give the CA a fight
to the finish."[25]

Reports from USMI contained similar warnings, that "Communism has
made great strides forward within the last two or three years." The Communists were particularly active in Minneapolis, where a "commodious" new
headquarters would house a radical bookstore. Communist Sunday Schools
and Young Workers' League meetings were well attended, and the discussion
of evolution was being pushed onto college campuses.

Even more threatening to USMI was the opening, on November 11, 1925, of
Communist schools throughout the country. This served "to show the energy
and determination of this revolutionary organization, and indicate[d] the systematic manner in which they are working from all possible angles."[26]

In Minneapolis, 150 party members were present at headquarters on
Fourth Avenue South to organize the new school. The USMI report on the
meeting listed the teachers of the Minneapolis school, which included

Clarence A. Hathaway, future teamster leader Vincent R. Dunne, and ousted IWW North High teacher Ole J. Arness. In addition to Communism, these radical instructors would teach public speaking and English for the foreign members to help them more effectively organize their compatriots. USMI also argued stridently against a *Minneapolis Tribune* editorial's dismissal of this threat. USMI concluded: "Communism is making headway. There is no doubt about that feature of the menace. The question is: What are we going to do about it, and how?" The leaders of the CA took this question very seriously.

The CA also faced an immediate political threat from the reorganized Farmer-Labor Party. In the spring of 1924, under the leadership of St. Paul Socialist William Mahoney, the Working People's Nonpartisan League (WPNPL) and the disintegrating NPL had merged into the Farmer-Labor federation. Abandoning the NPL strategy of running in the Republican primaries, the Farmer-Labor Party endorsed public ownership of transportation and public utilities, government control of banks, the abolition of the labor injunction, controls over the monopoly of Minneapolis milling interests, and a state insurance fund for workers' compensation. The political organization and widespread popularity of the Farmer-Labor Party and its candidates made the Socialist platform a grave danger to Minneapolis business interests. Obtaining intelligence regarding the membership, finances, and plans of the Farmer-Labor Party quickly became a high priority.[27]

On April 28, 1924, the NIB reported that the "Farmer-Labor Party has been built up during the past year by the Communists through their legal machinery known as The Workers' Party." Boyce claimed to have irrefutable proof that the Farmer-Labor Party was "originated and is controlled and dominated by the Communist Party, and that it is also financed by the Communists." Although a red smear campaign helped defeat the Farmer-Labor candidates in the 1924 election, the radical party's major candidates received over 350,000 votes. Two years later, the NIB still warned of the danger of the Communist Party and the Farmer-Labor Party.[28]

Any counterattack to the radical threat, of course, would have to be made by business interests from across the state, as represented by the Minnesota Employers' Association. Harry C. Wilbur, who had run the successful antiradical campaign of the Minnesota Sound Government Association (MSGA) in 1920, was still in charge of the MEA's general manager's department. The department, which was created to check up on "radical activities in the industrial, economic and political field," had maintained its vigilance at the strong urging of CA Vice President Strong and his St. Paul counterparts. When the special funding for Wilbur's intelligence work expired in 1921, the MEA paid for the department's work out of its own budget. With the help of "undercover" men and women, Wilbur was able to obtain advance information on the plans of both the Communist Party and the "Communist-dominated" Farmer-Labor Party during the 1924 campaign.[29]

As part of his mission, Wilbur cooperated with various United States Army departments, reported his findings to the president of the United States, and furnished reports, data, and copies of documents to different organizations, societies, and individuals, civil and military. Wilbur claimed that his department was "the *only* center in the Northwest to which those who are seeking to offset the attacks on America and American institutions can turn for accurate and authentic information that is kept strictly up-to-date."[30]

On the basis of his department's intelligence findings, Wilbur issued a stern warning to the leaders of the MEA and the CA. "It would be a mistake," he wrote in his 1924 annual report, "to adopt the attitude of 'It's all over.' That is exactly what was done in 1920, and you all know what it brought about." The MEA must "guard against over confidence and lack of vigilance." Wilbur's report suggested that the CA's best defense against radicals was the tireless efforts of an intelligence agency that could "tabulate the facts, analyze them, make clear their significance, and then go to the people constantly, whenever occasion demands, with the facts."

In effect, he was recommending a permanent version of the Minnesota Sound Government Association. With the encouragement of MEA leaders Strong, Washburn, and Warner, Wilbur had undertaken an initial survey of the state in 1923 and then outlined a skeleton program. A series of informational conferences were held to explain the "menace that confronted us." In March 1924, a special meeting of the organizing committee (Strong, Washburn, and Warner) reluctantly accepted the fact that the long delays and the failure of support from the business community made any future campaign untenable. In the estimation of business leaders, the negligible threat of a radical resurgence did not justify the expense of their defensive propaganda operations. The MEA and the CA abandoned their seven-year statewide campaign against radicals, ignoring the reports of their widespread intelligence network. Ten years later, the Farmer-Labor Party would control Minnesota's state government and the Communist-led Teamsters' union would control the streets of Minneapolis. Ignoring Wilbur's warning would bear a bitter fruit for the CA.

Although the Hennepin County Law Enforcement Association gradually faded away and the MEA relaxed its surveillance, the CA remained steadfastly vigilant. In 1926, the CA recruited private detective Lloyd M. MacAloon to run the Free Employment Bureau. MacAloon already had experience in hiring workers for Minneapolis Steel and Machinery with a bonus for "talking with employees, eavesdropping around shop conversations, and reporting the names of all employees heard to express dissatisfaction with wages, hours or working conditions." From his position as field commissioner of the CA in charge of the Employment Bureau, MacAloon could keep track of all union-organizing efforts.[31]

Three years later, he took charge of the CA's investigating agency, the Special Service. From this dual position, he controlled over one-quarter of the CA's operating budget and, with the help of Operative No. 11 and other agents, quickly became the CA's best-informed officer. The Minneapolis labor movement had acquired a powerful new enemy. By the mid-1930s, MacAloon, now also the CA's field agent, would direct the strike-fighting efforts of the CA and its member firms. As the head of the CA's Bureau of Industrial Relations after 1935, MacAloon continued to be organized labor's primary adversary.[32]

The targets of MacAloon's Special Service agents were very similar to those of the APL after World War I—radicals and trade unionists. With the emergence of the Farmer-Labor Party into the political mainstream, however, the CA's intelligence agency concentrated its efforts on the growing threat of the Communist Party. MacAloon's agents or their informants attended meetings of the Communist League, the Workers' Party, and the Unemployed Council of Minneapolis and were able to obtain valuable information on Communist plans. On November 5, 1934, for example, the Special Service reported on the merger of the Communist League and the American Workers' Party into the Workers' Party. The new Communist program would infiltrate the AFL and other labor organizations and promote the interests of the Workers' Party.[33]

Because the leadership of Teamsters' Local 574 belonged to this organization, these reports also contained strategic information on radical union activities. Although much of the intelligence generated by the Special Service was useless Communist rhetoric, announcing that "the mighty mechanism of capitalist society is crumbling in the sight of all," it also frequently warned the CA of impending Communist demonstrations. The specific local intelligence generated by MacAloon's Special Service was supplemented by a thorough clipping service from local and major city newspapers tracking the growth and spread of Communism on a national scale.[34]

More important in the battle for the open shop, the Special Service employed "investigators" in "virtually every bona fide union labor organization in the city." These agents attended union meetings, took part in deliberations, and had access to union correspondence and reports. CA agents, working their way up through the union ranks, even had agents at private meetings of the Central Labor Union, which only special delegates from each union attended. Reports from these highly placed agents allowed the CA to keep track of union membership, finances, and plans on both the local and state level. Agents like

Operative 11 received $250 per month and $50 for expenses. They reported back to MacAloon on Ediphone dictating machines. To protect the source of their information, secrecy was of paramount importance. When the CA received requests for information on their intelligence service from their allies across the nation, they did "not consider it wise to answer [the] question in an open letter."[35]

MacAloon's intelligence activities, however, were not limited to radicals and labor unions. He also kept a thorough listing of "persons of progressive thought, men and women in public life, college professors, lawyers, labor leaders, writers and persons of other walks of life." This list also gave basic statistical information on each person, attempted to show associations and attitudes, and even recorded personal histories and habits. Anyone with liberal leanings who might be a threat to the CA or might encourage others in anti-business activities or thoughts was watched by MacAloon and his agents."[36]

The Special Service, beginning in 1934, was assisted in its intelligence operations by the agents of the Hennepin County Law and Order League. A. W. Strong and E. S. Warner of St. Paul began planning and lobbying for a revival of the campaign against the forces of disorder in 1932. Their committee for a Minnesota Law Enforcement League warned that union agitators with Communist connections were becoming "a direct menace to the lives and property of Minnesota's law abiding citizens. . . . The whole structure of our great Minnesota commonwealth is threatened."[37]

Two years later, the Minnesota Law and Order League, formed and financed by the CA and the St. Paul CA, was ready to "support law and order and to arouse citizens to the necessity of combating outlawry of every kind, including racketeering, kidnapping, robberies and unlawful interference with natural human rights to life and property." The Farmer-Labor Party and the *Minneapolis Labor Review* correctly accused the Law and Order League of being a creature of the CA "created to crush labor, the Farmer-Labor Party and all socially minded and progressive movements." Although the state league would function primarily as an anti-labor propaganda tool, two-thirds of the Hennepin County chapter's budget of $15,000 went into intelligence activities. During 1934, six investigators sought information to bring prosecutions against "criminals, racketeers, enemies of society and organized lawless minorities." The results of these investigations undoubtedly reached MacAloon's desk and supplemented the work of the Special Service.[38]

The importance of the CA's Special Service became particularly critical in 1937 when the Farmer-Labor Party began a concerted attack on the Minneapolis business community's other intelligence sources, the private detective agencies. In Washington, D.C., Senator Robert LaFollette's Committee on

Civil Liberties had thoroughly investigated the activities of the largest national detective agencies. The committee found that they were primarily labor espionage services that provided strikebreakers, stole union records, and even spied on an assistant secretary of labor. In reaction, the Senate passed a resolution stating "that the so called industrial spy system breeds fear, suspicion and animosity, tends to cause strikes and industrial warfare and is contrary to sound public policy."[39]

At the request of Governor Elmer A. Benson, the LaFollette committee furnished detailed materials on the Pinkerton's Detective Agency, which the governor used to deny Pinkerton's a license to operate in Minnesota. The *New York Post* reported on July 31, 1937, that "Governor Benson of Minnesota becomes the first Governor of an American State to deny a license to a detective agency on the ground it allegedly took part in strike-breaking activities."[40]

The Burns National Detective Agency quickly followed Pinkerton's into exile. LaFollette committee records on Burns indicated "widespread planting of spies in union organizations for the purpose of providing employers with names of active members to be discharged" and "deliberate incitation to violence during labor disputes by Burns 'guards' illegally armed with deadly weapons." These practices were used in Minnesota in Burns's work for large Minnesota industrial concerns like General Mills and Honeywell Regulator Company, both CA members. Despite these setbacks, however, Minneapolis industry could still rely on the CA's Special Service, which, because it didn't operate openly as a private detective agency, did not require a state license.[41]

The intelligence coup of MacAloon's career, however, would come not from gathering intelligence, but from interpreting and disseminating it. By the late 1930s, he had established himself as the foremost expert on subversive activities in the Upper Midwest. The Special Service, the Free Employment Bureau, and the Law and Order League had spread the tentacles of his intelligence network into every labor or radical group. MacAloon's unique position had not escaped the notice of United States Military Intelligence officials. By tapping into intelligence produced by MacAloon's agents, USMI could keep a close watch on possibly revolutionary subversive movements and theoretically protect the security interests of the United States government. MacAloon cooperated fully, furnishing USMI with copies of his detailed reports and meeting regularly with MI officers stationed in St. Paul and Omaha. There is little doubt that MacAloon realized the advantages of his role as the USMI source in Minneapolis. His data, analysis, and interpretations of local subversives would in all probability become the intelligence and form the attitudes of USMI. He now had a direct pipeline to Washington, D.C., through which he could influence the actions of the United States government.[42]

Fortunately for MacAloon, the conservative interests of USMI closely paralleled the intelligence of the CA. USMI kept detailed dossiers on Farmer-Labor
Party officials in Governor Olson's administration. The governor's secretary,
Roger S. Rutchick, for example, was a "Russian Jew-Communist. Said to be the
dictator of personnel in State employ. Has absolute control of the Governor's
office." The dossiers of deputy state printer Jean Spielman detailed his activities as an IWW organizer twenty-five years earlier. It would be absurd to call
Governor Olson a "tool of the Third Internationale," Major Moore of the USMI,
reported:

> On the other hand, Gov. Olson's appointments of known communists to State
> office, his radical utterances, and the similarities in methods and aims between
> the Communist Party, the Farmer-Labor Party which he represents, and the
> League for Independent Political Action, with which he is affiliated, indicate
> some common bond. . . . The logical inference is that, standing with the more
> conservative and well organized of the radicals, and at the same time conceding
> to, encouraging, and affiliating with the more extreme groups, he [Olson] hopes
> to amalgamate all these elements into a third party, for which the national
> political situation seems ripe, and of which, in this section of the country, his
> position, strength and leadership make him the obvious Stalin.[43]

Of greater importance to the CA was the USMI interest in Teamsters' Local
574. As early as 1934, USMI reports asserted that the AFL union was dominated
by Communists. According to these alarmist reports, Communists were looking for ex-soldiers to teach classes in the use of Browning machine guns and
grenades. They knew the location of all ammunition and explosives at Fort
Snelling and secretly had members among the military guard units of the
Third Infantry. Dossiers were kept on the Dunne brothers, Carl Skoglund, Farrell Dobbs, and other leaders of Local 574. Their radical histories, connections
with the Communist Party, and even their character tendencies were carefully
compiled. Robley D. Cramer, the editor of the *Minneapolis Labor Review*, was reported to be "one of the most vitriolic and inflammatory speakers against capitalism" and had "rendered immeasurable assistance" to the 1934 Teamsters'
strike. Major Moore concluded that the 1934 strike "was communist planned
and 90 percent communist operated, the AFL being only the tool and 'front.'"
Although the CA failed to incite the United States government into action
against the Farmer-Labor Party or Teamsters' Local 574, MacAloon had
seeded an important relationship with USMI that would later flower in the
nourishing hysteria of World War II. [44]

15 *Financing the War on Labor*

THE YEAR 1903 was a prosperous one for the Minneapolis financial community. An excellent harvest throughout the Northwest would bring the usual flood of money into Minneapolis banks. *Commercial West* reported: "There is nothing now in the financial situation of the Northwest to indicate any change ahead." Northwestern (NW) National Bank stood solidly above its competitors on one million dollars capital and a surplus profit of more than $500,000. NW had survived the panics of the 1890s and solidified its position in the business community. Its prominent position was reflected in a move from its leased space on the second floor of the Guaranty Loan Building into its own building at 411 Marquette Avenue.[1]

Despite these reassuring circumstances, however, the death of Northwestern President James W. Raymond in 1903 brought dramatic changes in the bank's leadership and policies. The newly elected trio of President William H. Dunwoody, a prominent milling executive, and vice presidents Martin B. Koon, a judge with substantial milling interests, and Edward W. Decker, a longtime bank employee, would manage NW until 1912. More importantly for the future of Minneapolis and the Northwest, this trio helped organize and finance the Minneapolis Citizens Alliance. The financial backing of NW and other Minneapolis banks allowed the CA to suppress radicals and labor unions for the next forty years.[2]

The prosperity of Northwestern and other Minneapolis banks at the turn of the century rested primarily on the harvest and milling of the Northwest's wheat crop. By 1890, Minneapolis had become the primary wheat market of the world. In 1900, nearly one-third of the total value of Minnesota's industrial product came from flour milling. By 1905, this had increased to more than 40 percent. Dominated by two giants, Pillsbury-Washburn Company and Washburn-Crosby Company, Minneapolis millers under the leadership of W. H. Dunwoody organized a buying pool in 1876 that had a virtual monopoly over grain trading in Minnesota. Reorganized as the Minneapolis Chamber of Commerce in 1881, the millers controlled hundreds of country elevators and had the power to set prices and determine grades.[3]

With the chamber's power to exclude non-members from the grain exchange, a few large corporations had virtual economic control over the entire Northwest. In order to purchase and move the grain crops, enormous financial resources had to flow into the Northwest each fall during the wheat harvest. The milling interests, desiring favorable banking conditions, helped organize and—through their position as the largest source of banking income—control the principal Minneapolis banks. Minneapolis, the United States' grain marketplace, became the financial center for the Northwest.[4]

Northwestern National Bank opened for business in September of 1872 with a deposit by William H. Dunwoody. By steadily increasing its capital under the leadership of miller George A. Pillsbury, NW paid dividends every year while many underfunded banks were closed. This position was strengthened by a core of conservative professionals that revered liquidity and solvency and established a very conservative loan policy at NW. As 1903 approached, the bank's executive committee and its board of directors were dominated by members of the Minneapolis Chamber of Commerce. The immense wealth of NW's backers in the milling industry guaranteed its prosperity. During a 1907 financial panic, Washburn-Crosby executive and NW President Dunwoody personally deposited one million dollars to protect the bank against a run.[5]

The next year, NW launched an expansion drive, taking over the National Bank of Commerce with the help of Citizens Alliance President Frederick. E. Kenaston and the Swedish-American National Bank. These additions nearly doubled Northwestern's deposits. In 1909, Northwestern affiliated with Minnesota Loan and Trust Company, officially bringing CA founder Edmund J. Phelps into the bank. At the outset of World War I, NW was the Twin Cities' largest bank, with deposits of more than $33 million. NW could claim that "every important northwestern industry and business has its connection with this bank." The net worth of Northwestern depositors constituted a large share of the wealth of the Northwest.[6]

The interrelationship of Minneapolis business leaders was particularly evident in the interlocking directorships of Northwestern's leaders. President Dunwoody was elected to the board in 1876. While he served NW, he also was a vice president at Washburn-Crosby Company for twenty-five years and a director of the Great Northern Railway. Dunwoody's influence at Washburn-Crosby Company was substantial. In 1899, he personally purchased the Washburn-Crosby milling plants from the Washburn heirs to save them from an eastern takeover. Judge Koon became a director at NW in 1881 and served thirty-one years. He also served as a vice president at Minnesota Loan and Trust Company and a director at several large grain and milling companies. It was Judge Koon, fellow Minnesota Loan and Trust executive E. J. Phelps, and another distinguished member of the business community who grasped the significance of union organization and therefore organized and perfected the CA.[7]

It was, however, Edward W. Decker, who succeeded Dunwoody as Northwestern president in 1912, who became one of the most influential figures in Twin Cities' banking. Decker, born in Austin, Minnesota, in 1869, had worked his way up from messenger at Northwestern in 1887 to vice president in sixteen years. He was also president of Minnesota Loan and Trust, vice president of Twin City Rapid Transit Company, and a director of the Soo Line Railroad. Decker was also substantially responsible for bringing the Federal Reserve Bank to Minneapolis in 1914 and then served as a director. From his position at the top of Minneapolis's largest bank for a quarter-century, Decker would be a crucial link in the war on labor.[8]

After the formation of the Citizens Alliance in 1903, Northwestern, represented by Vice President Decker, joined three other major Minneapolis banks in the CA drive against labor unions. These banks held 63 percent of the city's bank deposits. By 1914, with the First National Bank on board, the CA financial team represented 95 percent of Minneapolis deposits and 58 percent of Twin Cities' deposits. A substantial portion of the financial resources of the Northwest were backing the CA. Without the money and influence of the flour mills and the financial community, however, it is doubtful that the CA would have become a powerful institution. This endorsement of CA principles related directly to Northwestern's shareholders and directors. Over half of the board of directors worked for the milling industry or in the bank itself. All twenty-one members of Northwestern's board worked for firms that were associated with the CA. As maintaining the open shop became a more and more complex and expensive operation in the 1920s and 1930s, Northwestern Bank and E. W. Decker would play critical roles.[9]

To maintain the Citizens Alliance's control over the Minneapolis industrial and commercial labor markets, the Minneapolis business community had to donate sufficient funds for the CA's operations. Leading the CA budget during the 1920s was the $20,000 salary of President Otis P. Briggs. Salaries for the rest of the full-time staff of ten cost a combined $25,000. The Employment Bureau and the Special Service, both essential CA services, cost approximately $10,000 and $5,000 respectively. Legal fees, production of the CA *Bulletin*, and the CA's watchman service rounded out the budget. During the 1920s, CA expenses exceeded $70,000 per year.[10]

The CA, however, was only a single cog in the business community's broad campaign in defense of its dominance. Leading the network of business organizations was the Minneapolis Civic and Commerce Association (CCA), the

parent of the CA. The CCA's program encompassed everything from advising
the Minneapolis City Council on tax levies to promoting the improvement of
local roads. Despite its many innocuous civic promotions, the CCA still actively
supported the CA's mission to defend the open shop. In 1924, the CCA's annual
budget reached $250,000. These funds had to come from the same business
interests that supported the CA.[11]

On the state level, the Minnesota Employers' Association (MEA), which was
controlled by CA members, functioned on a budget of $8,000 a year. Each sep-
arate industrial or commercial group within the business community also organized to support its particular interests. CA members such as Dayton's and
Donaldson's, for example, joined with sixty-six other Minneapolis stores to
form the Minneapolis Retailers' Association. In addition to regulating retail
competition, the Retailers' Association backed the fight for the open shop at a
cost to the members of $8,000 per year. In 1920, the Twin City Vehicle Manu-
facturers' Association (TCVMA) budgeted almost $2,400 in addition to its reg-
ular budget specifically to fight for the open shop. When the CA helped form the
Associated Business Organization (ABO) of Minneapolis in 1920 to provide a
united business front against unionism, twenty-four employer associations,
including the Builders Exchange and the Manufacturers' Club, joined their
effort.[12]

Many of the CA's labor-fighting functions were also supported by other less
visible organizations. In the intelligence field, for example, the Hennepin
County Law Enforcement Association (HCLEA) and a vast array of private detective agencies supported the CA's Special Service. These were labor-intensive
operations and therefore very expensive. The HCLEA employed forty-six part-
time agents at a yearly budget of $20,000. The large amount of funds pumped
into the city's sixteen detective agencies by CA members can only be roughly
estimated. The Northern Information Bureau, which specialized in watching
the Industrial Workers of the World (IWW), received $12,000 from CA mem-
bers. Large firms like Pillsbury and Washburn-Crosby bought intelligence from
the Marshall Service of Kansas City for $10,000 per year. The larger, nation-
ally based agencies like Pinkerton's fielded more than twenty-five agents at
much greater costs. With the inclusion of the CA's own intelligence expenditures, the business community expended in excess of $300,000 yearly for in-
formation on the organization and activities of radicals and labor unions.[13]

Defeating the Nonpartisan League, the Socialists, and later the Farmer-
Labor Party at the ballot box was vitally important for the success of the CA's
policies. Electing sympathetic, conservative mayors, governors, and judges
would determine who controlled the police, the National Guard, and the courts.
The Minneapolis business community, led by the CA, raised enormous sums of

money to defeat labor candidates. In the 1920 governor's race, for example, the CA and the Minnesota Employers' Association organized the Minnesota Sound Government Association (MSGA) to campaign against socialism. The successful effort to elect Governor Preus cost the business community $329,000. In the same campaign, the American Committee of Minneapolis raised another $400,000 and the Minneapolis Publicity Bureau another $40,000 from the same sources. Although this was probably an unusually expensive campaign, other examples (such as the $50,000 spent on Mayor George Leach's 1921 campaign and the $75,000 raised to elect Supreme Court Justice James H. Quinn) indicate that the political contributions of CA members were always a major part of the budget in the fight for the open shop.[14]

To effectively maintain the open shop in Minneapolis, the business community had to raise $1.5 to $2 million each year. Most of the various business organizations raised the majority of their operating funds through membership dues. These dues ranged from $12 to $60 per year at the Twin City Vehicle Manufacturers Association, from $5 to $250 at the Minnesota Employers' Association, from $50 to $750 at the Minneapolis Retailers' Association, and from $50 to $5,000 for corporate sustaining members at the CCA. In 1928, the CA had 655 dues-paying members in three classifications. Individuals and professional members paid $10 per year, small employers paid $25, and large employers $50. Slightly more than 60 percent of the $16,937 came from 430 small firms. This represented, however, only 23 percent of the CA's operating budget. The CA realized that a larger source of income was required to meet the labor threat during World War I.[15]

On August 15, 1917, Northwestern President Decker, a member of the CA board of directors, proposed a solution that would secure the future of the CA's operations and alter the power base within the CA. Decker and Edwin J. Cooper made a motion at the annual meeting that a guaranty fund of $50,000 be raised, $10,000 of which would pay a full-time salary for CA President Briggs. By 1928, pledges to the fund supported 76 percent of the CA's operating budget. Although the average contribution of the 204 firms pledging was $175, eighteen firms contributed 42 percent of the fund. Four major organizations contributed $2,500 each: Pillsbury, Washburn-Crosby, Minneapolis Street Railway Company, and the Minneapolis Clearing House, which primarily represented Northwestern Bank and the First National Bank. The major commitment flour millers and their banks forged to the open shop in the 1903 mill strike remained the strongest financial support of the CA twenty-five years later.[16]

In addition to the interlocking directorships and the common cause of maintaining the open shop, the various business organizations encompassed the same basic membership and therefore drew their financial support from the same sources. Small firms such as H. E. Wilcox Motor Car financially supported both the cca and the ca, the Minnesota Employers' Association, and the Twin City Vehicle Manufacturers Association, and its guaranty fund. Pillsbury and Washburn-Crosby paid membership dues in the three major organizations, supported the ca Guaranty Fund, and belonged to the Minneapolis Chamber of Commerce, which was also a ca supporter. First National Bank and nw had a similar arrangement. In 1928, they donated $8,000 to the cca and $2,500 to the ca in addition to each bank's membership dues. This outpouring of cash by hundreds of businesses enlarged the war chests of the cca and the ca and gave them the financial resources to wage a successful war on labor unions. Although the largest single source of financial support came from the millers, it was the banks, and particularly nw, that would provide the crucial financial power the ca would need in the turbulent 1930s.[17]

The conduit for moving banking cash into the ca and other organizations was the Minneapolis Clearing House. Formed in 1880 to clear each day's balances between the banks of Minneapolis and St. Paul, the Clearing House was also "in constant touch with affairs tending to the onward progress, not only of banking and business, but of the city itself," according to *Commercial West*. The Clearing House was controlled by representatives of nw and First National and closely associated with the ca. In fact, from 1926 through 1932, Charles B. Mills, the president of the Clearing House, was also the treasurer of the ca.[18]

In addition to financing the Civic and Commerce Association, the Citizens Alliance, and the Minnesota Employers' Association, the Clearing House donated $1,000 each year to the cca's intelligence arm, the Hennepin County Law Enforcement Association, which was a descendant of the Minneapolis branch of the American Protective League. To infiltrate and watch over the radical iww, the Clearing House paid $500 to the Northern Information Bureau. The Clearing House also supported various cca-sponsored publicity agencies. For the fight against the npl and socialism in the 1920 elections, the American Committee received $20,000. This amount, like other Clearing House donations, was apportioned among all the banks by the Clearing House manager. This effort continued in 1923 and 1924, when the Clearing House gave the Minneapolis Publicity Bureau $2,000 and paid $2,000 per year for a period of three years to support a radio station, with the call letters wcco, to be run by the Washburn-Crosby Company and the cca. The banks' support of the ca and its objectives was thorough and substantial. Northwestern acknowledged the results of these policies in a 1926 advertising flier in which it proclaimed Minneapolis to be "a city remarkably free from labor discontent."[19]

By 1928, Northwestern had grown to serve more than 110,000 customers and its resources had passed the $125 million mark. NW's 1,500 stockholders had received uninterrupted dividends since 1872. Through mergers and acquisitions, NW now had four separate offices and four branch banks in Minneapolis, in addition to its trust investment and securities affiliates—the Minnesota Loan and Trust Company and the Minnesota Company. Despite these extraordinary successes, the directors and officers of Northwestern spent 1928 planning the creation of Northwest Bancorporation (NW Banco), a group bank holding company that by 1931 would control 127 banks.[20]

The plan for the organization of Northwest Bancorporation was first discussed informally in early 1928 by a small, select group of Northwestern and Minnesota Loan and Trust officers. Although the idea was submitted to NW's board of directors, no corporate action was taken and no records kept. Apparently, President Decker and his fellow officers decided, as a group of influential individuals, to launch the NW Banco holding company, which was to absorb by ownership the capital stocks of strategic Northwest banks. The group banking plan had been necessitated by state and federal laws banning branch banking. When Decker and Clive T. Jaffray of First National Bank suspected that smaller Minneapolis banks were nearing failure in the early 1920s, they absorbed the banks and operated them as branches.[21]

In reaction to the possible dangers of this expansion of Minneapolis financial power, the Minnesota legislature unanimously authorized the liquidation of any state bank operating branch banks. In 1927, the United States Congress passed the McFadden Act, which allowed branch banks only in the same city as the head office and only if state laws permitted. Despite these restrictions, however, no state laws regulated the ownership of bank stock by a holding company. The expansion of NW's influence throughout the region could proceed without further legal difficulties.[22]

The consolidation of the financial resources of the Northwest into NW Banco and First Bank Stock Corporation beginning in 1929 marked a basic shift from industrial capitalism to financial capitalism. *Commercial West*, the financial weekly magazine with associations to the CA, claimed that the significance of these changes in the financial structure of the Northwest region to "the Twin Cities [was] little short of epochal." L. S. Donaldson executive and NW Director Joseph Chapman called it "the greatest step for the upbuilding of the Northwest on solid and substantial lines, that has been made since the railroads were first projected into this territory." These economic changes would also shift the power center within the CA. While the CA's ideological fervor had been generated from the machine shops and foundries of A. W. Strong and O. P. Briggs, the financial backing had initially come from the flour and lumber industries. The vast 1929 expansion of NW Banco marked the emergence of a new power behind the CA.[23]

NW President Decker advanced a number of rationales for his decision to launch NW Banco. Minneapolis businessmen feared that the expansion of "eastern interests" would eventually erode their control over local banks and industries. Decker believed, first, that the formation of NW Banco would "make the Northwest financially independent." The people of the Northwest would "retain control in their home district of the prosperous banks and industrial concerns." Secondly, Decker felt that the absorption of many of NW's correspondent country banks into NW Banco would stabilize these banks and protect them from the effects of the agricultural deflation of the 1920s. The chaotic disruption of rural communities, created by the closing of 2,333 banks in the Northwest during the 1920s, would be relegated to history.[24]

According to *Commercial West*, the broader aim of NW Banco was to strengthen and develop finance, farming, and industry. Decker at the time of organization stated, "What the businessman and farmer want is absolute safety and the most efficient and complete service." NW Banco would accomplish these goals through its added financial strength and its centralized administration of various banking and trust services. In addition to saving and revitalizing the Northwest, NW Banco's concentration of banking resources would promote foreign trade and strengthen its position as a world banker.[25]

Despite these laudable goals, the primary objective of NW Banco as a corporate entity was to make a profit. According to NW Banco's first annual statement, expected increased earnings would "result from the economies effected and from increased business obtained through group action; in increased financing operations and the underwriting and sale of investment securities; through the addition of trust departments to affiliated banks and the development of fiduciary business; through increased bank deposits, coming as a result of renewed public confidence and the ability of affiliated banks to render greater service."[26]

The expectation of market profits was also a strong force in organizing group banks. The stock of country banks, which had a very limited market value, would appreciate dramatically when they were exchanged for NW Banco shares. Without consolidation, of course, the loss of Northwestern's correspondent relationship with country banks to eastern interests would diminish profits. The prospect of these increased earnings would fuel the two engines of expansion: The desire of country banks to join NW Banco and exchange their stock for NW Banco stock, and the cash flow from stock sales.[27]

It was clear from the organization of NW Banco that a great financial power was being created. An ecstatic *Commercial West* editorialized that the businessmen of Minneapolis must assume responsibility over "the great empire that is spread out before us and of which we are the natural financial, banking, manufacturing and trade capital." Although President Decker and others applauded the great constructive force that NW Banco could exert, this influence also served the purposes of the CA.[28]

While the CA had effectively suppressed labor unions in Minneapolis, the spread of the Nonpartisan League into Minnesota in the early 1920s had nearly wrested political control of the state from the major political parties. A joint effort of Twin Cities' banks and businesses had been able to stem the tide of socialism in the Northwest, but Decker realized that "the farmer is isolated and unorganized and an easy prey for politicians." A vast financial "empire" would, the banks and the CA hoped, forestall any resurgence of radicalism. Leadership over the entire economic life of the region would also be vital to maintaining business unity in defense of the open shop. While NW Banco did not publicly explain these benefits of a financial empire, there is little doubt that Decker and other CA members were fully aware of them.[29]

On January 8, 1929, after a year of secret negotiations, NW officers publicly announced the formation of NW Banco, a new company that had already arranged to acquire Northwestern, First National Bank of Fargo, and First National Bank of Mason City. From this rather modest beginning, NW Banco expanded rapidly until its territory reached into eighty-four towns and cities in eight states. A little over a year after startup, the NW Banco group included 105 affiliated institutions with combined resources of $480 million. Most of the banks signing up in early 1929 were large, important, and profitable institutions: key banks in their communities such as First National Bank of Duluth, U. S. National Bank of Omaha, and Midland National Bank of Minneapolis. Belle Plaine, Luverne, and twenty-one other smaller rural Minnesota communities joined the group when the Union Investment Company agreed to an exchange of stock with NW Banco on October 6, 1929.[30]

By the fall of 1929, NW Banco already owned an astonishing 22.6 percent of Minnesota banking resources. By the end of 1931, NW Banco owned 127 banks, 9 investment companies, and 3 livestock loan companies, and the Northwest had the greatest concentration of banking resources of any region of the country outside of California. To remain competitive, First National and First National Bank of St. Paul joined to form First Bank Stock Corporation. By December of 1929, First Bank Stock Corporation had acquired seventy-eight banks in five states. Three years later, in the middle of the Depression, the new group bank owned 100 banks with total resources of $365 million. In less than a year, the two banking giants had permanently changed the financial structure of the Northwest.[31]

Although the early acquisitions were accomplished entirely by stock exchanges, NW Banco soon discovered that it needed cash to purchase stock of
affiliated banks, capitalize new banks, and strengthen NW Banco members. To
raise cash for these operations, NW Banco's first issue of stock was offered on
February 20, 1929, by its subsidiary, the Minnesota Company, for $50.35 per
share. To increase public confidence in the stock, NW Banco orchestrated a barrage of publicity. Full-page ads appeared in newspapers, magazines, and win-
dow displays stressing the profitability, diversification, and growing territory
that would earn stockholders an annual dividend of $1.80 per share.[32]

In order to increase stock sales and bank acquisitions, NW Banco reported
large earnings and paid dividends despite large losses. The *Minneapolis Tribune*,
closely affiliated with the business community, joined in with a stream of articles and editorials praising the coming of the new Minneapolis empire, NW
Banco. From July 20 to August 4, the *Minneapolis Journal*, a CA member, featured a fifteen-part series by Charles B. Cheney extolling the advantages of
group banking, all on page one in bold type. The public responded to NW
Banco's message, quickly buying the first issue of 100,000 stocks for
$5,000,000.[33]

When the seven top officers of NW and Minnesota Loan and Trust planned
for the organization of NW Banco, they also realized that maintaining local
control of NW Banco stock would require the revival of the old Minneapolis
Stock Exchange. During the final stages in late 1928, Henry D. Thrall, vice
president of Minnesota Loan and Trust and one of NW Banco's organizers,
headed a committee to organize the Minneapolis and St. Paul Stock Exchange. Twenty days after NW Banco opened, the new Twin Cities Exchange,
which would trade only local stocks, opened on the second floor of the
Roanoke Building in Minneapolis. Thrall, NW executive David R. West, and CA
treasurer Charles B. Mills each bought one of the fifty $1,000 seats on the
exchange.[34]

From the beginning, the Stock Exchange was dominated by NW Banco and
First Bank Stock Corporation. By September 1929, 68 percent of the stock sold
on the exchange represented sales by NW Banco or its affiliates. NW Banco
stock was sold by trading specialists of BancNorthwest Company, a subsidiary
of NW Banco run by Henry Thrall. From this unique position, NW Banco was
able to manipulate the price of its stock on the local exchange. While the
twenty million dollars raised through stock sales provided the cash, it was the
steady advance of stock prices that convinced many of the banks of the Northwest to join NW Banco. In less than three years, a financial empire had been
created, and, partly due to the Minneapolis and St. Paul Stock Exchange, it was
an empire which was primarily owned by Minnesotans.[35]

Fearing that the "menacing growth of these two holding company jugger-nauts" threatened their existence, a group of small banks met on May 9, 1929, and formed the Independent Banker's Association (IBA). Ben Dubois, secretary of the IBA, suggested that NW Banco and First Bank Stock Corporation planned on eliminating all independent banks in the region within three years. To counter these fears, NW Banco stressed in its literature that each member bank was to retain its unit structure and continue to operate on a local basis. While NW Banco would supervise and make policy recommendations, the final authority for loans, dividends, and so on, would rest with the directors of the local banks.[36]

Even NW Banco's "operating plan" concealed the real relationship between NW Banco and its widespread empire. At the Minnesota Commerce Department's hearings in 1933, NW Banco President Decker revealed that NW Banco owned 90 percent of the stock of its affiliated banks and that it was Banco directors who actually controlled the amount of all dividend payments. Banco's executive committee also controlled bank personnel, reserves, loan policies, and operating procedures. Inside NW Banco, the upper echelon of management came intact from Northwestern and Minnesota Loan and Trust. The board of directors, reduced to twenty after 1933, was dominated by members of the CA.[37]

To house this rapidly growing "financial empire," NW launched the construction of a new headquarters fronting on Marquette Avenue, between Sixth and Seventh streets. Following the policies of the CA, which NW had supported since 1903, the bank building would be constructed using open-shop labor. For the first time, NW would take its place on the front lines of the war on labor. In February 1929, NW let the contracts for what Edward Decker proudly called "the largest project of its kind ever undertaken in Minneapolis."[38]

Harry B. Waite, chairman of the building committee, announced that the materials, equipment, and labor would all come from Minneapolis. Nearly half of the six million dollars expended on the project would go to 3,000 Minneapolis workers. NW made sure that they would be non-union workers when it let the general construction contract to C. F. Haglin and Sons Company. The *Minneapolis Labor Review* accused Haglin, who was one of the founding members of the CA and had been on the CA board of directors since 1915, of being "for more than 30 years the most notorious non-union contracting concern in the N.W." The major subcontracts were also given to prominent CA firms such as Minneapolis Steel and Machinery and Strong and Scott Company, CA president Albert Strong's firm. NW's press announcements confidently predicted a March 1, 1930, opening for their new home.[39]

Long before the contracts were let, the building trades organization of Minneapolis notified the NW building committee that the leaders of the various construction locals had unanimously agreed that the bank job was to be either 100 percent union or 100 percent non-union. The Hoisting Engineers and Shovelmen's Union went on strike immediately and was joined by all of the Minneapolis building unions. Pickets began bannering the job in its first week and were still at it as the steel work went in place for the sixteenth and final story in November.[40]

To further damage NW's standing in the community, the *Minneapolis Labor Review* launched a yearlong publicity campaign to discredit NW and its project. From the onset of the wrecking crews, the *Labor Review* exposed the thirty-cents-per-hour non-union wages, the continuous stream of on-the-job injuries, the danger of shoddy work to the public, and the thirteen-dollar-per-week "starvation wages" paid to women working in the bank. The Central Labor Union of Minneapolis (CLU) also struck at what it perceived as the bank's Achilles' heel, its deposit base. On March 8, the CLU requested that the City Council remove funds from NW. At the same time, it asked union members to put their personal funds in other banks. The *Labor Review* claimed on May 3 that NW branch banks were "suffering terribly" from the loss of depositors. By mid-May, the *Labor Review* reported that union solidarity had put the bank construction twelve weeks behind schedule.[41]

Although Minneapolis was essentially an open-shop city and the CA had an effective strikebreaking capacity, the united union stand against NW and the extremely low wages paid by C. F. Haglin combined to create a shortage of skilled labor. Haglin, who had a history of bringing in non-union workers from outside the city, quickly found workers in St. Paul, Duluth, and Milwaukee. As late as January 31, 1930, Flour City Ornamental Iron Company, a CA stalwart, advertised for workers in the *Chicago Sunday Tribune*. By mid-May, the contractor was forced to raise wages to forty-five cents, and then fifty cents per hour, to keep non-union men on the job.[42]

At the same time, with the project three months behind, Horace B. Lowry, a member of the building committee and a CA leader, asked Governor Christianson for National Guard troops to guard the construction site, despite the lack of any violence. As job-related injury reports mounted, C. F. Haglin constructed a high board fence around the project. To counter union publicity, NW took out advertisements in Minneapolis papers, proclaiming the bank building a Minneapolis project. The greatest threat to NW, the threatened withdrawal of 1.5 million dollars in public funds, would have been less than a 1 percent loss of resources for the bank, even if it had been completely successful. Northwestern, obviously willing to weather the storm, ignored this threat.[43]

Despite the many difficulties, NW moved into its magnificent new home "on time almost to the day," on May 12, 1930—although they were two months behind the original schedule. The customer passed through a beautiful ornamental bronze gate to ascend wide marble staircases to the longest banking room in the country. Twenty-four immense pillars of Botticino marble rose thirty-nine feet to the ceiling. This magisterial effect was softened somewhat by six bronze pendant chandeliers. Along the outside walls were seventy-five open, caged tellers' stations for conducting the business of the bank and the trust company. The large director's room, with its four semicircles of chairs, was in two tones of gold with walnut furnishings. The final touch of opulence was reserved for NW President Decker's office, a beautiful Levanto marble fireplace. Above the public display of splendor, on the fourth floor, were the offices of the Northwest Bancorporation, efficiently incorporating the banks of the northwestern United States.[44]

The concentration of Minnesota banking resources in the hands of NW Banco and First Bank Stock Corporation allowed the CA to control much of the financial credit of the Northwest. When Minneapolis Steel and Machinery or Pillsbury-Washburn were overextended and faced financial failure, a flow of generous credit from these banking giants saved and strengthened two of the CA's staunchest members. The CA's enemies, however, found it exceedingly difficult to obtain any credit whatsoever.[45]

While NW Banco erected its headquarters in 1929, with non-union labor, a far more impressive structure was dominating the skyline and the front pages of the national press. The Foshay Tower, designed on the pattern of the Washington Monument and rising majestically thirty-two stories over Minneapolis, was the tallest building in the Northwest. Wilbur B. Foshay's utility empire extended to twelve states and five countries. After discussions with officials of the Minneapolis Central Labor Union, Foshay decided to construct his tower with union labor. Foshay's public endorsement of union labor and the huge "Foshay" chiseled into the top of the tower for all to see helped to enrage the CA. Foshay had also acquired options to buy out thirty-five Minnesota newspapers. It was clear that Foshay constituted a threat to the CA's maintenance of the open shop in Minneapolis.[46]

Foshay's utilities empire, however, had been built on the proceeds of securities sales and loans from local and eastern banks. In Minneapolis, Foshay had obtained funds from Metropolitan National Bank, Minneapolis Trust Company, Lincoln National Bank of Minneapolis, and Lincoln Trust and Savings Bank—all institutions associated with the CA. When NW Banco acquired Metropolitan National Bank in 1929, Foshay was forced to pay off his loans or submit to NW Banco terms. This left his $25 million empire $300,000 short when stock prices plunged in October, shortly after the celebration of the Foshay Tower completion. When the CA succeeded in shutting off any rescue from eastern financial interests, Foshay quickly went bankrupt. Joseph Chapman, a director of NW, was appointed receiver. When the receivers eliminated the common stock of the Foshay companies, Wilbur Foshay was left with less cash than his personal debts. The CA heralded this as a magnificent victory for the open shop and turned off the electricity to the blazing "FOSHAY" name on top of the tower.[47]

Financial credit from Minneapolis's major banks, NW Banco and First Bank Stock Corporation, was also an important tool with which the CA could enforce unity on its members during a strike. If an employer entered into an agreement with a union, his credit was cut off. This was particularly evident during the latter stages of the bitter and violent 1934 truckers' strike. In early August, the united front of the CA-run Employers' Advisory Committee began to crack as four small concerns agreed to recognize the Teamsters' union. The employers' leader addressed the city on WCCO radio and vowed never to surrender. NW Banco and First Bank Stock Corporation immediately used their financial influence to stem the tide of defection. A grocer who signed the Haas-Dunnigan plan was refused credit by his wholesaler; a contractor could not get any credit from any of the local cement companies. If a company was already heavily in debt before a strike, NW Banco's approach was more direct. During a strike at the Puffer-Hubbard box factory in 1939, NW Banco forced the company into receivership and then used their control over negotiations to demand a 10 percent wage cut and loss of seniority rights from the Furniture Workers' Union. NW Banco credit was an essential weapon in the CA's strike fighting arsenal.[48]

The financial strength of Minneapolis banks also exerted pressure on the CA's political enemies. While the CA fought the Nonpartisan League in the 1920 elections, Minneapolis banks strangled the resources of the NPL's Bank of North Dakota. When Minneapolis banks were approached by the Bank of North Dakota to float a desperately needed bond issue, the CA bankers first demanded that the NPL gut its socialistic programs and then refused to handle the bonds at all. The decline of the Bank of North Dakota and the defeat of NPL political candidates in Minnesota were both bought and paid for by the financial wealth of CA members.[49]

In Minneapolis, Northwestern and First National banks brought pressure to bear on local companies to enforce an advertising boycott on the *Minnesota Daily Star*. The *Star*, a staunch NPL supporter, fell deeper and deeper in debt until 1923, when it was forced to drastically water down its editorial policy to obtain advertising. When unemployment ravaged Minneapolis during the Depression, the city of Minneapolis appealed to NW Banco for loans to continue relief payments. At the same time, NW Director Chapman lobbied the city for a 10 percent pay cut for all city employees. President Decker brought city officials to his office and demanded the pay cut as a condition for any NW loans. When the City Council agreed, Mayor William A. Anderson twice vetoed the pay cuts, observing that the council's action "will be notice to private employers to make pay cuts." Despite a CA victory when Anderson's veto was overridden, however, NW refused to buy city bonds for relief.[50]

The rapid expansion of NW Banco and its successful anti-union efforts inevitably brought on a counterattack, led by Farmer-Labor Governor Floyd B. Olson. Olson, who had been a bitter enemy of the CA since 1923, instructed the Minnesota Commerce Commission to investigate the stock sales of NW Banco and First Bank Stock Corporation. In November 1933, the Securities Division of the Commerce Department began lengthy interrogations of President Decker and other NW Banco executives. The investigation concluded that NW Banco had fraudulently misrepresented its earnings and the value of its stocks and had manipulated the price of those stocks in order to sell its stock issues at inflated prices.[51]

Strangely, Governor Olson asked the Hennepin County attorney for indictments against NW Banco executives. Olson, who had been Hennepin County attorney a decade earlier, was fully aware that the CA dominated the county's grand juries. When the grand jury refused to return an indictment, Olson instructed Commissioner of Securities S. Paul Skahen to present evidence to the United States District Attorney for prosecution. In September 1934, J. Cameron Thomson, NW Banco vice president and general manager, went on trial in Clay County, where Governor Olson hoped to find a grand jury that was hostile to big business.[52]

The trial was a publicity disaster for NW Banco, as Minnesota newspapers reveled in the prosecution's description of NW Banco's scheme to "control the liquid banking resources of the Northwest." The defense, perhaps realizing that the jury was confused by the complicated financial testimony, rested its case without calling a witness. The jury agreed with the defense's contention that the prosecution had failed to prove its case. The second case, against NW Banco President Decker, was dropped after he resigned. The charges against the other eighteen defendants were dropped in 1936. Although many Farmer-Labor and rural newspapers charged that justice had been perverted, NW Banco escaped with its empire unscathed.[53]

Although NW Banco survived the attacks of the Farmer-Labor Party, the economic disaster of the Great Depression proved a far more devastating opponent. NW Banco deposits sank more than $50 million in 1932. Dividends on

NW Banco stock sank from $1.80 per share in 1929 to $1.10 in 1932 and were suspended in 1933 for six years. At the end of 1931, NW Banco had capital, surplus, and undivided profits of $52.4 million or $29.81 per share. A year later, the capital, surplus and undivided profits had shrunk to $29 million or $8.13 per share. Although all of NW Banco's affiliates survived the Bank Holiday of March 6, 1933, its liquidity continued to rapidly decline. It was clear that NW Banco had expanded too rapidly, using too much of the proceeds of their stock sales for acquisitions without establishing reserves for economic bad times.[54]

The organization that built NW Banco also suffered under New Deal legislation. The Banking Act of 1933 banned banks from owning investment affiliates and from making stock exchange loans or loans to officers. Government examiners were given the authority to inspect holding company books and the companies were required to possess free assets worth 12 percent of the value of their stocks. The Depression had both undercut NW Banco's assets and forced them to dismantle their system of market manipulation.[55]

New Deal legislation had also created the Federal Deposit Insurance Corporation (FDIC), which would not insure deposits unless the capital fund of a bank exceeded 10 percent of deposits. By 1933, with capital plummeting, few of NW Banco's banks could meet this requirement. Fortunately, the Emergency Bank Act of March 9, 1933, had also created the Reconstruction Finance Corporation (RFC). The RFC was to purchase issues of preferred stock from troubled national banks in order to strengthen their capital structure.[56]

In the fall of 1933, NW Banco sent General Manager Thomson and Directors Crosby and Heffelfinger to Washington, D.C., to negotiate with the RFC. On December 7, 1933, the RFC authorized the purchase of $22,995,000 in preferred stock and capital notes from NW Banco and a loan of three million dollars to the Union Investment Company. The holding company's capital structure and the stability of the Northwest's financial markets had been saved, but the United States government now controlled 70 percent of the net worth of NW Banco. Although NW Banco would survive and retire all of the RFC stock by 1941, the government's influence over NW Banco would have disastrous consequences for the CA.[57]

Despite the suspension of dividend payments and the government control of NW Banco stock, the bank's financial contributions continued to swell the coffers of Minneapolis's anti-union organizations. The Clearing House agreed to pay 5 percent of the cost of hiring extra policemen and deputies during the 1934 trucker's strike. In the years after the strike, the banks continued their generous contributions to the CA and the CCA. On December 17, 1936, the CA adopted a new constitution and changed its name to Associated Industries of

Minneapolis (AI). The daily operations continued to be run by J. W. Schroeder and paid for by the CA cash balance of nearly $30,000. Although AI now portrayed itself as an association to serve business needs in the field of employee relations, its board of directors, policies, and financial backers remained substantially intact.[58]

NW Banco continued to be represented on the board and donate to the Clearing House's $1,500 contribution. In 1938, AI and the CCA joined with other civic organizations to form the Minneapolis Civic Council. The council was to revitalize Minneapolis by acting on the Minneapolis Plan, a wide-ranging program that encompassed the basic goals of the CA and the CCA. The banks rerouted their contributions to the Civic Council, contributions that reached $10,000 each in 1945. Nearly 70 percent of the Civic Council's budget was transferred to the CCA and AI. NW Banco and its Clearing House partners also contributed $1,000 to support the Minnesota Law and Order League. The CA had formed the league to combat the Communist menace, which had become the "leading political working class force in this city." As the bombing of Pearl Harbor approached in December 1941, the AI and NW Banco continued to prosecute the war on labor that had begun forty years earlier.[59]

By the beginning of World War II, E. W. Decker's dream of a powerful financial empire encompassing the northwestern United States was still a reality. NW Banco had survived the Depression still affiliated with eighty-two banks in 100 communities. After suffering through the 1930s with no dividend payments, NW Banco ended 1942 with more than five million dollars in undivided profits and more than $700 million in deposits. The wealth and power of this banking giant was still controlled by a board of directors dominated by milling and banking executives associated with the CA and its offspring, AI.[60]

In 1940, NW Banco and First Bank Stock Corporation controlled 13 percent of the banks in the Northwest and an incredible 55 percent of the deposits. By 1954, NW Banco had capital, surplus, and deposits worth more than 1.5 billion dollars. These two banking groups, said Clive T. Jaffray, were able to "exert tremendous power in Minnesota, North Dakota, South Dakota and Montana." The anti-union crusade that had developed out of the 1903 mill strike and had kept Minneapolis an open-shop city for more than thirty years would continue to be backed by the greatest financial powers of the Northwest.[61]

16 A Social Agenda for an Open-shop City

THE SUPPRESSION OF LABOR UNIONS and political radicals absorbed most of the CA's energy during the open-shop drive of the early 1920s. At the same time, Minneapolis business leaders were also forced to grapple with the social problems that clouded the radiant success of their empire. The long hours worked by children in the nation's mills and, later, the massive unemployment and poverty of the Great Depression provoked radicals and reformists inside state and federal governments and on the floors of the nation's factories. Although the Roosevelt administration's New Deal programs alleviated the pressure for local private action, they were repugnant to Citizens Alliance members, with their concept of an America based on individual freedom and private property.

They were also, of course, a threat to private capital's domination of American life. As National Association of Manufacturers' (NAM) counsel James A. Emery observed, "Those who analyze and reflect will find lurking beneath a touching sentiment a determined endeavor to obtain a grant of power from the people, revolutionary in its effect upon their private life and government, and entirely unnecessary to accomplish an object which all desire." The first defense of the NAM, the Minnesota Employers' Association, and the CA was to convince the public that problems such as child labor were not really problems at all. During the Depression, when unemployment and poverty finally became undeniable, the country's conservative business elite faced a difficult choice: the overwhelming expense of private charity and new self-help organizations, or the much cheaper but un-American scourge of public relief.[1]

Ironically, one of the first postwar challenges to American industry's domination of the nation's work force was ignited in May 1922, when, for the second time, the United States Supreme Court struck down a congressional attempt to regulate child labor. Realizing the futility of federal legislation, a large collection of national social, civic, religious, and labor groups joined to write and advocate an amendment to the Constitution giving Congress the "power to limit, regulate, and prohibit the labor of persons under eighteen years of age." On April 26, 1924, the House adopted the resolution by an overwhelming vote of 297 to 69. A little over a month later, the Senate sent the amendment to the states for ratification on a 61-to-23 vote.[2]

With the support of both the Republican and Democratic parties and a favorable reaction from the nation's press, adoption of the amendment seemed assured. The National League of Women Voters (LWV), the American Federation of Labor (AFL), the American Federation of Teachers, the National Education Association (NEA), the National Child Labor Committee, the General Assembly of the Presbyterian Church, and a host of other national organizations joined the crusade to save the 400,000 children under fourteen years of age who worked in the factories, mills, mines, and canneries of the nation.[3]

Leaders of the League of Women Voters mistakenly assumed that "the organizations financially interested in cheap child labor, were in despair." On the contrary, defeat of the amendment became the NAM's primary objective for 1924. At its annual convention, the NAM passed a resolution disapproving "of this revolutionary grant of power to the Congress as repugnant to our traditional conception of local responsibility and self government." The amendment, "under the guise of protecting childhood, would authorize by necessary implication the control of all the minor life of the nation, the mode of its training and education, the duties of its parents and guardians and substitute the bureaucratic regulation of remote, expensive, and irresponsible authority."[4]

To counterbalance the widespread support for the bill's passage, the NAM organized the National Committee for the Rejection of the 20th Amendment. A member of the NAM's law department acted as secretary for the temporary Rejection Committee, which quickly became the propaganda headquarters for anti-amendment groups. MEA director James H. Ellison was chosen to represent Minnesota on the national committee. Following the NAM's lead, the National Founders' Association passed an identical resolution. Southern textile interests and the United States Chamber of Commerce quickly joined the NAM's campaign.[5]

The NAM propaganda campaign against the "so-called Child-labor amendment" was led by NAM general counsel James A. Emery. An examination of the amendment written by Emery and distributed by the NAM served as the ideological core of the attack. Emery claimed that the amendment proposed "a revolutionary transformation of the traditional relationship and respective function of local and federal government and the primary control of parents over the training and occupation of their children." The amendment was also completely unnecessary: According to Emery, only 77,485 children were employed in agriculture outside their home farm, and only 49,104 children from age ten to thirteen were in non-agricultural employment: "Can it be contended that the employment of 126,590 children out of 12,502,582 demand the grant of power to Congress which is sought? . . . There is no evidence that the employment is other than intermittent, is dangerous to health or morals, or to the extent that such is the fact, it will not be corrected by the states with the rapidity which has characterized their progress in dealing with this subject." These arguments, however, were unlikely to strike a chord of fear into the hearts of the American public.[6]

In agricultural regions across the country, but particularly in the South, children under eighteen were employed in fieldwork, many of them on their parents' farms. Emery argued that the language of the amendment and the publications of the National Child Labor Committee exposed the legislation's true purpose: To regulate and restrict the right of parents to the labor of their children on their own farms. The NAM, the National Committee for the Rejection of the 20th Amendment, and the *Southern Textile Bulletin* flooded the country with propaganda designed to convince farmers that the amendment was aimed at their children. The *Manufacturers' Record* warned that the amendment would prohibit farm children from "driving the cows to pasture, or hoeing the vegetables, or doing any work of that character, even for their own parents." Although proponents of the amendment, such as the Minnesota League of Women Voters president Marguerite Wells, claimed that "There is not the slightest ground for such fears," the campaign had a devastating impact. Farm organizations and farm journals apparently accepted the NAM's warning with few reservations, adding their voices to the growing sentiment against the amendment.[7]

The pivotal contest would be fought in Massachusetts, a state with strong child-labor laws of its own, where seventeen groups led by the League of Women Voters had prepared the way for a decisive victory. The league, however, had vastly underestimated the NAM and its local allies at Associated Industries of Massachusetts, and the strength of Emery's most effective argument. The NAM claimed that the amendment was "socialistic in its origin, philosophy and associations. . . . Every Bolshevik, every extreme Communist and Socialist in the U. S., is back of the measure." The proposed Twentieth Amendment was a "communistic, bolshevistic scheme, and a lot of good people, misled, are accepting it, not knowing the evil consequences which will result and the sinister purpose back of the measure."[8]

The head of Associated Industries of Massachusetts, who also served on the NAM's Committee for the Rejection of the 20th Amendment, formed the Citizens' Committee to Protect Our Homes and Children, to disseminate vast quantities of anti-Communist propaganda across the state. With the substantial aid of the Roman Catholic clergy, the amendment was overwhelmingly rejected on November 4, 1924. The NAM had conducted an amazingly effective educational campaign, which would have far-reaching consequences in the campaign for ratification of the child-labor amendment.[9]

Ten days after the Massachusetts victory, representatives of thirty-one state employer and manufacturer organizations met at the Hotel Astor in New York for the semiannual conference of the National Industrial Council (NIC). MEA general manager A. V. Williams and CA president Briggs listened respectfully as Emery, general counsel of both the NIC and the NAM, urged business leaders across the country to contact their state legislators on the proposed Twentieth Amendment. Of more practical benefit, the manager of the Associated Industries of Massachusetts reported in detail on the campaign to defeat the amendment in his state.[10]

At the next MEA board of directors' meeting, Otis Briggs and A. V. Williams reported back with a plan of action for defeating the child-labor amendment in Minnesota. After the report, Briggs, Ellison, MEA President Charles B. Mills, and Will O. Washburn were appointed to a committee to handle the MEA's campaign against the amendment. At the annual meeting on December 2, 1924, Williams read the amendment and discussed the far-reaching danger inherent in its ratification. It was the unanimous opinion of those present that the "Amendment was objectionable in every particular and should be opposed by the Association."[11]

The MEA's special committee served as the state's anti-amendment distribution center, responsible for circulating propaganda throughout the state to district organizations, the daily press, the Farm Bureau, and the legislature. The *Minneapolis Journal* supported the sentiments of Utah's Senator William H. King that the amendment was "a scheme to destroy the State, our form of government and to introduce the worst form of communism into American institutions." League of Women Voters President Wells wrote her local chairwoman that the league was swamped by the sudden flood of bitter propaganda against ratification of the child-labor amendment. The CA took an active role in the campaign, financing the appearance of an NAM lecturer in the Twin Cities and dedicating two issues of its monthly bulletin to the battle.[12]

While the CA continued to hammer away with Emery's arguments, particularly communism, Briggs took a more philosophical tack. He recalled "most vividly the genuine thrill of joy, happiness and pride which possessed his soul when, at the age of five, he was sufficiently educated to count up to six and could help his grandfather plant corn. . . . The very foundation of this nation is built upon countless numbers of its people who learned the habit of work long before they were eighteen. . . . The heritage of the American child has been the right to do things himself. . . . To deny a child the right to work is to stifle and thwart all ambition and incentive to become a useful citizen," said

Briggs. The amendment also posed a serious threat to society as a whole. "Ninety-nine times out of a hundred, the boy who has not learned to work before he is eighteen years old increases the idlers and street corner loafers, thieves and other criminals, and goes straight to perdition. . . . Which will you have—your children in the Devil's Workshop or in the Industrial Workshop? It is up to YOU to decide!"[13]

Despite an impressive campaign by the Minnesota League of Women Voters and the Minnesota Joint Ratification Committee for the Child-labor Amendment, the MEA's propaganda gradually altered perceptions across the state. On December 31, 1924, the Minnesota Farm Bureau Federation denounced the amendment as "un-American, a blow at agriculture and fundamentally wrong." Rural Minnesota was slowly leaning against ratification. On February 18, 1925, however, after a spirited public hearing before joint Senate and House committees, the House Public Welfare Committee sent the amendment to the floor on a ten-to-seven vote.[14]

The *Minneapolis Journal*, however, still considered defeat of the amendment inevitable: "Minnesota, it may be said without fear of contradiction, stands strongly against the amendment." Behind the scenes, Stillwater attorney R. G. Thoreen effectively lobbied for the MEA. On February 27, the public galleries of the legislature filled with applauding citizens, proponents and opponents of the bill debated heatedly for four hours before passing an amended resolution to reject the federal amendment by a sixty-eight-to-fifty-six vote. Of the sixty-eight legislators who voted to reject, only six came from Minneapolis, St. Paul, or Duluth. Joined by six country Farmer-Labor Party members, the conservative and agricultural forces had doomed Minnesota's attempt to ratify the child-labor amendment. There is little doubt that the MEA had played a crucial role.[15]

The Minnesota and Massachusetts experience was repeated across the country with only Arizona, Arkansas, California, and Wisconsin ratifying the amendment in 1924–1925. The battle in Minnesota, however, was not over. Although the House's vote had doomed the amendment for 1925, Attorney General Clifford L. Hilton ruled that failure to ratify was not final. Hilton added that, in fact, any future legislature could reopen the question and ratify the amendment. Opponents of the amendment, infuriated by Hilton's ruling, pushed for a Senate vote to reject so that the state could certify to Washington that Minnesota had rejected the amendment. Senator George H. Sullivan, who had led the MEA's fight in the Senate, offered a resolution to reject the amendment and demanded a vote. The *Minneapolis Journal* supported Sullivan's resolution, suggesting that "such action would probably be final, so far as Minnesota is concerned."[16]

On April 14, the Senate followed the House lead, passing a resolution of rejection by thirty-six to twenty-eight. Despite this resounding defeat, however, the Minnesota League of Women Voters resolved to continue its fight to save "young children from unsuitable labor." Eight years later, on December 14, 1933, the Minnesota legislature finally ratified the child-labor amendment. Although the MEA attempt to bury the issue in 1925 had failed, the NAM's national campaign had damaged the amendment beyond repair. The proposed child-labor amendment never became a part of the United States Constitution.[17]

The programs of President Roosevelt's New Deal, however, presented a more difficult challenge for the NAM. The National Industrial Recovery Act (NIRA), passed in June 1933, mandated the development of codes of fair competition for all branches of industry. Child labor became one of the main targets of the National Recovery Administration (NRA), set up to implement the NIRA. On July 9, the cotton textile mills, long a stronghold of child labor, accepted a code provision establishing a minimum working age of sixteen. Two weeks later, President Roosevelt expanded the code to other manufacturing industries. With a stroke of a pen, 100,000 children were removed from industry shops. In May of 1935, however, the Supreme Court unanimously found the NRA to be unconstitutional on the grounds that Congress overextended its authority over interstate commerce and had set up an administrative authority without specifying its powers.[18]

The NAM's respite from child-labor regulation, however, was brief. By 1938, the Supreme Court had ruled the National Labor Relations Act, which recognized the right of employees to organize unions, was constitutional, expanding its interpretation of interstate commerce and opening the door for federal child-labor legislation. The Fair Labor Standards Act, passed in June 1938, prohibited the interstate shipment of goods made in shops and factories in which children under sixteen worked. The NAM denounced the new law as "a step in the direction of communism, bolshevism and Nazism." Although the act was a significant defeat for the NAM, it did not have the impact of a child-labor amendment. In fact, only 25 percent of children working in nonagricultural occupations would be protected.

In 1933, however, the Minneapolis business community faced the far greater economic and social problems of the Great Depression. By 1932, 86 percent of the state's manufacturers were reporting operating losses. In Minneapolis, the number of factories decreased by nearly 25 percent between 1929 and 1933, while the value of retail goods sold dropped 45 percent. The effect of the economic collapse on the state's workers was dramatic. By 1933, the state's unemployment level had risen to 23.4 percent, while in Hennepin County an estimated 68,500 were jobless. At the same time, Minneapolis wages fell 27 percent and, as many plants went on part-time schedules, the workweek dropped below forty hours for over 45 percent of the city's workers.[19]

In the unstable and low-paying garment industry, unemployment for women workers reached over 65 percent. Fortunately for the CA, the city's food industries were not hit as hard. Leading financial backers of the CA, including Franklin M. Crosby, Charles S. Pillsbury, James Ford Bell, Jr., Harry A. Bullis, George D. Dayton, and Joseph Chapman still managed to increase their wealth. The mass of unemployed men, women, and children were not so fortunate. They were forced for their very survival to rely on the inadequate resources of private charity and the city's small, understaffed relief department.[20]

The problem of poverty had challenged the resources and conscience of Minneapolis's business leaders for over a half-century. In December 1884, George A. Brackett, George A. Pillsbury, and others like them who had "moulded the business, religious and philanthropic destiny of Minneapolis" met to establish an organization "to study, relieve and prevent poverty, and to reestablish families in independence and strength." Brackett, a former mayor, a leading miller, and a prominent member of the Minneapolis Business Union, first proposed the establishment of Associated Charities and presided over the growing institution for eleven years. The new organization pledged to diminish pauperism through encouraging thrift, self-reliance, industry, and better modes of life through friendly sympathy, advice, and employment. By 1909, Associated Charities had serviced 2,411 cases and given $16,793.19 in relief. It had established a visiting nurse committee, a medical inspection department, an anti-tuberculosis committee, children's camps, and a legal aid department. While the groundwork had been laid for future philanthropic work, Associated Charities also worked to arouse the social conscience of the city's business leaders.[21]

As the city grew, of course, the difficulty of financing and coordinating the work of providing charity taxed the capacities of Associated Charities. In 1915, the CCA organized the Council of Social Agencies to handle raising the rapidly expanding Community Fund, which by 1929 had reached $1,196,426, and to distribute this money to the sixty-five member social agencies. Associated Charities, now the Family Welfare Association, received the largest share of over $170,000. The Salvation Army, Union City Mission, Visiting Nurse Association, Infant Welfare Society, Children's Protective Society, Maternity Hospital, and the YWCA each received more than $40,000.[22]

The job of raising the Community Fund fell to First National Bank President Lyman E. Wakefield and a finance committee of twenty-four prominent leaders of the CA and the CCA, including CA treasurer Charles B. Mills. Publicity for the 1933 campaign was handled by Merrill Hutchinson, president of the Minnesota Law and Order League. Ironically, financial control of the city's social agencies charged with relieving poverty were in the hands of the open-shop employers of the CA.[23]

The form of Minneapolis relief policies during the unemployment crisis would inevitably be shaped by the philanthropic leaders of the CA. In the fall of 1921, the city faced a crisis of unemployed, homeless men. While private charities publicly accepted responsibility for the city's homeless, they had a very different attitude toward the unemployed. The CA tried to deny the very existence of the problem. When the city attempted to relieve the crisis, the CA argued against appropriations for the aid of the unemployed homeless, opposed procuring jobs for the registered unemployed, and insisted that work relief be paid depressed wages. The Council of Social Agencies advocated a work test for all unemployed relief recipients, either manufactured work on a rock pile or temporary jobs arranged through an unemployment bureau: "Without an adequate work test any city would be flooded with the undesirable type of dependent men and those who make their living by looking for work and failing to find it." Associated Charities' handling of the crisis reflected the views of its financiers. Applications from the unemployed were referred to the city relief department. Associated Charities refused to assume the financial burden of the unemployed and argued that simple unemployment was not properly within its field anyway.[24]

A decade later, the archaic system of private charity was once again overwhelmed. By the fall of 1930, the number of unemployed seeking aid from the Family Welfare Association was rising at an alarming pace. In early January of 1932, with public and private relief agencies serving more than 5,000 families, the *Minneapolis Tribune* still maintained that private charity could meet the community's needs. A month later, the Council of Social Agencies asked the city to take over the support of 2,600 families. The Community Fund agencies would now help only families with children under sixteen where the major problem was not unemployment. Federal, state, and city governments would now assume the responsibility of providing food, shelter, and clothing for the destitute unemployed. While private agencies had provided 54.3 percent of the city's relief in 1928, by 1935 their share had plummeted to 6.9 percent. The withdrawal of private charity from unemployment relief had a dramatic effect on city and charity budgets. The Family Welfare Association's allocation of funds dropped from $600,000 to $300,000 in 1938, while the city was forced to issue two million dollars in bonds to cover direct relief in 1932.[25]

As the city's leading employers and taxpayers, the business community expected public relief to meet the work ethic standards of the CA at the least possible cost. With the city issuing over two million dollars in bonds, the CA and the CCA pressed for a work requirement to make sure "the taxpayers would be getting something constructive and valuable for their relief fund expended" and an "immediate reduction of salaries and wages comparable to that which business generally found necessary to maintain its existence." Without a pay cut for city workers, the CA's conservative allies on the Board of Estimation and Taxation would block the issuance of city bonds to support relief. To appease the city's bankers, homeless men were frequently required to work on private property to receive their thirty cents per day. The CA quickly realized that public relief, if issued to strikers, might undermine its efforts to break union-led strikes and therefore endanger the open shop. During the Strutwear strike of 1935–1936, the CA lobbied to stop relief payments to all striking workers. A battle of attrition could be more easily won if the enemy did not receive government support.[26]

Relieved of the financial burden of supporting the unemployed, Community Fund agencies could now concentrate their resources on their efforts to take "the family off the relief line, build up its morale, and bring it back to ultimate independence." In an old building at 712 Fourth Avenue South, the Family Welfare Association put the CA's work ethic philosophy into practice. Two-hundred-and-fifty men and women came to "712" to "renew their trades, talents and abilities" and, of course, to earn their relief payments. In a building entirely remodeled by work relief, shoes were repaired, Red Cross cloth was sewn into garments, and government boxes were made into chairs. From 712, woodcutting crews went out to cut wood for the poor and drivers provided transportation for public and private social workers. In its first three years of operation, the work relief program baked 145,000 loaves of bread, salvaged material from 125 boxcars, and canned produce from municipal gardens. The economical program allowed $150,000 Community Fund dollars to do "double or triple duty" in 1933. The Community Fund publicized the program's outstanding advantages: "There is no blow to the pride in accepting aid which is paid for in service. A man who goes out to do a day's work for a day's wage has none of the rankling consciousness of accepting alms."[27]

Unemployment could also be combated by increasing the city's industrial job base. In 1925, the Industrial Department of the CCA had been split off into a supposedly separate institution, the Minneapolis Industrial Committee (MIC). Led by retired CCA President Arthur R. Rogers and CCA board member Alfred C. Godward, the MIC mission focused on selling the benefits of relocating businesses in Minneapolis. MIC publications touted a "Three-Billion Dollar Market," with one million people within fifty miles, abundant raw materials, an extensive railroad center, power facilities, excellent educational and park systems, and efficient and reliable labor at reasonable wages. MIC publication, *Facts about Minneapolis*, proclaimed: "Industrially, Minneapolis is open shop, being one of the leading open shop cities in the U. S. The nationality of the people, the working conditions, and training facilities provided, have made for efficient labor giving high production per worker at reasonable wages. It is because of these facts that Minneapolis is unusually free from labor disturbances."[28]

From January 1 to October 1, 1930, MIC chairman Rogers claimed to have brought seventeen new manufacturing industries and thirty-five wholesale, retail, and distributing organizations into the city, creating 984 new jobs with a total payroll of $1,314,200. In addition, Godward initiated a campaign for Minneapolis businesses to reemploy as many laid-off employees as possible. An MIC survey reported that nearly 1,000 workers had been rehired. Although Minneapolis newspapers applauded the MIC's efforts, they had little impact on the city's rising unemployment or the growing lines of the hungry.[29]

There was, however, another way to fight hunger. On May 19, 1931, CCA president Benjamin B. Sheffield called a conference to form an emergency garden program. Working in close cooperation with President Herbert Hoover's Emergency Commission in the Matter of Unemployment, the Emergency Garden Committee, which included George D. Dayton and Charles C. Webber, set out to alleviate the hunger of the unemployed. With the vast resources of the Minneapolis business community behind the program, $4,370 was proudly collected. A fifty-three-acre plot at Nicollet Avenue and Sixty-first Street was plowed by Minneapolis Moline Power Implement Company and harrowed by Deere and Webber Company.[30]

The Family Welfare Association screened applicants and assigned 90-by-90 foot plots where the needy families planted potatoes, corn, peas, beans, tomatoes, and other vegetables. Seeds, tools, fertilizers, and insecticides were furnished by the committee. A group canning factory was set up on the side in tents donated by Hoigaard's. The eighty-one families without home facilities canned 5,135 jars with stoves and gas donated by NW Blaugas Company. The Park Board, the Board of Education, and the Minneapolis Real Estate Board joined the numerous industrial benefactors offering support for the self-help program that was "vastly better than outright doles which may tend to undermine self respect and the will to work."[31]

The Emergency Garden Committee, however, did "not claim that its plan is a panacea for the unemployment problem." The garden plan was merely a stopgap measure "until the only adequate solution is reached—jobs for those who are willing and able to work." While the seeds sprouted in South Minneapolis, the CA unveiled "A Practical Plan of Unemployment Relief." The city's open-shop employers proposed job-a-week clubs to be organized immediately in the various neighborhoods to furnish odd jobs to unemployed heads of family. Each member would give a worker a few hours of work each week at a forty cents per hour minimum wage. The CA listed possible jobs: mowing lawns, beating rugs, scrubbing garages, washing windows, and so on. The CA Free Employment Bureau would be available to register and assign jobs. To jumpstart the "plan of relief," the CA recruited luncheon and service clubs to sponsor it. The CA's promotional pamphlet pointed out that if 500 members furnished three hours a week, a weekly payroll of $600 would be created. Faced with the massive unemployment of the Great Depression, the CA plan called for "aggressive and vigorous action."[32]

Ironically, in addition to trumpeting the benefits of capitalism, the Minneapolis Industrial Committee also supported the medieval barter and scrip economy created by the Reverend George H. Mecklenburg, pastor of the large downtown Wesley Methodist Church. For two years, Mecklenburg had carried on relief work through his church, only to be overwhelmed by the sheer weight of the starving people as the city's unemployment mounted. During the summer of 1932, after intensive study of medieval barter economies, Mecklenburg devised a plan for organizing the unemployed for self-help, using scrip money as the medium of exchange. Although Mecklenburg's primitive economic concept violated the basic capitalistic tenets of the business community, his fundamental belief in the value of work agreed closely with the moral precepts of the CA. The reverend wrote: "No family can live in idleness two years on city relief and maintain self respect and the proper attitude to society." Mecklenburg's new organization, The Organized Unemployed, Inc. (OUI), would be based on a fundamental philosophy of "Work. No charity. No dole. Productive, creative, respectable work."[33]

In mid-July 1932, Mecklenburg called a meeting to gather support from "executives and leaders of men." Two weeks later, The Organized Unemployed, Inc., was launched. The group's headquarters and most of its activities took place in the vacant Girls' Vocational High School at Fourth Avenue South and Eleventh Street, which was donated by the Board of Education. In the basement, hundreds of barrels of sauerkraut were canned, shoes and furniture repaired, toys constructed, and cereal milled. On the main floor, a staff of forty served 1,400 meals per day in the cafeteria, while 1,500 customers shopped for clothes and canned fruits and vegetables. Upstairs, fifty to sixty people manufactured women's, men's, and children's clothing.[34]

The most "spectacular activity," however, took place beyond headquarters. Four hundred men working on thirty crews cut over 5,000 cords of wood. The wood was then transported into the city in donated trucks, cut into one-foot lengths, and delivered to as many as 100 families a day. The workers were paid and purchased the various goods with scrip printed by the organization. The bank just inside the Grant Street doors handled $500,000 in denominations from five cents to ten dollars. Each day, $4,000 in scrip was paid out in salaries and could be used in the cafeteria or stores. In a matter of months, Mecklenburg had created an extraordinary new economy and given hope to hundreds of desperate families.[35]

The Organized Unemployed publicly claimed that 3,700 officers and leaders throughout the city aided over 7,000 families. In fact, the organization had only one leader, the Reverend Mecklenburg, who feared that the "unreliable" element among the unemployed might take over his project. At scrip wages of twenty-five cents per hour, fewer than 300 families received enough income to stay off relief. Speculation in scrip devalued it and led to shortages of staples in the Organized Unemployed stores. When outside businesses accepted scrip and began attempting to pay their workers with it, the Central Labor Union complained that the OUI was "breaking down wage scales and conditions and lowering living standards to a point where honest toil brings only the reward of the barest existence or even less." The United States Bureau of Labor concluded: "There are dangerous elements in this situation." The Bureau's report, of course, was excellent news from the perspective of the CA, aiding their campaign to lower the city's wages.[36]

The OUI's publicity had also proudly proclaimed its ability to be self-supporting. They would not ask the public for "something for nothing. . . . There will be no tag days or cash raising drives. Our members are not charity cases." Two months after the organization was industriously created, it was in financial trouble. Mecklenburg was forced to appeal to the CCA for financial aid. Funding was quickly arranged through the Minneapolis Industrial Committee. The cash would ultimately come from the same funding channels as for the CCA and the CA. The MIC's 1932 budget of $100,000 came from twenty industrial groups. The Minneapolis Clearing House, representing the city's banks, contributed $5,000. Mecklenburg, in return for contributions totaling $6,000, would have to accept the advice and counsel of the MIC. Four months later, realizing that the cash drain would continue indefinitely, the MIC advised that the OUI be liquidated. Mecklenburg refused, and by July 1 was again requesting aid. It was clear that the self-supporting, self-help institution was becoming a relief operation funded by the MIC.[37]

After consulting with its financial supporters, the MIC reluctantly supplied the OUI with another cash donation "so as to permit the organization to realize on their investment in growing crops." The business group also supported the OUI application for $30,000 in federal funds, arguing that "the services given by this organization in maintaining the morale of the unemployed and in giving relief service requiring a cash subsidy of only about 20 percent have justified its existence."[38]

The OUI financial problems, however, did little to reassure its benefactors. To receive continued local support and federal aid, the MIC took control of the organization's administrative operations. CCA director Godward acted simultaneously as MIC executive-engineer and special treasurer of the OUI. As federal funds began to pour in, however, the business community quickly relinquished the financial burden of self-help. By midsummer of 1934, the OUI had essentially become a state work-relief project that still relied on scrip and barter to justify its survival. A year later, the federal government disbanded the conservative experiment. The CCA and CA were free to pursue cheaper and simpler solutions to the continuing problem of unemployment and poverty.[39]

Governor Olson, on the other hand, believed that only massive government intervention could ensure a stable economy and alleviate unemployment. Led by the governor and the Farmer-Labor Party, an intensive campaign was mounted to push an unemployment insurance program through the 1933 legislature. Olson's legislation, substantially written by University of Minnesota professors, called for an annual tax of 4 percent on employer payrolls and was estimated to cost the state's employers one million dollars a month. With enough legislators authoring the bill to make passage possible in both the Senate and the House, the MEA and CA faced a serious threat. Governor Olson reminded them that "industry, as such, being concerned largely with the sole motive of profit, has concerned itself little with the welfare of its workers. . . . It now remains for the state to do what industries failed to do. . . . This proposal is an attempt, whether wisely or not, to patch up the so called capitalist system—to prevent the substitution of socialization of industry." As if this were not enough of a warning, the governor added: "If employers are not willing to take such steps—then inevitably some other system will have to be substituted."[40]

The MEA board of directors immediately passed a resolution authorizing opposition to any unemployment insurance legislation. Anticipating the problem three years earlier, MEA secretary A.V. Williams had sat on a committee of the National Industrial Council investigating unemployment insurance. The NAM then produced a report, in December 1933, for use in the 1933 legislative battles in twenty-five states. The NAM concluded that unemployment in-

surance would facilitate the "ultimate socialistic control of life and industry."
The National Metal Trades Association distributed a leaflet arguing that unemployment insurance would benefit only "the inefficient, the drifters, and the
unemployable." Such legislation was the "entering wedge" of socialism that
"threatens to transform a virile, self reliant, hard-working people into a nation
of dependents without initiative, enterprise, or desire to provide for themselves." The leaflet went on: "Embracing visionary promises of ease . . . may
well be the beginning to the downfall of our civilization." The MEA hired
lawyer R. G. Thoreen for $2,000 to lead the business community's lobby at the
1933 legislative session.[41]

The CA played an important role in the "program of opposition." In the critical period when the legislature was considering the bill, the CA provided substantial funds from its own treasury to fund the efforts of the MEA. Letters from
the influential industrialists on the CA's board of directors poured into the
offices of state legislators and the governor. James Struthers of the Strutwear
Knitting Company warned that the effect of the law's extra tax burden "would
be to eliminate industries from this state." The president of Crown Iron Works
Company wrote that his industry had "sustained heavy losses each of these
years and should further burdens be placed on our shoulders, the only alternative would be to close our doors." In an open letter to manufacturers and all
other employers of labor, the president of the Toro Manufacturing Company,
John S. Clapper, warned that passage of the measure "will surely wreck the entire economic structure of our institutions in this state." The burdens of unemployment insurance would force Toro to eliminate 20 percent of its employees or be forced to liquidate. In his impassioned appeal, Clapper added,
"There has never been a time in the history of this state that business of all
kinds was in such jeopardy as at present, and [it] needs the full and unqualified support of our legislature and governmental department to prevent failure resulting in untold misery."[42]

Clapper led a Minneapolis manufacturers' committee in a parade of opposition before the House committee considering the bill. They claimed that executives had already taken severe salary cuts and could not absorb any further
burdens. Others argued that passage should be delayed until better economic
conditions would ease the financial burden of establishing a reserve. Governor
Olson retorted that waiting and doing nothing was analogous to waiting during a plague "until we're all dead" before attempting to vaccinate the sick.
Despite amendments that split the contributions for unemployment insurance
between employers and employees, the supposedly progressive House killed
the bill sixty-eight to fifty-four. Infuriated, Olson stepped up his campaign to
pressure the legislature. From the Capitol steps, he told a crowd of the

unemployed: "The present system of local government would go right down to hell" if the state did not act. When the Senate restored the original bill and left it to die, the CA claimed a major role in the bitter fight. They were well aware, however, that the victory was only a temporary respite from the onslaught of the New Deal.[43]

In CA Secretary Jack Schroeder's opinion, the extremely radical "Farmer-Labor administration made an unemployment law inevitable." The CA immediately began studying other plans and collecting documents "so as to be prepared in the event of an emergency, to introduce a Bill that can be supported by the employers, rather than to take that which we are bound to get, and which will not be to our liking." In a January 16 letter to the secretary of the NAM, Schroeder apologized for the CA's position: "We wish to explain that it is not the intention of this organization to start agitation ahead of everybody else for Unemployment Insurance." While the CA held meetings to discuss its options, Chairman Strong attended the annual meetings of the National Industrial Council and the NAM, where he gathered extensive information to aid Minnesota employers in the coming fight. Although the CA had absolutely no desire for unemployment insurance, it was faced with the stark reality of Minnesota politics.[44]

After completing their study, however, CA members decided that the material could be more effectively presented by the MEA, which represented employers across the entire state. At the December 19, 1934, MEA board of directors meeting, Strong and CA director Willis C. Helm of the Russell-Miller Milling Company argued at length that a bill should be prepared "so that the proponents of that type of legislation could not say that the employers were not giving the matter consideration." A committee of ten chaired by CA director J. C. Buckbee of the Bureau of Engraving was created to consider the question. Material gathered by the CA and the MEA's legal counsel, R. G. Thoreen, would guide the committee in preparing an unemployment insurance bill favorable to employers. CA Secretary Schroeder and field agent Paul J. Ocken would continue to be closely involved in the process.[45]

The committee quickly produced a bill for the 1935 legislature that acknowledged that "unemployment has become an urgent public problem, nation wide in scope." In its declaration of public policy, the bill supported a limited reserve fund to alleviate the distress of unemployment and advocated an employer contribution, although the bill pointed out that employers were already taxed for public relief and substantially supported private charity. To help stabilize employment, employers and employees would make equal contributions of 1.5 percent. To spread the financial burden to as many employers as possible, the bill would affect any employer with four or more employees. Benefits were restricted to a maximum of ten dollars per week after a four-week waiting period. To help mitigate the effect of unemployment insurance on the open shop, strikers were disqualified.[46]

Although the 1935 legislature failed to pass an unemployment insurance bill, the pressure increased dramatically when Congress enacted the Social Security Act on August 13. Under the landmark federal legislation, employers of over eight employees would have to pay a federal unemployment fund tax of 1 percent of wages in 1936, 2 percent in 1937, and 3 percent in 1938 and after. A tax credit of up to 90 percent, however, would be available to employers in states with an acceptable state law. Thoreen and the MEA worked feverishly to present a new bill to a special session of the Minnesota legislature on December 4, 1935. In hopes of avoiding the harsher provisions of the federal act, Senate File 9 allowed employees to pay only half as much as the employers and raised the maximum benefit to $12.50 per week. The Senate quickly struck out employee payments and raised coverage to employers with eight employees, putting the bill in line with federal standards. The MEA considered these amendments "detrimental to employers, particularly members of this association." Sixty-five telegrams were sent out to important connections throughout the state, withdrawing the MEA's support and urging members to pressure their senators. The Senate voted the bill down thirty-seven to twenty-nine.[47]

A year later, after the death of Governor Olson from cancer, newly sworn-in Governor Hjalmar Petersen called another special session. With a December 31, 1936, federal deadline facing the states, a compromise bill was quickly passed, and Minnesota's unemployment insurance bill became effective on December 23, 1936. The law declared that "economic insecurity due to unemployment is a serious menace to the health, morals, and welfare of the people of this state." The MEA's determined campaign, first to reject unemployment insurance and then to make employees pay half of the fund, had failed. Employers alone would contribute at slightly below the federal standards. Benefits had been hiked upwards to a fifteen-dollar weekly maximum.[48]

The benefit regulations were also a direct threat to the CA's open-shop policies: the eligible unemployed could not be forced to break strikes by taking jobs vacated by strikers. Of equal importance, strikers could receive unemployment benefits. The inclusion after the first year of all employers of one or more employees represented the MEA's only substantial victory. In the MEA's annual report in the fall of 1937, President H. E. Wade meekly informed members that the MEA "did give very helpful service to the Committees of the Legislature in charge of the preparation of that legislation and aided in enacting the present unemployment compensation act."[49]

For Minnesota employers, the bad news emanating from Washington continued to mount in 1937, when the United States Supreme Court reversed an earlier decision and validated minimum wage laws for adults. Minnesota's first minimum wage law was passed in 1913 to protect the health of women and minor workers. A 1914 commission established a nine-dollar-per-week minimum for mercantile, office, waitress, and hairdressing occupations in the state's major cities. In 1923, however, the minimum wage law of the District of Columbia was declared unconstitutional by the United States Supreme Court on grounds of denial of the right of contract. MEA attorneys reported to the board of directors that "There was no question but what the minimum wage law of Minnesota could be successfully attacked on the same grounds." The MEA executive committee delayed any action until after the 1925 legislature. On June 8, 1925, however, the Minnesota attorney general wrote to the Industrial Commission that "it would not be possible for the state to enforce a minimum wage law in the case of women over 18 years of age." For the next twelve years, the state's minimum wage law would be enforced only for girls under eighteen and boys under twenty-one.[50]

On April 16, 1937, the Minnesota attorney general informed the Industrial Commission that, because of the recent Supreme Court decision, it was now its duty to enforce the entire minimum wage law. Wage order No. 12, promulgated in 1920, set the minimum wage rate for adult women in the large cities at twelve dollars per week. Recognizing the inadequacy of seventeen-year-old standards, the Industrial Commission asked the Minnesota Employers' Association and the Minnesota State Federation of Labor to each select five members for an advisory board to set new minimum wages. The MEA selected William E. Parmeter of the Dayton Company and representatives from the Minnesota Canners' Association, the Minnesota Hotel and Restaurant Association, Minnesota Mining and Manufacturing Company (3M), and West Publishing Company.[51]

The advisory board gathered extensive material from the United States Department of Labor and the Department of Agriculture. Of particular value was a study of the budgets of 175 women making less than twenty dollars per week. In a series of fourteen meetings, the board considered expenses: lodging, board, clothing, and lesser but important expenses for laundry, recreation, insurance, and so on, and finally arrived at a figure of fifteen dollars per week minimum wage. Before acting on the recommendations, the Industrial Commission solicited critical briefs from state employers.[52]

On April 9, 1938, MEA President Wade asked the Industrial Commission to postpone action "until something like normal conditions in business, industrial and labor would be restored." Wade argued that "the economic situation and business outlook is worse than it was at the depth of the Depression in 1932. . . . Unfortunately many industries have found it necessary to release large numbers of men and women from service. Naturally this decreases purchasing power and seriously affects our whole economic and industrial situation." The Depression in 1938 had rendered the advisory board's recommendations obsolete. Wade claimed that living costs were actually less than in 1921: "When conditions improve it will be time for the Industrial Commission to exercise its function under the minimum wage law." Wade added that these reservations did not "indicate that the MEA opposes reasonable wages for employees." The MEA's objections and a public hearing two days later had little effect on the Industrial Commission. Minimum Wage Order 13 was adopted on April 25, 1938.[53]

The MEA's complicity in establishing new minimum wage standards had enraged many CA members and even members of its own executive committee. Munsingwear Secretary-Treasurer Charles L. Pillsbury, a CA director who received the highest taxable income in the state in 1938, wrote MEA secretary Williams: "The order is so obviously unfair and discriminatory that, in our opinion, the MEA should have openly and vigorously opposed it while it had the opportunity before [it was] officially proclaimed." Pillsbury particularly objected to the variance of rates for cities of different sizes. Munsingwear and fourteen other employers in the needlework industry, mostly AI (the former Citizens Alliance) members, joined with employers in the laundry, restaurant, and telegraph industries to sue the Minnesota Industrial Commission and stop the implementation of Order 13. AI attorney Levy, hired by Munsingwear, Strutwear Knitting, and others, argued that they had been denied their Fourteenth Amendment right to due process of law. Leaving nothing to chance, Levy continued to solicit campaign contributions from his clients for the four incumbent district court judges not hearing the case while the case was still being deliberated.[54]

The Hennepin County District Court found that the advisory board held no public hearings, that no material evidence was presented at the single public hearing held by the Industrial Commission, and that employers were not afforded a full opportunity to present their case. On August 27, 1938, the court found that Order 13 would cause the plaintiffs "substantial injury" and issued a temporary injunction. Two months later, Levy wrote Munsingwear to report that the Industrial Commission had admitted the invalidity of Order 13. Until a new order could be promulgated, Order 12 was once again in effect. Levy's victory, however was short-lived. Minimum wage Order 15, essentially the same as Order 13, was quickly adopted and went into effect March 1, 1939.[55]

One of the primary objections of the business community to Farmer-Labor social legislation, of course, was the threat of new taxes to pay for them. Early in 1923, several members of the Real Estate Board of Minneapolis claimed that "the manner for spending public money" threatened the prosperity of the city and county. Assisted by important business leaders, they organized the Taxpayers' Association on May 26, 1924, to "reduce taxes, to keep public bonded debt within bounds and to stop wasteful and unnecessary expenditure of public funds." Two years later, the local group was expanded to form a statewide coalition, the Minnesota Taxpayers' Association (MTA). Minneapolis would provide 37 percent of the $10,000 budget, over half of the 100-member advisory board, and the executive secretary, H. J. Miller. From its inception, the MTA would appear before the legislature to oppose the enactment of any new taxes that would not permanently replace a current tax. "Unemployment and financial Depression are children of deadening taxation and unwise public and private spending," according to the MTA. By the late 1930s, the MTA had affiliates in eighty counties, a membership of 52,000, and, more importantly, was backed by the major financial and industrial interests of the CA.[56]

The ultimate challenge to the MTA came when then-Representative Hjalmar Petersen introduced a statutory income tax bill on January 19, 1933. The proposed income tax allowed a $1,000 exemption for individuals and businesses and a graduated rate of 1 percent to 5 percent for all net income over $10,000. Businesses would be allowed a credit for business expenses up to 15 percent of their net incomes. CA and MTA members lobbied for the adoption of a competing bill that would require that income tax revenues be used for real estate tax relief. The *Minneapolis Journal* claimed that the people of the state had rejected a constitutional amendment in the previous election because it was a "free spending scheme" similar to Petersen's income tax bill. "The people of the state should realize that their wishes are being thwarted and their mandates defied," the *Journal* warned.[57]

Resolutions from the local groups associated with the MTA flooded the Capitol demanding that the income tax must provide permanent real estate tax relief. CA Director Clapper of the Toro Manufacturing Company brought Wisconsin Taxpayers' Alliance officials to testify before the legislature: "The tax will become just another tax. . . . The revenue will be squandered in new spending. . . . The property owners will receive little or no benefit in the way of relief from their tax burdens" unless safeguards were enacted. Despite repeated protests by proponents of the statutory income tax, the *Journal* continued to hammer at the proposed law as just another "tax spending bill."[58]

In more prosperous times, the anti-income tax movement might have prevailed. In the early spring of 1933, however, the state and the nation were in a state of crisis. President Roosevelt spoke of the "nameless, unreasoning, un-justified terror" that gripped the nation and then declared a national bank holiday to save the financial structure of the economy from collapse. On March 25, 1933, the House passed the statutory income tax by a vote of 104 to 11, after amending it to allocate the funds to school districts. On April 12, Governor Olson addressed the Minnesota Bonus Expeditionary Force and warned that if the legislature did not pass relief bills, he would declare martial law and confiscate private wealth. Hours later, under intense pressure, the Senate voted forty-nine to seventeen in favor of the income tax.[59]

In the first year, the Minnesota income tax collected $1,805,542. Because a majority of the state's large incomes came from Minneapolis and St. Paul, the Twin Cities contributed 73 percent of the total. Leading backers of the CA, such as John S. Pillsbury, Robert F. Pack, James F. Bell, Sr., and James F. Bell, Jr., all with substantial incomes, were now forced to pay the bill for the social consequences of the Depression. MTA supporter Charles Pillsbury was hit with a $9,096 bill. Forty-five percent of the income tax receipts came directly from corporations. The businesses of CA members paid a substantial portion of the state's corporate income tax. The Dayton Company, for example, paid $44,279 in 1935, while companies such as Munsingwear Corporation, Deere and Webber Company, and Minneapolis Honeywell Regulator Company paid over $10,000 each. It was clear both on the profit sheets and in the pocketbooks of CA members that the MTA, MEA, and CA had failed to protect their interests.[60]

Despite its inability to forestall the income tax, the MTA was not disbanded. With the organization of the Minneapolis Civic Council in 1938, the MTA became formally aligned with the CCA and the CA (which became the AI in 1937). With an enlarged budget (about 40 percent of AI's budget), the MTA would continue to lobby to prevent increased taxation, stop new bond issues, and lower property taxes. The MTA's first priority in 1939 was to lower the cost of relief by transferring the administration and financing of relief to local governments. MTA publications argued that only local officials could successfully segregate those in distress from those capable of partial or complete self-support.

Unfortunately, with seemingly unlimited federal and state funds, local officials had very little motivation to curtail their relief programs. Despite an improving economy, the costs of relief continued to grow. The social policies of the CA and the CCA and the financial policies of the MTA were simply two sides of the same coin. The overarching umbrella of the Civic Council had now brought the three allied business institutions together.[61]

17 The CA and the 1934 Teamsters' Strike

BY EARLY 1933, the CA, protected by its elaborate system defending the open shop, had survived both the first term of Farmer-Labor Governor Floyd B. Olson and the first four years of the Depression. On June 16, 1933, however, President Roosevelt signed the National Industrial Recovery Act (NIRA) into law, commenting: "History probably will record the NIRA as the most important and far-reaching legislation ever enacted by an American Congress." Over the strenuous objections of the National Association of Manufacturers (NAM) and the United States Chamber of Commerce, section 7(a) of the act stated: "Employees shall have the right to organize and bargain collectively through representatives of their own choosing, and shall be free from the interference, restraint, or coercion of employees of labor, or their agents, in the designation of such representatives."[1]

United.Mine Workers President John L. Lewis said, "From the standpoint of human welfare and economic freedom we are convinced that there has been no legal instrument comparable with it since President Lincoln's Emancipation Proclamation." The independent existence of employee organizations, which the CA had vigorously opposed for three decades, was now a federally protected right. The CA recognized instantly that Section 7(a) would be a dangerous weapon in the hands of "unscrupulous, prejudiced union walking delegates." The NIRA contained "real dynamite" that all the members of the CA agreed was "obnoxious and undesirable."[2]

The response of American unions to their new Magna Carta was dramatic. One-fourth of the unions in the American Federation of Labor doubled their membership. The United Mine Workers, with only 60,000 members in 1932, added 300,000 workers within a few months. A wave of strikes erupted across the country as newly strengthened unions demanded recognition. CA members faced a similar onslaught in Minneapolis. The Amalgamated Clothing Workers quickly organized over half the workers at the Robitshek-Schneider Company and went on strike for union recognition on July 20. At the same time, the Upholsterers' union was rapidly recruiting over two-thirds of the workforce at Minneapolis furniture factories. On October 12, Local No. 61 demanded that CA stalwarts Brooks Parlor Furniture, Davis Manufacturing Company, Levin Brothers, and four other members sign a closed-shop contract. Eight days later, the revitalized union shut down Minneapolis's furniture industry. CA Executive Vice President John W. Schroeder stated that "It has been demonstrated again and again that all the labor trouble we are having in Minneapolis is a direct result of Section 7-A."[3]

In November, the CA's intelligence system discovered ominous signs of organization in the lifeless General Drivers Local 574. CA leaders had realized since 1902 that a citywide drivers' strike was the one way that union labor could force the closed shop on Minneapolis. Except for a brief revival in the spring of 1924, which the CA had quickly squashed, the Teamsters' union had been dormant since the great 1916 strike. The union's membership had vacillated between fifty and one-hundred-and fifty during the 1920s and represented only a small fraction of the city's drivers. Recognizing their new opportunity, a group of workers from the coal yards approached Local 574 with a proposal to organize the industry. Within weeks, the union had several hundred new members and was planning a campaign to force the closed shop on the city's coal yards. The opening wedge into the CA's open shop fortress was quietly driven home.[4]

In New York, Harry A. Bullis, vice president of CA member General Mills, and his fellow directors at the NAM had a dramatically different interpretation of Section 7(a). NAM *Employment Relations Bulletins*, which were distributed to employers across the country, argued that:

- The law required negotiations with unions but did not compel union recognition or a union contract.
- The closed shop was illegal, that seniority was to be recognized only when seniority and merit do not conflict.
- Companies were not compelled to rehire union workers after a strike.
- Section 7(a) recognized the principle of the open shop.

Any other interpretation would threaten the "basic principle underlying American employment relations . . . the square deal" and undermine fifty years of industrial progress.[5]

To forestall the threat of union organization, companies across the country formed company-controlled unions to bargain with and fulfill the legal requirements of the new law. As the NAM's policies were adopted by employers across the country, the growth in membership of company unions actually exceeded that of trade unions. When strikes erupted, the federal government created the National Labor Board (NLB) to "adjust and settle differences and controversies that may arise through differing interpretations of the President's re-employment agreement." Quoting a statement of NLB chairman Senator Robert F. Wagner, the NAM informed its members that the NLB could not "render enforceable decisions. . . . It relies upon voluntary action." By November 1933, the NAM had launched a campaign against the NLB. Employers across the country, following the NAM's legal advice, began to defy NLB decisions.[6]

To thwart union expansion, the CA quickly developed a plan that was in close harmony with the national policies that it had helped formulate at the National Industrial Council and the NAM. On June 6, 1933, before President Roosevelt had signed the NIRA, the CA circulated a "suggested plan of employee and employer organization" that was essential for every CA member unless he wanted "to leave the organization of his employees to the known enemies of industry, the closed shop unions." To control this company union, management should make sure that "tried and true employees assume the leadership of this work of organization."[7]

Over the next year, the CA perfected a more thorough "Uniform Employment Relations Policy" that specified: "No contract will be signed with any labor union or committee, whether or not the closed union shop is demanded." The company was to retain complete control over hiring and firing workers, and seniority would be used only when it did not conflict with merit. The CA's guide, "Rules and Regulations Governing Employment," allowed the discharge of employees for organizational activities during working hours or for participating in any action that tended "to create discord between employees or between Management and employees." To avoid these problems, management was advised to select only employees who would help the company maintain a "spirit of friendliness and harmony" between employees and the management. It was clear that the CA's open shop would not tolerate unions, union organizers, or union members. The CA was determined to undermine the influence of Section 7(a).[8]

The success of the CA's defiant strategy depended on the rulings of the Minneapolis-St. Paul Regional Labor Board (RLB) and the ability of the government agency to enforce its decrees. The first confrontation erupted when the Robitshek-Schneider Company, guided by the CA, refused to bargain with or recognize the Amalgamated Clothing Workers Union. When the United States Department of Labor sent a conciliator, the company, represented by CA lawyer Sam Levy, would negotiate with the government only after making it clear that it did not intend to in any way recognize the union.[9]

On November 6, after months of futile negotiations, the union appealed to the Regional Labor Board that the firm had "used coercion and violated Section 7(a)." At conferences called by the RLB, Levy "stated emphatically that they had nothing to arbitrate and nothing to discuss." Despite the union's naive agreement to abide by the RLB's decision, the company, undoubtedly familiar with the NAM's analysis of the NLB's lack of authority, refused. On December 27, 1933, the Labor Board ordered that the Clothing Workers' strike be declared called off and that the company reemploy the strikers first. The company's blatant defiance of Section 7(a) was dismissed on a technicality, giving the CA's policy its first victory.[10]

A week later, the RLB intervened in the bitter strike of the Upholsterers Local 61 at seven of the city's major furniture manufacturing companies. The union, which was restricted by a district court injunction and slowly losing a battle of attrition as it ran out of money to support strikers, agreed to submit to arbitration. The employers, represented by Sam Levy, stated that they would "reserve all their legal and constitutional rights" and refused. On January 9, the Regional Labor Board ruled that the strike be called off and that elections be held in each plant. The Labor Board, however, agreed with the NAM's interpretation of Section 7(a), that the National Industrial Recovery Act did not recognize the closed shop. Non-union employees were entitled to their own representatives even if they were in the minority.[11]

Although the RLB set wages at fifty-five cents an hour and mandated the reemployment of strikers, it ignored the question of piece rates and workers hired during the strike. Under Levy's direction, Brooks Parlor Furniture Company led the defiance of the board's order, refusing to return all union men to work, discharging workers for union activities, continuing its company-union organizing, and refusing to pay the fifty-five cents wage. The company then ignored the board's efforts to force it to comply. On March 2, the RLB, finally convinced that further efforts were useless, referred the case to the National Labor Board. When Local 61 won elections in February at six out of the seven plants, the companies, backed by the CA, refused to sign contracts or recognize the union. The NAM's prediction that the NLB lacked any powers of enforcement had been confirmed. The CA's strategy for coping with the obnoxious New Deal legislation had worked perfectly. Another challenge, however, was looming in the city's coal yards.[12]

By January 1, 1934, committees from the various coal yards organized by the truck drivers, Teamsters' Local 574, had prepared and ratified demands for union recognition, increased wages, shorter hours, overtime pay, improved working conditions, and a seniority system. The RLB, in an attempt to head off a threatened strike, arranged negotiations between union members and representatives of the Twin City Coal Exchange (TCCE), a longtime ally of the CA. The CA, finally realizing that a strike was imminent, recommended a wage survey of all coal dealers and the establishment of a higher industry-wide wage scale.[13]

On February 1, the TCCE and the coal dock dealers posted a new wage scale, raising the seasonal truck drivers' hourly wage to sixty cents an hour. The union continued to threaten a strike if its demands for recognition were not met. By late January, the negotiations were complicated by the entrance of J. B. Beardsley of the Pittsburgh Coal Company. Beardsley, a member of the CA's board of directors, refused to even meet with union representatives, stating that they meant "just exactly nothing to me." While the CA was willing to avoid a strike with a wage increase, it could not countenance the recognition of Local 574. The CA recommended that businesses across the city stock up on coal and counted on the RLB to quickly end any strike. Although the CA realized that the new union threat was led by "a number of militant communists," they had little reason to expect an effective strike.[14]

At 7:00 A.M. on Wednesday, February 7, the coal truck drivers, their helpers, laborers, and yard workers struck the city's sixty-seven coal dealers. Within three hours, the union's 600 pickets had closed down sixty-five yards "as tight as a bull's eye in fly time." The Minneapolis police quickly mobilized and attempted to remove all pickets from one of the larger yards. When two trucks broke through the picket lines, their loads were dumped in the streets. To harass and shut down any trucks that escaped, pickets operated their own cars to spot and block any coal movements. Any trucks caught in the net of cruising pickets were boarded and the coal shoveled into the streets.[15]

Despite brisk winds and temperatures near zero, the picketing continued through Wednesday night into Thursday. As coal stocks across the city dwindled, desperate citizens beseeched the police department, demanding protection. Although the overmatched police were able to protect a few cars, the city's coal yards remained shut. By late Thursday, many large office buildings, hotels, stores, and factories were running short of fuel. Mayor Alexander G. Bainbridge admitted that the exhausted police were very close to losing complete control of the situation. CA attorney Levy wrote the RLB, warning, "An emergency exists in this city, whereby the life and safety of the public is menaced and endangered." As Minneapolis's coal supply quickly burned down, the CA realized that it had grossly underestimated Teamsters' Local 574.[16]

Facing the threat of a major Teamster victory, the CA stepped in to control negotiations. On their advice, forty coal companies petitioned the RLB on the first day of the strike, seeking the board's intervention because the "health, comfort, business and life of the citizens of Minneapolis are seriously menaced." Levy would represent the coal dealers in all RLB negotiations. After meeting with both sides the next day, the Labor Board ruled that the strike be called off immediately and all men be rehired without discrimination. Elections would be held immediately to select representatives for collective bargaining purposes. Pending elections, Local 574 would represent union employees in the coal yards. The board added, following the CA's interpretation of Section 7(a), that the rights of individual employees to bargain for themselves would not be affected.[17]

Recognizing that Levy had obtained the same non-binding, anti-closed-shop ruling as in the earlier rulings, the coal dealers signed an agreement with the RLB. The union response was delayed by the impassioned objections of the more radical members, who realized that the employers had not really recognized the union, negotiated on any of the wage or seniority demands, and were unlikely to ever sign a contract with Local 574. To put pressure on the unions to settle, the CA made arrangements on Thursday night to move trucks at 1:00 P.M. Friday afternoon and threatened that these new employees would not work "as 'strikebreakers,'" but as regular and permanent employees." A majority of the strikers voted to accept the very limited union recognition contained in the RLB ruling.[18]

On Saturday morning, a flood of calls from members prompted the CA to issue a special bulletin reassuring Minneapolis businessmen that no contract had been signed with Local 574 and that there would be no closed shop. On February 13, the day before elections, the coal yards informed their employees that, while they would "recognize any duly accredited representative of our employees," they were not "required by law, to agree to any particular contract."[19]

Local 574 swept the coal yard elections. Five days later, on February 19, the CA developed a Uniform Employment Relations Policy for the coal dealers that would strip the union victory of any immediate practical importance. The policy stipulated that "no contract will be signed with any labor union or committee, whether or not the closed shop is demanded," and that "hiring and discharging of employees shall continue to be vested solely in the management" and based on merit. The CA's only acknowledgment of the union's election victory was to "give courteous recognition to employees, listen to all grievances, and give due consideration to the welfare of employees . . . in an effort to promote fair dealing and harmonious employment relations." This strategy, however, could not obscure the basic fact that Local 574's picket line had successfully paralyzed the city and stalemated the CA.[20]

Local 574's radical organizing committee quickly capitalized on its success, signing up over 2,000 drivers by April 1. The CA belatedly realized that Local 574 intended to organize "every truck driver in Minneapolis, including those employed by retail stores, oil companies, transfer companies, produce firms and all private concerns." It was clear by early April that Local 574 was planning to strike for "closed union shop control of all primary transportation."[21]

The CA, still not completely aware of the danger, followed its well-developed strategies. With winter over, seasonal layoffs in the coal yards were used to clean out union organizers and destroy Local 574's strongest position in Minneapolis industry. The CA also launched an investigation of Local 574 that revealed that five of the union's seven organizers were active members of the Communist League of America, and two of them served on the national committee. This Communist plot was revealed at a March CA organizing rally where CA leaders assured the business community that the CA, in cooperation with the mayor and the police, would save the city. In hopes of forestalling this battle, the CA organized a series of meetings with transfer and warehouse firms and urged the employers to adopt a fifty-cents-per-hour minimum wage scale, 11 percent above the national NIRA code wage scale. Although the entire trucking industry agreed to put the new wage into effect by May 1, the CA's strategy had little effect on Local 574.[22]

On April 6, the CA's *Special Weekly Bulletin* announced that Governor Olson would speak on "The Right to Organize" at a mass meeting at the Shubert Theater on April 15. At a packed, enthusiastic meeting, the governor's private secretary, Vincent Day, read a message from the governor applauding "the union idea," saying that "without it the status of labor would be pitiful." Olson recommended that the workers of Minneapolis "band together for your own protection and welfare." Galvanized by the governor's endorsement, Local 574's membership quickly shot past the 3,000 mark. The CA's strategies were clearly not working.[23]

By the first week in May, Local 574 was ready to demand a closed-shop contract throughout the trucking industry. While the union prepared for a possible strike, the CA quickly organized the trucking industry. Two representatives of each industry employing truck drivers, each with the power to act for members of its group, joined to form the Employers' Advisory Committee (EAC). An elected steering committee headed by CA Director Joseph Cochran would handle all negotiations. In reality, however, the CA would run every aspect of the employers' fight with Local 574. CA President Albert Strong would direct the EAC, advised by attorney Levy. Executive Vice President Schroeder and Vice President MacAloon would run the EAC strikebreaking efforts in the streets.[24]

On May 1, Cochran and two other EAC representatives attended a Regional Labor Board conference with Local 574, where they sidestepped the closed-shop issue and demanded proof that Local 574 represented their employees. The union reciprocated, demanding a list of firms represented by the Advisory Committee. The Citizens Alliance stated that the EAC would represent 166 firms, two-thirds of which were in the transfer, lumber, or food industries. While the majority of CA members were protected from direct engagement in the coming conflict, the EAC included enough firms without any union members to support the contention that Local 574 did not represent its employees.[25]

On May 7, the Employers' Advisory Committee wrote the Regional Labor Board that the demand for a "closed shop agreement is hereby definitely rejected." The EAC firms were committed to open-shop operations in accordance with Section 7(a) of the NIRA. The EAC set up a strike headquarters in Room 126 of the West Hotel, ignoring RLB attempts to continue negotiations. The RLB reported "no conciliatory move of any kind whatsoever at any time by employers." The union, on the other hand, agreed to the RLB's suggestion to drop its insistence on the closed shop. The RLB's last recommendation, however, still called for a signed agreement between the union and the employers. The EAC rejected the proposal and waited for the inevitable strike vote.[26]

On the morning of May 16, the CA received a devastating shock. Operating from a garage at 1900 Chicago Avenue, Local 574 picketed the city with military precision. The *Minneapolis Tribune* reported on May 17: "With nearly 3,000 picketers blocking every entrance to the city and massed about the gates of every large fleet owner, they succeeded in halting most of the ordinary trucking movements." At union headquarters, reports that flowed in over the telephones, by short-wave radio, and by motorcycle couriers were used to quickly dispatch pickets with the union's fleet of private cars and trucks. Cruising squads swept each district of the city searching for truck movements. Any commercial trucks caught by picket squads were escorted back to 1900 Chicago Avenue.[27]

Hennepin County Sheriff John P. Wall admitted that "they had this town tied up tight, you could not move a truck." When the growing army of pickets ignored Police Chief Michael J. Johannes's threats of arrests, he begged the City Council for 500 special police officers. The CA quickly realized that it was totally unprepared for the magnitude of a strike that was "crippling our industries and is greatly inconveniencing our citizens. . . . A group of men have virtually seized our city and are attempting to dictate to a half-million people, how, when and where we can secure even the bare necessities of life." With the city's food supply rapidly dwindling, a mass meeting of "citizens" was organized by the CA to deal with the emergency.[28]

Hundreds of Citizens Alliance members crowded into the West Hotel on the strike's third day and issued a call for action to break the strike. The meeting's first resolution was a demand "that law and order must prevail." Wild cheering interrupted the program when a local businessman suggested: "We'll volunteer as deputies if the authorities have not got the necessary manpower, and we'll raise all the money they need." A Citizen's Committee for Law and Order, which was appointed by the meeting's chairman Charles C. Webber, appointed a subcommittee to organize a voluntary force of deputies.[29]

The plan for recruiting and operating this force was formulated by Sheriff Wall, Police Chief Johannes, and the subcommittee of CA members. Faced with a desperate situation, any non-union Minneapolis male was a likely recruit. CA Vice President MacAloon concentrated on former police officers, while Johannes recruited inmates from the city jail. Businessman Totten P. Heffelfinger asked his own friends—doctors, lawyers, and other businessmen. The largest contingent of the rapidly growing army, however, were clerks and salesmen employed by CA members. Heffelfinger recruited Colonel Watson, a military man who had had experience in handling mobs, to reorganize the employers' army. Watson was assisted by Major Perry G. Harrison, who had led the Civilian Auxiliary during the 1917 streetcar strike. Headquarters was established at 1328 Hennepin Avenue with a commissary, hospital, and barracks. Across town, CA member J. R. Clark's Woodenware Company manufactured wooden saps to arm the CA's army. Within a couple of days, Watson had over 700 volunteers for his amateur army. Unlike the Civilian Auxiliary of 1917, however, the CA's 1934 army had no firearms, little time for training, and faced a large, determined, and well-organized union force.[30]

The plan to break the union's control over Minneapolis streets was revealed the next day, Saturday, May 19, when two trucks were loaded at the Bearman Fruit Company under the armed guard of Minneapolis policemen and newly recruited special deputies. When the unarmed pickets attempted to talk to the driver, they were beaten unconscious with clubs and pipes. The Minnesota Police Association said, "When the smoke of battle cleared they had the situation well in hand. Unfortunately for the CA, however, only two trucks had been moved.[31]

That evening, Burns Agency detective James O'Hara, who had infiltrated union headquarters for the police department, dispatched two truckloads of pickets to the alley behind the *Journal* and *Tribune* newspapers, where a squad of police and special deputies waited in ambush. At O'Hara's instigation, about thirty women joined the ill-fated mission. Trapped in the narrow alley, the pickets were viciously beaten. Twenty of the blood-covered women were hospitalized, several with broken legs or unconscious. The CA's army had won its second battle. By carefully controlling the site of each skirmish, the employers' army had used superior forces and weapons to brutally defeat its enemies. It had also forewarned the union of the nature of the coming war. Local 574 leaders told their angry pickets, "We'll prepare for a real battle, and we'll pick our own battleground next time." The CA's attempt to win a military victory would now face a serious challenge.[32]

On Monday, the CCA sent out a special appeal proclaiming that "MAN POWER IS OUR ONLY SAFETY! . . . In the face of property destruction . . . and a general condition of rioting existing in Minneapolis as a result of professional agitators and communists, the welfare and safety of Minneapolis and its citizens is at stake. . . . This appeal is to you, personally, and through you to any friends, relatives, neighbors, or business associates or employees personally known to you for their integrity." Every citizen of this kind was asked to report to the headquarters of the CA's army at 1328 Hennepin Avenue where they would be sworn in as special police officers or deputy sheriffs. They were instructed to wear rough clothes and to be ready for service. Unlike the Civilian Auxiliary in 1917, they were not issued military uniforms, rifles, or bayonets, and had received no training. In the rush to field an army, the CA had failed to make the preparations that had proved effective in 1917. Local 574 would make them pay dearly for their omissions.[33]

At 9:00 A.M. Monday, six trucks were backed up to the loading dock at the Gamble-Robinson Company in the market district. The Citizens Alliance was now confident that trucks could be moved. Several hundred police officers supported by a similar force of special deputies were stationed in the street, ready to convoy the trucks and break the strike. When the first truck started to move, over 500 club-swinging pickets charged into police lines. The employers' army and Local 574 supporters were finally locked in ferocious hand-to-hand combat. While the battle raged, another 600 strikers marched into the market area in military formation to join the battle. The injured bodies of deputies, policemen, and strikers soon littered the pavement.[34]

Outnumbered and losing ground, the police were forced to bring out their riot guns. When the police held their fire momentarily, a truck loaded with pickets smashed its way into their midst to resume their close-in battle. Unable to fire, Johannes ordered the retreat of the CA's army and brought in night shift officers to reinforce police positions. When the fighting died out, thirty policemen along with a number of special deputies had been hospitalized. The union wounded were treated at strike headquarters, except for several men with broken bones. More important for the CA, no trucks had moved. In Minneapolis's most brutal taste of class warfare, the huge crowds had jeered the CA's army and cheered Local 574. The well-organized ferocity of the union and the sympathetic response of onlookers portended an ominous future for the CA.[35]

The next morning, Tuesday, May 22, a peculiar calm hung over the market as the two separate forces gathered. Police Chief Johannes, obsessed with keeping the streets of Minneapolis open, assembled over three-quarters of the police force in the market district, while the CA's army commander Colonel Watson sent nearly 1,000 special deputies. Unlike the day before, each group of special deputies, armed with clubs, would be paired with regular police officers. They were met by a huge throng of pickets and thousands of onlookers. By mid-day, the market district had erupted into an immense battleground. Armed with almost every conceivable improvised weapon, from large stones and machine bolts to baseball bats and wagon wheel spokes, the strikers concentrated their attack on the easily identifiable special deputies. Blood-soaked men fell to the street as the carnage quickly mounted. The employers' soldiers, outnumbered and beaten, fled for their lives, tossing their nightsticks and badges into the street. The regular Minneapolis police hung back and refused to fire their weapons.[36]

Although the battle lasted less than an hour, union pickets continued to track down and attack special deputies through the evening. At CA army headquarters, Colonel Watson and Major Harrison managed to escape a threatening crowd by brandishing shotguns and sidearms. The Battle of Deputies Run, as it came to be called, was a complete rout. CA Director Arthur Lyman lay dead from a fractured skull. The CA's army was defeated, never to regroup. The private militia that had carried the day in October of 1917 had failed miserably in 1934. Instead, the Teamsters' union temporarily controlled the streets and, once again, no trucks had moved. The CA could no longer rule Minneapolis by brute force. It had fought a civil war and lost.[37]

At noon on Tuesday, with sporadic fighting still breaking out in the streets, representatives of Local 574 and the Employers' Advisory Committee met with Governor Olson, Police Chief Johannes, and Sheriff Wall and hammered out a twenty-four-hour truce that suspended all picketing and all transportation by EAC firms and closed the market district. Later that afternoon, the RLB, after a day-and-a-half of hearings, issued a ruling that reaffirmed Section 7(a) of the NIRA, returned all strikers to their jobs without discrimination, established seniority rights, maintained the current fifty-cents-per-hour wage for a year, and established arbitration for future conflicts. The ruling ignored the central issue of the strike—recognition of the union by a signed contract directly with the employers. In fact, the RLB's order was very similar to the employers' original proposal.[38]

Governor Olson, perhaps realizing that the RLB ruling was only the first step of negotiations, called a conference that evening at the Nicollet Hotel. Police Chief Johannes and the CA, always quick to spot opportunity, swore out warrants for the arrest of the union leaders and stationed 150 police and guards at the Nicollet Hotel. The union committee, "taking no chances with the bosses," approached the trap under the guard of a large force of pickets. CA attorney Sam Levy waited in front of the hotel to "welcome" the union committee. Governor Olson, who must have been aware of the large concentration of police, was forced to withdraw the police before the union would agree to negotiate. With tension and hostility at a fever pitch, Olson was also forced to shuttle from room to room between representatives of the two warring classes. Minneapolis waited for its fate to be decided.[39]

At noon Wednesday, when it seemed apparent that negotiations would fail and that the truce would not be extended, Governor Olson mobilized the National Guard to aid the civil authorities of Hennepin County and Minneapolis. By the next morning, over 3,000 state troops were concentrated in the Twin Cities. Much to the disappointment of Adjutant General Walsh and the CA, Governor Olson ordered that the troops would not be used to convoy trucks. Unless serious warfare resumed, the National Guard would stay off the streets. The CA lobbied the White House through its channels, urging that under a new law the president take charge of all troops for industrial purposes. If the commanding officer at Fort Snelling was put in charge of the militia, the CA hoped that law and order and the movement of trucks would be restored.[40]

Although some of the employers had reservations, the EAC, generally pleased that the union would not be recognized, accepted the RLB plan. Recognizing the similarity of the RLB proposal to the employers' original offer, the union unanimously rejected the ruling: "Until such time as the employers see fit to recognize officially . . . local #574, the strike will continue." The union suggested that the board's recommendation that contracts be signed after employers and employees agreed on terms be changed to an order. All parties knew that the CA and its EAC negotiators would never consent to these conditions. Renewed confrontation in the streets seemed inevitable.[41]

While Governor Olson met with employers, Levy, and union officials all day and into Thursday night, 5,000 building trades workers went out on a sympathy strike. The CA countered with meetings of the EAC and the Law and Order Committee to consider how to resume trucking operations. Chief Johannes announced that trucks would move at 9:00 P.M., guarded by police and National Guard. With pressure mounting and no chances of forcing the CA into a direct contract, the union demanded that inside workers be included in the terms of the RLB ruling. The CA, realizing that this would vastly expand the impact of the strike and dramatically increase Local 574's influence, adamantly refused. When the union walked out of negotiations, Governor Olson changed the wording to "persons as are ordinarily engaged in trucking operations." Olson then gave the skeptical union leadership his personal guarantee that this vague statement included inside workers. The CA had a very different interpretation. On Friday evening, Local 574 reluctantly voted to accept the compromise. Meeting at the same time at the West Hotel, EAC employers also agreed to sign. Although a truce had been signed, the strike was far from over.[42]

The *Minneapolis Labor Review* triumphantly proclaimed: "GENERAL DRIVERS SMASH Lines of Citizen's Alliance, Victory Held Greatest in City History." Local 574 leaders realized that it was a very limited and transient victory. The union had gained seniority rights, a non-discrimination clause, and the right to organize, but, as the CA relayed to its members, "Under the final order terminating this strike, there is no closed shop nor is there any signed agreement with the union." The Communist Party attacked the agreement as a "Trotskyite sellout" to the CA. Federal conciliator B. M. Marshman succinctly wrote: "The big point at issue was the fact that the union demanded a signed agreement with the employers. This, of course, the employers refused." Trotskyite leader James P. Cannon reflected that "realistic leaders do not expect justice from the capitalists, they only strive to extract as much as possible for the union in the given situation and strengthen their forces for another fight."[43]

Although Governor Olson undoubtedly lied to union leaders on the inside workers issue to get them to accept the settlement, he was merely giving them and the CA a face-saving way to defuse the violent civil war and consolidate their forces. The CA and Local 574 both realized that the ruling was a temporary truce. Neither side had any intention of honoring a disagreeable compromise. Both sides also knew that the significance of the May strike was not the settlement—it was the Battle of Deputies Run. The CA would never again rule the city with an army of its own.[44]

The immediate problem for the CA following the settlement of the May strike was raising funds to pay the expenses of the EAC, particularly the employers' army. In the haste of recruiting special deputies and police, the CA had agreed to pay their salaries. On Monday, May 21, while the first market square battle was being fought, the CA cranked its financial network into high gear. CA secretary Paul Ocken appealed to the Minneapolis Clearing House for $5,000 as its share of a $75,000 to $100,000 fund for paying the employers' mercenary army. The city's major bankers, all CA members, agreed to pay their customary 5 percent and jointly wrote an initial check for $2,000 to EAC treasurer George Stricker, a CA director. The wholesale division and the other seven major industrial groups contributed the rest of the fund. The trucking companies, which were suffering the most direct financial losses of the strike, were not solicited. When an attempt was made by conservative City Council members to pay for the special police from Minneapolis city funds, Farmer-Labor aldermen demanded that the CA pay for its own army. The indirect cost of lost business to the employers of Minneapolis, of course, was a far greater expense, estimated at $1,900,000. The CA also solicited funds from the St. Paul business community to help offset the enormous cost of the strike.[45]

By mid-June, the May settlement was starting to break down. The employers, under pressure from the CA, began firing senior union employees from lists collected and distributed by the CA and cutting back the work and wages of others. When Local 574 complained to the RLB, the EAC claimed it was in full accord with the settlement despite the fact that the union was, in effect, still carrying on the strike "by a course of threats, intimidation and in some instances, assaults upon and towards employees who are not members of this Local Union." The union's call for arbitration in nearly 700 disputes was summarily rejected. The EAC had agreed to arbitration with its employees or their representatives but "many of our employers had no employees who were members of the union; . . . local 574 did not represent their employees."[46]

More importantly, the employers refused to allow Local 574 to represent inside workers and expand its power base into the city's warehouses. When the union asked for a ruling on the inside worker clause of the May settlement, the RLB ruled that the union could represent only drivers, helpers, and platform workers "directly engaged in loading and unloading trucks." Local 574, denied the right to represent half of its members, set a July 11 deadline for a strike vote.[47]

CA Secretary Schroeder, realizing that "the employers had been caught napping in May," prepared the city and the police for the coming battle. Police Chief Johannes admitted that the performance of his force during the May strike had been a "disgrace" and asked for 400 more police officers and a police school. The police "must be trained just like an army to handle riots." The officers also must be armed like an army. Johannes's expanded budget request included $1,000 for machine guns and funds for 800 rifles with bayonets, 800 steel helmets, 800 riot clubs and 26 motorcycles. The CA and their staunch ally Johannes were determined not to repeat the disaster of Deputies Run. In the hands of highly trained police units, these new weapons would ensure victory for the forces of law and order. Johannes's vow to move trucks would have a first-class army to back it up.[48]

At the same time the EAC opened up a blitzkrieg campaign in Minneapolis newspapers to turn the public against the Teamsters' union and the coming second strike. In the July 1 *Minneapolis Journal,* the EAC claimed that employers were living up to the letter and the spirit of the Labor Board's order: They were maintaining the wage scale, rehiring strikers, and seeking arbitration on all matters of dispute. The "wholly unwarranted and undeserved hardships" facing the citizens of Minneapolis would be the responsibility of the truck driver's union.[49]

In an attempt to undermine Local 574 and divide the city's union movement, the EAC blamed the May strike on the Teamster local's Communist leadership. In the July 3 *Minneapolis Star,* the EAC asked, "Are the Communists insidiously taking over the union labor organizations—most of which are reputable and patriotic—to achieve the Russianizing of Americans?" The EAC claimed that "a super-government has been set up in Minneapolis by the Communist leaders of the truck drivers." In an attempt to arouse a torpid populace, the EAC asked, "How do you like having Our Minneapolis Streets in the Control of Communists?" and, "Is this still a free country and a free city?" and, finally, "Will Minneapolis citizens submit to such domination by Communists?" When Local 574 finally met on July 11 and voted to strike on July 16, the CA told its members that the majority of the 1,200 present were not truck drivers at all, "but members of the Communist Unemployed Councils and other Communist organizations." If the EAC could isolate the union and particularly its leadership, the weakened union force would be easy prey for Johannes's highly trained, heavily armed police force.[50]

On July 16, the Teamsters went out on strike again. A steady stream of cars was dispatched from union headquarters with coded instructions to blanket the city. A strategic decision was made to leave all weapons at headquarters. The responsibility for any renewed violence would rest on the police. On the strike's first day, the city streets were devoid of trucks except those permitted by the union, which included trucks carrying ice, milk, bakery, or brewery goods. According to the EAC, "bands of roving picket cars violently assaulted drivers of trucks, destroyed property, and successfully bottled up all vehicle transportation of industry."[51]

Sheriff Wall and Mayor Bainbridge, fearing that "various disturbances, tumults and riots may occur" and "impair the lives, health and property of the citizens," requested military assistance the next day. Governor Olson once again called out the National Guard "to create and maintain order, preserve the general welfare, protect property and bring about a restoration of peace and law and order" in Minneapolis. While arrangements were made to move the Ninety-second Infantry Brigade from Fort Ripley to Minneapolis, a provisional battalion was mobilized in the Minneapolis Armory under the command of Lieutenant Colonel Stewart G. Collins, a former Civilian Auxiliary officer and a close confidant of CA General Manager Jack Schroeder.[52]

On the third day of the strike, National Labor Relations Board (NLRB) negotiator, the Reverend Francis J. Haas, after a day of consultation with Labor Department conciliator Eugene H. Dunnigan, met with the Employers' Advisory Committee. Haas was informed point-blank that the EAC "refused to negotiate with these Communist leaders." In addition, the EAC claimed that of the 4,400 workers employed by the EAC's 166 firms, only 309 were actually on strike. At 120 of these firms, no one was on strike.[53]

The EAC was willing to accept wage arbitration by the RLB under its May 31 order. This would allow the question of representation of inside workers of produce and fruit warehouses to be decided by a comparison of payrolls with paid-up union membership. Any agreement would be by RLB stipulation without any union contract. The union wanted wages of fifty-five cents per hour for drivers and forty-five cents for inside workers and a signed contract with the market companies. Local 574 contended that the effectiveness of the May strike had already proved that market employees were represented by the union. Father Haas, recognizing that both sides were intractable on the issue of representation, submitted a proposal that set new wages but avoided any definition of inside workers and settled the strike by RLB stipulation without a contract. Haas felt "sanguine that we are going to settle this strike without much more delay." The Citizens Alliance, however, had very different plans for ending the strike.[54]

That night a large meeting of employers pressured Police Chief Johannes to preserve the "liberty of the streets." The next morning, despite promising Father Haas that no police protection would be given to the trucking companies, Johannes ordered the convoy of trucks to begin moving under heavily armed police protection. At 2:00 P.M. on July 20, a delivery truck escorted by at least twenty-five cars of police backed up to the loading dock of the Slogum-Bergren Company. Over fifty policemen armed with riot guns and Thompson submachine guns leaped from the cars to guard the truck from market district pickets. A few sacks of oatmeal and cartons of cornflakes were loaded as the pickets watched in the 90-degree heat. When the delivery truck attempted to leave the market district, it was cut off by a union truck carrying a sign, "Rid the city of rats," on its side. The police took direct aim at the unarmed pickets in the union truck and fired to kill.[55]

In the slaughter that followed, sixty-seven strikers were shot, over forty of them in the back as they were running from the police. Two union pickets, Henry Ness and Jack Belor, died from their wounds. While the fighting was still in progress, the Provisional Battalion of the 151st Field Artillery was called for riot duty. Lieutenant Colonel Collins's men rushed to the market area in trucks armed with machine guns. Within fifteen minutes, they marched forward in two separate waves, flanked by officers carrying Thompson machine guns and anchored by a gas squad. Any possibility of a union counterattack was defused by their deliberate and impressive show of force. The CA's carefully staged police attack on Local 574 had been backed up by its friends in the National Guard. In the aftermath of the strike, CA Secretary Schroeder could "definitely see that the strike was breaking," adding, "And if the troops had not come in and interfered, the strike would have been soon over. Because there are very few men who stand up in a strike when it's a question of they themselves getting hurt and killed." It was now clear to the governor and the federal negotiators that the CA wanted to fight out the strike.[56]

With a tense, eerie calm hanging over the city and National Guard trucks cruising the congested areas of the city, Haas and Dunnigan tried to find a common ground for settling the strike. The EAC agreed to have two group elections for the twenty-two market firms, one for the truck drivers and another for inside workers, but it took a hard line on other issues. A provision for not reinstating strikers "found guilty of violence in connection with the present strike" would allow the EAC to weed out union members before elections were held. The employers also insisted that elections would be held in the other 144 firms only if a question of representation arose. If their contention that no union members were on strike in 120 of these firms was accepted, elections would be held in only twenty-four non-market firms. When negotiations failed, the Advisory Committee agreed to an arbitration board whose deciding member would be chosen by mutual consent or by the Labor Board. Local 574 insisted on the reinstatement of all strikers, the representation of inside workers in all firms, and the settlement of the wage question before ending the strike. Negotiations were clearly deadlocked.[57]

Haas and Dunnigan, frustrated at their inability to bring the two sides together, broke off discussions and conferred with Governor Olson. At noon on July 25, they publicly released the Haas-Dunnigan Plan. This plan met union demands for the full reinstatement of strikers, election at all 166 firms, selection of the fifth arbitrator by the NLRB, and establishment of minimum wages as a basis for arbitration. Governor Olson threatened to declare martial law and permit the movement of trucks only with special military licenses if both sides did not agree. Adjutant General Walsh ordered the Ninety-second Infantry to the Minnesota State Fair Grounds and designated as commander Brigadier General Frank E. Reed, a Hennepin County District Court judge and CCA member.[58]

Local 574 accepted the proposal immediately after an overwhelming majority vote. The EAC replied that "under the circumstances we cannot deal with this communistic leadership; as it represents only a small minority of our employees. . . . This whole strike is the result of misrepresentation, coercion and intimidation." Joseph R. Cochran, chairman of the Employers' Advisory Committee and a member of the CA's board of directors, insisted that the union pickets "do not, in any way, represent the real truck drivers of Minneapolis."[59]

Ignoring the Haas-Dunnigan Plan, the EAC continued to insist that it would not rehire violent strikers or accept elections in firms where there was no employee dispute. The employers suggested that the friendly district court select the fifth arbitrator and ridiculed the minimum wage stipulation, which would only "pave the way for a repetition of the *same lawlessness* a few weeks or months hence, which would plunge our city into new turmoil." Two days later, the EAC tersely restated its contention that "the leadership of Local 574 is Communistic" and "does not represent the employees of our firms." Cochran demanded immediate elections "in each firm where there is any dispute between any firm and its employees."[60]

When the employers rejected a federal mediation plan, Governor Olson made good on his threat on July 26, assuming military command of Minneapolis "because of a state of riot, violence and insurrection." Taking over as troop commander, General Walsh declared: "It is believed that the indiscriminate operation of commercial trucks will cause violence and precipitate riot. To preserve order and prevent rioting, only the movement of such trucks as transport common necessities will be permitted at this time." Minneapolis employers could now move only the merchandise necessary for business if they obtained a truck permit from the National Guard. If the permit system was enforced, the National Guard, under Olson's direction, would shut down the city almost as tightly as the Teamsters' Union and put the CA in an extremely tenuous position.[61]

General Reed, realizing that the National Guard could not be used to ruthlessly restore law and order, resigned in protest. Representatives of the CA moved quickly to circumvent the permit system, meeting almost continually with General Walsh and frequently Governor Olson to press for the movement of trucks and goods in Minneapolis. Within four days, the National Guard Permit Bureau had allowed over 7,500 trucks to resume operations. Although its original mission was to restore peace and allow a minimal flow of essential goods, the National Guard was quickly and effectively breaking the strike.[62]

When union pickets attempted to slow the flood of trucks, a stockade was erected at the State Fairgrounds to hold violators of General Walsh's anti-picketing edict. The union pickets were then quickly tried in military court (because the city was under martial law) by Captain John Derrick, a counsel for CA members. Despite Governor Olson's avowed hatred for the CA, the National Guard was now supporting the alliance's efforts to defeat the Teamsters' union. The CA, however, was not satisfied with the movement of 65 percent of the city's trucks. Cochran lambasted Governor Olson for not upholding the lawful use of Minneapolis's streets. The CA threatened Olson with legal action.[63]

Local 574 leaders, realizing that the truck permit system of the National Guard would soon break the strike, held a mass meeting at the Parade Grounds to rally union support. The Teamsters threatened to resume unrestricted picketing the next day and told General Walsh: "Get your soldiers off the streets or we'll fight them." This public threat to the authority of the state apparently removed the last of Governor Olson's restraints on the National Guard. As the skies were becoming gray with the early light of dawn on August 1, three battalions of infantry marched through the streets in the searchlights of National Guard trucks to converge and surround the union's strike headquarters. While Provost Marshal Colonel Elmer W. McDevitt led into the building a "strong guard of husky soldiers" with bayonets drawn, a machine-gun company set up four mobile machine guns opposite the entrance. Without a shot being fired, Teamsters' leaders were arrested, their weapons and cars were confiscated, and, after all strikers were removed, the headquarters was put under military guard.[64]

By the next day, however, it was clear that Governor Olson's attempt to destroy the resistance of the Teamsters' Union had failed miserably. The *Organizer* (which was published by the Teamsters) announced: "Never before in our time has such a direct and outright act of strike breaking by military force been witnessed." While the *Organizer* stirred public sentiment against Olson and the National Guard, the union's picket commanders set up a series of control points, mainly at filling stations. Cruising picket squads directed by these scattered dispatchers were soon harassing and stopping trucks all across the city. Leaderless and without a headquarters, the union still defied the National Guard. Unwilling to order a blood bath and realizing that his political position was untenable, Governor Olson quickly capitulated, releasing the arrested leaders and returning the headquarters to the union. Although the Farmer-Labor governor had gone far beyond the CA's expectations in supporting law and order, it was now clear that the National Guard, when controlled by a hostile administration, would not slaughter strikers in the streets to maintain law and order. For better or for worse, the National Guard was a political organization limited by the political aspirations of its commander, Minnesota's governor.[65]

Reeling from the political repercussions of the raid on Local 574, Governor Olson ordered a raid on the CA's headquarters, ostensibly to obtain military intelligence on the CA's attempts to subvert a settlement of the strike. Olson secretly assigned the task to two men: The head Securities Commission investigator in the Northwest Banco case, William E. G. Watson, and the only National Guard officer with loyalties to the governor and the Farmer-Labor Party, Lieutenant Kenneth C. Haycraft. Under Commander Walsh's direct orders, Watson and Haycraft synchronized their watches and stealthily crept into the Builders' Exchange Building. None of Haycraft's squad of National Guardsmen knew what the target of their raid was to be.[66]

Despite the governor's precaution, however, word of the raid had leaked from Walsh's headquarters to Lieutenant Colonel Collins of the 151st Field Artillery in Minneapolis and to Jack Schroeder, secretary of the CA. When the National Guard arrived at the CA offices, four suitcases of sensitive records had already been removed. The CA's influence in the National Guard had allowed it to preserve the identity of its intelligence operatives in the labor movement.[67]

The next day, however, Governor Olson revealed in a public statement what the remaining CA files contained: Evidence of Citizens Alliance control of the Employers' Advisory Committee running the anti-strike effort and of CA "stool pigeons" in various labor organizations. A. W. Strong, chairman of the CA, publicly categorized the governor's raid as "part of his persistent effort to paint the CA as some mysterious 'big bad wolf' with which to 'scare the children,' (and the voters)." Although the CA had suffered a public relations setback, most of the revelations were already common knowledge to the readers of the *Minneapolis Labor Review.*[68]

Governor Olson's command of the National Guard became more threatening to the CA on August 6, when he issued an Executive Order revoking all permits and restricted truck movement to vehicles transporting milk, ice, bread, fuel, and gasoline; emergency vehicles; vehicles used in interstate commerce; and trucks operated by employers who agreed to a strike settlement proposal of federal mediators. With the National Guard shutting down most commercial transport, the CA claimed that the situation was "becoming unbearable and desperate, causing us very serious losses and forcing us to lay off more and more men."[69]

Pushed into a corner, the department stores and transfer company members of the CA applied for an injunction in Hennepin County District Court to stop the governor from interfering with the movement of motor trucks. CA attorney Sam Levy argued that, by refusing them permits, the National Guard and the governor had deprived the employers of their constitutional rights. Governor Olson, representing the state, argued that it was his constitutional duty to command the National Guard to restore law and order in an emergency. Although the court disagreed with Olson's attempt to force employers to accept the federal mediator's plan and felt that martial law was uncalled for, they were unwilling to force a confrontation between the court and the chief executive of the state during the serious crisis that existed in Minneapolis: "Military rule is preferable under almost any circumstances to mob rule." Although disappointed by the court's ruling, the CA undoubtedly realized that the court's reservations might stifle the governor's use of the National Guard during a more normal strike.[70]

While the CA waited for the court's decision, the EAC launched a propaganda campaign on WCCO radio to create public pressure on Governor Olson to rescind his August 6 Executive Order. EAC chairman Cochran introduced the anti-Communist theme of the broadcasts on August 6. If the employers gave in, "Other unions would be seduced by the Communists and shortly all or most of Minneapolis union labor would be Communized. . . . Communism's objective is a national peril, centered by this strike in Minneapolis. The Communists hope that this strike is the beginning of a revolution that will overthrow all existing government."[71]

EAC member Ralph M. Beckwith reiterated Cochran's domino theory two days later, warning that the Communist intention was to "upset the whole American economic and governmental system and replace it eventually with the Soviet State." The propaganda barrage tried to separate the majority of the *bona fide* truck drivers, who were "upright and law abiding citizens," from the "Communistic gangster type which destroys property, and murders and maims citizens, under the disguise of picketing." In the fourth radio program, *Minneapolis Journal* publisher George C. Jones accused Local 574 of aiming for "that one big union we all know Communist agitators have been trying to foist on the country for a number of years." The final appeal was to the purity of America, "where freedom and liberty and opportunity have been offered as in no other country since the world began. A communist snarls; an American does not. A communist seeks to tear down; an American seeks to build. Let us approach the solution of this strike from now on as Americans." In less than a week, Governor Olson received a report that "the radio talks of the Employers' Association are turning sentiment against the strikers by using the charge of Communism."[72]

With Governor Olson's authority upheld, the CA was forced to use the permit system to move trucks. While the court deliberated, a number of small transfer companies signed the Haas-Dunnigan federal mediation proposal. They immediately received military permits and began hauling goods for CA firms. Other CA companies received permits under the interstate commerce provision. After the court's ruling, the permit system loosened further, with National Guard troops actually helping market companies load their trucks. The Dayton Company repainted its older trucks and obtained military permits through dummy owners. When the union uncovered extensive misuse of the permits system, General Walsh warned them: "You have no right to stop trucks and examine their contents, nor even to examine permits on the trucks."[73]

By the third week in August, it was clear to Local 574 and the CA that the National Guard would let as many trucks roll as it could and that Governor Olson, facing a fall reelection campaign, would never allow the citizens of Minneapolis to go without the necessities of life. With thousands of trucks running and possibly 5,000 people back at work, the union's strike effort was beginning to unravel. A trickle of disheartened strikers was returning to work. The CA was very slowly winning a war of attrition. It was clear that trucks would roll and the CA would do business even with a Farmer-Labor commander of the National Guard.[74]

Late in the afternoon of August 8, however, the CA's strengthening position in the strike was shattered when Haas and Dunnigan met with First Bank Stock Corporation President Clive T. Jaffray and Northwest Banco President Theodore Wold. Under discussion was a strike settlement in the context of the weakening collateral of the $23 million purchase of Northwest Banco preferred stock by the Reconstruction Finance Corporation (RFC). Earlier that morning, Governor Olson had met with President Roosevelt in Rochester, Minnesota, and suggested that the RFC use its bailout of Northwest Banco as leverage to force the CA to end the strike. Within hours, RFC Chairman Jesse Jones called Haas and suggested that perhaps "prominent men" such as Jaffray and Wold could help with strike negotiations.[75]

Jaffray and Wold must have recognized instantly the magnitude of the thinly veiled threat. Northwest Banco had been created and developed to serve as the financial foundation of the industrial empire that encompassed most of the Minneapolis business community, including milling giants Pillsbury and General Mills. If the federal government drove Northwest Banco into bankruptcy, the shock wave would decimate many of the city's most important merchants and manufacturers. The CA's desperate defense of the open shop would have little relevance if most of those shops were financially destitute. But would the RFC really dare to undermine the economy in such a drastic fashion?

Although Jaffray initially told Haas that there was nothing he could do, negotiations were now handled by Jaffray, Northwest Banco's John W. Barton, who was also the regional RFC director of loans to industry, and CA President Strong. Representing the real power behind the EAC, the three business leaders continued to insist on elections only where disputes existed, retaining newly hired strikebreakers, and wage arbitration without any minimum scale. Barton suggested that Haas bypass union leaders and submit these proposals directly to the men. When this ploy failed, the EAC finally agreed on August 15 to permit elections in all 166 firms.[76]

Haas immediately wired the NLRB and requested that they order an election. This apparent breakthrough was exposed as a hoax the next day when the *Organizer* printed a letter that the EAC had sent to each firm. In an attempt to bypass Local 574, the EAC instructed each firm to immediately call eligible employees together to select candidates from among them for the election. Father Haas considered the EAC's maneuver as "equivalent to a conspiracy to steal the election." The deceit was the last straw for RFC Chairman Jones. It was clear that the bankers still considered the federal threat a bluff. Jones called Haas on August 16 and told him to "knock their heads together." Jaffray was infuriated when Haas intensified the pressure on him. The First Bank president threatened to call the employers together and call a mass meeting of citizens to demand the recall of Haas and Dunnigan.[77]

That afternoon, backed into a corner by Haas, Dunnigan, and the officials of the RFC, the EAC, the CA, and its bankers appealed to President Roosevelt to intervene on its behalf. An organized telegram campaign was launched on August 16. A. W. Strong, Jr., described the strike as "nothing but a communist uprising." His brother, Lucian, vice president of the Strong-Scott Manufacturing Company, added that it "should have been stamped out long ago." Strong stated the CA's opinion "that your mediators Haas and Dunnigan are actually doing more harm than good and we ask their immediate recall." George D. Dayton, treasurer of the Dayton Company, advised Roosevelt in a telegram that the "Minneapolis situation is desperate, rapidly growing worse Haas-Dunnigan unable or unwilling to effect a settlement" and urged that the president use his "influence and order individual elections." C. T. Jaffray, as the president of the Minneapolis, St. Paul, and Sault Ste. Marie Railway (Soo Line), who had been in on negotiations with the RFC as one of the CA's principal bankers, wrote President Roosevelt. Jaffray pleaded for the jobs of the railway's 2,000 employees and "urgently requested that you have an election called." He also suggested that "new representatives from Washington would be more worth while because of present impasse which mediators are now in." The CA's only hope was that Roosevelt was unaware of the RFC's role in the negotiations or that the president somehow did not comprehend the gravity of the strike. If Roosevelt removed Haas and Dunnigan and reined in the RFC, Local 574 might still be crushed. No answer ever came to this last-minute appeal. Federal negotiators and the RFC continued to tighten the financial noose around Northwest Banco.[78]

Under the combined pressure of the RFC, the NLRB, and the CA's leading financial backers, President Strong finally cracked Saturday evening, August 18. The iron-willed leaders of the CA "were so worn out, the tension was so great that they were willing to do almost anything to get the thing out of the way." CA Executive Vice President Schroeder, who believed that the CA was close to victory, complained bitterly of Strong's weakness. At 2:30 the next afternoon, Barton, Strong, and Williams met with government representative

P. A. Donoghue to offer whatever concessions were necessary to end the strike. They agreed to drop the violence clause for returning strikers, to allow the RLB to supervise elections within ten days, and to set minimum wages of forty cents per hour for inside men and fifty cents per hour for drivers. Donoghue was given assurances that the employers would sign whatever agreement he suggested.[79]

That evening, Haas and Donoghue worked until 1:00 A.M. writing an agreement that varied only slightly from the July 25 Haas-Dunnigan Plan. The employers were given several minor concessions: Minimum wages had been lowered 2.5 cents-per-hour and elections and the choice of a fifth arbitrator would be handled by the Regional Labor Board instead of the National Labor Relations Board. On August 21, both the union and the employers signed the consent order of the NLRB. On August 22, Jesse Jones wired President Roosevelt that the men were back at work and added that the "employers have made substantial concessions in the general interest." The strike was over![80]

The *Organizer* proclaimed "VICTORY" in its one-word August 22 headline. Strike leader Vincent Dunne believed that the settlement was "substantially what we have fought for and bled for since the beginning of the strike." Actually, strike leaders had received a "roasting" from union members when they presented the Donoghue proposal. Many of Local 574 rank and file wanted to fight the strike to the bitter end. The consent agreement guaranteed elections, but not a single employer was required to or had signed a union contract. The Communist Party condemned the "treacherous leadership of Local 574" for an agreement that was "a guarantee of victory for company unionism and for the employers." The agreement threw overboard the 2.5-cent raise of the Haas-Dunnigan Plan, recognized inside workers in only twenty-two firms, and established an arbitration system that would be "dominated by the CA."[81]

The *Journal* attempted to minimize the union victory and portray the settlement as "a fair compromise" that was essentially what the employers had wanted. The EAC issued a similar statement and contended that the entire "month of rioting, disorder, military rule, public disgrace, bitterness, and hatred could and should have been avoided." Union leader Farrell Dobbs later remarked: "Although the settlement provided much less than the workers deserved, it was as much as we could get at the time. On the whole the gains that were being registered provided a solid basis from which to go forward with the union-building job." Looking back on events several years later, CA leader Schroeder commented that "all our troubles date from 1934."[82]

Both the EAC and Local 574 claimed that the post-strike elections were a victory for their cause. Local 574 trumpeted the majority votes that entitled it to represent the employees of sixty-two firms. This included sixteen of the marketplace wholesale fruit and produce companies and twenty-two firms in the critical transfer and warehouse industry. In all, 61 percent of the employees in the general trucking industry voted for Local 574. The EAC claimed that only 695 employees voted for 574, a fraction of the "flamboyant claims of the communist leaders."[83]

Despite 574's victories, employees of 103 firms did not vote for the union. Because the union's goal was the complete unionization of the trucking industry, the union's victory was partial at best. Although the EAC claimed to have no quarrel with its employees, it was determined to continue its "opposition to Communist domination of business and industry." With the support of every employer in the state, the CA hoped to eventually win back the ground that it had lost.[84]

The imposing Minneapolis Club, where CA leaders gathered to socialize and decide the future of their city, at Second Avenue South and Eighth Street, ca. 1908

A sample of wealth and status: Fair Oaks, the W. D. Washburn residence, Steven and Twenty-second, Minneapolis

St. Anthony Falls and the Minneapolis Milling District, ca. 1905. The backing of the powerful milling and lumber industries was essential to the CA's success as an employers' union.

A machine shop at the Dunwoody Industrial Institute, May 1928

A machine shop at the Dunwoody Industrial Institute, March 1931

The St. Paul Street Railway Company Strike, 1917

Crowds in St. Paul during the railway strike.
A parallel strike in Minneapolis was quickly shut down by the CA, which offered
reinforcements to squelch strikers in St. Paul, where businesses and law enforcement
were less prepared to deal with a strike of this magnitude.

Braving the cold to uphold law and order: members of the Home Guard
posed with their riot sticks and rifle in front of the St. Paul Public Library, 1917

Why Minneapolis Stands for the

Because—

It brings the employer and employe closer together.

It protects the employe in his right to work unmolested.

It establishes relations of mutual confidence and respect.

It protects the liberty and independence of employe and employer.

It promotes individual initiative and ambition with greater reward for greater effort.

It protects the employe from the dictation and domination of third parties.

It secures free exercise by employe and employer of their natural and constitutional rights.

IT INSURES JUSTICE AND A SQUARE DEAL.

Associated Business Organizations of Minneapolis

Citizens' Alliance
Composed of the People who are interested in the welfare of Minneapolis

Minneapolis Hotel & Restaurant Keepers' Association
Composed of all the leading Hotels and Restaurants.

Minneapolis Retailers' Association
Composed of the down-town Retail Stores.

Minneapolis Auto Trade Association
Composed of Wholesale and Retail Dealers in Automobiles, Trucks and Accessories.

Minneapolis Master Builders' Ass'n.
Composed of the Master Builders.

Minneapolis Real Estate Board
Composed of all Realtors in the City

Minneapolis Transfer Men's Ass'n.
Composed of the Transfer Companies.

Manufacturers' Club of Minneapolis
Composed of all the leading Manufacturers.

Builders' Exchange
Composed of Contractors, Builders, Material Men and Manufacturers.

Northwestern Coal Dock Operators' Association
Composed of the Coal Dock Operators.

Twin City Coal Exchange
Composed of Retail Coal Dealers.

Minneapolis Launderers' Association
Composed of the Laundry Companies.

Minnesota Warehouse Men's Assn.
Composed of Warehouse and Storage Houses.

Minneapolis Garage Owners' Ass'n.
Composed of Garages and Repair Shops.

Minneapolis Apartment House Owners and Managers
Composed of Owners and Managers of Apartment House Associations.

Twin City Foundrymen's Association
Composed of the Foundrymen.

Twin City Association of Employers of Machinists
Composed of the Machine Shops.

Sheet Metal Contractors' Association
Composed of the Contractors in the Sheet Metal Business.

Minneapolis Building Material Exchange
Composed of the Retail Lumber Dealers.

Minneapolis Wood Workers' Ass'n.
Composed of the Manufacturers and Dealers in Wood Work.

Pattern Jobbers' Association
Composed of the Pattern Makers.

Twin City Vehicle Manufacturers Association
Composed of the Manufacturers and Painters of Auto Bodies and Tops.

Minneapolis Association of Building Owners and Managers
Composed of Owners and Managers of Office Buildings.

Propaganda distributed by the CA and reprinted in the *Iron Trade Review*, March 17, 1921: "Why Minneapolis Stands for the Open Shop." An example of prevailing attitudes among Minneapolis employers.

Members of the Minnesota Commission of Public Safety,
set up during World War I to coordinate the activities of all public peace and
prosecuting officers of the state. Judge John F. McGee (farthest right),
a prominent CCA member, used the Minnesota Home Guard and the
Minnesota Secret Service to suppress labor unions.

From a CA publication: "A Quiet Afternoon at Our Free Employment Bureau."
In order to get a job, many of these men had to agree to
spy on other workers in Minneapolis industries.

Picketing at the New National Theater in Minneapolis on November 15, 1917.
Workers sought recognition of the union and its demands.

Mass picketing by strikers at Robitshek-Schneider Co., a Minneapolis clothing
manufacturer, August 21, 1933. The strikers demanded union recognition.

THE STRIKER

The courts were often friendly to the CA, issuing injunctions that stopped strikes
in their tracks and permitted employers to enforce the non-union shop.
Cartoon from the *Minneapolis Labor Review*, October 23, 1936.

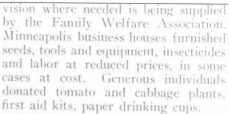

vision where needed is being supplied by the Family Welfare Association. Minneapolis business houses furnished seeds, tools and equipment, insecticides and labor at reduced prices, in some cases at cost. Generous individuals donated tomato and cabbage plants, first aid kits, paper drinking cups.

Owing to the lateness of the season, great speed was necessary in order to get the project under way, and during the first three difficult weeks the committee was fortunate in having as su-

pervisor E. W. Norcross, who resigned at the end of that period to accept a permanent position with the University of North Dakota. He was succeeded by George Wickham. Kenneth W. Smith is assistant supervisor.

Certain skeptical observers of the committee's efforts triumphantly reported that garden workers, supposedly destitute, were arriving in expensive automobiles. Upon investigation, the "expensive" cars dwindled to one: a man who was formerly a chauffeur for a stock market victim had been told by

beans, radishes, rutabaga, squash, cabbage, tomatoes, and other optional vegetables.

The project is a shining example of team work. Community-minded citizens donated the use of their land

The "Emergency Garden Committee" was the Minneapolis business community's "stopgap measure" for the unemployed during the Great Depression. Needy families planted potatoes, corn, peas, beans, tomatoes, and other vegetables, canning the produce for their own consumption. From *Minneapolis: Metropolis of the Northwest*, August 1931.

Strikebreakers hide their faces from the crowd during the Minneapolis Strutwear Plant strike, 1935. Strutwear's owners maintained that there was no dispute between the management and employees of the plant, but that the strike was run entirely by "outsiders."

Damage to the Flour City Company Building during the Ornamental Iron Strike in Minneapolis, 1935. Flour City's owners, too, insisted that none of its employees were on strike, but that the picketing of the plant was the work of "outsiders."

The 1934 Teamsters' Strike

Strikers with friendly policeman, Minneapolis, 1934. The complicity of the police during the "Battle of Deputies Run" infuriated members of the CA.

Deputy Sheriff George Hansen, his face bloodied from the fighting, converses with a police officer during the Teamsters' strike in Minneapolis, May 1934.

Police open fire on strikers who rammed a truck guarded by police, Minneapolis, July 20, 1934

The 1934 Teamsters' Strike

National Guard officers ensure the safe loading of a truck during the Teamsters' Strike in Minneapolis, 1934. Governor Olson called upon the Guard to "maintain order" when negotiations between employers and the union broke down.

"The other side": a pamphlet from the unions' perspective exhorts workers to "Support this Strike" and fight the CA's brutality against workers who "ask for a living wage."

Picketing at the Lincoln Manufacturing Company in Minneapolis on July 29, 1929. Workers' demands were simple, but CA policy precluded negotiation with unions.

The battle against socialism: Deputy United States marshals raid the Socialist Workers Party headquarters at 919 Marquette Avenue. *Minneapolis Morning Tribune*, June 28, 1941.

18 Regrouping for Labor's Second Onslaught

THE EXTRAORDINARY EVENTS OF 1934 focused a glaring spotlight on the inadequate preparations of the Citizens Alliance in the coal yards and loading docks of the city. The executive committee of the CA was convinced that a new department, "devoted to rendering more direct service to employers with respect to employment relations problems" was needed. On June 1, 1934, the Minneapolis Bureau of Industrial Relations (MBIR) was established to promote "harmonious employment relations" and prevent "serious industrial disputes which result from misunderstanding." Under this thinly veiled cover, Lloyd MacAloon would direct the CA's defense of the open shop.[1]

MacAloon, who had run the intelligence operation of the CA's Free Employment Bureau and Special Service and directed strike-fighting activities in the field, seemed a perfect choice for the task of halting the advance of unionism from the beachhead established by Local 574. With the aid of the NAM's legal department and the National Industrial Conference Board, MacAloon and the Bureau of Industrial Relations, operating out of their own office in the Plymouth Building, would attempt to guide the CA "through this wilderness of recovery, reform and social change."[2]

To establish a solid line of employer resistance, the MBIR developed and copyrighted a guide called "Employment Relations Policies and Rules and Regulations Governing Employment" for CA members. In accordance with the CA's open-shop philosophy, the MBIR's principles dictated that company management would be in complete control of all property, business, and the "direction and supervision of the working force," which included "the hiring, discharging, suspending and transferring of employees." The MBIR declared itself in "unalterable opposition to the closed shop," which was "an invasion of the constitutional rights of the American workman." In a direct attack on the Socialist Workers' Party leadership of Local 574, the policy denied employment to "any person whose principles or expressed beliefs are in opposition to the Constitution of the United States of America or the American principles of government."[3]

Advertised by the CA's *Special Weekly Bulletins* and a series of pamphlets, the MBIR principles quickly worked their way into the labor relations programs of Minneapolis companies. Despite the CA's lip-service acknowledgment of Section 7(a) giving employees the right to bargain collectively, the MBIR principles made it clear that the Minneapolis business community's war on union labor would continue unabated without regard for federal statutes or the realities of the 1934 Teamster strikes.[4]

Although the MBIR principles were really only a revision of the basic open-shop philosophy of the CA, its rules and regulations were an attempt to strengthen the anti-union position of every company. MacAloon realized that the surest defense against union organization was to eliminate the infiltration of organizers into the open-shop industries of the city. The MBIR tried to establish a "Basic Employment Relationship," under which management would "select new employees very carefully, not only from the stand point of skill and adaptability, but also considering personal make-up and congeniality, so that a spirit of friendliness and harmony may exist among employees and between employees and the Management." Each new employee was required to sign an "agreement of hire" acknowledging and consenting to the MBIR program.[5]

If personnel control methods failed, employees could be terminated for "violation of any law . . . any habits, demeanor, characteristics, action or course of action that make him objectionable to other employees, the public or to the management." Other reasons for termination included "union organization during working hours, conspiracies to slow down work or preaching or advocating doctrines of communism." If MacAloon could effectively introduce and maintain the MBIR programs throughout Minneapolis industry, the 1934 gains of the union movement would be stopped and eventually destroyed.

MacAloon set up the MBIR program in 140 businesses in four months, then developed an elaborate support system. To assess the most effective strategies, MacAloon designed and distributed a thorough questionnaire to determine the status of every employer with the following questions:

- Did their business operate across state lines and therefore fall under the purview of federal statutes?
- How did it deal with labor unions?
- Did it have a company union?
- What were its sources of labor supply?
- How did it handle its employees?
- What benefits did employees receive?[6]

More importantly, the bureau set up a complete personnel service for employers that did not maintain a personnel department. The records and experience of the CA Free Employment Bureau were used to supply open-shop workers and weed out union activists. The bureau also handled all cases before the National Labor Relations Board and dealt with the arrangements and procedures of NLRB-mandated elections. To avoid elections, the bureau helped draft constitutions and bylaws for employee representation plans. In the five months following the settlement of the 1934 strikes, MacAloon set up forty-four company unions. He had also advised the management of sixty-three companies involved in or threatened with strikes. In fact, MacAloon, with eight years of detailed union fighting behind him, would now lead the CA in its efforts to establish and maintain a consistent employment relations policy.[7]

MacAloon's efforts were aided dramatically on May 27, 1935, when the United States Supreme Court declared the National Recovery Administration unconstitutional. The right to organize that unions had acquired in Section 7(a) of the NIRA no longer existed. The union movement across the country quickly lost ground, with hundreds of thousands of new members deserting the ranks. Unemployment increased, hours of work lengthened, and wages dropped.[8]

The respite, however, was short-lived. In July of 1935, despite a determined lobbying campaign by the NAM, the National Labor Relations Act, also known as the Wagner Act, was passed. The new law protected the right of employees to organize and bargain through the representatives chosen by the majority. The act outlawed several unfair employer practices, including interference with employees' guaranteed rights, the support of company unions, and the refusal to bargain collectively with union representatives. A National Labor Relations Board (NLRB) was created to investigate problems with the power to issue orders against employers. The orders were enforceable by the United States Circuit Court of Appeals. MacAloon's labor relations program would now have to contend with a new set of laws weighted toward the continued existence of labor unions.[9]

Direct conflict between the growing union movement and companies following the policies of the MBIR was inevitable. At Flour City Ornamental Iron, Vice President Walter Tetzlaff, an important CA member, had successfully followed MacAloon's strategy. Under an employment policy agreed to with other ornamental iron manufacturers, the Flour City plant was operated on an open-shop basis with layoffs governed by employee merit. Using CA intelligence agents infiltrated into the plant, Tetzlaff was able to identify and discharge any suspected union sympathizers. Despite the difficulties of openly organizing in these hostile conditions, International Association of Machinists' (IAM) Ornamental Metal Workers Local 1313 demanded that Tetzlaff recognize the union, grant a forty-hour week, time-and-a-half overtime, seniority rights, and a wage raise. When negotiations failed, Local 1313 called a strike on July 11, 1935. That morning, only twelve employees were able to get through the mass of nearly 100 pickets stationed in front of the plant. The next day, Tetzlaff shut down the plant. MacAloon's policies were about to meet their first serious challenge.[10]

In an attempt to mediate the strike, United States Department of Labor Commissioner J. E. O'Connor met with MacAloon. The MBIR director advised O'Connor that the employers would never directly or indirectly make an agreement with the union. MacAloon concluded that any mediation effort would fail because of the manner in which Haas and Dunnigan had "shoved a settlement" down the throats of employers during the 1934 strike. When O'Connor suggested that various government contracts made a settlement imperative, MacAloon replied that he didn't give a damn about that.[11]

Reluctantly, MacAloon finally arranged a meeting in his office between eleven iron manufacturers and O'Connor in which the entire contingent insisted that no strike existed. E. R. Baker, the group spokesman, then unleashed "a tirade of abuse against the mayor, Governor Olson and President Roosevelt" and concluded "that goddamned old lady Perkins [Secretary of Labor Frances Perkins] sent you here to [Hermann] Husman [national representative for the IAM] and this gang [the union] so you are wasting your time trying to talk to us." After this well-rehearsed performance, the entire group walked out. It was clear that MacAloon's thinly veiled labor relations policy contained the same anti-union philosophy that the CA had enforced since 1903.

Adjusting strike strategy to the employee representation requirements of New Deal legislation, plant foremen and employees loyal to the company filed suit in Hennepin County District Court. Having failed in their attempt to get the NLRB to intercede, the employees charged that Local 1313 would cause great and irreparable injury to employees' rights and properties if it were not restrained. Flour City Vice President Tetzlaff testified that seventy-five employees had stated that "they are not out on strike, that the gangs of men outside the plant threatened them and prevented them from going to work." Tetzlaff insisted that "no strike whatsoever exists." The pickets, "all strangers to the business," had denied employees the right to work with "various assaults, intimidation and abuses."[12]

Although Judge Winfield W. Bardwell was on his summer vacation, he quickly issued a typical blanket restraining order that restricted pickets from using physical force or violence to intimidate Flour City workers or in any way restricting the access of workers to the plant. Unlike MacAloon's superficial adjustments to CA strategy, the union realized that the 1934 strike had changed the rules of the battle. The CA reported to its members that "violence and intimidation continued in defiance of the court's order. Because of the extremely large number of strangers on the picket lines, violators could not be identified and contempt proceedings could not be brought." The *Minneapolis Labor Review* reported: "The only effect of the injunction has been to strengthen and increase the picket lines at the Flour City."[13]

In an attempt to rally public opinion in the company's favor and put pressure on Thomas E. Latimer, Farmer-Labor mayor of Minneapolis, Tetzlaff placed a large ad in the Wednesday, July 24 edition of the *Minneapolis Journal*. Its headline announced: "NO STRIKE . . . BUT PICKETS FORCE PLANT TO CLOSE." Tetzlaff accused Local 1313 of calling the strike although "Not a single employee of our company went out on strike!" On July 11, an "organized mob of 150 or more pickets besieged our place of business, prevented our employees from going to work, threatened and assaulted them."[14]

Despite assurances from the mayor and police chief that the plant could reopen on July 22, another mob surrounded the plant and prevented all but five or six employees from entering the plant. Tetzlaff complained that the police had failed to protect "Minneapolis workmen in their right to earn a living for themselves and families," compelling Flour City Ornamental Iron Company to shut down its plant "until these employees can be given the protection they are entitled to against invasion of their rights by this union, which does not represent these employees and certainly has no right under our laws to prevent them from earning a living." The ad, however, had no immediate impact.

The next day, July 25, with picket lines holding, the Flour City employee group appealed to Mayor Latimer to restore law and order. At the invitation of the mayor, sixty employees met in his office and voted by secret ballot that they were completely satisfied with their jobs. The next day, Mayor Latimer, apparently impressed by the orchestrated appeal, and sixty-eight police officers safely escorted thirty workers into the plant. The CA had finally obtained the police protection that it had demanded.[15]

When word of Latimer's "treacherous deed" reached Teamsters' Local 574, the union quickly set its strike machinery in motion. By 4:30 P.M., over 1,000 pickets, many of them unemployed turned out by the union's Federal Workers Section, had formed a gauntlet along Twenty-seventh Avenue to greet the departing Flour City workers. The large police contingent was completely outnumbered and "powerless to cope with the mob." As the shaken workers were escorted away from the plant, their cars were stoned from all sides. To complete their intimidation of the management, the crowd also stoned police cars and the plant windows. Faced with a superior force, MacAloon and Tetzlaff closed the Flour City plant for a second time.[16]

With the Flour City plant shut down and trouble brewing at the Strutwear Knitting Company, the Citizens Alliance realized that its propaganda efforts following the 1934 strike had been inadequate. The Latimer administration would provide adequate police protection only if its hand were forced by public opinion. On August 14, the CA published the first issue of its *Industrial News Service (INS)* bulletin, which was "devoted exclusively to recording events and activities in the field of industry and business which do not ordinarily come to the attention of the average citizen." Because "anything which retards the progress and development of business and industry or interferes with its operation has a more direct effect upon the well-being and prosperity of all classes of citizens than is generally realized," the public had a right and need to be informed. The nine issues of INS published in 1935 attempted to focus public attention on the lawless violence that unions had let loose on the city at the Flour City and Strutwear strikes. Responsibility for this wave of anarchy was placed on the doorstep of the Communist leaders of Teamsters' Local 574. In addition to a mailing list of 10,000, copies of *INS* issues were sold to employers for two cents each for distribution to their employees.[17]

While the Flour City strike remained deadlocked, the Struthers family, represented for several years on the CA board of directors, discovered that a union-organizing nuisance at the Strutwear Knitting Company was rapidly escalating into a crisis. Carefully following the labor policies of the CA and the MBIR, the Strutherses had expanded from a small family business in 1916 to a thriving factory employing 1,133. Directed by MacAloon, the open shop and company union had enabled the company to maintain profits by depressing the wage scale to 30 percent below that of other cities. When union organizers arrived during the summer of 1935, company President Florence Struthers personally directed surveillance of the meetings. Strutwear knitters were called in to the company offices one by one and warned that any further union activity would bring the penalty of discharge. Between May and July, the leading spirits in the union drive were fired while other employees were placated with one dollar-a-week raises. Unable to have any impact on what Minneapolis labor activists felt was "one of the most infamous sweatshops in the city of Minneapolis," the Hosiery Workers' Union Local 38 struck on August 16.[18]

Claiming that "there was no dispute between Strutwear Knitting Company and its employees," Florence Struthers, advised by MacAloon, was determined to keep the plant operating. There would be no negotiations with "outsiders." When Strutwear employees showed up for work Friday morning, August 16, a large, belligerent crowd met them at the gates. Although the company had requested police protection, only eight police officers were present. Intimidated by the threatening pickets and the memory of Flour City, only fifty employees managed to enter the plant. Struthers and MacAloon, apparently unaffected by these threats, announced during the day that the company would reopen on Monday morning. Inexplicably, they had given Hosiery Workers' Local 38 and their allies an entire weekend to organize for the confrontation. Either MacAloon's intelligence system had failed to appreciate the Teamsters' policy of combating the CA in every strike, or he still felt that the Minneapolis Police Department could handle any situation.[19]

At 6:30 Monday morning, Strutwear employees arrived at the plant to find 400 to 600 pickets completely blocking Sixth Street in front of the factory. The Hosiery Workers' Union had been reinforced by the unemployed auxiliary of Teamsters' Local 574, Iron Worker's Local 1313 from the Flour City plant, and striking lathers. Using their clubs to clear the sidewalks, nearly 100 policemen managed to get several hundred workers into the plant. In the melee, Teamster leader Ray Dunne was isolated, beaten, and arrested. As news of the arrest and the morning battle spread, reinforcements swelled the picket line to a thousand union supporters. Strutwear described the day in newspaper ads as "the continued presence of a hostile and disorderly mob of several hundred, who surrounded our plant and virtually kept it in a state of siege throughout the entire day, terrified employees in the plant, causing two women to collapse from hysteria and fright." The other employees "were so frightened they could not work."[20]

MacAloon and the company conceded that they would have to close the plant. But first they had to clear the beleaguered employees from the plant. At 3:00 P.M., the Strutwear workers marched four abreast down Seventh Street towards the downtown department stores where it was hoped they would be able to escape. Although they were escorted by police to Seventh and Nicollet, the picket line moved with them, "jeering and hurling vile epithets and abuse at them." Local 574, anticipating the company's plan, stationed a picket detachment inside Dayton's Department Store. As Strutwear's male employees were escorted into the store, they were assaulted by the determined pickets. The Minneapolis Police Department had once again been unable to cope with the city's militant labor movement. Strutwear was forced to close.[21]

With two major plants shut down by union pickets, the open-shop regime of the CA was in danger of crumbling. Tetzlaff, desperate to start work on a million-dollar United States government contract, met with CA officials to work out a plan for reopening the Flour City plant. A committee was formed to investigate the feasibility of housing heavily guarded workers inside the plant, despite a 1933 city ordinance prohibiting this tactic. At 4:30 A.M. on Friday, September 6, a railroad car was pushed across the tracks into the back of the plant. Inside were thirty men, many of whom were private detectives from the Bergoff Agency in Chicago, plus guns, munitions, beds, and food, sent in as an advance guard to restart production and break the strike. Although Tetzlaff and the CA publicly announced the restart of production, the small force was better suited to prolonged siege warfare. When the union demanded that Mayor Latimer enforce the city ordinance and arrest Tetzlaff's troops and clear the plant, Tetzlaff appealed to Hennepin County District Court for an injunction on the grounds that the ordinance was unconstitutional. On Monday morning, Judge Edmund A. Montgomery issued a temporary order restraining the police chief from any interference. The CA had successfully made a direct challenge to Local 574's domination of the strike. The union's reply would not be long in coming.[22]

That evening, Local 1313 held a small demonstration, pelting the plant with bricks and rocks while police looked on. Tetzlaff and the CA, having learned of plans for an "even more violent riot" the next night, appealed to Mayor Latimer for police protection. Tuesday night several thousand men and women held a rally in a vacant lot across from the plant. Shortly before midnight the police attempted to disperse the crowd. An armored car drove into the street and fired a volley of tear gas into the rally. The pickets fled into adjoining streets but quickly rallied and attacked police along a block-long front. Freely swinging their clubs, police advanced against a barrage of stones and bricks. Casualties mounted as fallen pickets were trampled by the surging battle. After thirty minutes of vicious hand-to-hand combat, the area was vacated and quiet. The next morning, the *Minneapolis Journal* reported that the "Attempt to Storm Factory Where 25 Workers Are Lodged Fails" after "Police Rout Strike Attack With Tear Gas." Although fifty-five Minneapolis citizens had been injured in the pitched battle, the police had forcibly protected the company's property and its right to do business. MacAloon's gamble appeared to be working. The defeat, however, had only set the stage for a resurgence of labor's determination.[23]

As thousands of pickets and union sympathizers streamed into the area around the plant the next night, over 100 policemen reinforced with six armored cars grimly prepared for battle. By 10:00 P.M., the huge crowd had jammed Twenty-seventh Avenue, blocking streetcar traffic. An hour later, police inspector Fritz Ohman ordered his troops into action. The six armored cars revved their engines as they moved slowly up and down the street, forcing the crowd back and laying down a barrage of tear gas. The crowd scattered and then regrouped to rain stones down on the police and the plant. "About 11:30 P.M. firing broke out and police, armed with pistols and riot guns, set out to drive the pickets from the vicinity of the plant," according to the newspaper reports, "The injured were dropping all along 26th avenue." The appearance of ambulances and the stench of tear gas finally broke up the battle. For the next two hours, police fought to clear the streets around the plant. In the chaos of guerilla warfare, bullets whizzed through local alleys, often finding innocent victims. Frank Vinette was shot in the arm while sitting on his porch. One youth was shot dead on his way home from a church social; another high school student was cut down while watching from the curb. At General Hospital, "the corridors were literally running with blood for a time, as a steady flow of persons, bleeding from wounds, came in for treatment."[24]

Reaction to the carnage of Wednesday night's battle was immediate and dramatic. Local 574 declared: "Murder has been committed on the streets" of Minneapolis and blamed Tetzlaff, the CA, and Mayor Latimer. The *Minneapolis Labor Review* decried the deaths of two young men, "victims of the greed and violence that today has the social system in its grip." Governor Olson mobilized 300 National Guardsmen in St. Paul in case of continued violence and suggested that "the plant be closed immediately." Mayor Latimer issued this statement: "I have ordered police to clear all men out of the plant of Flour City Ornamental Iron Works. The presence of workmen and guards in the plant was one of the provocative causes of the riot." The CA complained bitterly that the plant had been "closed for the THIRD Time!" and continued to argue that there was no strike and no dispute between the management and the employees. Whatever violence and death occurred was entirely the fault of the Communist leaders, whose "inflammatory speeches" inspired the "riotous demonstrations." Although the violent tactics of the police had once again cleared the streets, the blood-soaked streets of Minneapolis had forced Mayor Latimer to abandon his support of "law and order" and relinquish victory to the determined forces of Local 574.[25]

One week after the deadly confrontation at the Flour City plant, Mayor Latimer announced that the Minneapolis Employer-Employee Board (MEEB) would attempt to mediate the city's industrial disputes. The MEEB's mission was to "act the role of a friendly, unbiased mediator seeking to be of help to the contending parties." It would not "take sides on a 'closed shop-open shop' issue." Local 574 immediately labeled the purportedly conciliatory MEEB a "Full-Blown Union-Busting Machine." The MEEB's credibility was further undermined by the conservative nature of its members. Under the influence of the CCA, Mayor Latimer had appointed three conservative union representatives, who were joined by the presidents of three companies which were long-time CA members: Donald Davis of General Mills, Robert F. Pack of NSP, and Sheldon Wood of Electric Steel. The board would be chaired by Charles A. Prosser, director of the Dunwoody Institute.[26]

An attempt to portray Prosser as impartial and Davis and Pack as independent of and out of sympathy with the CA had little effect. The *Northwest Organizer* identified Prosser as the "Director of Dunwoody Institute which had turned out scabs to work in opposition to the building trades mechanics, printers, and the machinists." Pack was accused of resorting "to every possible means of intimidation, including the time worn red scare, in his efforts to defeat unionization in his plants." Davis and General Mills had "for 15 years nurtured a company union in its plants." Wood was identified as a representative of the NAM, "which was widely recognized as the most vicious toward labor of any employer group." In addition, the MEEB was organized at the CCA's offices and the CCA funded its operations. There was little doubt as to which side of the labor-employer struggle the board would favor. Local 574 openly refused to submit any dispute to the board because it had no voice in selecting the labor representatives, who were all ultra-conservative, and because Dr. Prosser was an open-shop advocate.[27]

Despite Local 574's hostility, less-radical Minneapolis unions submitted over forty disputes to the board in its year of operation. The MEEB claimed to have averted nineteen strikes and settled twelve. During the fall of 1935, the board settled a strike at Minneapolis candy factories and was instrumental in preventing a strike of filling station employees on September 22, which had been rumored "to be the fuse for a general strike in this area." Less than a week after its creation, on September 6, the board offered its services to the officials of Flour City Ornamental Iron Works and the Strutwear Knitting Company. Tetzlaff responded that employees at Flour City "are conducting no strike against our company. Complete harmony exists between our employees and our firm." He then offered to supply the facts to the board to prove his assertions. The Strutwear Company informed the board that its plant had "been forcibly closed by outsiders through unlawful mass picketing and violent disturbances." Strutwear would consider employee grievances only after its employees, who have "no quarrel or dispute with us," are "permitted to exercise, and be protected in, their right to work."[28]

Despite Tetzlaff's hostility to mediation, the pressure to complete its large government-contracted orders was mounting at Flour City. The fatal September conflicts had made it clear that the company would not forcibly reopen its plant. Ignoring the board, MacAloon bargained directly with union attorney, John Goldie. Within days, Flour City and eight other ornamental iron companies filed an agreement with the NLRB. The employment policy of Ornamental Iron Manufacturers of Minneapolis "provided for the return of strikers, a minimum wage scale close to union demands, a forty hour week with time and a half for overtime and hiring and discharges based on seniority." The union filed a similar agreement that added the return of workers discharged for union activity before the strike.[29]

On Monday, September 23, the plant resumed operations. In that week's issue of the *Industrial News Service*, the CA informed the public: "No agreement was entered into between the ornamental iron companies and the union. The union voluntarily called off the strike." Although Local 574 realized that "the agreement leaves much to be desired," it suggested that "there is provided an excellent foundation from which a live union with aggressive shop committees can go forward to great gains." Faced with the immediate prospect of more deadly violence, both sides had decided to postpone the battle. The CA had denied the union recognition but had allowed the enemy to remain entrenched inside the iron industry's plants.[30]

With the Flour City strike settled, the CA was free to concentrate its efforts on the stalemate at Strutwear Knitting Company. The only way to reopen the plant was to obtain adequate protection from the Minneapolis Police Department. MacAloon and CA President George K. Belden devised a complex campaign to force the mayor's hand. First, the CA's friends on the City Council would attempt to secure a law-and-order resolution. Second, Strutwear would threaten to move its 1,100 jobs and its $25,000 weekly payroll to another city. Third, Belden would orchestrate a businessmen's committee to publicly pressure Latimer; and fourth, Strutwear workers would form a "club" to publicly plead for their jobs. Although Local 574 had shown no qualms in battling Minneapolis police in the streets in the past, a firm show of force by a Farmer-Labor mayor might yet provide a military victory and reopen the Strutwear plant.

The campaign was kicked off October 12, when conservative City Council members introduced a resolution claiming that strikes were giving Minneapolis "a very bad reputation throughout the nation and its business and industrial future is being seriously jeopardized." The resolution demanded that the mayor "take such action as will proclaim to the people of this city, state and nation that Minneapolis is determined to preserve the rights of its citizens and to again make this city a good place in which to live, work and to do business." If the situation continued, Strutwear Knitting Company could be expected to "accept one of the many offers made to them by cities in other states who are desirous of building up their industries and are offering unusual inducements, including several years free taxes, free rent and other attractive conditions." Finally, the resolution called for the mayor to provide the necessary police protection for the reopening of the Strutwear plant. Unfortunately for the CA, the council, on a thirteen-to-twelve vote, referred the matter to its police committee. When a large crowd gathered on October 21 to witness the deliberations, the committee, concerned about the City Council's lack of jurisdiction, voted four to one to table the resolution. The CA would have to find another venue to put pressure on Mayor Latimer.[31]

Several weeks later, the CA board of directors, along with several business leaders closely associated with the CA, formed a sponsoring committee to organize the business community to deal with the crisis. As a separate organization, a "citizens' committee" could disassociate itself from the anti-union record of the CA and pretend to consider the Strutwear problem from an impartial position. A mass meeting of approximately 300 Minneapolis business people was held at the Radisson Hotel on November 13 "for the purpose of considering ways and means of bringing about a reopening of the Strutwear Knitting Company plant." A committee of eleven was appointed "to call upon the mayor to maintain law and order and to provide such protection as to enable the Strutwear plant, in case it reopened, to continue operations."[32]

The committee was also to ask Strutwear to reopen and reemploy all workers as fast as possible and to confer with employees or their representatives about any grievances. CA President Belden was chosen to chair the "Citizens' Committee" in its effort to save Minneapolis from the "great danger" of losing the Strutwear Company to some other, more favorable locality. Within two days, Mayor Latimer had agreed in principle to the reemployment policy that the company had received from the Citizens' Committee. The union, afraid that its new members would be culled from the plant once they returned to work, refused to end its strike before it received recognition. At a second meeting on November 20, the Citizens' Committee resolved to continue its efforts to pressure Mayor Latimer.[33]

To intensify the out-of-state threat to Minneapolis industry, Strutwear quickly set up a dummy corporation in St. Joseph, Missouri. The Peacock Knitting Company, owned by the same people who owned Strutwear, brought an action in federal court to recover $5,000 of its goods from the Strutwear plant. When the writ was granted, it became the duty of the United States Marshal to move goods out of the closed Strutwear plant. In this unusual manner, MacAloon had maneuvered the United States government into a position of aiding the CA to break the strike. On Wednesday, November 7, trucks bearing signs that read, "This truck and its contents in the custody of the United States Marshal," drove into the Strutwear plant. The loading and movement of the property, primarily hosiery and underwear, was guarded by 100 Minneapolis policemen, sheriffs' deputies, and United States Marshal's deputies.[34]

Unfortunately for the CA, the trucks were furnished by Minneapolis transfer firms. When Local 574 threatened to strike the offending firms, the trucks were withdrawn from the operation. Two days later, the United States Marshal completed the move with trucks from the non-union Winona Dray Line. In spite of the heavy guard, "A comparatively small number of pickets vigorously stoned the trucks, smashing windshields," breaking over 100 plant windows, and injuring four Winona truck drivers. Armored cars were finally brought in to disperse the pickets so that the loading could continue. The business people's committee quickly used the move to pressure Mayor Latimer. F. H. Stinchfield, chairman of the November 13 meeting, told the *Journal* that "the decision of the company to move its supplies and machinery to St. Joseph made it appear that further work on the part of the committee would be useless." Three days later, after the threat had hopefully softened the mayor's stance, the committee reassured the city that the plant had not been moved: "There is the same hope the city has always had that some basis can be reached whereby the plant will reopen and this large army of employees given the work many of them so desperately need."[35]

A large delegation of Strutwear employees was also present at the November 13 meeting to announce that 900 employees had signed cards asking to return to work. With Mayor Latimer refusing to buckle under pressure, MacAloon devised a scheme to break the strike. The company organized a Back-to-Work Club that supposedly represented 900 of Strutwear's 1,100 employees. The club contended that the union represented "a very small minority of the employees," and was "causing distress and suffering to them and to their families." A committee representing the club petitioned the NLRB for a plant-wide election on November 21. On November 25, while the NLRB deliberated, Strutwear, wanting "to do everything possible to aid employees in securing their moral and legal rights," agreed to cooperate with a plant-wide election. Hosiery Workers' Local 38, which had a majority of the hosiery department employees, knew that it would lose in a plant-wide election.[36]

Regional Labor Board Director Robert M. Gates became suspicious of the Back-To-Work Club when he realized that letters from the club committee and the company were typed on the same typewriter. The committee chairman also told Gates: "I will get in touch with the company and find out from them definitely whether they want us to go on with this." Gates contended that the group, whether or not they really represented 900 workers, was not interested in bargaining collectively, was asking the NLRB to act as strikebreakers, and was acting in concert with the company. On December 16, the NLRB officially rejected the petition for investigation and certification. MacAloon's scheme had failed because of its obvious transparency.[37]

While MacAloon waited for an NLRB decision, Strutwear officially opened a branch in St. Joseph and began moving equipment into a four-story building. On December 7, Minneapolis newspapers announced that seventy-five employees from Minneapolis would open the new plant in a week. With pressure mounting, the Citizens' Committee held a series of "very satisfactory" conferences with Mayor Latimer. Finally, on December 9, the mayor gave in, writing the committee "to assure the citizens of Minneapolis that I will give them all of the protection necessary to conduct their business in a lawful and peaceful manner." The Farmer-Labor mayor endorsed the right-to-work principles of the open shop and promised: "When the plant is reopened I will use all the facilities of my office to see that law and order is maintained."[38]

Despite the mayor's surprising assurances, Strutwear President Florence Struthers reacted cautiously, stating that management was "anxious to reopen the plant here just as soon as possible, but that some of the manufacturing and sales operations have been moved to a branch plant in St. Joseph, Missouri where operations got under way today." Undoubtedly realizing that Latimer would also face increasing pressure from Minneapolis unions and the Farmer-Labor Party, MacAloon had decided to maintain the threat of losing the Strutwear plant.[39]

On Christmas Eve, the Citizens Alliance's patience finally ran out. The Strutwear Company broke off all negotiations and announced that the plant would be reopened under non-union conditions the day after Christmas. On December 26, thirty-five Strutwear maintenance workers attempting to ready the plant for reopening were greeted by hundreds of pickets. A rain of stones broke plant and car windows as an outnumbered police squad unsuccessfully attempted to protect the maintenance workers. The next morning, the CA Businessmen's Committee issued a statement deploring that "mob rule and brute force has prevailed as demonstrated by the violence and disorder which occurred at the plant Thursday night" and calling on Mayor Latimer "to take such steps as are necessary to bring about the maintenance of law and order." Latimer claimed that the Minneapolis police force was "entirely too small to effectively handle such a situation as has arisen" and would not be able to "prevent injury to persons, possibly resulting in death and damage to property." Latimer and Sheriff Wall requested that Governor Olson call out the National Guard to "take charge of the district."[40]

Within hours, a platoon of seventeen soldiers from the 135th Infantry under the command of Captain Owen J. Trainor entered the plant and announced that it was now closed. Mayor Latimer told military authorities that the only way to prevent disorder and destruction of life and property was to close the plant. Captain Trainor and a detail of sixty-five guardsmen were left to guard the empty plant. Only two maintenance men per shift were allowed in with military passes. The National Guard was now being used to defeat the CA's support of one of its staunchest members.[41]

Florence Struthers, president of Strutwear, demanded "free and unlimited access to and use of our own property by our firm and its employees" and threatened legal action for the "unlawful seizure of our plant." The Businessmen's Committee met at the Radisson Hotel and unanimously formed a committee to aid Strutwear's legal battle. CA Chairman Belden, who was also a member of the Businessmen's Committee, declared that "law and order does not exist in Minneapolis" and that "the forces of government . . . are being used . . . to oppress law abiding citizens." Within three weeks, a bill of complaint was served in United States District Court on the governor and the mayor, ordering them to appear before a three-judge court on January 25, 1936. Before Mrs. Struthers received her day in court, however, the state and the city argued among themselves about who was in charge of the National Guard troops in the Strutwear plant. The adjutant general's counsel informed the mayor that the troops "were there under the direction of the Sheriff and the mayor," while the city attorney claimed that the commander-in-chief had to take ultimate responsibility. In the face of Strutwear's litigation and the mayor's evasive responses, Governor Olson ordered the withdrawal of the National Guard on January 27, 1936.[42]

With the National Guard removed from the strike, MacAloon was ready to resume negotiations and continue pressure on Local 38 and Mayor Latimer. By the end of January, over $150,000 worth of machinery and goods had been trucked to St. Joseph, Missouri. Nearly 100 Strutwear employees had been transported to St. Joseph, where they were put up in the city's best hotel, met by representatives of the Welcome Wagon, and given charge accounts with local merchants. On February 8, Belden and his committee again met with Latimer and were again secretly assured that the mayor would, within two or three days, "take steps to stop violence and lawlessness and give these employers protection."[43]

Five days later, twenty Strutwear employees entered the plant and started operating some of the machinery. For their safety and protection, the workers were housed inside the plant. On Monday, February 17, pickets paraded around the plant shouting threats and breaking plant windows with rocks. Belden informed the mayor that "the reasons for our Committee withholding publicly no longer exist. Unless you forthwith enforce the law, suppress disorder and permit the orderly operation of this business, as you have repeatedly promised, you are deliberately misleading our Committee and the public, and are working hand in hand with the forces of disorder."[44]

The Strutwear Company also initiated an aggressive legal campaign. One suit sought $101,500 in damages from the governor and adjutant general for the National Guard's forced closing of the plant. On February 24, the company also applied for a temporary injunction against Local 38, Teamsters' Local 574, and ninety-six individual defendants "to enjoin mass and mob picketing at the Strutwear plant" so that employers could return to work and "have free access to the plant without being subjected to intimidation or physical violence."[45]

Strutwear lawyers also requested restraint against "hurling any missile" at the plant, addressing to employers "any vile, indecent, or insulting epithets of any kind," and placing employees in fear of bodily harm. Through the March trial, local labor papers reported the sensational testimony of Strutwear employees "satisfied" with thirteen-dollar-per-week wages and their fear of joining a union without company approval. Florence Struthers testified to the similarity of workers to jungle animals and to the honesty of MacAloon. The reason for the failure of negotiations became apparent when Mrs. Struthers declared that she saw "no reason why we should deal with an organization that is not legally an organization in this country or in any state." Despite the negative publicity, the company continued to insist that it would reopen soon.[46]

As the injunction hearing wore on, the absolute intransigence of the company, the union's distrust of the courts, and the impending reopening of the plant finally eroded the union's insistence on union recognition. MacAloon, sensing the union's weakened stance, used the assistance of federal labor conciliator Robert Mythen to convince Struthers to put her earlier offers into an official statement. On April 3, she wrote the union to announce that the plant would reopen April 6, 1936. All employees as of August 15 would be returned to work without discrimination because of membership or non-membership in a labor union; arbitration would determine the status of the eight discharged workers; and "the Company will meet at any reasonable time with any employee or representative of employees for the purpose of discussing any complaint affecting employee's employment with the Company." The next day, the union officially capitulated to an agreement that had been on the table for the entire strike. Local 38 would now once again attempt to organize in a hostile open-shop environment. The CA informed its members that its representatives had "worked diligently and patiently to bring about a termination of this deplorable situation."[47]

Within two weeks of the union's capitulation, the Strutwear Company announced that the settlement did not mean it would be operating a union or closed shop and set a new policy for union activities: "The management cannot permit rivalries and controversies to be built up among employees over the question of unionism. The management must demand a harmonious and friendly relationship as between and among employees as well as between employees and management. Any employee who conducts himself in any other manner will be summarily dealt with. . . . Union organization activities must be carried on outside of working hours and off the premises of the company."[48]

It was clear that MacAloon and Strutwear had no intention of honoring the no-discrimination clause of the settlement. Within two months, however, the NLRB had stepped in to stop the company's "open campaign of coercion and intimidation." Strutwear denied these charges but admitted that intense rivalries between union and non-union employees might make it necessary "to take some very definite action against those responsible." Stymied, the company immediately renewed their threat to move to St. Joseph.[49]

In reviewing the final six months of 1935, the CA blamed the strikes on the "complete failure of the duly constituted authorities to maintain law and order." Although the CA had emerged victorious from both the Flour City and the Strutwear strikes, the violent upheavals had buoyed the fighting spirit of the city's unions and undermined the confidence of CA members. While these battles raged, other firms quietly avoided a similar conflict by signing union contracts. Particularly threatening was the organization of Minneapolis Moline, the second-largest manufacturing firm west of Chicago and an important CA member. When faced with the fact that Machinists' Local 382 had organized over 1,000 men on an industrial basis, the company quickly signed a contract to avoid a strike. Local 574 continued to expand and solidify its leadership of the growing union movement.[50]

By May of 1936, the Teamsters' local had organized 90 percent of the transport industry and appeared ready to continue its assault on the CA's domination of Minneapolis industry. Its success, however, had angered International Brotherhood of Teamsters (IBT) President Daniel J. Tobin. Local 574's radical and independent actions had violated both Tobin's conservative craft union philosophy and the power structure of the IBT. On April 15, Local 574 had received the news that their charter as a union in the IBT and AFL had been revoked. They would have to proceed as an isolated, independent union. In November, AFL representative Meyer Lewis had come to Minneapolis to purge the labor movement of Communists, particularly "a small group of communists using 574 as a shield to work behind." The CA, fresh from two stirring victories, faced the future with the same determination that it had displayed since 1903.[51]

19 *The Birth of Associated Industries*

BY THE SUMMER OF 1936, ominous clouds had once again begun to threaten the CA's position. Teamsters' Local 544 (formerly 574) had made peace with the American Federation of Labor and had been accepted back into the fold in a body. Despite a so-called Red purge, 544 leaders Miles Dunne, Farrell Dobbs, Carl Skoglund, and William Brown had retained their leadership positions and would now lead an intensive state-wide campaign of union expansion. In addition, the union announced that it would cooperate with all other unions involved in labor controversies.[1]

Within days of its July 20 reinstatement in the AFL, Local 544 had "fink" squads combing the city, pressing all truck drivers to join the union. The CA accused the union of strong-arm tactics and increased its own organizing, signing up 126 new business firms in the first six months of 1936. By early August, the CA reported to its members that the leaders of Local 544 were boasting that "they are going to make Minneapolis the strongest closed-shop union town in the country. To this end, Communist and AFL leaders are working hand in hand." These leaders "do not fear, nor anticipate any restraining influence by law enforcement agencies. Sheer force will be relied upon to force the closed union shop upon both employers and workers." Attempting to ignite the fighting spirit of the Minneapolis business community, the CA asked, "Is Minneapolis ready to accept closed union shop dictatorship?"[2]

On July 24, Local 544 sent written demands to wholesale grocers insisting upon a closed-shop contract, the representation of inside workers, and an immediate wage raise. The wholesale grocery firms, many of which had fought the bitter 1934 strike against the Teamsters, refused to even negotiate with a union committee. Although several grocery firms showed a desire to avoid confrontation, threats of financial reprisals from the CA's bankers tightened the ranks of the CA members under attack. Despite the companies' complaint that none of their workers belonged to Local 544, the union went out on strike on August 20. According to the CA, Local 544 employed its usual "rule or ruin" policy in its attack on the food industry.[3]

Local 544, which considered the strike "the gravest crisis that has confronted it since the 1934 strikes," began picketing the struck firms with its usual efficiency. Cruising squads shut off the resupply of the wholesale firms. With their employees intimidated by Local 544 pickets, Minneapolis Allied Grocers, Inc., was compelled to close its warehouse "in order to avert loss of life, bodily injury, and damage to property such as occurred in the strike of 1934." Sixteen other wholesalers, including Red Owl and National Tea and the suppliers of Piggly Wiggly and IGA stores, quickly followed suit and closed their doors. Except for milk, bread, meat, and vegetable and produce supplies, Local 544 had shut off the resupply of the city's non-union grocers.[4]

The CA's warning of a coordinated attack against Minneapolis employers was confirmed when the Flour, Cereal, Feed and Elevator Workers' Local 19152 struck the terminal grain elevators on the same day as the start of the grocery strike. Local 19152 had asked for a ten-cent wage increase, union recognition, and the closed shop. Although some flour mills agreed to the wage raise, most of them preferred to close their plants before negotiating with the union. The major mills, Washburn-Crosby and Pillsbury, refused to even bargain collectively with the union.[5]

Within a week, the union had forced all terminal elevators, the Russell-Miller Milling Company, the Minneapolis Milling Company, the linseed mills, and four or five feed mills to close. The elevator owners publicly claimed that their employees were not union members and that outside agitators were once again causing the trouble. The strikers briefly allowed the Archer-Daniels-Midland (ADM) linseed mill to reopen on August 28 but then forcibly reentered the plant three days later, shut off the power, and warned workers to stay away. On September 3, union pickets surrounded the Pillsbury "A" Mill, one of the largest flour mills in the country, preventing the day shift from entering the mill. Mill managers, expecting little or no "assistance from the city administration and police force in preventing violence on the picket lines," shut down Minneapolis's milling industry. *The Northwestern Miller* and the CA claimed that Teamsters' Local 544 was involved in organizing the strike and manning the picket lines. *The Northwest Organizer* considered the strike "one of the most significant events in local labor struggles. Owners of mills and terminal elevators rank as the financial giants of the northwest." They also formed the financial backbone of the CA. The defeat of Local 19152 quickly became a critical last stand in the CA's defense of the open shop.[6]

The CA, recognizing the leverage that the Teamsters' union could exert on the food industry, quickly directed a counterattack. Hoping to turn public opinion against the strikers, a series of full-page advertisements intended to scare the public were placed in the *Tribune* and the *Journal*. The thick, dark letters headlining the ads proclaimed: "Food Shortage. The avenues of food distribution have been lawlessly choked off by picketing activities and threats of violence" by "a handful of men who are attempting to force all Minneapolis business concerns to operate under permit from them." Another ad warned, "If this small band of agitators succeeds in gaining its selfish ends in the present food strike, then it is too late for citizens to protect themselves. Other strikes are certain to follow and these agitators will set themselves up as dictatorial rulers of all Minneapolis business." The Hennepin County Farmers' Protective Association, which the labor papers and the Farm Holiday Association labeled a pseudo-organization controlled by the CA, claimed that "our products are in the fields rotting." *The Northwest Organizer* counterattacked, proclaiming that "Local 544 Shows That Food Is Plentiful Here Despite Bosses' Lies." The *Minneapolis Labor Review* listed the grocery stores that had signed union contracts and were fully stocked.[7]

The CA sent out invitations for a mass meeting the same week, asking business and professional people, "Are you an American Citizen?" and "Have You Red Blood in Your Veins?" and "Should Minneapolis be rid of the Communist leaders of the group which is attempting to force its selfish demands on an otherwise peaceful and prosperous society?" On Monday, August 31, hundreds of CA faithful gathered in the Gold Room at the Radisson Hotel to take steps toward restoring industrial peace. CA attorney Arnold L. Guesmer, who presided over the meeting, urged all Minneapolis citizens to come to the aid of the food industry, declaring that control of the food supplies means virtual control of the city. Guesmer accused Local 544 of "carrying on an organized campaign of terrorism, riots, violence, assaults and extortion."[8]

Civic and Commerce Association President Herbert J. Miller complained that "an irresponsible element had gained control of an organization which could eliminate it and set up a dictatorship not only over business but over the city government." Two specific demands emerged from the three-hour meeting. First, that Mayor Thomas Latimer enforce the laws which protect the rights of business owners to operate their companies and employees their right to work; and, second, that businesses and law-abiding citizens support the city to help labor purge its ranks "of the lawless, irresponsible leadership."[9]

In another attempt to end Local 544's assault on the food industry, the Minneapolis Employer-Employee Board announced on August 27 that it would mediate the dispute only if the union drivers returned to work and the wholesale grocers reopened by 9:00 A.M. the next Monday. Local 544, which had repeatedly refused to submit controversies to the board in the past, stated: "We attempted negotiations several weeks before the strike was called and we will not give in now until our demands are met." For the Teamsters' local, the key issue was union recognition, and it was not debatable.[10]

The CA quickly used the Local 544 refusal to accept this supposedly neutral mediation as a propaganda weapon against the union. When Governor Petersen held conferences with representatives of the wholesale grocers on September 5, they cited Local 544's refusal to accept mediation as the reason for the strike. Although it had fifteen other cases pending, the MEEB voted unanimously to resign because the board was "unable to perform its proper function of mediation and conciliation. . . . This situation resulted from the refusal of certain groups in the organized labor movement to cooperate with the board by asking or accepting its help before calling strikes." The CCA-sponsored effort to short-circuit the Teamsters' direct-action tactics had been frustrated at every turn by Local 544's refusal to cooperate. Recognizing failure, MEEB Secretary Frank J. Miller resigned from the board on September 8, only to show up at the bargaining table representing the wholesale grocery firms the next day.[11]

During the second week of September, Governor Petersen held a series of conferences with state and city law enforcement agencies and representatives of both the employers and employees. Harrison H. Whiting, president of Pillsbury Flour Mills, was informed that the governor would not call out the National Guard. Lack of support from the state Farmer-Labor administration, however, was hardly a surprise and had little impact on the CA. Frank Miller informed federal conciliator Mythen that he would definitely not recommend that the grocers sign a contract with Local 544, and on September 14 stated that the "employers just intended to fight it out." At 7:00 A.M. the next day, twenty-five police officers were on duty at the linseed mill of prominent CA member Archer-Daniels-Midland at Twenty-ninth and University Avenue South East. About sixty non-strikers were escorted into the plant before pickets arrived. At 9:30, several more automobile loads of non-strikers were convoyed in to help reopen the plant. As the picket line tightened and scuffles broke out, additional replacement workers were turned back. ADM President Shreve M. Archer announced that he would discuss problems with employees but that the company did not "care to negotiate through the union." The stage was once again set for an escalation into violence.[12]

At General Mills, company president Donald Davis had had enough. In disgust at the impotence of the MEEB, Davis had tendered his resignation to Mayor Latimer. Now, with flour production at a standstill, violence threatened the industrial production of Minneapolis for the third straight year. On September 15, Davis met with federal conciliator Robert Mythen. The next day, 450 employees reopened the great Washburn-Crosby mill without union interference. Union representative Meyer Lewis announced that the union had "no controversy with Washburn-Crosby Co, the management and the employees are sitting down together to discuss the situation." The baffled CA reported to its members that Washburn-Crosby had reached some arrangement but that the CA had no idea what it was.[13]

In fact, Davis had agreed with the United States Department of Labor to negotiate with the union and sign a contract reflecting the results. Conferences between the company and the union to discuss wages, hours, and working conditions were started immediately. Within a week Charles C. Bovey, chairman of Washburn-Crosby Company, had signed a stipulation with the Department of Labor. Without consulting the CA, one of its primary financial backers for thirty-three years, Washburn-Crosby, had agreed to recognize the union. The company, perhaps recognizing the inevitable, had abandoned its twenty-year-old company union program. Davis announced that General Mills' new labor policy would be to negotiate "under such procedures and methods as might be determined by the employees themselves or through representatives of their own choosing."[14]

The day after Davis's momentous decision, the tense standoff at the ADM linseed oil mill exploded when a railway coach, filled with heavily armed special guards deputized by Sheriff Wall at the request of the CA, was pulled into a siding. Over 600 pickets swarmed forward up an embankment, hurling rocks through the smashed windows of the coach. A burst of shotgun fire from the coach quickly drove the attackers back. Although Sheriff Wall claimed that the deputies shot in the air, one picket was hit in the leg by a shotgun slug.[15]

Within an hour, the pickets had reorganized and charged again. This time, however, flaming torches were thrown into the coach. While a switch engine tried desperately to move the car, the fire quickly caught hold, forcing the deputies to flee for their lives. A police detail rushed forward to escort the deputies through the picket lines and into the plant while the flames consumed the rest of the coach. Despite their lack of munitions, the union pickets had dispersed the sheriff's special deputies in a show of violent force. The sheriff's vow to "give protection to those who ask" had done little to save ADM's rail coach or the numerous plant windows broken in a rain of stones.[16]

As midnight approached on Monday, the plant was surrounded by 500 pickets. Using heavy slingshots, two-man crews shot rocks and pieces of metal at the plant windows and searchlights illuminated the perimeter of the grounds. While special deputies and police guarded the gates, gasoline-soaked rags were tossed inside a tank and machine shop and ignited. By 12:45 A.M., the interior was ablaze and flames shot through the roof. Although the crowd held its fire while firefighters fought the fire, an unconscious searchlight operator and two other guards were taken away by ambulance. One strike sympathizer was taken to General Hospital with scalp wounds. At 2:00 A.M., the tense standoff continued between the large crowd of pickets and Minneapolis police. The next morning, newspapers reported that Sheriff Wall would ask for the National Guard "if there is any more trouble."[17]

Apparently reassessing the situation overnight, Sheriff Wall wrote Governor Petersen on September 22 requesting National Guard troops to aid in the preservation of law and order. Wall claimed that "rioting had been rampant in Minneapolis . . . impairing the lives, health and property of the citizens." He cited gunshots the previous night at ADM and the closing of a "large number of both wholesale and retail grocery stores. . . . Due to the closing of these stores, a number of people have been unable to obtain food in the city of Minneapolis and the situation is rapidly growing acute." Wall informed the governor that the situation was "beyond the control of the present civil authorities." Herbert Miller, CCA president, Shreve Archer of ADM, and Edwin Lindello, secretary of the Minnesota Law and Order League, accompanied the sheriff to the Capitol to lobby for troops to enforce the CA's defense of the open shop.[18]

Governor Petersen, after meeting with union and business leaders, ordered Adjutant General Colonel Nelson to "hold in readiness a sufficient force of the National Guard to meet any emergency." Nelson mobilized 400 National Guardsmen, 150 of whom were in the 151st Field Artillery in the Minneapolis Armory. The force would be under the command of Brigadier General George E. Leach, former mayor of Minneapolis. Despite Sheriff Wall's appeal, however, the troops remained in the St. Paul and Minneapolis armories. Governor Petersen called for a quick settlement of the strike and refused to reopen the mills under the protection of the National Guard.[19]

As the troops mobilized, the CA pressed its demands for law and order. The Hennepin County Chapter of the Law and Order League, closely associated with the CA, attacked Mayor Latimer for "shirking responsibilities" during the strike. At the same time, Pillsbury Flour Mill officials met with United States mediators and union representative Meyer Lewis. Within hours, Pillsbury President Harrison H. Whiting and Chairman of the Board John S. Pillsbury had signed a stipulation with the United States Department of Labor agreeing to meet with union representatives "for the purpose of establishing labor relations policies governing wages, hours and working conditions and to carry out the policies duly adopted at such conferences."[20]

By June 1, 1937, Pillsbury had signed a contract with the AFL to recognize the union in all its plants where union members were in the majority. The same day, Flour, Cereal, Feed and Elevator Workers' Local 19152 signed an agreement governing wages in the company's Minneapolis mills. Pillsbury had joined General Mills in abandoning the non-union shop policies of the CA. The flour-milling giants of the Northwest that had been the backbone of the CA for thirty-three years had abandoned the open shop.[21]

The defection of CA members from the fold continued to mount the next day when Shreve Archer of ADM met with Mythen and Governor Petersen. Although Archer had been willing to lead the CA's fight to reopen his mill, two days of violence had apparently changed his mind. Before leaving the meeting, Archer signed a stipulation similar to the Washburn-Crosby and Pillsbury agreements. ADM would discuss labor policies with union representatives and abide by the results of the negotiations. On September 25, 900 men returned to work in ADM mills and elevators where deputy sheriffs and pickets had battled four days earlier. Governor Petersen declared that the "mobilization of the Guard immediately restored peace and order and brought to a head negotiations" and demobilized the Guard.[22]

That evening, the governor went on the radio to pronounce that "all recognize certain fundamental rights have now been established. Among these are, First: The right to organize. Secondly: The right of labor to bargain collectively through its own representatives. . . . If the employers, whether in Minneapolis or elsewhere, will live up to the law of the land and recognize these elementary rights of labor, we will avoid most of these difficulties." With the capitulation of ADM and the removal of the National Guard, the CA's future looked increasingly bleak.[23]

Despite the capitulation of the major flour mills, most Minneapolis grain elevators and feed mills remained closed. After additional conferences with the governor and Robert Mythen, these employers also agreed to the Washburn-Crosby settlement. The union, however, perhaps realizing its growing power, now rejected the proposal. New conditions, demanding official union recognition, seniority rights, all workers returned to work at once, no discrimination against union workers, and collective bargaining, were submitted to Cargill Elevator Company and other companies. Outraged, the employers demanded the same terms as those of the flour-mill operators.[24]

While Mythen tried to reconcile the two sides, the employers sent their employees a letter falsely implying that Mythen had given his assurance that picketing would end once the companies posted a notice similar to the settlement agreed upon at the flour mills. Ignoring this devious attempt to avoid negotiation, Mythen developed his own compromise settlement, which he submitted to the employers on October 5. The CA, desperately trying to hold the line, managed to convince its members to reject the proposal. The mill strike negotiations had once again deadlocked.[25]

The struggle between Local 544 and the grocery industry had also intensified during September. With employers still refusing to negotiate, the Teamsters had voted to shut down all deliveries to chain stores in the neighborhoods. Without milk, ice, meat, or groceries by the last week in September, Thomas and Piggly Wiggly shut down their chain stores. When the smaller, independent grocery wholesalers tried to settle, CA bankers threatened financial reprisals to force them to reconsider. The effective picketing of Local 544 showed no signs of weakening. When grocery store managers tried to resupply their stores, they were attacked by pickets and the merchandise destroyed. A strikers' commissary fed 150 workers daily, while money to support the strike poured in from other unions and farmers' organizations. Although conferences between Local 544 and the employers continued, little progress was made. Both sides still apparently thought that they were winning the war of attrition, while the grocery industry was slowly being strangled.[26]

On October 1, in an attempt to break the deadlock, Governor Petersen and conciliator Mythen drafted a compromise proposal that would return all strikers to work without discrimination, recognize the International Brotherhood of Teamsters, and set up negotiations for determining hours, wages, and other conditions of employment. The next day, the employers agreed with the provision that they could also negotiate with other duly chosen representatives of their employees. The union met this thinly disguised attempt to legitimize company unions with a demand for the specific recognition of Local 544 and seniority rights. On October 5, Governor Petersen and Mythen finally convinced the employers to recognize Local 544 and begin negotiations.[27]

Three days later, a chastened CA reported the settlement to its members without comment. The wholesale grocers had recognized Local 544, agreed not to discriminate against union members, granted seniority rights, included inside workers and warehousemen, limited hours to forty-four to forty-eight per week with time-and-one-third for overtime, set drivers' minimum pay at sixty cents per hour, and granted one week paid vacation. *The Northwest Organizer* declared it "one of the most important victories achieved by General Drivers Union since August of 1934." Within a short time, employers in the coal and transfer industries signed contract renewals and the big department stores signed an agreement for the first time. Once again, a successful Teamsters' strike was rippling across Minneapolis industry.[28]

The defection of the wholesale grocers and Governor Petersen's push for a settlement of the mill strike brought an immediate and desperate reaction from the mill operators. On October 6 and 7, the Twin City Trading Company and the Pioneer Steel Elevator Company reopened their elevators despite continued picketing. Plans to reopen other elevators were quickly drawn up.

Sheriff Wall moved deputies into the plants to provide protection. Predictably, violence erupted at both plants their first night back in operation. At Twin City Trading Company, a lead pipe "bomb" exploded near a transformer. Wall and the Minnesota Law and Order League immediately asked Governor Petersen for troops "in the interest of law and order and for the protection of citizens in their normal lawful activities." If the National Guard intervened, the Citizens Alliance might be able to break the strike and maintain the open shop.[29]

While Sheriff Wall's deputies prepared for a final confrontation, officials of the King Midas Mill Company, the Russell-Miller Milling Company, several feed mills, and the remaining terminal elevators continued negotiations. On October 8, the Flour, Cereal, Feed and Elevator Workers' Union voted to accept a proposal for the employers to post notices of their willingness to return all strikers to work without discrimination, to meet with the duly chosen representatives of the employees to establish labor relations policies, and to hold elections to determine representation if requested by the employees. The employers agreed to be bound by the results of any elections and to deal and bargain collectively with the representatives of the majority of the employees. More than 1,200 men returned to work in forty plants. All grain elevators and flour and feed mills were operating for the first time since August 19.[30]

With the defection of the flour mills and grocery industry, the CA was faced with a stark fact: Minneapolis employers would now negotiate and even sign contracts with labor unions. Five weeks later, his life's work shattered, A. W. Strong suddenly fell ill and had an abdominal operation on November 19. Six days later, the CA's leader was dead. In a memorial in a *Special Weekly Bulletin,* the CA said that it "deeply mourns his loss. We shall miss his judgment and sound advice at the council table, as well as his courageous leadership." A founding member and longtime director of the Citizens Alliance, the Civic and Commerce Association, and the Minnesota Employers' Association, Strong had dedicated himself to the destruction of labor unions and the establishment of a society dominated by business. Strong had commanded the respect and fear of business people and manufacturers in Minneapolis and had been influential with national business leaders in Washington. While evangelizing the cause of individualism, Strong had ruthlessly unified the Minneapolis business community into a thirty-three-year crusade against the organization of Minneapolis working men and women. The relentless organizational assault of Teamsters' Local 544, however, had destroyed the basic tenet of Strong's philosophy. Labor unions were now an indisputable part of Minneapolis industrial life. If the Minneapolis employers were to maintain their dominance of the city's economic life, a new anti-union strategy would have to be developed. With the fateful death of Albert W. Strong, the CA was poised on the edge of a new era.[31]

CA President George K. Belden took quick and decisive action. On December 17, a new constitution and bylaws were adopted and the name of the Citizens Alliance was changed to Associated Industries (AI) of Minneapolis. On January 7, a press release announced the formation of a "new organization to meet present day trends" and simultaneously that the CA had "passed out of existence." The press release failed to mention that the officers, board of directors, members, financial balance, and offices of the two organizations were identical. The new AI was "to take a leading part in promoting and encouraging industrial peace and in placing Minneapolis industry at least on a par with its competitors in other cities."[32]

Industrial peace, of course, did not include the acceptance of Local 544 or its Communist leadership. AI was "pledged to a policy of protecting to the fullest extent, both labor and industry against racketeering." The rest of its labor relations program was cooperation with proper mediation boards and seeking cooperation of the public through the formation of an advisory committee of representative citizens to advise the board of directors. The committee would convey the true facts concerning industrial disputes to the public and also "assist in the solution of such problems." Proclaiming a mission of peace, the CA—now called AI—would now attempt to disassociate itself from its thirty-three-year history of often-violent union suppression.[33]

The new AI constitution reflected the adjustments of the business community to the harsh realities of union organization. While the original CA constitution stated simply that its object was "to uphold the principle of the Open Shop," AI proclaimed four lengthy principles dealing with employee rights. Employees had the right to

1. "Bargain collectively, free from coercion, intimidation or interference from any source,"
2. "Remain at work of their own free will, free from interference, intimidation and violence, when others have abandoned their jobs,"
3. "Seek, secure and retain employment, free from coercion or interference from any source, regardless of religious, political or labor affiliation," and
4. "Deal with employer and employees as individuals, on a basis mutually beneficial and satisfactory."[34]

The principles of the AI constitution, in essence, were exactly the same as those of the CA, the principles of the open shop. The practical reality of their application, however, was quite different. For three decades, the CA's open-shop principle had functioned as a thinly disguised rationale for the *non-union* shop. By 1937, however, unions were an established fact of industrial life in Minneapolis. The AI constitution, in fact, recognized the right of employees to strike, although this "should be the right to peacefully strike, not the right to resort to violence or intimidation." The new principles expressed the CA's fear of the closed union shop and defined the strategy that AI would now employ. While the open shop had only been a rationalization for the CA's anti-union policies, it would now become the goal of AI in its defensive battle against the Teamster-led onslaught of union organization.[35]

The new constitution also revealed some of AI's strategies for slowing the union advances of the previous three years. To maintain industrial peace and prosperity, "every possible effort should be exerted to avoid strikes or lockouts and to compose difficulties in an amicable and peaceful manner. . . . To prevent or adjust actual labor disputes, in the interest of public welfare," AI approved of "voluntary arbitration dealing with the facts, not the principles." When agreements were reached, the AI constitution favored legislation to make contracts legally binding on unions. Dealing directly with the threat of Local 544, principle twelve stated that "racketeering in the field of labor relations, under which either employee or employer is subjected to force, fear or intimidation must be vigorously opposed."

To enforce its defense against the Trotskyite-led Teamsters, AI asked that "state laws and city ordinances, passed for the protection of life and property, must be impartially enforced at all times by duly constituted authorities." Although Local 544 was never mentioned by name, the Teamsters' success in challenging the CA had forced the creation of AI and necessitated the new, more elaborate, and carefully cloaked constitution. The leaders of Teamsters' Local 544 were not fooled by the new organization. On January 14, a *Northwest Organizer* editorial announced "The Leopard Changes Its Spots." The "defunct" CA believed in "head on collisions with labor organizations and believed in beating the unions down with brute force." But *The Northwest Organizer* pointed out: "Minneapolis is now an ORGANIZED TOWN," the CA would have to devise "a newer, more subtle and more sinister method of dealing with labor unions." The new policy of AI would call for "a small army of trained employer representatives, labor conciliators and employer relations directors. Their policy will be to outmaneuver the unions in negotiations, write union agreements with double meanings and buy off union representatives with money or favors."[36]

Although AI was made up of the same personnel, the same employers, and the same "labor haters . . . whose only outlook is to wreck, destroy and defeat the trade union movement," the success of Local 544 had forced them to adopt new strategies. Teamster leaders had not only seen through the CA's transparent change of name, they had predicted the anti-union strategy of Minneapolis employers for decades to come.

The first task for AI President Belden and General Manager Schroeder was reorganizing and reenergizing a business community that was demoralized by the often violent and extremely successful three-year campaign of Local 544. During the first nine months of 1937, AI set up an organization called Industries Council for the "stabilization of employment relations, and the maintenance of industrial peace, through coordination of the various business interests." Each industrial group in the city would appoint two representatives to the council. Belden communicated directly with the Minneapolis Retailers' Association and other industrial groups, convincing them that unity would strengthen their position.[37]

By October, twelve groups had selected members to serve on the council. The organizing campaign was undoubtedly aided by the assistance that AI was giving to employers in twenty-eight industries in their collective bargaining negotiations during the summer of 1937. AI promoted the Industries Council for its "facilities for cooperative action between business and industry groups to promote uniformly sound collective bargaining procedures and exchange of information." In a June 17, 1937, editorial, *The Northwest Organizer* reported that "Minneapolis employers are better organized at this time than they have been since 1934." AI "had done a splendid job in organizing the bosses." It had "built up the morale of the employers to the point where it appears that they are determined to resist" union demands.[38]

The goal of Industries Council in assisting the various industrial groups was to "modify to a very pronounced degree the demands originally made upon them, and thus to avert strike situations" and limit the damage of the contract. While employers had generally accepted the principle of collective bargaining, AI hoped to counteract union pressure and forestall the closed shop. Over the summer of 1937, the majority of contracts signed by the twenty-eight employer groups assisted by AI managed to include the fundamental principles of the open shop in the following provisions: 1) the union would be recognized as the bargaining agent for its members; 2) discrimination against non-union employees would be banned; 3) union activities on company time or property would be banned; 4) all employees would abide by company rules; 5) seniority would be allowed if it did not conflict with the "efficient operation of a department"; 6) strikes or lockouts would be forbidden unless the contract is violated.[39]

In many other industries, however, major employers felt compelled to sign closed-shop contracts. By the fall of 1937, Northern States Power (NSP), Minneapolis Gas and Light, and the city's major bakeries had joined Strutwear

Knitting Company in the closed-shop camp. The hard-fought strikes of the three previous years had forced AI to adopt a policy of avoiding the major confrontations that each strike involving the Teamsters had become. AI General Manager Schroeder was convinced "that strikes and lockouts are no longer necessary to settle labor differences. . . . Labor disputes have to be settled sometime and the sooner the better and the cheaper the better is our motto." Despite the somewhat limited success of their negotiations, AI declared that "there is a stronger tendency manifested in this city by various industry groups to present a united front in opposition to radical demands than has been the case in many years."[40]

The increased unity initiated by the Industries Council had an immediate impact on negotiations in the laundry industry. When contracts expired on October 31, 1937, the AFL Laundry Wagon Drivers' Union demanded a ten-dollar-per-week wage increase, a closed union shop, and checkoff of union dues by the employer. The laundry employers suggested arbitration, but this suggestion was rejected. Finally, the laundries as a group offered a 5 percent wage raise, plus a week's vacation pay if the union would drop its other demands. All laundries agreed to close down operations and remain closed until the union dropped its demand for the closed shop. Within forty-five days, the union withdrew its demands and reached a new contract agreement, "an open shop agreement," which also provided for wage increases. Although AI firms had granted concessions, they had pressured the Laundry Wagon Driver's Union into delaying their demands for the closed shop for another year.[41]

The most effective policy for avoiding union gains and maintaining the open shop remained the employee representation plans that MacAloon had instituted through the Minneapolis Bureau of Industrial Relations. Strong company unions like the Munsingwear Employees' Association, voluntarily organized in 1933, were carefully designed to "conform to the principle for 'self organization' for collective bargaining or other mutual aid or protection." Although unions were able to eliminate several company unions that had been established for years in local public utilities, a number of new "independent employee groups" were set up. To meet national labor law standards, these groups were always presented as employee-initiated organizations, but they were usually organized by the employers with the assistance of AI.[42]

During the summer of 1937, over twenty groups of workers, through their committees, consulted with the director of Labor Relations of AI about their rights to organize. The formation of a number of these groups indicated to AI "that there are many workers who do not wish to become involved with either the CIO or the AFL, and want to organize for their own protection." With a strong company union program, assisted by AI's careful personnel policies and practices, AI hoped to forestall union-organizing activities before they could establish a presence in open-shop companies. When AI policies of appeasement failed, however, they stood ready to assist their members in fighting strikes and combating picketing.[43]

Although union avoidance and negotiations were the primary focus of AI, it also continued and elaborated on the array of services that the CA had initiated and the MBIR had expanded. To provide up-to-date information on labor legislation, NLRB rulings, and the state of local contract negotiations, AI published a biweekly newsletter. The AI library and staff also helped each employer set up thorough employer-employee relations plant programs which included shop rules, insurance programs, apprenticeship rules, thrift plans, recreational programs, health and welfare programs, incentive plans and piecework, vacation and holiday practices, and in-house employee communications programs. These programs decreased in-plant friction and promoted job satisfaction, both vital to curtailing union organization.[44]

To aid Minneapolis employers in maintaining competitive operations, AI made periodic wage and cost-of-living surveys, which it then published and distributed to members. Expert staff at AI, with the aid of the NAM's legal department, also endeavored to keep members abreast of the complicated requirements of state and federal labor laws. When employers were faced with state or federal conciliation hearings or arbitration, AI experts would intercede to represent their members. With its vast array of services and experienced staff, AI advertised "how it helps to save you money, time and work in solving every kind of EMPLOYEE RELATIONS problem."[45]

The growing unity fostered by AI was, however, threatened by serious dissension within the organization. Lloyd MacAloon had closed his private detective agency in 1926 to join the CA and run both its Free Employment Agency and its Special Service. When the Minneapolis Bureau of Industrial Relations was formed in 1934, MacAloon was promoted to direct the CA's union-fighting service from separate offices. By 1936, his role in the city's industrial conflicts had eclipsed that of CA General Manager Jack Schroeder. In a move made allegedly to save money, the MBIR's separate office was closed on May 21, 1936, once again placing MacAloon under Schroeder's direct command. When AI was formed in December 1936, MacAloon, still vice president and director of Employment Relations, demanded complete and exclusive control over AI's labor-relations activities. Schroeder and the board of directors refused MacAloon's request. Unwilling to continue in a position subservient to Schroeder, MacAloon left AI in April 1937 to form his own organization— Lloyd M. MacAloon Industrial and Labor Relations Service. He set up operations in his old MBIR offices in the First National-Soo Line Building.[46]

Even more divisive for AI, MacAloon took an impressive list of CA members with him. Thirteen retail stores defected, including industry leaders Dayton Company, L. S. Donaldson Company, J. C. Penney, Powers, Young-Quinlan, Woolworth's, and Warner Hardware. The Atwood, McGarvey, and Nash coffee companies and eighteen retail furniture stores, including Boutell Brothers and New England Furniture Company, joined MacAloon's client list. In fact, the city's department stores, furniture stores, and coffee companies had defected *en masse* and would continue to be represented by MacAloon for years to come.[47]

Particularly devastating for AI was the defection of the Dayton Company, an important CA member since its origin in 1903. In addition, Dayton's was an influential leader of the Minneapolis Retailers' Association and an important financial contributor to the CA. One can only assume that its experience with MacAloon during the 1934 strike and in his role as director of the MBIR had overshadowed long-time loyalties with the CA. Fortunately, new cooperative financial operations arranged by the CCA and AI still funneled money from these firms into the AI budget. Although the competition of MacAloon's firm cut into AI membership and diluted the unity of Minneapolis industry, it did not undercut AI's primary position or its funding.[48]

Although MacAloon was now operating independently, his labor relations policies closely paralleled the policies at AI, policies that MacAloon had developed as director of labor relations. In early 1937, the Minneapolis Credit Exchange, advised by MacAloon, still operated under a system that allowed the company to control all management functions, acknowledged the open shop, and refused to employ any person "whose principles or expressed beliefs are in opposition to the Constitution of the U. S. and the American principles of government."[49]

MacAloon, like AI, would fight Minneapolis unions one by one on whatever level and with whatever weapons were available. At Gray and Company and Robitshek-Schneider Company, where company unions were still in existence, MacAloon developed strategies to disguise the management-led organizations as independent labor unions. Contracts were designed to copy the appearance of labor union contracts and, when necessary, to negotiate with international unions and therefore maintain their independence. When strong unions existed, MacAloon maneuvered to avoid closed-shop contracts or to weaken their enforcement. At Scott-Atwater, the company signed an exclusive bargaining agreement with IAM Local 382, but would agree only to recommend that new employees join the union after thirty days. In the department stores, where Teamsters' Local 544 controlled the drivers, however, MacAloon bowed to the reality of a strongly entrenched union and negotiated contracts that recognized the union, granted seniority rights, a week's vacation pay, the eight-hour day, and time-and-a-half for overtime.[50]

Two years after MacAloon set up his competing industrial relations firm, AI secretary Paul J. Ocken also defected. Ocken had joined the CA as its field secretary in 1929, after serving as executive secretary of the Citizens' Club for five years. At this time, Ocken believed "wholeheartedly in the principles" of the CA and felt that its work "in resisting the efforts of radicals to gain a foothold in our city is of inestimable value." In his position as secretary of AI, Ocken worked closely with industrial groups that President Belden recruited for his Industries Council. By October 28, 1937, the Minneapolis Typothetae, representing the printing industry, unanimously approved two representatives to sit on the Industries Council "to handle joint labor relations." In August of 1939, the Minneapolis Typothetae hired Ocken as general manager of the association. The former AI secretary quickly assumed the responsibility of negotiating labor contracts for Typothetae members. By 1942, Ocken, as vice president and general manager of the reorganized Graphics Arts Industry, Inc., represented more than 200 business firms in all collective-bargaining negotiations with seventeen labor unions. Another crack had appeared in the iron structure of industrial unity envisioned by George Belden.[51]

When Local 544 pressed for across-the-board wage increases for all Minneapolis companies employing drivers in 1942, however, it was AI that quickly organized over 300 Minneapolis employers. Industries Council brought AI clients back together with the department stores, furniture dealers, and coffee companies represented by MacAloon, the graphic arts companies represented by Ocken, the transfer and warehouse companies represented by Ferris Martin, the lumber dealers represented by Thomas Vennum, and the building material companies represented by Arthur Egan. In March of 1942, these groups joined the Minneapolis Employers' Negotiating Committee (ENC) and agreed to let the ENC handle all negotiations with Local 544 as a single entity with one common labor policy. Seventeen Minneapolis industries had been reunited by AI in what the Civic Council called "the outstanding use of employer cooperative action in the history of Minneapolis."[52]

As the wage cases wound their way through the state conciliation process and the War Labor Board appeals, the ENC and AI counsel handled all hearings and paperwork. Recognizing the new threat represented by a unified business community, Local 544 refused to accept the ENC as the single bargaining agent for seventeen industries. To prevent the Teamsters from using gains at some employers to force similar concessions at others, AI hoped to use the ENC to set up a standard contract for Local 544 that would be used for all Minneapolis employers. The results at the War Labor Board, however, were far from encouraging. The Teamsters received significant raises in several separate cases over the vehement objections of the ENC. While the new, unified business community might be effective in local negotiations, it apparently did not impress federal officials. Despite these setbacks, however, AI had clearly demonstrated its position as the leading labor relations firm of the 1940s.[53]

20 Taming the Red Menace

THE LEADERS OF THE Minneapolis business community realized that the new labor relations stance of Associated Industries (AI) was a defensive strategy that would only delay the inevitable unionization of the city. As long as the Communist leaders of Local 544 were organizing the city's labor force, direct confrontation in the streets was the only alternative to a series of endless concessions. In 1920, the Minnesota Employers' Association had organized the Minnesota Sound Government Association (MSGA) to save the state from the Nonpartisan League. It was time to revive the network of organizations to once again save capitalism. The CA had failed in its attempts to redbait and depose the leaders of Local 544. Now a broader, more intensive campaign was required on both the local and national levels. Communism and its radical influence on the labor movement must be defeated.

AI and its allies also realized that Local 544 relied on the direct confrontation of sit-down strikes, massive picketing, and boycotts to win favorable union contracts. If a new system of government mediation could be installed, backed with laws that eliminated the tools of direct confrontation, the radical and effective Teamsters' union would be neutralized. Although the job would require an immense financial commitment, a thorough organization, and a complete dedication to the cause, the AI, the Civic and Commerce Association, the Minnesota Employers' Association, and the NAM pressed forward to reestablish their vision of capitalism.

One of the first steps was to end the civic isolation of Associated Industries. When the CA was formed as a secret committee to suppress union organization in 1903, a conscious decision was made to operate the CA as a separate entity: The CA fought for the open shop, while the Minneapolis Commercial Club and the CCA pursued a wide range of civic development and improvement functions. While this kept the larger civic bodies above the industrial warfare waged by the CA, it also isolated the CA and gradually created a focal point for the hatred of the Minneapolis working force. The CA's public image had become a source of organizational strength for the Teamsters' union and had helped neutralize the anti-radical propaganda of the daily newspapers. Although the

creation of Associated Industries attempted to create a new public image, business leaders realized that, to succeed, AI must be identified with the broader
and more acceptable image of the CCA. It was finally time for the CCA to bring
its warrior child into the fold of respectable civic organizations. With this new
identification, AI would attain a credibility and, it was hoped, a new effectiveness in its campaign against the Communist leadership of the Teamsters.

Shortly after the 1934 strike, business leaders proposed a plan for a Special
Emergency Citizens' Committee to serve as a united front for the coordinated
activities of the CCA, the CA, the Law and Order League, and the Council of Civic
Clubs. The committee must "take a strong position with reference to 544 and
its efforts to unionize this city. This must be done immediately. And must be
done publicly." This joint stand "would have tremendous force . . . [to] stimulate
those already fighting this menace, it would give loyal citizens a rallying point.
. . . It would announce to the radical enemy, that the forces arrayed against
them are now UNITED," and it would relieve the burden of the CA and give them
the allies they need against "these labor racketeers." The committee would create an educational department to "re-sell the capitalistic system of government
to the voters of Hennepin County and to assist all interested groups in perpetuating the original spirit of America." The committee would serve as the pol-
icy-making body for all the conservatives of the city, providing a leadership that
had been sadly missing at this critical moment in the city's history.[1]

The plan languished through 1935 and 1936 as the business community
frantically reacted to the crisis created by the aggressive organizing of Local
544 on a strike-by-strike basis. With the advent of AI in 1937 and a new long-
term approach to labor relations, the business leaders of AI and the CCA tack-
led the serious task of organizing a federation of civic groups, the Minneapolis Civic Council (CC). By April, 1938, the Civic and Commerce Association and
AI had been joined by the Better Business Bureau, the Hennepin County Good
Roads Association, the Minneapolis Safety Council, Minneapolis United, and
the Minneapolis Taxpayers' Association in the Civic Council's drive to "improve and unify the Industrial and Civic work done by the various organizations." The CC would finance all of its members in one joint funding campaign,
develop a Minneapolis plan of activities, and assign each project to the appropriate member. Although each organization would retain its own identity and
board of directors and would continue with most of its current activities, leadership and direction would now be guided by the Civic Council. AI, the only
member involved in labor-relations activities, would, of course, continue to
handle these problems for the CC. The close relationship of the CCA and AI was
finally a publicly acknowledged fact.[2]

The labor policies of Minneapolis industry were now to be controlled by the board of directors of the Civic Council. AI, however, had little to fear from this apparent shift of power. The new board was almost entirely composed of the same business leaders who had run the CA and now directed Associated Industries. AI President George Belden was joined on the board by prominent businessmen Henry J. Doerr, Jr., Frank P. Heffelfinger, Sumner T. McKnight, Charles L. Pillsbury, J. S. Pomeroy, and CCA President Herbert J. Miller. The Civic Council bylaws were carefully engineered to assure that the organization remained in the control of the city's largest, most powerful employers. At least half of the board represented firms that contributed over $500 to the CC. This put companies such as NSP, Northwest Banco, First Bank, Northwestern Bell Telephone, General Mills, Minneapolis Honeywell, and the Dayton Company in the secure position of determining the city's civic policies. Teamsters' Local 544 observed in *The Northwest Organizer* that "the Associated Industries crowd are in full charge of the 'new' outfit, except for a few dummies and none-too-bright stooges who provide a new 'front.'"[3]

Civic Council literature announced a dual mission: The "greatest goal" was "civic unity." While a united business front was the core element of civic unity, the Civic Council decided that the city must have "unity, integration, the working together of all the people and all their institutions toward their common goals. . . . Over and above the apparent strife and controversy among groups there is a community of interests." Labor and capital must be "interested primarily in peace, prosperity and progress. Law and order and the democratic process must prevail, not violence.[4]

The intertwined corollary mission was the defense of the American economic system, "a system based on free and individual enterprise that has done much to make this nation the finest place on earth in which to live and do business. The Council stands for a continuance of this system. . . . While not a red-baiting organization, [it] is definitely opposed to all 'isms' and departures from democracy and free enterprise." The Civic Council had evaluated "certain fundamental issues that now confront us," and had devised one simple objective— neutralize and destroy Teamsters' Local 544.[5]

To establish a comprehensive program, a special committee held citywide clinics and distributed questionnaires to city leaders. Over 3,000 suggestions were tabulated that made clear that the most serious problem facing Minneapolis, according to business, civic, and political leaders, was employer-employee relations. The CC quickly developed the "Minneapolis Plan" to attack the question of labor strife, along with the lesser problems of sound government, taxation, and public apathy. The plan included these elements:

First, Minneapolis labor relations needed a "workable procedure and a body of governing policies and principles fair and equitable as to management and labor."

Second, the city needed an accumulation of factual information on labor laws, past and current disputes, wage levels, and union and open-shop contracts.

Third, the city needed an authoritative labor service to provide counsel to businesses, to discourage unfair employer or employee practices, to provide an unbiased source of information, and to provide expert personnel for negotiating agreements and for arbitrating disputes.

AI, of course, was to provide this service for the Civic Council and find the solutions to the city's labor problems.[6]

When Associated Industries and the Civic and Commerce Association joined the Civic Council, the task of raising and distributing funds for their operations became the responsibility of the CC. The massive funding campaigns of the Civic Council raised well over $200,000 in 1938 and nearly $400,000 by 1950. Associated Industries, which had raised $36,693 by itself in 1937, received $51,235 in 1945–22 percent of the CC budget. The CCA received over 48 percent. The unified financial appeal widened the base and size of subscriptions for both organizations. AI had 500 contributors in 1937, but by 1945 3,859 business and financial firms had subscribed to CC. This wide response, however, was somewhat deceptive. In 1949, for example, over one-half of the subscriptions came from only 49 members. The funds from these major contributors had increased significantly after 1938 and were distributed to additional civic organizations. General Mills, for example, had contributed less than $4,000 to four organizations in 1937; in 1945, its contribution of $8,000 was distributed to the seven-member agencies of the Civic Council.[7]

As part of its financial campaigns and to advance its civic missions, the Civic Council spent most of its non-administrative budget on publicity. The CC arranged conferences on citizenship, parades celebrating the city, and town hall meetings to spread its message. In March 1939, it launched a monthly newsletter, *Minneapolis Civic Activities,* to report on its current work and the progress of its program and to explain in detail the "yeoman work" being done by the various agencies. Associated Industries, the agency directly involved in handling the city's most difficult problem, received lengthy and detailed publicity in numerous CC pamphlets and in its monthly bulletin. A 1947 article explained that AI "promotes industrial peace and friendly employer-employee relations." AI President Belden was quoted, "It is the joint responsibility of employers and employees to settle such disputes on a fair and equitable basis, keeping the public interest in mind." In serving the public interest, and, of course, the open shop, AI assisted 925 companies in their 1946 labor negotiations. Three times as many employers were served as in 1936. Under the wing of the Civic Council, AI would expand and flourish.[8]

While the restructuring of Associated Industries and the CC had been delayed until 1937, the leaders of the CA had recognized the resurgent dangers of radicalism even before the 1934 strike. Unemployed and relief marchers led by Communists had fought Minneapolis police and threatened City Hall in May of 1931 and again in November of 1932. The Farm Holiday strikes had closed down state highways into Minneapolis, and workers from Minneapolis furniture factories were mobbed and beaten. It was clear to the business community that Minneapolis faced a threat reminiscent of the Nonpartisan League a decade earlier. In 1919, Eli S. Warner of the St. Paul CA and Albert W. Strong had sat on the MEA's committee of three that had organized the Minnesota Sound Government Association. They realized that the time to fight radicalism had now returned.[9]

In the fall of 1933, Strong and Warner formed a committee of directors from the Twin Cities' CAs to organize the Minnesota Law Enforcement League. In a call to action, the committee warned: "The actions of these agitator groups are a direct menace to the lives and property of Minnesota's law abiding citizens. . . . The whole social structure of our great Minnesota Commonwealth is threatened. . . . It is time that public sentiment for law enforcement was aroused." The committee beseeched "red blooded Americans" to cooperate with "this movement to protect the lives and property of the good people of Minnesota." While Local 544 began organizing Minneapolis truck drivers, the CA was reinventing the Sound Government Association. For the next eight years, it would battle for the allegiance of the people of the city.[10]

On January 10, 1934, the first annual meeting of the renamed Minnesota Law and Order League was held in St. Paul. By March 10, 1934, Steele County had perfected the first county Law and Order unit. In September, shortly after the violent summer of 1934, the league was incorporated "to build up respect and a sense of individual responsibility for law and order and to support and encourage public officers in the performance of their official duties in maintaining the supremacy of law." By November of 1934, Charles W. Drew, secretary of the league, reported definite organizational plans in twelve counties and contacts with groups in twenty-one other counties.[11]

In Hennepin County, the CA quickly began recruiting directors and distributing membership pledge cards that read: "Believing in the American system of government, I pledge my best efforts to build up and maintain interest in and respect for law." The officers and directors of the Hennepin County chapter included CA allies George C. Jones of the *Minneapolis Journal*, General Mills executive Harry A. Bullis, and Judge W. W. Bardwell. Hennepin County Chapter President Merrill Hutchinson, later replaced by University of Minnesota Dean Edward E. Nicholson, sought the support and membership of business and civic organizations. In the league's first year, it received endorsements from the Minneapolis Retailers' Association, the American Legion, many Rotary, Kiwanis, Elks, and commercial clubs, and clubs affiliated with the Minnesota Federation of Women's Clubs. By 1936, the league claimed several thousand members, considerably less than the stated goal of several hundred thousand.[12]

The program of the Law and Order League, like the Sound Government Association (SGA) in 1920, was primarily the "dissemination of dependable information to the citizens of the state." League pamphlets extolled the virtues of "GOOD GOVERNMENT and HONEST GOVERNMENT," and sought to ignite the outrage of the great majority of citizens who would demand "active enforcement of our ordinances and laws by public officers against criminals, racketeers enemies of society and organized lawless minorities." The CA, directing the campaign from behind the scenes, considered Teamsters' Local 544 to fit into all four categories of evil. If the citizens wanted truly efficient law enforcement, league pamphlet "Law and Order" suggested enacting the recommendations of the last three crime commissions and creating an adequately equipped and trained system of state police. By creating a "robust civic sentiment dominated by a sense of justice," the league propaganda would encourage victims of racketeering to seek police protection and give jurors the courage to convict criminals. If successful, the league program would combat those forces "breeding a spirit of lawlessness that is permeating every rank of society and which, if permitted to continue, will destroy the foundation of sound government."[13]

The league message was distributed to 480 Minnesota newspapers through the facilities of the Associated Press, the United Press, and the news service of the Minnesota Editorial Association. The league's clipping files indicated that at least three news stories or editorials were in state papers every day through the summer and fall of 1934. A speakers' bureau was coordinated from league headquarters in the Endicott Building in downtown St. Paul. During 1934, speakers representing the league gave 100 addresses before service clubs and other organizations across the state. In addition, sixteen weekly radio programs were broadcast over WCCO. Although these programs were temporarily suspended during the political campaign in the fall of 1934, they had stirred inquiries into the league's program from twelve states. Looking to the future, the league realized that it also needed to arouse the boys and girls of the state. Arrangements were made with the Department of Education to hold an essay contest in Minnesota high schools to "rebuild respect for the law among the youth of our State."[14]

Although the league educational campaign was not as expansive as the SGA's in 1920, generating and widely distributing its literature was still an expensive proposition. Eli S. Warner, who had fund-raising experience with the MSGA, was appointed chairman of the finance committee. Although voluntary contributions were solicited with membership pledges, the large funds required would once again come from the Twin Cities's industrial groups. In Hennepin County, Merrill Hutchinson, league chapter president, and Charles Drew, chapter secretary, met with various business associations, described the league program, and requested donations for a $15,000 fund. After listening to Hutchinson's presentation, the Minneapolis Retailers' Association donated $1,000, as did the banks represented by the Minneapolis Clearing House. Separate donations were given to the state league. The CA also collected funds directly from its members. Deere and Webber Company, for example, donated $750. With the financial might of the Minneapolis business community supporting it, the league had little difficulty raising funds for its activities.[15]

The revision of Minnesota statutes to facilitate the conviction and incarceration of criminals became the league's top priority. It held conferences with Harold E. Stassen, president of the Minnesota County Attorneys' Association, and meetings with a committee appointed by Stassen to make recommendations for alterations in the criminal code because "the present code is alleged to give undue advantage to the criminal." State league president Donald J. Cowling, president of Carleton College, was appointed to a state Bar Association committee to make a new study of crime conditions in Minnesota. Cowling announced that "by the time the committee completes its study the Minnesota Law and Order League, composed of a large body of leading citizens of the State, will be in position to aid materially in carrying out the recommendations of the Committee." When the 1935 legislature met to consider the recommendations of the Minnesota Crime Commission, the league exhorted its members to contact their representatives in support of law and order. Charles Drew wrote: "We believe that the most important single contribution we can make to the war on crime at this time is our active aid in enacting the thirty-six recommendations of the Minnesota Crime Commission."[16]

The decisions of grand juries had been important to the CA for over thirty years and might still be influential. The league also worked closely with the Association of Former Grand Jury Foremen. Hennepin County secretary Drew arranged several dinners for grand jurors where they could receive information and instruction from University of Minnesota Dean of Student Affairs E. E. Nicholson, who was president of the Hennepin County League and president of the Association of Former Grand Jury Foremen. The Central Labor Union accused the league of tampering with the jury and demanded that the Former Grand Jury Association be dissolved. The Minneapolis City Council passed a resolution calling for Nicholson's resignation. District Court Judge Vince Day, former secretary to Governor Floyd Olson, publicly attacked "the interference of any super-legal organization, whether it be a law and order league or any other lawful or unlawful organization." When the Minnesota State Federation of Labor asked Governor Petersen to investigate this attempt to control Hennepin County grand juries, Charles Drew resigned as secretary of the league.[17]

Although the Law and Order League worked closely with the Minnesota Crime Commission, the County Attorneys' Association, and the State Police Officers' Association, and lobbied for a state police, it emphatically announced that it would "NOT MAINTAIN ANY SPECIAL OR AUXILIARY POLICE FORCE!" The league, however, stood ready to be of service to any community that would organize vigilante groups. Leading citizens of Minnetonka and White Bear Lake, in close contact with the league, had organized vigilante groups to "make it difficult for gangsters to establish hide-outs in their respective areas." With aroused and alert citizens keeping their communities under close observation, racketeering would be discouraged. The league provided speakers for these groups and cooperated in every possible way in their development. In this way, the league could help vigilante groups flourish without having any official role in their operations.[18]

At the offices of the NAM in New York City, the successes of the Minneapolis Teamsters' Union and the erosion of law and order were viewed as symptoms of a far wider and much deeper problem. The NAM recognized that "as a by-product of the depression, serious doubts had been raised among the people as to the desirability of maintaining free enterprise as the keystone of our economy. . . . In the midst of widespread distress and unemployment, industry's voice was lost in a welter of economic fantasies and seductive theories." The NAM admitted that, "For years the industrialists of this country have defaulted public opinion to those who menace the system upon which our modern civilization has been built." Demagogues of the left had made industry the scapegoat of the Depression. An NAM survey had revealed that three-quarters of the public believed that industry had failed in its social and economic responsibilities. In the country's colleges, half of the instructors felt that the forces of education should be directed toward "a more thoroughly socialistic order of society." The NAM was faced with "a vital question of national policy," which it stated as: "Was the American economy to be motivated by private initiative or by some form of regimentation under the domination of an all-powerful State?" The NAM told the American business community: "Unless industry rallies, unless it vigorously undertakes a nation-wide, unremitting campaign of education, . . . it may find it has moved too late." The NAM proclaimed itself the one organization that "had the vision to see this and the breadth of support to undertake this job for all industry."[19]

NAM President Bardo assigned the task of educating the American public and saving capitalism to Harry A. Bullis, chairman of the Public Relations Committee and vice president of General Mills. Bullis had joined Washburn-Crosby shortly after World War I and had quickly reorganized the mill's archaic administrative practices and broadened its employee welfare programs. When company executives conceived an enormous consolidation eight years later, it was Bullis who traveled the country, "the prophet of the idea" that became General Mills on June 22, 1928. As Bullis's influence grew, he became Minneapolis's primary emissary to the NAM. In 1931, he was appointed to an NAM-sponsored National Advisory Board to develop programs for "reestablishing business confidence" in the American public. A year later, he was elected to the NAM's board of directors.[20]

In Minneapolis, Bullis's executive position in General Mills provided him with important influence in the councils of the CA. After the disastrous 1934 Teamsters' strike, Bullis took a more active role in defending local industry, joining the board of directors of the Hennepin County Chapter of the Minnesota Law and Order League. In accepting his massive and vital task at the NAM, Bullis proclaimed, "Today, our American system needs defenders—or crusaders, if you will. We cannot sit back and depend upon the message of time and dead reckoning to maintain the equilibrium of the American people—to keep them on the right course. . . . Industry faced the grim realization that it had to get up on its feet and square off in its own defense." Harry Bullis would organize the charge.[21]

Bullis realized that transforming 128 million people into a patriotic community that believed implicitly in the American Way—individual liberty, representative democracy, and private enterprise—was a monumental task. Only a carefully planned, coordinated, and financed program in every state and in thousands of cities and towns, relentlessly driving home the facts about industry, day after day, week after week, could turn back the tide of radicalism. The NAM public relations campaign had to be skillfully integrated so as to blanket every form of media with its message. Bullis felt that public opinion, in the final analysis, entrenched itself in the hometowns and neighborhoods of America. The general principles of industrial progress must be filtered into the grassroots. The program would encompass newspapers, motion pictures, educational booklets for high schools and colleges, billboards, employee newsletters, radio shows, a speakers' bureau, and regional conferences on a scale never before attempted. The NAM message, however, was not to be delivered in the dull pedantic language of economists or business people, but "in a human interest and entertaining manner" and in plain terms for plain people. To the accusation that the NAM campaign was propaganda, Bullis remarked, "If this be propaganda, make the most of it."[22]

To run the campaign, the NAM hired James Selvage, a former Associated Press reporter on the Washington beat. Selvage immediately established an Industrial Press Service (IPS), which sent a five-page weekly clipsheet of news, cartoons, columns, and editorials to 3,200 weekly and small newspapers in its first year. By 1939, the IPS reached over 6,000 papers, 122 of them in Minnesota, and was an important factor in helping small-town editors mold public opinion. The cartoon service was particularly popular with its 3,500 regular subscribers. One cartoon, "The Pocketbook of Knowledge," devoted itself to the benefits of industry, the terrors of taxes (a horned imp labeled "Hidden Taxes" peeps out of a loaf of bread and chortles, "I'm in the dough"), and the miseries of foreigners living in non-industrial countries. The IPS was augmented by a series of columns by six outstanding economists titled, "You and Your Nation's Affairs"; a special industrial news service to 200 foreign-language papers; and an *Industrial Information Bulletin* for the editorial writers and columnists. Concentrating on enhancing the understanding of industry in rural regions, the IPS's massive output gradually established the NAM as the accepted voice of American industry.[23]

The NAM also took its "American Way" propaganda onto the nation's airwaves. "American Family Robinson" was heard over 270 radio stations across the country. The plot revolved around a fictional average American family that lived in Centerville and faced the problems of everyday Americans. Luke Robinson, editor of the *Centerville Herald*, espouses a fair deal for business and industry; "there's Betty and Dick in love to bring romance in; Professor Broadbelt, prototype of the panacea peddler, organizer of Arcadians, Inc.; and Mrs. Robinson, who always brings to bear the leveling influence of a woman's judgment." In later episodes, the Robinsons start a table relish factory, demonstrating the possibilities of industry for the average American family. The popularity of this down-to-earth propaganda brought "American Family Robinson" into American homes during prime hours of the evening and Sunday afternoon. A series of short films, called "Frontiers of the Future," supplemented the radio campaign. The four films actually played opposite "Snow White and the Seven Dwarfs" for nine days at Radio City Music Hall. By 1939, the NAM's films had played to an estimated 20 million viewers and were booked six months in advance.[24]

The Bullis plan also targeted specific segments of the American public. The NAM felt that "women with their natural interest in homes, jobs and the preservation of stable free government represent one of the greatest single forces in our society." A Women's Division was created to tap into this social "force." By 1946, 39,000 women's club leaders received the NAM's "Program Notes" each month. The nation's schools were also ripe ground for propaganda. A School Division distributed 2.5 million copies of eight different "You and Industry" booklets as texts in high schools and colleges. In addition, 35,000 teachers and educators received a monthly newsletter, *Trends in Education-Industry Cooperation*.

Any group with a perceived influence over the American public needed to be cultivated and given the NAM's message. A special quarterly publication, *Understanding*, offered a cooperative hand in social betterment to 12,000 clergymen of all faiths. Constantly seeking to expand the campaign, a New Groups Contacts Division cultivated patriotic organizations, Parent-Teacher Associations, and clubs of all varieties. A speakers' bureau provided skilled voices of industry to service the new contacts and spread the NAM's version of the "American Way."[25]

To finance the educational campaign and to distribute the propaganda, the NAM sponsored the National Industrial Information Committee (NIIC), a group of leaders "who occupy positions of great responsibility in American enterprise." The NIIC combined executives from the country's major manufacturers—Standard Oil, Phillips Petroleum, Anaconda Copper, and Westinghouse—with the presidents of *Newsweek*, McGraw-Hill, and McFadden Publications to form a high-powered propaganda machine. They were joined by Harry Bullis and Frederick K. Weyerhaeuser from Minnesota. As chairman of the Minnesota branch of the NIIC, Bullis was responsible for soliciting donations from Minnesota business.[26]

The task was substantial, as the NIIC's budget rose from nearly one million dollars in 1940 to $1.7 million five years later. While a substantial part of Minnesota's contribution came directly from the large milling companies, smaller companies such as Paper Calmenson Company of St. Paul and Williams Hardware of Minneapolis also contributed. By 1946, over $25,000 in checks passed through Bullis's office on their way to the NAM. NIIC Chairman J. Howard Pew, president of Sun Oil, complimented Bullis for his "magnificent job" of fund raising. In the 1946 campaign, 159 companies had raised $1,607,000 "to carry the vital story of the private enterprise system to more millions of Americans."[27]

The state and local financial organization also was used to gather educational material and served as a distribution conduit to local news and educational sources. As chairman of the Public Relations Committee, Bullis had carefully planned state educational committees to give the NIIC program "local standing and intimate personal consideration of leaders in each community throughout the United States" As chairman of the Minnesota branch, Bullis implemented his program locally through a state speakers' bureau, Minnesota newspapers, and Twin City radio stations. When the NAM instituted a series of public relations conferences across the country to instruct local manufacturers on effective public relations techniques, Bullis organized the Industrial Commission of Minnesota.[28]

Assisted by the presidents of Associated Industries, the Civic and Commerce Association, the Minnesota Employers' Association, and the St. Paul Committee on Industrial Relations, the 1946 conference at the Radisson Hotel featured the discussion of effective industrial propaganda by Bullis, President Robert Wason of the NAM, and editors from the *St. Paul Pioneer Press, St. Paul Dispatch, Minneapolis Tribune, Minneapolis Star,* the *Duluth Herald,* and the *Duluth News Tribune.* A similar effort went into the Northwest Education and Industry Conference in 1942, at which the leaders of AI, the Civic Council, and the MEA met with representatives of the state Department of Education, the University of Minnesota, the National Education Association, and the Minneapolis Public Schools.[29]

While the Minneapolis Civic Council, the Minnesota Law and Order League, and the NAM mounted a massive campaign to sell capitalism to the American public, the CA, on a more modest scale, directly attacked the Communist leadership of Teamsters' Local 544. In a pamphlet released in 1935 and titled, *The Real Menace to Industrial Peace in Minneapolis,* the CA traced in great detail the activities of the Socialist Workers' Party (SWP) during the 1934 strikes: "Those who are familiar with the background of the men who inspired, instigated and directed these strikes, know that they were nothing more or less than a deliberate attempt of the Communist League of America to stir up class warfare in this community." The aim of the Workers' Party was to "lead the working class of the United States in revolution. . . .This would be accomplished first by the Communists' subtle and insidious infiltration of the labor movement and then to foment strife and discord among our working people in furtherance of their revolutionary activities." The CA considered it a duty to inform the people of Minneapolis that Communists were attempting to destroy their city, their country, and the American way of life itself.[30]

Although Bullis and his colleagues believed that they were turning the tide of the nation away from Communism, the local, state, and national propaganda programs were having very little local impact. The SWP members still retained leadership of Local 544 and continued to challenge AI's dominance of

Minneapolis industry. A new local strategy was required. The plant-by-plant organization of company unions supported by the workers of the Free Employment Bureau was no longer an effective counter to the massive efforts of Local 544. In the fall of 1937, the AI's Free Employment Bureau, part of the CA's anti-union strategy since 1919, was discontinued. At the same time, the NAM sent an agent to Minneapolis to organize a new, broader form of company union, Associated Independent Unions (AIU). Supported by Minneapolis business people, AIU was to organize across craft and company lines in competition with the AFL and the CIO. Separate AIU locals were set up for carpenters, plumbers, bricklayers, decorators, mechanics, and, most importantly, truck owners and drivers. By December 1938, AIU claimed to directly represent 2,000 Minneapolis workers and to have affiliates with nearly 10,000 members.[31]

As *The Northwest Organizer* pointed out, Associated Independent Unions was a very strange labor union. The AIU supported "the right of individual decision," the open shop, and the right of employers to organize for collective bargaining purposes. Any union's right to picket or to strike violated the AIU basic philosophy "that all grievances arising in the industry, shall be adjusted in a peaceful and orderly manner." Contrasting itself to Local 544, the AIU claimed to "be an American movement first, last and all the time, there will be no place in it for the gangster, racketeer, thug or Communist." The AIU would "promote goodwill, mutual understanding, harmony and cordial cooperation between employer and workers, instead of the distrust, suspicion, hatred and disorganization that now prevails." The leaders of Local 544 were described as "self seeking racketeers" and "Communistic labor organization dictators." The Teamsters, having little difficulty recognizing the signs of a company union, accused the AIU of subverting the union movement and working hand in hand with Associated Industries.[32]

The AIU's primary target, of course, was Teamsters' Local 544. Spearheaded by its own Minnesota Mutual Truck Owners and Drivers Association Local No. 1, AIU attempted to undermine the legitimate unions and lure their members into the company union fold. Local No. 1's chief spokesman, Floyd L. ("Forced Labor") Taylor, raged against Local 544 before business clubs, American Legion posts, and church audiences. It was the Christian duty of fellow church members to rid the city of Local 544. Local No. 1 President A. C. Hubbard publicly accused the Teamsters of harboring "thugs and racketeers" and unleashing "personal and brutal attacks" on union members. The AIU plans, however, went beyond the usual anti-union propaganda. Minnesota Mutual organizers infiltrated Local 544 meetings and urged the members to "join a good union." Despite offering membership for only "two bits" (twenty-five cents) rather than Local 544's "penalty of $2 a month plus assessments," the employer-backed group had little success luring union members into "an American Institution with American-Ideas."[33]

On February 16, 1938, five AIU members embedded inside Teamster Local 544, backed by Mayor Leach and undoubtedly financed by the business community, filed a suit in Hennepin County District Court asking for a complete financial disclosure and accounting of the drivers' union. The suit accused Local 544 of forcing Minneapolis employees to sign closed-shop contracts, which denied all workers the right to work, of illegally picketing jobs with Local No. 1 members, and of intimidating the city into "paying out large sums of money for relief." The AIU plaintiffs asked the court to tie up union funds, appoint a receiver to take over the union, stop the union from interfering with non-union trucks, and permit plaintiff attorneys to inspect all the records of Local 544.[34]

On July 27, 1938, Judge Frank E. Reed ordered Local 544 to turn over its books to the court. When the case finally came to trial two years later, the AIU attorney Arthur H. Anderson charged the Teamsters with illegal elections, financial irregularities, and encouraging threats, force, and violence to attain "their ends." Accusations of Communist activities became the sensational center of attention in daily reports in Minneapolis newspapers. Ironically, the Teamster leaders were saved by a technicality. Although Judge Paul S. Carroll ruled that the union charter denied membership to members of the Communist Party, testimony proved that Local 544 officials were followers of Trotsky, and, in the case of Carl Skoglund, had actually been expelled from the Communist Party. When the headlines finally faded, Teamster officials had to repay a little over $6,000, and Skoglund, who was not a United States citizen, was removed from office. The union had survived with the rest of its leadership intact.[35]

But a more violent threat to the Teamsters' union was organizing secret councils in Minneapolis during the summer of 1938. The fascist Silver Shirts had returned to Minneapolis under William Dudley Pelley's battle cry, "Down With the Reds and Out With the Jews." First organized in 1933, Pelley's radical organization had reached a national membership of 25,000 in 1934 and then faded from national attention. Revived in 1936, one organizer claimed 6,000 members in Minnesota, where Silver Shirts hoped to segregate all Jews in one city.[36]

In August of 1938, Pelley sent his top lieutenant, Roy Zachary, from North Carolina to Minneapolis with a list of Silver Shirt contacts and instructions to enlist 3,000 to 5,000 new members. Minneapolis, one of the most anti-Semitic cities in the country, provided an excellent environment for the spread of Pelley's doctrines. Among Zachary's Minnesota contacts were James F. Gould, who had run the American Committee of Minneapolis in 1919, Roy F. Dunn, secretary of the state Republican Party, Jay C. Hormel, president of the Hormel Packing Company in Austin, and Al C. Hubbard, president of Minnesota Mutual Truck Owners and Drivers Association. One of Zachary's primary targets in his organizational meetings was the Communist racketeers of Teamsters' Local 544. He disclosed to an August 4 meeting that the Silver Shirts were infiltrating Minneapolis labor unions, particularly Local 544. One Silver Shirt speaker called for vigilante bands to raid the headquarters of Local 544 and destroy them.[37]

These threats were undoubtedly music to the ears of Associated Industries President George Belden, who attended Silver Shirt meetings after learning that they were intent on exposing Communism. Belden sympathized with Zachary's call for getting rid of racketeers and felt that the Silver Shirts "have some ideas that are good." When Rabbi Albert I. Gordon publicly exposed Belden's attendance at Silver Shirt meetings, Belden responded: "I am unalterably opposed to secret organizations or un-American groups of any kind that foster and attempt to promote racial or religious hatred or that attempt to pit class against class."[38]

Following this theme, the *Minneapolis Journal* called the Silver Shirts racketeers and made an obvious attempt to categorize Local 544 and the fascist organization as "Hate Crusades." Two days later, Belden told the *Minnesota Leader* that there were "some good things about" the Silver Shirts. Zachary's contact with A. C. Hubbard also brought AIU organizers to the Silver Shirt meetings where they were allowed to distribute literature and recruit new members. The close association of Associated Industries, the AIU, and the Silver Shirts, combined with the threat of paramilitary strikes against Teamster headquarters, provoked a hasty reaction from Local 544.[39]

The Dunne brothers realized that "no one can defend labor but labor." In August and September of 1938, a Union Defense Guard (UDG) was formed to defend "the union picket lines, headquarters and members against anti-labor violence." Ray Rainbolt of the Local 544 staff was elected commander of the force of 600 union men. In squads of five men, each wearing "544 Union Defense Guard" armbands, the UDG could be mobilized in an hour. Two .22 caliber pistols and two .22 caliber rifles were purchased for target practice. If weapons were necessary, the UDG would have to rely on the hunting guns of its members.[40]

In an attempt to warn the Silver Shirts, *The Northwest Organizer* publicized the UDG's activities. When Pelley arrived in Minneapolis to address a Silver Shirt rally at Calhoun Hall, UDG units showed up in force and intimidated the audience. Confronted with a determined and superior force, Silver Shirt activity quickly subsided. With the Silver Shirt threat removed, the UDG's activities subsided into policing union picnics and rallies. Three years later, however, the formation of a paramilitary force by the leaders of the Minneapolis Socialist Workers' Party would have devastating consequences. With war clouds gathering in Europe, AI and Lloyd MacAloon, remembering the suppression of the International Workers of the World during World War I, waited for their next opportunity.[41]

By the summer of 1940, war in Europe had radically altered the political climate in Washington. In June1940, the Alien Registration Act (Smith Act), sponsored by notorious anti-labor congressman Howard W. Smith of Virginia, sailed through the House by a 382-to-4 vote despite one representative's warning that the bill was "an attempt to break the labor movement." Despite the ACLU's protest that the Smith Act "would become an instrument of oppression against unpopular minorities and organized labor," on June 28, 1940, President Roosevelt signed the first federal peacetime anti-sedition and conspiracy law since 1798. The Smith Act defined three offenses: Knowingly advocating the overthrow of the United States by force; knowingly helping to organize a society that engages in such advocacy or becoming a member of such a society; and conspiring with others to commit either of these offenses. The United States government had served notice on the country's radicals: Wartime dissent would not be tolerated. Lloyd MacAloon, well aware of the SWP's anti-war position, now had a tool with the potential to destroy Local 544.[42]

On June 4, 1940, with the Smith Act moving quickly through Congress, MacAloon had lunch and spent the afternoon discussing subversive activities in Minneapolis with officials of the United States Department of Justice and United States Military Intelligence (USMI). MacAloon, no doubt aware of the successful intelligence operations and subsequent prosecutions of the IWW during World War I, had now formed an alliance with federal intelligence agencies to gather and distribute information on the SWP and the Communist Party. The SWP's anti-war posture had put the leaders of Local 544 in a legally vulnerable position—a position that MacAloon and AI would attempt to take advantage of. For the next year, often working through the night, MacAloon would generate a stream of reports on subversive activities, particularly inside Local 544. MacAloon was joined in the field by FBI agents Noonan, Notesteen, and Perrin. As intelligence operations intensified in 1941, he met weekly with Colonel Michael J. Mulcahy, a Military Intelligence officer on assignment with the Minnesota National Guard. Colonel Mulcahy would then forward MacAloon's reports to the FBI, G-2 in Omaha, Nebraska, and G-2 at the War Department in Washington, D.C. Although MacAloon would continue to lead the Minneapolis business community's intelligence operations against Local

544, by September of 1940 Associated Industries had also begun to collect subversive material on the Socialist Workers' Party.[43]

Reports originating in Minneapolis gradually built up files on Communist and SWP activities in local unions. The chief danger, of course, came from the "fearless and outspoken" Trotskyite Communists who led Local 544, according to reports by MacAloon to USMI Lieutenant Colonel W. T. Bals. United States Military Intelligence's observer predicted a labor flare-up, "which will probably be accompanied by violence and possibly by assassinations," which would undoubtedly disrupt the armament program. Local radical union leaders were supposedly planning "a campaign of violence directed primarily at the armament program." Local 544 had gone so far as to demand a contract clause denying reemployment to any employee who volunteered for military service. To fund its activities, Local 544 was reportedly diverting union funds to further "their Communistic doctrine." Minneapolis was "rapidly becoming a clearing house for the coordination of activities by subversive groups" and radical Minneapolis leaders were preparing for "taking over control of the community upon departure of the National Guard with special regard to power, communication and transportation."[44]

Of vital importance for any prosecutions under federal sedition statutes, United States Military Intelligence gathered information on the mainly ceremonial Union Defense Guard of Local 544. To a complete list of Defense Guard captains was added a list of members who had secured pistol permits on November 26, 1937. With supposedly credible reports of a radical, armed paramilitary force, MacAloon, AI, the FBI, and USMI were in a position to both push for indictments and provide evidence for the prosecutions that followed. Bals, who met frequently with MacAloon, realized, of course, that his observer's "views are somewhat colored by his close association and for that reason the dangers foreseen are believed to be somewhat exaggerated." These possible exaggerations, however, were to have very little effect on the government's use of MacAloon's intelligence.[45]

Ironically, despite the obvious intent of using MacAloon's reports in Smith Act prosecutions, they were first to become a tool for the International Brotherhood of Teamsters (IBT) President Daniel J. Tobin. Tobin, who had been trying to oust Local 544's Trotskyite leadership for half a decade, now had federal allies. In February 1941, FBI agents, armed with MacAloon's detailed reports on the Socialist Workers' Party, began working within Local 544 in an attempt to overthrow the union's radical leadership. Agent Perrin and his associates took part in organizing the Committee of 100, a small, dissident faction inside Local 544, providing the group with intelligence and advising them on strategies for neutralizing and dividing the union's leadership. After receiving charges against the Dunne brothers from the Committee of 100, on April 8 Tobin appointed a commission to investigate.[46]

On June 3, the charges that Local 544's leadership was "communistic, alien, and grossly negligent and inefficient" was repeated before the IBT's executive council in Washington, D.C., where Tobin read aloud from FBI reports: "The main specific task of the Socialist Workers' Party is the mobilization of the American masses for struggle against American capitalism and for its overthrow." Tobin then demanded that all union members disassociate themselves from the SWP and accept a receivership to control policies of the local. Realizing that Tobin intended to either take over Local 544 or destroy it, the drivers' union disaffiliated with the IBT and the AFL and joined the CIO. It was a drastic decision that quickly brought a drastic reaction.[47]

On June 13, Tobin telegraphed President Roosevelt to report that Local 544's "affiliation with the CIO is indeed a regrettable and dangerous condition." Tobin believed that "while our country is in a dangerous position, those disturbers who believe in the policies of foreign, radical governments, must be in some way prevented from pursuing this dangerous course." The president instructed his secretary to "immediately have the government departments and agencies interested in this matter notified, and to point out that this is no time, in his opinion, for labor unions, local or national, to begin raiding one another for the purpose of getting memberships or for similar reasons." At 3:00 P.M. on June 27, FBI agent Perrin and two deputy United States marshals climbed the stairs at 919 Marquette Avenue to the second-floor offices of the SWP, where they browsed in the book room and purchased a copy of the *Communist Manifesto* and a copy of the *Declaration of Principles of the Fourth International*. Thirty minutes later, they returned with a search warrant and seized bushels of leaflets, pamphlets, and books. The boxes were actually carried downstairs and loaded into a truck by the drivers of the Skellet Company, a loyal Associated Industries transfer firm.[48]

According to Special Assistant United States Attorney General Henry A. Schweinhaut, neither SWP records nor membership lists were confiscated. A longtime accumulation of such evidence by MacAloon and the FBI made their seizure irrelevant. Although the raid seized primarily publicly available material, it was a marvelous public relations extravaganza to announce the coming criminal prosecutions for alleged "seditious conspiracy to advocate overthrow of the government of the United States by force and violence," as the *Tribune* reported.[49]

Within three weeks, a United States District Court indicted the leaders of Local 544 on two counts: one based on a seditious conspiracy act passed in 1861, and the other on the recently passed Smith Act. Count one accused the twenty-nine indicted SWP members of conspiracy "to overthrow, put down, and to destroy by force the Government of the United States. The defendants would seek to bring about an armed revolution when the time seemed propitious. They would accomplish their seditious plan by first taking over the trade unions in all major industries in order to paralyze the country. The revolution would be consummated by the infiltration of the United States military and the formation of armed and organized militia units."[50]

Count two, based on the Smith Act, was a much more general charge, accusing the defendants of advising, counseling, and teaching the duty, necessity, desirability, and propriety of overthrowing and destroying the government of the United States by force and violence. Like the 1917 Minnesota Syndicalism Act, used to suppress the IWW during World War I, the Smith Act required only that the government prove the distribution of ideas. The sedition charges, on the other hand, suggested that the initial planning and actions to carry out a real revolution had taken place. The government would rest its sedition case on Local 544's formation of the Union Defense Guard. Minneapolis newspapers, which were Associated Industries members long critical of Local 544, plastered their front pages with dramatic photos and accounts of the nest of traitors running the union. Minneapolis employers, of course, viewed the raid and indictments as an "unalloyed blessing." Local 544's time was definitely running out.[51]

When the trial began on October 27, it became clear that Local 544's Union Defense Guard would be the smoking gun that proved that the SWP was actively engaged in a seditious conspiracy. The bulk of this case came from members of the Committee of 100 who were strong supporters of Tobin's campaign against Local 544. The prosecution witnesses testified that the UDG had marched unarmed to the Gayety Theater, had policed various picnics, and had had several target practices with .22 caliber revolvers and rifles. All the government witnesses except one testified that the UDG had been organized to defend the union against possible attacks of the fascist Silver Shirts. One witness, who had attended practically all the meetings of the UDG, testified that the last meeting, a party with sandwiches and coffee, was in 1940.[52]

With their case already proven by the prosecution, the defense called only six witnesses, who testified briefly on the UDG issue. The final blow came when District Judge Matthew M. Joyce instructed the jury that mere advocacy or teaching of revolution was not enough, but that they must find an actual conspiracy to overthrow or destroy the government. The prosecution's case, resting on the overt actions of the UDG, disintegrated. The jury acquitted all defendants on count one, seditious conspiracy to overthrow the government. One defendant, however, did not escape. Grant Dunne, a World War I veteran who had long suffered from the effects of shell shock and had been physically ill for years, committed suicide on October 4, 1941. One enemy of Associated Industries had been removed.[53]

The charge under the Smith Act, however, only necessitated proving that the defendants conspired to undermine the loyalty of United States military forces and published material advocating the overthrow of the government. To do this, the prosecution simply exhibited the vast collection of SWP materials taken in the June 27 raids. The *Communist Manifesto* crowned a large assortment of pamphlets and essays by Trotsky, Lenin, and Marx. Copies of *The Militant, The Northwest Organizer,* and even the *Minneapolis Labor Review* were also entered into evidence next to the SWP's "Declaration of Principles and By Laws." The SWP aided the prosecution by establishing an obligatory policy that party members must defend themselves in a way that was "worthy of our movement and our tradition: No attempt to water down or evade our revolutionary doctrine, but on the contrary, to defend it militantly."[54]

The defense did contend, however, that an SWP revolution would be accomplished by radicalizing the majority and not through violence. The argument had little effect on the judge or the jury. Eighteen defendants, including Local 544 leaders Vincent Dunne, Farrell Dobbs, Carlos Hudson, and Carl Skoglund were found guilty under the Smith Act with a recommendation for leniency. That December, twelve defendants were sentenced to sixteen months in federal prison and six others received terms of a year and a day. On December 31, 1943, having exhausted all appeals, fifteen of the eighteen defendants assembled at Minneapolis SWP headquarters and marched side by side through the streets to the Federal Courthouse to begin serving their sentences. A decade after the radical leadership of the Teamsters' Union had begun organizing Minneapolis coal drivers and changed the Minneapolis union movement, the leaders of Associated Industries watched the cell doors of Hennepin County jail clang shut on their most resourceful and feared enemies.[55]

21 Creating a New Era

WITH THE DRAMATIC ASCENDANCY of the Farmer-Labor Party and Teamsters' Local 544, the Minneapolis business community and its conservative political allies in St. Paul had suffered through the Depression with their economic and political power neutralized. Only the Republican Party's control of the state Senate had allowed them to slow the tide of radicalism sweeping the state. Even before the violent summer of 1934, however, the seeds of change were being sown within the conservative political community. Racked by malcontents and defections, the Republican Party created a statewide Young Republican organization on December 20, 1931. Aspiring toward independence, the new group quickly issued a new challenge to the old guard leadership. The GOP hoped that new, more progressive policies might attract more moderate voters away from Governor Olson's radicalism.[1]

At General Mills, where executives controlled the flow of cash from the Minneapolis business community into the Republican Party, John Crosby wrote that "our best hope for decent government in this state lies in your group and as I wrote young Russell Bennett I am sure that now you have started to work you will not drop it." He was not to be disappointed. Younger members of the Citizens Alliance quickly assumed significant roles in the new movement. While Crosby and General Mills legal advisor Sydney Anderson worked behind the scenes, Frank P. Leslie of the Leslie Paper Company, an important CA member, served as treasurer of the Republican State Central Committee, while also enlisting in the party's youth movement. He was joined by CA members Russell H. Bennett on the Young Republican League (YRL) advisory board and Totten P. Heffelfinger as Fifth District congressional chairman. Two years later, Heffelfinger would play a significant role in organizing the CA's army during the 1934 trucker's strike. The duties of operating the YRL fell on Secretary Edwin L. Lindell, who was also secretary of the Minnesota Law and Order League. Although some of the old guard criticized this new movement, Crosby "heard among the older and responsible men many expressions of commendation" for what the young men had done.[2]

Three years later, the Young Republican League finally emerged as a serious organization. On November 1, 1935, 150 young Republicans from thirty counties held their first convention in Minneapolis. Within two months, the fledging group had established offices in St. Paul, hired a full-time organizer, distributed a "Suggested Plan for County Organizations," and issued a ten-point statement of objectives titled "Our Call to Youth." The YRL promised "to oppose such fantastic and vicious plans as cooperative commonwealth" and "to oppose oppressive political dictatorship on the one hand and ruthless financial tyranny on the other."[3]

Dakota County Attorney Harold E. Stassen was elected to lead the YRL's efforts "to preserve our American System by striving to correct its abuses." The twenty-eight-year-old chairman confidently stressed the independence of his small cadre. The YRL would cooperate with the senior party organization while "carefully avoiding domination by any group outside of our membership." Stassen sought a program "that would correct the abuses of today without returning to the inequalities of yesterday." The YRL program was cleverly designed to appeal to youth "from all walks of life, laborers, farmers, merchants and professional men." The Farmer-Labor Party had been issued a serious challenge.[4]

On November 18, 1937, Stassen opened his primary campaign for governor in Hastings, saying, "The flames of industrial warfare present one of the most serious problems facing Minnesota. The twin stokers that feed these flames are the few reactionary industrialists on the one hand and the few irresponsible, radical labor agitators on the other." After decisively defeating old guard leader Martin Nelson and Minneapolis Mayor George Leach in the June primary, Stassen developed a labor peace plan for the general election campaign against Governor Benson. Stassen's labor plank called for "a labor relations act drafted with the cooperation of sound labor leaders and progressive employers to protect the rights of labor and avoid premature strikes, violence, lockouts and caveman tactics in industrial disputes. The very successful laws in Sweden, Norway and Denmark offer constructive models for such an act." On a more ominous note for Local 544, Stassen also promised to oppose class hatred, fascism, and Communism.[5]

As the fall campaign heated up, Republican allies of Stassen picked up on the divisive issues of the Farmer-Labor primary. Former state auditor Ray P. Chase led the attack on Governor Benson, attempting to reveal a Jewish-Communist conspiracy within the state administration. While his Republican soldiers redbaited Benson, Stassen campaigned for responsible government, a civil service merit system, more jobs for Minnesota, and "the enactment of a sound labor relations code to lessen the economic and social repercussions of strikes and lockouts."[6]

On September 13, 1938, in a bold incursion into a Farmer-Labor strong-hold, Stassen addressed the Minnesota Farmer-Labor convention in Mankato. Stassen reached out to labor conservatives, contending that improved relations between labor and capital could best be secured "by full recognition of the rights of labor to organize and to bargain collectively through representatives of its own choice." In a shocking departure from Republican tradition, Stassen announced that "we shall never permit the National Guardsmen's bayonets to be used as an employer's weapon to crush those who labor, and neither shall we give to the irresponsible left wing of labor the support of the state government in its attempt to undermine the sound labor movement built through years of constructive leadership." Although Benson received the Minnesota Farmer-Labor Party's endorsement, Stassen's message of labor peace had brought him the support of 20 percent of the Farmer-Labor delegates. Two months later, in the November election, with 59 percent of the vote, Stassen became Minnesota's governor. While Associated Industries' campaign to win the minds of the Minnesota people had not yet led to the downfall of the radical Teamsters, it had certainly helped swing the mood of the state in a conservative direction. With Republican control of the state House and Senate, a comprehensive reform of the state's labor laws seemed inevitable.[7]

With a new governor committed to legislative reforms in labor relations, the state Bar Association, the Farmer-Labor Party, and the CIO all rushed to prepare bills for the 1939 legislature. Confident in their influence with a Republican legislature and state house, attorneys at the MEA quickly wrote an employers' bill. The directors of AI and the St. Paul CA had good reasons for their optimism. The presidential political ambitions of Governor Stassen and the reelection campaigns of the legislators were almost totally dependent on the financial contributions of the open-shop employers of Minneapolis and St. Paul.[8]

Influential members of the AI and its St. Paul counterpart were secretly organized into the "A" Luncheon Group by General Mills executive John Crosby, long-time General Mills legal advisor Sydney Anderson, and Frank P. Leslie of the AI's Leslie Paper Company. Eighty-three percent of the Minnesota Republican Party funds came from the "A" Luncheon Group and the smaller businesses of the "B" group. Checks were collected by AI director Lucian S. Strong and passed on to the Republican State Central Committee, the Republican National Committee, Republican campaign funds, or the Newspaper Publicity Fund. Major contributions came from the executives of General Mills, Pillsbury Company, Peavey, Cargill, Honeywell, Dayton's, the *Star Journal,* and the *Tribune* in Minneapolis, and 3M, West Publishing, and First National Bank in St. Paul. Although Leslie tried to restrain the direct commands of the business community, there is little doubt that Republican office holders, including Governor Stassen, knew who was paying the party's bills and were told what business expected for its money.[9]

Under the direction of AI leaders, Minnesota Employers' Association attorney Charles Elmquist prepared a radical bill that would serve the interests of the state's employers. A new Minnesota Labor Relations Board (MLRB) would be created to mediate disputes and, with the backing of the district courts, to enforce the other Draconian provisions of the law. The measures that would put teeth into the law were listed in two sections of unfair labor practices. Employers were deemed unfair if they spied on employees or blacklisted union members. Of course, these transgressions were difficult to detect and almost impossible to prove in court.

More importantly, employers were restricted from entering "into a closed-shop agreement or check-off of union dues by which employees are prevented from either joining or not joining a union, thereby depriving him of his liberty of action and which therefore constitutes a discrimination in favor of a particular labor organization." Other unfair labor practices included compelling any person to work or not to work, or joining a union or not joining a union by threat or intimidation to any employee, family members, or their property. Elmquist was boldly attempting to make the open shop the law of the state.[10]

The unfair labor practices for employees would, if enacted, severely limit the activities that Local 544 had successfully used to challenge the CA's dominance of Minneapolis industry. Unions were prohibited from

- Seizing property to win a labor dispute (that is, waging a sit-down strike),
- Calling a strike at all unless a majority of workers in the bargaining unit approved by the MLRB voted in a secret ballot conducted by the board to strike,
- Committing a misdemeanor or felony in connection with a labor dispute,
- Striking for any reason except for better wages or conditions of employment,
- Picketing or boycotting by anyone other than the employees of a struck plant,
- Unlawfully interfering with any person in his or her employment, and
- Interfering "in any way with the movement of articles of commerce by motor vehicle or teams upon the public roads, streets, alleys, and highways in the state."

Any employee who committed any of these unfair labor practices could be fired and any union suspended. The law would override the 1933 anti-injunction act and allow the courts to enjoin any violation. If passed into law,

Elmquist and the MEA would strip the Teamsters of the effective strategies that had paralyzed various industries of the city during the numerous strikes of the 1930s. The roving pickets of 1934 and the massive picketing of the Strutwear strike would be outlawed. But would Local 544 obey restrictions that would neutralize direct action and render the union defenseless?

With the conservative International Brotherhood of Teamsters and the MSFL already in a vicious struggle with Local 544 and the CIO for the allegiance of the state's workers, the easiest answer was to isolate Local 544 from the rest of the union movement. In a case of remarkable prescience, Elmquist and the leaders of AI recognized the primary importance of establishing a government-regulated process of certifying the bargaining agent. Whenever a question concerning the representation of employees was raised by an employee, union, employer, or AI, the MLRB would investigate and designate the proper representatives. Any strike or picketing by an uncertified union would, of course, be an unfair labor practice. AI was confident that the MLRB Governor Stassen would appoint would favor the conservative MSFL in any controversy with Local 544 or the CIO. In addition to neutralizing Local 544's tactics and outlawing the closed shop, Elmquist's bill would isolate the Teamsters by essentially declaring them a non-union.

Realizing that a blatant Twin Cities employers' bill would garner little statewide support, the MEA chose five conservative rural legislators to sponsor its bill. The supposedly rural Vance-Myre bill, a barely concealed attack on unions, quickly drew the support of four major farm organizations: Land O'Lakes Creamery, the Minnesota Farm Bureau Federation, the Central Livestock Cooperative, and the Twin City Milk Producers Association. The rural bloc lobbied successfully across the state, asking newspaper editors to support the bill to "give the man who wants to work a chance to work and curb the labor racketeers who have done so much to disturb the conditions in our state in recent years."[11]

By March 1, the farm bloc claimed to "have organized labor in Minnesota backed against the wall," with enough votes to pass the Vance-Myre bill over a Stassen veto, if necessary. The inclusion of Helmer Myre as a bill sponsor, however, was a strategic mistake. As state CIO director Joe Van Nordstrand revealed over WCCO radio, Myre, as Freeborn County sheriff in 1937, had "deputized 200 men to lead a vicious assault upon the picket line and the union headquarters." The Minnesota labor movement had little difficulty realizing both the intent of the bill and the real organization behind it. Battle lines were clearly drawn in a critical contest to determine the future of Minnesota labor relations.[12]

The Vance-Myre bill and the intense lobby for its passage both focused on outlawing the activities of Local 544. The farm bloc was particularly interested in preventing any interference with the movement of their products on the highways. A March 15 *Minneapolis Journal* editorial supported the bill because "we have had enough of sit-down strikes, smashing windows, . . . seizure of highways and intimidation of farmers, . . . destruction of property by lawless mobs, . . . labor union strong-arm men going about the city like wolves telling workers to pay tribute to the unions or else."[13]

Minneapolis employers lobbied Governor Stassen with a detailed analysis of the atrocities of Local 544 and how these excesses would be curbed by the bill's unfair labor practices. They reported case after case where Local 544 had refused to move any goods past any picket line; where violence had erupted when the Teamsters supported a strike; or where truck drivers hauling farm goods were stopped and assaulted. The employers contended that "experience has proven conclusively that a State Labor Relations Act, if it is to successfully minimize industrial strife, promote industrial peace and bring about orderly collective bargaining," must designate these as unfair labor practices[14]

Despite labor protests, the Vance-Myre bill moved quickly through the House Committee on Labor and the Committee on Civil Administration with only minor changes. By March 28, it appeared that the MEA bill would become the law of the state. The Draconian measure, however, would be a political and public relations disaster for Governor Stassen, who had been elected on the promises of fairness and industrial peace. There was also a distinct danger that the restrictive features of the law would provoke the "lawless violence" that it supposedly sought to prevent. Without even the barest pretext of fairness, the public might support a return to the streets by the still-influential Teamsters' Union.[15]

In St. Paul, William H. MacMahon, managing director of the St. Paul Committee on Industrial Relations since its inception in 1920, recognized the problem and conceived a simple solution. MacMahon wrote Governor Stassen suggesting that "legislation should provide that there should be a waiting period of at least thirty days after the presentation of demands before a strike is instituted. Such a waiting period would give all interested parties and the public an opportunity to conciliate and mediate; it would give both sides to the controversy an opportunity to present to the public the facts involved in the situation." If enacted, MacMahon's idea would provide the governor with a peace plan to showcase his political ambitions, while its less public provisions would still eviscerate labor's defensive weapons. MacMahon even suggested repealing the state prohibition on the Highway Patrol's involvement in strikes. More importantly, the peace plan would isolate Local 544, reinforcing the conservative public perception that direct action in the streets had gone too far.[16]

With the Vance-Myre bill nearing passage, Governor Stassen arranged a conference with the authors of the bill, representatives of labor, farm, and employer organizations, and some University of Minnesota faculty. Stassen's objective was to write a new bill providing "every possible means of peaceful settlement before difficulty arises," while still preventing unlawful acts "that have brought reflection upon the entire labor movement on the one hand and upon employers as a whole on the other." The administration bill, supposedly modeled after the national Railway Labor Act and the labor laws of Norway, Sweden, and Denmark, provided a ten-day waiting period before a strike or lockout during which a state labor conciliator appointed by the governor would conduct hearings and negotiations. If the businesses involved invoked a substantial public interest, a further thirty-day waiting period was mandated, during which a three-person commission would hold hearings and issue a report on the controversy.[17]

Minnesota legislators and employers accepted these "peace" provisions quickly. They closely resembled McMahon's proposals, restricting the ability of unions to strike quickly when an issue was hot and allowing companies to prepare for conflict. If the conciliator failed to bring about a compromise, however, both the company and the union maintained their right to strike or lock out. In the final analysis, the "peace" plan would shift the balance slightly toward the members of AI.[18]

Stassen, however, also insisted on eliminating the Vance-Myre bill's prohibition on the closed shop. Associated Industries, of course, was adamantly opposed to the closed shop and had fought against it for nearly four decades. AI attorney Sam Levy explained to Governor Stassen that a "closed-shop agreement discriminates against employees who do not desire to belong to or pay tribute to a labor union. . . . Any attempt on the part of governmental authority to legalize a closed shop is unconstitutional." If the closed shop were legalized, Levy suggested that unions striking for union recognition be designated as an unfair labor practice unless a majority of the employees had voted for the union.[19]

These stipulations, which were already a part of the Vance-Myre bill, were included in Stassen's compromise package. In order to pass a bill over the opposition of the MEA, however, Stassen needed strong support from rural legislators. To entice the farm vote, the Stassen "peace" bill included a provision that prohibited interference with motor vehicles whose owners or operators were not parties to strikes or labor disputes. After an intensive lobbying effort by the administration, both houses of the legislature passed the amended bill and, on April 22, 1939, Governor Stassen signed the Minnesota Labor Relations Act into law.[20]

AI quickly arranged a clinic on the new law at the Radisson Hotel, where President Belden told 300 business people that it was a "pretty good law." AI's attorney then explained the law's provisions and answered questions in great detail. In conclusion, he listed the many benefits that employers would reap from Stassen's evenhanded compromise: Prohibiting "quickie strikes"; outlawing sit-down strikes; allowing employers to request that the labor conciliator certify union representation; declaring a number of union practices unfair and a number others unlawful; providing injunctive relief for violations; and directing "public opinion . . . towards a means that now exists for mediation and conciliation."[21]

How would these benefits affect the balance of power between Associated Industries and Local 544? Although Levy did not answer directly, union contracts in the critical transfer industry were due to expire in two weeks. AI decided to challenge the Teamsters immediately. Local 544 proposed an hourly wage increase to make up for a federally mandated cutback in the workweek from forty-eight to forty-four hours and demanded a week's vacation. The trucking employers proposed across-the-board wage cuts and waited for Local 544's reaction.[22]

At an emergency members' meeting, *Labor Review* editor Robley Cramer told the truck drivers that fear had driven the employers to pass the "Stassen Slave Act." Ray Dunne told union members that "We are going to observe the law in the way it deserves to be observed." On June 7, with negotiations stalled, Local 544 filed the required ten days' notice of its intention to strike. State Labor Conciliator Lloyd Haney, a conservative union man who had campaigned for Stassen, invoked the public interest clause of the law and asked the governor to appoint a three-man commission to investigate. When Stassen appointed three more men from his campaign, Local 544 challenged Haney's certification. District Judge Luther W. Youngdahl, after studying the case, finally upheld the governor, commenting that he "cannot help but feel that if the transfer industry is put out of business for, say, 30 days, it would seriously affect the public interest." While the court ruling buoyed the governor and AI, however, the Teamsters' Local had received an unprecedented strike endorsement from the executive board of the IBT. Local 544 was carefully playing the employers' new labor relations game.[23]

After considering evidence and testimony from union representatives, AI attorney Levy, and Minneapolis Transfermen's Association Secretary Ferris Martin, the commission ruled that there was no cost-of-living increase to justify the requested wage raise. In addition, vacations for hourly workers were rejected because it "virtually amounts to an increase in pay." AI's support of labor relations reform and the Republican Party appeared to be paying immediate dividends. Local 544 announced that the entire report was unacceptable to the union and was biased toward the employers. It refused to base negotiations on the commission's report or to conduct negotiations through Stassen's conciliator. Local 544 would negotiate only directly with the employers. As if to dramatize their stance, the union representatives picked up their briefcases and left the conciliator's office without a further word to Conciliator Haney. Labor peace on AI's terms had failed. Now the new laws would be tested in a direct conflict between AI and Local 544.[24]

At a private negotiating session that afternoon, the Transfermen's Association finally agreed to raise the hourly wage to the same weekly wages but stated that "they would absolutely refuse any vacations at this time." Shortly after the meeting, employers reported the Teamsters' threat to strike back to the now-powerless labor conciliator. Governor Stassen scolded Local 544 for its "chip-on-your-shoulder" attitude and hoped that the local would be more responsible in the future. Early the next morning, Stassen's conciliator was awakened by the Transfermen's Association secretary reporting that Local 544 had pulled workers out of Pratt's Express and Security Warehouse.[25]

The stage was set for a major strike, which would be fought under the restrictive new labor laws written by the MEA. Minneapolis employers, however, were well aware that the Teamsters were still a formidable opponent that had earned the loyalty of the city's workers. Within two weeks, the employers quietly gave in to the demands for a week's vacation and an hourly wage raise. The *Northwest Organizer* reported that "The merits of a union negotiating committee versus a boss commission were never better shown than in the present transfer dispute." Faced with a direct challenge, AI had blinked. There was plenty of time for the "peace plan" to erode the strength of labor's resolve.[26]

AI quickly mounted a public relations campaign based on "its policies to promote peace in labor relations." Minnesota experienced a dramatic decline in strikes during the first three years of the Stassen administration, from 15,865 striking workers each year in 1936–1938 to only 4,684 per year in 1939–1940. In April of 1940, *Nation's Business* reported: "No part of the country has been a brighter spot on the labor map than Minnesota." In Minneapolis, where most of Minnesota's strikes had occurred, only 13 percent of the days of work that were lost in 1936 to 1938 were lost in 1939. AI pointed out that the drop in strikes had actually begun before the passage of the Minnesota Labor Relations Act (MLRA). In the first six months of 1939, Minneapolis experienced only eight strikes involving 1,463 employees.[27]

In its quest to subvert Local 544 and its confrontational leadership of the Minneapolis union movement, AI claimed to have helped negotiate 266 collective bargaining agreements between January and June 1939. The *Civic*

Councilor added, "Few things are calculated to contribute better to Minneapolis development and prosperity than an established system to promote harmony in employer-employee relations." Not to be outdone in promoting labor peace, the Minneapolis Central Labor Union claimed that its Policy Committee intervened in seventy-nine threatened strikes in 1940, settling far more disputes than Stassen's labor conciliator. The gradual isolation of the Trotskyite-led Teamsters' union was moving inexorably forward.[28]

While Governor Stassen acknowledged the contributions to labor peace made by employers and unions, he credited the new law, which had "implemented in a practical and effective manner the desire for labor peace," for changing the "atmosphere" of the state. Within two months of passage, Stassen took his "labor peace" plan to the Governors' Conference, pronouncing that Minnesota was "laying a foundation for reducing to a minimum labor difficulties, which is one of the obstacles in the path of our economic readjustment." In fact, the "Count Ten" law would be a cornerstone for Stassen's future political campaigns for governor and president of the United States.[29]

The national spotlight on Stassen's program received a boost on August 1, 1940, when Senator Ernest Lundeen's plane crashed at the foot of the Blue Ridge Mountains, killing all aboard. Stassen appointed his confidante, reporter Joseph Ball, who agreed closely with the governor's labor positions. Ball quickly became the national spokesman for the "Minnesota miracle." Ball thought that the answer to the nation's labor difficulties was "to require a waiting period, with impartial government investigation and publicity of issues and recommended settlements in extreme cases." On January 31, 1941, the freshman senator from Minnesota brashly introduced a bill that proposed a ten-day notice for conciliation and a thirty-day waiting period for the intervention of a special mediation board appointed by the president. Although Ball's 1941 bill failed to pass, the Minnesota "peace plan" and Stassen's national political aspirations had been launched. The legislation authored by the MEA was succeeding and spreading far beyond the expectations of AI.[30]

The fairness of Stassen's labor peace act would depend on the administration of the office of labor conciliator. For the law's first decade, the Republican governors traditionally chose conservative AFL union officials who disliked Local 544. Stassen, of course, was determined to create industrial peace by delaying, settling, or stifling strikes. While the law called for fact-finding commissions in disputes affecting the public interest, the state conciliator's office interpreted this to mean any defense-related industry. In 1941, fact-finding commissions were appointed in seventy disputes. During the act's first ten years, commissions were appointed in the hotel and restaurant industry, newspapers, optical firms, laundries, the delivery of concrete, and, perhaps the most far-fetched example, a brewery. Minnesota employers, of course, favored these appointments because they delayed strikes and usually weakened the union's position. By the summer of 1941, it was clear to both AI and Local 544 that Stassen's labor peace was to be established on a playing field tilted decidedly toward Minneapolis employers.[31]

Stassen's labor peace act had also opened up some advantageous loopholes for AI members. Although employees were guaranteed the right to bargain collectively through their chosen representatives, it was not an unfair labor practice if the employer simply refused to negotiate. In a similar fashion, it was not an unfair labor practice for an employer to set up a company union. Although the conciliator was forbidden from certifying any organization "dominated, controlled or maintained by an employer," nothing prevented an employer from recognizing or signing a contract with a company union.[32]

Hoping to use this loophole, AI attorney Levy applied for an injunction in district court to ban Minneapolis construction unions from picketing job sites of Associated Independent Unions. When CLU attorneys prepared an employer-dominated union case for the state labor conciliator and the NLRB, however, he quickly abandoned the case. When the CIO's United Electrical Workers Local 1145 began organizing the Minneapolis Honeywell plants, an Employees' Association suddenly appeared. The association claimed to be an independent union freely chosen by Honeywell employees who were "*loyal* to the United States." During a heated campaign, the CIO local repeatedly accused the association of being a company union. When the NLRB supported this claim, the association suddenly disbanded, urging its members to join the AFL. This crude deception was shunned by Minneapolis AFL officials and, by 1942, the CIO had won employee elections at Honeywell. The promise of company unions encouraged by Stassen's labor peace act was rapidly waning.[33]

The true brilliance of the MEA legislation, however, now administered by Stassen's second handpicked conciliator, was revealed in the summer of 1941. When Local 544 withdrew from the AFL and accepted a CIO charter in June, Minneapolis became the focus for a national jurisdictional struggle for control of the nation's trucking industry. IBT president Tobin quickly mobilized several hundred "organizers" to defend the AFL's position in Minneapolis. Over 200 "labor huskies," many from Michigan, cruised the warehouse district, beating up any workers who refused to pledge allegiance to the new 544-AFL.[34]

Promised protection by District Attorney Goff and the chief of police, Tobin's campaign of intimidation quickly forced the leaders of 544-CIO to proclaim a policy of passive resistance. If threatened by "goons," individual union members were to sign AFL pledge cards under protest, but continue to wear their 544-CIO buttons. Wearing two buttons, however, was no protection from

Tobin's organizing squads. Ironically, 544-CIO sought protection from the courts under the Stassen Labor Relations Act, obtaining a court order enjoining the AFL from "interfering with the free and uninterrupted use of the streets" or "attempting through force and violence to compel workers to join the AFL union." The massive street warfare of 1934 that had built the Minneapolis union movement was now abandoned for a new policy of passive resistance and an appeal to law and order. It was a forlorn and fatal mistake.[35]

On June 17, AI's researcher Ward Stevenson issued the employers' position on the AFL-CIO struggle over WLOL radio. Associated Industries feared that the struggle, "if permitted to continue, may ultimately disrupt truck transportation in every state of the union and vitally cripple the nation's gigantic defense program." Stevenson reported that both union factions claimed to represent Minneapolis truck drivers and warned employers not to negotiate with the other side: "Minneapolis employers of truck drivers are now caught in the middle because of circumstances over which they have no control." With Local 544-CIO unable to sign any new contracts, Tobin would gradually force the city's truck drivers back into the AFL. Anticipating a last-ditch wave of strikes from Local 544-CIO, AI attorney Levy obtained from District Court Judge Luther W. Youngdahl a restraining order requiring a ten-day strike notice and prohibiting picketing for 150 businesses in the warehouse, trucking, coal, concrete block, paper, and grocery industries.[36]

Fully aware of its desperate situation, Local 544-CIO called for an immediate strike where strike notices had already been validated by Labor Conciliator Alfred P. Blair in May. The seven largest firms were shut down tight within hours, bolstering the union's claim to represent the city's drivers and inside workers. Within hours, Lloyd MacAloon, who represented most of the struck firms, appeared before Judge Youngdahl, arguing that the May 24 strike notice had been filed by 544-AFL and that 544-CIO had not filed any notice—therefore the strike was invalid under the labor relations act. Of course, this disingenuously ignored the fact that 544-AFL of May 24 and 544-CIO as of June 19 were the exact same union.[37]

Judge Youngdahl, a prominent Republican whom Stassen would consider as an appointee to the governorship the next year, issued a restraining order June 17, outlawing the strike and banning picketing shortly after MacAloon left the witness stand. While copies of the injunction were served on pickets the next morning, employers gave strikers written notice that they would be fired if they did not return to work by June 19. With 544-CIO stymied, the IBT announced that its own Local 544-AFL would now begin negotiations with all employers previously under contract with the union.[38]

Within hours of Judge Youngdahl's injunction, AFL and IBT general counsel Judge Joseph A. Padway held a strategy conference with AI attorney Sam Levy. That afternoon, AFL attorneys appeared in Youngdahl's court seeking an order for Local 544-CIO to turn over its books and assets to the IBT. The judge once again solidified the assault on the renegade union, ordering them to turn over their "headquarters at 257 Plymouth Av. and all furniture, fixtures, utensils, books, records, documents or things located therein" to Tobin's newly appointed trustee of Local 544-AFL. Several Hennepin County deputy sheriffs, backed up by a detail of Minneapolis police officers, were immediately dispatched to seize the union's headquarters. They arrived seconds too late and watched as the defendants piled into waiting cars, arms loaded with books and documents.[39]

Anticipating Tobin's move, Local 544-CIO had already acquired and opened a new headquarters two blocks away and safely removed its cash reserves. Padway and Levy's clever plan was completed four weeks later, when a Hennepin County grand jury indicted Miles Dunne and three other union leaders on charges of embezzlement and grand larceny for removing their members' money. With Judge Youngdahl's assistance, the noose was tightening around the enemies of AI.[40]

Outslugged in the streets and on the shop floors by Tobin's "organizers," and stripped of their legitimacy by Judge Youngdahl in the courts, Local 544-CIO filed petitions with Stassen's labor conciliator asking for industry-wide elections. On June 30, only days after federal raids on Minneapolis SWP headquarters, Conciliator Blair opened hearings on the request. He was met with a parade of workers testifying that the AFL had used threats and intimidation to make them sign pledge cards. At the same time, they had freely signed on with the CIO. IBT lawyers countered that the election of June 9 had been rigged and that the move of Local 544 into the CIO was illegal. On August 2, after several delays, Blair finally issued his first decision, denying elections in the furniture industry because Local 544 was guilty of an unfair labor practice—striking the furniture industry on June 17, "without giving notice as required in the state labor relations act." It was clear that Stassen's labor conciliator would follow Judge Youngdahl's lead.[41]

Even more ominous for the radicals of Local 544-CIO, the AFL had petitioned Blair three days earlier asking for his certification of the AFL as the bargaining agent for the entire Minneapolis trucking industry without an election. Even the *Minneapolis Star,* an AI member, reported that it was a move "without precedent since the state labor relations act was passed." While Blair repeatedly postponed the hearings to decide which union should represent employees, he conducted negotiations between AI members and Local 544-AFL. Discovering this deception, the Teamsters' CIO local filed strike notices against the wholesale grocers, coal dealers, and paper companies represented by AI.[42]

Stassen immediately delayed the strikes by invoking the thirty-day, public interest, cooling-off period of the Minnesota Labor Relations Act. Four days later, the IBT began signing contracts with the trucking companies. The *Industrial Organizer* quickly distributed copies of the wholesale grocers' contract, which made concessions on wages, overtime, vacations, and job protection. On August 29, a Stassen commission invalidated the Local 544-CIO strike notices because the union should have waited for Blair's certification decision and because Local 544-AFL had entered into a working agreement with the employers on August 14, 1941. The commission also accepted in detail AI attorney Levy's evidence that employees of the wholesale grocery firms were predominately dues-paying members of the AFL. The commission reported in its conclusion that the representatives of Local 544-CIO "have no respect for the Minnesota Labor Relations Act."[43]

On September 19, 1941, Stassen's labor conciliator certified Local 544-AFL as the bargaining agent for twenty-four groups of employers representing 570 firms and 5,500 drivers and helpers. Blair's ruling contended that "to effectuate the purposes of the Minnesota Labor Relations Act and to promote and preserve industrial peace and to safeguard the continued flow of commerce, it is essential there be one and only one bargaining agent for the general drivers and helpers of the Minneapolis area." In certifying the AFL unit that, according to Blair, had been representing Minneapolis drivers for the past five years, he dismissed the men who had led the Minneapolis labor movement for seven years, pretending that they represented only 172 men. AFL general counsel Padway called it "a just, fair and momentous decision," which would end the "loud clamoring of the men." In the September 25 issue of the *Industrial Organizer*, Local 544-CIO bitterly commented that "democracy is all right to talk about and to send abroad on the tips of bayonets. But democracy is beyond the reach of Minneapolis drivers."[44]

Local 544-CIO had been stripped of all its bargaining rights and deprived of its right to strike. Its leaders faced federal charges of sedition and local charges of embezzlement and grand larceny. The AFL had successfully forced the Teamsters to the fringe of the Minneapolis union movement. Trotskyite union leader Farrell Dobbs recognized the brutal truth of their situation: "As a result of these combined factors, what had previously been a dynamic organization with great ability to defend the workers' interest was reduced to little more than a union in name only." Realizing the "pointless risk of further victimization," the bitter leaders of 544-CIO urged its members to retain their jobs and join the AFL. The ferocious union that had waged a seven-year war against the CA and its successor, AI, had lost the final battle and disbanded. Unable to destroy Local 544 in the streets, AI had rewritten Minnesota labor law and then, with the aid of the Stassen administration, had used that law to behead its enemy.[45]

The eruption of a radical union movement had taken seven hard years to extinguish. The businessmen of AI were determined that it would never happen again. The core strength that had sustained Local 544 through the years of attack sprang from a battle-hardened loyalty inspired by the union's Trotskyite leaders. When any Minneapolis union was under attack, Local 544 was there to help defend it, with their blood if necessary. This industrial warfare solidified the working class and focused its energy and anger on the business firms of AI. The MLRA had slowed the direct action of Local 544 to a crawl and then allowed the Stassen administration to decertify the union into oblivion, but it might not stop another strong union from rebuilding the union solidarity that had come close to toppling the industrial dominance of Associated Industries. Clearly, the MLRA must be amended to outlaw Minnesota unions giving assistance to other unions that were on strike.

In early August of 1944, the officers of AI and the St. Paul Committee on Industrial Relations (SPCIR) held a conference with MEA President Otto F. Christenson. The Twin Cities business organizations were determined to amend the MLRA and wanted the MEA to once again channel the legislation through the Minnesota legislature. The same month, representatives of AI, SPCIR, the MEA, the Duluth Business Council, and several Minnesota farm groups met at the St. Paul Athletic Club to analyze the deficiencies of the MLRA and recommend changes. Leavitt R. Barker and Henry Haliday, both from the law firm of Dorsey, Colman, Barker, Scott and Barber, presented the recommendations of AI, and William H. MacMahon represented the SPCIR. Haliday then drafted the preliminary legislation. By the December meeting of the MEA board of directors, the council for AI had drafted a bill prohibiting secondary boycotts for the 1945 legislature. The allied farm groups included a provision in the bill outlawing supposed intimidation tactics used by drivers' union organizers to force farmers into the union. Plans were laid for the representatives of industrial and farm groups to meet with and advise Republican Governor Edward J. Thye before the measure was introduced to the legislature.[46]

The 1945 secondary boycott bill quickly became the controversial focal point of the legislative session. Minnesota State Federation of Labor President Robert Olson testified before a House labor committee, stating, "Anyone who even tells his storekeeper he will trade elsewhere because the storekeeper is selling products of a concern unfair to organized labor can be thrown into jail for a year and be fined $1,000." Another provision made it mandatory for a county attorney to prosecute anyone reported by the labor conciliator to be in violation of the law. MEA President Christenson countered that employers did not "object to anyone asking others not to patronize a place of business. What we do object to is putting a union picket in front of an innocent business establishment. Then truck drivers will refuse to deliver ice, fuel, merchandise or anything else and that innocent man's business can be destroyed." Despite union claims that "It was the Reichstag that passed a secondary boycott law and helped break the German unions," the bill passed the Senate by a thirty-six to eleven vote on March 6 and sailed through the House eighty-one to forty-seven in early April.[47]

Republican Governor Thye, who had suggested off the record that the anti-labor legislation might swing the pendulum too far in the other direction, came under intensive pressure to sign the bill into law. A flood of telegrams from rural editors and farmer and labor delegations urged him to sign. Republican legislators threatened to undermine the governor's other legislation and even jettison him in the next election if he vetoed the measure. Frank Leslie, who raised most of the money for Thye's campaign from AI members, and John Crosby spent the entire night trying to persuade the governor to sign the bill. On April 12, Governor Thye held his ground and vetoed the MEA's secondary boycott bill. Leslie immediately received angry ultimatums from a number of Minneapolis industrialists. One of the major contributors announced, "I'm through. Don't ask me for any more money." Leslie went straight to the man's office and told him, "You said you were through—you should remember—you're *never* through. Any man in your position is never through." Thye's veto was a setback, but AI would fight on until the battle was won.[48]

Two years later, with another Republican governor at the Capitol, Luther Youngdahl, the MEA had a streamlined bill reintroduced in the state legislature. Strongly backed by employer and farm groups, the rewritten measure would eliminate jurisdictional and organizational picketing in addition to outlawing the secondary boycott. Fairly sure of a favorable vote in both the House and the Senate, the MEA decided to forego the ferocious committee hearings that had characterized the 1945 fight. The MEA enthusiasm for quick Senate passage, however, was tempered by Governor Youngdahl's demand for milder legislation that employer groups felt would permit most of the boycotts they were seeking to outlaw. Ignoring the governor's veto threat, the House passed the MEA legislation with little change. Once again, Frank Leslie pulled on the Republican Party purse strings in an attempt to influence the governor's decision. On April 23, Youngdahl signed the bill into law, remarking that he "could not have looked Frank Leslie in the eye if he hadn't." More importantly, of course, he needed Leslie's fund-raising machine to continue his political career.[49]

The MEA's executive vice president Christenson happily announced: "Industry and business in Minnesota will be glad to learn this bill has been enacted. We commend Governor Youngdahl for signing it. It is a step toward industrial peace and will improve the already good labor relations for which Minnesota is outstanding." AI had good reason to be pleased. The organizational picketing that Local 544 and other unions had used at Strutwear and Flour City Ornamental Iron in 1935 was now unlawful. Of even greater importance, the Teamsters could no longer legally refuse to deliver goods to employers where employees were out on strike. Local 544 had fostered a strong and united union movement by using its critical position in Minneapolis industry to aid almost any union in its struggle for recognition. The Teamsters' ability to shut down the city's flow of goods had proved to be a formidable weapon. Under the banner of labor peace, the MEA and AI had finally destroyed its enemy's most effective weapon. At the same time, employers had retained their own right to break a strike by sending their work to another AI member who was not on strike. Stassen's labor peace was to be established at the expense of the union movement. The specter of another challenge to Associated Industries' industrial empire had been extinguished.[50]

The influence of MEA labor legislation, however, was not limited to Minnesota. In Washington, D.C., Senator Ball was leading the Senate toward a new national labor relations law modeled on the policies that the Minnesota Employers' Association had pioneered in Minnesota. In June 1945, Ball and Senators Burton and Hatch introduced a bill based on the Railway Labor Act and the Minnesota Labor Relations Act that included cooling-off periods, mediations, and fact-finding boards. The bill also attempted to amend the Wagner Act to include employee unfair labor practices that would have severely restrained union activities. When a compromise bill finally emerged from the Seventy-ninth Congress, Senators Ball, Taft, and Smith offered amendments to reinstate the unfair labor practices and outlaw the secondary boycott. Although President Truman vetoed the legislation on June 11, 1946, a new, powerful, anti-labor coalition was coalescing in the Senate Committee on Education and Labor.[51]

The next January, the three Republican senators introduced a revised draft of the vetoed Case bill. The provisions of the bill, however, did not go far enough for Minnesota's Senator Ball, who *Business Week* called the Labor and Education Committee's most implacable foe of big labor. On January 21, 1947,

Senator Ball detailed his own plans for national labor legislation to the MEA at the St. Paul Hotel. Ball warned that unions "are tremendously wealthy and powerful organizations whose policies and actions have terrific repercussions on our whole economy."[52]

Of primary importance to the MEA were Ball's proposals to prohibit the secondary boycott and the closed union shop. In language that the MEA could applaud, Ball argued that the closed shop turns over to the union "absolute control over the individual's right and opportunity to work and earn a livelihood." In six years, Ball's proposals had followed the legislative proposals of AI, from the MLRA to the 1947 amendments. The senator's speech echoed the legislation that he had introduced between January 6 and 10. In one week, Ball's Senate bills S.733, S.55, and S.105 called for the prohibition of industry-wide bargaining, the secondary boycott, and the closed shop. If the industrial leaders of AI had ever had reason to doubt their financing of the Minnesota Republican Party, those doubts evaporated in the spring of 1947.[53]

Ironically, the most forceful voice of moderation at the Taft committee hearings was Minnesota's former governor, Harold Stassen. Stassen interrupted his presidential campaign to attack Senator Ball's proposals to outlaw the closed shop and industry-wide bargaining. Stassen testified that anti-closed-shop legislation would "inject an element of instability in many stable, fair, and constructive labor relationships. It will be a major factor in so weakening the structure of labor as to place labor at a disadvantage in reasonable collective bargaining with management." In a bitter quarrel over industry-wide bargaining, Stassen told Ball that his proposed ban would allow employers to "pick off one union at a time."[54]

Ball, who had managed Stassen's presidential campaign three years earlier, argued that "The closed shop is much more a device to increase the power of union leaders over the employees than it is to increase the power of employees in relationship to the employer." He added that Stassen's statements in favor of industry-wide bargaining were merely "the classic argument for monopoly whenever it occurs." In the heat of the argument, Ball blurted out: "Collective bargaining is an interference with a completely free market." Stassen quickly capitalized on the explosive exchanges, publishing the testimony in a book, *Where I Stand,* that detailed his proposed presidential policies. Despite his more moderate stance, however, Stassen still voiced his full support for a ban on mass picketing, jurisdictional strikes, and secondary boycotts in conjunction with a system of cooling-off periods and mediation similar to the MLRA.[55]

Senator Ball's campaign to radically alter national labor policy received substantial support from the NAM, which had been organizing pressure against the Wagner Act since its passage in 1935. In preparation for the Eight-

ieth Congress, the NAM adopted labor relations policies that called for the prohibition of the closed shop, industry-wide bargaining, mass picketing, jurisdictional and sympathy strikes, strikes for recognition of an uncertified union,
and the secondary boycott. At a December 1946 convention of manufacturers, NAM board chairman Ira Mosher advised that industrial peace could come
through elimination of four "root causes" of strikes: Industry-wide bargaining, the closed shop, the secondary boycott, and mass picketing. In early 1947,
the NAM threw the massive resources of its propaganda machine into the fight.
Ads were launched with provocative headlines: "How about Some Pro-Public
legislation?"; "Industry Wide Bargaining is No Bargaining For You"; and
"Who Wants the Closed Shop?" The long NAM campaign for a "fair" program
for industrial harmony, which would be "good for all," gradually increased the
pressure on Congress to pass pro-business labor legislation.[56]

While Stassen and Ball dramatically argued over Senate legislation, the
NAM quietly influenced the direction of the House. Each member of the House
Education and Labor Committee received a personalized leather-bound copy
of the NAM's labor program. Chairman Fred Hartley and Republican committee members then worked out the legislation "behind closed doors." According to Representative Klein, the Hartley bill was actually written with the assistance of lawyers from the NAM and the United States Chamber of
Commerce. Although the NAM released a public statement denying the accusation, the final legislation, which passed by a large majority on April 17, bore
a remarkable resemblance to the NAM's program, including the prohibition of
the closed shop and industry-wide bargaining and new powers of injunction
for employers. Despite the tough pro-business stance of the Hartley bill, Minnesota's representative on the committee, George E. MacKinnon, claimed that
it would provide "democracy to all unions that is now provided by the best
unions" and would protect workers' "freedom of speech and political freedom
and protect them from intimidation." The AFL's William Green declared "Hartley will be classified as one of labor's chief enemies."[57]

On June 23, 1947, the United States Senate followed the House and voted
sixty-eight to twenty-five to override President Truman's veto of the Taft-
Hartley bill. Business Week declared that the Labor Management Relations Act
(LMRA) of 1947 was "A New Deal for America's Employers." The "license" of
the vast union movement "to operate almost without check has now been revoked." Although Senator Ball and the NAM were frustrated in their attempt
to ban industry-wide bargaining, the LMRA of 1947 initiated profound new restrictions on union labor's ability to defend itself. In an attempt to equalize the
law, the new federal law banned secondary boycotts and the closed shop. Although the union shop was legal after an NLRB election, more restrictive state

laws were legalized. Strikes or boycotts to force employers to cease business with another employer or to recognize or bargain with an uncertified union were now unfair labor practices and unlawful. Jurisdictional strikes or boycotts were also unfair labor practices. If disputes arose, the NLRB would decide the appropriate bargaining unit.[58]

The crucial Minnesota statute that Stassen had used to decertify Local 544 was now a national law. If a union was guilty of unfair labor practices, employers could seek court injunctions and sue for damages in federal court even if the actions of union members or agents were unauthorized. A union's right to strike was now restricted during a sixty-day negotiation period for collective bargaining. In the case of a strike that might imperil the national welfare, the president could enjoin the union from striking for eighty days. As a final blow against radical unions, all union officials had to file an affidavit swearing that they were not Communists.[59]

Governor Stassen believed that the new national labor law would be a success because it was "very similar in its basic principles to the MLRA of 1939." In fact, the establishment of cooling-off periods, unfair labor policies for employees, and the restrictions on boycotts and jurisdictional strikes can be traced from AI and the MEA to the Minnesota legislature and Republican governors Stassen, Thye, and Youngdahl, to Senator Ball and the Taft-Hartley Act. The Minnesota law and the national act were both written with the express purpose of restricting the power of labor unions and realigning the balance of power in American industry. The nation's union press labeled it "a law designed to smash all labor." An AI newsletter answered that the new law primarily "*protects the right and liberty of the individual worker*; attempts to safeguard him against abuse and coercion from *any source*; endeavors to protect the public interest and to make both parties in collective bargaining equal before the law; while at the same time preserving most of the gains for unions provided in the Wagner Act and granting others. The claim that this will smash all labor unions and enslave American workers, is clearly untenable."[60]

AI, of course, knew what it was writing about. The new labor relations era, conceived to thwart the power of Minneapolis Teamsters' Local 544, was meant to stabilize a conservative union bureaucracy and isolate the union movement from the threatening leadership of the country's radical movements while neutralizing the immense power of the country's workers. In less than a decade, the business community of Minneapolis had gone through an amazing metamorphosis and, in the process, had helped change the face of American labor relations.[61]

Epilogue

FIFTY-THREE YEARS AFTER Governor Youngdahl signed the final piece of the labor relations program created by Associated Industries and the Minnesota Employers' Association, the rules governing the conflict between Minnesota's employers and labor unions remain virtually unchanged. The direct-action strategies that enabled Teamsters' Local 574 to break the iron grip of the CA's non-union-shop industrial empire are still outlawed. Unions must still give ten days' notice of their intent to strike and wait thirty days while a commission investigates disputes affecting the public interest. In jurisdictional controversies, a labor referee decides which union represents employees and "will best promote industrial peace," based on the "past history of the organization, harmonious operation of the industry, and most effective representation for collective bargaining." The 2000 labor relations law proscribes the sit-down strike; interfering with the movement of employees entering or leaving a place of business; interfering with the operation of vehicles not directly involved in a strike; and interfering with the transport of agricultural products. In addition, jurisdictional, organizational, and secondary boycotts continue to be prohibited. The prohibitions on direct action that destroyed the radical Teamsters' union in the 1940s continue to restrict the activities of Minnesota labor unions in the twenty-first century.[1]

Employers, however, did not suffer under the same restraints. Although the 1935 Wagner Act protected the rights of workers to join unions and strike and prohibited employers from firing strikers, the United States Supreme Court in 1938 ruled that an employer had a right to "protect and continue his business by supplying places left vacant by strikers. And he is not bound to discharge those hired to fill the places of strikers" if the striking workers return to work. Employers can replace striking union workers with a larger group of non-union workers under the 1947 Taft-Hartley Act, and then request a decertification election that they will almost certainly win. If the employer waits out the strike for over twelve months, the striking workers no longer have a right to vote for continued union representation. The legal tools for the destruction of union labor were in place by 1950. Political repercussions and the power of the country's major unions, however, kept the use of these strategies in check.[2]

A new era in labor relations was heralded in 1981, however, when President Ronald Reagan fired the nation's striking air-traffic controllers. Four years later, United States employers were threatening to hire permanent replacements in 31 percent of strikes. Unions quickly learned that these were not idle threats. The Government Accounting Office found that permanent replacements were actually hired in 17 percent of 1985 strikes. Major companies like Phelps Dodge, International Paper, Hormel, Eastern Airlines, and Greyhound began to end their labor disputes by hiring permanent replacements to take strikers' jobs. In 1989, a House committee estimated that 21,000 workers had lost their jobs by "replacement." With employers taking direct action to destroy their company's unions, picket lines were reduced to a tragic display of futility. Facing the imminent, permanent loss of their jobs, workers' participation in strikes and membership in unions declined dramatically. The employer offensive of the 1980s was clearly successful.[3]

In Minnesota, the Employers' Association of Greater Minneapolis (formerly Associated Industries and the Minneapolis Citizens Alliance) and the St. Paul Employers' Association (formerly the St. Paul Citizens Alliance) merged in 1985 to form the Employers' Association, Inc. (EA), which followed the national trend. On June 20, 1983, 300 lithographers at Viking Press, Bureau of Engraving, Meyer Printing, John Roberts Company, and four other printing companies, all EA members, went on strike. Meyer Printing advertised for permanent replacements even before the strike began, and printers from Missouri, Ohio, and New York quickly brought the plant back up to a full staff. The strike was declared over on August 30, 1984, when the final employer, the Bureau of Engraving, voted to decertify the union.[4]

Six years and sixteen strikes later, on October 2, 1989, EA member Quality Tool hired permanent replacements several days after union workers struck its St. Paul plant on October 2, 1989. Eighteen months later, the picket lines were gone and all twenty-seven strikers had lost their jobs. Quality Tool president William ("Bill") Rowe looked forward to a bright, union-less future. Late in 1991, the labor relations department at EA intensified its campaign, warning unions before they struck at LSI Corporation of America and General Resources Corporation that permanent replacements would be hired. The Carpenters' and Teamsters' unions quickly found out that the EA was not bluffing.[5]

In January 1991, the Minnesota AFL-CIO, the Minnesota Teamsters, and the Minnesota Farmers' Union sought legislation to prohibit employers from hiring permanent replacements for strikers during an economic strike or lockout. As the companion bills worked their way through the House and Senate, the

MEA, now renamed the Minnesota Chamber of Commerce (MNCC), and the EA lobbied intensively to defeat the measures. The MNCC wrote senators, arguing that "Removing or restricting one side's use of its economic power would radically shift the delicate balance of power in collective bargaining disputes in favor of labor unions." The EA distributed an "Issue Brief" to its members, arguing that HF 304 "essentially abandons the policy of (government) neutrality in economic strikes first laid down by the United States Supreme Court in 1938 and leaves employers no effective recourse but to accede to union demands or curtail/cease operations." Even EA members without labor unions would be threatened, as the proposed change "would also enhance unions' ability to organize."[6]

On May 17, the Senate followed the House's lead and passed Senate File 597 by a forty-one-to-twenty vote. The EA quickly sent a "Veto Alert!!!" telling members that it was "imperative" that they urge Governor Arne Carlson to veto HF 304. Ironically, when Republican Governor Carlson failed to return his veto to the legislature within the constitutional three-day limit, Minnesota became the first state in the nation with a law prohibiting permanent replacements for striking or locked-out workers. The state's business leaders predicted ominous results and promised a legal challenge to the dangerous statute.[7]

When the Business Partnership, made up of the heads of ninety-five of the state's largest firms, and the MNCC declined to accept the challenge, EA president Tom Ebert stepped forward. The EA had the resources to accept the expense of a possibly long court battle. It was supported by corporate giants Norwest Bank, General Mills, and Dayton Hudson, which had financed the open-shop goals of the CA since its organization in 1903, and claimed more than 1,200 members statewide in 1991. Because the new law directly affected the labor relations operations of the EA, it represented the business community's best chance for a successful test case. While the Business Partnership and the MNCC were primarily lobbying organizations, EA had labor relations specialists available to handle contract negotiations and to assist employers in repelling union organization campaigns for over 200 of its members throughout Minnesota. Labor relations memberships were held by organizations such as KTCA-TV, Hamline University, the City of Hudson, Hoigaard's, Inc., Kowalski's Markets, the Minneapolis Institute of Arts, Northwestern Casket Company, Walker Lumber Company, and the Williams Steel and Hardware Company.[8]

On September 1, 1991, EA president Ebert and labor relations director Tom Rinne agreed that they would support a member challenge to the law, but only in an economic dispute, "not anti union." A month later, frustrated by the lack of a good case that "may be months away," Rinne suggested that the EA challenge the law itself on behalf of its membership. Fortunately, the current contract between Northern Hydraulics, Inc., which had an EA labor relations membership, and the United Steel Workers of America (USWA) expired on September 13, 1991.[9]

While union members engaged in informational picketing, EA specialist Len Grannes negotiated with the union on behalf of the company. On September 30, Grannes informed the union that Northern Hydraulics would hire permanent replacement workers if the union went out on strike. The union representative responded that the Minnesota Striker Replacement Law prohibited the threatened actions. The effect of the law on their members' negotiations with unions was now obvious and presented the opportunity that Ebert and Rinne had been waiting for. After receiving approval from the EA's board of directors, they hired the Dorsey and Whitney law firm in Minneapolis, which had been associated with open-shop employers for over fifty years, to file a lawsuit challenging the constitutionality of the Striker Replacement Law in Minneapolis federal district court.[10]

On December 2, 1991, Dorsey and Whitney attorney Douglas R. Christensen filed a complaint against the USWA in federal court. A week later, union protesters rallied on the front steps of the prestigious law firm's offices in the First Bank Building. Christensen asked the court for a summary judgment, ruling that the Striker Replacement Law was preempted by federal labor law and therefore contravened the Supremacy Clause of the United States Constitution. The EA's arguments were supported by amicus briefs from the MNCC and the Labor Policy Association, a national business-lobbying group brought into the case by an EA board member. District Court Judge James M. Rosenbaum concluded: "It is well-established labor law that an employer may hire permanent replacement workers during a lawful lockout of employees or during an economic strike." Minnesota's Striker Replacement Law "forbids actions which federal law clearly permits. Therefore the Court finds that the Striker Replacement Law is contrary to federal labor law and is preempted. The Act seeks to deny to an employer its protected right to resort to economic weapons should more peaceful measures not avail." On October 1, 1992, Judge Rosenbaum granted the EA's motion for a summary judgment declaring the law unconstitutional.[11]

Nine months later, the EA presented its arguments to the United States Court of Appeals for the Eighth Circuit's hearing on the USWA's appeal of Judge Rosenbaum's order. The case, now halfway through its second year, was making a serious impact on the EA's budget. Ebert solicited contributions from EA members and quickly covered all legal expenses. While the case was delayed in federal court, the Minnesota Supreme Court overturned an earlier state court ruling in a similar case, finding that "the decision to regulate the use of economic weapons or to continue to permit their unfettered use is for Congress. . . . In either event the decision is pre-empted by federal labor law." On March 11, 1994, the Minnesota Supreme Court agreed with Judge Rosenbaum that the Striker Replacement Law was unconstitutional. EA president Ebert said the association is "very pleased that Minnesota employers are no longer affected by this onerous law." In August of 1994, the Eighth Circuit Court affirmed Judge Rosenbaum's decision.[12]

The Minnesota Striker Replacement Law was finally dead. Ebert thought it "a victory for labor law that has been effective since the 1930s and helps both sides achieve equality." The EA had extinguished the first serious threat to the labor relations laws that it had written fifty-five years earlier. It had reestablished an "equality" that allowed its members to permanently replace strikers and decertify their unions. The threat of direct actions by the EA to destroy unions would once again wring concessions out of negotiations with unions and stifle union organization. Now entering the twenty-first century and its approaching 100th anniversary, the EA continues to defend the open shop.[13]

Appendixes

Appendix A   *Citizens Alliance Founders, 1903*

L. J. Bardwell	Bardwell, Robinson Co.
George K. Belden	W. I. Gray and Co.
Otis P. Briggs	Minneapolis Steel and Machinery Co.
William I. Gray	W. I. Gray and Co.
H. S. Gregg	Minneapolis Iron Store
Samuel A. Harris	National Bank of Commerce
Frederick E. Kenaston	Minneapolis Threshing Machine Co.
Owen B. Kinnard	Kinnard and Haines Co.
Martin B. Koon	Koon, Whelan and Bennett
Benjamin F. Nelson	B. F. Nelson Mfg. Co.
Edmund J. Phelps	Minnesota Loan and Trust Co.
Alexander M. Robertson	Minneapolis General Electric Co.
Fred R. Salisbury	Salisbury and Satterlee Co.
James D. Shearer	Belden, Jamison and Shearer
Albert W. Strong	Strong and Scott Mfg. Co.
Charles D. Velie	Deere and Webber Co.
Thomas B. Walker	T. B. Walker
John F. Wilcox	Wilcox Motor Car Co.

Appendix B *Citizens Alliance and Associated Industries Boards of Directors*

Name	Company	Organization and/or Dates
Clifford Anderson	Crown Iron Works	AI
E. L. Anderson	Crown Iron Works	1932
A. C. Andrews	Andrews Grain Co.	1932
L. S. Ashley	Northwestern Casket Co.	AI–1936
David E. Babcock	Dayton's	AI
M. Badenoch	General Mills, Inc.	AI–1945
Walter L. Badger	N. W. Terminal Co.	1930s
E. P. Baker	Baker Iron Co.	AI–1936
L. J. Bardwell	Bardwell, Robinson Co.	1915
Leavitt R. Barker	Dorsey, Colman, Barker, Scott and Barber	AI–1945
Charles E. Bateman	Old Tyme Bakeries	1915
J. B. Beardslee	Pittsburgh Coal Co.	1930s
Daniel Belcher	Bemis Bros. Boiler and Mfg. Co.	1932
George K. Belden	W. I. Gray and Co.	AI–1936
Judson Bemis	Bemis Bros. Bag Co.	AI–1947
T. N. Bergquist	Gray Co., Inc.	AI
H. T. Bertsch	Northome Furniture Industry, Inc.	1920s
Otis P. Briggs	H. E. Wilcox Motor Co.	1915
Edwin R. Booth	Regan Bakeries, Inc.	AI
Anson S. Brooks	Brooks-Scanlon Lumber Co.	1932
Bernard M. Bros	William Bros Boiler and Mfg. Co.	1915
Raymond J. Bros	William Bros Boiler and Mfg. Co.	AI–1945
J.C. Buckbee	Bureau of Engraving	1930s
B. S. Bull	Washburn-Crosby Co.	1918
A. P. Burris	Electric Machinery Mfg. Co.	AI
C. Cameron	Cameron Transfer and Storage Co.	1919
Albert Carlson		1929

Francis A. Chamberlain	First National Bank	1932
Harlow H. Chamberlain	Boyd Transfer Co.	1929
L. M. Chamberlain	Boyd Transfer Co.	1915
William R. Chapman	Midland National Bank	AI
Homer A. Childs	Super Value Stores, Inc.	AI
W. P. Christian	Northern Bag Co.	1932
John S. Clapper	Toro Mfg. Co.	1930s
A. E. Clerihew	Forman Ford and Co.	1918
Joseph R. Cochran	Cameron Transfer and Storage Co.	1932
J. N. Collins	J. N. Collins Co. (candy)	1929
R. N. Connors	Chase Bag Co.	1930s
George Cook	Pike and Cook Co.	1929
Franklin M. Crosby	Washburn-Crosby Co.	1915
William W. Cullen	Carr-Cullen Co.	AI–1945
H. L. Day	H. L. Day	1915
Kingsley Day	Southside Lumber	AI–1936
Edward W. Decker	Northwestern National Bank	1932
Marshall J. Diebold	Northrup, King and Co.	AI
Henry Doerr, Jr.	Minneapolis Drug Co.	AI–1936
George A. DuToit, Jr.	Minneapolis Honeywell Regulator Co.	AI–1945
J. E. Eckstrom		1919
Soren A. Egekvist	Egekvist Bakeries	AI–1947
L. A. Eggleston	David C. Bell Investment Co.	AI
J. W. Falconer	Northern Bag Co.	1918
Walter H. Feldman		AI–1947
T. W. Findley	Findley Electric Co.	1929
E. A. Forgeot	LaBelle Transfer Co.	1915
William A. French	William A. French and Co.	1932
Roscoe J. Furber	Northern States Power	AI
Ross Gamble	Gamble-Robinson Co.	1918
F. H. Gahre	Bardwell Robinson	1932
Herbert M. Gardner	Gardner Hardware Co.	1915
C. T. Gibson		AI–1947
George M. Gillette	Minneapolis Steel and Machinery Co.	1915
E. M. Goldsborough	W. S. Nott Co.	1929
R. W. Goodell	Commander-Larabee Corp.	1930s
James A. Graham	Studebaker Corp. of America	1918
William I. Gray	W. I. Gray and Co.	1929
F. W. Greaves	Gateway State Bank	1918
H. S. Gregg	Gregg Mfg. Co.; Minneapolis Iron Store	1932

William T. Greig	Bureau of Engraving	AI–1936–
Charles F. Haglin	C. F. Haglin and Sons Co.	1932
Lloyd Hale	G. H. Tennant Co.	AI
George E. Hall	Hall Hardware Co.	1932
Henry Halladay	Dorsey, Owen, Marquart, Windhorst and West	AI
Philip B. Harris		AI–1947
T. G. Harrison	Winston and Newell Co.	1930s
Willis C. Helm	Russell-Miller Milling Co.	AI–1936
J. S. Hernlund	Crown Iron Works	1918
J. W. Hernlund	Crown Iron Works	1915
C. J. Hoigaard	Hoigaard's, Inc.	AI
C. L. Holt	Holt Motor Co.	AI–1945
Charles H. Hornburg	Deere and Webber Co.	1930s
Charles C. Ingraham	Hart-Carter Co.	1930s
Charles H. Jensen	Jensen Printing Co.	1932
William C. Jensen	Jensen Printing Co.	AI
C. B. Jordan	Jordan-Stevenson Co.	AI–1936
Walter Jordan	W. B. Jordan Co.	1918
Frederick E. Kenaston	Minneapolis Threshing Machine Co.	1915
Ron Kennedy	F. H. Peavey and Co.	AI
Hubert Kennedy	Cedar Lake Ice and Fuel Co.	AI–1945
Claude D. Kimball	Kimball and Storer Co.	1915
C. H. Kinnard	Kinnard and Haines Foundry and Machine Co.	1915
Owen B. Kinnard	Kinnard and Haines Foundry and Machine Co.	1915
E. C. Kischel	Kischel Auto Co.	1919
F. W. Lagerquist	Gust Lagerquist and Sons	1932
M. A. Lehman	Pillsbury Mills Co.	1932
E. E. Leighton	H. N. Leighton Co.	1915
A.W. Leslie	John Leslie Paper Co.	AI–1945
Gordon B. Loomis	Conklin-Zonne-Loomis Co.	1930s
George H. Lugsdin	G. H. Lugsdin Co.	1932
C. Arthur Lyman	American Ball Co.	1932
F. W. Lyman	Lyman, Eliel Drug Co.	1915
F. R. Lyon	Lyon and Co.	1915
Pat Lyon	Janney, Semple, Hill and Co.	1915
Martin C. Madsen	Madsen Construction Co.	1932
Fred Malcolmson	Pence Auto	1929

C. C. Massie	Northrup, King and Co.	AI–1945
J. H. Mayhew	Hart-Carter Co.	1932
Lloyd L. McBurney	Tescom Corp.	AI
H. Clay McCartney	Toro Mfg. Co.	AI
J. L. McCaull	McCaull-Webster Grain Co.	1918
Fred L. McClellan	McClellan Paper Co.	1915
John M. McClure		AI–1947
Silas McClure	Electric Machinery Mfg. Co.	1930s
J. F. McDonald	J. F. McDonald Lumber Co.	1919
J. G. McHugh	Chamber of Commerce	1932
Frank E. McNally	B. F. Nelson Mfg. Co.	1932
J. G. McNutt	Ford McNutt Glass Co.	1930s
F. R. McQueen	Barnett and Record Co.	1929
J. E. McReavy	McReavy Bros. Transfer Co.	1932
A. M. Melone	Melone-Bovey Lumber Co.	1929
Charles B. Mills	Midland National Bank	1929
Howard Mithun	Minneapolis Star and Tribune	AI
L. R. Molan	Regan Bros. Co.	1930s
E. J. Moles	Janney, Semple, Hill and Co.	1915
Alan H. Moore	First National Bank	AI–1945
Gerry E. Morse	Minneapolis Honeywell Regulator Co.	AI
Guilford A. Morse	Custom Laundry	1932
W. W. Morse	Security Warehouse Co.	1918
J. A. Mull	Central Elevator Co.	1929
C. T. Naugle	Naugle-Leck, Inc.	1932
Henry J. Neils	Flour City Ornamental Iron Works	AI–1945
F. L. Neilson	Cargill Warehouse Co.	1930s
Benjamin F. Nelson	B. F. Nelson Mfg. Co.	1915
Ben F. Nelson	B. F. Nelson Mfg. Co.	AI–1945
N. W. Nelson	N. W. and W. A. Nelson Co.	1915
W. E. Nelson	B. F. Nelson Mfg. Co.	1929
A. W. Nevins	Fuller Laundry	1915
Ed Norblom	Landers, Morrison, Christensen Co.	1918
Rodger L. Nordbye	Archer-Daniels-Midland Co.	AI
W. G. Northrup, Jr.	North Star Woolen Mill Co.	1932
E. J. O'Brien	O'Brien Realty	1929
Allan G. Odell	Burma-Vita Co.	AI–1945
R. W. Page	Quaker Creamery Co.	1919
Leonard Paulle	Showcase Mfg. Co.	1915
Edmund J. Phelps	Minnesota Loan and Trust Co.	1915

Charles L. Pillsbury	Munsingwear Corp.	1932
J. S. Pomeroy	First National Bank and Trust Co.	1933
H. M. Porter	Belden-Porter Co.	1930s
Merwin Porter	Belden-Porter Co.	1929
Donald F. Pratt	Durkee-Atwood Co.	AI
E. C. Prewitt	Minneapolis Paper Co.	AI–1936
H. M. Puffer	Puffer-Hubbard Mfg. Co.	1915
James L. Record	Minneapolis Steel and Machinery Co.	1929
William Regan	Regan Bros. Co.	1915
Edwin F. Ringer	Foley Mfg. Co.	AI
Harlan P. Roberts	lawyer	1915
Alexander M. Robertson	Minneapolis General Electric Co.	1915
J. L. Robinson	J. L. Robinson Co.	1918
A. K. Roehl	Pittsburgh Coal Co.	1932
George Root	Root and Hageman, Women's Garment Store	1919
D. D. Ryerse	Thompson Lumber Co.	AI
Fred R. Salisbury	Salisbury and Satterlee Mattress Co.	1915
Maurice E. Salisbury	Salisbury and Satterlee Mattress Co.	1929
Willis D. Salisbury	Salisbury and Satterlee Mattress Co.	AI
W. R. Salisbury	Salisbury and Satterlee Mattress Co.	AI–1945
A. W. Saunders	Northwestern Fuel Co.	1918
Maurice Schumacher	Piper, Drake and Schumacher Inc.	1932
Thomas Skellet	Skellet Fuel Co.	1918
John A. Skinner	Chase Bag Co.	1932
H. C. Smith	McLeod and Smith	1915
F. M. Steiner	American Linen Co.	1932
C. P. Stembel	Standard Steel Car Corp.	1932
H. Stewart		1915
Arthur Stremel	Stremel Bros. Mfg. Co.	1915
George W. Strieker	Janney, Semple, Hill and Co.	1930s
Albert W. Strong	Strong and Scott Mfg. Co.	1930s
Lucian S. Strong	Strong and Scott Mfg. Co.	AI
James A. Struthers	Strutwear Knitting Co.	1932
William A. Struthers	Strutwear Knitting Co.	1933
C. J. Swalen	Pako Corp.	AI
H. W. Sweatt	Minneapolis Honeywell Regulator Co.	1929
Edward K. Thode	General Mills, Inc.	AI–1947
A. R. Thompson	Thompson Lumber Co.	1930s
Walter Thorp	Minneapolis Knitting Works	1915

Harry Tuttle	North American Telegraph Co.	1915
C. D. Velie	Deere and Webber Co.	1915
Archie D. Walker	Red River Lumber Co.	1930s
Glen M. Waters	Waters-Genter Co.	1920s
H. R. Weesner	Wabash Screen Door Co.	1932
Frederick B. Wells	F. H. Peavey and Co.	1929
W. O. Wells	Wells-Lamont-Smith Corp.	1930s
John F. Wilcox	Wilcox Motor Car Co.	1915
James T. Williams	The Creamette Co.	1929
H. H. Williams	Northrup, King and Co.	1930s
L. H. Williams	Williams Hardware Co.	1932
W. R. Winter	Williams Hardware Co.	AI
Robert C. Wood	Minneapolis Electric Steel Castings Co.	AI
S. V. Wood	Minneapolis Electric Steel Castings Co.	1932
R. C. Woodworth	Cargill, Inc.	AI
R. B. Wrigley	R. B. Wrigley Co.	1929
Edgar F. Zelle	Jefferson Highway Transportation Co.	1932
A. E. Zonne	Conklin-Zonne-Loomis Co.	1932

Appendix C *Citizens Alliance 1904 Membership List (by industry)*

Agricultural Implements

Walter Gregory	Advance Thresher Co.
J. P. Hale	Bement-Darling Co.
	Bradley-Clark Co.
W. J. Dean	Dean and Co.
Charles C. Webber	Deere and Webber Co.
J. A. Shephard	Gaar-Scott Co.
C. H. Ganglehoff	Ganglehoff Bros.
M. Schibsby	J. I. Case Implement Co.
B. G. Baker	J. I. Case Threshing Machine Co.
Owen B. Kinnard	Kinnard and Haines Foundry and Machine Co.
M. H. Davis	LaCrosse Implement Co.
T. B. Lindsay	Lindsay Bros.
A. C. Barber	Minneapolis Moline Plow Co.
Frederick E. Kenaston	Minneapolis Threshing Machine Co.
	Monitor Drill Co.
William K. Marshall	N. W. Implement and Wagon Co.
L. F. Mercord	Robinson-Miller Co.
L. W. Zimmer	Smith and Zimmer

Bankers

F. A. Chamberlain	Security Bank
Edward W. Decker	Northwestern National Bank
S. A. Harris	National Bank of Commerce
E. A. Merrill	
E. M. Stevens	Wells-Atkinson Co.

Bag and Barrel Manufacturers

Chester Simmons	Bemis Bag Co.
	Hardwood Mfg. Co.
	McVoy Tub Pail and Package Co.
	Minneapolis Cooperage Co.

378

Boiler Manufacturers

William Bros Boiler and Mfg. Co.

Building Material

S. J. Hewson

Brick

G. W. Higgins

Belting and Rubber Goods

W. S. Nott Co.

Building Contractors

A. Cedarstrand

Cooper, Barclay Building Contractors

J. and W. A. Elliot Building Contractors

John Engquist

Charles F. Haglin

T. P. Healy

Henry Ingham

H. N. Leighton

Leck and Prince

Libbey and Nelson Building Contractors

Frank G. McMillan

Pike and Cook Co.

J. L. Robinson

John Wunder

Cigars

W. Hooker

Lundgren Bros.

Wuom Watt Co.

Candy

McKusick-Towle Co.

Paris-Murton Factory

Caskets and Hearses

Northwestern Casket Co.

Decorators
John S. Bradstreet and Co.

Drayage, Transfer, and Storage
F. H. Armstrong
Boyd Transfer Co.
C. Cameron   Cameron Transfer and Storage Co.
P. F. Dubay

Leonard and Montague
McReavy Bros. Transfer Co.
W. W. Morse   Security Warehouse Co.

Drugs
F. W. Lyman   Lyman, Eliel Drug Co.
Voegli Bros. Drug Co.

Dry Goods
George D. Dayton
George H. Partridge   Wyman, Partridge Co.
O. C. Wyman   Wyman, Partridge Co.

Dust Collectors
H. L. Day

Electrical
George K. Belden   W. I. Gray and Co.
W. J. Chapman   Minnesota Electric Co.
William I. Gray   W. I. Gray and Co.
Gugler Electric Co.
Hartig and Hellier
Minneapolis Electric and Construction Co.
A. M. Robertson   Minneapolis General Electric Co.
John Trevor

Engravers
Bramblett and Beygeh
Minneapolis Engraving Co.

Fireproof Doors
Fire Proof Door Co.

Fruits, Wholesale

      E. P. Stacy Co.

Fuel

N. S. Coffin   Pioneer Fuel Co.

      Holmes and MacCaughey

Furniture Manufacturers

      Barnard, Cope Mfg. Co.

      Luger Furniture Co.

      McLeod and Smith

      Minneapolis Office and School Furniture Co.

      Minneapolis Furniture Co.

Gasoline Engines

F. A. Valentine   Valentine Bros.

Glass

F. W. Currier   Pittsburgh Plate Glass Co.

      Forman, Ford and Co.

Grain

George C. Christian

H. F. Douglas   Great Western Elevator Co.

W. D. Gregory   Gregory Jennison and Co.

Fred E. Hargenberg   National Milling Co.

C. M. Harrington   Van Dusen-Harrington Co.

W. H. Hastings   Northwestern Consolidated Milling Co.

J. V. McHugh   McHugh-Christensen Co.

J. L. McCaull   McCaull-Webster Grain Co.

E. J. Phelps   Belt Line Elevator Co.

G. F. Piper   G. F. Piper Co.

Alvin H. Poehler   H. Poehler Co.

P. B. Smith   St. Anthony and Dakota Elevator Co.

Fred G. Van Dusen   Van Dusen Harrington Co.

John Washburn   Washburn-Crosby Co.

Frederick B. Wells   F. H. Peavey and Co.

Grocers, Wholesale

      G. E. Higgins

      Anthony Kelly and Co.

Hardware

	Gardner Hardware Co.
H. S. Gregg	Minneapolis Iron Store
T. B. Janney	Janney, Semple, Hill and Co.
	W. K. Morison and Co.
Arthur Stremel	Stremel Bros. Mfg. Co.
L. H. Williams	Williams Hardware Co.

Hardwood Flooring

G. H. Tennant Co.

Heating and Ventilating

J. R. Foster

T. M. Maguire

Moore Heating Co.

Pond and Hasey Co.

W. F. Porter and Co.

William Schupp and Co.

E. T. Tunstead   Tunstead Heating Co.

Ice

E. P. Capen	Boston Ice Co.
D. M. Chute	Cedar Lake Ice Co.
C. O. Lampe	City Ice Co.

Jewelry

H. M. Carpenter   Minneapolis Jewelry Co.

Knitting Works

C. E. Ovenshire   Minneapolis Knitting Works

Laundries

A. W. Nevins   Fuller Laundry

S. H. Towler   Minneapolis Steam Laundry

Lawyers

Benjamin Davenport

Martin B. Koon

Harlan P. Roberts

Lime and Cement
M. Christenson
J. C. Landers

Livery Stables
A. W. Harwood

Liquor
Benz Bros.
J. C. Oswald and Co.

Lumber
William C. Bailey
S. H. Bowman Lumber Co.
D. F. Brooks
H. E. Day
Day Lumber Co.
DeLaittre Lumber Co.
Mississippi and Rum River Boom Co.
B. F. Nelson
C. F. Osborne
C. A. Smith
C. A. Smith Lumber Co.
Thomas B. Walker
Willis J. Walker

Machinery, Machinists, and Founders
Otis P. Briggs
Minneapolis Steel and Machinery Co.
Electric Machinery Mfg. Co.
S. T. Ferguson
Northwestern Foundry Co.
J. W. Hernlund
Crown Iron Works
William Kampff
Enterprise Machine Co.
Olson, Ottin, Standard Foundry Co.
James L. Record
Minneapolis Steel and Machinery Co.
H. H. Smith
Diamond Iron Works
Albert W. Strong
Strong and Northway Manufacturing Co.

Mantels, etc.
Northwestern Mantel Co.

Mattress and Bedding Manufacturing
Minneapolis Bedding Co.
Fred B. Salisbury
Salisbury and Satterlee

Millinery, Wholesale

Bradshaw Bros.
Patterson and Stevenson

Newspapers
Herschel V. Jones

Ornamental Iron Works
Eugene Tetzlaff   Flour City Ornamental Iron Works

Painters and Paperhangers

E. M. Drisko and Co.

Paper, Wholesale
John Leslie

McClellan Paper Co.
E. J. Stilwell   Minneapolis Paper Co.

Plumbers and Gasfitting

Allen Black and Co.
R. C. Black and Co.
James C. Fay and Co.
Garrett A. Kelly   H. Kelly and Co.
Miles Sherin

Plumbers and Steamfitter Supplies
H. F. Hodge   National Brass and Metal Co.
Kellogg-Mackay-Cameron Co.
Plumbing and Steamfitting Supply Co.

Printers
A. D. Axtell
A. C. Bausman

Cootey Litho and Printing Co.
William R. Dobbyn and Son
A. B. Farnham and Co.
Hall, Black and Co.
Harrison and Smith Co.
Kimball and Storer Co.
Kohlstedt Printing Co.

Miller-Davis Printing Co.
Minnesota Blank Book Co.
Mitchell Printing Co.
Munson Stationery Co.
Periodical Press Co.
Printers' Electroptyping Co.
Publishers' Typesetting Co.
Swinburne and Co.
University of Minnesota Press

Quarries

Kettle River Quarries Co.
Langdon Stone Co.

Real Estate

Walter L. Badger
F. P. Chute
L. P. Chute
T. A. Jamieson
O. M. Laraway
Edmund G. Walton

Restaurants

Charles E. Bateman   The Old Tyme Bakerie
W. E. Bateman   The Grill
William Crombie
W. A. Mather
William Regan
Fred Schick

Safes

J. A. Modisette

Sash and Door Manufacturers

L. J. Bardwell   Robinson Co.
Aaron Carlson

City Sash and Door Co.
Curtis and Yale Co.
Eddy Sash and Door
Fulton and Libbey Co.

H. S. Johnson Co.

Minneapolis Sash and Door Co.

J. F. Wilcox

J. T. Wyman   Smith and Wyman

Seeds

Northrup, King and Co.

Shoes, Wholesale

Grimsrud Shoe Co.

C. B. Heffelfinger   North Star Shoe Co.

Walter W. Heffelfinger   North Star Shoe Co.

Showcase Manufacturers

Leonard Paulie

Sign Painters

H. B. Cramer

Stationers

E. R. Williams

Stove Repairs

J. B. Elliot

Great Western Stove Repair Co.

Tinners

John Middlemist and Son

Wagon and Carriage Manufacturers

A. C. Atkinson

John M. Norris

Roeller Carriage Works

F. H. Wellcome

Windstacker Manufacturers

S. N. Sorenson   Fosston Windstacker Co.

Appendix D *Minneapolis Civic and Commerce Association Founders*

Howard W. Baker
George A. Brackett
J. W. Bragdon   Winston, Harper, Fisher Co.
Aaron Carlson   Capitalist
F. A. Chamberlain   Security National Bank
Joseph Chapman   Northwestern National Bank
F. W. Clifford   Cream of Wheat Co.
J. F. Conklin   Conklin-Zonne-Loomis Co.
A. A. Crane   National Bank of Commerce
Thomas E. Cullen   Church of the Immaculate Conception
Edward W. Decker   Northwestern National Bank
John DeLaittre   Bovey-DeLaittre Lumber Co.
Henry J. Doerr   Minneapolis Drug Co.
W. A. Durst   Gross Co.
W. A. Frisbie   *Daily News*
Lewis S. Gillette   Electric Malting Co.
Calvin G. Goodrich   Twin City Rapid Transit Co. (TCRTC)
C. Grimsrud   Grimsrud Shoe Co.
W. L. Harris   New England Furniture Co.
Perry G. Harrison   Winston, Harper, Fisher Co.
N. F. Hawley
H. M. Hill   Janney, Semple, Hill and Co.
George B. Howley   State Federation of Labor
Clive T. Jaffray   First National Bank
Thomas B. Janney   Janney, Semple, Hill and Co.
Lowell E. Jepson
W. S. Jones   *Minneapolis Journal*
E. C. Kischel   Northwestern Glass Co.
Erle D. Luce   Electric Short Line
John L. Lynch
J. L. McCaull   McCaull-Dinsmore

A. A. McRae   Southside State Bank
H. L. Moore   Moore Heating Co.
George R. Newell   George R. Newell and Co.
S. G. Palmer   S. G. Palmer Co.
George H. Partridge   Wyman, Partridge Co.
E. Pennington   Minneapolis, St. Paul, and Sault Ste. Marie Railway
George W. Porter   Minnekota Elevator Co.
F. M. Prince   First National Bank
James L. Record   Minneapolis Steel and Machinery Co. (MSM)
Arthur R. Rogers   Rogers Lumber Co.
Fred R. Salisbury   Salisbury and Satterlee Co.
Albert M. Sheldon   Imperial Elevator Co.
Fred B. Snyder   Snyder and Gale
Edward P. Wells   Wells and Dickey Co.
H. E. White   Minneapolis Paper Co.
A. M. Woodward   Chamber of Commerce
James T. Wyman   Smith and Wyman Co.
O. C. Wyman   Wyman, Partridge Co.

Appendix E *Minnesota Employers' Association Founders, 1908*

George M. Gillette	Minneapolis Steel and Machinery Co.
Eli S. Warner	McGill, Warner Co., St. Paul
C. S. Sulzer	Red Wing Advertising Co.
Horace N. Leighton	H. N. Leighton and Co., Minneapolis
L. Sargent	Stillwater Manufacturing Co., Stillwater
P. W. Herzog	Herzog Iron Works, St. Paul
H. P. Leach	E. M. Leach and Sons Lumber Co., Faribault
J. W. L. Corning	Greiner and Corning, Chaska
Z. D. Scott	Scott-Graff Co., Duluth
John F. Wilcox	J. F. Wilcox Manufacturing Co., Minneapolis
H. R. Armstrong	National Iron Co., Duluth

Appendix F *Minnesota Employers' Association Charter Members*

American Hoist and Derrick Co., St. Paul
Bemis Bros. Bag Co., Minneapolis
Boyd Transfer and Storage Co., Minneapolis
William Bros Boiler and Manufacturing Co., Minneapolis
Brown and Bigelow, St. Paul
Connolly Shoe Co., Stillwater
Cream of Wheat Co., Minneapolis
Crown Iron Works, Minneapolis
Deere and Webber Co., Minneapolis
L. S. Donaldson and Co., Minneapolis
Eagle Roller Mill Co., New Ulm
Farwell, Ozmum, Kirk and Co., St. Paul
Fidelity Storage and Transfer Co., St. Paul
Fisher Paper Box Co., Minneapolis
Flour City Ornamental Iron Co., Minneapolis
S. B. Foot and Co., Red Wing
General Mills (Washburn Crosby Co.), Minneapolis
Heywood Manufacturing Co., Minneapolis
George A. Hormel and Co., Austin
John Leslie Paper Co., Minneapolis
Luger Furniture Co., Minneapolis
McGill-Warner Co., St. Paul
McKesson and Robbins (Minneapolis Drug Co.), Minneapolis
Minneapolis Iron Store, Minneapolis
Nicols, Dean and Gregg, St. Paul
North Star Granite Corporation, St. Cloud
Northern Malleable Iron Co., St. Paul
Northern States Power Co., St. Paul.
Northwestern Bell Telephone Co., St. Paul
Northwestern Casket Co., Minneapolis
N. W. Hanna Fuel Co., St. Paul

Nutting Truck Co., Faribault
Powers Mercantile Co., Minneapolis
Red Wing Sewer Pipe Co., Red Wing
Jacob Ries Bottling Co., Shakopee
Rock Island Lumber Co., St. Paul
F. J. Romer Construction Co., St. Paul
Russell-Miller Milling Co., Minneapolis
St. Paul Engineering and Manufacturing, St. Paul
Scheffer and Rossum Co., St. Paul
H. M. Smyth Printing Co., St. Paul
Stillwater Manufacturing Co., Stillwater
Stilwell-Minneapolis Paper Co. (Minneapolis Paper Co.), Minneapolis
Strong-Scott Manufacturing Co., Minneapolis
Twin City Rapid Transit Co. (TCRTC), Minneapolis
Wabash Screen Door Co., Minneapolis
Charles Weinhagen and Co., St. Paul
West Publishing Co., St. Paul
Winston and Newell, Minneapolis

List of Abbreviations

ABO	Associated Business Organizations
ACM	American Committee of Minneapolis
ADM	Archer-Daniels-Midland
AEI	Associated Employers of Indianapolis
AFA	America First Association
AFL	American Federation of Labor
AI	Associated Industries (of Minneapolis)
AIU	Associated Independent Unions
APL, A-P-L	American Protective League
AWO	Agricultural Workers Organization
CA	Citizens Alliance
CC	Civic Council (Minneapolis)
CCA	Civic and Commerce Association (Minneapolis)
CIA	Citizens Industrial Association
EA	Employers' Association, Inc.
EAC	Employers' Advisory Committee
ENC	Employers' Negotiating Committee (Minneapolis)
FEB	Free Employment Bureau
HCLEA	Hennepin County Law Enforcement Association
IAM	International Association of Machinists
IBA	Independent Banker's Association
IBT	International Brotherhood of Teamsters
ILL	Independent Labor League
INS	*Industrial News Service*
IPS	Industrial Press Service
IWW	Industrial Workers of the World
LEA	Law Enforcement Association
LMRA	Labor Management Relations Act
MBEA	Minnesota Building Employers' Association
MBIR	Minneapolis Bureau of Industrial Relations
MCPS	Minnesota Commission of Public Safety

MEA   Minnesota Employers' Association
MEEB   Minneapolis Employer-Employee Board
MIC   Minneapolis Industrial Committee
MLRA   Minnesota Labor Relations Act
MLRB   Minnesota Labor Relations Board
MNCC   Minnesota Chamber of Commerce
MRA   Minneapolis Retailers' Association
MSFL   Minnesota State Federation of Labor
MSGA   Minnesota Sound Government Association
MSM   Minneapolis Steel and Machinery Company
MTA   Minnesota Taxpayers' Association
NAM   National Association of Manufacturers
NFA   National Founders' Association
NIB   Northern Information Bureau
NIC   National Industrial Council
NIIC   National Industrial Information Committee
NIRA   National Industrial Recovery Act
NLB   National Labor Board
NLRB   National Labor Relations Board
NMTA   National Metal Trades Association
NPL   Nonpartisan League
NRA   National Recovery Administration
NW   Northwestern (National Bank)
NWLB   National War Labor Board
OUI   Organized Unemployed, Inc.
RFC   Reconstruction Finance Corporation
RLB   Regional Labor Board (Minneapolis-St. Paul)
SPAC   St. Paul Association of Commerce
SPCIR   St. Paul Committee on Industrial Relations
SS   Secret Service (Minnesota)
SWP   Socialist Workers Party
TCCE   Twin City Coal Exchange
TCRTC   Twin City Rapid Transit Company
TCVMA   Twin City Vehicle Manufacturers' Association
UDG   Union Defense Guard
USMI   United States Military Intelligence
USWA   United Steel Workers of America
WPNPL   Working People's Nonpartisan League
YRL   Young Republican League

Notes

NOTES TO CHAPTER 1

1. Bertha L. Heilbron, *The Thirty-second State: A Pictorial History* (St. Paul: Minnesota Historical Society, 1966), 203; William W. Folwell, *A History of Minnesota*, 3 (St. Paul: Minnesota Historical Society, 1969), 253; *Commercial West*, April 13, 1901, p. 5, and May 18, 1901, p. 14; Charles B. Kuhlmann, "The Influence of the Minneapolis Flour Mills upon the Economic Development of Minnesota and the Northwest," *Minnesota History* 6 (June 1925), 149; Minneapolis Civic and Commerce Association, *Minneapolis Golden Jubilee* (Minneapolis: Minneapolis Tribune Job Printing Co, 1917), 37; D. Jerome Tweton, "The Business of Agriculture," in *Minnesota in a Century of Change: The State and Its People Since 1900*, ed., Clifford E. Clark (St. Paul: Minnesota Historical Society, 1989), 265.

2. Kirk Jeffrey, "The Major Manufacturers from Food and Forest Products to High Technology," in *Minnesota in a Century of Change*, 224; Tweton, "The Business of Agriculture," 266; Robert Morlan, *Political Prairie Fire: The Nonpartisan League, 1915–1922* (St. Paul: Minnesota Historical Society Press, 1985), 6; James Gray, *Business without Boundary: The Story of General Mills* (Minneapolis: University of Minnesota Press, 1954), 34; Charles R. Walker, *American City: A Rank-and-File History* (New York: Farrar and Rinehart, 1937), 19. Sixty percent of Minnesota flour milling was done in Minneapolis by twelve establishments, which were owned by four proprietors; *U.S. Census, 1900, Manufacturers*, 2:442, 456.

3. William J. Powell, *Pillsbury's Best: A Company History from 1869* (Minneapolis: Pillsbury Co., 1985), 41–73; *Northwestern Miller*, April 12, 1899, p. 687.

4. Charles B. Kuhlmann, *The Development of the Flour Milling Industry in the United States, with Special Reference to the Industry in Minneapolis* (Boston: Houghton-Mifflin, 1929), 167–69.

5. Powell, *Pillsbury's Best*, 63–64; Washburn-Crosby to Messrs. Wilkinson, Gaddis and Co., April 14, 1899, William Dunwoody Papers, Minnesota Historical Society (MHS).

6. Kuhlmann, *Development of the Flour Milling Industry*, 169–70; *Northwestern Miller*, April 12, 1899, pp. 687–88.

7. Albert K. Steigerwalt, *The National Association of Manufacturers, 1895–1914* (Ann Arbor: University of Michigan, 1964), 104, 105, 107; U.S. Commissioner of Labor, *Strikes and Lockouts*, 1906, pp. 490–91; Bruno Ramirez, *When Workers Fight* (Westport, CT: Greenwood Press, 1978), 10; Steigerwalt, *National Association of Manufacturers*, 107.

8. Joseph S. Smolen, *Organized Labor in Minnesota: A Brief History* (Minneapolis: Labor Education Service of the Industrial Relations Center and University of Minnesota General Extension Division, 1964), 2; *Minnesota Executive Documents*, 1902, vol. 2: 1064; George W. Lawson, *History of Labor in Minnesota* (St. Paul: Minnesota State Federation of Labor, 1955), 9, 10, 117.

9. Minnesota Bureau of Labor Statistics, *Biennial Report*, 1903–04 (St. Paul: Great Western Printing Co., 1904), 295; *Minnesota Executive Documents*, 1902, pp. 1039, 1045, 1069; U.S. Commissioner of Labor, *Strikes and Lockouts*, 1906, p. 533; Heilbron, *The Thirty-second State*, 209; *U.S. Census, 1900, Manufacturers*, 2: 442, 444, 456–57; Jeffrey, "The Major Manufacturers," 229.

10. Minnesota State Federation of Labor, *Proceedings*, 1901, p. 1; *The Union*, Aug. 30, 1901, p. 5.

11. *Commercial West*, Aug. 17, 1901, p. 5.

12. Joseph G. Rayback, *A History of American Labor* (New York: The Free Press, 1966), 213; David P. Nord, "Socialism in One City" (master's thesis, University of Minnesota, 1972), 50; William F. Willoughby, "Employers' Associations For Dealing with Labor in the United States," *Quarterly Journal of Economics* 20 (Nov. 1905): 120; John H. M. Laslett, *Labor and the Left* (New York: Basic Books, Inc., 1970), 156; Mark Perlman, *The Machinists: A New Study in American Trade Unionism* (Cambridge, MA: Harvard University Press, 1961), 17–28.

13. *Minnesota Executive Documents*, 1902, p. 945; *The Union*, Feb. 9, 1900, p. 1 and April 26, 1901, p. 3.

14. Marion D. Shutter, *History of Minneapolis: Gateway to the Northwest* (Chicago: S. J. Clarke Publishing Company, 1923): 3: 545, 546; CA, *Bulletin*, Dec. 1925, Jan.–Feb. 1929.

15. *Minneapolis Tribune*, Jan. 1, 1929, p. 6; *Minneapolis Journal*, Dec. 31, 1928, p. 1; *Commercial West*, March 24, 1928, pp. 19–20; Minneapolis Steel and Machinery Co., *Articles of Incorporation and By Laws*, 1910, in Minneapolis Moline Company Papers, MHS.

16. CA, *Bulletin*, Jan.–Feb. 1929.

17. Clarence E. Bonnett, *Employers' Associations in the United States* (New York: Macmillan Co., 1922), 68–69.

18. Bonnett, *Employers' Associations*, 64, 103–4; CA, *Bulletin*, Jan.–Feb. 1929; Dec. 1925; Willoughby, "Employers' Associations," 119; Bonnett, *Employers' Associations*, 92, 128, 103–4; National Metal Trades Association (NMTA), *Bulletin: Convention Proceedings, 1903* (Cincinnati: NMTA, 1903), 453, 460, 477, 583, 596, 613.

19. Willoughby, "Employers' Associations," 119–21; Perlman, *The Machinists*, 26–27; Nord, "Socialism in One City," 51.

20. Marguerite Green, *The National Civic Federation and the American Labor Movement, 1900–1925* (Washington, D.C.: The Catholic University of America Press, 1956), 21; Perlman, *The Machinists*, 27; *Chicago Tribune*, May 20, 1901, p. 1; May 21, 1901, p. 4.

21. *Minnesota Executive Documents*, 1902, 1039–40; *Minneapolis Journal*, May 20, 1901, p. 6; *The Union*, May 24, 1901, p. 3; *The Union*,

June 14, 1901, p. 5; *Minneapolis Journal*, May 20, 1901, p. 6.

22. Walker, *American City*, 187, 188; *Minneapolis Tribune*, May 20, 1901, p. 5, May 21, 1901, p. 2, May 23, 1901, p. 7, and May 28, 1901, p. 7; *Minnesota Executive Documents*, 1902, p. 1039; CA, *Bulletin*, April–May 1928.

23. A. W. Strong to Adjutant General, June 17, 1918, War Records Commission Records, MHS; Walker, *American City*, 187; Holcombe, *History of Minneapolis*, 521; Winfield S. Downs, ed., *Encyclopedia of American Biography* (New York: American Historical Society, 1934), 420; Minnesota Employers' Association (MEA), Board of Directors, *In Memory of Albert W. Strong*, Dec. 15, 1936, in Minnesota Association of Commerce and Industry (MACI) Papers, MHS.

24. *Minneapolis Tribune*, May 21, 1901, p. 2; *Minneapolis Journal*, May 22, 1901, p. 6.

25. *Minneapolis Journal*, May 22, 1901, pp. 1, 6, May 23, 1901, p. 6; *Minneapolis Tribune*, May 22, 1901, pp. 1, 7; May 24, 1901, p. 1, May 25, 1901, p. 9.

26. *Chicago Tribune*, May 25, 1901, p. 3, May 30, 1901, p. 1; *Minneapolis Tribune*, May 22, 1901, pp. 1, 6l, May 28, 1901, p. 7, May 29, 1901, p. 10.

27. *New York Times*, June 2, 1901, p. 10; NMTA, *Bulletin* (July 1903) 2:7a (back page); *Minneapolis Journal*, June 1, 1901, p. 2; *Chicago Tribune*, May 31, 1901, p. 3.

28. *Minneapolis Tribune*, June 1, 1901, p. 9; June 8, 1901, p. 9; Green, *The National Civic Federation*, 21.

29. Perlman, *The Machinists*, 27.

30. *Minneapolis Tribune*, June 9, 1901, p. 11, June 23, 1901, p. 5; *The Union*, June 21, p. 4, July 19, 1901, p. 4; *Minneapolis Journal*, June 7, 1901, p. 6.

31. *Minnesota Executive Documents*, 1902, p. 1039; *The Union*, July 5, 1901, p. 4; *Minneapolis Tribune*, July 1, 1901, p. 5, July 21, 1901, p. 7; *Minneapolis Journal*, July 3, 1901, p. 6.

32. *Minneapolis Journal*, July 3, 1901, p. 6; Walker, *American City*, 188.

33. CA, *Policy and Principles of the Citizens Alliance*, pamphlet, n.d., CA Papers, MHS; Rayback, *History of American Labor*, 212; Coal Strike Commission, *Report to the President on the Anthracite Coal Strike of May–Oct., 1902*

(Washington, D.C.: Government Printing Office, 1903), 75. The "common sense and common law" quotes were used frequently in Citizens Alliance publications for the next thirty-three years.

34. CA, *Policy and Principles.*

35. *New York Times*, June 2, 1901, p. 10; Walker, *American City*, 186–92; Coal Strike Commission, *Report*, 64.

36. A. J. Hain, "Twin Cities Team for Open Shop," in *The Iron Trade Review*, May 17, 1921, pp. 764, 767 (copy in the CA Papers).

37. Hain, "Twin Cities Team for Open Shop," 767; CA, *Bulletin*, Dec. 1920, p. 1.

38. CA, *The Open or Closed Shop—Which?* Dec. 15, 1920; CA, "Law and Order," Feb. 1927, both in CA Papers.

39. CA, *Bulletin*, Jan.–Feb. 1929, June 1929; CA, "Open or Closed Shop."

40. CA, "Law and Order"; *The Union*, July 29, 1904, p. 4.

41. *The Union*, July 29, 1904, p. 4; Hain, "Twin Cities Team," 762.

NOTES TO CHAPTER 2

1. Horace B. Hudson, ed., *A Half Century of Minneapolis* (Minneapolis: Hudson Publishing Company, 1908), 527; Minneapolis Board of Trade, "Address of President Phelps," *Annual Report*, 1883 (Minneapolis: Johnson, Smith & Harrison, 1884), 7; *The Minneapolis Business Union*, pamphlet, n.d., Thomas B. Walker Papers, Minnesota Historical Society (MHS), St. Paul.

2. Hudson, ed., *Half Century*, 527; Minneapolis Board of Trade, *Trade and Commerce of Minneapolis* (Minneapolis: Johnson, Smith & Harrison, 1885), 101.

3. Board of Trade, *Annual Report*, 1883, 4–7.

4. John G. Rice, "The Old Stock Americans," June D. Holmquist, ed., *They Chose Minnesota: A Survey of the State's Ethnic Groups* (St. Paul: MHS Press, 1981), 55–72 (quotations on 58 and 59); Lucile M. Kane, *The Falls of St. Anthony: The Waterfall that Built a City* (St. Paul: MHS Press, 1987).

5. Hudson, *Half Century*, 527; Minneapolis Chamber of Commerce and Minneapolis Board of Trade, *Joint Annual Report*, 1882 (Minneapolis: Tribune Job Rooms Print, 1883), 5; Chamber of Commerce, *Third Annual*

Report, 1886 (Minneapolis, 1886), 151; *Annual Report*, 1890 (Minneapolis, 1891), 222–33. Fifteen Minneapolis Chamber of Commerce members sat on the forty-five-member board of directors of the Board of Trade.

6. *Minneapolis Journal*, April 11, 1889, p. 1.

7. *Minneapolis Journal*, April 11, 1889, p. 1, April 12, 1889, p. 1, April 13, 1889, p. 1; *Minneapolis Tribune*, April 12, 1889, p. 1. Lowry had just returned from the East where he had met with streetcar officials from New York, Brooklyn, and Rochester. Strikes also erupted in these cities after these meetings.

8. *Minneapolis Journal*, April 12, 1889, p. 2; Helen Asher, "The Labor Movement in Minnesota, 1850–1890" (unpublished paper, Hamline University, 1925), 33; *Minneapolis Journal*, April 13, 1889, p. 1.

9. Asher, "The Labor Movement in Minnesota," 34; *Minneapolis Journal*, April 12, 1889, p. 2, April 13, 1889, p. 2, and April 16, 1889, p. 1; Chamber of Commerce, *Annual Report*, 1890, p. 227.

10. *Minneapolis Journal*, April 13, 1889, p. 2.

11. *Minneapolis Journal*, April 13, 1889, p. 1, April 15, 1889, p. 1, April 17, 1889, p. 1.

12. *Minneapolis Journal*, April 18, 1889, p.1, April 19, 1889, p.1, April 22, 1889, p. 1, April 23, 1889, p. 1, April 24, 1889, p. 1, April 27, 1889, p. 1; *Minneapolis Tribune*, April 23, 1889, p. 5.

13. Joseph S. Smolen, *Organized Labor in Minnesota: A Brief History* (Minneapolis: University of Minnesota, Labor Education Service of the Industrial Relations Center and General Extension Division, 1964), 9.

14. Smolen, *Organized Labor in Minnesota*, 9; Lawson, *History of Labor in Minnesota*, 14.

15. E. J. Phelps et al., notice, "The Minneapolis Business Union," n.d.; report of committee, "The Mid-Continent City," n.d.; Business Union (MBU) report, "This Association," 1890, p. 2; MBU, List of Committees, 1890; MBU, *Treasurer's Annual Report*, Jan. 10, 1894—all in Thomas B. Walker Papers, MHS; *Minneapolis City Directory*, 1891. Two-thirds of the board of directors of the MBU would later be associated with the Citizens Alliance.

16. Phelps et al., *Minneapolis Business Union*; "This Association," 2, both in Walker Papers.

17. Hudson, *Half Century*, 527; *Minneapolis City Directories*, 1890–96; MBU, "This Association," 2, 3; MBU, "For a number of years," 1890, p. 4, all in Walker Papers.

18. MBU, "For a number of years," 6; "This Association," 3–5, in Walker Papers.

19. Hudson, *Half Century*, 527; Commercial Club, Articles of Incorporation, 1903, 7.

20. Amasa C. Paul et al., to Commercial Club members, May 21, 1901, Walker Papers; Commercial Club, *Annual Report*, 1904. The advisory committee included leaders from the Board of Trade and the Business Union who would also play a prominent role in the Citizens Alliance. The advisory committee was, in fact, dominated by future CA members.

21. Hudson, *Half Century*, 527; Paul et al., to Commercial Club members, May 21, 1901; Commercial Club, *Annual Report*, 1903, p. 27, both in Walker Papers; *Minneapolis Tribune*, July 16, 1901, p. 5.

22. *Minneapolis Journal*, April 28, 1901, p. 6; *Minnesota Executive Documents*, 1902, p. 1039.

23. Boyd Transfer and Storage Co. to CA, May 12, 1905, CA Papers; *The Union*, Nov. 7, 1902, p. 1, Dec. 19, 1902, p. 9, and Dec. 26, 1902, p. 1.

24. *Minneapolis Tribune*, May 24, p. 8; Boyd to CA, May 12, 1905, Papers, MHS; *The Union*, May 23, 1902, p. 5.

25. *Minneapolis Journal*, May 26, p. 6; Boyd to CA, May 12, 1905; lists of CA Boards of Directors, 1915–19, both in CA Papers; Commercial Club, Convention Committee to Members, 1902, in Walker Papers; Commercial Club, *Annual Report*, 1903, pp. 28, 31.

26. Commercial Club, *Annual Report*, 1904, p. 4; CA, *Bulletin*, Nov. 1923.

27. Board of Trade, *Annual Report*, 1885; letter from F. H. Forbes to T. B. Walker, n.d., Walker Papers; Shutter, *History of Minneapolis*, 2:117; Commercial Club, *Annual Report*, 1904, p. 4, and *Annual Report*, 1905, p. 10; Belt Line Elevator Company, Directors' Meeting, Jan. 13, 1900, Peavey Company Records, MHS.

28. Holcombe, *History of Minneapolis and Hennepin County*, 209. The following seventeen men are listed in Citizens Alliance documents as founders of the organization: Edmund J. Phelps, Judge Martin B. Koon, Otis P.

Briggs, Owen B. Kinnard, Albert W. Strong, Fred. E. Kenaston, Fred R. Salisbury, Lamont J. Bardwell, William I. Gray, J. F. Wilcox, Charles D. Velie, George K. Belden, Alexander M. Robertson, James D. Shearer, Samuel A. Harris, Benjamin F. Nelson, and Hiram S. Gregg. Although historians have frequently considered the alliance an autonomous organization, considerable evidence suggests that it was an arm or committee of the Public Affairs Committee (PAC) of the Minneapolis Commercial Club. Fourteen of the seventeen founders were Commercial Club members and ten were directors or committee members of the Public Affairs Committee. In addition, Secretary Nye of the PAC supervised the recruitment of the original members of the CA from the Commercial Club's membership. Even after adding new recruits in 1904, the vast majority of CA's membership came directly from its parent group. CA, *Bulletin*, April–May 1932; List of CA founders, n.d., and Fred R. Salisbury to George K. Belden, July 28, 1903, both CA Papers; Commercial Club, *Annual Reports*, 1903–8; *The Union*, July 29, 1904.

29. A. J. Hain, "Twin Cities Team for Open Shop," *Iron Trade Review*, March 17, 1921, p. 764; National Metal Trades Association (NMTA) to Otis P. Briggs, June 29, 1903; *Bulletin of the NMTA*, July 1903; NMTA *Proceedings of the 5th Annual Convention*, 487; CA, *Constitution*, 1903, all in CA Papers.

30. CA, *Constitution*; Horace N. Leighton to E. J. Phelps, Aug. 15, 1903; J. Bryan Bushnell to O. P. Briggs, Aug. 26, 1903; CA, *By Laws*, 1903, all in CA Papers.

31. Salisbury to Belden, July 28, 1903, and May 15, 1905; C. D. Velie to G. K. Belden, July 28, 1903, all in CA Papers; *The Union*, July 29, 1904, p. 4. See Appendix for the list of all CA members as of July 29, 1904.

32. Briggs to Belden, Oct. 12, 1903; W. C. Thompson to Belden, May 16, 1903; Salisbury to Belden, May 15, 1905, all in CA Papers.

33. CA, *By Laws*; J. B. Bushnell to O. P. Briggs Aug. 26, 1903. The first officers of the CA were E. J. Phelps, president; F. E. Kenaston and Thomas B. Walker, vice presidents; O. P. Briggs, Treasurer; G. K. Belden, secretary.

34. J. B. Bushnell to O. P. Briggs, Aug. 26, 1903; A. M. Robertson to J. A. Elliot, Oct. 17, 1905; *Annual Reports*, 1915–19, CA, *Bulletins*,

Annual Meeting Issues, 1920–36, all in CA Papers; *Minneapolis City Directories*, 1904–14.

35. *The Union*, Sept. 26, 1902, p. 1; William C. Edgar, *The Medal of Gold* (Minneapolis: The Bellman Company, 1925), 226.

36. Edgar, *Medal of Gold*, 227–29; *The Union*, Oct. 3, 1902, p. 1.

37. *The Union*, Nov. 6, 1903, p. 1; Minnesota Bureau of Labor, *Biennial Report*, 1903–4, p. 260; Edgar, *Medal of Gold*, 230; W. H. Dunwoody to Thomas C. Jenkins, Sept. 25, 1903, William H. Dunwoody Papers, MHS. The exact date on which the various flour milling companies joined the CA is unclear. However, they joined the National Association of Manufacturers in June 1903. The NAM was closely associated with the CA and, under the leadership of Parry, was heavily involved in the 1903 open-shop drive across the United States. The mills were important members and financial supporters of the CA for the next thirty-three years.

38. Edgar, *Medal of Gold*, 231; *Minneapolis Journal*, Sept. 24, 1903, p. 1.

39. *Northwestern Miller*, Sept. 30, 1903, p. 727; *The Union*, Nov. 6, 1903, p. 1; *Minneapolis Journal*, Sept. 24, 1903, p. 1; *Minneapolis Tribune*, Sept. 30, 1903, p. 1; Dunwoody to Jenkins, Sept. 28, 1903, Dunwoody Papers.

40. *The Union*, Nov. 6, 1903, p. 1; *Northwestern Miller*, Sept. 30, 1903, p. 728; *Minneapolis Journal*, Sept. 26, 1903, p. 1; MSfl, *Proceedings*, 1904, p. 19.

41. *The Union*, Oct. 2, 1903, p. 4; *Minneapolis Journal*, Sept. 25, 1903, p. 1, Sept. 26, 1903, p. 1; *Minneapolis Tribune*, Sept. 27, 1903, p. 1.

42. *Minneapolis Tribune*, Sept. 27, 1903, p. 1, and Sept. 28, 1903, p. 5; *Minneapolis Journal*, Sept. 25, 1903, p. 1, Sept. 26, 1903, p. 1, and Sept. 28, 1903, p. 1; *Northwestern Miller*, Sept. 30, 1903, p. 728.

43. *Northwestern Miller*, Sept. 30, 1903, p. 728, and Oct. 7, 1903, p. 781; *Minneapolis Journal*, Oct. 2, 1903, p. 6 (Harding quote); Dunwoody to Wilson, Oct. 9, 1903, Dunwoody Papers.

44. *Northwestern Miller*, Oct. 14, 1903, pp. 837–38; *Minneapolis Journal*, Sept. 25, 1903, p. 1.

45. *Northwestern Miller*, Oct. 7, 1903, p. 781, and Oct. 14, 1903, pp. 837, 838; *Min-*

neapolis Journal, Sept. 28, 1903, p. 1; *Minneapolis Tribune*, Oct. 3, 1903, p. 5, Oct. 6, 1903, p. 7; Dunwoody to J. W. Raymond, Oct. 20, 1903, Dunwoody Papers.

46. *Minneapolis Journal*, Oct. 6, 1903, p. 6, Oct. 8, 1903, p. 9, Oct. 9, 1903, Oct. 10, 1903, p. 7, Oct. 12, 1903, p. 6, Oct. 15, 1903, p. 7; *Minneapolis Tribune*, Oct. 5, 1903, p. 5, Oct. 6, 1903, p. 7, Oct. 8, 1903, p. 9, Oct. 12, 1903, p. 6, Oct. 16, 1903, p. 6, Oct. 17, 1903, p. 7; *The Union*, Oct. 9, 1903, p. 1, Nov. 6, 1903, p. 1. The unions expected very little help from outside Minneapolis. In addition, Washburn-Crosby had shut down for the summer, leaving workers short of cash.

47. MSfl, *Proceedings*, 1904, p. 44; *Minneapolis Tribune*, Oct. 26, 1903, p. 6; Edgar, *Medal of Gold*, 235; Dunwoody to James Bishop, Nov. 11, 1903, and Dunwoody to Raymond, Oct. 20, 1903, both in Dunwoody Papers.

48. *The Union*, July 29, 1904, p. 4; Thompson to Belden, May 16, 1905, CA Papers.

49. *The Union*, July 29, 1904, p. 4.

NOTES TO CHAPTER 3

1. Here and below, *The Union*, Nov. 20, 1903, p. 1.

2. Bonnett, *Employers' Associations*, 291, 292 (quotation), 367–72.

3. Bonnett, *Employers' Associations*, 367, 368; Robert A. Brady, *Business as a System of Power* (New York: Columbia University Press, 1943), 193.

4. Here and below, National Association of Manufacturers (NAM), *Proceedings of the Annual Convention*, 1903 (Indianapolis: Century Press, 1903), 17, 50, 58.

5. NAM, *Proceedings*, 1903, pp. 58, 165–66; Bonnett, *Employers' Associations*, 368.

6. Bonnett, *Employers' Associations*, 308–12.

7. Bonnett, *Employers' Associations*, 308–9; *The Union*, July 3, 1903, p. 1.

8. MSfl, *Proceedings*, 1904, pp. 19, 48; E. J. Phelps to W. R. Cray, June 29, 1903; O. P. Briggs to W. R. Cray, July 15, 1903; CA, *Law and Order*, pamphlet, n.d.; CA, *The Open Shop*, pamphlet, Feb. 1927, all in CA Papers, MHS; Bonnett, *Employers' Associations*, 308–9.

9. Here and below, Bonnett, *Employers' Associations*, 336–39, 341, 353–55.

10. NAM, *Proceedings of Annual Convention*, 1903, p. 169.

11. Selig Perlman and Philip Taft, *History of Labor in the United States, 1896–1932*, vol. 4, *Labor Movements* (New York: MacMillan Co., 1935), 134.

12. Perlman and Taft, *Labor Movements*, vol. 4, 134–35; CIA to Record, Oct. 31, 1905, CA Papers; Marguerite Green, *The National Civic Federation and the American Labor Movement, 1900–1925* (Washington, D.C.: Catholic University of America Press, 1956), 102.

13. Perlman and Taft, *Labor Movements*, vol. 4, 136.

14. William F. Willoughby, "Employers' Associations for Dealing with Labor in the United States," *Quarterly Journal of Economics* 20 (Nov. 1905): 130–31; Bonnett, *Employers' Associations*, 64. This agreement was modeled after the Chicago agreement between the NMTA and the IAM.

15. Bonnett, *Employer's Associations in United States*, 90, 92; NFA, "Outline of Policy," in *The Review*, May 1905, pp. 3–20.

16. "NFA," *The Review*, Dec. 1905; Bonnett, *Employer's Associations in United States*, 90; Stecker, "The NFA," 384–85.

17. Bonnett, *Employer's Associations in United States*, 78.

18. NFA, "Outline of Policy," *The Review*, Dec. 1905; Stecker, "The NFA," 384; Bonnett, *Employers' Associations*, 86–87; Briggs, *Policy of Lawlessness*, 24; CA, *Law and Order*, pamphlet, CA Papers.

19. Here and below, "NFA," *The Review*, June 1905, pp. 9, 11, 13–14; Dec. 1905, p. 28.

20. Stecker, "The NFA," 382–83 (quotation 383); Briggs, *Policy of Lawlessness*, 21–22; Bonnett, *Employers' Associations*, 79, 80.

21. Briggs, "Acceptance Speech," *The Review*, Dec. 1905, p. 91.

22. Bonnett, *Employers' Associations*, 74–76.

23. Stecker, "The NFA," 362, 363; Bonnett, *Employers' Associations*, 74, 75.

24. Bonnett, *Employers' Associations*, 75, 76.

25. *Minneapolis Journal*, Nov. 28, 1905, p. 6.

26. *Minneapolis City Directories*, 1904–1907.

27. In 1904, the Citizens Alliance executive committee had hired George O. Eddy to run its affairs; Belden to Walker, March 8, 1904, Walker Papers, MHS. *Minneapolis Labor Review*, July 18, 1907, p. 4; Sept. 26, 1907, p. 3, Jan. 9, 1908, p. 4; May 26, 1911, p. 1, and June 2, 1911, p. 1; MSFL, *Proceedings*, 1904, p. 45. Ward served simultaneously as agent for the Builders' and Traders' Exchange in its 1908 open-shop drive.

28. Belden to Walker, Jan. 14, 1904, Walker Papers; *Minneapolis Labor Review*, Sept. 21, 1906, p. 4, June 13, 1907, p. 8, Oct. 17, 1907, p. 3, Nov. 21, 1907, p. 3, June 9, 1911, p. 4; *The Union*, Feb. 17, 1905, p. 1, June 23, 1905, p. 5.

29. *Minneapolis Labor Review*, July 25, 1907, p. 7, Aug. 15, 1907, p. 8, Sept. 12, 1907, p. 5, Nov. 21, 1907, p. 3, May 5, 1911, p. 1, June 2, 1911, p. 1, and June 9, 1911, p. 4. The 1912 building trades strike and the 1914 upholsterers' lockout were both precipitated by employer open-shop drives; Minnesota Bureau of Labor, *Fourteenth Biennial Report* (Minneapolis: Syndicate Printing Co., 1914), 209; *Minneapolis Labor Review*, Jan. 9, 1914, p. 1; Bureau of Labor, *Thirteenth Biennial Report*, 436. In the 1905 printers' strike and the 1907 machinists' strike, union demands for shorter hours and higher wages were used by the Citizens Alliance to initiate open-shop drives; *Minneapolis Labor Review*, April 25, 1907, p. 13; *Minneapolis Tribune*, Oct. 2, 1905, p. 7.

30. *Minneapolis Labor Review*, June 6, 1907, p. 3, July 4, 1907, p. 10, July 11, 1907, p. 5, Aug. 15, 1907, p. 8.

31. Although skirmishes between pickets and CA plant guards occasionally erupted, they were usually isolated incidents, often initiated by the CA guards; MSFL, *Proceedings*, 1904, p. 45; *Minneapolis Journal*, Nov. 25, 1905, p. 7; *Minneapolis Labor Review*, June 27, 1907, p. 6. In the major open-shop drive conflicts of the CA's first decade, injunctions were sought in the 1905 printers' strike, in the 1907 machinists' and sheet metal strikes, and in the 1914 upholsterers' strike.

32. *Minneapolis Labor Review*, May 30, 1907, p. 1; Belden to T. B. Walker, May 20, 1907, Walker Papers.

33. *The Union*, July 29, 1904, p. 4, June 23, 1905, p. 5; *Minneapolis Labor Review*, June 2, 1911, p. 1, June 9, 1911, p. 4.

34. *Minneapolis Journal*, Oct. 5, 1905; Minneapolis Typothetae, signed agreement, Sept. 12, 1905; and *Minute Book One*, 183, undated, both in Minneapolis Typothetae (MT) Papers, MHS.

35. Minneapolis Typothetae, *Minute Book One*, 183, MT Papers; CA membership list compiled by author, in possession of author; *Minneapolis Tribune*, Oct. 3, 1905, p. 6; Oct. 5, 1905, p. 8. Typothetae members who belonged to the CA employed two-thirds of the Typothetae's total work force; *Minneapolis Journal*, Oct. 5, 1905, p. 6.

36. *Minneapolis Journal*, Oct. 11, 1905, p. 11; *The Union*, April 13, 1906, p. 1.

37. *Minneapolis Tribune*, Oct. 2, 1905, p. 7, Oct. 3, 1905, p. 6; *Minneapolis Journal*, Oct. 2, 1905, p. 6.

38. *Minneapolis Journal*, Oct. 2, 1905, p. 6, Oct. 4, 1905, p. 6; *Minneapolis Tribune*, Oct. 3, 1905, p. 6; *The Union*, Feb. 13, 1908, p. 9.

39. *Minneapolis Journal*, Oct. 4, 1905, p. 6; *Minneapolis Tribune*, Oct. 5, 1905, p. 8.

40. *Minneapolis Tribune*, Oct. 6, 1905, p. 6, Oct. 7, 1905, p. 6, Oct. 10, 1905, p. 7; *The Union*, April 13, 1906, p. 1; *Minneapolis Journal*, Oct. 4, 1905, p. 6, Oct. 7, 1905, p. 6.

41. *The Union*, Oct. 13, 1905, p. 4, Oct. 20, 1905, p. 4, Dec. 8, 1905, p. 4, Feb. 9, 1906, p. 4; *Minneapolis Tribune*, Oct. 3, 1905, p. 6, Oct. 10, 1905, p. 7.

42. *Minneapolis Tribune*, Oct. 10, 1905, p. 7; *The Union*, Nov. 24, 1905, p. 4, Dec. 15, 1905, p. 5, Dec. 22, 1905, p. 5, Jan. 26, 1906, p. 4; *Minneapolis Labor Review*, April 25, 1907, p. 3, Oct. 17, 1907, p. 3.

43. *Minneapolis Labor Review*, Oct. 17, 1907, p. 3.

44. *Minneapolis Labor Review*, April 25, 1907, p. 13, May 2, 1907, p. 6, May 9, 1907, p. 6, May 30, 1907, pp. 3, 5, July 25, 1907, p. 7, and Sept. 12, 1907, p. 5.

45. *Minneapolis Labor Review*, July 25, 1907, p. 7, Aug. 15, 1907, p, 8, Oct. 24, 1907, p. 13, Nov. 7, 1907, p. 10, and May 28, 1908, p. 20.

46. Minnesota Bureau of Labor, *Biennial Reports*, 1905–14; *Tenth Biennial Report*, 1906, p. 364; Minnesota Department of Labor, *14th Biennial Report*, 1914, p. 205.

47. *Minneapolis Labor Review*, Sept. 21, 1906, p. 4; CA, *Bulletin*, April–May 1932, CA Papers.

NOTES TO CHAPTER 4

1. *Minneapolis Labor Review*, July 14, 1916, p. 3.

2. *Minneapolis Tribune*, Feb. 11, 1912, p. 1; Minnesota Employers' Association (MEA), *48th Annual Meeting*, April 25, 1956.

3. "Documents, Reports, and Legislation—Industries and Commerce," *American Economics Review* 4 (Sept. 1914): 701; Harwood Lawrence Childs, *Labor and Capital in National Politics* (Columbus: Ohio State University Press, 1930), 8–9, 66–67.

4. Joseph S. Smolen, *Organized Labor in Minnesota: A Brief History* (Minneapolis: University of Minnesota, Labor Education Service of the Industrial Relations Center and General Extension Division, 1964), 10; MEA, *Minutes*, Dec. 14, 1908, in Minnesota Association of Commerce and Industry (MACI) Papers, MHS; *St. Paul Pioneer Press*, March 19, 1934, p. 14. The ten men were George M. Gillette (Minneapolis CA); Eli S. Warner, (St. Paul CA); C. S. Sultzer, Red Wing Advertising Co., Red Wing; Horace N. Leighton, H. N. Leighton and Co. (Minneapolis CA); L. Sargent, Stillwater Mfg. Co., Stillwater; Philip W. Herzog, Herzog Iron Works (St. Paul CA); H. P. Leach, E. M. Leach and Sons Lumber Co., Faribault; J. W. L. Corning, Corning, Greiner, and Corning, Chaska; Z. D. Scott, Scott-Graff Co. (Duluth CA); John F. Wilcox, J. F. Wilcox Mfg. Co. (Minneapolis CA); H. R. Armstrong, National Iron Co. (Duluth Commercial Club). Seven of the eleven businessmen at the Dec. 14, 1908, meeting were associated with open-shop organizations. Minneapolis Steel and Machinery Co. was one of the original CA members and was associated with the CA until it was merged into Minneapolis Moline, which also supported the CA.

5. MEA, *48th Annual Meeting*, April 25, 1956; MEA, Articles of Incorporation and Bylaws, MEA, in *Minute Book*, MACI Papers; Deborah L. Gelbach, *From This Land: A History of Minnesota's Empires, Enterprises, and Entrepreneurs* (Northridge, CA.: Windsor Pub., 1988), 250.

6. MEA, *48th Annual Meeting*, April 25, 1956; MEA, *Minutes*, Jan. 11, 1909; MEA, Membership Assessment List, MACI Papers.

7. MEA, *Minutes*, Dec. 13, 1911, and Dec. 15, 1914; Membership Assessment List, all in MACI Papers. A complete membership list of

the St. Paul Citizens Alliance is not available. However, 53 percent of the St. Paul contingent in the MEA served on the St. Paul CA board of directors. Over 70 percent of the Duluth MEA contingent belonged to the Duluth CA or its parent, the Duluth Commercial Club. See Chapter Eight for more on these organizations. E. S. Warner to "Dear Sir" [Members of St. Paul CA], June 7, 1929, Great Northern Railway Co. Records, MHS; CA of St. Paul, "Five Years," 1925, pamphlet; St. Paul Committee on Industrial Relations, "Finding the Right Answers," 1948, pamphlet; St. Paul Association Yearbook, 1918, Charles W. Ames Papers, MHS; CA, Duluth Open Shop Companies, Jan. 1929, CA Papers; Duluth Herald, Oct. 3, 1919, p. 6; The Labor World, Sept. 18, 1920, p. 1; L. C. Harris to Gentlemen [members of the Duluth CA] Aug. 4, 1922, Robert A. Olson Papers, MHS. A number of MEA proxy lists are in the MACI Papers, several of which list the firms whose proxies were CA representatives.

8. MEA, Minutes, Jan. 11, 1909, March 15, 1911, MACI Papers. Shearer was paid $400 per year for his services for the MEA; Shutter, History of Minneapolis, 2:208; Robert Asher, "The Origins of Workers' Compensation in Minnesota," Minnesota History 44 (winter 1974): 150.

9. Gillette to Members, June 23, 1913; MEA, Weekly Bulletin No. 1, Jan. 6, 1917; both in MACI Papers; Minnesota State Federation of Labor (MSFL), Proceedings, 1911, pp. 16–17.

10. MSFL, Proceedings, 1911, pp. 16–17; MEA, Weekly Bulletin No. 1, Jan. 6, 1917; MEA, Minutes, Jan. 11, 1909; Dec. 14, 1911; all MEA items in MACI Papers.

11. MSFL, Proceedings, 1911, pp. 15–16; MEA, Minutes, Dec. 15, 1914, MACI Papers. An excellent example of a concerted letter-writing campaign can be found in Rep. William I. Nolan's papers pertaining to S. F. 290 and H. F. 406, bills on workers' compensation, in W. I. Nolan Papers, MHS. The MEA had a close connection with the NAM from which it received extensive information. The NAM legal department corresponded regularly with the MEA on pending national legislation; MEA, Report of the Secretary, 1925, MACI Papers.

12. Gillette to Members, June 23, 1913; MEA, Weekly Bulletin No. 1, Jan. 6, 1917, both in MACI Papers.

13. Gillette to Members, June 23, 1913; MEA, Weekly Bulletin No. 1, Jan. 6, 1917, both in MACI Papers.

14. MEA, Bulletin No. 15, May 15, 1917, MACI Papers. In 1913, the MEA handled seventy general measures. By 1917, this had grown to 123; Gillette to Members, June 23, 1913, MACI Papers.

15. Minneapolis Labor Review, June 16, 1911, p.1, MEA, Minutes, Dec. 15, 1914; Dec. 11, 1916; Feb. 13, 1917; Weekly Bulletin No. 1, Jan. 6, 1917; all MEA items in MACI Papers.

16. MEA, Weekly Bulletin No. 1, Jan. 6, 1917, MACI Papers.

17. Minneapolis Labor Review, March 26, 1908, p. 5.

18. MEA, Minutes, Jan. 12, 1910, MACI Papers; Minneapolis Labor Review, March 26, 1908, p. 5.

19. Asher, "Origins of Workers' Compensation in Minnesota," 144; Asher, "Workers' Compensation in the United States, 1880–1935" (Ph.D. thesis, University of Minnesota, 1971), 422; MACI, Public Hearings: Employers' Liabilities Act, Feb. 10–11, 1909, p. 38, MACI Papers; Minnesota Bureau of Labor, Twelfth Biennial Report, 1909–10, pp. 154–55; Minneapolis Steel and Machinery Co., Sixth Annual Report, Dec. 31, 1908. Asher's article and Ph.D. thesis contain a detailed description of the MEA's role in the creation of a workers' compensation system in Minnesota.

20. Bureau of Labor, Twelfth Biennial Report, pp. 154–55; Asher, "Origins of Workers' Compensation in Minnesota," 143–44, 146; Bureau of Labor, Public Hearing, Employers' Liability Act, pp. 40–41.

21. MEA, Minnesota Workmen's Compensation Law, Oct. 1, 1913; MEA, Minutes, Jan. 11, 1909; April 13, 1909; June 10, 1909; all in MACI Papers; Asher, "Origins of Workers' Compensation in Minnesota," 144–45.

22. Asher, "Origins of Workers' Compensation in Minnesota," 146; MSFL, Proceedings, 1911, p. 15.

23. Asher, "Workers' Compensation in the United States," 439, 442; MEA, Minutes, June 14, 1910, MACI Papers.

24. Asher, "Origins of Workers' Compensation in Minnesota," 146, 150.

25. MEA, Minutes, June 14, 1910; Dec. 14, 1911, both in MACI Papers; Asher, "Workers'

Compensation in the United States," 448–49; Asher, "Origins of Workers' Compensation in Minnesota," 148.

26. MEA, *Minutes*, Dec. 29, 1911, March 15, 1912, Aug. 2, 1912, all in MACI Papers.

27. MEA, *Minutes*, Dec. 29, 1911, Aug. 2, 1912, March 15, 1912; MEA, Draft of Workers' Compensation Bill, 3, 10, all in MACI Papers; Asher, "Origins of Workers' Compensation in Minnesota," 152.

28. MEA, Draft of Workmen's Compensation Bill, 10, 11; Gillette to Members, March 1, 1913 (quotation), both in MACI Papers; Asher, "Origins of Workers' Compensation in Minnesota," 150.

29. Gillette to Members, March 1, 1913; MEA, *Minutes*, March 14, 1913, both in MACI Papers; *Minneapolis Labor Review*, April 11, 1913, p. 1. Numerous examples of material from this campaign, dated from Feb. 14 to March 8, 1913, are in the Nolan Papers, MHS.

30. Minneapolis Trades and Labor Assembly, "To Whom It May Concern," March 4, 1913, Nolan Papers; Asher, "Workers' Compensation in the United States," 486; MEA, Draft of Workmen's Compensation Bill, 3; MEA, Minnesota Workmen's Compensation Law, Oct. 1, 1913, p. 14; *Minneapolis Tribune*, March 19, 1934, p. 1; *St. Paul Pioneer Press*, March 19, 1934, p. 14.

31. MEA, Summary of 1913 Legislature, June 23, 1913; Gillette to Members, April 23, 1913, both in MACI Papers; Asher, "Radicalism and Reform: State Insurance of Workers' Compensation in Minnesota, 1910–1933," *Labor History* 14 (winter 1973), 20; Asher, "Workers' Compensation in the United States," 486.

32. Gillette to Members, April 23, 1913, MACI Papers; Asher, "Radicalism and Reform," 19–41.

33. *Minneapolis Tribune* Dec. 7, 1911, p. 1; Northwestern National Bank, *The First 75 Years* (pamphlet); Marion D. Shutter, *History of Minneapolis: Gateway to the Northwest* (Chicago: S. J. Clarke Publishing Co., 1923), 3:607–8. Wells was president of Wells-Dickey and chairman of the board of Russell-Miller Milling Co. The other CA members were William S. Jones, *Minneapolis Journal*; William J. Murphy, *Minneapolis Tribune*; Horace M. Hill, Janney, Semple, Hill Co.; John L. Record, Minneapolis Steel and Machinery Co.; W. L. Har-

ris, New England Furniture and Carpet Co.; and lawyer Fred B. Snyder.

34. Civic and Commerce Association (CCA), address of President A. R. Rogers, in CCA *Reports*, 1912–14, pp. 40, 41, 117. A majority of the incorporators of the CCA were CA members.

35. *Minneapolis Tribune*, Dec. 10, 1911, p. 1; CCA, Articles of Incorporation, *Reports*, 1912–14, p. 19.

36. CCA, "Rogers' Address," 117; *Minneapolis Tribune*, Feb. 11, 1912, p. 1.

37. *Minneapolis Tribune*, Feb. 11, 1912, p. 1.

38. CCA, Articles of Incorporation, 21, 22, 38. The executive committee included the president and seven board members. The membership committee included the president and five board members.

39. CCA, Articles of Incorporation, 19–21, 22–23, 30–33; CCA *Third Annual Report*, p. 13; Millikan, CA membership list, in possession of author; *Minneapolis Tribune*, Feb. 11, 1912, p. 1; James H. Collins, "Running a Town with a Club," *Saturday Evening Post*, Jan. 1, 1916, p. 23; *Minneapolis Labor Review*, July 14, 1916, pp. 1, 3.

40. CCA, "Report of the Board of Directors," CCA *Reports*, 1912–14, pp. 55–56; *Minneapolis Tribune* Feb. 11, 1912, p. 1; CA, *List of Founders*, CA Papers.

41. *Minneapolis Tribune*, Feb. 11, 1912, p. 1.

42. CCA, Membership Roll; CCA *Second Annual Report*, 1914, pp. 137–60; Millikan, CA membership list.

43. CCA, *Bylaws*, 37; *Fourth Annual Report*, 1916, pp. 72–75; R[eturn] I. Holcombe, *Compendium of History and Biography of Minneapolis and Hennepin County* (Chicago: Henry Taylor and Co., 1914), 509; *Fifth Annual Report*, 65, 69.

44. CCA, *Fifth Annual Report*, 72; CA *Bulletin*, April–May 1932; *Minneapolis Labor Review*, Jan. 9, 1914, p. 1; Jan. 16, 1914, p. 1; Jan. 23, 1914, p. 1; Feb. 13, 1914, p. 1; Feb. 20, 1914, p. 1; March 13, 1914, p. 1.

45. CCA, *Fourth Annual Report*, 80–81.

46. CCA, *Fourth Annual Report*, 80–81 (paternalism quotation); James Gray, *Business without Boundary: The Story of General Mills* (Minneapolis: University of Minnesota Press, 1954), 294–96, 298–99 (future development quotation).

47. CCA, *Fourth Annual Report*, 66–71, 132.

48. CCA, *Fourth Annual Report*, 132, 133, 134–35.

49. CCA, *Third Annual Report*, 87; *Minneapolis Tribune*, April 10, 1916, p. 1.

50. CCA, *Third Annual Report*, 88–91.

51. CCA, *Fourth Annual Report*, 93–94; *Fifth Annual Report*, 87, 89, 92; *Minneapolis Tribune*, April 10, 1916, p. 1. In 1915, the CCA's Committee on Municipal Research had eight CA members: F. A. Bovey, William Y. Chute, John Crosby, James F. Conklin, George H. Elwell, N. F. Hawley, M. Schumacher, and Fred B. Snyder. CCA, *Fifth Annual Report*, 87; Millikan, "List of CA Members."

52. *Minneapolis Tribune*, Feb. 11, 1912, p. 1.

53. CCA, *By Laws*, 38; *Fourth Annual Report*, 82–83; *Fifth Annual Report*, 44–45, 62.

54. O. B. Kinnard to Gentlemen, Sept. 1, 1906, Walker Papers.

55. *Minneapolis Journal*, Nov. 3, 1912, p. 1 (quotation); *Commercial West*, Nov. 2, 1912, p. 8. Of the twenty-two advisors who influenced Gould's withdrawal, twenty-one were either CA or CCA members. Of the twenty-eight members of the Citizen's Non-Partisan Committee, at least twenty-two were CA or CCA members.

56. David Paul Nord, "Minneapolis and the Pragmatic Socialism of Thomas Van Lear," *Minnesota History* 45 (spring 1976): 6. See Chapter Nine of this book for the story of the 1920 MEA campaign to save Minnesota from socialism.

57. *Minneapolis Labor Review*, July 14, 1916, p. 1.

58. *Minneapolis Labor Review*, July 14, 1916, p. 1; Childs, *Labor and Capital*, 11; St. Paul Association of Commerce, *Sixth Year Book*, 1917, p. 56; CCA, *Report*, 1912–14, p. 45. Official literature of the U.S. Chamber of Commerce claimed that the organization grew from a call by President William H. Taft for a national business organization in early 1912. It is clear from examples in Minnesota, however, that local organizational preparation for the Chamber of Commerce was under way throughout the United States in 1911. Chamber of Commerce of the U.S.A. (hereafter abbreviated USCC), *Yearbook*, 1917 (Washington, D.C.: W. F. Roberts Co., 1918), 5.

59. *Minneapolis Journal*, Aug. 3, 1919, p. 12; USCC, *8,000 Chambers of Commerce throughout the World* (Washington, D.C., 1936).

60. USCC, *Yearbook*, 1917, pp. 11–12, 14; St. Paul Association of Commerce (SPAC), *Sixth Year Book*, 56; CCA, *Fifth Annual Report*, 16; "Documents, Reports, and Legislation," *American Economic Review*, 4 (Sept. 1914): 703; USCC, *Yearbook*, 1917, pp. 11, 12, 14, 42, 90–91, 97–98, 106; Sidney L. Gulick, "A New Immigration Policy," *The Nation's Business*, May 15, 1914, p. 10. Each member organization received at least one vote. Larger organizations received more votes, according to their size, with a limit of ten.

61. "A Most Solemn Protest of Business Men," *The Nation's Business*, July 15, 1914, p. 8; USCC, *Yearbook*, 1917, p. 44; USCC, *Policies Advocated by the Chamber of Commerce of the United States* (Washington, D.C.: 1937), 38–39.

62. "Documents, Reports and Legislation," p. 705; Childs, *Labor and Capital*, 187–89.

63. Childs, *Labor and Capital*, 203, 205.

64. Childs, *Labor and Capital*, 184; USCC, *Yearbook*, 1917, p. 34.

65. Here and below, Childs, *Labor and Capital*, 217–19, 225, 227, 229.

NOTES TO CHAPTER 5

1. Report of the [Massachusetts] Commission on Industrial and Technical Education (Boston, 1906), 4–5; U.S. Bureau of the Census, *Historical Statistics of the United States* (Washington, D.C., 1975), 666; James W. Van Cleave, *Industrial Education as an Essential Factor in Our National Prosperity* (New York: NAM, 1908), 5; Paul C. Violas, *The Training of the Urban Working Class* (Chicago: College Publishing Co., 1978), 132; Bureau of the Census, *Historical Statistics*, 139, 142.

2. Charles A. Prosser, "The Evolution of the Training of the Worker in Industry," *Journal of Proceedings and Addresses of the National Education Association* (Ann Arbor: NEA, 1915), 302.

3. Prosser, "Training the Worker," 301; Violas, *Urban Working Class*, 130.

4. Prosser, "Training the Worker," 302; Violas, *Urban Working Class*, 136–37; Colleen A. Moore, *Corporation Schools: 1900–1930* (Akron: University of Akron, 1980), 7, 11, 16; Violas, *Urban Working Class*, 132, 135; Moore,

Corporation Schools, 15; *Commercial West*, Feb. 11, 1911, p. 8.

5. Bonnett, *Employers' Associations*, 319; Moore, *Corporation Schools*, 9; Bernice M. Fisher, *Industrial Education: American Ideals and Institutions* (Madison: University of Wisconsin Press, 1967), 116; "The Vocational Education Age Emerges, 1876–1926," *American Vocational Journal* (May 1976), 49, 50.

6. Moore, *Corporation Schools*, 14; Lewis Anderson, *History of Manual and Industrial School Education* (New York: D. Appleton & Co., 1926); Bonnett, *Employers' Associations*, 26, 123, 132; Moore, *Corporation Schools*, 20.

7. Arthur B. Mays, *The Problem of Industrial Education* (New York: Century Co., 1927), 100; "Vocational Education Age," 48, 49.

8. Mays, *The Problem of Industrial Education*, 100, 113.

9. Mays, *The Problem of Industrial Education*, 101, 105; Anderson, *History of Manual and Industrial School Education*, 229–33; Bureau of the Census, *Historical Statistics*, 139.

10. Fisher, *Industrial Education*, 118–19; "The Vocational Education Age Emerges," 52; Melvin L. Barlow, *History of Industrial Education in the United States* (Peoria, IL: Charles A. Bennett Co., Inc., 1967), 53–54, 55; Bonnett, *Employers' Associations*, 123.

11. Charles A. Bennett, *History of Manual and Industrial Education, 1870–1917* (Peoria, IL: Chas. A. Bennett Co., Inc., 1937), 545–46.

12. *Commercial West*, June 17, 1903, p. 10.

13. U.S., *Census, 1920, Manufacturing*, 9:738; *Minneapolis Labor Review*, Feb. 27, 1908, p. 8; MSFL, *Convention Proceedings*, 1908, p. 5; Homer J. Smith, *Industrial Education in the Public Schools of Minnesota* (Minneapolis: University of Minnesota, 1924), 8; See Chapter Three on the machinists' strike.

14. *Commercial West*, Feb. 25, 1905, pp. 9, 10.

15. *Minneapolis Labor Review*, April 9, 1908, p. 4, Dec. 3, 1908, p. 6; Smith, *Industrial Education in Minnesota*, 4, 8.

16. MSFL, *Convention Proceedings*, 1910, p. 19; MSFL, "Report of the Committee on Education," *Convention Proceedings*, 1919, p. 2.

17. *Minneapolis Labor Review*, April 9, 1908, pp. 3, Sept. 3, 1908, pp. 4, 5.

18. *Commercial West*, Nov. 9, 1912, p. 7.

19. *Dunwoody News*, Dec. 10, 1954; North-western *Miller*, Dec. 16, 1936, p. 714; Will Carl Wachtler, "W. H. Dunwoody—A Portrait of Service" (master's thesis, University of Minnesota, 1963), 55; Jeffrey, "The Major Manufacturers," 224; Tweton, "The Business of Agriculture," 266.

20. *Northwestern Miller*, Dec. 16, 1936, p. 714; Washburn-Crosby Co. to Messrs. Wilkinson, Gaddis & Co., April 14, 1899; W. H. Dunwoody to Thomas C. Jenkins, Aug. 22, 1899, both in William H. Dunwoody Papers, MHS.

21. Dunwoody to Jenkins, Sept. 25, 1903, Sept. 28, 1903, Oct. 22, 1903; Dunwoody to James Wilson Oct. 9, 1903; Dunwoody to R. E. Kidder, Oct. 16, 1903; Dunwoody to Joseph Raymond, Oct. 20, 1903; Dunwoody to James Bishop, Nov. 11, 1903, all in Dunwoody Papers, MHS; *Dunwoody News*, Dec. 10, 1954; Charles S. Popple, *Development of Two Bank Groups in the Central Northwest* (Cambridge, MA: Harvard University Press, 1944), 51; Edward W. Decker, *Busy Years*, ed. Winthrop Chamberlain (Minneapolis: Lund Press, 1937), 73.

22. *Commercial West*, Feb. 21, 1914, p. 8; Wachtler, *Dunwoody*, 73, 74; Dunwoody to R. V. Martin, April 2, 1899; Booker T. Washington to Dunwoody, Sept. 23, 1904; Stanley R. Yarnall to Dunwoody, April 26, 1912, letters all in Dunwoody Papers, MHS.

23. *Commercial West*, Feb. 11, 1911, p. 7, Dec. 19, 1914, p. 8; W. H. Dunwoody Institute, *50th Anniversary*, pamphlet, 1964; *Commercial West*, Feb. 21, 1914, p. 8; Chapman to Dunwoody, June 12, 1912; Dunwoody to Chapman, June 11, 1912, both in Dunwoody Papers; Wachtler, *Dunwoody*, 74; Probate of W. H. Dunwoody Will, 1913, Hennepin County Court Records (File E16127).

24. William H. Dunwoody, Last Will & Testament, 1913, p 23–24, Hennepin County Court Records.

25. *Minneapolis Journal*, Feb. 15, 1914, p. 1; Dunwoody, Last Will, 24.

26. Dunwoody, Last Will, 24; Dunwoody to James Wallace, 1901, Dunwoody Papers; Minneapolis Clearing House, *Minutes*, Nov. 3, 1927, Northwest Bancorporation Papers, MHS; John W. Schroeder to T. B. Walker, Jan. 7, 1921, and O. P. Briggs to T. B. Walker, Jan. 21, 1922, both in Walker Papers. The Minneapolis Clearing House was a banking institution run

by the leading banks. It cleared checks between the various banks. See Chapter 15 on the financing of the Citizens Alliance.

The twelve men on the first board of trustees were the following, all from Washburn-Crosby Co.: John Washburn and James S. Bell, presidents; Fred G. Atkinson, vice-president; John Crosby, secretary and treasurer; William H. Bovey, superintendent; William G. Crocker, Charles Cranston Bovey, and Franklin M. Crosby, all directors of Washburn-Crosby Co. In addition, the board included Elbridge C. Cooke, president, Minneapolis Trust Co.; Robert W. Webb, vice-president of Minneapolis Trust Co.; Joseph W. Chapman and Edward W. Decker, both officers at Northwest Bank. Minneapolis Trust Co. was held by the identical stockholders as First National Bank, then First and Security National Bank.

27. *Northwestern Miller*, Dec. 16, 1936, p. 713; Wachtler, *Dunwoody*, 77, 78.

28. *Dunwoody News*, Dec. 12, 1924, p. 1; Dunwoody Institute, "To the Boys of Minnesota," pamphlet, 1914, Dunwoody Papers.

29. Dunwoody Institute, *12th Annual Commencement Exercises*, program, 1926; "To the Boys of Minnesota," both in Dunwoody Papers; *Dunwoody News*, March 27, 1928, p. 3.

30. Dunwoody Institute, *The Artisan*, Jan. 1916, pp. 13, 24–25; "To the Boys of Minnesota," Dunwoody Papers; *Dunwoody News*, Dec. 12, 1914, p. 1. The Citizens Alliance had launched open-shop drives in the printing industry in 1905, in the machinist industries in 1907, and in the building trades in 1911. See Chapters One and Three for these accounts.

31. Dunwoody Institute, *The Artisan*, Jan. 1916, p. 12; *Dunwoody News*, Dec. 12, 1924, p. 1; Feb. 23, 1945, p. 6; *12th Commencement Exercises*, 1926, all in Dunwoody Papers; U.S. Bureau of Labor, *Proceedings of Employment Managers' Conference*, 1916 (Washington, D.C.), p. 47. See Chapter Three for a discussion of the 1905 printing strike and Chapter Ten for discussion of the CA and the press.

32. *Dunwoody News*, Dec. 12, 1924, p. 1; Dunwoody Institute, *12th Commencement Exercises*.

33. Wachtler, *Dunwoody*, 79, 80, 81–82; *The Union*, July 29, 1904, p. 4; Dunwoody Institute, *Day School Bulletin No. 1*, pamphlet, n.d., in Dunwoody Papers.

34. *Minneapolis Star Journal*, May 15, 1945, p. 1; *Minneapolis Star*, Dec. 27, 1952, p. 1; Dec. 29, 1952, p. 8

35. *Minneapolis Star Journal*, May 15, 1945, p. 1; Dunwoody Institute, *The Artisan*, Jan. 1916, p. 1; U.S. Bureau of Labor, *Proceedings*, 47.

36. Dunwoody Institute, *The Artisan*, Jan. 1916, p. 1; Peter Rosendale, *Dunwoody Institute*, June 1936, unpublished report in Minneapolis Collection, Minneapolis Public Library (MPL); *Minneapolis Star Journal*, May 15, 1945, p. 1.

37. "The Vocational Education Age Emerges," 56–58.

38. *Dunwoody News*, March 14, 1924, p. 2; March 28, 1924, p. 2; Jan. 30, 1925, p. 2.

39. *Dunwoody News*, April 18, 1924, p. 2; Jan. 30, 1925, p. 2.

40. *Minneapolis Labor Review*, May 6, 1920, p. 1; numerous documents in the Twin City Vehicle Manufacturers' Association Papers (TCVMA), MHS.

41. George Schuler to O. P. Briggs, Aug. 21, 1920; TCVMA, *Minutes*, April 5, 1920; H. L. Soderquist, secretary, to Dear Sir, Sept. 8, 1920; CA, *Law and Order*, Feb. 1927, p. 7, pamphlet in CA Papers.

42. *Minneapolis Journal*, April 23, 1920, p. 13; TCVMA, unsigned intelligence report titled "Confidential," April 1920; Schuler to Briggs, Aug. 21, 1920; Soderquist to Minneapolis Steel and Machinery Co., April 17, 1920; Mitsch Heck to TCVMA, April 8, 1920, all TCVMA items in TCVMA Papers; CA, *Law and Order*, pamphlet, Feb. 1927, p. 7, CA Papers; *Minneapolis Labor Review*, April 23, 1920, p. 1.

43. *Minneapolis Labor Review*, May 6, 1920, p. 1; May 18, 1920, p. 1; May 25, 1920, p. 1; TCVMA, *Minutes*, April 12, 1920; Soderquist to Prosser, April 13, 1920, both in TCVMA Papers.

44. TCVMA, *Minutes*, April 19, 1920; Minneapolis Garage Owners' Association to Members, Sept. 3, 1920, both in TCVMA Papers.

45. Prosser, Memo 76, May 12, 1920; Memo 88, May 29, 1920 (summaries of meetings between Prosser and TCVMA); TCVMA, "Learn While You Earn," three-page typed manuscript, June 1920, all in TCVMA Papers.

46. Prosser, Memo 89, June 1, 1920, TCVMA Papers.

47. Prosser, Memo 88, May 29, 1920, TCVMA Papers.

48. Prosser, Memo 76, May 12, 1920; Memo 88, May 29, 1920; Kavel to Soderquist, Sept. 15, 1920, all in TCVMA Papers.

49. Prosser, "The New Apprenticeship as a Factor in Reducing Labor Turnover," *Proceedings of Employment Managers Conference*, Jan. 19–20, 1917 (Washington, D.C., 1917), 46.

50. Prosser, "The New Apprenticeship," 47, 51.

51. Prosser, "The New Apprenticeship," 50.

52. Minneapolis Civic and Commerce Association (CCA), "Dunwoody Opens Door of Opportunity," *Minneapolis: Metropolis of the Northwest*, Aug. 1931, p 10.

53. CCA, "Dunwoody Opens Door," 10; Dunwoody Institute, *12th Commencement Exercises*, Dunwoody Papers; U.S. Bureau of the Census, *Historical Statistics of the U.S.*, 139; *Census, 1920, Manufacturing*, 9:739; *Commercial West*, Dec. 19, 1914, p. 8.

54. CCA, "Dunwoody Opens Door." Other companies included Westinghouse, Stromberg Carburetor Co., Bendix Brake Co., Western Electric Co., Northern States Power Co., Oakland Automobile Co., and Bell Telephone Co.

55. CA, *Law and Order*, CA Papers; *Special Weekly Bulletin No. 228*, April 11, 1923, Walker Papers, MHS.

56. *Minnesota Building Trades School, Inc.*, pamphlet, n.d., CA Papers; CA, *Special Weekly Bulletin No. 132*, July 8, 1921, Walker Papers, MHS.

57. CA, *Special Weekly Bulletin No. 132*; *Commercial West*, May 2, 1924, p. 8.

NOTES TO CHAPTER 6

1. Charles S. Popple, *Development of Two Bank Groups in the Central Northwest* (Cambridge, MA: Harvard Univ. Press, 1944), 144–45.

2. Here and below, William C. Edgar and Loring M. Staples, *The Minneapolis Club* (Minneapolis: Minneapolis Club, 1974), 7–23, 24–27, 30–34, 57, 59, 66, 75–76, 129–33, 147–61.

3. Edgar and Staples, *Minneapolis Club*, 58–59, 69; Minneapolis Club, *Annual Report*, Dec. 31, 1921, copy in Longyear Co. Records, MHS. The cigar budget equaled the separate

wages paid for the clubhouse employees and the restaurant employees.

4. Edgar and Staples, *Minneapolis Club*, 5.

5. Edgar and Staples, *Minneapolis Club*, 38, 51, 84–85; Helen De Haven Bush, *The History of Northrup Collegiate School* (Minneapolis: Harrison and Smith Co., 1978), 14. See Chapter Eight for the full story of the Civilian Auxiliary and the 1917 streetcar strike.

6. Here and below, Minikahda Club, *Minikahda Club*, 4–6, 12, 52–64.

7. Benjamin M. Sherman, *The Blake School* (Minneapolis: Colwell Press, 1975), 10–11, 238–39. Nearly half of Blake's graduates attended eastern private colleges.

8. Sherman, *The Blake School*, 11, 20. Guarantors C. C. Bovey, James Ford Bell, F. M. Crosby, John Crosby, and W. H. Dunwoody were all Washburn-Crosby executives; Elbert L. Carpenter, Shevlin-Carpenter Lumber Co.; George B. Clifford and Frederick W. Clifford, both of the Cream of Wheat Co.; Charles S. Pillsbury, Pillsbury Flour Mills; David D. Tenney, Tenney Co.; E. C. Gale, Snyder, Gale and Richard Law Firm; Charles M. Case, Atlantic Elevator Co.; Charles D. Velie, Deere and Webber Co.; Frederick B. Wells, F. H. Peavey and Co.; C. T. Jaffray, First National Bank; S. S. Thorpe, Thorpe Bros. Realty; T. B. Janney, Janney Lumber Co. These men were all members of the Citizens Alliance or the Civic and Commerce Association. F. M. Crosby, Velie, and Wells all served on the CA Board of Directors.

9. Here and below, Sherman, *The Blake School*, 11, 15, 16, 20, 42, 43, 238–39.

10. Bush, *Northrup Collegiate*, 12–13, 14, 15.

11. Bush, *Northrup Collegiate*, 15; newspaper clipping, n.d., Northrup Collegiate School clipping file, Minneapolis Collection, MPL.

12. Brooklyn Institute of Arts and Sciences, *The American Renaissance, 1876–1917* (New York: Pantheon Books, 1979), 19, 21, 111.

13. *American Renaissance*, 58, 68, 64.

14. Walker Art Center, *The Walker Art Center*, pamphlet, n.d., 6; T. B. Walker, typescript, n.d., giving his opinions of Walker Art Center, beginning p. 2, "Corner of 8th and Hennepin . . ." 5, both in Walker Papers; Benidt, *Library Book*, 15, 27, 32, 34.

15. Benidt, *Library Book*, 27, 29–34; Walker typescripts, "As there is now a delay . . ." 1, and "As this action on my part . . ." 1918, 1, Walker Papers.

16. Minneapolis Athenaeum, *Minneapolis Athenaeum*, 10; Benidt, *Library Book*, 28, 30, 34. Other businessmen backing the Athenaeum included: Charles A. Pillsbury, H. G. Harrison, C. M. Loring, H. T. Welles, S. C. Gale, and Dorilus Morrison; *Minneapolis Golden Jubilee*, 42.

17. Here and below, Benidt, *Library Book*, 36–38, 48–49, 93, 95–96, 97.

18. Benidt, *Library Book*, 98; *Minneapolis Golden Jubilee*, 43.

19. Here and below, *The Walker Art Center*; Walker, typescript, essay on art; Eugen Neuhaus, "The T. B. Walker Art Collection," report, n.d., both in Walker Papers.

20. Minneapolis Society of Fine Arts (MSFA), Articles of Incorporation, Jan. 31, 1883, copy in Edward C. Gale Papers; William Watts Folwell, "Historical Sketch of the Minneapolis Society of Fine Arts," Oct. 1923, unpublished manuscript; *The Minneapolis Society of Fine Arts*, pamphlet, 1920, both in Walker Papers; Jeffrey A. Hess, *Their Splendid Legacy: The First 100 Years of the Minneapolis Society of Fine Arts* (Minneapolis: Society of Fine Arts, 1985), 5–11.

21. *The Minneapolis Society of Fine Arts*; Thomas Lowry to T. B. Walker, Sept. 1, 1892, both in Walker Papers; list of Guarantors of School Fund, Gale Papers.

22. Folwell, *Historical Sketch*; Hess, *Their Splendid Legacy*, 21–23.

23. Hess, *Their Splendid Legacy*, 22–27, 86; MSFA, Report on Meeting, Jan. 10, 1911, Gale Papers.

24. Hess, *Their Splendid Legacy*, 26–27; Walker, essay on art, Walker Papers; *Minneapolis Journal*, Feb. 15, 1914, p. 1; MSFA, pamphlet, 1920; Dunwoody Fund Report, Gale Papers.

25. *The Walker Art Center*; Walker, essay on art; Briggs to Walker April 21, 1925; James Leck Co., memo on Walker Art Gallery contract, April 6, 1926; and "Amounts expended on Construction of Art Gallery," all in Walker Papers.

26. Thomas F. Russell, "Minneapolis Symphony Orchestra," June 1936, unpublished report, Minneapolis History Collection, MPL; John K. Sherman, *Music and Maestros: The*

Story of the Minneapolis Symphony Orchestra (Minneapolis: University of Minnesota Press, 1952), 49.

27. Sherman, *Music and Maestros*, 52; *Minneapolis Tribune*, Aug. 14, 1927, p. 12; List of Guarantors: W. S. Nott, O. C. Wyman, Healy C. Akeley, Samuel H. Bowman, T. B. Janney, George W. Peavey, C. J. Martin, William L. Harris, Walter D. Boutell, Henry Little, Charles Pillsbury, Hovey C. Clarke, Edward P. Wells, Benjamin F. Nelson, Thomas Lowry, Frank T. Heffelfinger, George H. Partridge, Francis A. Chamberlain, John S. Pillsbury, Jr., George Harrison, Journal Printing Co., Times Newspaper Co., Tribune Printing Co., Maurice L. Rothchild, L. T. Jamme, W. H. Dunwoody, F. B. Wells, H. J. Burton, L. S. Donaldson, Calvin G. Goodrich, Perry G. Harrison, T. H. Shevlin, C. A. Smith, W. Y. Chute, Fred Fayram, Marion W. Savage, J. E. Carpenter, E. M. Stevens, E. J. Carpenter, and William L. Martin.

28. *Minneapolis Tribune*, Aug. 14, 1927; Sherman, *Music and Maestros*, 52–53.

29. Sherman, *Music and Maestros*, 56–62; Russell, "Minneapolis Symphony Orchestra."

30. Sherman, *Music and Maestros*, 66, 68, 70.

31. *Minneapolis Journal*, June 1, 1924, editorial section, p. 1.

32. Frederick Platt, *America's Gilded Age: Its Architecture and Decoration* (South Brunswick, NJ: A. S. Barnes, 1976), 253, 280; Donald R. Torbert, "Minneapolis Architecture and Architects, 1848–1908" (Ph. D. thesis, University of Minnesota, 1953), 106.

33. Arnold Lewis, *American County Houses of the Gilded Age* (New York: Dover Public, Inc., 1982) House No. 72; Lucile M. Kane, *The Falls of St. Anthony: The Waterfall that Built a City* (St. Paul: MHS Press, reprint edition, 1987), 91.

34. Lewis, *American County Houses*, House No. 72.

35. Here and below, Wachtler, *Dunwoody*, 32–35.

36. Charles W. Nelson, "Minneapolis Architecture for the Elite: A View of the Gilded Age of the 1880s," *Hennepin History* 52 (winter 1993): 12.

37. Torbert, "Minneapolis Architecture," 64.

38. Lists of Open-Shop Buildings; CA Membership List, both in CA Papers.

39. Here and below, Torbert, "Minneapolis Architecture," 80, 426.

40. Lists of Open-Shop Buildings, CA Papers.

NOTES TO CHAPTER 7

1. CA, *Bulletin*, April–May 1932; A. J. Hain, "CA Has Kept Minneapolis Open Shop," *The Iron Trade Review* (March 17, 1921): 764.

2. For example, Minneapolis Steel and Machinery (MSM), one of the largest and most influential CA members, had net earnings in 1916 ten times what it had earned in 1913. MSM, *Annual Reports* 1913 and 1916, Minneapolis Moline Papers, MHS; Rayback, *History of American Labor*, 259; Minnesota Department of Labor, *Fifteenth Biennial Report* (Minneapolis: Syndicate Printing Co., 1916), 165, 167, 172.

3. *Commercial West*, Nov. 2, 1912, pp. 7, 8 (quotations); David Paul Nord, "Minneapolis and the Pragmatic Socialism of Thomas Van Lear," *Minnesota History* 45 (spring 1976): 4.

4. *Minneapolis Labor Review*, March 31, 1916, p. 1; *New Times*, April 1, 1916, p. 1; Norman Francis Thomas, *Minneapolis Moline* (New York: Arno Press, 1976), 231–34; *Commercial West*, March 24, 1928, p. 19; Jeffrey, "The Major Manufacturers," 230–31; MSM, *Annual Report*, 1916.

5. *Minneapolis Labor Review*, April 21, 1916, p. 1; *New Times*, April 1, 1916, p. 1; MSM, *Annual Reports*, 1913–16; Shutter, *History of Minneapolis*, 2:166–67.

6. *Minneapolis Labor Review*, March 31, 1916, p. 1 (union-hating quotation); CA, Minutes of Annual Meeting, 1916, CA Papers; National War Labor Board (NWLB), Minneapolis Steel and Machinery Case, statement of J. L. Record, pp. 1, 2 (non-union shop quotation), 5, 6, Spielman Papers, MHS.

7. *Minneapolis Labor Review*, March 31, 1916, p. 1, and April 28, 1916 p. 1; *New Times*, April 1, 1916, p. 1, April 8, 1916, p. 1.

8. *New Times*, April 1, 1916, p. 1; *Minneapolis Labor Review*, March 31, 1916, p. 1.

9. *Minneapolis Labor Review*, March 31, 1916, p. 1; *New Times*, April 8, 1916, p. 1, April 1, 1916, p. 1; NWLB, Minneapolis Steel and Machinery Case, testimony of George M. Gillette, 17, in Minnesota Commission on Public Safety (MCPS) Papers, MHS.

10. Here and below, *New Times*, April 1, 1916, p. 1; *Minneapolis Labor Review*, March 31, 1916, p. 1

11. *New Times*, April 1, 1916, p. 1; MSfl, *Proceedings*, 1916, p. 58.

12. *New Times*, April 1, 1916, p. 1; June 2, 1916, p. 1; *Minneapolis Labor Review*, March 31, 1916, p. 1, April 14, 1916, p. 1, May 5, 1916, p. 1, June 2, 1916, p. 1; MSM, *Annual Report*, 1916.

13. *Minneapolis Labor Review*, April 7, 1916, p. 1, April 20, 1917, p 1, April 28, 1916, p. 1, May 19, 1916, p. 1, June 30, 1916, p. 1.

14. CA, *Bulletin*, May–June 1928; Jean E. Spielman, speech at Teamsters' mass meeting, June 26, 1916, Spielman Papers, MHS.

15. Spielman speech, June 16, 1916, Spielman Papers; *Minneapolis Journal*, May 3, 1916, p. 22; CA, *Bulletin*, May–June 1928; Hain, "Twin Cities Team for Open Shop," 764.

16. *Minneapolis Journal*, May 3, 1916, p. 22; *Minneapolis Labor Review*, May 12, 1916, p. 1, May 19, 1916, p. 1, June 9, 1916, p. 1, June 11, 1916, p. 4, June 16, 1916, p. 1; CA, *Law and Order*, pamphlet, 1927, CA Papers.

17. *Minneapolis Labor Review*, June 9, 1916, p. 1, June 23, 1916, p. 1; *New Times*, June 10, 1916, p. 2; *Minneapolis Journal*, June 11, 1916, p. 4, June 14, 1916, p. 17.

18. *Minneapolis Labor Review*, June 16, 1916, p. 1; Minneapolis City Council, *Proceedings*, June 9, 1916; Civic and Commerce Association (CCA), membership list, *Second Annual Report*, 1912, p. 152. In 1903, Mayor Nye was secretary of the Public Affairs Committee of the Commercial Club. In this position he was intimately involved in the organization of the CA; Fred Salisbury to George K. Belden, July 28, 1903, CA Papers; Minneapolis Commercial Club, *Annual Report*, 1903; *Minneapolis Journal*, June 11, 1916, p. 4.

19. Minneapolis City Council, *Proceedings*, June 13, 1916, p. 611; *Minneapolis Journal*, June 14, 1916, p. 17. City police officers were not withdrawn until July 3, when the strike was essentially broken. *Minneapolis Labor Review*, June 16, 1916, p. 1; CA, *Law and Order*, CA Papers.

20. *Minneapolis Journal*, June 18, 1916, p. 3; *Minneapolis Labor Review*, June 23, 1916, p. 1; Minneapolis Trades and Labor Assembly, "The Story of the Teamsters' Strike," n.d., Spielman Papers, MHS.

21. "The Story of the Teamsters' Strike"; *Minneapolis Labor Review*, June 30, 1916, p. 1; *Minneapolis Tribune*, June 29, 1916, p. 11.

22. CA, *Bulletin*, April–May 1932; *Minneapolis Tribune*, June 28, 1916, p. 9.

23. *Minneapolis Tribune*, June 28, 1916, p. 9.

24. *Minneapolis Tribune*, June 28, 1916, p. 9; CA, *Bulletin*, April–May 1932; Hain, "Twin Cities Team for Open Shop," 764.

25. *Minneapolis Journal*, June 28, 1916, p. 17; *New Times*, July 15, 1916, p. 1; CA, *Minutes of Annual Meetings*, 1915–19, CA Papers; CA, *Bulletin*, April–May 1932.

26. "The Story of the Teamsters' Strike"; *Minneapolis Journal*, July 1, 1916, p. 6, July 8, 1916, p. 1; *Minneapolis Tribune*, June 29, 1916, p. 11.

27. "The Story of the Teamsters' Strike"; *Minneapolis Journal*, July 2, 1916, p. 7.

28. *Minneapolis Tribune*, July 1, 1916, p. 8.

29. *Minneapolis Journal*, July 1, 1916, p. 8, July 2, 1916, p. 7; *Minneapolis Labor Review*, July 21, 1916, p. 1; *New Times*, July 8, 1916, p. 1; *Minneapolis Tribune*, July 1, 1916, p. 8.

30. *Minneapolis Journal*, July 2, 1916, p. 7, July 3, 1916, p. 11, July 9, 1916, p. 1; Hain, "Twin Cities Team for Open Shop."

31. CA, *Bulletin*, May–June 1928.

32. CA, *Bulletin*, Oct. 1918.

33. Minnesota Department of Labor, *Fifteenth Biennial Report*, 1916, pp. 168–69; *New Times*, July 1, 1916, p. 1; Neil Betten, "Riot, Revolution, Repression in the Iron Range Strike of 1916," *Minnesota History* 41 (summer 1969): 83–85.

34. Betten, "Riot, Revolution, and Repression," pp. 83–85; *New Times*, July 1, 1916, p. 1.

35. *New Times*, July 1, 1916, p. 1; Betten, "Riot, Revolution, and Repression," 83–85, 88; Michael Brook, "Voices of Dissent: The Minnesota Radical Press, 1910–1920," unpublished paper written for the Minnesota Radicalism Conference, Minnesota Historical Society (MHS) Symposium, 1989.

36. Betten, "Riot, Revolution, and Repression," 90, 93.

37. Minnesota House of Representatives, Committee of Labor and Labor Legislation, Hearings, Jan. 30, 1917: testimony of the following: Horace Wood, Labor Troubles in Northern Minnesota, 11, 113, 122; William Pe-

terson, 199, 201; Archie Sinclair, 149, all in John Lind Papers, MHS; John E. Haynes, "Revolt of the Timber Beasts," *Minnesota History* 42 (spring 1971): 164; *New Times*, Jan. 27, 1916, p. 1.

38. Haynes, "Revolt of the Timber Beasts," 165, 169.

39. Haynes, "Revolt of the Timber Beasts," 170; House of Representatives, Labor Committee, "Labor Troubles in Northern Minnesota," testimony of Sinclair, 146.

40. Haynes, "Revolt of the Timber Beasts," 171–73.

41. International Workers of the World (IWW), "The Preamble of the Industrial Workers of the World," *One Big Union of the I.W.W.* (Chicago: IWW, n.d.), 26.

42. L. W. Boyce to Captain Fitzhugh Burns, Sept. 27, 1918; Burns to Director of Military Intelligence, Sept. 25, 1918 and Oct. 4, 1918, Boyce to Burns, Sept. 27, 1918, Burns to Director, Sept. 25, 1918, all in U.S. Military Intelligence (USMI) Files (microfilm, Wilson Library, University of Minnesota).

43. *Commercial West*, Aug. 12, 1916, p. 8; Philip Taft, "The I.W.W. in the Grain Belt," *Labor History* 1 (winter 1960): 59; Haynes, "Revolt of the Timber Beasts," 166; Taft, "The I.W.W. in the Grain Belt," 60–61; "The Militant Harvest Workers," *International Socialist Review* (Oct. 1916): 230.

44. *Commercial West*, Sept. 23, 1916, p. 8.

45. *Minneapolis Journal*, June 26, 1916, p. 1.

46. Robert L. Morlan, *Political Prairie Fire: The Nonpartisan League, 1915–1922*, (Minneapolis: University of Minnesota Press, 1985), 87–89, 100–108, *Commercial West*, Feb. 3, 1917, p. 8; Fred B. Snyder to Sen. Knute Nelson, Aug. 18, 1917, Nelson Papers, MHS; *St. Paul Pioneer Press*, April 20, 1918, p. 1.

47. *New Times*, March 18, 1916, p. 1, June 24, 1916, p. 1; David Paul Nord "Minneapolis and the Pragmatic Socialism of Thomas Van Lear," *Minnesota History* 45 (spring 1976): 3–10.

48. *New Times*, March 18, 1916, p. 1. For a complete account of Thomas Van Lear's union and political career, see Nord, "Socialism in One City" (master's thesis, University of Minnesota, 1972).

49. *Minneapolis Tribune*, Sept. 24, 1916, p. 6. The committee included many of the city's most important industrialists such as John S. Crosby, John Washburn, and John S. Pillsbury and leading bankers C. T. Jaffray and Charles B. Mills. Former CA President F. E. Kenaston led a CA and CCA contingent that numbered at least thirty-nine out of fifty-three committee members; *New Times*, Sept. 29, 1916, p. 1, Oct. 28, 1916, p. 1; *Minneapolis Journal*, Sept. 24, 1916, p. 1.

50. *Minneapolis Labor Review*, Sept. 29, 1916, p. 2; *New Times*, Oct. 21, 1916, p. 1.

51. *Minneapolis Labor Review*, Oct. 6, 1916, p. 1.

52. Nord, "Hothouse Socialism: Minneapolis, 1910–1925," in *Socialism in the Heartland*, ed., Donald T. Critchlow (Notre Dame, IN: University of Notre Dame Press, 1986), 133–66; *Minneapolis Journal*, Nov. 8, 1916, p. 3; *New Times*, Dec. 30, 1916, p. 1.

53. Nord, *Socialism in One City*; Nord, "Thomas Van Lear"; *New Times*, Dec. 30, 1916, p. 1. See Chapter Nine on the 1917 streetcar strike.

NOTES TO CHAPTER 8

1. Minnesota, *Laws*, Chapter 261, S. F. 1006, Sections 3, 9, April 16, 1917; Minnesota Commission of Public Safety (MCPS), *Report*, 1919. There are a number of excellent sources on the MCPS: Carl H. Chrislock, *Watchdog of Loyalty: The Minnesota Commission of Public Safety during World War I* (St. Paul: Minnesota Historical Society Press, 1991); William W. Folwell, *A History of Minnesota*, 3:556–75; Charles S. Ward, "The Minnesota Commission of Public Safety in World War I" (master's thesis, University of Minnesota, 1965); Ora A. Hilton, "The Minnesota Commission of Public Safety in World War I, 1917–1919," *Oklahoma Mechanical College Bulletin* 48, No. 14.

2. MCPS, *Mobilizing Minnesota* (Minneapolis, 1918), 55; MCPS, *Report*, p. 11, both in Minnesota Commission of Public Safety Papers (hereafter MCPS Papers), MHS.

3. Ambrose Tighe to Charles Farnham, March 29, 1917; Farnham to James Clark, April 4, 1917, p. 1, Patriotic League Papers; Willis H. Raff, "Civil Liberties in Minnesota during the World War I Period" (thesis, University of Minnesota, 1950), 41; CCA, *Reports*, 1912–18; *Minneapolis City Directory*, 1917; CA, *Annual Meeting*, 1915–18, in CA Papers; Lucian Swift to George K. Belden, April 11, 1917, Knute Nelson Papers; Chrislock, *The Progressive Era*, 132; MCPS, *Report*, 9.

Ambrose Tighe was a lawyer for Twin City Rapid Transit Company. TCRT executives were all members of the CCA. Vice president Edward W. Decker (also president of Northwest National Bank) was an influential member of the Civic and Commerce Association's (CCA) financial committee and the Citizens Alliance (CA) board of directors. All of the executives of the Journal Printing Co.—publisher of the *Minneapolis Journal*—Herschel V. Jones, C. R. Adams, and W. M. Hones, were CCA members. The *Journal* had actively supported the CA as early as 1905.

4. *Minneapolis Journal*, March 29, 1917, p. 14; *St. Paul Daily News*, April 4, 1917, p. 1; *Commercial West*, Aug. 25, 1917, p. 8, April 24, 1915, p. 7; McGee to Nelson, April 11, 1917, Nelson Papers; Chrislock, *The Progressive Era*, 132.

5. McGee to Nelson, April 11, 1917, Nelson Papers.

6. MCPS, *Report*; MCPS Organizational Chart and Minutes, May 21, 1917, both in MCPS Papers; George M. Stephenson, *John Lind of Minnesota* (Minneapolis: University of Minnesota Press, 1935), 334; Tighe to Farnham, March 29, 1917; Farnham to Clark, April 13, 1917, St. Paul Patriotic League Papers, MHS; McGee to Nelson, April 11, 1917, Nelson Papers; President's Mediation Commission, *Report on Minneapolis*, 1918, University of Minnesota Library, microfilm.

7. Here and below, MCPS, *Report*, 13, 57, 74; MCPS, *Mobilizing Minnesota*, 9; MCPS, *Minutes*, April 24, 1917, all in MCPS Papers; Franklin F. Holbrook and Livia Appel, *Minnesota in the War with Germany*, vol. 2 (St. Paul: MHS, 1932), 228; Franklin F. Holbrook, ed., *St. Paul and Ramsey County in the War of 1917–1918* (St. Paul: Ramsey County War Records Commission, 1929), 221; John Lind to William W. Folwell, letter received Dec. 12, 1924, William Watts Folwell Papers, MHS; CCA, *Annual Report*, 1917, p. 112. Snyder also drafted the CCA constitution and was its first secretary: Marion D. Shutter, *History of Min-*

neapolis: Gateway to the Northwest (Chicago: S. J. Clarke Publishing Co., 1923), 3:462. Cross-reference of the following sources indicates the preponderance of CCA members in these groups: Minneapolis Civilian Auxiliary, membership list, Edward Karow Papers, MHS; Minnesota Home Guard Motor Corps, membership list; Hennepin County in World War I, scrapbook, Minneapolis Public Library; *Minneapolis City Directory*, 1917; CCA, *Annual Reports*, 1912, pp. 7–18, 1913, pp. 7–12, 1914, pp. 11–16. The Minneapolis Civilian Auxiliary became the Thirteenth Battalion of the Minnesota Home Guard on Feb. 21, 1918, and then the Third Battalion of the First (later Fourth) Regiment of the Minnesota Infantry National Guard on July 1, 1918; Karow to Henry A. Bellows, Sept. 6, 1918, Karow Papers.

8. C. W. Ames to J. F. McGee, July 11, 1917, Ames Papers.

9. MCPS, *Report*, 13, 75–76, 215; MCPS, List of State Peace Officers; List of Minneapolis Peace Officers; James Markham to Henry W. Libby, March 5, 1918, R. A. Gantt to Libby, July 30, 1918; American Protective League, membership lists; MCPS, *Mobilizing Minnesota*, 10, all in MCPS Papers; Minnesota, *General Statutes*, 1913, p. 1991; APL, Operative No. 71, *Summary and Report of War Service* (Minneapolis: APL, 1919), 5; CCA, *Annual Report*, 1917, p. 112; 1918, p. 13.

10. Tighe to McGee, Oct. 14, 1918, p. 8; David C. Adie to John S. Pardee, May 15, 1917, May 31, 1917; MCPS, *Minutes*, May 22, 1917, May 30, 1917; MCPS, *Mobilizing Minnesota*, 11, all in MCPS Papers; *Minnesota Laws*, 1917, Chapter 215, S.F. 942, "An Act Defining Criminal Syndicalism"; *Minnesota Senate Journal*, 1917, p. 1198; CCA, *Annual Reports*, 1912–14, CCA Papers; *Commercial West*, April 14, 1917, p. 8.

11. MCPS, *Mobilizing Minnesota*, 12; MCPS, *Minutes*, April 24, 1917, MCPS, *Report*, 1919, pp. 37, 72; Tighe to McGee Oct. 14, 1918, p. 8, all in MCPS Papers.

12. MCPS, *Report*, 1919, pp. 35, 38; MCPS, *Mobilizing Minnesota*, 12; MCPS, *Minutes of Special Meeting*, June 21, 1917, all in MCPS Papers; W. S. Jones to Burnquist, June 18, 1917; George M. Gillette to Burnquist, June 20, 1917, both in J. A. A. Burnquist Papers, MHS.

13. MCPS, *Minutes of Special Meeting*, June 21, 1917; Tighe to John Lind, June 23, 1917; copy of proposed Vagrancy Ordinance; Ward, MCPS, *Report*, 1919, p. 37, all in MCPS Papers; Hilton, "The CPS in World War I," 64. According to informants' reports in USMI files, the vagrancy statutes so infuriated the IWW that they planned firebomb attacks on the property of individuals belonging to the CA; USMI, Report of T. E. Campbell, June 29, 1917.

14. MCPS, Secret Service (SS) Agent "D. J. G.," Reports, July 24, 1917, July 25, 1917, SS Files, MCPS Papers. D. J. G. suggested that the fire was accidental. Sherman Bailey to Burnquist, July 25, 1917; Graham M. Torrance to Pleva, Feb. 9, 1918; Residents of Beltrami County to Burnquist, July 25, 1917, all in Burnquist Papers; newspaper clippings, July 25, 1917, July 26, 1917, Charles W. Ames Papers, MHS.

15. MCPS, *Minutes*, May 22, 1917, May 30, 1917, MCPS Papers; Lind to Burnquist, May 16, 1917; June 4, 1917; Salo to Lind, July 16, 1917; Pleva to Lind, July 16, 1917, all in Burnquist Papers.

16. MCPS, *Minutes*, May 22, 1917, May 30, 1917; Hatfield to Winter, June 26, 1917; newspaper clipping, n.d.; MCPS, SS Agent D. J. G., Reports, July 6, 1917, SS Files, MCPS Papers; T. G. Winter to Ames, Sept. 20, 1917, Ames Papers; SS Files, MCPS Papers. The reports of Hatfield's agents are filed in the Secret Service Files of the MCPS.

17. Newspaper clipping, n.d.; Winter to Pardee, June 30, 1917, July 18, 1917, Sept. 1, 1917; Pardee to Winter, July 19, 1917; Winter to Hatfield, July 18, 1917; Hatfield to Pardee, July 26, 1917; Aug. 15, 1917; O. R. Hatfield, Reports, June 16, 1917, all in MCPS Papers; newspaper clipping, n.d., Ames Papers; Winter to Ames, Sept. 20, 1917, Burnquist Papers. In the Secret Service Files, most agents mention O. R. Hatfield as their chief in at least one of their reports.

18. Hatfield to Winter, June 26, 1917; Agent No. 45, Reports, Aug. 14, 1917, Aug. 17, 1917, Aug. 19, 1917; MCPS, SS Agent D. J. G., Reports, July 25, 1917, MCPS Papers; Winter to Ames, Sept. 20, 1917, Burnquist Papers; Winter to Ames, Sept. 20, 1917, Ames Papers.

19. Winter to Pardee, June 27, 1917; Hatfield to Winter, June 26, 1917, both MCPS

Papers; translation of Swedish-language newspaper, *Allarm*, June 1, 1917 issue, Ames Papers.

20. Winter to Pardee, July 17, 1917; Hatfield to Winter Aug. 2, 1917; E. T. O. Reports, July 10, 1917; MCPS, SS Agent D. J. G. Reports, July 15, 1917; MCPS, SS Agent C. M. R., Reports, July 15, 1917; all in MCPS Papers. According to the USMI files, Ahlteen was arrested and released to try to provoke him into personally taking part in radical illegal acts; T. E. Campbell Report, July 26, 1917; USMI Files, MCPS Papers. Other reports are in Secret Service and Northern Information Bureau (NIB) files, MHS.

21. Carlos Avery to Winter, July 23, 1917; Don D. Lescohier to Pardee, July 18, 1917; Pardee to Lescohier, July 19, 1917; C. A. Prosser to Winter, Aug. 7, 1917; Edward Karow to Winter, Oct. 10, 1917, Oct. 29, 1917; W. S. Jones to Winter, Oct. 10, 1917; Pardee to Burns Detective Agency, July 14, 1917; H. Johnson to Winter, Aug. 31, 1917; W. H. Kelley to McGee, May 24, 1917; Pardee to Alfred Jacques, July 6, 1917; director, Norman County, to Pardee, Aug. 12, 1917, all in MCPS Papers.

22. White to Burnquist, July 14, 1917; Pardee to White, July 17, 1917; both MCPS Papers; Lt. Col., General Staff, Chief, Military Intelligence, to Winter, July 27, 1917; regarding IWW activities, Virginia, Minn. and Vicinity, July 20, 1917; L. W. Boyce to Capt. Fitzhugh Burns, Sept. 27, 1918; director, Military Intelligence to Intelligence Officers, St. Paul, Minn., Oct. 29, 1918, all in USMI Files. The NIB agent acted as secretary for both the Minneapolis and St. Paul branches of the IWW. Burns to director of Military Intelligence, Oct. 4, 1918; M. Churchill to Bruce Bielaske, Oct. 11, 1918; both USMI Files.

23. Winter to C. W. Ames, Sept. 20, 1917; Charles D. Frey to Winter, July 14, 1917; MacMartin to Winter, July 18, 1917; Nov. 6, 1917; A. M. Sheldon to Winter, Aug. 9, 1917; MacMartin to Winter, Nov. 24, 1917; MCPS, List of Minnesota Peace Officers, all in MCPS Papers; APL, Operative No. 71, *Summary Report of War Service*, 1–3; CCA, *Annual Report*, 1918, p. 13; Charles G. Davis to C. W. Shirk, Sept. 18, 1922, Hennepin County War Records Committee Papers, MHS; American Protective League (APL), booklet, n.d., 9, War Records Commission.

24. Winter to Pardee July 9, 1917, Aug. 16, 1917, Aug. 27, 1917, MCPS Papers; Lind to W. B. Wilson, July 31, 1917, John Lind Papers.

25. Michael R. Johnson, "The IWW and Wilsonian Democracy," *Science and Society* 28 (summer 1964): 267; Thorstein Veblen, Memorandum: Farm Labor and the IWW—Veblen, n.d., LeSueur Papers; report of T. E. Campbell, July 12, 1917; report of John F. McGovern, n.d., both USMI Files; MCPS to A. T. VanScoy, July 9, 1917, MCPS Papers.

26. MCPS, SS Agent H. H. C., Reports, June 26, 1917, MCPS Papers; J. M. Hannaford to Howard Elliot, Oct. 25, 1917, Northern Pacific Railway Papers, MHS; Pardee to the Sheriff, Aug. 16, 1917, Ames Papers.

27. Pardee to Lind, July 20, 1917, MCPS Papers; MCPS, Report on IWW Raid, Burnquist Papers.

28. Hinton G. Clabaugh to Winter, July 14, 1917, MCPS Papers; Clabaugh to Ames, Aug. 1, 1917, Ames Papers; MCPS, Report on IWW Raid, Burnquist Papers; Lind to Gregory, July 26, 1917, Lind Papers.

29. Lind to Gregory, July 26, 1917, Lind Papers.

30. Tighe to Lind, Aug. 5, 1917; Tighe to Burnquist, July 31, 1917; MCPS, Report on IWW Raid, all in Burnquist Papers.

31. Johnson, "The IWW and Wilsonian Democracy," 257–61; T. E. Campbell, Report, Sept. 6, 1917, USMI Files; *Minneapolis Tribune*, Sept. 6, 1917, p. 1; MCPS, *Report on IWW Raid*, Burnquist Papers.

32. Report of T. E. Campbell, Sept. 6, 1917, USMI Files; *Minneapolis Journal*, Sept. 5, 1917, p 1; Winter to Pardee, Sept. 5, 1917, MCPS Papers; Michael Brook, *Allarm*, (unpublished paper written for MHS seminar, 1989), 6–7, MHS Research Division. The source did not explain why liquids and acids of various kinds were found, but perhaps they were used to make false documents.

33. MCPS, Report on IWW Raid, Burnquist Papers; Winter to M. M. Booth, Oct. 3, 1917, both MCPS Papers; T. E. Campbell, Reports, Sept. 10, 1917, Nov. 24, 1917, USMI Files.

34. L. W. Boyce to J. F. Gould, Oct. 28, 1919, NIB Papers, MHS.

35. Nord, "Hothouse Socialism," 150; McGee to Nelson, Nov. 15, 1916, Knute Nelson Papers, MHS.

36. McGee to Nelson, May 31, 1917, Nelson Papers; Chrislock, *Watchdog of Loyalty*, 87–88.

37. MCPS, SS Agent C. H., Reports, June 3–8, 1917, MCPS Papers; *New Times*, June–Dec. 1916, usually p. 1; Nord, "Minneapolis and the Pragmatic Socialism of Thomas Van Lear," 3–10.

38. MCPS, SS Agent C. H. Reports, June 6, 1917, June 7, 1917, June 8, 1917, MCPS Papers.

39. *New Times*, June 16, 1917, p. 1; Report on Socialist Meeting at Ada, Minn., Aug. 16, 1917, USMI Files.

40. *New Times*, July 14, 1917, p. 1, July 21, 1917, p. 1.

41. *New Times*, Sept. 15, 1917, p. 1.

42. Newspaper clipping, n.d.; Newspaper clippings, Aug. 20, 1917, Oct. 20, 1917, all in MCPS Papers; *Minneapolis Labor Review*, April 16, 1920, p. 2.

43. *Minneapolis Journal*, Aug. 29, 1917, p. 16; *Bulletin of the People's Council of America*, Aug. 16, 1917, pp. 1, 4, Ames Papers; *New Times*, Aug. 25, 1917, p. 1; Nord, "Hothouse of Socialism," 147; Chrislock, *Watchdog of Loyalty*, 147–50.

44. Mayor's Statement Concerning Meeting of People's Council, Aug. 24, 1917, Burnquist Papers; *New Times*, Aug. 25, 1917, p. 1; *Minneapolis Journal*, Aug. 29, 1917, p. 16; *Minneapolis Tribune*, Aug. 26, 1917, p. 1, Aug. 29, 1917, p. 1.

45. Mayor's Statement Concerning Meeting of People's Council, Aug. 24, 1917, Burnquist Papers, MHS.

46. Burnquist to Otto Langum, Aug. 27, 1917; Sheldon to Burnquist Aug. 28, 1917; CCA, "Resolution of the board of directors," Aug. 28, 1917, all in Burnquist Papers; *Minneapolis Journal*, Aug. 29, 1917, p. 16; For a complete explanation of the organization and use of the Minneapolis Civilian Auxiliary, see Chapter Nine. In addition to Sheldon, the committee included CCA vice presidents Karl De Laittre and W. S. Dwinnell (also a state senator from Minneapolis), CA financier Edwin J. Cooper, and CA lumber magnate John Leslie.

47. MCPS, *Minutes*, Aug. 28, 1917, MCPS; Gov. Burnquist, *Proclamation*, Aug. 28, 1917, Burnquist Papers.

48. Chrislock, *Watchdog of Loyalty*, 133–56, 200–201; Lind to Folwell, Nov. 19,

1924, Folwell Papers; *St. Paul Daily News*, Dec. 24, 1917.

49. *New Times*, Feb. 23, 1918, p. 1; Minneapolis Typothetae (MT), Board of Governors, *Minutes*, Feb. 19, 1918, MT Papers, MHS.

50. *New Times*, April 6, 1918, p. 1; Nov. 1918, p. 1; Nord, "Hothouse of Socialism," 151–52.

51. Morlan, *Political Prairie Fire*, 110, 166.

52. MCPS, SS Agent G. W. S., Reports, July 13, 1917, MCPS Papers.

53. *Nonpartisan Leader*, Nov. 30, 1918; MCPS, "The State and the Citizen," Gilman Papers, MHS. The MCPS papers contain numerous letters from county officials reporting on the seditious nature of NPL meetings. The Secret Service kept files on thirty-five socialists and twenty-nine "Wobblies." There are NPL files only on A. C. Townley, Executive Secretary Henry C. Teigen, and three other NPL members. Compared to the surveillance of these other groups and the German community, the Secret Service reports on NPL meetings are quite limited. The NPL was clearly given a low priority by T. G. Winter.

54. Morlan, *Political Prairie Fire*, 145; MCPS, *Report*, 1919, p.163, MCPS Papers; Chrislock, *Watchdog of Loyalty*, 282. Ames was an active member of the St. Paul Association, St. Paul's counterpart of the CCA. The association went public with its open-shop policy during the spring of 1920. Ames was also active in the organization of the St. Paul Citizens Alliance in 1920 and served on its board of directors; St. Paul Association, *Yearbook*, 1918; *Minnesota Union Advocate*, March 26, 1920, p. 4; St. Paul CA, *Five Years*, pamphlet, 1925; Paul N. Myers to Ames, Oct. 11, 1919, Ames Papers.

55. Ames to John Lind, Oct. 17, 1917, Ames Papers.

56. Millikan, "In Defense of Business," 8; F. G. Thornton, "Order Forbidding Seditious Meetings," Feb. 16, 1918, MCPS Papers.

57. J. A. A. Burnquist, address, March 7, 1919; Organization Agent to L. Binshoof, Oct. 5, 1917, both in MCPS Papers. MCPS files contain considerable correspondence between county officials and the MCPS, in which the MCPS explained the responsibility of each county during the current crisis.

58. "Meeting of Representative Americans, Oct. 7, 1917, America First Association

(AFA) of St. Paul Papers, MHS; *Nonpartisan Leader*, Nov. 1, 1917, p. 18.

59. "To Our Fellow Citizens of Minnesota," n.d.; F. W. Murphy to Fellow Americans, Oct. 29, 1917; Northwest Loyalty Meeting, *Minutes*, Nov. 16, 1917, all in AFA Papers; *Nonpartisan Leader*, Nov. 1, 1917, p. 18.

60. AFA, *Meeting of Officers*, Nov. 25, 1917, AFA Papers; F. W. Murphy to Elmer E. Adams, Feb. 6, 1919, Adams Papers, MHS.

61. F. W. Murphy, "Americans, Do Your Duty," Nov. 14, 1919, AFA Papers.

62. AFA, *Meeting of Officers*, Nov. 25, 1917; County Chairmen for America First Body, Nov. 17, 1917; AFA, Executive Committee, Feb. 7, 1919, all in AFA Papers; CCA, *Yearbook*, 1912–14, 1918, p. 5; CCA, *Minneapolis Golden Jubilee*, 1917, pp. 29–30; On The Square Publishing Co. (OTSP), *Contract*, Dec. 29, 1917, OTSP Papers.

63. AFA, Executive Committee, Feb. 7, 1919, AFA Papers.

64. OTSP, *Contract*, Dec. 29, 1917; Charles Patterson to H. M. Van Hoesen, Oct. 10, 1917; Patterson, "Statement of Minnesota Conditions," all in OTSP Papers; County Chairmen for American First Body, Nov. 17, 1917, AFA Papers. Patterson, owner of Patterson Street Lighting Co., later served on the St. Paul Citizens Alliance board of directors.

65. OTSP, *Contract*, Dec. 29, 1917; Patterson to Van Hoesen, Oct. 10, 1917; Van Hoesen to Patterson Dec. 28, 1917; Van Hoesen to Beardsley, March 22, 1918, all in OTSP Papers; *Nonpartisan Leader*, Aug. 19, 1918, p. 8. A series of letters in the OTSP files in the MHS notifying the backers of On The Square Publishing Co. of changed financial conditions include letters to a number of prominent CCA and CA members: George H. Partridge of Wyman Partridge Co.; Fred B. Snyder, Hennepin County Public Safety Director; Henry Doerr, vice president of the Industrial Division of the CCA; and CCA treasurer Joseph Chapman of Northwest Bank.

66. Van Hoesen to CCA three-member committee, Dec. 29, 1917, OTSP Papers; Patterson to Ames, Oct. 18, 1918, Ames Papers; Patterson to Charley, June 27, 1918, NIB Papers.

67. *Nonpartisan Leader*, Jan. 21, 1918, p. 6.

68. *On The Square*, May 1918, pp. 7, 8, 29; June 1918, p. 28.

69. Van Hoesen to Phile Hall, June 4, 1918, OTSP Papers; *Nonpartisan Leader*, Aug. 19, 1918, p. 8.

70. Ames to Burnquist, Feb. 25, 1918, Burnquist Papers; Ames letter, Feb. 22, 1918; Alex C. King to F. B. Lynch, May 1, 1919, both in Ames Papers.

71. Ames to Charles O. Erbaugh, June 29, 1918, July 20, 1918, Oct. 4, 1918; Ames to Miller, Aug. 18, 1919; Miller to Ames, Aug. 18, 1919; copy of speech of C. B. Miller in Minnesota House of Representatives, June 8, 1918; C. W. Ames, mailing list, n.d.; King to Lynch, May 1, 1919, all in Ames Papers. Erbaugh and Ames conducted a lengthy correspondence that is in the Ames Papers.

72. Millikan, "In Defense of Business," 8; Morlan, *Political Prairie Fire*, 199.

73. Millikan, "In Defense of Business," 8.

74. MCPS, *Aiding the Enemies of Our Nation*, 1918, Burnquist Papers; MCPS, *The State and the Citizen*, n.d., Gilman Papers; MHS.

75. *Nonpartisan Leader*, Jan. 14, 1918, p. 14, April 1, 1918, p. 1, Nov. 30, 1918, n.p., clipping in Lind Papers; Carol Jenson, "Loyalty As a Political Weapon: The 1918 Campaign in Minnesota," *Minnesota History* 43 (summer 1972): 47, 50, 55.

76. Morlan, *Political Prairie Fire*, 200.

NOTES TO CHAPTER 9

1. Sumner T. McKnight to Civilian Auxiliary Members, April 9, 1917, War Commission Records, MHS; Paul H. Struck to Carroll K. Michener, July 14, 1918, Edward Karow Papers, MHS; CCA, *Annual Report*, 1917, pp. 33–34.

2. R[eturn] I. Holcombe, *Compendium of History and Biography of Minneapolis and Hennepin County* (Chicago, 1914), 356; Holbrook, *St. Paul in the War*, 76; CCA, *Annual Report*, 1917, pp. 33–34; Earnest H. Davidson to Franklin F. Holbrook, March 1921, War Commission Records; St. Paul Association to CCA of Sault St. Marie, Aug. 27, 1917, both in War Records Commission Papers, MHS; *St. Paul Pioneer Press*, April 7, 1917, p. 12.

3. Struck to Michener, July 14, 1918, Karow Papers.

4. Here and below, *A Statement of the Striking Streetcar Men to the Public*, pamphlet, 1917, Charles W. Ames Papers, MHS.

5. Harlow H. Chamberlain to Knute Nelson, July 3, 1918, Knute Nelson Papers, MHS; President's Mediation Commission, Report on Minneapolis, 1918, p. 4, copy in John Lind Papers, MHS; *Statement of Striking Streetcar Men*; Secretary of TCRT, *History of Labor Difficulties with the Trainmen of Twin City Lines in Minneapolis and St. Paul and the strike which occurred as a result*, n.d., Ames Papers.

6. Struck to Michener, July 14, 1918; Civilian Auxiliary to Members, Sept. 11, 1917, both in Karow Papers.

7. Mpls. Civilian Auxiliary, *Report*, Sept. 11, 1917; Sheriff Otto Langum to Minneapolis Civilian Auxiliary Members, Sept. 25, 1917, both in Karow Papers.

8. *Minneapolis Labor Review*, Oct. 5, 1917, p. 1; Otto Langum to J. A. A. Burnquist, Oct. 7, 1917, Burnquist Papers; First Battalion, Mpls. Civilian Auxiliary, Location of Units, Oct. 1917; Civilian Auxiliary, War Map, Oct. 1917; Company B, Mpls. Civilian Auxiliary, Method of Mobilization, Oct. 1917; Civilian Auxiliary, Assignments of Posts, Oct. 5, 1917, all auxiliary items in Karow Papers; *Minneapolis Journal*, Oct. 6, 1917, p. 1.

9. Civilian Auxiliary, Method of Mobilization, Oct. 1917, Karow Papers; *Minneapolis Directory*, 1917, Karow to Henry A. Bellows, Sept. 6, 1918, Civilian Auxiliary, Assignment of Posts, Oct. 5, 1917, Karow Papers.

10. Karow to Bellows, Sept. 6, 1918, Karow Papers; *Minneapolis Journal*, Oct. 6, 1917, p. 1; *St. Paul Pioneer Press*, Oct. 7, 1917, sec. 2, p. 2.

11. Karow to Bellows, Sept. 6, 1918, Karow Papers.

12. *St. Paul Pioneer Press*, Oct. 7, 1917, sec. 2, p. 1.

13. *St. Paul Pioneer Press*, Oct. 8, 1917, p. 1; Davidson to Holbrook, March 1921, War Records Commission; *St. Paul Pioneer Press*, Oct. 9, 1917, p. 2; *Minneapolis Tribune*, Oct. 10, 1917, p. 7.

14. MCPS, *Report*, 1919, pp. 38–40; MCPS, *Minutes*, Oct. 9, 11, and 12, 1917, all in Lind Papers.

15. *Minneapolis Labor Review*, Oct. 12, 1917, p. 1; Horace Lowry to Col. Perry Harrison, Oct. 10, 1917, Karow Papers; *St. Paul Daily News*, Nov. 11, 1917, p. 1.

16. Trainmen's Cooperative and Protective Association, *Constitution and By Laws*, 1917, Trainmen's Cooperative and Protective Association, *Membership Card*, 1917, MCPS Papers; *Minneapolis Labor Review*, Nov. 9, 1917, p. 1.

17. *Minneapolis Labor Review*, Nov. 9, 1917, p. 1; Proceedings of a meeting between Gov. Burnquist and Union Representatives, Nov. 1, 1917; excerpts of Henry W. Libby, Oct. 30, 1917, Ames Papers.

18. MCPS, *Minutes*, Nov. 2 and 6, 1917, Lind Papers; Robert Jamison to MCPS, Nov. 5, 1917, in MCPS Papers; CCA, *Annual Reports*, 1912–14, University of Minnesota, Wilson Library; newspaper clipping, n.d., CA Papers; List of Hamline Board of Trustees, n.d., Hamline Archives, Hamline University, St. Paul; CA, *Annual Meetings*, 1915–18, CA Papers; MCPS Special Committee, *Report*, ca. Nov. 1917, Jean Spielman Papers, MHS. Kerfoot biographer Mirion A. Morrill, commenting on Kerfoot's strident anti-radicalism, discusses the perpetual conflict between the church's obligation to survey all truth and its heavy financial burden in maintaining the institutions by which it lives; Morrill, "The Era of Consolidation," Charles Nelson Pace, ed., *Hamline University* (St. Paul, 1939), 53–59.

19. Karow to Bellows, Sept. 6, 1918; Civilian Auxiliary, *Service Manual*, 1918; Col. Harrison to Civilian Auxiliary Members, Nov. 12, 1917, all in Karow Papers; newspaper clipping, n.d., CA Papers; Leslie Sinton to Burnquist, Nov. 24, 1917, Burnquist Papers; *Minneapolis Labor Review*, Nov. 16, 1917, p. 1.

20. Here and below, MCPS Special Committee, *Report*, Nov. 19, 1917, Spielman Papers; MCPS, *Minutes*, Nov. 20 and Nov. 27, 1917, Lind Papers; TCRT, *History of Labor Difficulties*, Nov. 30, 1917, Ames Papers. McGee had suggested that the original CPS button recommendation be an order but "a pussy-footing request" by Lind swayed the CPS to make it a recommendation only; McGee to Burnquist, Nov. 30, 1917, Burnquist Papers.

21. United States, President Woodrow Wilson's Mediation Commission, *Report*, Feb. 14, 1918, Lind Papers; *St. Paul Dispatch*, Nov. 26, 1917, p. 1.

22. *St. Paul Dispatch*, Nov. 26, 1917, p 1; MCPS, *Report*, 1919, pp. 38–40, 146–47; "State-

ment of St. Paul Organized Labor," Dec. 2, 1917, Spielman Papers.

23. CA *Bulletin*, Sept. 1917; Oct. 1917; Jan.–Feb. 1929.

24. Chamberlain to Knute Nelson, July 3, 1918, Nelson Papers; MCPS, *Minutes*, Nov. 20, 1917, Lind Papers.

25. A. W. Strong to Burnquist, Dec. 1, 1917; Louis F. Post to Burnquist, Dec. 1, 1917, both in Burnquist Papers. There were over fifty telegrams to Burnquist from CCA members. It was clearly an organized campaign to reassure and congratulate Burnquist.

26. Burnquist to Post, Dec. 1, 1917, Burnquist Papers; *St. Paul Dispatch*, Nov. 27, 1917, p. 1, Nov. 28, 1917, p. 1.

27. *St. Paul Pioneer Press*, Dec. 3, 1917, p. 1; *Minneapolis Tribune*, Dec. 3, 1917, p. 1; Davidson to Holbrook, March 1921, War Records Commission Papers.

28. Nicholson to Adjutant General, March 11, 1918; E. P. Towne to Adjutant General, Sept. 27, 1918; Fifth Battalion Minnesota Home Guard, *Report*, n.d.; Seventh Battalion Minnesota Home Guard, *Historical Resume*, n.d.; J. R. Snow to T. Glenn Harrison, Sept. 26, 1918; all in Minnesota Adjutant General Papers, MHS; Davidson to Holbrook, March 1921. The term "the War of St. Paul" was used within the Home Guard. J. N. Nicholson to Adjutant General, March 11, 1918, and Feb. 14, 1918, both in Adjutant General Papers.

29. Karow to Bellows, Sept. 6, 1918; Karow to Harrison, Dec. 19, 1917, both in Karow Papers; *Minneapolis Labor Review*, Dec. 7, 1917.

30. The Nonpartisan League supported the striking streetcar men both financially and in the field with a massive publicity campaign. The IWW, already decimated by government suppression, was content to let the Minnesota State Federation of Labor take the heat for backing the strike; *Report on Union Meetings*, Jan. 13–14, 1918, Ames Papers; T. E. Campbell, *Report- In re:* IWW, Dec. 13, 1917, USMI Files, Wilson Library, University of Minnesota; Newton D. Baker to Burnquist, Dec. 4, 1917, Nelson Papers.

31. Alex M. Robertson to Nelson, Dec. 4, 1917; Nelson to Roberts, Dec. 4, 1917; McGee to Nelson, Dec. 5, 1917, all in Nelson Papers; *St. Paul Pioneer Press*, Dec. 5, 1917, p. 1.

32. *Minneapolis Labor Review*, Dec. 7, 1917, pp. 1, 2; Resolutions of a Trade Unionist Convention, Dec. 5, 1917, Spielman Papers; Campbell, *Report-In Re:* IWW, Dec. 13, 1917, USMI Files; *Minneapolis Labor Review*, Dec. 7, 1917, p. 2.

33. *St. Paul Daily News*, Dec. 4, 1917, p. 1; *Minneapolis Journal*, Dec. 4, 1917, p. 1; St. Paul Trades and Labor Assembly, *Truth About the Streetcar Strike*, 4, MCPS Papers; O. A. Hilton, "The Minnesota Commission of Public Safety in World War I," *Oklahoma Mechanical College Bulletin*, 48:22; Davis to Libby, Dec. 8, 1917, MCPS Papers.

34. Davis to Libby, Dec. 8, 1917, MCPS Papers.

35. *Minneapolis Journal*, Dec. 12, 1917, p. 1; *St. Paul Pioneer Press*, Dec. 14, 1917, p. 1; *St. Paul Daily News*, Dec. 13, 1917, p. 1.

36. *St. Paul Daily News*, Dec. 13, 1917, p. 1; *Minneapolis Labor Review*, Dec. 14, 1917, p. 1; Burnquist to Baker, Dec. 13, 1917, Nelson Papers.

37. *Minneapolis Journal*, Dec. 20, 1917, p. 12, Dec. 19, 1917, p.1; *St. Paul Pioneer Press*, Dec. 19, 1917, p. 1, Dec. 20, 1917, p. 1.

38. *St. Paul Pioneer Press*, Dec. 19, 1917, p. 1; Lowry to Nelson, Dec. 21, 1917, Nelson Papers.

39. President's Mediation Commission, *Report*, Feb. 14, 1918, copy in Lind Papers; Union pamphlet, *Twin City Rapid Transit Is Charged With Hampering War*, Feb. 14, 1918; Lowry to MCPS, Feb. 21, 1917, MCPS Papers; CCA, *Summary of War Activities*, 1917; State Employment Office Records, 1917; both in WRC Papers.

40. President's Mediation Commission, *Report*, Feb. 14, 1918, copy in Lind Papers; Lowry to MCPS, Feb. 21, 1917; Baker to MCPS, Feb. 15, 1917; both in MCPS Papers; Harlow H. Chamberlain to Nelson, July 3, 1918, Nelson Papers.

41. Lowry to MCPS, n.d. [late Feb. 1918]; Chamberlain to Nelson, July 3, 1918, Nelson Papers.

42. J. H. Walker to Joseph Colgan, March 13, 1918, Spielman Papers; President's Mediation Commission, *Minneapolis Report*, 1918; Briggs to Nelson, March 18, 1918, Nelson Papers; McGee to Harry A. Garfield, March 11, 1918, MCPS Papers.

43. Union pamphlet, Feb. 14, 1918, MCPS Papers; *Minneapolis Labor Review*, March 15, 1918, p. 1.

44. Chrislock, *Watchdog of Loyalty*, 252; President Woodrow Wilson, *Presidential Proclamation*, April 8, 1918, copy in Lynn Haines Papers, MHS. The controversy between federal and state labor policies, particularly the MCPS role in protecting the CA, is more fully explained in Chrislock's *Watchdog of Loyalty*, Chapter Twelve, "Defending the Status Quo Ante."

45. Wilson, *Presidential Proclamation*, April 8, 1918; MCPS Arbitration Order No. 30, MCPS Papers.

46. Regular correspondence from Briggs to Gov. Burnquist is found in the Burnquist Papers. Raymond Swing and Herbert R. Brougham, *Report of An Investigation of the Minneapolis Steel and Machinery Company*, ca 1918, p. 4.

47. Swing and Brougham, *Report of An Investigation*, 4, 36.

48. Briggs to Gov. Burnquist, April 16, 1918, Burnquist Papers; Swing and Brougham, *Report of An Investigation*, 4–5; MCPS, *Report*, 1919, pp. 108–9.

49. Swing and Brougham, *Report of An Investigation*, 23; Minnesota Board of Arbitration to Minneapolis Street Railway Company, June 10, 1918; Lowry to Minnesota Board of Arbitration, June 10, 1918, both in Minnesota Labor and Industry Dept. Records, MHS.

50. State Board of Arbitration, *Award In the Matter of the Controversy Between Twin City Rapid Transit Company and Certain of Its Former Employees*, June 12, 1918; Lowry to Board of Arbitration, June 10, 1918; both in Minnesota Labor and Industry Dept. Records, MHS; Lowry to Minnesota Board of Arbitration, June 13, 1918, copy in Swing and Brougham, *Report of an Investigation*, 27, 28.

51. Swing and Brougham, *Report of an Investigation*, 10, 11, 14–15, 36, 38–42; *Minneapolis Labor Review*, Dec. 20, 1918, p. 1.

52. Swing and Brougham, *Report of an Investigation*, 50.

53. Swing and Brougham, *Report of an Investigation*, 7, 8; *Minneapolis Labor Review*, Oct. 4, 1918, p. 1, Oct. 11, 1918, p. 1.

54. Swing and Brougham, *Report of an Investigation*, 3–8.

55. *Minneapolis Labor Review*, Oct. 11, 1918, p. 1; NWLB, *Decision Docket 46 and 196*, Nov. 22, 1918, copy in Lynn Haines Papers, MHS; Minnesota Employers' Association (MEA), *Statement and Resolutions*, Oct. 8, 1918, Minnesota Association of Commerce and Industry (MACI) Papers, MHS.

56. NWLB, *Decision Docket 46 and 196*, Nov. 22, 1918, copy in Lynn Haines Papers; MEA, *Statement and Resolutions*, Oct. 8, 1918, in Haines Papers; *Minneapolis Labor Review*, Oct. 11, 1918, p. 1.

57. NWLB, *Decision Docket 46 and 196*, Nov. 22, 1918; Chrislock, *Watchdog of Loyalty*, 266.

58. NWLB, *Decision Docket 46 and 196*, Nov. 22, 1918; *Minneapolis Labor Review* April 18, 1919, p. 1.

59. Minnesota Board of Arbitration, *Report for 1917–1918*, Dec. 20, 1918, 13–17; Board of Arbitration to National Industrial Conference Board, April 28, 1919; Board of Arbitration, Report to MCPS, Sept. 1, 1917 to May 18, 1918, all in Minnesota Labor and Industry Dept. Records.

60. *Minneapolis Labor Review*, April 18, 1919, p. 1.

61. Chrislock, *Watchdog of Loyalty*, 267–68; *Minneapolis Morning Tribune*, Dec. 10, 1925, clipping, n.p., in Minneapolis Moline Papers, MHS; Arthur LeSueur to Frank Morrison, Dec. 24, 1920; LeSueur to Glenn P. Turner Jan. 7, 1924, Arthur LeSueur Papers, MHS.

62. *Minneapolis Morning Tribune*, Dec. 10, 1925, p 33; *Minneapolis Journal*, May 1, 1920, p. 5.

NOTES TO CHAPTER 10

1. Gene Slanchfield to The Local Unions, Feb. 1918; Minneapolis Trades and Labor Assembly, "Report of Committee on Platform," Feb. 23, 1918, both in Central Labor Union (CLU) of Minneapolis Papers, MHS; Nord, "Hothouse Socialism," 149–52.

2. Minneapolis Trades and Labor Assembly, "Platform Committee," Feb. 23, 1918, CLU Papers; Nord, "Hothouse Socialism," 149–52.

3. American Committee of Minneapolis (ACM), "Declaration of Principles" and "A Call to Citizens," both dated May 12, 1919, ACM Papers, MHS; *Minneapolis Journal*, June 22, 1919, p. 1.

4. ACM, *Fall In! The U.S. Needs You*, pamphlet, May 12, 1919, ACM Papers; *Minneapolis Journal*, June 22, 1919, p. 1.

5. *Minneapolis Journal*, June 22, 1919, p. 1; Shutter, *History of Minneapolis*, 3: 249, 548; CCA, *1918 Yearbook*; Special Senate Investigating Committee, *Report to the Senate*, 1923, p. 7, MHS; *Minneapolis Journal*, June 22, 1919, pp. 1, 16; *Minneapolis Labor Review*, Aug. 29, 1919, p. 4. Ellison, one of the original CA members, was a director of the First National Bank and vice-president of Cedar Lake Ice Company. Chamberlain had served both as president and chairman of First National Bank and as president of the Minneapolis Threshing Machine Co.

6. *Minneapolis Labor Review*, Aug. 29, 1919, p. 4.

7. ACM, *Fall In! The U.S. Needs You*; ACM, Application for Membership, both ACM Papers; J. F. Gould to E. J. Longyear Co., Nov. 5, 1919; F. A. Chamberlain to E. J. Longyear, July 22, 1919, both in Longyear Co. Records, MHS; Minneapolis Clearing House, *Minutes*, July 8, 1919, NW Banco Papers; *Minneapolis Labor Review*, Aug. 29, 1919, p. 4.

8. Rev. Marion D. Shutter, D. D., "From Constitution to Chaos in Russia," March 1919, MHS; *Minneapolis Journal*, Sept. 19, 1936, p. 3; *Who's Who in Minneapolis*, 122.

9. Shutter, "From Constitution to Chaos in Russia." In 1922 Shutter edited a three-volume *History of Minneapolis*. Volumes 2 and 3 were glowing biographical studies of the community and business leaders of Minneapolis, most of whom were CCA members. CCA members not only made history, they wrote it.

10. Gould to Longyear, July 29, 1919, Longyear Co. Records, MHS; ACM Secretary to J. F. Walker, Dec. 5, 1919, NIB Papers, MHS. MHS has five pamphlets written by Dr. Shutter and issued by the ACM.

11. Shutter, *Socialism and the Family*, *Patriotism*, and *The Work of Our Fathers*.

12. Shutter, *The Menace of Socialism*; *Socialism and the Family*.

13. Peter W. Collins, "Why Socialism is Opposed to the Labor Movement," ACM Papers.

14. Collins, "Why Socialism is Opposed to the Labor Movement," ACM Papers.

15. The Northern Information Bureau Papers at MHS contain lengthy files of the correspondence between Boyce and Gould in Gould's position as secretary of the ACM. Numerous letters discuss surveillance and activities of the IWW, NPL, and labor radicals. Boyce to Gould, Nov. 25, 1919, Dec. 2, 1919, both NIB Papers.

16. Gould to Boyce, Dec. 5, 1919, Dec. 20, 1919, March 22, 1920; April 13, 1920, April 24, 1920; Gould to NIB, Oct. 9, 1919, Jan. 5, 1920, April 26, 1920, May 5, 1920; E. E. Noble to Gould, March 11, 1920; Boyce to Hon. Walter H. Newton, Oct. 20, 1919; Boyce to Gould, Feb. 19, 1920, all in NIB Papers.

17. Boyce to Gould, Oct. 28, 1919, Jan. 19, 1920, both in NIB Papers.

18. Boyce to Gould, Sept. 8, 1919; Sept. 15, 1919; Sept. 19, 1919; Oct. 31, 1919; all in NIB Papers.

19. Boyce to Gould, Oct. 17, 1919; Boyce to Hon. W. H. Newton, Nov. 18, 1919, both in NIB Papers.

20. *Minneapolis Labor Review*, Jan. 30, 1920, p. 1; March 12, 1920, p. 1.

21. Working People's Nonpartisan League (WPNPL), *Declaration of Principles and Platform of Organized Labor in Minnesota*, July 20, 1919, CLU Papers; Morlan, *Political Prairie Fire*, 262–63; Nord, *Socialism in One City*, 149–55.

22. Morlan, *Political Prairie Fire*, 262–63; Nord, *Socialism in One City*, 149–55.

23. WPNPL, *Declaration of Principles*; Preus Biography, n.d., 1, Preus Papers; Boyce to Gould, Nov. 25, 1919; Oct. 31, 1919 (two different letters, same date), NIB Papers.

24. Boyce to Gould, Nov. 3, 1919; Dec. 31, 1919, NIB Papers.

25. Morlan, *Political Prairie Fire*, 279; WPNPL, Convention, March 25, 1920, Farmer-Labor Association Papers, MHS. All members of the press were excluded from these proceedings except representatives of the *Daily News* and the *Daily Star*; Harold L. Nelson, "The Political Reform Press: A Case Study," *Journalism Quarterly* 29 (summer 1952): 295.

26. F. J. McPartlin to W. I. Nolan, Feb. 2, 1920; Theodore Christianson to Nolan, Oct. 23, 1919, both in W. I. Nolan Papers, MHS.

27. Preus Biography, 3; Preus speech, June 3, 1920, pp. 4, 16, 19; Preus to W. I. Norton, May 6, 1920, all in J. A. O. Preus Papers, MHS; Charles S. Marden to Nolan, Jan. 30, 1920; Christianson to Nolan, Feb. 4, 1920, both in

Nolan Papers. The CA exerted a powerful influence on the Republican Party leadership of
the period. Edward E. Smith, unofficial "boss"
of the party, secretly received $41,000 be-
tween 1916 and 1921 from Twin City Rapid
Transit Co., a powerful CA member since 1903.
H. M. Olmsted, "Twin Cities and the Holding
Co.: The Minneapolis Street Railway Story,"
National Municipal Review (July 1923): pp.
376–80; M. H. Hedges, "Who Corrupts Our
Politics?" *The Nation*, July 19, 1922, pp. 66–68.
The WPNPL did have connections with the Socialist Party. WPNPL President Mahoney and
Secretary-Treasurer Van Lear were both ex-
Socialist office holders. Domestic policies of
the two groups were very similar. Their pri-
mary disagreement was over war policy; Morlan, *Political Prairie Fire*, 262; Nord, *Socialism
in One City*, 149–59; Preus speech, June 3,
1920, p. 15, Preus Papers.

28. CA membership list, compiled by author and in author's possession; Edward C.
Gale, "Herschel V. Jones," *Minnesota History*
10 (March 1929): 29; Commercial Club, letterhead 1902, James Gray Papers, MHS.

29. Lucian Swift to George K. Belden, April
11, 1905, CA Papers; Gale, "Herschel V. Jones,"
29; Hon. James Manahan, "Who Owns the
Journal?" *Congressional Record*, May 8, 1914,
MHS; Walter A. Eggleston to Elmer E. Adams,
Aug. 8, 1908, E. E. Adams Papers. Various
sources point to James J. Hill and Minneapolis
financial interests as the backers for Jones's
purchase of the *Journal*.

30. *Minneapolis Journal*, Oct. 12, 1920,
p. 18.

31. *Minneapolis Journal*, June 11, 1920, p.
14, Oct. 10, 1920, p. 1, Oct. 12, 1920, Oct. 21,
1920, p. 4, Oct. 22, 1920, p. 29, Oct. 24, 1920,
p. 3.

32. *Commercial West*, May 22, 1920, p. 8.

33. *Commercial West*, Jan. 24, 1920, p. 8.

34. C. W. Ames to John Crosby, July 8,
1919, Crosby to Ames, July 9, 1919, Ames Papers.

35. Harry Curran Wilbur, *The Red Menace
in Minnesota* (St. Paul: 1923 [?]), 6–17; this
"open letter to friends of constitutional
government in Minnesota" included a transcript of the testimony before the Senate investigating committee of Wilbur and W. O.
Washburn.

36. MEA, Executive Committee Meeting
Minutes, May 29, 1919, Oct. 2, 1919; MEA,
Board of Directors Minutes, Aug. 11, 1919;
MEA, Annual Meeting, Dec. 5, 1922, all in MEA
Papers; O. P. Briggs to T. B. Walker, Oct. 13,
1920, Walker Papers; Wilbur, *The Red Menace
in Minnesota*, 4.

37. Frank E. Putnam, et al., to E. E.
Adams, Jan. 19, 1920; E. E. Adams to P. C.
Frazee, March 10, 1920, both in E. E. Adams
Papers, MHS.

38. MSGA, "Declaration of Principles and
By-Laws," Jan. 30, 1919; *Minnesota Issues*,
March 1, 1920. The treasury of the official
MSGA handled only $6,039,77, which repre-
sented a membership of approximately 1,208
at five dollars per membership; Senate Special
Investigating Committee (SSIC), Report to the
Senate, April 18, 1923.

39. E. E. Adams to P. C. Frazee, March 10,
1920; E. E. Adams Papers; MEA Executive Committee, *Minutes*, Jan. 7, 1920, MEA Papers; SSIC,
Testimony, 397–99, 605; SSIC, Report to the
Senate, April 18, 1923, copy in Preus Papers.

40. Wilbur, *The Red Menace in Minnesota*,
27; E. E. Adams to Frazee, March 10, 1920;
Preus to Adams, June 30, 1920; Frazee to
Adams, March 21, 1920, May 11, 1920, all letters in Adams Papers; *The Labor World*, May 8,
1920, p. 4; *Minnesota Union Advocate*, May 14,
1920, p. 5.

41. *Who Was Who in America*, p. 634; SSIC,
Report, 12, 13; SSIC, Testimony, 359–62, 374,
397, 401–2, 496, 501. Noel G. Sargent lec-
tured for both the ACM and the MSGA in addition to writing pamphlets for both organizations; *Who Was Who in America, 1969–1973*, p.
634; Noel Sargent, *Socialism—The Farmer—the
NPL, MSGA* pamphlet; Sargent, NPL *Leaders
Work with IWW, MSGA* pamphlet, copy in National NPL Papers, MHS; Sargent, IWW *Preach
Violence*, ACM pamphlet, copy in CA Papers.
Sargent would run the open shop Industrial
Relations Department until 1932 when he
formed and headed the National Association
of Manufacturers (NAM) economic research
department. After fourteen years as secretary
of the NAM, he was elected to the position of
executive vice-president in 1947; *St. Paul Pioneer Press*, July 7, 1947.

42. Wilbur, *The Red Menace in Minnesota*,
7–8; SSIC, Report, 11; Morlan, *Political Prairie*

Fire, 279; *Minnesota Issues*, Feb. 15, 1920, p. 1, March 1, 1920, p. 1, March 15, 1920, p. 1.

43. *Minnesota Issues*, Feb. 15, 1920, p. 1, March 1, 1920, March 15, 1920.

44. *Minnesota Issues*, Oct. 10, 1920; Minnie J. Nielson, "A Message to Minnesota Womanhood" (St. Paul: Minnesota SGA, 1920).

45. *The Union*, Nov. 2, 1906, p. 4; *Labor Digest*, Jan. 1908, pp. 5, 13, Feb. 1908; "Principles of the Labor Digest," *Labor Digest*, Jan. 1919, p. 2; CA to T. B. Walker, Feb. 9, 1921; Briggs to Whom It May Concern, Feb. 5, 1925; and E. E. Stevens to T. B. Walker, Nov. 25, 1925, all in Walker Papers. In reaction to this change in editorial policy, the Minneapolis Trades and Labor Assembly organized the *Minneapolis Labor Review* in April 1907, "the only publication in Minnesota owned and controlled in every department by organized labor"; *Minneapolis Labor Review*, April 4, 1907, p. 7.

46. *Labor Digest*, Jan. 1920, March 1920, June 1920.

47. *Northwestern Appeal*, Sept. 17, 1920, p. 3, Nov. 5, 1920, p. 1; T. B. Walker to R. A. Long, Feb. 8, 1921; O. P. Briggs to T. B. Walker, Oct. 4, 1920; Report on Speech of F. G. R. Gordon, June 10, 1921; Lewis R. Hovey to J. R. Forbes, n.d., all in Walker Papers.

48. Briggs to Walker, Oct. 16, 1920; Walker to R. A. Long, Feb. 8, 1921, both in Walker Papers; *Northwestern Appeal*, Sept. 17, 1920, p. 3; Sept. 24, 1920, p. 3; Nov. 5, 1920, p. 1.

49. *Northwestern Appeal*, June 26, 1920, p. 1; Minnesota, *Legislative Manual*, 1921, pp. 100–101; *Minnesota Issues*, July 4, 1920, p. 3.

50. Minnesota, *Legislative Manual*, 1921, p. 526–27; *Minnesota Issues*, Nov. 24, 1920, p. 3; *Northwestern Appeal*, Nov. 5, 1920, p. 1.

51. *Legislative Manual*, 1921, pp. 526–27; *Minnesota Issues*, March 1921, p. 5; untitled report, Nov. 1, 1922, Intelligence Report on Alexis Georgian, Feb. 1923, CA Papers.

52. Untitled Report, Nov. 1, 1922, CA Papers; *Minnesota Laws*, 1921, p. 53. On evidence provided by the American Protective League (APL) and other agencies, Georgian was ordered deported on June 19, 1921, but Russia would not take him. He was extradited to Michigan to face syndicalism charges. Throughout legal proceedings the Communist Party paid his bail and, as of March 1, 1923, he was free and still in Minneapolis.

53. *Minneapolis Labor Review*, June 10, 1921, p. 1; George E. Leach, "The Personal History of Major General G. E. Leach," 30, George E. Leach Papers, MHS.

54. Nord, "Socialism in One City," 167–73; *Commercial West*, June 18, 1921, p. 7; F. G. R. Gordon to T. B. Walker, Sept. 18, 1922, and June 11, 1923, both Walker Papers.

NOTES TO CHAPTER 11

1. Lewis L. Lorwin, *American Federation of Labor: Policies and Prospects* (Washington, D.C.: The Brookings Institution, 1933), 187–88; *New York Times*, Sept. 9, 1923.

2. Minnesota Department of Labor, *17th Biennial Report*, 1919–20, pp. 133, 135–48; Hain, "CA Has Kept Minneapolis Open Shop," 765; CA, "The CA—Its Aims, Its Policies, Its Accomplishments," manuscript, n.d., Great Northern Railway Records, MHS; CA, "Law and Order and The Open Shop," CA Papers; CA, *Bulletin*, May 1928.

3. Bonnett, *Employers' Associations*, 84, 87, 89, 296, 336.

4. Jacob Nathan, "The Open Shop Primer," 1918; Employers' Assn. of Washington, "Story of Detroit Open Shop," 1916, both in CA Papers; Bonnett, *Employers' Associations*, 126–27.

5. Bonnett, *Employers' Associations*, 76, 369; *Minneapolis Labor Review*, March 13, 1914, p. 1.

6. Bonnett, *Employers' Associations*, 93, 130, 499–544; Employers' Assn. of Washington, "Story of Detroit Open Shop," CA Papers.

7. Bonnett, *Employers' Associations*, 130, 371.

8. Bonnett, *Employers' Associations*, 499–544; 517.

9. A. J. Hain, "Nation Swinging to Open Shop," *Iron Trade Review*, Sept. 23, 1920, pp. 847–48, copy in CA Papers; Bonnett, *Employers' Associations*, 539–40; Associated Employers' of Indianapolis (AEI), *Special Bulletin*, March 8, 1920, copy in CA Papers. Both the literature of the open-shop movement and historical studies of it suggest that the open-shop movement exploded spontaneously across the country (see Allen M. Wakstein, "The Origins of the Open Shop Movement, 1919–1920," *The*

Journal of American History 51[Dec. 1964]:
460–75). An examination of the educational
and organizational efforts of the AEI indicate a
more likely inspiration. The remarkably similar ideology, constitutions, methods, and so
on, also suggest an interconnected movement.

10. Roll 13 of the microfilm of the CA Papers contains literature from across the country distributed during the 1919–20 open-shop
campaign. CA, "The Citizens Alliance of Minneapolis—Its Policy and Principles," March
18, 1919, Spielman Papers; *Duluth Labor
World*, May 14, 1921, p. 1.

11. *Duluth Labor World*, May 14, 1921, p. 1;
William Millikan, "Maintaining Law and Order in Minneapolis: The Citizens Alliance in
the 1920s," *Minnesota History* 51 (summer
1989): 220.

12. CA, "Law and Order and The Open
Shop," Feb. 1927, CA Papers; CA, *Bulletin*, Feb.
1918, Aug. 1918, Feb. 1919, Sept. 1919, Dec.
1920; also, see Citizens Alliance *Bulletins* from
1917 to 1922 for how the CA spread the gospel
of the open shop.

13. CA, "Law and Order and The Open
Shop," Feb. 1927, CA Papers. The CA continued
to publish the *Weekly Bulletin* through the end
of 1936. In 1935, the CA also began publication of the *Industrial News Service*, which
served a very similar purpose and contained
similar information. CA, "Review of CA Activities Since Jan. 1, 1921," CA, *Special Weekly Bulletin No. 66*, April 2, 1920, *No. 128*, June 10,
1921, *No. 132*, July 8, 1921, *No. 120–33*, April
15–July 15, 1921, *No. 243*, Aug. 24, 1923, *No.
290*, July 18, 1924; CA, "Review of CA Activities since Jan. 1, 1921," all in Walker Papers.

14. CA, "The CA Free Employment Bu-
reau," April 1932, p. 2, CA, "List of Founders";
Fred R. Salisbury to George K. Belden, July 28,
1903; CA, *Bulletin*, March 1929, all in CA Papers. Salisbury was a member of the Commercial Club's Public Affairs Committee when it
organized the CA in 1903. In 1904, he became
president of the Commercial Club. He was also
president of the Twin City Merchants' Assn.
and the Minneapolis Furniture Manufacturers' Assn. He took over the presidency of Salisbury and Satterlee, Minneapolis's primary
mattress manufacturer in 1898 and ran the
company under the open shop until his death;
Commercial Club Finance Committee to Dear

Sir, May 21, 1901, Walker Papers; Minneapolis
Commercial Club, *Yearbook*, 1904; Salisbury
and Satterlee Co., *Sixty Years*, Salisbury Co.
Papers.

15. CA, "The CA Free Employment Bureau," CA Papers.

16. CA, *Bulletin*, Sept. 1919, March 1929;
CA, "The CA Free Employment Bureau," CA
Papers.

17. CA, "The CA Free Employment Bureau," 70, CA Papers. The intelligence function
of the bureau is discussed in Chapter Fourteen.

18. CA, *Special Weekly Bulletin No. 146*, Oct.
14, 1921, Walker Papers; CA, *Bulletin* Sept.
1919; CA, "The CA Free Employment Bureau,"
CA Papers.

19. CA, *Bulletin*, March 1929; CA, "The CA
Free Employment Bureau," CA Papers.

20. Minneapolis Retailers' Association
(MRA), *Minutes*, Sept. 9, 1919, Feb. 10, 1920,
MRA Papers; Associated Business Organizations (ABO) of Minneapolis, *Rules and Regulations*, n.d., Alexis Caswell to Twin City Vehicle
Manufacturers' Assn. (TCVMA), April 14, 1920,
both in TCVMA Papers. Each association had to
vote to support the open shop before it was
granted membership.

21. MRA, *Minutes*, Aug. 27, 1919, Feb. 10,
1920, March 2, 1920, March 12, 1912, June
17, 1916, Sept. 9, 1919, all in MRA Papers; Minneapolis Clearing House, *Minutes*, Feb. 25,
1920, Northwestern Bancorporation Papers.
See Chapter Fifteen, "Financing the War on
Labor," for a detailed account of the relationship of Minneapolis banks to the CA. The
Clearing House minutes state that joining the
ABO would be incompatible with the Clearing
House constitution and bylaws. The *Minneapolis Labor Review* suggested that the banks
wanted to avoid the publicity of openly joining
the ABO, while still supporting the open-shop
fight behind the scenes. The banks' role in the
CA indicates that the *Labor Review*'s suggestion
was probably correct; *Minneapolis Labor Review* April 9, 1920, p. 2.

22. CA, "Law and Order and the Open
Shop," Feb. 1927, CA Papers; TCVMA, *Minutes*,
April 5, 1920; TCVMA letterhead, 1920, both in
TCVMA Papers; Briggs to Nelson, Dec. 31, 1917,
Nelson Papers.

23. TCVMA, *Minutes*, April 12, 1920,
Caswell to TCVMA, April 14, 1920; Caswell to

Harvey B. Smith, May 18, 1920, all in TCVMA Papers. The other ABO members were: Minneapolis Auto Trade Assn.; Minnesota Garage Owners Assn.; Minneapolis Hotel & Restaurant Keepers Assn.; Minneapolis Launderers Assn.; Minneapolis Master Builders Assn.; Minneapolis Real Estate Board; Minneapolis Transfermen's Assn.; Minneapolis Wholesalers and Manufacturers Assn.; Minneapolis Woodworkers Assn.; Minnesota Warehousemens Assn.; Pattern Jobbers Assn.; Sheet Metal Contractors Assn.; Twin City Assn. of Employers of Machinists; Twin City Coal Exchange; and Twin City Foundrymen's Assn.

24. Caswell to Smith, May 18, 1920; Caswell to Secretaries, Constituent Organizations, July 28, 1920, both in TCVMA Papers.

25. Caswell to Secretaries of Member Organizations, June 15, 1920; ABO, *Special Notice*, [date crossed out], 1920; ABO, *Important Notice*, May 26, 1920, all in TCVMA Papers.

26. Caswell to C. J. Gotshall, April 14, 1920, TCVMA Papers; MRA, *Minutes*, March 2, 1920, MRA Papers.

27. *Minneapolis Journal*, April 24, 1920, p. 5, May 1, 1920, p. 5; *Minneapolis Tribune*, April 5, 1920.

28. "Wage Earners: Are you making the most of these Good Times?" clipping, n.d.; "Prosperity For Minneapolis Through the Open Shop," clipping, n.d., both in CA Papers; *Minneapolis Journal*, May 1, 1920, p. 5.

29. *Duluth Labor World*, Oct. 11, 1919, p. 4, May 29, 1920, p. 4, Sept. 18, 1920, p. 1; *Duluth Herald*, Oct. 3, 1919, p. 6; Briggs to Our Members, March 25, 1920, Walker Papers. The officers of the Duluth CA and at least six of seven members of the executive committee were prominent members or officers of the Commercial Club; Duluth Commercial Club, *Annual Reports*, 1917–18; L. C. Harris to Gentlemen, Aug. 4, 1922, Robert A. Olson Papers.

30. *Duluth Labor World*, Oct. 11, 1919, p. 4, Sept. 18, 1920, p. 1; *Duluth Herald*, Oct. 3, 1919, p. 6; Duluth CA, *Bulletin*, Feb. 8, 1922, Davidson Co. Records, MHS; Harris to Gentlemen, Aug. 4, 1922, Robert A. Olson Papers. The 1919 board of directors included officers or directors of the following Duluth organizations, by type: Its four largest banks—First National, American Exchange National, Northern National, and the City National;

wholesalers—Duluth Crushed Stone Co., Scott Graff Lumber Co., Marshall Wells Co., Gowan Lenning Brown Co.; manufacturers—Clyde Iron Works, Diamond Calk Horseshoe Co., De-Witt-Seitz Co.; and mining—John H. Savage Co., Oliver Mining Co.; *Duluth Herald*, Oct. 3, 1919, p. 6; Duluth Commercial Club, *Annual Reports*, 1911–18; Duluth Board of Trade.

31. *Duluth Labor World*, Sept. 18, 1920, p. 1.

32. Duluth CA, *Bulletin*, Feb. 1922, copy in Davidson Co. Records; *Duluth Labor World*, Aug. 20, 1921, p. 6.

33. *Duluth Labor World*, May 28, 1921, p. 1, July 30, 1921, p. 1, July or Aug. 1921.

34. Duluth CA, *Bulletin*, Feb. 1922; *Minneapolis Labor Review*, Jan. 13, 1922.

35. CA, *Special Bulletin* (Duluth), April 1, 1921, Robert A. Olson Papers; *Duluth Herald*, April 28, 1921, p. 2.

36. Duluth CA, *Bulletin*, Feb. 1922; *Duluth Herald*, May 3, 1921, p. 3; *Duluth Labor World*, Aug. 20, 1921, p. 6. During 1921, the *Duluth Labor World* carried frequent articles with very similar statements relating to the open shop by the Builders' Exchange, Employing Printers, and the CA.

37. *Duluth Labor World*, May 15, 1920, p. 4; W. H. Everett to All Building Trades Councils and Labor Assemblies, March 18, 1921, Duluth Federated Trades and Labor Assembly Papers, MHS.

38. Griggs to E. J. Phelps, Sept. 24, 1903; E. H. Davidson to Elliot H. Goodwin, Sept. 6, 1918; Bigelow to the Board of Directors, Feb. 24, 1916; all in Davidson Co. Records; CA, *Annual Meetings*, 1915–19, CA Papers; Paul N. Myers to Charles W. Ames, Oct. 11, 1919, Dec. 16, 1919, both Charles W. Ames Papers. In 1903, St. Paul businessmen formed the St. Paul Citizens' Association of St. Paul based on principles similar to the Citizens Alliance. Frank T. Heffelfinger of the CA helped the new group establish itself. Alexander M. Robertson of Minneapolis reported on his investigation of the Business Men's Association of Omaha. See St. Paul Citizen's Assn. Papers.

39. St. Paul Citizens Alliance, *The American Plan*, Feb. 1, 1922, Davidson Co. Records; St. Paul CA, *Five Years*, in CA Papers.

40. St. Paul CA, *Five Years*; St. Paul CA, *Bulletin*, Jan. 1924, both in CA Papers; *The Ameri-

can Plan, Feb. 1, 1922, Davidson Co. Records; Charles Patterson to C. W. Ames, March 19, 1920, Ames Papers. Patterson, in addition to his role in fighting the Nonpartisan League (NPL), was on the Jobbing, Manufacturing, and Trade Extension Committee of the St. Paul Association; St. Paul Association, *Official Bulletin*, Feb. 21, 1919, Hiram D. Frankel Papers.

41. *Minnesota Union Advocate*, March 26, 1920, p. 4; William H. MacMahon, "The Open Shop Workman," June 1930, W. H. MacMahon Papers. MacMahon was the employment manager of the CA of Ramsey and Dakota Counties in 1923 and by 1929 had become general manager; E. H. Davidson to Dear Sir, Oct. 20, 1923, LeSueur Papers; Membership Committee to Dear Sir, June 7, 1929, Great Northern Railway Co. Records, MHS.

42. Davidson to My Dear Sir, June 25, 1920, Ames Papers.

43. St. Paul CA, *Five Years*; Minnesota Employers' Association (MEA), *Minutes*, Jan. 11, 1909.

44. MEA, *Minutes*, Jan. 11, 1909; Frank P. Donovan, Jr., and Cushing F. Wright, *The First Through A Century* (St. Paul: Webb Publishing Co., 1954), 125, 131; Roy W. Clark to George R. Martin, Feb. 17, 1926, Great Northern Railway Records; *Minnesota Union Advocate*, Jan. 20, 1921, p. 1, and Nov. 17, 1921, p. 1; *Minneapolis Labor Review*, April 27, 1923, p. 1; Davidson to Dear Sir, Oct. 20, 1923, LeSueur Papers.

45. CA of Ramsey and Dakota Counties, *Five Years*; Minnesota Building Employers' Association, pamphlet, *Minnesota Building Trades School*, n.d., CA Papers; CA, *Bulletin*, Jan. 1924.

46. CA of Ramsey and Dakota Counties, *Special Weekly Bulletin No. 6*, June 18, 1920; *Special Weekly Bulletin No. 24*, Oct. 22, 1920, Ames Papers; CA, "The Employment Department," n.d.; "The Open Shop Workman," June 1930, both in MacMahon Papers.

47. "The Employment Department," n.d.; "The Open Shop Workman," both in MacMahon Papers.

48. "The Open Shop Workman"; "The Employment Department," n.d., both in MacMahon Papers.

49. *The American Plan*, Dec. 1, 1920, p. 4.

50. *St. Paul Pioneer Press*, May 11, 1921, p. 7; *The American Plan*, Dec. 1, 1920, p. 4.

51. *The American Plan*, Dec. 1, 1920, p. 4; CA of Ramsey and Dakota Counties, *Special Weekly Bulletin No. 1*, May 14, 1920, Ames Papers.

52. Duluth CA, *Bulletin*, Feb. 1922, Davidson Co. Records; CA of Ramsey and Dakota Counties, "The Printing Industry," MacMahon Papers; CA, *Bulletin*, Jan. 1924; *Minnesota Union Advocate*, Sept. 1, 1921, p. 12; *Duluth Labor World*, Feb. 12, 1921, p. 1; Feb. 19, 1921, p. 1; *The American Plan*, Feb. 1, 1922; Duluth CA, *Bulletin*, Feb. 1922, Davidson Co. Records.

53. CA, "Review of CA Activities since Jan. 1, 1921, Walker Papers; CA membership list, compiled by author, in possession of author; Electrical Worker's Union 292, "A Statement to the Contractors and General Public," Feb. 1921, Robley D. Cramer and Family Papers.

54. CA, *Bulletin*, Jan. 1924; CA, "Review of CA Activities," Walker Papers; CA, "A Few Outstanding Buildings erected under open-shop conditions previous to 1927," List, CA Papers. The following buildings are examples of those built by CA member firms during this period: University of Minnesota Stadium, James Leck Co.; Nicollet Hotel, C. F. Haglin and Sons Co.; Walker Art Center, L. S. Donaldson Co., Pike and Cook Co.; Ritz Hotel, H. N. Leighton Co.; Lincoln Bank Building, J. L. Robinson Co.

55. Duluth CA, *Special Bulletin*, April 1, 1921, Robert A. Olson Papers; *Duluth Labor World*, Feb. 26, 1921, p. 1, March 19, 1921, p. 6, April 16, 1921, p. 1, April 30, 1921, p. 1.

56. L. C. Harris to Gentlemen, Jan. 15, 1923, Robert A. Olson Papers; *Duluth Labor World*, April 30, 1921, p. 1, May 28, 1921, p. 1; Duluth CA, *Bulletin*, Feb. 1922, Davidson Co. Records; CA, *Special Weekly Bulletin No. 118*, April 1, 1921, Walker Papers; *Duluth Herald*, May 2, 1921, p. 5; Federated Trades Assembly to Duluth Business and Professional Men, Sept. 30, 1924, Duluth Federated Trades and Labor Assembly Papers.

57. CA of Ramsey and Dakota Counties, "St. Paul stands at the threshold of better days," unpublished manuscript, n.d., MacMahon Papers; *Minnesota Union Advocate*, Sept. 1, 1921, p. 12.

58. *Minnesota Union Advocate*, March 3, 1921, p. 1, Sept. 1, 1921, p. 12; CA of Ramsey

and Dakota Counties, "St. Paul stands . . . ," MacMahon Papers; *St. Paul Pioneer Press*, May 9, 1921, p. 14, May 13, 1921, p. 5, May 18, 1921, p. 2.

59. CA of Ramsey and Dakota Counties, *The American Plan*, Feb. 1, 1922; "The printing industry," MacMahon Papers; CA, *Special Weekly Bulletin No. 120*, Walker Papers.

60. "Indorse American Plan League," *The Iron Trade Review*, Nov. 11, 1920, pp. 1339, 1342, copy in CA Papers.

61. "Indorse American Plan League"; "A Stand on Labor Principles," *The Nation's Business*, Sept. 1920, pp. 16–17; Allen M. Wakstein, "Origins of the Open Shop Movement, 1919–1920," *The Journal of American History* 51 (Dec. 1964): 473.

62. NAM, *National Convention, 1921*, pp. 33–35, 124–26; Wakstein, "The Origins of the Open Shop," 471.

63. Bonnett, *Employers' Association in United States*, 266; Perlman and Taft, *History of Labor in the United States*, 4: 497; Industrial Commission of Minnesota (ICM), *First Biennial Report*, 1921–22, p. 103; ICM, "Strike of the Printing Crafts," 101–2; CA, "Review of CA Activities," Walker Papers; Minneapolis Typothetae, *Minutes of the Joint Industrial Relations Committee*, Jan. 7, 1921; *Minutes of January Typothetae Meeting*, Jan. 19, 1921; Minneapolis Typothetae to Gentlemen, Jan. 20, 1921, all Typothetae items in Minneapolis Typothetae Papers (hereafter referred to as MT), MHS.

64. H. S. Hodges to Gentlemen, March 16, 1921; Hodges to Minneapolis Typothetae Union 42, March 29, 1921; MT, *Minutes of Special Meeting of Board*, March 27, 1921; *Minutes of Board Meeting*, April 4, 1921, all in MT Papers; ICM, *First Biennial Report*, 102.

65. MT, *Minutes of Trade Relations Joint Committee Meeting*, April 5, 1921; *Minutes of Board Meeting*, March 28, 1921, May 17, 1921, May 23, 1921, June 6, 1921, all in MT Papers; CA, *Special Weekly Bulletin No. 120*, April 15, 1921, Walker Papers.

66. MT, "An Excessive Demand that Vitally Effects Your Business," and "Obstructing a return to Normal Business"; MT, "The 48 Hour League of Minneapolis," *Bulletin No. 1*, n.d., all in MT Papers.

67. *Minneapolis Journal*, June 1, 1921, p. 2, June 2, 1921, p. 17; CA, *Special Weekly Bulletin*

No. *127*, June 3, 1921, Walker Papers; MT, *Minutes of 48-Hour League Meeting*, June 1, 1921, MT Papers; CA, *Special Weekly Bulletin No. 127*, June 3, 1921, Walker Papers.

68. CA, *Special Weekly Bulletin No. 127*, June 3, 1921, Walker Papers; MT, *Minutes of Board Meeting*, June 6, 1921, MT Papers; *Minneapolis Labor Review*, June 10, 1921, p. 1, June 17, 1921, p. 1, June 24, 1921, p. 1.

69. Perlman and Taft, *History of Labor in the United States*, 498–99; *Minneapolis Labor Review*, June 10, 1921, p. 1; CA, *Special Weekly Bulletin No. 128*, June 10, 1921, Walker Papers.

70. CA, *Special Weekly Bulletin No. 131*, July 1, 1921, No. *132*, July 8, 1921, Walker Papers; Hennepin County District Court (HCDC), Case 190, 546, *Frank Huff vs. Minneapolis Typographical Union, Local No. 42, Complaint*, June 25, 1921, MHS; *Affidavit of Frank Huff*, June 25, 1921, HCDC files, MHS.

71. CA, *Special Weekly Bulletin No. 131*, July 1, 1921; HCDC, Case 190, 546, June 25, 1921, MHS.

72. *Minneapolis Journal*, July 6, 1921, p. 2; CA, *Special Weekly Bulletin No. 133*, July 15, 1921, Walker Papers; Industrial Commission of Minnesota, *First Biennial Report*, 105–6. Minnesota House File No. 349, which created the Industrial Commission, provided only for "voluntary arbitration, mediation and conciliation of disputes between employers and employees in order to avoid strikes, lockouts, boycotts, blacklists, discriminations and legal proceedings in matters of employment."

73. MT, amendment to Bylaws of the Minneapolis Typothetae, Aug. 6, 1921, Walker Papers; MT, Hodges's letter, Aug. 4, 1921, MT Papers; CA, *Special Weekly Bulletin No. 132*, July 8, 1921; CA, "Review of CA Activities," both Walker Papers.

74. CA, *Special Weekly Bulletin No. 136*, Aug. 5, 1921; No. *290*, July 18, 1924, Walker Papers; MT, *Minutes of Board Meeting*, July 25, 1921, MT Papers.

NOTES TO CHAPTER 12

1. Charles O. Gregory, *Labor and the Law* (New York: W. W. Norton and Co., 1979), 99–104.

2. Bonnett, *Employers' Associations in the United States*, 80, 89, 90, 309.

3. Gregory, *Labor and the Law*, 99–104.

4. Gregory, *Labor and the Law*, 159–74, Bonnett, *Employers' Associations of the United States*, 92, 308, 456–57.

5. *The Union*, June 6, 1902, p. 1; July 3, 1903, p. 1; CCA membership list (*see* Appendix G).

6. CCA membership list; Ben Chernov, "The Labor Injunction in Minnesota," *Minnesota Law Review*, 24 (May 1940): 761–63.

7. Edmund J. Phelps to W. R. Cray, July 15, 1903, Cray Papers, MHS; MSfl, *Proceedings*, 1904, pp. 45–49; Chernov, "The Labor Injunction in Minnesota," 761–69.

8. *The Union*, Jan. 26, 1906, p. 4; James D. Shearer to Hon. A. O. Eberhardt, Nov. 21, 1912; E. J. Phelps to A. O. Eberhardt, Nov. 13, 1912, both in Governor's Records, MHS. Governor Eberhardt appointed six judges to the Hennepin County District Court. Three of them, Edward F. Waite, Joseph W. Molyneaux, and Daniel Fish, would play important roles in the CA's legal battles with Minneapolis labor unions.

9. *Minneapolis Labor Review*, Oct. 22, 1920, p. 1; Aug. 1, 1924, p. 1. By 1922, Eberhardt's appointments were joined by pro-business judges Edmund A. Montgomery, Winfield W. Bardwell, and Mathias Baldwin. Along with Judge Horace D. Dickinson, appointed by Republican Gov. Samuel R. Van Sant, the court was now dominated by judges who would use the labor injunction to suppress union activities. The five most active anti-labor judges, Dickinson, Waite, Montgomery, Bardwell, and Baldwin, each averaged twenty-five years on the court.

10. Chernov, "The Labor Injunction in Minnesota," 770–74.

11. CA, "Law and Order and The Open Shop," CA Papers; Hennepin County District Court, Civil Case File #158061, John J. Campbell testimony, 2, 3, 17, 21, 22, 37, 41, 42. The *Labor Review* suggested, and it seems likely, that Campbell also consulted with the CA. When defense attorney Finney asked this question, Campbell's attorney, CA lawyer Nathan Chase objected. The judge sustained, so we do not know Campbell's answer. However, the CA bankrolled and controlled Campbell's defense from the beginning. HCDC Case #158061, Campbell Testimony, 6, 36; CA

"Law and Order and the Open Shop," CA Papers.

12. HCDC Case #158061. James E. Liedoff testimony, 86; Campbell Testimony, 15, 28, 32, 33, 35; Emmett T. Dillon testimony, 75, 78. Minneapolis Socialist Mayor Thomas Van Lear had appointed Socialist Lewis Harthill as police chief. Harthill had vowed not to use police in any labor disturbances. This might have affected the police response to the Wonderland controversy. *Minneapolis Tribune*, Jan. 26, 1918. The police asked Campbell to take his banner down, but did not ask the union to take its down. Apparently they felt the theater's banner caused more disturbances; Campbell Testimony, p. 48.

13. Minnesota Supreme Court Civil Case 22200, Opinion, 3–5; *Minneapolis Labor Review*, July 16, 1920, p. 1; HCDC Case 158061, Fannie Bronson testimony, 65; Dillon testimony, 75; Campbell Testimony, 8, 34; Liedoff Testimony, 98.

14. Campbell's prosperity in June 1917 might have been the result of an influx of CA money rather than from theater attendance. Campbell testified that he had not consulted with the CA in over a year when his lawyer at the trial, Nathan Chase, was the CA lawyer and was being paid by the CA. HCDC Case 158061, Campbell Testimony, 44; *Minneapolis Labor Review*, June 9, 1922, p. 1; CA, "Law and Order and the Open Shop," CA Papers; CA, *Bulletin*, Aug. 1920.

15. CA, *Bulletin*, Aug. 1920, April–May 1932; Holcombe, *Compendium of Minneapolis History*, 228; *The Union*, July 29, 1904, p. 4; *Minneapolis Labor Review*, July 16, 1920, p. 1; Aug. 1, 1924, p. 1.

16. Holcombe, *Compendium of Minneapolis History*, 228; CCA, *Annual Report*, 1914; *Minneapolis Labor Review*, Oct. 22, 1920, p. 1. The *Minneapolis Labor Review* for Oct. 29, 1920, argued that CA control over the courts was so complete that they knew ahead of time what the court's ruling would be.

17. Here and below, CA, *Bulletin*, March 1922.

18. CA, *Bulletin*, March 1922; *Minnesota Statute* 17c 493 s-2 4257; Gregory, *Labor and the Law*, 159–74.

19. CA, *Bulletin*, Sept. 1920; Bureau of Labor, *Report*, 1919–20, p.148; *Minneapolis Labor*

Review, Sept. 17, 1920, p. 1; Jean E. Spielman, "The Open Shop via the Injunction Route," Spielman Papers, MHS. Government-estimated living expenses for a family of four in 1919 were $2,632. Employers of electrical workers in Minneapolis were pushing for a 20 percent wage reduction on a maximum yearly income of $2,080; Electrical Workers' Union, "A Statement to the General Public," Feb. 1921, Robley D. Cramer Papers, MHS.

20. *Minneapolis Labor Review*, Aug. 13, 1920, p. 1, Aug. 20, 1920, p. 1; Sept. 17, 1920, p. 1; *Minneapolis Journal*, Aug. 14, 1920, p. 3; National Information Bureau (NIB) Report, Aug. 12, 1920, Hannon Papers, MHS.

21. CA, *Bulletin*, Sept. 1920.

22. *Minneapolis Labor Review*, Aug. 27, 1920, p. 1.

23. *Minneapolis Labor Review*, Sept. 3, 1920, p. 1, Sept. 17, 1920, p. 1.

24. *Minneapolis Labor Review*, Sept. 5, 1920, p. 1, Sept. 10, 1920, p. 1, Sept. 24, 1920, p. 1, Oct. 15, 1920, p. 1, Nov. 5, 1920, p. 1.

25. *Minneapolis Journal*, Sept. 22, 1920, p. 1, Nov. 3, 1920, p. 1, Nov. 12, 1920, p. 1, Jan. 27, 1922, p. 1, June 17, 1922, p. 3; *Minneapolis Labor Review*, Oct. 29, 1920, p. 1; *Minneapolis Daily News*, Nov. 12, 1920, clipping in CA Papers; *Minneapolis Tribune*, Oct. 12, 1921, p. 21, Nov. 12, 1920, p. 1.

26. *Minneapolis Tribune*, Oct. 12, 1921, p. 21; *Minneapolis Labor Review*, Oct. 14, 1921, p. 1.

27. *Minneapolis Labor Review*, Feb. 10, 1922, p. 1; *Minneapolis Journal*, Jan. 27, 1922, p. 1. Justices James H. Quinn, Andrew Holt, and Chief Justice Calvin L. Brown voted in the majority; Justices Oscar Hallam and Homer B. Dibbell dissented. *Minneapolis Labor Review*, Feb. 10, 1922, p. 1; *Biographical Sketches of the Justices of the Minnesota Supreme Court from Territorial Days to the Present* (St. Paul: West Publishing Co., 1976), 17.

28. Minnesota Supreme Court, Civil Case File #22200, Opinion, 7, 10, 11; *Minnesota Law Review*, 6:334; Three decisions by the anti-labor United States Supreme Court emasculated the protections enumerated in the anti-injunction provisions of the Clayton Anti-Trust Act (1914). *Truax vs. Corrigan* (1921), 257 (United States) 312, stated that denial of injunction protection was a violation of equal protection. In *American Steel Foundries vs. Tri-City Central Trades Council* (1921) 257 (United States) 184, the court defined legal picketing as that involving one man at the plant entrance. *Duplex Printing Press Co. vs. Deering* (1921) 254 (United States) 443, stated that only employees of an employer could take action against that employer, and this applied to only legal actions, which would be defined by the courts. Gregory, *Labor and the Law*, 158–74, Rayback, *History of American Labor*, 295–96.

29. Minnesota Supreme Court, Civil Case File #22200, Opinion, 13, 14; CA, *Bulletin*, March 1922.

30. HCDC Case # 210558, Affidavit of Sander Genis, April 6, 1923, *E. G. Vashro vs. Twin City Joint Board Amalgamated Clothing Workers of America, Complaint*, March 29, 1923.

31. HCDC Case # 210558, *Complaint*, March 29, 1923, Affidavit of David B. Rosenblatt, March 27, 1923; Affidavit of Emma O. Johnson, March 27, 1923. Accused union business agent Joseph Daniels denied that this assault took place; HCDC Case #210558, Affidavit of Joseph Daniels, April 4, 1923; CA "Law and Order and the Open Shop," 1927, CA Papers.

32. CA "Law and Order and the Open Shop," 1927, CA Papers.

33. HCDC Case #210558, *Order to Show Cause and Restraining Order*, March 29, 1923; *Order for Temporary Injunction*, April 13, 1923; *Findings of Fact and Conclusion of Law*, June 27, 1923; CA, *Special Weekly Bulletin, No. 223*, April 6; *No. 224*, April 13; *No. 225*, April 20, 1923, in Walker Papers.

34. CA, *Bulletin*, July 1923, Walker Papers.

35. HCDC Case #258980: Affidavit of Irving Melamed, Nov. 30, 1926; Zuckerman to Central Labor Union of Minneapolis, Nov. 23, 1926, CLU Papers, MHS.

36. HCDC Case #258980: Affidavit of Melamed; Sam Smoliak, Nov. 30, 1926, and Nathan Hoffman, Nov. 30, 1926; transcript of assault trial of Lawrence Horowitz in Minneapolis Municipal Court, copy in HCDC Case # 258980; Affidavit of L. MacAloon, Dec. 9, 1926; *Complaint*; CA, "Law and Order and The Open Shop," CA Papers.

37. HCDC Case #258980: *Complaint; Order to Show Cause; Restraining Order*, Nov. 26,

1926; CA, *Bulletin*, May–June 1927; CA, *Special Weekly Bulletin*, 429, March 18, 1927, Walker Papers.

38. HCDC Case #258980, *Findings of Fact in Permanent Injunction*, March 4, 1927.

39. *Minneapolis Labor Review*, Aug. 26, 1927, p. 1; HCDC Case #269804: *Notice of Motion*, Sept. 27, 1927. The CA frequently used court injunctions to halt union activities. In the preceding year, Nathan Chase had secured injunctions in strikes at the Davis Manufacturing Co. on Nov. 16, 1926 (HCDC Case #257944) and the T. W. Stevenson Manufacturing Co. on Dec. 29, 1926, (HCDC Case #258980); HCDC Case #269804: *Complaint and Order*; Fred Keightly to H. L. Kerwin, Oct. 1, 1977, National Archives R. G. (NARG) 280 File #170-4179.

40. *Minneapolis Labor Review*, Jan. 6, 1928, p. 1, Oct. 21, 1927, p. 11.

41. Barbara Stuhler, *Ten Men of Minnesota and American Foreign Policy* (St. Paul: MHS, 1973), 78–79; Chrislock, *The Progressive Era in Minnesota*, 183–88; *Minneapolis Labor Review*, March 18, 1927, p. 1; CA, *Bulletin*, June 1928.

42. *Minneapolis Labor Review*, Feb. 24, 1928; subcommittee of the Committee on the Judiciary, United States Senate, 70th Congress, 1st Session, *On Senate 1482* (Washington, D.C., 1928), 53. Emery officially represented the National Association of Manufacturers, the National Founders' Association, and the Minnesota Employers' Assn. The Citizens Alliance had close ties to all three organizations; CA, *Bulletin*, Aug.–May 1925, April–May 1929. U.S. Senate File 2497, Confidential Committee Print United States Senate, Dec. 4, 1929, copy in Shipstead Papers, MHS.

43. J. W. Schroeder to CA members, May 15, 1930, Shipstead Papers; *New York Herald Tribune*, May 5, 1930, p. 31; *Minneapolis Labor Review*, July 4, 1930, p. 4.

44. *House Journal*, 1929, p. 638; House File 994, copy in CA Papers; Secretary of MEA, *Annual Report*, Nov. 30, 1929, MEA Papers.

45. Minnesota House of Representatives, Labor Committee, *Minutes*, March 27, 1929; MEA, "Notice on Important Injunction Bill," March 21, 1929, MEA Papers; *Minneapolis Star*, April 3, 1929, p. 7; *House Journal*, April 16, 1929, p. 1236; *Senate Journal*, April 18, 1929, p. 1154, April 20, 1929, p. 1352.

46. Shipstead, *Labor*, pamphlet, Feb. 11, 1928–Feb. 19, 1946, Shipstead Papers; Gregory, *Labor and the Law*, 184–99.

47. United States House of Representatives, Report No. 821 (Washington, D.C.: United States Government Printing Office, 1932), 2.

48. Minnesota House File 1255, House Records; *Journal of the House*, March 22, 1933, pp. 1110–11; McClintock, "Minnesota Labor Disputes Act," *Minnesota Law Review* (May 1937): 619–21; Secretary, MEA, *Annual Report*, Nov. 30, 1931, *Annual Report*, Nov. 30, 1933, MEA Papers. In 1937, the MEA defeated an attempt to reinstate the federal provision requiring collective bargaining by employers. The bill passed the House but was defeated in the Senate. The inability of the Farmer-Labor Party to control the Minnesota Senate doomed much of the progressive legislation of the 1930s; Secretary of MEA, *Annual Report*, Nov. 30, 1937, MEA Papers.

49. *Minneapolis Labor Review*, April 21, 1933, p. 4; Secretary, MEA, *Annual Report*, Nov. 30, 1933; *Senate Journal*, April 17, 1933, p. 1495; House File 1255.

50. Chernov, "The Labor Injunction in Minnesota," *Minnesota Law Review*, 791–93; House File 1255.

51. Sander Genis to William W. Hughes, Nov. 6, 1933; NLRB, Robitshek-Schneider case, Docket No. 1, National Archives Records Group (NARG) 25; HCDC Case 342518, *Findings of Fact*, Oct. 9, 1933.

52. J. W. Schroeder to Our Members, July 25, 1933, R. D. Cramer and Family Papers, MHS; Genis to Hughes, Nov. 6, 1933; HCDC Case #342518, *Benjamin Bueck vs. Twin Cities Amalgamated Clothing Workers of America*, Affidavit of H. A. Snead, Sept. 12, 1933, LeSueur Papers, MHS.

53. HCDC Case #342518, Affidavit of H. A. Snead, Sept. 12, 1933; testimony of Sander Genis in *Memorandum for the Defendants, Bueck vs. Twin City Joint Board*, Sept. 1933, both in LeSueur Papers, MHS.

54. HCDC Case #342518: *Order To Show Cause and Restraining Order*, Aug. 25, 1933, *Bueck vs. Twin City Joint Board, Amalgamated Clothing Workers of America*; Senate File 1255, 1933.

55. HCDC Case #342518, *Findings of Fact and Conclusions of Law*, Oct. 9, 1933; *Notice of*

Motion, Sept. 11, 1933; *Memorandum For The Defendants*, n.d., copy in LeSueur Papers.

56. HCDC Case #342518: *Findings of Fact and Conclusions of Law*, Oct. 9, 1933; *Minneapolis Labor Review*, Sept. 29, 1933, p. 1.

57. *Minneapolis Labor Review*, Sept. 29, 1933, p. 1, Oct. 13, 1933, p. 1.

58. HCDC Case #344692: *Affidavit of Arthur P. Wilcox, Wilcox vs. Local No. 61 Upholsters International of North America, Complaint*, Nov. 13, 1933; *Order to Show Cause and Restraining Order*.

59. HCDC Case #344692: *Amended Restraining Order*, Nov. 22, 1933; *Minneapolis Labor Review*, Dec. 8, 1933, p. 1.

NOTES TO CHAPTER 13

1. Manufacturers' Club of Minneapolis, Inc., *Bulletin*, n.d.; Karow to Adjutant General, March 17, 1919; Karow to Drew, July 31, 1919; Karow to Bellows, "History of Company B," Sept. 6, 1918, all in Karow Papers, MHS; William Millikan, "Defenders of Business: The Minneapolis Civic and Commerce Association versus Labor During W.W.I.," *Minnesota History* 50 (spring 1986): 1; *Minneapolis Daily News*, Aug. 29, 1919. Civilian Auxiliary officer Edward B. Karow was instrumental in forming the Manufacturers' Club, which was controlled by members of the CA board of directors. Karow was an executive assistant of Horace Lowry, president of Twin City Rapid Transit Co. The Transit Company was defended by the Civilian Auxiliary during the 1917 streetcar strike.

2. *Minneapolis Tribune*, Oct. 21, 1914, p. 3; newspaper clipping, "Light Infantry in a Reunion," n.d., in Minnesota National Guard Papers (hereafter referred to as MNG Papers), MHS.

3. "Light Infantry in a Reunion," in MNG Papers; *Minneapolis Tribune*, July 9, 1886, p. 4; letterheads in correspondence, MNG Papers.

4. *Minneapolis Tribune*, Oct. 6, 1912, p. 18, Oct. 21, 1914, p. 9.

5. "Light Infantry in a Reunion," MNG Papers; newspaper clipping, "Company A Holds Reunion," n.d., MNG Papers. Over the winter of 1893–94, growing economic distress and mass unemployment brought formation of scattered groups of jobless men into "armies." The best known was "Coxey's Army," led by Populist Jacob S. Coxey of Massillon, Ohio. These "armies" called upon the unemployed to march upon Washington and deliver demands for relief to Congress. Although many small detachments of the "army" started out from various points throughout the country, only about 400 reached the nation's capital.

6. Adjutant General, *Annual Report*, 1892, pp. 928, 981; *Vermillion Iron Journal*, June 23, 1892, p. 1; *Duluth Evening Herald*, June 18, 1892, p. 7, June 20, 1892, p. 5.

7. *Duluth Evening Herald*, May 2, 1894, p. 1, May 3, 1894, p. 5, May 4, 1894, p. 1, May 5, 1894, p. 1; *Vermillion Iron Journal*, May 3, 1894, p. 1; Adjutant General, *Annual Report*, 1894, pp. 6–7, 86–87, 105.

8. *Minneapolis Journal*, March 5, 1918; Bellows to Company Commanders, Feb. 16, 1918, Karow Papers. On the recommendation of Rhinow, Minnesota Public Safety Commissioner McGee (also a CCA member) moved that this transfer take place. The MCPS passed the motion; MCPS, *Minutes*, Feb. 19, 1918, John Lind Papers, MHS. During the period that Minnesota was controlled by the MCPS, prominent CCA member Judge McGee was a dominating influence on Governor Burnquist and the MCPS. McGee was immediately put in charge of the Military Dept., which would oversee the organization of the Home Guard to protect the state. Current Adjutant General Fred B. Wood was shuttled into draft duties under a cloud of financial mismanagement. The MCPS then brought in Rhinow as the Governor's Military Secretary in May of 1917 to act as adjutant general. Rhinow pursued an investigation of Wood until Wood resigned (he was never convicted). Rhinow was officially appointed adjutant general on Sept. 1, 1917. He was undoubtedly McGee's choice to lead the state's militia. MCPS, "Mobilizing Minnesota," 1917, pp. 9, 55, in MCPS Papers; Hilton, "The MCPS in World War I," 4; Holbrook, *Minnesota in the War with Germany*, 1:76–78; Lind to Folwell, Dec. 12, 1924, Folwell Papers, MHS; Burnquist, *Minnesota and Its People*, 1:451

9. MCPS, Order No. 3, April 28, 1917, MCPS Papers, MHS; The Chief, Militia Bureau, to Adjutants General of All States, May 4, 1918, MNG Papers.

10. *Minneapolis Journal,* May 2, 1918, p. 1; June 28, 1918, p. 9; Bellows to Karow, May 3, 1918; Bellows to Commanders, June 21, 1918, both in Karow Papers. The Civilian Auxiliary men were required to drop their commission as special deputy sheriffs, which eliminated the flexibility of having them under the local control of Sheriff Langum when necessary; Bellows to Company Commanders, July 5, 1918, Karow Papers.

11. *Minneapolis Tribune,* Aug. 19, 1917, p. 12.

12. Report on the Motor Corps, n.d., Burnquist Papers; *Minneapolis Tribune,* Nov. 24, 1918, p. 14.

13. *Minneapolis City Directory,* 1924; *Minneapolis Tribune,* Sept. 20, 1918, p. 8, Nov. 24, 1918, p. 14; *Minneapolis Daily News,* June 21, 1918; *St. Paul Pioneer Press,* Nov. 25, 1918, pp. 1, 6; *Minneapolis Journal,* Jan. 28, 1919, p. 1.

14. *Minnesota Legislative Manual,* 1921, p. 603; Minnesota, S. F. 330, 1919, MHS; *Senate Journal,* Feb. 5, 1919, p. 251.

15. Wverzinger to Leslie Sinton, Oct. 19, 1916; Sinton to Members, 1916, CLU Papers; E. E. Adams to Pierce Butler, April 16, 1921, Adams Papers, MHS; *Minneapolis Journal,* Feb. 11, 1919, p. 10; *Minneapolis Tribune,* Feb. 12, 1919, p. 6; *Senate Journal,* 1919, p. 1839.

16. *Minneapolis Journal,* March 28, 1919, p. 1; *Commercial West,* Nov. 22, 1919, p. 7.

17. *Minneapolis Tribune,* June 14, 1919, p. 20; Oct. 18, 1919, p. 1; Lt. Carroll K. Michener, "National Guard," *Northwest Warriors Magazine,* Nov. 1919, p. 66, Karow Papers; Officers' List, 1919, Karow Papers.

18. Leach, Bellows, and Karow, "Legislative Suggestions," Dec. 29, 1919, Karow Papers.

19. E. M. McMahon to Dear Sirs, June 30, 1919; St. Paul Association, *Official Bulletin,* Sept. 13, 1919, both in Hiram D. Frankel Papers, MHS.

20. *Commercial West,* March 19, 1921, p. 8, Dec. 18, 1920, p. 8; *Monticello Times,* Feb. 9, 1922, p. 1; bill for a Department of State Police, 1921, Preus Papers.

21. Bill for a Department of State Police, 1921, Preus Papers; S. F. 703, 1921; *Commercial West,* March 19, 1921, p. 8, March 26, 1921, p. 7; *Senate Journal,* 1921, p. 765.

22. Minnesota, S. F. 703, 1921; *Minneapolis Labor Review,* April 8, 1921, p. 8; *Minnesota House Journal,* 1921, p. 1189.

23. *Minneapolis Journal,* Dec. 7, 1921, p. 1, Dec. 8, 1921, p. 1; *Minnesota Statutes,* 1921, Chapter 12, Sec. 2404, 2407; George M. Lawson to Leslie Sinton, Jan. 7, 1922, CLU Papers; *Labor World,* Dec. 10, 1921, p. 1; *Minnesota Union Advocate,* Dec. 15, 1921, p. 1; *Commercial West,* Dec. 10, 1921, p. 9; American Civil Liberties Union (ACLU) to Governor Preus, Jan. 12, 1922, Governors' Records.

24. *Minnesota Daily Star,* Sept. 13, 1922, p. 1; CA, *Bulletin,* April–May 1924; CA, *Special Weekly Bulletin, No. 263,* Jan. 11, 1924, Walker Papers.

25. George W. Lawson to All Central, Jan. 23, 1922, CLU Papers; *Minneapolis Labor Review,* March 14, 1924, p. 1; *Minnesota Daily,* March 8, 1924, pp. 1, 3.

26. Minnesota Crime Commission, Report, Jan. 1923, pp. 5, 6, 17, Governors' Records; *Commercial West,* Dec. 9, 1922, p. 8, Jan. 6, 1923, p. 7; *House Journal,* 1923; *Senate Journal,* 1923. No state police bill was introduced in 1923. Senator Putnam, who was also vice president of the Minnesota Sound Government Association (MSGA), introduced S. F. 987, which would have created a Bureau of Crime Prevention and Identification but no action was taken; *Senate Journal,* 1923, p. 600.

27. E. G. Hall, *Speech,* June 21, 1922 (St. Paul, 1922), 7, 10.

28. *Commercial West,* April 11, 1925, p. 8, Oct. 17, 1925, p. 8; MSfl, *Minutes,* Feb. 11, 1925, p. 3, CLU Papers; *Senate Journal,* 1925, p. 914. Sec. 33 of Senate Files 776 containing provisions for a highway patrol was defeated 29 to 28 on April 3, 1925.

29. *Commercial West,* June 6, 1925, p. 7, Jan. 2, 1926, p. 8.

30. Minnesota S. F. 269; H. F. 315, 1927; *Minneapolis Daily Star,* Jan. 22, 1927, p. 10; *Minneapolis Tribune,* Feb. 10, 1927, p. 1.

31. Gov. Christianson statement creating the 1926 Crime Commission; W. T. Coe to Gov. Christianson, Feb. 1, 1926, both in Governors' Records; *Minneapolis Journal,* Feb. 21, 1927, p. 1; Minnesota Crime Commission, Fourth Public Statement, 1926, p. 1, Crime Commission Records, MHS.

32. *House Journal*, 1927, p. 1036; *Senate Journal*, 1927, p. 938; H. F. 1158, 1927; *Minneapolis Tribune*, Dec. 19, 1930, p. 1.

33. Hennepin County Grand Jury, "Bombings" Report, April 1927, CA Papers; *Minneapolis Journal*, May 19, 1926, p. 21; CA, *Special Weekly Bulletin*, Oct. 9, 1925, May 21, 1926, CA Papers.

34. CA, *Special Weekly Bulletin*, Oct. 9, 1925; *Minneapolis Labor Review*, Dec. 23, 1921, p. 1, March 12, 1926, p. 1; list of Grand Jurors drawn Dec. 4, 1926; Grand Jury Lists, 1926, 1928; CA, Hennepin County Grand Jury, "Bombings" Report, April 1927, CA Papers; *Minnesota Daily Star*, April 7, 1922; *Minneapolis Labor Review*. The mystery of these bombings was never solved. The CA claimed that its Secret Service had discovered that the eighteen sticks of dynamite taken from Richmond Labor Hall in 1921 were part of an undertaking in which the entire executive board of the Minneapolis Trades and Labor Assembly took part (Report on Bombings, Nov. 22, 1921, CA Papers). The *Labor Review* referred frequently to a controversy in 1923 when Hennepin County Attorney Floyd B. Olson denounced the CA and O. P. Briggs for hiring the Gleason Detective Agency to investigate the 1922 bombings. Gleason, with Briggs's full knowledge and financial support, hired a "dopefiend" named Meyers to persuade a drunken ex-union officer named Mahady to purchase dynamite. Gleason then had Meyers and Mahady arrested. Briggs denied the frame-up attempt charges. Gleason's detective license was revoked by the state on Dec. 16, 1924; statement of Floyd B. Olson, Jan. 8, 1927, R. D. Cramer Family Papers, MHS; *Minneapolis Journal*, Jan. 9, 1923, p. 6; Governors' Detective License Records, Governors' Records.

35. *Minneapolis Journal*, March 4, 1927, p. 1; CA, *Special Weekly Bulletin No. 170*, March 3, 1922, CA, *Bulletin*, May–June 1927, both in Walker Papers; CA, Hennepin County Grand Jury, "Bombings" Report, April 1927. It is unlikely that the CA with its many intelligence sources failed to realize until 1927 that the Minneapolis Police were affiliated with the Minneapolis Central Labor Union. This affiliation began in 1917, and Mayor Leach was

aware of it in 1921. He undoubtedly would have notified his supporters, the CA. The role of the Minneapolis Police in opposing all state police bills and Mayor Leach's gradual shift of allegiance toward labor are a more likely reason for this 1927 attack on the police union.

36. Fred Keightly to H. L. Kerwin, Sept. 26, 1927, File 170-4158, NARG; CA, *Bulletin*, Nov. 1927; *Minneapolis Labor Review*, Oct. 14, 1927, p. 1; excerpt from Grand Jury Report, Nov. 7, 1927, CA Papers; *Minneapolis Journal*, Nov. 14, 1927, p. 11. A union member was acquitted in one gas attack. Labor implicated the CA in the New Logan bombing, which took place when a settlement of the strike was imminent. Mayor Leach and the City Council offered to mediate the controversy, but a solution satisfactory to both sides was reached on Oct. 26, 1927. The *Labor Review* reported that the CA had offered its services to the theater owners and had been turned down; *Minneapolis Labor Review*, Nov. 11, 1927, p. 1, Oct. 28, 1927, p. 1, Oct. 14, 1927, p. 1.

37. *Minneapolis Journal*, Nov. 8, 1927, p. 18; *Commercial West*, Nov. 24, 1927, p. 6; Briggs to Gov. Christianson, Nov. 9, 1927, Governors' Records; Leach to Frank Morrison, Jan. 3, 1928, CLU Papers; *Minneapolis Labor Review*, Nov. 18, 1927, p. 1.

38. *Minneapolis Labor Review*, Nov. 11, 1927, p. 1; *Minneapolis Journal*, Nov. 14, 1927, p. 1, Dec. 9, 1927, p. 1; *Minneapolis Daily Star*, Nov. 26, 1927, p. 1.

39. Unidentified newspaper clipping, n.d., CA Papers; *Minneapolis Labor Review*, Dec. 23, 1927, p. 1; CA, *Bulletin*, Dec. 1927.

40. *House Journal*, 1929, pp. 978, 1519; H. F. 447, 1929.

41. *Commercial West*, Aug. 17, 1929, p. 6; *Princeton Union*, Oct. 22, 1931, p. 1; *Minneapolis Journal*, April 6, 1931, p. 15.

42. *Minneapolis Daily Star*, Aug. 9, 1929, p. 1; editorial clippings from *St. Cloud Journal-Press*, *Brainerd Dispatch*, *Duluth Herald*, *Hastings Gazette*, *Elk River Star News*, and others in Earle Brown Papers, MHS; *Minneapolis Journal*, Aug. 17, 1929, p. 4.

43. Christianson to Edward E. Sheagreen, Aug. 23, 1930, Governors' Records; *Minneapolis Tribune*, Dec. 19, 1930, p. 1; *Minneapolis Tri-*

bune, Dec. 19, 1930, p. 1; *St. Paul Pioneer Press*, Dec. 19, 1930, p. 1; *Minnesota Statutes*, 1930, Chapter 13, Sec. 2554, sub. 18 (a), Chap 93A, Sec. 9950-6 and 7.

44. John L. Shover, *Cornbelt Rebellion: The Farmers' Holiday Association* (Urbana: University of Illinois Press, 1965), 67, 70.

45. *Minneapolis Journal*, Oct. 7, 1932, p. 1, Oct. 12, 1932, p. 1, Oct. 16, 1932, p. 1, Oct. 19, 1932, p. 1; also *Minneapolis Journal*, Oct. 7–20, 1932, usually p. 1; *Anoka Union*, Oct. 1, 1932, p. 1.

46. *Minneapolis Journal*, Oct. 20, 1932, p. 1; *Minnesota Statutes*, 1932, 626–33l.

47. *Minneapolis Journal*, Oct. 21, 1932, p. 1, Oct. 22, 1932, p. 1.

48. *Minneapolis Labor Review*, April 23, 1937, p. 1. A Special Emergency Citizens' Committee composed of representatives of the CCA, the CA, the Minnesota Law and Order League, and the Council of Civic Clubs was formed. The committee's first priority was to "take a strong stand with reference to 544 and its efforts to unionize the city. This must be done immediately"; Special Emergency Citizens' Committee, Plans, n.d., CA Papers.

49. *Minneapolis Labor Review*, April 23, 1937, p. 1, April 30, 1937, p. 1, May 14, 1937, p. 1.

50. Findings and Opinion of Court of Inquiry, March 9, 1938, Governors' Records.

51. *Minneapolis Labor Review*, Feb. 18, 1938, p. 1, Feb. 25, 1938, p. 1; *The Union*, July 29, 1904, p. 4; *Northwest Organizer*, Feb. 10, 1938, p. 1, Feb. 17, 1938, p. 1; Benson to Ellard A. Walsh, Feb. 15, 1938, Elmer A. Benson Papers, MHS. The CA was renamed Associated Industries in 1936. MacAloon had been a field agent since 1926.

52. Affidavit of Benson, Loyalty and Security Investigation File, Kenneth Haycraft, U.S. Army, in possession of author; Haycraft to Gov. Benson, Feb. 19, 1938; Findings and Opinion of Court of Inquiry, March 9, 1938; statement of National Guardsman Robert Peterson, Feb. 18, 1938; newspaper clipping, n.d., "Two Guard Officers to be Court Martialed"; newspaper clipping, n.d., "Guard Inquiry Discloses Man Hired for Plant Duty"; Memo on Northwestern Casket Co. strike, n.d.; newspaper clipping, "Guard List Kept Secret by Officers," n.d.; Haycraft to Governor, Feb.

19, 1938, all but Benson affidavit in Governors' Records; *St. Paul Pioneer Press*, Feb. 24, 1938.

53. Findings and Opinion of Court of Inquiry, March 9, 1938; newspaper clipping, "Guard List Kept Secret by Officers," n.d.; Haycraft to Governor, Feb. 19, 1938; Adjutant General Walsh to Gov. Benson, March 14, 1938, all in Governors' Records; *Minneapolis Labor Review*, March 4, 1938, p. 1; J. R. Clark to Furniture Workers Union Local 1859, Feb. 11, 1938, MacAloon Papers, MHS.

54. Interviews of Frank E. McNally and Jack Schroeder by Charles Walker, n.d.; interview of Schroeder by Charles Walker, April 1939, Charles Walker Papers, MHS; memo for Record, John G. Adams interview of Harold E. Stassen, March 10, 1954, copy in Loyalty and Security Investigation of Kenneth Haycraft, U.S. Army.

NOTE TO CHAPTER 14

1. American Protective League (APL), Operative 71, *Summary and Report of War Service*, APL Minneapolis Division; APL, *Operatives Booklet*, n.d., copy in War Records Commission (WRC) Papers, MHS.

2. APL, *Operatives Booklet*.

3. APL, Operative 71, *Summary and Report of War Service*.

4. Mayor J. E. Meyers to My Dear Mr. . . . , Jan. 17, 1919; Committee of Thirteen, Meeting Minutes, Jan. 22, 1919, Committee of Thirteen, Program, n.d.; H. G. Irving to Gilman, Jan. 29, 1919, all in Gilman Papers, MHS; List of Minnesota APL directors, in Adjutant General's Papers, MHS.

5. *Minnesota Daily Star*, March 15, 1923, p. 1; Committee of Thirteen, Annual Report, Aug. 15, 1921, Gilman Papers.

6. Committee of Thirteen, *Annual Report*, Aug. 15, 1921, Gilman Papers; Committee of Thirteen, Board of Directors' list; Davis to James S. Cady, APL member, Feb. 18, 1919; E. C. Hilliweg to Judge Charles F. Amidon, Jan. 23, 1919; Davis to Gardner, May 17, 1919; Gardner to Davis, May 20, 1919; Davis to all A-P-L Operatives, Sept. 6, 1919, all in WRC Papers; *Minnesota Daily Star*, March 15, 1923, p. 1; *Minneapolis Daily News*, March 9, 1923, p. 1.

7. Minneapolis Clearing House, *Minutes*, Feb. 4, 1925, Northwest Bancorporation (NW

Banco) Papers, MHS; newspaper clipping, Oct. 13, 1922, CA Papers; T. E. Campbell to Davis, Sept. 4, 1919, WRC Papers; *Minnesota Daily Star* March 7, 1923, p. 1, March 15, 1923, p. 1.

8. *Minneapolis Journal*, May 14, 1920, p. 1; Committee of Thirteen, *Annual Report*, Aug. 15, 1921, Gilman Papers; *Minneapolis Labor Review*, May 21, 1920, p. 2.

9. Committee of Thirteen, *Annual Report*, Aug. 15, 1921.

10. Committee of Thirteen, *Annual Report*, Aug. 15, 1921; Law Enforcement Association (LEA) of Hennepin County, *Manager's Quarterly Report*, June 8, 1922, Gilman Papers; Davis to Gardner, May 17, 1919; Gardner to Davis, May 20, 1919, both in WCR Papers.

11. Newspaper clipping, Oct. 13, 1922, CA Papers; Davis to Gilman, Sept. 23, 1921; Gardner to Gilman, Sept. 23, 1921; Gilman to Davis, Jan. 25, 1922, all in Gilman Papers.

12. George E. Leach, manuscript, 59, Leach Papers, MHS; *Minnesota Daily Star*, March 9, 1923, p. 2. In the 1927 election, Leach was backed by organized labor against CA candidate Alderman O. J. Turner. *Minneapolis Daily News*, March 6, 1923, p. 1, March 9, 1923; *Minneapolis Tribune*, March 9, 1923, p. 13.

13. Marshall Service to A. C. Loring, July 23, 1920; Marshall Service to John Crosby, July 23, 1920; Marshall Service, Standard Contract, July 15, 1920; A. J. Esplin to Marshall Service, Aug. 4, 1920; Esplin to Dear Bill, Aug. 14, 1920, and Aug. 15, 1920; Esplin to Mr. Marshall, Aug. 24, 1920; Marshall Service to Esplin, Aug. 7, 1920, Aug. 11, 1920; Marshall Service Investigator No. 10, Reports, Aug. 24, 1920; Kansas City Investigator No. 14, Reports, Aug. 18, 1920, Aug. 21, 1920; all in Spielman Papers.

14. List of Subscribers to Northern Information Bureau (NIB), n.d.; L. W. Boyce to Edward J. Fisher, Nov. 28, 1921, both in NIB Papers.

15. Boyce to J. A. Reid, May 18, 1921; John G. McHugh to Boyce, Nov. 12, 1925; Boyce to Edward J. Fisher, Nov. 28, 1921; List of Subscribers to NIB; NIB to Frank E. Brunskill, March 9, 1926; Boyce to J. S. Bangs, Dec. 23, 1919, all in NIB Papers.

16. A large file of reports from inside the Butcher Workers' Union is in the NIB Papers. Boyce to J. S. Edwards, Aug. 12, 1919; NIB, Re-

ports, Nov. 11, 1919, Aug. 24, 1920, and Sept. 14, 1920, all in NIB Papers.

17. Boyce to Edwards, Aug. 12, 1919, NIB Papers; NIB, Report, Aug. 30, 1920, in John Hannon Detective Agency Papers, MHS.

18. CA, *Bulletin*, Sept. 1919, March 1929; CA, "The CA Free Employment Bureau," April 1, 1932, CA Papers; Boyce to J. F. Gould, Jan. 27, 1920, NIB Papers.

19. Boyce to Gould, Jan. 27, 1920, and Jan. 28, 1920, both in NIB Papers; CA, *The Citizens Alliance of Minneapolis*, pamphlet, n.d., CA Papers.

20. U.S. Senate Special Investigating Committee, Testimony, 1923, pp. 158, 234; *Minneapolis Journal*, July 12, 1922, p. 1, July 1, 1922, p. 1; series of agent reports to Adjutant General, July 13, 1922, Governors' Records; Robert G. Watts to Adjutant General, July 13, 1922. National Guard intelligence agent Charles E. Depew was a CCA member. Agent James F. Gould served as secretary of the Republican State Central Committee while he was a full-time National Guard intelligence agent; Depew to Adjutant General, July 13, 1922, Governors' Records; Senate Special Investigating Committee, Testimony, 1923, pp. 151, 154, 157–59.

21. W. D. Long to Dear Sir, Oct. 16, 1922, CA Papers; Director of Military Intelligence (MI) to Capt. Fitzhugh Burns, Dec. 18, 1918; Burns to Director of MI, Nov. 22, 1918; Reports of T. E. Campbell to USMI, June 29, 1917, Aug. 1, 1917, Aug. 2, 1917, Oct. 17, 1917; USMI, Report on Radical Activities, Nov. 12, 1925, all in USMI files; Boyce to Gould, Jan. 27, 1920, NIB Papers; MEA, *Annual Report of General Manager*, 1924, MEA Papers.

22. U.S. Army Recruiting Officer to Director of MI, Dec. 14, 1920, USMI files; Boyce to Frank C. Cross, Feb. 25, 1926, NIB Papers.

23. CA, *Special Weekly Bulletin*, Jan. 4, 1924, Jan. 2, 1925, in T. B. Walker Papers; CA, *Law and Order and The Open Shop*, pamphlet, Feb. 1927, CA Papers; Boyce to Cross, Feb. 25, 1926, NIB Papers.

24. U.S. Army Recruiting Officer to Director of MI, Dec. 14, 1920; NIB, Report on IWW and other Radical Organizations, Feb. 4, 1924; NIB, Report on IWW, Communist Party, and Other Radical Organizations, April 28, 1924; NIB, Report on IWW College at Duluth, Minnesota, Dec. 9, 1924, all in NIB Papers.

25. NIB, Report on IWW College at Duluth, Minn., Dec. 9, 1924; NIB, Report on IWW and Other Radical Organizations, Feb. 4, 1924; NIB, Report on Communist Party Activities, Dec. 29, 1924; NIB, Report on Radical Organizations, July 13, 1925, all in NIB Papers.

26. Here and below, USMI, Report on Radical Activities, Nov. 12, 1925, USMI files.

27. Millard L. Gieske, *Minnesota Farmer-Laborism: The Third Party Alternative* (Minneapolis: University of Minnesota Press, 1979), 65–95; Report of the Farmer-Labor Federation Convention, March 12–13, 1924; Farmer-Labor Party of Minnesota, Declaration of Principles and Platform, 1924, both in William Mahoney Papers, MHS.

28. NIB, Report on IWW, Communist Party and other Radical Organizations, April 28, 1924; NIB to Sveinbjorn Johnson, Feb. 24, 1926; NIB to Frank C. Cross, Feb. 25, 1926, all in NIB Papers; Gieske, *Minnesota Farmer-Laborism*, 92. See Gieske, 65–95, for a less-inflammatory description of Communist participation in the early Farmer-Labor Party.

29. Harry C. Wilbur, *Annual Report of General Manager of* MEA, Dec. 1, 1924; MEA, *Minutes*, Dec. 5, 1922, Dec. 20, 1922, Oct. 20, 1924, in MEA Papers.

30. Here and below, Wilbur, *Annual Report of General Manager of* MEA, 1924; MEA, *Minutes*, Oct. 20, 1924, both in MEA Papers.

31. Walter Wold and Co. to CA, Oct. 30, 1929, Audit of CA, CA Papers; *Minneapolis Labor Review* May 25, 1923, p. 1. The Hennepin County LEA continued to receive funding from CA banks until 1929; Northwestern Banco Papers.

32. Wold to CA, Oct. 30, 1929, Audit, CA Papers. For one example of MacAloon's service, see Lois Quam and Peter J. Rachleff, "Keeping Minneapolis an Open Shop Town: The CA in the 1930s," *Minnesota History* 50 (fall 1986): 105–17. For an example of MacAloon's role as labor adversary, see the J. R. Clark Co. 1938 file in the MacAloon Papers, MHS.

33. CA, Special Service Reports, Jan. 24, 1934, Nov. 5, 1934, Feb. 25, 1935, March 4, 1935, all in CA Papers.

34. CA, Special Service Reports, Jan. 24, 1934, Nov. 5, 1934, CA Papers. The CA papers contain a large collection of clipping files on Communist activities.

35. W. G. Watson (legal advisor to Gov. Olson) and Abe Harris (editor of the Farmer-Labor newspaper), CA Activities, Aug. 1934, Floyd B. Olson Papers, MHS; American Federation of Hosiery Workers to Dear Fellow Workers, Sept. 5, 1935; CA, *Special Weekly Bulletin*, No. 659, Aug. 21, 1931; Approximate Expenditures of Minneapolis Unions during 1928; Wold Co., Audit of CA, Oct. 30, 1929, all in CA Papers.

36. Watson and Harris, CA Activities, Olson Papers.

37. Minnesota LEA to J. W. Schroeder, Nov. 18, 1932, CA Papers.

38. CA, *Basis for Organization of Minnesota Law and Order League*, pamphlet, n.d., CA Papers; Watson and Harris, CA Activities, Olson Papers; Minneapolis Clearing House, *Minutes*, May 24, 1935, July 2, 1935, July 20, 1937; "Report of the Committee Appointed to Investigate the Hennepin County Law and Order League," n.d., Allen N. Sollie Papers, MHS. A more complete discussion of the activities of the Minnesota Law and Order League is in Chapter 20.

39. Gov. Benson to J. O. Camden, July 26, 1937, Governors' Records, MHS; Asher Rossetter to David C. Thornhill, April 20, 1937, Elmer A. Benson Papers, MHS.

40. Roger S. Rutchick to Robert M. LaFollette, Aug. 24, 1937, Benson Papers; *New York Post*, July 31, 1937 (copy), both in Benson Papers.

41. "Reasons for Denying Renewal of Minnesota License to Burns Detective Agency," 1938, Benson Papers; "Violations of Free Speech and Rights of Labor," hearings before a Subcommittee of the Committee on Education and Labor, U.S. Senate, 75th Congress, 1st Session, Senate Resolution 266, March 8 and 9, 1937, Part 8, p. 3075. Undoubtedly to the surprise and dismay of the CA, and despite lobbying of CA firms, Gov. Stassen also rejected applications from Burns and Pinkerton's for Minnesota licenses; Gov. Stassen, Executive Order In the Matter of the Application of the William J. Burns International Detective Agency, April 4, 1939; W. F. Davidson to Gov. Stassen, Jan. 20, 1941; Bradshaw Mintener to Gov. Stassen Jan. 9, 1941, all in Gov. Stassen Papers.

42. Lloyd M. MacAloon Industrial and Labor Relations Service, "General Drivers,

Helpers and Inside Workers Union Local No. 544," July 31, 1940, USMI files; Daily Reports, 1940–41, MacAloon Papers, MHS. USMI was aware of the fact that reports from Minneapolis were exaggerated because of their observers' close association with the situation. The extreme dangers foreseen were unlikely unless a major general strike occurred; Lt. Col. W. T. Bals to Asst. Chief of Staff, G-2, War Dept., Nov. 8, 1940, USMI files.

43. Major J. M. Moore, Special Report on Communism in Minneapolis, n.d.; USMI report, "The Farmer Labor Party," n.d., both in USMI files.

44. Assistant Chief of Staff, G-2, Omaha, Nebraska, to Asst. Chief of Staff, G-2, War Department, June 27, 1939, USMI files.

NOTES TO CHAPTER 15

1. *Commercial West*, Sept. 5, 1903, p. 40, June 10, 1939, p. 82; Charles S. Popple, *Development of Two Bank Groups in the Central Northwest* (Cambridge, MA: Harvard University Press, 1944), 42–50.

2. Edward W. Decker, *Busy Years*, 76; Northwestern National Bank of Minneapolis, *The First 75 Years*, 1949, pamphlet, 16–18; R[eturn] I. Holcombe, *Compendium of History and Biography of Minneapolis and Hennepin County* (Chicago: Henry Taylor and Co., 1914), 191; Personnel file of E. W. Decker, Northwest Bancorporation (NW) Papers, MHS; CA, *Bulletin*, Nov. 1923; *The Union*, July 29, 1904, p. 4; Minneapolis Clearing House Minutes, 1904–64, in NW Papers; CA, Audit, 1936, p. 15, CA Papers.

3. Charles B. Kuhlmann, "The Influence of the Minneapolis Flour Mills Upon the Economic Development of Minnesota and the Northwest," *Minnesota History* 6 (June 1925): 149; Folwell, *A History of Minnesota*, 3:252; *Minnesota's 50th Anniversary* (1908); Kirk Jeffrey, "The Major Manufacturers," 224; and Jerome Tweton, "The Business of Agriculture," 226, both in Clifford E. Clark, Jr., ed., *Minnesota in a Century of Change: The State and its People since 1900* (St. Paul: MHS, 1989).

4. Robert Morlan, *Political Prairie Fire*, 6; Walker, *American City*, p. 19; Kuhlmann, "The Influence of the Minneapolis Flour Mills," 143, 150; *Commercial West*, Sept. 5, 1903, p. 40.

5. NW *National Bank of Minneapolis*, pamphlet, 1926; *The Northwestern Banks*, pamphlet, n.d.; *Northwestern Banks*, pamphlet, 1927; *The* NW *National Bank and the Minnesota Loan and Trust Co.*, pamphlet, 1930; NW, *The First 75 Years*; all in NW Papers; Popple, *Two Bank Groups*, 46–47, 50–51; Decker, *Busy Years*, 68, 73; Minneapolis Civic and Commerce Association (CCA), *Annual Reports*, 1912–14; *Minneapolis City Directories*, 1903–14; *The Union*, July 29, 1904.

6. Popple, *Two Bank Groups*, 52; *Commercial West*, Sept. 26, 1914; NW *National Bank of Minneapolis*, 1926, NW Papers.

7. *Northwestern Banks*, pamphlet, n.d.; NW, *The First 75 Years*, 16–17; Decker, *Busy Years*, 74, 75, 92; Holcombe, *History of Minneapolis and Hennepin County*, 191; *The* NW *National Bank and the Minnesota Loan and Trust Co.*; CA, *Bulletin*, Nov. 1923.

8. NW Banks, E. W. Decker Personnel file, NW Papers; Popple, *Two Bank Groups*, 45; Decker, *Busy Years*, 86; *Commercial West*, June 10, 1939.

9. *The Union*, July 29, 1904, p. 4; *Commercial West*, Sept. 5, 1903; Sept. 26, 1914; CCA, *Annual Reports*, 1912–14; *Minneapolis City Directories*, 1903, 1914; *The Northwestern Banks*, 1927; *The* NW *National Banks and The Minnesota Loan and Trust Co.*, both in NW Papers.

10. *Minneapolis Labor Review*, Nov. 14, 1924, p. 1; CA, Audit, 1929, p. 6, *Minneapolis Labor Review*, Nov. 14, 1924, p. 1.

11. Millikan, "Maintaining Law and Order," 219–20; CCA, "Organized Minneapolis: The Enlarged Program for 1924," 4–20, Albert J. Chesley Papers, MHS.

12. Minneapolis Retailers' Association (MRA), *Constitution and By Laws*, 1916, *Annual Report of the Secretary of the* MRA; *Annual Report of the Treasurer of the* MRA, in MRA Papers, MHS; TCVMA, *Minutes*, April 5, 1920; Alexis Caswell to Harvey B. Smith, May 18, 1920, both in TCVMA Papers, MHS; CA, *Bulletin*, 1920. Minneapolis CA members dominated the MEA membership and its board of directors. In one yearly meeting, for example, 54 out of 129 proxy votes were controlled by CA officer A. W. Strong; Williams to Bullis, Dec. 3, 1936, Harry A. Bullis Papers, MHS; membership list of MEA; Proxy list, both in MACI Papers.

13. *Minneapolis Tribune*, March 8, 1923, p. 1; Minneapolis Clearing House, *Minutes*, Jan. 15, 1924, NW Papers. The Clearing House con-

sidered banking industry's fair share of funds raised by the business community for special purposes to be 5 percent; Minneapolis Clearing House, *Minutes*, May 21, 1934, Nov. 23, 1927, NW Papers; CA, Audit, 1929, CA Papers; *Minneapolis City Directory*, 1920; L. W. Boyce to Capt. Fitzhugh Burns, Sept. 27, 1918, USMI Records; Marshall Service to Pillsbury, Sept. 12, 1921; Marshall Service to Washburn-Crosby, Sept. 12, 1921, both in Spielman Papers. Minnesota Secret Service agents, who in May and June of 1917 were Pinkerton's agents, sent initialed or number-identified reports to the MCPS. Twenty-five different agents reported through O. R. Hatfield of the Twin Cities Pinkerton's office; Minnesota Secret Service agent reports, MCPS Papers, MHS. The CA's Secret Service was probably supplemented by information from the workers of the CA Employment Office. Both operations were run by former private detective Lloyd MacAloon; Millikan, "Maintaining Law and Order," 229.

14. Minnesota, Special Committees, 1923, Senate Committee Investigating Republican State Central Committee, *Minutes*, 606; Minneapolis Clearing House, *Minutes*, July 8, 1919, April 24, 1923, NW Papers; Millikan, "Maintaining Law and Order," 223, 226, which discusses the CA's activities in the legal and political arena.

15. Two examples are: The Minneapolis Retailers' Association, which raised 78 percent of its funds through memberships, and the CCA, which raised 98 percent of its budget from dues; MRA, Bylaws, 1939, MRA Papers; CCA, *Annual Reports*, 1914–15, p. 114. CCA, *Annual Reports*, 1912–14; TCVMA, *Minutes*, April 5, 1920, TCVMA Papers; MRA, Bylaws, 1939, MRA Papers; MEA, Financial Report, n.d., MACI Papers; CA, Audit, 1929, p. 6, CA Papers; CA, Application for Membership, Cramer and Family Papers. The commissioner of Internal Revenue had allowed businesses to deduct CA membership fees from their taxes; CA, *Special Weekly Bulletin*, Feb. 8, 1924, Walker Papers, MHS; CA, Audit, 1929, pp. 6, 12, CA Papers.

16. CA, 12th Annual Meeting, May 27, 1915; CA, Special Meeting of the Board of Directors, April 3, 1919, both CA Papers. CA, Annual Meeting Minutes, 1915–17; CA, Audit, 1929, p. 10, both in CA Papers; Minneapolis Clearing House, *Minutes*, Nov. 3, 1927, NW Pa-

pers; J. W. Schroeder to T. B. Walker, Jan. 7, 1921; O. P. Briggs to Walker, Jan. 21, 1922, both in Walker Papers. Decker was also on the 1917–18 Finance Committee of the CCA, raising funds for the Minneapolis Civilian Auxiliary, a private army, that helped win the 1917 streetcar strike; CCA, *Seventh Annual Report*, 1918; Millikan, "In Defense of Business: The Minneapolis CCA Versus Labor During W.W.I.," *Minnesota History* 51 (spring 1986).

17. CCA, *Annual Reports*, 1912–14; TCVMA, *Minutes*, April 12, 1920, TCVMA Papers; CA, "Top Business Leaders Among Founders of First Organization," 1903; CA, Audit, 1929, p. 12, both in CA Papers; *The Union*, July 29, 1904, p. 4; Minneapolis Clearing House, *Minutes*, Dec. 4, 1928, Nov. 23, 1927, NW Papers.

18. *Commercial West*, June 10, 1939, pp. 30–31. The controlling Clearing House committee had three members. In 1926, for example, NW Bank, First National, and Midland National Bank and Trust each had one representative. Midland was affiliated with NW and C. B. Mills was a NW director. The Midland representative, C. B. Mills was also president. The manager of the Clearing House for the 1920s and 1930s, J. S. Pomeroy, came from First National. His predecessor from 1885 to 1916, Perry Harrison, was the commander of the Minneapolis Civilian Auxiliary during the WWI streetcar strike; Clearing House, *Minutes*, Jan. 19, 1926, and Jan. 20, 1925, both in NW Papers; *Commercial West*, June 10, 1939, p. 30; Shutter, *History of Minneapolis*, 2: 153; CA, *Bulletin*, May–June 1929; NW, *First Annual Report*, Dec. 31, 1929; Minneapolis Clearing House, *Minutes*, Jan. 19, 1926, Aug. 3, 1932, both in NW Papers.

19. Millikan, "Maintaining Law and Order," 225, 228–29; Minneapolis Clearing House, *Minutes*, July 8, 1919, Sept. 29, 1920, April 24, 1923, Jan. 15, 1924, Aug. 20, 1924, Feb. 4, 1925, Feb. 10, 1926, July 1, 1926, Feb. 3, 1928, March 7, 1929, all in NW Papers; L. W. Boyce to Capt. Fitzhugh Burns, Sept. 27, 1918, USMI Files; NW *National Bank of Minneapolis*, 1926.

20. *The Northwestern Banks*, 1927; Minnesota Commerce Department (MCD), Investigation of NW, 1933, testimony of Decker, 7, 8, in Minnesota Securities Division Papers (hereafter referred to as MCDSD) Papers, MHS; Harold

Chucker, *Banco at Fifty: A History of Northwest Bancorporation, 1929–1979* (Minneapolis: 1979), 12, NW Papers.

21. MCD, Investigation of NW, 4, 5, 7–10, in MCDSD Papers; NW, *First Annual Report*, Feb. 26, 1930, p. 3, NW Papers.

22. *Minnesota Statutes*, 1990, Sec. 48.34, 1923; *House Journal*, March 20, 1923, pp. 828, 1313; *Senate Journal*, 1923, April 4, 1923, p. 934; Gaines T. Cartinhour, *Branch, Group and Chain Banking* (New York: Macmillan Co., 1931), 203, 286. When Midland National Bank joined NW Banco in Sept. 1929, the Minnesota State Federation of Labor petitioned the state to revoke the charter of NW and dissolve NW Banco; *Minneapolis Labor Review*, Sept. 27, 1929. Decker still hoped that branch banking would eventually be legalized. Several bills to liberalize branch banking regulations were introduced in the 1933 legislature but both died without a vote. As of this writing, branch banking is still restricted in Minnesota; Decker, *Busy Years*, 82; *House Journal*, 1933, pp. 1705–6, 2309; *Commercial West*, April 1, 1933, p. 17, Jan. 28, 1933, p. 11.

23. Popple, *Two Bank Groups*, 124; Millikan, "Maintaining Law and Order," 226; *Commercial West*, Jan. 12, 1929, p. 36, July 13, 1929, p. 6.

24. *Commercial West*, Jan. 12, 1929, p. 9; Chucker, *Banco at Fifty*, 7, 19; Investigation of NW, 9, MCDSD Papers; Chucker, *Banco at Fifty*, 4. NW Banco did increase the Northwest's banking stability during the Depression. All affiliates opened immediately after the 1933 Bank Holiday and no depositor ever lost a dollar from an affiliate. However, group banks were less liberal in granting local loans than independent banks; Russell A. Stevenson, *Type Study of American Banking* (Minneapolis: University of Minnesota Press, 1934), 34; NW, *Ten Years After*, pamphlet, 1942, p. 37.

25. *Commercial West*, Jan. 12, 1929, p. 6, Nov. 30, 1929, p. 8; NW Banco, *First Annual Statement*, Feb. 26, 1930, p. 5.

26. Cartinhour, *Branch, Group and Chain Banking*, 132; NW Banco, First Annual Statement, 9.

27. W. Ralph Lamb, *Group Banking* (New Brunswick, NJ: Rutgers University Press, 1961), 88–89; Popple, *Two Bank Groups*, 330.

A 1934 study actually showed rural banks to be a source of losses rather than profits to group banks; Stevenson, *Type Study of American Banking*, 37; Chucker, *Banco at Fifty*, 8.

28. *Commercial West*, Jan. 12, 1929, p. 6, July 13, 1929, p. 6, Aug. 10, 1929, p. 35.

29. Millikan, "Maintaining Law and Order," 225. See Morlan, *Political Prairie Fire*, for the story of the NPL in Minnesota.

30. Popple, *Two Bank Groups*, 179, 200; NW Banco, *First Annual Report*, Feb. 26, 1930, pp. 3, 16. The number of institutions affiliated with NW Banco, by state, were Minnesota, 54; South Dakota, 11; North Dakota, 10; Iowa, 4; Montana, 9; Nebraska, 8; Wisconsin, 7; Washington, 3. NW Banco, *First Annual Report*, p. 3; Popple, *Two Bank Groups*, 200, 204; Chucker, *Banco at Fifty*, 12. NW Banco tried to acquire a major St. Paul bank, First National. Negotiations were nearly completed when Merchants National Bank of St. Paul interceded and arranged a merger of St. Paul's two major banks; Popple, *Two Bank Groups*, 181–82. Midland National was the third-largest bank in Minneapolis with resources of $24,580,196; C. B. Mills, Midland's president since 1919 was treasurer of the CA.

31. *Commercial West*, Nov. 30, 1929, p. 8; Popple, *Two Bank Groups*, 199, 208; *Business Week*, Sept. 10, 1930, p. 24; Interview of Clive T. Jaffray, April 1956, MHS; Stevenson, *A Type Study of American Banking*, 32, 37.

32. NW Banco, *Ten Years After*, 11, 12; Popple, *Two Bank Groups*, 186–87; MCD, Investigation of NW, 458; Investigator Report, Nov. 23, 1933, both in MCDSD Papers.

33. Independent Banker's Association (IBA), *How a "Great Financial Empire" Was Built* (Sauk Centre, 1933), 7, 13–15. Investigator Report, MCDSD Papers; *Minneapolis Journal*, July 20 through Aug. 4, 1929, all p. 1; Popple, *Two Bank Groups*, 187. In 1930, NW Banco paid $742,000 in dividends on earnings of $11,000. In 1931, NW Banco reported earnings of $5,740,000 on an actual loss of $4,461,000.

34. MCD, Investigation of NW, 4, MCDSD Papers; *Commercial West*, Dec. 22, 1928, p. 9, Feb. 2, 1929, p. 22.

35. MCD, Investigator Report, Nov. 23, 1933; MCD, Investigation of NW, 458, both in MCDSD Papers; *Commercial West*, Sept. 14,

1929, pp. 36–37; IBA, *How a "Great Financial Empire" Was Built*, 15, 16; NW Banco, *Ten Years After*, 11–12; Popple, *Two Bank Groups*, 194; NW Banco, *First Annual Report*, 7. Sixty-seven percent of NW Banco stock was held by Minnesotans, 90 percent by people living in the Northwest. The stock ownership of NW Banco reflects the rationale that NW Banco would foster independence from eastern interests. However, Chase Manhattan National Bank of New York held a three million dollar mortgage on the new NW building and land; *Minneapolis Labor Review*, May 23, 1930.

36. Ben Dubois, "Spreading 'Main Street' Philosophy," clipping, n.d., Dubois Papers, MHS; Chucker, *Banco at Fifty*, 9, 24; Popple, *Two Bank Groups*, 260–61.

37. Chucker, *Banco at Fifty*, 24; MCD, Investigation of NW, 153–54; J. Cameron Thomson to C. B. Mills, Nov. 24, 1931, Nov. 10, 1931; J. C. Thomson to Member Banks, n.d., and Sept. 28, 1932, all in MCDSD Papers; NW Banco, *The NW Banks*, 1927; NW Banco, *First Annual Report*, 10. Decker was president of NW National and NW Banco. NW Banco vice president and general manager J. C. Thomson, vice president and treasurer, Robert E. MacGregor, and secretary David R. West all came from NW National Bank of Minneapolis; NW Banco, *Ten Years After*. Eleven of twenty members of the board were affiliated with the CA. Of these, five represented the grain industry and five NW National Bank of Minneapolis

38. Popple, *Two Bank Groups*, 206; IBA, *How a "Great Financial Empire" Was Built*; *Minneapolis Labor Review*, Feb. 22, 1929, p. 1; *Minneapolis Journal*, Feb. 16, 1929, p. 2.

39. *Commercial West*, Feb. 23, 1929, pp. 11, 12; *Minneapolis Journal*, Feb. 16, 1929, p. 2; CA, Board of Directors' Lists, 1915, 1930; CA, list of early leaders; CA, Audit, 1929, p. 15, all in CA Papers; *The Union*, July 29, 1904, p. 4; *Minneapolis Labor Review*, Feb. 22, 1929, p. 1; *Minneapolis Journal*, Feb. 16, 1929, p. 2; CA Papers.

40. Minnesota State Federation of Labor (MSfl) Proceedings, Executive Council Meeting, May 12, 1929, p. 28; and Resolution 10, Aug. 20, 1929, p. 37; *Minneapolis Labor Review*, March 1, 1929, p. 1; Nov. 1, 1929, p. 1; *Commercial West*, May 10, 1930, p. 15.

41. *Minneapolis Labor Review*, March 1, 1929, p. 1, March 8, 1929 p. 2, April 5, 1929,

p. 1, April 19, 1929 p. 1, April 26, 1929 p. 1, May 3, 1929 p. 1, May 17, 1929 p. 1, Nov. 29, 1929, p. 1.

42. *Minneapolis Labor Review*, Sept. 20, 1929, p. 1, Feb. 22, 1929, p. 1; *Minneapolis Labor Review*, Jan. 31, 1930, p. 1; MSfl Proceedings, Executive Council Meeting, May 12, 1929, p. 28.

43. *Minneapolis Labor Review*, March 29, 1929, p. 1, May 10, 1929, p. 1, May 17, 1929, p. 1, Sept. 20, 1929, p. 1; CA, list of top business leaders, CA Papers.

44. *Commercial West*, May 10, 1930.

45. Jaffray Reminiscences, April 1956, pp. 59, 60, 65–67, MHS. As mentioned earlier, Pillsbury was a major financial backer of the CA. CA President Briggs was a Minneapolis Steel and Machinery executive. Longtime president of the MEA George Gillette was also president of Minneapolis Steel and Machinery. After reorganization, Minneapolis Steel and Machinery merged with Minneapolis Moline.

46. *The Foshay Tower*, pamphlet, 1929, pp. 6, 23; *Fortune 13*, April 1936, p. 193; George D. Tselos, "The Minneapolis Labor Movement in the 1930s" (Ph.D. dissertation, University of Minnesota, 1970), 34–35; *Minneapolis Labor Review*, Nov. 8, 1929, p. 1; Marcy Francis McNulty, "Wilbur Burton Foshay: The Saga of a Salesman" (masters thesis, Creighton University, 1964), 86–88, MHS; *Minneapolis Journal*, Nov. 1, 1929, p. 1.

47. *The Foshay Spotlight*, Sept. 1929, p. 43; *Foshay Tower*, 27; CCA, *Annual Reports*, 1912–14; *Minneapolis Labor Review*, Nov. 8, 1929, p. 1; "Revolt in the Northwest," *Fortune Magazine* 13.2, April 1936, pp. 112–19; p. 1; McNulty, "Wilbur Burton Foshay," 92. The Lincoln Banks were acquired by NW in 1922; Shutter, *History of Minneapolis*, 1:297. The Minneapolis Trust Co. was owned by the identical stockholders as the First National Bank of Minneapolis and First National Bank and Trust Co. of Minneapolis; see *75 Years of Service*, Dec. 12, 1939, p. 19.

48. Tselos, "The Minneapolis Labor Movement," 22, 256; Walker, *American City*, 189–91; Minnesota Industrial Commission, Fifth Biennial Report, "Report of Temporary Board of Mediation and Arbitration," 1929–30, p. 284; *Minneapolis Labor Review*, Aug. 10,

1934, p. 1; *Minneapolis Tribune*, Aug. 8, 1934, p. 1; NW *Organizer*, Aug. 11, 1934, p. 1, Sept. 14, 1939, p. 1, Nov. 16, 1939, p. 1; *Minneapolis Labor Review*, Nov. 10, 1939, p. 1, Nov. 17, 1939, p. 1. See Thomas E. Blantz, C. S. C., "Father Haas and the Minneapolis Truckers' Strike of 1934," *Minnesota History* 42 (spring 1970).

49. *Commercial West*, Sept. 18, 1920, p. 8, Feb. 19, 1921, p. 40; *The Nation*, March 2, 1921, p. 330; Millikan, "Maintaining Law and Order," 225. As an influential member of the Minneapolis Federal Reserve Bank, NW helped deny the Bank of North Dakota membership. Also, in league with flour-milling and elevator companies, it used an injunction to delay the Bank of North Dakota from selling bonds; Chucker, *Banco at Fifty*.

50. *Minneapolis Labor Review*, Nov. 8, 1929, p. 1, April 1, 1932, p. 1, April 8, 1932, p. 1, April 9, 1932, p. 2, July 1, 1932, p. 1; Harold L. Nelson, "The Political Reform Press: A Case Study," *Journalism Quarterly* 29 (summer 1952): 294–302; *Minneapolis Tribune*, April 9, 1932, p. 2.

51. George H. Mayer, *The Political Career of Floyd B. Olson* (Minneapolis: University of Minnesota Press, 1951), 26; Chucker, *Banco at Fifty*, p. 29; transcripts of Securities Division hearings, MCDSD Papers, MHS; S. Paul Skahen to U.S. District Attorney George F. Sullivan, Sept. 7, 1934, MCDSD Papers.

52. Chucker, *Banco at Fifty*, p. 30; Mayer, *Floyd B. Olson*, p. 26; Millikan, "Maintaining Law and Order," 229; Olson to Skahen, June 30, 1934, MCDSD Papers. Evidence of the CA's active interest in this particular grand jury surfaced when the Minnesota National Guard raided the CA headquarters during the 1934 Truckers' Strike; Memo on Seized Evidence, n.d., Olson Papers.

53. Chucker, *Banco at Fifty*, 30–33; Transcript of Thomson Trial, 2, MCDSD Papers; *Fortune 13*, April 1936, p. 194. Affidavits in the trial files indicate that there was an organized effort to illegally influence the jury; Robert Greenberg to Skahen, May 14, 1935 (two letters on same day), MCDSD Papers.

54. NW Banco, *Ten Years After*, 16, 17; Chucker, *Banco at Fifty*, 15, 19–20.

55. Popple, *Two Bank Groups*, 256–57, 272.

56. Popple, *Two Bank Groups*, 253–54, 272; Chucker, *Banco at Fifty*, 20.

57. NW Banco, *Ten Years After*, 28–30, 35; Popple, *Two Bank Groups*, 272. Both John Crosby and Frank T. Heffelfinger were grain executives; Crosby was director of General Mills and Heffelfinger was president of F. H. Peavey Co.; NW Banco, *First Annual Report*, 11–12. *Minneapolis Labor Review* editor R. D. Cramer appeared before the Commerce Dept. hearings and asked the state to join labor in asking the RFC not to loan money to NW Banco. The bank organization was an important member of the CA, which was preventing settlement of a bitter, eight-week upholsterers' strike. Labor representatives in the Minnesota House introduced a resolution asking the RFC to suspend assistance; MCD, Investigation of NW Banco, 95–96, MCDSD Papers; *House Journal*, Dec. 12, 1933, p. 4.

58. Minneapolis Clearing House, *Minutes*, May 21, 1934, April 19, 1935, p. 167, Aug. 5, 1936, p. 198, all in NW Papers; CA, Audit, 1936, pp. 3, 9, 15, CA Papers; E. T. Iserman to Charles L. Pillsbury, Nov. 21, 1942, Munsingwear Papers, MHS; *Associated Industries of Minneapolis* (AI), pamphlet, n.d.; *Sunday Worker*, June 6, 1937. AI's constitution still objected repeatedly to closed-shop unionism. During World War II, AI lobbied Gov. Stassen for a no-strike policy, which echoed the CA's status quo policy during World War I; J. W. Schroeder to Lester Badger, Nov. 24, 1941, Gov. Stassen Records, MHS; *Sunday Worker*, June 6, 1937.

59. *Associated Industries of Minneapolis* (AI); Minneapolis Clearing House, *Minutes*, July 2, 1935, April 20, 1938, April 20, 1939, and 1963, NW Papers (the banks were still supporting AI with $2,500 as late as 1963); Minneapolis Civic Council, "What is the Minneapolis Plan?" 1938, Elmer A. Benson Papers, MHS; Minneapolis Civic Council, Memorandum on Civic Council Campaigns, Dec. 9, 1945; Minneapolis Civic Council, Statement of Income Received and Appropriations Made, 1946 Civic Fund, March 31, 1947, all in Arnuf Ueland, Sr., Papers, MHS; McNally, "The Real Menace to Industrial Peace in Minneapolis," Feb. 8, 1935, Cramer and Family Papers; Minnesota Law and Order League, "A Statement," n.d., Bullis Papers; Summary of CA Papers Taken in National Guard Raid, Olson Papers.

60. NW Banco, *Ten Years After*, 36, 39.

61. Popple, *Two Bank Groups*, 332; Jaffray Reminiscences, 34.

NOTES TO CHAPTER 16

1. James A. Emery, *An Examination of the Proposed Twentieth Amendment to the Constitution of the U.S.* (New York: National Association of Manufacturers, pamphlet, 1924).

2. Walter I. Trattner, *Crusade for the Children: A History of the National Child Labor Committee and Child Labor Reform in America* (Chicago: Quadrangle Books, 1970), 163, 167, 168.

3. Louise M. Young, *In the Public Interest: The League of Women Voters, 1920–1970* (New York: Greenwood Press, 1989), 97; Women's Committee for the Children's Amendment, *The Children's Amendment*, pamphlet, n.d., Minnesota League of Women Voters (MLWV) Papers, MHS.

4. Marguerite M. Wells to Dear Member of Legislature, Jan. 23, 1925, MLWV Papers; Albion Guilford Taylor, *Labor Policies of the National Association of Manufacturers* (Urbana: University of Illinois, 1928), 131; NAM, *Convention Proceedings, 1924*, p. 215.

5. Taylor, *Labor Policies*, 132–33; MEA, Report of Secretary, 1925, Minute Book 2, MACI Papers, MHS; *New York Times*, Nov. 21, 1924, p. 3; Young, *In the Public Interest*, 97.

6. Emery, *An Examination of the Proposed Twentieth Amendment*; Trattner, *Crusade for the Children*, 166.

7. Trattner, *Crusade for the Children*, 173, 174; Taylor, *Labor Policies*, 131; Wells to My Dear Member, Jan. 6, 1925, MLWV Papers.

8. Trattner, *Crusade for the Children*, 175; Young, *In the Public Interest*, 97; Walter F. Dodd, ed., "Legislative Notes and Reviews," *American Political Science Review* 19 (Feb. 1925): 69–72; Emery, *An Examination of the Proposed Twentieth Amendment*.

9. Trattner, *Crusade for the Children*, 175; *American Political Science Review* (Feb. 1925): 67–72.

10. Briggs and Williams, Report to MEA, Nov. 28, 1924, MACI Papers.

11. MEA, Minutes of Board of Directors, Dec. 1924; MEA, Minutes of Annual Meeting, Dec. 2, 1924, both in MACI Papers.

12. MEA, Secretary's Annual Report, 1925, MACI Papers; *Minneapolis Journal*, Dec. 23, 1924, p. 4, copy in CA Papers; Wells to My Dear Local Chairman, Jan. 22, 1925, MLWV Papers; CA, *Bulletin*, Feb. 1925, Jan. 1925.

13. CA, *Bulletin*, Feb. 1925.

14. Clara Ueland to E. E. Adams, Oct. 1, 1924, Elmer E. Adams Papers, MHS; Wells to Member of Legislature, Jan. 23, 1925; Minnesota Joint Ratification Committee, "Why the 18 year limit is not too high," Feb. 25, 1925; Sadie Quamme to Dear Member, Feb. 13, 1925, Jan. 31, 1925, all in MLWV Papers; *Minneapolis Journal*, Dec. 31, 1924; Feb. 18, 1925, p. 1.

15. *Minneapolis Journal*, Feb. 20, 1925, p. 12, Feb. 28, 1925, p. 1; MEA, Secretary's Annual Report, 1925; *St. Paul Pioneer Press*, Feb. 27, 1925, p. 1.

16. Gertrude Zimand, *Child Labor Facts* (New York: National Child Labor Committee, 1940), copy in Gilman Papers, MHS; *Minneapolis Journal*, Feb. 20, 1925, p. 12, Feb. 27, 1925, p. 1, Feb. 28, 1925, p. 1.

17. Barbara Stuhler, *Gentle Warriors: Clara Ueland and the Minnesota Struggle for Woman Suffrage* (St. Paul: MHS Press, 1995), 200; MLWV, Board of Directors Minutes, Feb. 1925, MLWV Papers; William Phillips to Governor of Minnesota, Dec. 18, 1933, Governors' Records. Fourteen additional states ratified the amendment in 1933. Although a majority (76 percent) of the U.S. population favored ratification in 1937, only twenty-eight states ratified the amendment; Zimand, *Child Labor Facts*, 1940.

18. Here and below, Trattner, *Crusade for the Children*, 190–212.

19. Kirk Jeffrey, "The Major Manufacturers," 238; Elizabeth Faue, *Community of Suffering and Struggle* (Chapel Hill: University of North Carolina Press, 1991), 58–59, 64; Tselos, *Minneapolis Labor Movement*, 65–66.

20. Faue, *Community of Suffering and Struggle*, 104; Jeffrey, "The Major Manufacturers," 238; List of individuals paying largest tax, 1935, Benson Papers, MHS.

21. Associated Charities of Minneapolis, "A Quarter-Century of Work Among the Poor," Dec. 31, 1909; Shutter, *History of Minneapolis*, 1:191, 192, 677; Kane, *The Falls of St. Anthony*, 99, 106; Minneapolis Business Union

(MBU), Treasurer's Annual Report, Jan. 10, 1894, Walker Papers.

22. Shutter, *History of Minneapolis,* 1:191–94, 213–17; *Minneapolis Community Fund,* March 1929, report by Community Fund in Minneapolis Collection, MPL.

23. *Minneapolis Community Fund, 1929* and *1933; Minneapolis Labor Review,* Oct. 30, 1931, p. 1.

24. Philip Klein, *The Burden of Unemployment: A Study of Unemployment Relief Measures in Fifteen American Cities, 1921–22* (New York: Russell Sage Foundation, 1923), 45, 86, 140, 171–73, 180, 236.

25. Raymond L. Koch, "Politics and Relief in Minneapolis During the 1930s," *Minnesota History* 41 (winter 1968): 153–54; Tselos, *Minneapolis Labor Movement,* 147; Faue, *Community of Suffering and Struggle,* 202; Community Fund, "Let's Get This Straight," n.d.; Minneapolis Family Welfare Association, "Family Service," 1936, both in Minneapolis Collection, MPL; Koch, "Politics and Relief," 155–56.

26. Koch, "Politics and Relief," 155–60; Tselos, *Minneapolis Labor Movement,* 141, 149–62; *Minneapolis Labor Review,* June 24, 1932, p. 1; Faue, *Community of Suffering and Struggle,* 119–20.

27. Community Fund, "Let's Get This Straight"; *Minneapolis Tribune,* March 5, 1934; *Minneapolis Community Fund, 1933.*

28. *Minneapolis Journal,* Nov. 5, 1928; MIC, *A Logical Location for You,* pamphlet, Aug. 1929, pp. 2–3, Aug. 1931, p. 3, Minneapolis Collection, MPL; CCA, *Bulletin,* Jan. 8, 1924; *Minneapolis Tribune,* Oct. 11, 1928. Gov. J. A. O. Preus became the first manager of the MIC after his term as governor; *Minneapolis City Directories,* 1924–36; MIC, *Facts About Minneapolis,* 1932, pp. 27, 48.

29. A. R. Rogers, "Minneapolis Industrial Progress is Extended," *Minneapolis: Metropolis of the Northwest* (Minneapolis: CCA, 1931), 20; *Minneapolis Tribune,* Jan. 14, 1930 or 1931, clipping in Alfred C. Godward file, Minneapolis Collection, MPL.

30. J. C. Lawrence, "Garden Aid Unemployment," *Minneapolis,* August 1931, p. 26; "Emergency Gardens for Unemployed provide 20,000 jars of produce," *Minneapolis,* Nov. 1932, p. 18; "What Emergency Gardeners Think About," *Minneapolis,* 17; B. B. Sheffield

to Gov. Olson, May 15, 1931, Governors' Records.

31. "What Emergency Gardeners Think About," 17; "Emergency Gardens for Unemployed."

32. "Emergency Gardens for Unemployed"; CA, "A Practical Plan of Unemployment Relief," Aug. 31, 1931, Great Northern Railway Co. Records, MHS.

33. George Tselos, "Self-Help and Sauerkraut: The Organized Unemployed, Inc., of Minneapolis," *Minnesota History* 45 (winter 1977): 308, 318; Tselos, Organized Unemployed, Inc., Minneapolis, Minnesota, various documents collected by Tselos in MHS, hereafter referred to as Tselos Collection, MHS.

34. Tselos, "Self-Help and Sauerkraut," 309, 311; Floor Plan of Organized Unemployed, newspaper clipping, Organized Unemployed (OUI) file, Minneapolis Collection, MPL; Langland Report to State Board of Control, May 19, 1934, Tselos Collection.

35. Tselos, "Self-Help and Sauerkraut," 311; OUI report, "The Organized Unemployed, Inc.," in Tselos Collection.

36. Newspaper clipping, n.d., OUI file, Minneapolis Collection; Tselos, "Self-Help and Sauerkraut," 316; Jacob Baker to Harry L. Hopkins, Aug. 8, 1933, Tselos Collection.

37. Tselos, "Self-Help and Sauerkraut," 318; D. B. MacKenroth, George H. Rogers, and A. C. Godward to Federal Emergency Administrator and the Board of Control, Oct. 13, 1933, Tselos Collection; Minneapolis Clearing House, Special Meeting, Feb. 8, 1932, NW Banco Papers.

38. MacKenroth, et al., to Federal Emergency Relief Administrator (FERA), Oct. 13, 1933, Tselos Collection; Tselos, "Self-Help and Sauerkraut," 318.

39. Tselos, "Self-Help and Sauerkraut," 318; Mecklenburg to FERA, March 6, 1924; Langland Report to State Board of Control, May 19, 1934, both in Tselos Collection; Tselos, "Self-Help and Sauerkraut," 319–20.

40. MEA, *1933 Legislative Bulletin,* MACI Papers; John S. McGrath and James J. Delmont, *Floyd B. Olson: Minnesota's Greatest Liberal Governor* (St. Paul: McGrath and Delmont, 1937), 234.

41. MEA, *Annual Report,* Nov. 30, 1935, MACI Papers; Anthony J. Badger, *The New Deal:*

The Depression Years, 1933–1940 (New York: The Noonday Press, 1989), 229; Arthur M. Schlesinger, *The Coming of the New Deal* (Boston: Houghton Mifflin Co., 1958), 311; NMTA, "Unemployment Insurance? What You Can Do," Jan. 1933, copy in Governors' Records; MEA, *Annual Report*, Nov. 10, 1936, MACI Papers.

42. W. E. G. Watson and Abe Harris, "CA Activities as Disclosed From Evidence Gathered in National Guard Raid," Aug. 1934, Olson Papers; James A. Struthers to All Members of the Minnesota State Legislature, March 8, 1933; E. L. Anderson to Gov. Olson, Feb. 21, 1933; J. S. Clapper to Manufacturers, Feb. 16, 1933, all in Governors' Records.

43. Mayer, *The Political Career of Floyd B. Olson*, 135–36; McGrath and Delmont, *Floyd B. Olson*, 235; "CA Activities Disclosed From Evidence," Olson Papers.

44. Schroeder to Secretary of Milwaukee Employers' Council, Feb. 19, 1934; Schroeder to Secretary of the NAM, Jan. 16, 1934, both in "CA Activities Disclosed From Evidence," Olson Papers; MEA, Board of Directors Meeting, Dec. 19, 1934, MACI Papers.

45. MEA, Board of Directors' Meeting, Dec. 19, 1934; MEA, Executive Committee Minutes, Jan. 29, 1935, March 6, 1935, all in MACI Papers.

46. MEA, *Special Bulletin: Unemployment Reserves*, 1935, MACI Papers.

47. NAM, *Labor Relations Bulletin*, Aug. 1935, copy in CA papers; MEA, *Annual Report*, Nov. 30, 1935; *Annual Report*, 1936, both in MACI Papers.

48. MEA, *Special Bulletin: Minnesota Unemployment Insurance Law*, 1936, MACI Papers.

49. MEA, *Special Bulletin: Minnesota Unemployment Insurance Law*; MEA, Report of H. E. Wade, Nov. 30, 1937, both in MACI Papers.

50. Minnesota Department of Labor and Industry, *Twenty-Sixth Biennial Report*, 1938, pp. 200–215; MEA, Minutes, Minute Book 2, 1925–26, MACI Papers.

51. MEA, Minutes, Minute Book 2, 1925–26, MACI Papers; Williams to Members, Feb. 17, 1938, Munsingwear Papers, MHS.

52. Williams to Members, Feb. 17, 1938, Munsingwear Papers.

53. Wade to Industrial Commission of Minnesota (ICM), April 9, 1938, Munsingwear

Papers; Minnesota Department of Labor and Industry, *Twenty-Sixth Biennial Report*, 1938, pp. 200–215.

54. Minnesota, [apparently a state agency report to the governor], "Net Incomes over $100,000," 1935, Benson Papers; Pillsbury to Williams, July 27, 1938; Pillsbury to ICM, March 2, 1938; Levy to Dear Friend, Aug. 24, 1938, Sept. 7, 1938, all in Munsingwear Papers; U.S. Fourth District Court, *Western Telegraph Co. vs. Industrial Commission of Minnesota, Decision*, Aug. 27, 1938.

55. *Western Telegraph Co. vs. Industrial Commission of Minnesota, Decision*, Aug. 27, 1938; Levy to Gentlemen, Oct. 24, 1938, Munsingwear Papers; Index of Procedures In the Adoption of Wage Orders, 1938–39, ICM Records, MHS.

56. Minnesota Taxpayers' Assn. (MTA), *The Taxpayer's Association*, Oct. 15, 1924; "Minnesota Taxpayers' Assn.," 1927; Program of MTA, n.d.; *Tax Thoughts for Minnesota*, 1939; MTA Advisory Board, 1938, all in Ray P. Chase Papers; MTA, Advisory Board, 1938, Harry A. Bullis Papers, MHS.

57. Steven J. Keillor, *Hjalmar Petersen of Minnesota: The Politics of Provincial Independence* (St. Paul: MHS, 1987), 90; *Minneapolis Journal*, Jan. 19, 1933, p. 1, March 7, 1933, p. 10.

58. *Minneapolis Journal*, Feb. 18, 1933, p. 14, March 3, 1933, p. 17, March 8, 1933, p. 10.

59. Keillor, *Petersen*, 90–95.

60. MTA, *Minnesota Taxes*, 1934, Chase Papers, MHS; "Net Incomes Over $100,000," 1938; "Corporations Having a Net Income Assigned to Minnesota over $100,000," 1935, both in Benson Papers; MTA, Advisory Board, Feb. 8, 1938, Bullis Papers.

61. Minneapolis Civic Council (MCC), "Memorandum on Civic Council Campaign," Dec. 9, 1945, Arnulf Ueland Papers, MHS; MCC, "What is the Minneapolis Plan?" April 1938, Benson Papers; MTA, *Tax Thoughts*, 1939, Chase Papers.

NOTES TO CHAPTER 17

1. Arthur M. Schlesinger, Jr., *Coming of the New Deal* (Boston: Houghton Mifflin Co., 1958), 99, 102, 137.

2. Schlesinger, *Coming of the New Deal*, 139; CA, "Suggested Plan of Employee and Employer Organization," June 6, 1933, CA Papers; Walker, *American City*, 81, 82; "CA Activities as Disclosed from Evidence Gathered in National Guard Raid," [Aug. 1934], Floyd B. Olson Papers, MHS.

3. Rayback, *History of American Labor*, 328; Schlesinger, *Coming of the New Deal*, 145; Sander Genis to W. W. Hughes, Nov. 6, 1933; Regional Labor Board, "In the Matter of Robitshek-Schneider Co.," Dec. 27, 1933, Robitshek-Schneider Case; both in Docket No. 1; Mpls.-St. Paul Regional Labor Board Executive Secretary to National Labor Board, Jan. 4, 1934; Minneapolis-St. Paul Regional Labor Board (hereafter referred to as RLB), "Data relating to strike of Upholsterers," both in Docket No. 2, all in Record Group (RG) 25, National Archives (NA); Levy and Allen L. Dretchko to W. H. Rodgers, Oct. 17, 1933, CA Papers; Schroeder to J. S. Clapper, April 12, 1933, confiscated in National Guard raid on CA headquarters, Aug. 3, 1934, quoted in "CA Activities as Disclosed from Evidence."

4. CA, *The Real Menace to Industrial Peace in Minneapolis*, pamphlet, Feb. 8, 1935, Cramer Papers, MHS; Boyd to CA, May 12, 1905, CA Papers; Charles Walker interview of John W. Schroeder, vice president of CA, n.d., Charles R. Walker Papers, MHS (hereafter referred to as C. Walker Papers); CA, *Special Weekly Bulletin*, No. 267, Feb. 8, 1924, and No. 281, May 16, 1924; Howard Y. Williams, Report to Committee, May 1, 1935, Williams Papers, MHS.

5. Robert L. Lind to Harry A. Bullis, Nov. 18, 1932; NAM, "Employment Relations, Industrial Disputes," 40–41, both in Bullis Papers; NAM, *Employment Relations Bulletin*, Nov. 17, 1933, CA Papers.

6. Schlesinger, *Coming of the New Deal*, 144–45, 148; Rayback, *History of American Labor*, 329; NAM, *Employment Relations Bulletin*, Nov. 17, 1933.

7. CA, *The Real Menace*; CA, "Suggested Plan of Employee and Employer Organization."

8. CA, "Uniform Employment Relations Policy," 1934; CA, "Employment Relations Policies and Rules and Regulations Governing Employment," 1934, both in CA Papers.

9. Genis to Hughes, Nov. 6, 1933; John W. Schroeder to Industrial Association of San Francisco, Jan. 24, 1934, quoted in "CA Activities as Disclosed from Evidence"; RLB, "In the Matter of Robitshek-Schneider."

10. Genis to Hughes, Nov. 6, 1933; RLB, "In the Matter of Robitshek-Schneider."

11. RLB, "In the Matter of Upholsterers vs. Brooks Parlor," Jan. 9, 1934, Docket No. 2, Furniture Manufacturing, Box 1, RG 25, NA.

12. RLB, "In the Matter of Upholsterers vs. Brooks Parlor"; Neil M. Cronin to NLB, March 2, 1934, Docket No. 60, Box 3, Brooks Parlor, RG 25, NA; Tselos, *Minneapolis Labor Movement*, 198, *Minneapolis Labor Review*, May 18, 1934, p. 1.

13. Farrell Dobbs, *Teamster Rebellion* (New York: Monad Press, 1972), 20–21; RLB, "Report of Contemplated Twin City Coal Handlers' Strike," Feb. 1, 1934, NLB, Docket No. 32, Coal Dealers, RG 25, NA; *Minneapolis Journal*, May 1, 1920, p. 5; CA, *The Real Menace*.

14. CA, *The Real Menace*; CA *Special Weekly Bulletin*, No. 788, Feb. 2, 1934; NLB Docket No. 32, "Report of Contemplated Twin Cities Coal Handlers' Strike"; RLB, Report, Feb. 1, 1934 and Feb. 1, 1935; and TCCE to Gentlemen, Jan. 23, 1934, all in RG 25, NA; Dobbs, *Teamster Rebellion*, 21; newspaper clipping, "Parley of Coal Dealers," Feb. 8, 1934, CA Papers.

15. Coal Dealers to RLB, Feb. 7, 1934, RLB Docket No. 32, RG 25, NA; Dobbs, *Teamster Rebellion*, 22; Walker, *American City*, 90; newspaper clipping, Feb. 8, 1934.

16. Newspaper clipping, Feb. 8, 1934; *Minneapolis Star*, Feb. 9, 1934, p. 1; Levy to Cronin, Feb. 9, 1934; Bainbridge to Cronin, Feb. 9, 1934, both in RLB Docket No. 32.

17. General Committee to Coal Dealers of Minneapolis, April 25, 1934, Teamsters' Local 574 Papers, MHS; CA, *The Real Menace*; Coal Companies to RLB, Feb. 7, 1934, RLB, Docket No. 32; General Committee to Coal Dealers, April 25, 1934; RLB, Ruling, Feb. 8, 1934, CA Papers.

18. Committee for Employers to Cronin, Feb. 8, 1934; Levy to RLB, Feb. 9, 1934, all in RLB Docket No. 32; Dobbs, *Teamster Rebellion*, 23–24; CA, *Special Weekly Bulletin*, Feb. 10, 1934, Local 574 Papers.

19. CA, *Special Weekly Bulletin*, Feb. 10, 1934; Coal Employers to Employees, Feb. 13, 1934, both in Local 574 Papers.

20. Uniform Employment Relations Policy of Coal Dealers, Feb. 19, 1934, CA Papers.

21. Thomas E. Blantz, *A Priest in Public Service* (Notre Dame, IN: University of Notre Dame Press, 1982), 111; Dobbs, *Teamster Rebellion*, 60–66; CA, *Special Weekly Bulletin*, April 6, 1934, May 11, 1934, both in Local 574 Papers.

22. Dobbs, *Teamster Rebellion*, 61–62; EAC, "The Truth About the Truck Drivers' Strike"; Dobbs, *Teamster Rebellion*, 66; CA, *The Real Menace*.

23. CA, *Special Weekly Bulletin*, No. 797, April 6, 1934, Local 574 Papers; Floyd Olson to William Brown, April 13, 1934, Vince Day Papers, MHS; EAC, "The Truth About the Truck Drivers' Strike"; Dobbs, *Teamster Rebellion*, 64–66.

24. Dobbs, *Teamster Rebellion*, 64–66; CA, *Special Weekly Bulletin*, No. 802, May 11, 1934, and No. 804, June 1, 1934, both in Local 574 Papers; Father Haas, Diary, July 18, 1934, in Dept. of Archives and Manuscripts, Catholic University of America; William W. Hughes to P. A. Donaghue, Sept. 1, 1934; F. J. Miller to Benedict Wolf, Dec. 19, 1934, both NLRB Case No. 38; "CA Activities as Disclosed From Evidence."

25. EAC, "Truth About the Truck Drivers' Strike"; NLB, "General Drivers' Strike, April and May 1934," NLRB Case No. 38; EAC to W. W. Hughes, May 7, 1934, CA Papers; *Organizer*, Aug. 7, 1934, pp. 1, 2.

26. EAC to Hughes, May 7, 1934; CA, *Special Weekly Bulletin*, May 11, 1934; RLB, Report, May 15, 1934, NLRB Case No. 38.

27. Walker, *American City*, 97–98; Dobbs, *Teamster Rebellion*, 74–75.

28. Sheriff Wall, interview by Charles R. Walker, C. Walker Papers; *Minneapolis Star*, May 18, 1934, p. 1. Although the meeting was supposedly spontaneous, it was chaired by CA member C. C. Webber and the resolutions considered were drafted by a group of five CA members (two of them on the board of directors). The twenty-six representatives Webber selected to attend the meeting were either associated with the EAC or the CA. At the time of the strike, most Minneapolis businessmen were CA members.

29. *Minneapolis Star*, May 18, 1934, p. 1.

30. CA, *Special Weekly Bulletin*, No. 804, June 1, 1934, Local 574 Papers; Olson, et al., signed statement, "Early this morning," May

17, 1934, Allen N. Sollie Papers, MHS; U.S. Senate, Committee on Education and Labor, Subcommittee Hearings, 74th Congress, 2nd sess., 1936, statement of Grant J. Dunne, "Violations of Free Speech and Other Rights," April 10–23, 1936, p. 44; interview of Totten Heffelfinger by Charles Walker, C. Walker Papers; Walker, *American City*, 109; List of Special Deputies, May 19–22, 1934, Local 574 Papers; Walker, *American City*, 109, 111, 119.

31. Dobbs, *Teamster Rebellion*, 78–79; U.S. Congress, Senate Committee on Education and Labor, Grant Dunne statement; Minnesota Police Association, *Bulletin*, June/July 1934, p. 59.

32. U.S. Congress, Senate Committee on Education and Labor, Grant Dunne statement, "Violations of Free Speech and Other Rights"; Walker, *American City*, 107–8; Dobbs, *Teamster Rebellion*, 79–80.

33. *Minneapolis Labor Review*, May 23, 1934, p. 1.

34. Dobbs, *Teamster Rebellion*, 82–86; *Minneapolis Journal*, May 21, p. 1; Walker, *American City*, 113–16.

35. *Minneapolis Journal*, May 21, 1934, p. 1; Dobbs, *Teamster Rebellion*, 83–84, 86; Walker, *American City*, 116.

36. *Minneapolis Star*, May 22, 1934, p. 1; Walker, *American City*, 117, 118; memorandum from Stephen Early, assistant secretary to the president, May 23, 1934, RG 25, NA; Minnesota National Guard, "Minnesota National Guard, Civil Disturbances," Adjutant General Papers, MHS; *Minneapolis Star*, May 22, 1934, p. 1; George Van Allen, "Recent Strike Disorder in Minneapolis," in Minnesota Police Association, *Bulletin*, June/July 1934, p. 59. For a description of the battle, see Prologue.

37. Van Allen, "Recent Strike Disorder in Minneapolis"; Farrell Dobbs, *Teamster Power* (New York: Monad Press, 1973), 88; Walker, *American City*, 119, 120, 121.

38. *Minneapolis Labor Review*, May 23, 1934, p. 1; NLRB, Ruling, May 22, 1934, Docket No. 77; General Drivers' Strike, April and May 1934, Summary, Case No. 38, both in RG 25, NA; Benedict Wolf, Re: Minneapolis Trucking, May 22, 1934, NLB Case No. 38; *Minneapolis Journal*, May 24, 1934, p. 1.

39. Dobbs, *Teamster Rebellion*, 95–96; Walker, *American City*, 123–24.

40. "Minnesota National Guard, Civil Disturbances"; W. L. M., "Memorandum for Mr. McIntyre," May 24, 1934, file 407B, Franklin Delano Roosevelt (FDR) Papers, FDR Library, Hyde Park, NY.

41. *Minneapolis Journal*, May 24, 1934, p. 1.

42. "General Drivers' Strike: April and May 1934," NLB Case No. 38; Marshman to Kerwin, May 25, 1934, File No. 176-1539, RG 280, NA; *Minneapolis Journal*, May 24, 1934, p. 1; Dobbs, *Teamster Rebellion*, 96–97; Walker, *American City*, 125–26; NLRB, Docket No. 77, May 25, 1934, copy in Haas Papers.

43. *Minneapolis Labor Review*, June 1, 1934; Dobbs, *Teamster Rebellion*, 96–100; CA, *Special Weekly Bulletin* No. 804, June 1, 1934, Local 574 Papers; Marshman to Kerwin, May 31, 1934.

44. Minnesota Historical Society (MHS), "20th Century Radicalism in Minnesota," interview with Jack Maloney, 110, Oral History Project, MHS 70.

45. *Minneapolis Star*, May 23, 1934, p. 6; Minneapolis Clearing House, Meeting, June 1930, Special Meeting, May 21, 1934, both in NW Banco Papers; M. E. Salisbury to Dear Sir, Aug. 3, 1934, C. Walker Papers; EAC to Gentlemen, July 23, 1934, Cramer Papers; *Minneapolis Star*, May 25, 1934, p. 4; Local 574, Report, July 6, 1934, p. 4, Local 574 Papers.

46. Dobbs, *Teamster Rebellion*, 101; MHS, Maloney interview, 70; EAC to W. W. Hughes, June 16, 1934, CA Papers; J. W. Schroeder to Gentlemen, June 14, 1934, Local 574 Papers.

47. Dobbs, *Teamster Rebellion*, 102, 114.

48. Walker, *American City*, 155, 158.

49. *Minneapolis Journal*, July 1, 1934, p. 4, copy in CA Papers; *Minneapolis Tribune*, July 7, 1934, p. 5.

50. *Minneapolis Star*, July 3, 1934, p. 5; *Minneapolis Journal*, July 20, 1934; CA, *Special Weekly Bulletin*, No. 810, July 13, 1934, Local 574 Papers.

51. Dobbs, *Teamster Rebellion*, 119–21; J. R. Cochran to President Roosevelt, Aug. 7, 1934, NLRB Case No. 38.

52. Gov. Olson, Executive Order No. 4, July 17, 1934, Adjutant General Records; Minnesota National Guard, "Minnesota National Guard, Civil Disturbances"; Stewart G. Collins to War Work Division, CCA, Oct. 31, 1917, War Records Commission; Affidavit of William E.

G. Watson, Dec. 15, 1954, in Security and Loyalty Investigation File of Kenneth Haycraft, U.S. Army Archives and copy in author's possession. Collins, a real estate agent, was also a CCA member; Collins to vice president in charge of War Activities, CCA, Nov. 7, 1917, War Records Commission.

53. Dunnigan to Kerwin, July 19, 1934; EAC, "The Truth About the Truck Drivers' Strike," 9, C. Walker Papers.

54. Dunnigan to Kerwin, July 19, 1934; Haas, "Memorandum of Agreement," July 19, 1934, NLRB Case No. 38; *Minneapolis Journal*, July 19, 1934, p. 1.

55. Haas, Diary, July 19, 1934, Haas Papers; NLB, Memorandum, "Minneapolis Truck Drivers," July 20, 1934, NLRB Case No. 38; MHS, Maloney interview, 75; "Minnesota National Guard, Civil Disturbances"; Dobbs, *Teamster Rebellion*, 127.

56. Walker, *American City*, 165–69; "CA Activities as Disclosed from Evidence"; MHS, Maloney interview, 73–76; "Minnesota National Guard, Civil Disturbances"; Schroeder interview, C. Walker Papers; Haas, Diary, July 21, 1934.

57. "Minnesota National Guard, Civil Disturbances"; Cochran to Haas, July 21, 1934; William Brown to Haas and Dunnigan, July 23, 1934, both in NLRB Case No. 38; Cochran to Haas, July 23, 1934, Haas Papers.

58. Haas and Dunnigan to EAC, Local 574 and General Public, July 25, 1934, NLRB Case No. 38; Mayer, *Floyd B. Olson*, 211; Dobbs, *Teamster Rebellion*, 148; "Minnesota National Guard, Civil Disturbances."

59. "Minnesota National Guard, Civil Disturbances"; Cochran to Haas, July 25, 1934, Haas Papers.

60. Cochran to Haas, July 25, 1934, Haas Papers; Cochran to Haas, July 27, 1934, Case No. 38.

61. Gov. Olson, Executive Proclamation, Aug. 22, 1934; Brig. General Ellard A. Walsh, *Proclamation*, July 26, 1934, both in Adjutant General Papers.

62. *Minneapolis Star*, July 28, 1934, p. 1; July 31, 1934, p. 1; "Minnesota National Guard, Civil Disturbances"; *Minneapolis Star*, July 31, 1934.

63. *Organizer*, July 28, 1934, p. 1; "Minnesota National Guard, Civil Disturbances."

See William Millikan, "The Red-Baiting of Kenneth C. Haycraft," *Minnesota History* 54 (winter 1994); *Minneapolis Star*, July 30, 1934, p. 5.

64. *Minneapolis Star*, July 30, 1934, p. 5; *Organizer*, Aug. 1, 1934, p. 1; Dobbs, *Teamster Rebellion*, 151; *Minneapolis Journal*, Aug. 1, 1934, p. 1; "Minnesota National Guard, Civil Disturbances."

65. "Minnesota National Guard, Civil Disturbances"; *Organizer*, Aug. 1, 1934, p. 1; Dobbs, *Teamster Rebellion*, 154; Herbert Solow to *The New Republic*, Oct. 1, 1934, C. Walker Papers. Col. Elmer W. McDevitt objected to returning the strike headquarters to the union. He argued that it would damage the morale of the troops. Olson's close adviser Vincent Day counseled that public sentiment was strongly in favor of the demands of the truck drivers for fair wages and decent hours of employment; memo, Aug. 6, 1934, Vincent Day Papers, MHS.

66. *Organizer*, Aug. 2, 1934, p. 1; *Minneapolis Journal*, Aug. 4, 1934, p. 1; Affidavit of Adjutant General J. E. Nelson, Jan. 7, 1954, Affidavit of Major General Ellard A. Walsh, Jan. 10, 1955, Affidavit of William E. G. Watson, Dec. 15, 1954, all in U.S. Army Loyalty and Security Investigation of Kenneth C. Haycraft; Haycraft to author, June 4, 1992, in possession of author; Commander-in-Chief, Minnesota National Guard, to Lt. Kenneth Haycraft, Aug. 3, 1934, copy in C. Walker Papers.

67. Richard M. Valelly interview of Kenneth C. Haycraft, June 1, 1981, copy in author's possession; affidavit of Watson, Dec. 15, 1954; Haycraft to author, June 4, 1992; William E. G. Watson and Abe Harris, "Citizens Alliance Activities as Disclosed From Evidence."

68. Valelly interview of Haycraft, June 1, 1981; *Minneapolis Journal*, Aug. 4, 1934, p. 1.

69. *Minneapolis Journal*, Aug. 4, 1934, p. 1; Gov. Olson, Executive Order No. 7, Aug. 6, 1934, C. Walker Papers.

70. J. C. Buckbee to Pres. Roosevelt, Aug. 16, 1934, RG 31, NA; U.S. District Court of Minnesota, 4th Division, Equity Case No. 2775, *Powers Mercantile Co. et al. vs. Floyd B. Olson*, Aug. 11, 1934, Governors' Records, MHS.

71. *Powers Mercantile Co. et al. vs. Floyd B.*

Olson, Aug. 11, 1934; Charles Walker, Report on Red Scare, n.d., C. Walker Papers.

72. *Minneapolis Journal*, Aug. 8, 1934, p. 3, Aug. 9, 1934, p. 11, Aug. 10, 1934, p. 2, Aug. 11, 1934, p. 3; Vince Day, memo to the Governor, Aug. 10, 1934, p. 3, Day Papers.

73. *Organizer*, Aug. 9, Aug. 13, Aug. 15, Aug. 20, 1934, all p. 1.

74. Dobbs, *Teamster Rebellion*, 126; MHS, Maloney interview, 97.

75. Haas, Diary, Aug. 8, 1934. Both the Minnesota State Federation of Labor and the Minneapolis Central Labor Union had been lobbying the NLRB and President Roosevelt from July 28 to August 8 to use their leverage over the Minneapolis financial group to force a strike settlement. The timing of the Jesse Jones call to Haas suggests that Olson's visit with Roosevelt finally precipitated the federal action; memorandum for Secretary Frances Perkins, July 31, 1934, and CLU officials for Colonel Louis Howe, Aug. 8, 1934, both in FDR Papers, file 407B; Emery C. Nelson to Lloyd Garrison, July 28, 1934, and George W. Lawson to Garrison, July 30, 1934, both in NLRB Case No. 38.

76. Haas Diary, Aug. 9, Aug. 11, Aug. 15, 1934; Benedict Wolf, Memorandum, Re: Telephone conversation with Father Haas, Aug. 8, 1934; Memorandum Re: Minneapolis Trucking Strike, Aug. 11, 1934, both NLRB Case No. 38.

77. Haas to Garrison, Aug. 15, 1934; Haas Diary, Aug. 16, Aug. 17, Aug. 18, 1934; EAC to 166 firms, Aug. 15, 1934, all in Haas Papers.

78. A. W. Strong, Jr., to Pres. Roosevelt, Aug. 16, 1934, FDR Papers file 407B; Lucian S. Strong to Roosevelt, Aug. 16, 1934; George N. Dayton to Roosevelt, Aug. 16, 1934, both in NLRB Case No. 38; Clive T. Jaffray to Roosevelt, Aug. 16, 1934, NA 25 RG.

79. Haas Diary, Aug. 18, 1934; Memorandum Re: Minneapolis Trucking Strike, Aug. 20, 1934, NLRB Case No. 38; Charles Walker interview with McNally and Schroeder; interview with Schroeder, both in C. Walker Papers.

80. Minneapolis RLB Docket No. 112, consent order, Aug. 21, 1934, Case No. 38; Haas and Dunnigan to EAC, July 25, 1934, Haas Papers; Jones to the President, Aug. 22, 1934, FDR Papers, file 407B.

81. *Organizer*, Aug. 22, 1934, p. 1; Thomas E. Blantz, "Father Haas and the Minneapolis Truckers' Strike of 1934," *Minnesota History* 42 (spring 1970): 14; MHS, Maloney interview, 99; Statement of Communist Party, District 9, n.d., copy in C. Walker Papers.

82. *Minneapolis Journal*, Aug. 23, 1934, p. 14, Aug. 22, 1934, p. 2; Dobbs, *Teamster Rebellion*, 179; Walker interview of Schroeder, C. Walker Papers.

83. Dobbs, *Teamster Rebellion*, 181; EAC, "Truth About the Truck Drivers' Strike," 16.

84. EAC, "Truth About the Truck Drivers' Strike."

NOTES TO CHAPTER 18

1. CA, "Minneapolis Bureau of Industrial Relations, Its Purposes and Functions," Feb. 8, 1935, Cramer Papers; CA, "Employment Relations Program," Sept. 1934, CA Papers. Other CA documents suggest an earlier date of late 1933; Minneapolis Bureau of Industrial Relations (MBIR), "Industrial and Employment Relations Questionnaire," CA Papers.

2. CA, "MBIR, Purposes and Functions," Feb. 8, 1935, Cramer Papers.

3. MBIR, "Employment Relations Policy," 1934, CA Papers.

4. Strutwear Knitting Co., "General Policies and Principles," May 2, 1934, CA Papers; CA, *Special Weekly Bulletin*, No. 824, Nov. 2, 1934, Cramer Papers.

5. Here and below, MBIR, "Employment Relations Policy," 1934.

6. CA, "MBIR, Purposes and Functions"; MBIR, "Industrial and Employment Relations Questionnaire."

7. CA, "MBIR, Specific Activities of MBIR," n.d., in CA Papers.

8. Rayback, *A History of American Labor*, 341–46.

9. Harry A. Millis and Emily C. Brown, *From the Wagner Act to Taft-Hartley* (Chicago: Univ. of Chicago Press, 1950), 281–82; Emily Brown, *National Labor Policy: Taft-Hartley after Three Years* (Washington, D.C.: Public Affairs Institute, 1950), 11–14.

10. Dobbs, *Teamster Power*, 90; Ornamental Iron Manufacturers of Minneapolis, "Employment Policy of Ornamental Iron," Aug. 26, 1935; J. E. O'Connor to H. L. Kerwin, Sept. 9, 1935, both in File 182-935, RG 280, NA; Or-

namental Iron Workers Local 1313 Strike Committee, "The Facts of the Flour City Ornamental Iron Strike," n.d., CA Papers; *Northwest Organizer*, Aug. 8, 1935, p. 1; *E. M. Brusig, et al. vs.* IAM *Twin City Ornamental Metal Lodge 1313*, July 1935, "Deposition of Walter Tetzlaff."

11. Here and below, O'Connor to Kerwin, Sept. 9, 1935; *Brusig, et al. vs.* IAM *Twin City Ornamental Metal Lodge 1313*, July 1935, "Order to Show Cause" and "Deposition of Walter Tetzlaff."

12. *Minneapolis Labor Review*, July 26, 1935, p. 1; *Brusig, et al. vs.* IAM *Local 1313*, "Order to Show Cause" and "Restraining Order," July 19, 1935; "Affidavit of Walter Tetzlaff," in CA Papers; CA, *Industrial News Service*, No. 4, Sept. 16, 1935; issues 1–9 can be found in the Minneapolis Collection, MPL, and in the R. P. Chase Papers, MHS.

13. "Restraining Order," *Brusig, et al. vs. Local 1313*, July 19, 1935; CA, *Industrial News Service*, No. 4, Sept. 16, 1935; *Minneapolis Labor Review*, July 26, 1935, p. 1.

14. Here and below, *Minneapolis Journal*, July 24, 1935, p. 4.

15. CA, *Industrial News Service*, No. 4, Sept. 16, 1935; *Northwest Organizer*, Aug. 1, 1935, p. 1.

16. Dobbs, *Teamster Power*, 90–91; "Mob Violence Prevents Us From Working," advertisement, File 182-264, RG 280, NA; CA, *Industrial News Service*, No. 4, Sept. 16, 1935.

17. CA, *Industrial News Service*, No. 1; No. 3, Aug. 29, 1935, No. 6, Oct. 3, 1935, No. 7, Oct. 24, 1935, No. 9, Dec. 2, 1935; CA, "The Citizens Alliance of Minneapolis: Its Purpose and Activities," Jan. 28, 1936, CA Papers.

18. James A. Struthers served on the CA Board of Directors from 1931 to 1932; William Struthers served from 1933 to 1934. Strutwear Knitting Co., "That The Public May Know," n.d., CA Papers; Strutwear Knitting Co., "General Policies and Principles," May 2, 1934, CA Papers; Robert M. Gates, Memorandum for file: Strutwear Knitting Co., Oct. 10, 1935, NLRB Case XVIII-R-2, Entry 155, Box 310, RG 25, NA; John W. Schroeder interview with Charles R. Walker, C. Walker Papers; U.S. Senate, Committee on Education and Labor, Hearings: "Violation of Free Speech and Other Rights," Testimony of Katz, 222–23; Gates Memorandum, Oct. 10, 1935; *Northwest Orga-*

nizer, Aug. 21, 1935, p. 1; Lois Quam and Peter J. Rachleff, "Keeping Minneapolis an Open-Shop Town: The Citizen's Alliance in the 1930s," *Minnesota History* 50 (Fall 1986): 110.

19. "Strutwear Knitting Co. Case," 1935–36, CA Papers; Schroeder interview by Walker, C. Walker Papers; Quam and Rachleff, "Keeping Minneapolis an Open-Shop Town," 112; Walker, *American City*, 248; *Industrial News Service*, No. 2, Aug. 21, 1935; MHS, Maloney interview, 110.

20. *Industrial News Service*, No. 2, Aug. 21, 1935; Dobbs, *Teamster Power*, 92; Strutwear, "That The Public May Know."

21. *Industrial News Service*, No. 2, Aug. 21, 1935; Maloney interview, 112; Dobbs, *Teamster Power*, 93.

22. *Northwest Organizer*, Aug. 14, 1935, p. 1; *Industrial News Service*, No. 4, Sept. 16, 1935; U.S. Congress, Hearings before a Senate Committee on Education and Labor, 1936, Grant Dunne statement, "Violation of Free Speech," 45–46; *Minneapolis Journal*, Sept. 12, 1935, p. 1. The *Minneapolis Labor Review* (Sept. 20, 1935, p. 1) stated that twenty of twenty-six men were private detectives armed with rifles. The CA claimed eighteen were workers and said they were armed only with tear gas.

23. *Industrial News Service*, No. 4, Sept. 16, 1935; *Minneapolis Journal*, Sept. 11, 1935, p. 1; *Northwest Organizer*, Sept. 11, 1935, p. 1.

24. *Minneapolis Journal*, Sept. 12, 1935, p. 1; *Minneapolis Tribune*, Sept. 12, 1935, p. 1; *Industrial News Service*, No. 4, Sept. 16, 1935.

25. *Northwest Organizer*, Sept. 18, 1935, p. 1; *Minneapolis Labor Review*, Sept. 20, 1935, p. 1; *Minneapolis Journal*, Sept. 12, 1935, p. 1; *Industrial News Service*, No. 4, Sept. 16, 1935.

26. *Minneapolis Star*, Sept. 7, 1935, p. 1; *Northwest Organizer*, Sept. 11, 1935, p. 1; CCA, *Bulletin on Employer-Employee Cooperation*, Oct. 1, 1934; P. W. Chappell to H. L. Kerwin, Oct. 17, 1935, File 182-935, RG 280, NA; Victor A. Johnston, "Employer-Employee Board Meets Success," *Junior Executive*, Aug. 1936, copy in CA Papers; *Northwest Organizer*, Sept. 11, 1935, p. 1.

27. Chappell to Kerwin, Oct. 17, 1935; *Northwest Organizer*, Sept. 11, 1935; *Minneapolis Journal*, Sept. 9, 1935.

28. George D. Tselos, "Minneapolis Labor Movement in the 1930s," (Ph.D. thesis, University of Minnesota, 1970), 405; L. A. Knapp to Charles Fahy, Nov. 5, 1935, and Robert M. Gates to NLRB, Oct. 1, 1935, both NLRB Case XVIII-R-2, Entry 155, Box 310, NA; *Minneapolis Journal*, Sept. 19, 1935, p. 1; Strutwear Knitting Co. to MEEB, Sept. 25, 1935, copy in file on Strutwear Strike file, Minneapolis Collection, MPL.

29. *Northwest Organizer*, Sept. 25, 1935, p. 1; Gates to NLRB, Oct. 1, 1935.

30. *Industrial News Service*, No. 5, Sept. 24, 1935, Chase Papers; *Northwest Organizer*, Sept. 25, 1935, p. 1.

31. *Minneapolis Tribune*, Oct. 12, 1935, p. 1. An offer for a free manufacturing plant with no taxes for three years had been made by St. Joseph, MO, the previous week; Gates to NLRB, Oct. 7, 1935.

32. *Minneapolis Journal*, Nov. 13, 1935, p. 1, Dec. 9, 1935, p. 1; George K. Belden "Report of Citizens' Committee," Jan. 7, 1936, in Strutwear Strike File, Minneapolis Collection. In addition to CA President Belden, five other members of the CA board of directors were assigned to the committee of eleven. The other five were also CA or CCA members.

33. *Minneapolis Journal*, Dec. 9, 1935, p. 1; Belden "Report of Citizens' Committee," in Minneapolis Collection, MPL.

34. Gates to Wolf, Nov. 29, 1935, NLRB Case XVIII-R-2; *Minneapolis Journal*, Nov. 27, 1935, p. 1; *Northwest Organizer*, Dec. 4, 1935, p. 1.

35. CA, *Industrial News Service*, No. 9, Dec. 2, 1935; *Northwest Organizer*, Dec. 4, 1935; *Minneapolis Tribune*, Nov. 30, 1935, p. 1; *Minneapolis Journal*, Nov. 27, 1935, p. 1, Dec. 2, 1935, p. 1.

36. *Minneapolis Journal*, Nov. 13, 1935, p. 1; Gates to NLRB, Dec. 13, 1935; Strutwear Knitting Co., Back-to-Work Club committee to NLRB, Nov. 21, 1935 and Nov. 25, 1935, NLRB Case XVIII-R-2.

37. Gates to NLRB, Dec. 13, 1935.

38. Order Denying Petition for Investigation, and Certification, Dec. 16, 1935, both in NLRB Case XVIII-R-2, Entry 155, Box 310; *Minneapolis Star*, Dec. 7, 1935, p. 1; *Minneapolis Journal*, Dec. 7, 1935, p. 1; *Minneapolis Tribune*, Dec. 10, 1935, p. 6; Belden, Report of Citizen's Committee, Jan. 7, 1936.

39. *Minneapolis Journal*, Dec. 9, 1935, p. 1.

40. *Minneapolis Labor Review*, Dec. 27, 1935, p. 1; Quam and Rachleff, "Keeping Minneapolis an Open-Shop Town," 114; *Minneapolis Journal*, Dec. 27, 1935, p. 10; Businessmen's Committee, Statement for the Press, Dec. 27, 1935, copy in Strutwear Strike File, Minneapolis Collection; Latimer and Wall to Gov. Olson, Dec. 27, 1935, Adjutant General's Records.

41. U.S. Fourth District Court, Complaint, Equity Case 2909, Jan. 16, 1936 Governors' Records.

42. *Minneapolis Journal*, Dec. 31, 1935, p. 1, Jan. 7, 1936, p. 1; Frederic D. McCarthy, Lt. Col., Judge-Advocate General's Dept., to Commander-in-Chief, Jan. 27, 1936, in Minnesota National Guard (MNG) Papers, MHS; Commander-in-Chief Olson, Executive Order 1, Jan. 27, 1936, Governors' Records.

43. CA, *Special Weekly Bulletin*, No. 884, April 7, 1936; Belden to Latimer, Feb. 18, 1936, both in CA Papers; *Minneapolis Tribune*, Jan. 20, 1936, p. 1; George O. Pratt, director of 17th Region, NLRB, to NLRB, Memo on Strutwear Knitting Co., Feb. 3, 1936, RG 25, Case XVIII-R-2.

44. CA, *Special Weekly Bulletin*, No. 877, Feb. 18, 1936; Belden to Latimer, Feb. 18, 1936.

45. CA, *Special Weekly Bulletin*, No. 878, Feb. 25, 1936.

46. Notice of Motion, *Strutwear Knitting Co. vs. A. F. of Hosiery Workers Local Branch 38*, CA Papers; *Northwest Organizer*, March 25, 1936, p. 3; *Minneapolis Labor Review*, March 20, 1936, p. 1, March 27, 1936, p. 1; newspaper clipping, March 25, 1936, Strutwear Strike file, Minneapolis Collection; F. R. Struthers, letter, Feb. 29, 1936, MacAloon Papers.

47. Robert E. Mythen to H. L. Kerwin, April 4, 1936; Struthers to Francis Cloutier, April 3, 1936; Cloutier to Struthers April 4, 1936, all in RG 280, File 182-748; CA, *Special Weekly Bulletin*, No. 884, April 7, 1936, CA Papers.

48. Strutwear Knitting Co., Statement, April 20, 1936, MacAloon Papers.

49. Nathaniel S. Clark, Weekly Report, June 27, 1936, RG 25, Case XVIII-R-2; Strutwear to NLRB, May 29, 1936, MacAloon Papers.

50. CA, *Special Weekly Bulletin*, No. 872, Jan. 14, 1936, No. 899, July 21, 1936, both in CA Papers; *Minneapolis Labor Review*, Aug. 2, 1935; *Northwest Organizer*, July 31, 1935; Dobbs, *Teamster Power*, 56–64.

51. CA, *Special Weekly Bulletin*, No. 872, Jan. 14, 1936, No. 899, July 21, 1936.

NOTES TO CHAPTER 19

1. CA, *Special Weekly Bulletin*, No. 899, July 21, 1936.

2. Dobbs, *Teamster Power*, 135; CA, *Special Weekly Bulletin*, No. 899, July 21, 1936, No. 901, Aug. 4, 1936, No. 903, Aug. 19, 1936.

3. CA, *Special Weekly Bulletin*, No. 904, Aug. 26, 1936, No. 908, Sept. 24, 1936; a Mr. Slocum, "Notes on Conference Held Sept. 5, 1936," with Slocum representing wholesale grocers; the governor; Herman Hanson, president of the Retail Grocers' Assn.; and a Mr. Faber, president of the Hennepin County Farmers' Protective Assn., in Governors' Records; *Minneapolis Tribune*, Aug. 26, 1936, p. 7; *Northwest Organizer*, Aug. 7, 1934, p. 1, Aug. 26, 1936, p. 1; Dobbs, *Teamster Power*, 136; Harry Martin to Gov. Petersen, Aug. 25, 1936, Gov. Petersen Records; N. S. Clark, Preliminary Report of Commissioner of Conciliation, Re: 17 Wholesale grocery firms, Minneapolis, to NLRB, Sept. 2, 1936, File 182-1727 RG 280, NA.

4. Tselos, "Minneapolis Labor Movement in the 1930s," 364; Dobbs, *Teamster Power*, 136–37; Martin to Gov. Petersen, Aug. 25, 1936; *Northwest Organizer*, Aug. 26, 1936, p. 1; *Minneapolis Tribune*, Aug. 26, 1936, p. 7.

5. *Northwestern Miller*, Aug. 19, 1936, p. 487, Aug. 26, 1936, p. 546; Charge against Washburn-Crosby Co., Sept. 17, 1936, NLRB Case XVIII-c-42; Charge against Pillsbury Co., Sept. 17, 1936, Case XVIII-c-37, both NA.

6. *Northwestern Miller*, Aug. 26, 1936, p. 546, Sept. 2, 1936, p. 620, Sept. 9, 1936, p. 696, Sept. 10, 1936, p. 1; CA, *Special Weekly Bulletin*, No. 905, Sept. 2, 1936.

7. *Northwest Organizer*, Aug. 26, 1936, p. 1; *Minneapolis Labor Review*, Sept. 4, 1936, p. 1; *Minneapolis Journal*, Aug. 25, 1936, p. 9, Aug. 27, 1936, p. 13; *Minneapolis Tribune*, Aug. 25, 1936, p. 1, Aug. 26, 1936, p. 7.

8. *Northwest Organizer*, Sept. 3, 1936, p. 1; *Minneapolis Tribune*, Sept. 1, 1936, p. 1. The *Tribune* reported an attendance of 800 while

The Northwest Organizer estimated 200; *Minneapolis Tribune*, Sept. 1, 1936, p. 1.

9. *Minneapolis Tribune*, Sept. 1, 1936, p. 1.

10. *Minneapolis Star*, Aug. 26, 1936, copy in CA Papers; *Minneapolis Tribune*, Aug. 27, 1936, p. 1; Dobbs, *Teamster Power*, 137.

11. Robert E. Mythen to Hugh L. Kerwin, Sept. 14, 1936; Clark, Preliminary Report, Sept. 2, 1936, both in file 182-1727, RG 280, NA; Notes on Conference, Sept. 5, 1936, Gov. Petersen Records; *Minneapolis Tribune*, Sept. 12, 1936, p. 1; *Minneapolis Journal*, Sept. 9, 1936.

12. *Northwestern Miller*, Sept. 16, 1936, p. 756; Mythen to Kerwin Sept. 14, 1936; *St. Paul Dispatch*, Sept. 14, 1936, copy in CA Papers.

13. *Northwestern Miller*, Sept. 16, 1936, p. 768; Clark, Preliminary Report; *St. Paul Dispatch*, Sept. 16, 1936; *St. Paul Daily News*, Sept. 16, 1936, p. 1; CA, *Special Weekly Bulletin*, No. 907, Sept. 17, 1936.

14. NLRB, Cases Closed, Case XVIII-c-42, Report, Sept. 26, 1936, RG 25, NA; C. C. Bovey to Robert Mythen, Sept. 21, 1936; Gray, *Business without Boundary*, 298.

15. *Minneapolis Labor Review*, Oct. 2, 1936, p. 1; *Minneapolis Tribune*, Sept. 18, 1936, p. 1; *Minneapolis Journal*, Sept. 18, 1936, p. 1.

16. *Minneapolis Journal*, Sept. 18, 1936, p. 1.

17. *Minneapolis Tribune*, Sept. 22, 1936; CA, *Special Weekly Bulletin*, No. 908, Sept. 24, 1936; *St. Paul Daily News*, Sept. 22, 1936, copy in CA Papers.

18. John P. Wall to Gov. Petersen, Sept. 22, 1936, Gov. Petersen Records; *Minneapolis Journal*, Sept. 23, 1936, p. 1.

19. Hjalmar Petersen statement, Sept. 22, 1936; Wall to Petersen Oct. 1, 1936, both in Gov. Petersen Records.

20. *St. Paul Pioneer Press*, Sept. 24, 1936, p. 6; Whiting to Mythen, Sept. 23, 1936, NLRB Case XVIII-c-37, RG 25, NA.

21. William J. Powell, *Pillsbury's BEST: A Company History from 1869* (Minneapolis: Pillsbury Co., 1985), 125; *Minneapolis Journal*, Sept. 25, 1936, p. 1; copy of Gov. Petersen radio talk, Sept. 25, 1936; Mythen to Kerwin, Oct. 30, 1936, both in File 182-1766, RG 280, NA.

22. Mythen to Kerwin, Sept. 25, 1936, Oct. 30, 1936; Gov. Petersen radio talk, Sept. 25,

1936; Gov. Petersen statement on the demobilization of the National Guard, n.d., Gov. Petersen Records.

23. Gov. Petersen radio talk, Sept. 25, 1936.

24. Mythen to Kerwin, Oct. 30, 1936; Robert E. Walsh to Cargill Elevator Co., Sept. 28, 1936, Gov. Petersen Records.

25. *Minneapolis Journal*, Oct. 4, 1936, p. 12; Mythen to Kerwin, Oct. 10, 1936.

26. Dobbs, *Teamster Power*, 138–39; Mythen to Kerwin, Oct. 30, 1936; *Northwest Organizer*, Oct. 1, 1936, p. 1; CA, *Special Weekly Bulletin*, No. 908, Sept. 24, 1936.

27. Petersen and Mythen to Gentlemen, Oct. 1, 1936; Wholesale Grocers and Chain Store Warehouse Operators to Gov. Petersen and Robert Mythen, Oct. 2, 1936; Carl Skoglund, Oct. 3, 1936; Mythen to Kerwin, Oct. 30, 1936, all in File 182-1727, RG 280, NA.

28. CA, *Special Weekly Bulletin*, No. 910, Oct. 8, 1936, CA Papers; *Northwest Organizer*, Oct. 8, 1936, p. 1; Dobbs, *Teamster Power*, 139.

29. CA, *Special Weekly Bulletin*, No. 910, Oct. 8, 1936; *Minneapolis Journal*, Oct. 8, 1936, p. 1; Charles W. Drew to Gov. Petersen, Oct. 7, 1936, Gov. Petersen Records.

30. *Minneapolis Journal*, Oct. 8, 1936, p. 1; *Northwestern Miller*, Oct. 14, 1936, p. 117; Exhibit, statement of flour mills, grain elevators, and feed mills, Oct. 5, 1936, Farm Services Administration (FSA), 14, File 182-1727 RG 280, NA; *Northwestern Miller*, Oct. 14, 1936, p. 117.

31. *Minneapolis Tribune*, Nov. 26, 1936, copy in CA Papers; CA, *Special Weekly Bulletin*, No. 917, Nov. 27, 1936; MEA Board of Directors, "In Memory of Albert W. Strong," Dec. 15, 1936, MEA Papers.

32. CA, 1936 Audit, CA Papers; AI, Press Release, Jan. 7, 1937, Cramer Papers.

33. AI, Press Release, Jan. 7, 1937.

34. CA, Constitution, 1903, CA Papers; AI, Press Release, Jan. 7, 1937.

35. Here and below, AI, Press Release, Jan. 7, 1937.

36. *Northwest Organizer*, Jan. 14, 1937, p. 4.

37. Minneapolis Retailer's Association (MRA), Minutes, Sept. 7, 1937, Jan. 13, 1938, MRA Papers.

38. MRA, Minutes, Oct. 14, 1937, MRA Papers; AI, Report to National Industrial Council

(NIC), Sept. 15, 1937, CA Papers; Minneapolis Civic Council (MCC), "Minneapolis Civic Activities," Nov. 28, 1947, p. 3, Minneapolis Collection, MPL; *Northwest Organizer*, June 17, 1937.

39. AI, General Status of Union Activity in Minneapolis, 1937, CA Papers; AI, Report to NIC, Sept. 15, 1937.

40. Tselos, "The Minneapolis Labor Movement in the 1930s," 369–87; MCC, "Civic Councilor," March 1940; AI, "The labor situation in Minneapolis as of Nov. 15, 1937," CA Papers.

41. AI, "The labor situation in Minneapolis."

42. Munsingwear Co., "Program of Employment Relationship between Management and Employees," Jan. 1935, Munsingwear Papers; AI, General Status of Union Activity, 1937.

43. AI, Report to NIC, Aug. 15, 1937, CA Papers; AI, "Associated Industries of Minneapolis," ca. 1950s, MHS; MCC, "Minneapolis Civic Activities," Nov. 28, 1947; MCC, newsletter, Oct. 1941.

44. MCC, "A Report to the Stockholders," Nov. 1941; MCC, "Minneapolis Civic Activities," Nov. 28, 1947; AI, "Associated Industry of Minneapolis."

45. AI, "Associated Industries of Minneapolis."

46. CA, 1936 Audit, CA Papers; author interview with Bertram Locke, director of AI from 1943 to 1962, June 22, 1992, in possession of author; Historical notes, Employer's Association, Inc.; MacAloon to Governor Edward J. Thye, Aug. 10, 1943, Governors' Records. AI merged with its St. Paul counterpart in 1982 to form Employer's Association, Incorporated.

47. MacAloon client list, Joint Employers' Committee Files, MacAloon Papers.

48. MacAloon client list; *The Union*, July 29, 1904, p. 4; MRA, Minutes, ca. 1930s, MRA Papers. One-third of MacAloon's early clients had been members of the Employers' Advisory Committee during the 1934 Teamsters' strike; MacAloon client list; *Northwest Organizer*, Aug. 7, 1934, p. 1. AI income in 1937 was $36,693. Eight years later it received $51,235 through the allocations of the Minneapolis Civic Council's joint financial campaign. The Dayton Co. in that time had raised its donation to the seven-member organizations of the Civic Council from $7,500 to $12,000. Of this, 22 percent, or $2,640, still went to AI despite the fact that they were represented by MacAloon; MCC, "Memorandum on Civic Council Campaigns," Dec. 9, 1945, Arnulf Ueland Papers, MHS.

49. Minneapolis Credit Exchange, Employment Relations Policy, Jan. 7, 1937, MacAloon Papers.

50. MacAloon to R. A. Johnson, May 15, 1937; Gray Co., Agreement, Dec. 23, 1937; Scott-Atwater, Agreement, May 26, 1937, and Agreement, June 3, 1937; Retail Dept. Stores, Agreements, 1937, 1938, 1939, and 1941, all in MacAloon Papers.

51. Minneapolis Typothetae (MT) Minutes, Sept. 29, 1937, Oct. 28, 1937, Aug. 5, 1939, Oct. 11, 1939, all in MT Papers; *Minneapolis Journal*, April 30, 1929, p. 11.

52. Graphic Arts Industry, Inc., to Hennepin County Local Draft Board, 15, Nov. 7, 1942, MT Papers; MCC, *Newsletter*, Oct. 1942; Employers' Negotiating Committee (ENC), Report on Representation, 1942, "Proposed Program of Cooperative Action," 1942; ENC, Authorization Form, March 18, 1942, all in MacAloon Papers; MCC, *Newsletter*, Oct. 1942.

53. MCC, *Newsletter*, Oct. 1942; S. V. S. to MacAloon, Memorandum, May 5, 1942, MacAloon Papers; MCC, Civic Council Activities, *Newsletter*, Jan. 13, 1945, March 30, 1945, June 1, 1945; National War Labor Board (NWLB), Brief in Summation of Retail Dept. Stores and Retail Furniture Stores of Minneapolis; Trucking Commission Case, 111-8197-D, July 21, 1944, RG 202, NA.

NOTES TO CHAPTER 20

1. "Proposed Plan of Action," n.d., Cramer Family Papers.

2. MRA, Annual Meeting, Oct. 14, 1937, MRA Papers; Minneapolis Civic Council (MCC), "What is the Minneapolis Plan?" April 1938, Benson Papers; *Minneapolis Tribune*, April 5, 1938, p. 1.

3. MCC, Constitution and Bylaws, both Sept. 3, 1948; "What is the Minneapolis Plan?"; MCC, Memorandum on Civic Council Campaign, Dec. 9, 1945, all in Ueland Papers; *Northwest Organizer*, April 14, 1938, p. 4.

4. MCC, Memo on Civic Council Campaign, Dec. 9, 1945; MCC, *Civic Councilor*, April 1939.

5. MCC, *Civic Councilor*, April 1939.

6. MCC, *Statement of Program of the Civic Council*, pamphlet, in MCC file, Minneapolis Collection, MPL.

7. MCC, "Agreement Between Civic Council and _____," Nov. 24, 1948; Memo on Civic Council Campaign, Dec. 9, 1945; MCC, Statement of Income and Expenditures, March 31, 1950, all in Ueland Papers.

8. Statement of Income Received and Appropriations Made, March 31, 1947, March 31, 1950, Ueland Papers; MCC, *Action*, pamphlet, 1940; *Civic Councilor*, March 1939; MCC, "Minneapolis Civic Activities," June 13, 1947.

9. *Minneapolis Journal*, May 2, 1931, p. 2; *Minneapolis Tribune*, Nov. 22, 1932, p. 9; Minn. Law Enforcement League Organizing Committee to J. W. Schroeder, Nov. 18, 1933, CA Papers; MEA, Executive Committee Minutes, May 29, 1919, MEA Papers.

10. Law Enforcement League Organizing Comm. to Schroeder, Nov. 18, 1933; *Bulletin*, No. 1, Nov. 27, 1934, CA Papers; Minnesota Law and Order League (hereafter referred to as MLOL), Hennepin County Chapter, *A Statement: Law and Order*, n.d., pamphlet, MHS. After the MLOL was organized, Warner became chairman of the Finance Committee and Strong served as a state director from MLOL, Hennepin County Chapter.

11. MLOL, Basis for Organization of Minn. Law and Order League, n.d.; and Secretary's Report, Nov. 16, 1934, both in CA Papers; MLOL, *Official Bulletin*, No. 1, March 10, 1934; and Articles of Incorporation, Sept. 21, 1934, both in Bullis Papers.

12. "CA Activities as Disclosed from Evidence Gathered in National Guard Raid," 1934, Floyd B. Olson Papers; MLOL, Membership Pledge; and MLOL, Hennepin County Chapter, *A Statement: Law and Order*, June 1936; MRA, Board of Directors Meeting Minutes, Jan. 11, 1934, June 4, 1935; and Secretary's Report, Nov. 16, 1934, both in MRA Papers; MLOL, *Official Bulletin*, No. 1, March 10, 1934.

13. MLOL, Hennepin County Chapter, *A Statement: Law and Order*, Bullis Papers; MLOL, Hennepin County Chapter, *Law and Order*,

June 1936; CA, *The Real Menace to Industrial Peace in Minneapolis*, Feb. 8, 1935, Cramer Papers; MLOL, "A Basis for Organization," CA Papers.

14. MLOL, *Official Bulletin*, No. 1, March 10, 1934; Secretary's Report, Nov. 16, 1934, CA Papers; The Endicott building was owned by the Davidsons. L. H. Davidson was the managing director of the St. Paul CA; Davidson Company Records, MHS.

15. MLOL, *Bulletin*, No. 1, Nov. 21, 1934, CA Papers; MLOL, Membership Pledge, Bullis Papers; MRA, Board of Directors Minutes, June 4, 1935, MRA Papers; Minneapolis Clearing House, Special Meeting Minutes, May 24, 1935, July 20, 1937, both in NW Banco Papers; "CA Activities as Disclosed From Evidence Gathered in National Guard Raid," Olson Papers.

16. MLOL, *Official Bulletin*, No. 1, March 10, 1934; Drew to Members, Feb. 8, 1935, CA Papers; Drew to Bullis, Dec. 4, 1934, Bullis Papers.

17. "Report of the Committee Appointed to Investigate the Hennepin Co. Law and Order League," n.d., Sollie Papers, MHS; *Minneapolis Star*, Jan. 7, 1937, p. 1. Fifteen members of the sitting grand jury were sent invitations using league stationery. *Northwest Organizer*, Dec. 3, 1936, p. 1; *Minnesota Leader*, n.d., copy in Vince Day Papers, MHS; *Minneapolis Labor Review*, Dec. 11, 1936.

18. MLOL, Hennepin County Chapter, *A Statement: Law and Order*; and *Official Bulletin*, No. 1, CA Papers.

19. NAM, "Digest of National Industrial Information Committee (NIIC) Activities," 1944; NAM, *Re-Selling The American Way to America*, n.d., pamphlet; Ernest T. Weir to "Mr. American Businessman," May 20, 1935, all in Bullis Papers; Howard Wood, "Business Must Sell Itself," *Nation's Business*, Jan. 1938, p. 27.

20. H. A. Bullis, "Public Relations Activities of NAM," Dec. 4, 1935; James N. MacLean to Bullis, Dec. 9, 1931; Robert L. Lund to Bullis, Nov. 18, 1932, all in Bullis Papers; Gray, *Business without Boundaries*, 91–92, 139–41.

21. Merrill Hutchinson to Bullis, Sept. 8, 1934; Bullis, "Public Relations Activities of NAM," Dec. 4, 1935, both in Bullis Papers.

22. Bullis, Speech at Congress of American Industry, Dec. 9, 1936; Bullis, "Public Re-

lations Activities of NAM," Dec. 4, 1935; Bullis, Educational Outline, n.d.; NAM, *Re-Selling the American Way*, n.d.; NAM, "Digest of NIIC Activities," 1944; Bullis, "On Winning Public Good Will," April 9, 1935, all in Bullis Papers.

23. Bullis, "Public Relations," *Fortune* (March 1939): 110; Bullis, "On Winning Public Good Will," April 9, 1935; NAM, "Digest of NIIC Activities"; NAM, "A Look Ahead," n.d.; NAM, *Re-Selling the American Way*; Bullis, "Public Relations Activities of NAM," all in Bullis Papers.

24. "Public Relations," *Fortune* (March 1939): 110; NAM "A Look Ahead"; Bullis, "Public Relations Activities of NAM."

25. NAM, *Re-Selling The American Way*; NAM, "Leadership: The Strength of Industry's Program," 1946, Bullis Papers.

26. NAM, "Digest of NIIC Activities," 1944; NAM, *Re-Selling the American Way*; Bullis to Those Who Contributed For 1935," June 15, 1937, all in Bullis Papers.

27. C. M. Chester to Bullis, Dec. 28, 1940; Alfred P. Sloan to Bullis, Feb. 20, 1945; Weisenburger to Bullis, July 19, 1935; J. Howard Pew to Bullis, Jan. 18, 1946, all in Bullis Papers.

28. NAM, Educational Outline, n.d.; NAM, *Re-Selling the American Way*; Minnesota Industrial Conference, Program, Oct. 8, 1946, Bullis Papers.

29. NAM, *Re-Selling the American Way*; Northwest Education and Industry Conference, Roster of Participants, Nov. 5, 1942, both in Bullis Papers.

30. CA, *The Real Menace to Industrial Peace in Minneapolis*, Feb. 8, 1935, Cramer Papers.

31. Northwest Organizer, *Behind the 544 Suit: The Truth about the Fink Suit against the Minneapolis General Drivers' Union* (Minneapolis: Northwest Organizer, 1940), foreword by Miles Dunne, 1–38; Albert R. Bell to Harold E. Stassen, Dec. 29, 1938; A. Chase to Harold E. Stassen, Dec. 27, 1938, both in Governors' Records.

32. *Behind the 544 Suit*; "From the President," *Independent Labor News*, March 1939, June 1939, Sept. 1939; *Minneapolis Labor Review*, May 27, 1938; reprint from a national magazine, July 9, 1938, copy in CA Papers.

33. *Northwest Organizer*, March 24, 1938; Minnesota Mutual Truck Owners' and Dri-

vers' Association, Local No. 1, "A Challenge to the Officials and Citizens of Minneapolis," n.d., CA Papers; *Behind the 544 Suit*, 15–17.

34. *Behind the 544 Suit*, 7–8; James M. Shelton to Asst. Chief of Staff, G-2, "Subversive Activities," April 18, 1938, USMI, Surveillance of Radicals, Wilson Library, University of Minnesota, Minneapolis.

35. *Behind the 544 Suit*, 10; *Minneapolis Star Journal*, April 2, 1940, p. 17, April 3, 1940, p. 1, April 13, 1940, p. 1; Dobbs, *Teamster Bureaucracy*, 70–71.

36. *Minneapolis Tribune*, Aug. 3, 1938, p. 8; *Minneapolis Journal*, Sept. 11, 1936, p. 1; Report on William Dudley Pelley, n.d., Jewish Community Relations Council Papers, MHS.

37. *Minneapolis Tribune*, Aug. 3, 1938, p. 8; Report on Pelley; *Minneapolis Labor Review*, Aug. 5, 1938, p. 1.

38. *Minnesota Leader*, Aug. 6, 1938; *Minneapolis Tribune*, Aug. 4, 1938, p. 1.

39. *Minneapolis Journal*, clipping, n.d. (probably Aug. 4 or 5, 1938), CA Papers; *Minnesota Leader*, Aug. 6, 1938; *Behind the 544 Suit*, 27; Dobbs, *Teamster Politics*, 139–48.

40. Dunne, *Behind the 544 Suit*.

41. Dobbs, *Teamster Politics*, 141–45; Dobbs, *Teamster Bureaucracy*, 180–81.

42. Rayback, *A History of American Labor*, 382; George E. Novack, *The Bill of Rights in Danger* (New York: Civil Rights Defense Committee, 1941), 12; Thomas L. Pahl, "G-String Conspiracy, Political Reprisal or Armed Revolt? The Minneapolis Trotskyite Trial," *Labor History* 8 (winter 1967): 31.

43. Lloyd M. MacAloon Industrial and Labor Relations Service, Daily Reports Book, 1940–41, MacAloon Papers; USMI, Surveillance of Radicals; Major Mulcahy, Report on Subversive Activities of Local 544, July 31, 1940, USMI, Surveillance of Radicals; SWP Trial Transcript, 1941, p. 602.

44. Report on Subversive Activities to War Dept., Oct. 3, 1940, USMI, Surveillance of Radicals; Report of W. T. Bals on Subversive Activities to War Dept., Sept. 14, 1940, Nov. 8, 1940; MacAloon, Report on Subversive Activities of Local 544, July 31, 1940, all in USMI Surveillance of Radicals.

45. Report on Union Defense Guard (UDG), Oct. 14, 1940, USMI Surveillance of Radicals; Bals, Report, Nov. 8, 1940.

46. *U.S. vs. Vincent Raymond Dunne et al.*, No. 7256, Trial Transcript, 570–72, 575, 753, microfilm copy in MHS.

47. Pahl, "G-String Conspiracy," 32, 35–37; Dobbs, *Teamster Bureaucracy*, 115–16.

48. Civil Rights Defense Committee, "American Civil Liberties Union Blasts Federal Indictment of '29,'" Aug. 20, 1941; SWP Trial 1941, 242–46, both in SWP Papers, MHS; *Minneapolis Morning Tribune*, June 28, 1941, p. 1. In contrast, in 1935, CA transfer firms had been too afraid of Local 544 to remove equipment from the Strutwear Company.

49. *Minneapolis Morning Tribune*, June 28, 1941, p. 1, June 30, 1941, p. 1.

50. Pahl, "G-String Conspiracy," 32–33; Indictment No. 7256, SWP trial, July 15, 1941, p. 5–13.

51. Pahl, "G-String Conspiracy," 42; Novack, "Bill of Rights," 9; SWP Trial Transcript, 535, 693; Albert Goldman, *In Defense of Socialism* (New York: Pioneer Publishers, 1942), 60.

52. SWP Trial Transcript, 693; Pahl, "G-String Conspiracy," 33; Grace Carlson to Comrade Natalia, Oct. 20, 1941, Carlson Papers, MHS; Dobbs, *Teamster Bureaucracy*, 162.

53. SWP Trial Transcript, Judge's Summation, 1164; Pahl, "G-String Conspiracy" 33.

54. Grace Carlson to Comrade Natalia, Oct. 20, 1941; Dobbs, *Teamster Bureaucracy*, 162; SWP Trial Transcript, 250.

55. *Minneapolis Star Journal*, Nov. 24, 1941, p. 15; Pahl, "G-String Conspiracy," 33; Dobbs, *Teamster Bureaucracy*, 273.

NOTES TO CHAPTER 21

1. Mayer, *The Political Career of Floyd B. Olson*, 93.

2. John Crosby to Frank Leslie, Nov. 17, 1932; E. L. McMillan to Leslie, Nov. 10, 1932; Edwin L. Lindell to Leslie, April 25, 1932, all in Frank Leslie Papers, MHS; Interview of Totten P. Heffelfinger, C. Walker Papers; Minnesota Law and Order League (MLOL), *Bulletin* No. 1, Nov. 27, 1934, CA Papers.

3. Young Republican League (YRL), News Release, Sept. 15, 1962; YRL, *1936 Report*; YRL, "Our Call to Youth," Nov. 27, 1935, all in YRL Papers, MHS.

4. "Our Call to Youth," Nov. 27, 1935, YRL, *1936 Report*, both in YRL Papers.

5. Ivan Hinderaker, "Harold Stassen and Developments in the Republican Party in Minnesota, 1937–1943," (Ph.D. dissertation, University of Minnesota, 1949), 464; "Stassen's Ten Point Program," newspaper clipping, n.d., YRL Papers.

6. Ray P. Chase, "Are They Communists or Catspaws? A Redbaiting Article," Chase Papers, MHS; "Stassen's Ten Point Program"; Wayne E. Gilbert, "The Rise of Harold Stassen," typescript, 1970, MHS.

7. Stassen, address at Minnesota Farmer-Labor Convention, Mankato, MN, Sept. 13, 1938, Sollie Papers; Gilbert, "The Rise of Harold Stassen."

8. *Minnesota Law Review*, Jan. 1940, pp. 217–21; MEA, Secretary's Report, Dec. 1, 1939, MACI Papers.

9. List of "A" Luncheon Group; Stassen to Leslie, Oct. 20, 1947; Leslie to G. Nelson Dayton, Nov. 11, 1946; Leslie to Gentlemen, n.d.; Leslie to Crosby, Sydney Anderson, and Lucian Strong, May 17, 1945; Sources of Money, April 25, 1946; George C. Jones to Lucian Strong, Oct. 18, 1946, Nov. 6, 1946; John Cowles to Leslie, May 1, 1946; Major "A" subscriptions in recent election years and in 1945, April 25, 1946; Leslie to Sydney Anderson, Aug. 12, 1945; Warren E. Burger to Leslie, May 14, 1947; Leslie to Harold Knutson, March 18, 1946; Lucian Strong to Leslie, June 27, 1947; all in Leslie Papers.

10. Here and below, Minnesota House File 352, "A Proposed State Labor Relations Act," n.d. (introduced Jan. 31, 1939), CA Papers.

11. *Minneapolis Star*, March 24, 1939, p. 12; *St. Paul Pioneer Press*, March 20, 1939, p. 1; Henry E. Vance, et al., to Mr. Editor, Feb. 16, 1939, CA Papers.

12. *Minneapolis Star*, March 1, 1939, p. 1; *St. Paul Pioneer Press*, March 22, 1939, p. 1, March 24, 1939, p. 1; Dobbs, *Teamster Politics*, 149–51.

13. *Minneapolis Star*, March 1, 1939, p. 1; *Minneapolis Journal*, March 15, 1939, copy in CA Papers.

14. "Reasons For Designating Unfair Labor Practices in Proposed State Labor Relations Act, HF 352," Feb. 17, 1939, Governors' Records.

15. *Minneapolis Star*, March 24, 1939, p. 1; *Minnesota Law Review*, Jan. 1940, pp. 222–24.

16. William H. MacMahon, *Minnesota Labor Laws, 1939*, Governors' Records.

17. *Minneapolis Journal*, March 30, 1939, p. 1; *Minneapolis Tribune*, March 30, 1939, p. 1; *St. Paul Dispatch*, March 29, 1939, p. 1.

18. *St. Paul Dispatch*, March 29, 1939, p. 1.

19. *St. Paul Dispatch*, March 29, 1939, p. 1; Levy to Stassen, Jan. 17, 1939, Levy to Morris B. Mitchell, Jan. 16, 1939, both in Governors' Records.

20. *St. Paul Dispatch*, March 29, 1939, p. 1; Dobbs, *Teamster Politics*, 152–53; William H. Kelty, "Minnesota's Year of Labor Peace," *Nation's Business*, April 1940, p. 30.

21. *Minneapolis Star*, May 19, 1939; AI, "New Minnesota Labor Relations Law Clinic," May 18, 1939, CA Papers.

22. *Northwest Organizer*, June 27, 1939, p. 1; Alfred P. Blair to Gov. Stassen, Commission Report, July 1, 1939, Governors' Records; Dobbs, *Teamster Politics*, 155–56.

23. Dobbs, *Teamster Politics*, 155–56; Lloyd J. Haney to Gov. Stassen, June 6, 1939, Governors' Records; St. Paul Committee on Industrial Relations, "St. Paul Shop Talk," July 12, 1939, p. 1.

24. Blair, Commission Report, July 1, 1939; Haney to Gov. Stassen, "Confidential Report," July 6, 1939, Governors' Records; Dobbs, *Teamster Politics*, p. 158.

25. Haney to Stassen, July 7, 1939; Stassen to Carl Skoglund, July 8, 1939, both in Governors' Records; Dobbs, *Teamster Politics*, 158.

26. *Northwest Organizer*, July 20, 1939, p. 1.

27. *Civic Councilor*, Sept. 1939, p. 3; "The Minnesota Labor Peace Plan," Governors' Records; Kelty, "Minnesota's Year of Labor Peace"; Jack W. Stieber, "Ten Years of the Minnesota Labor Relations Act," University of Minnesota Press, *Bulletin* 9, April 1949, p. 2. AI acknowledged that its figures did not include the 1939 WPA strike, citing the federal nature of that strike. The AI had no involvement in or impact on this strike.

28. *Civic Councilor*, Sept. 1939, p. 3; *Minneapolis Labor Review*, Jan. 17, 1941, p. 1.

29. Stassen, *Where I Stand* (Garden City, NY: Doubleday and Co., 1947), 73–153; Hinderaker, "Harold Stassen," 479; "The Minnesota Labor Peace Plan," Governors' Records.

30. Hinderaker, 605–24; Sen. Joseph Ball, "Notes From Washington," Feb. 6, 1941; U.S. Senate, Bill 683 (copy), 77 Congress, 1 Session, Jan. 31, 1941, both in Ball Papers.

31. Stieber, "Ten Years," 11, 17–18, 24, 31; Minnesota Labor Conciliator, Annual Report, 1941, Governors' Records.

32. Stieber, "Ten Years," 17–18, 24.

33. *AIU vs. Asbestos Workers, et al.*, Aug. 3, 1940, Henn. Co. District Court; Goldie and Carlson, to Central Labor Union, Nov. 1, 1940, CLU Papers; Local 1145, "Who Makes Gains For Employees?" June 25, 1941; Honeywell, "Attention: Honeywell Workers," May 26, 1941, and numerous other flyers; UE 1145, "Hundreds Join Local 1145," July 31, 1941; "Open Meeting Wednesday" July 29, 1941, all in Governors' Records; George D. Tselos, "The Minneapolis Labor Movement in the 1930s" (Ph. D. thesis, University of Minnesota, 1970), 520–21.

34. *Minneapolis Tribune*, June 13, 1941; *Milwaukee Journal*, June 15, 1941; *The Industrial Organizer*, Sept. 12, 1941; *Minneapolis Times*, June 20, 1941, p.1; Dobbs, *Teamster Bureaucracy*, 131–32; Tselos, "The Minneapolis Labor Movement," 535.

35. Tselos, "The Minneapolis Labor Movement," 535; Dobbs, *Teamster Bureaucracy*, 131, 132.

36. *Minneapolis Times*, June 17, 1941, p. 17; *Minneapolis Tribune*, June 14, 1941, p. 1.

37. Dobbs, *Teamster Bureaucracy*, 133; *Minneapolis Times*, June 17, 1941, p. 17, June 20, 1941, p. 1.

38. Frank Leslie, Memoirs, unpublished mss, n.d., Leslie Papers; *Minneapolis Times*, June 17, 1941, p. 17; Dobbs, *Teamster Bureaucracy*, 134.

39. *Minneapolis Morning Tribune*, June 18, 1941, p. 1; *Minneapolis Times*, June 17, 1941, p. 17.

40. Dobbs, *Teamster Bureaucracy*, 134, 144–45.

41. *The Industrial Organizer*, Sept. 12, 1941; Dobbs, *Teamster Bureaucracy*, 141; *Minneapolis Times*, July 1, 1941, p. 10.

42. *The Industrial Organizer*, Sept. 12, 1941.

43. *The Industrial Organizer*, Sept. 12, 1941; Dobbs, *Teamster Bureaucracy*, 154–55; Commission Appointed to Conduct Hearings on

Local 544-CIO, Report to Stassen, Aug. 29, 1941, Governors' Records.

44. *Minneapolis Star Journal*, Sept. 19, 1941, p. 1; Dobbs, *Teamster Bureaucracy*, 159.

45. Dobbs, *Teamster Bureaucracy*, 160.

46. MEA, Minutes, Annual Meeting, Aug. 2, 1944; MEA, Minutes, Board of Directors, Sept. 6, 1944; MEA, Minutes, Board of Directors, Dec. 6, 1944, all in MACI Papers; *Minneapolis Star Journal*, Jan. 18, 1945, p. 1.

47. *Minneapolis Star Journal*, Feb. 8, 1945, p. 1, Feb. 9, 1945, p. 1, April 6, 1945, p. 1; *St. Paul Pioneer Press*, March 7, 1945, p. 1.

48. *Minneapolis Star Journal*, April 6, 1945, p. 1, April 10, 1945, p. 1, April 12, 1945, p. 1; Leslie, Memoirs.

49. *St. Paul Pioneer Press*, Feb. 6, 1947, p. 6, Feb. 13, 1947, March 18, 1947, p. 2, March 19, 1947, pp. 1, 2, April 2, 1947, p. 1, April 7, 1947, April 12, 1947, p. 13, April 24, 1947, p. 1; Leslie, Memoirs.

50. *St. Paul Pioneer Press*, April 24, 1947, p. 1; Stieber, "Ten Years of the MLRA," 28.

51. Harry A. Millis and Emily C. Brown, *From the Wagner Act to Taft-Hartley* (Chicago: University of Chicago Press, 1950), 358–62; Senators Ball, Taft, and Smith, Minority Views (to accompany HR 4908), Labor Disputes Act of 1946, April 9, 1946, Senate Committee on Education and Labor, 79 Congress, 2 session, copy in Ball Papers.

52. "Congressional Hopper Choked With Labor Proposals," *Business Week*, Jan. 11, 1947, p. 18; "Senate Brews Strong Medicine," *Business Week*, April 12, 1947, p. 94.

53. Ball, Speech to MEA, Jan. 21, 1947, Ball Papers; Senate Committee on Labor and Public Welfare, 80 Congress, 1 Session, 1947, Senate 133, S. 55, S. 105.

54. Stassen, *Where I Stand*, 99–100; Alfred Friendly, "Taft, Ball Hit Stassen Labor Plan," *Washington Post*, Feb. 8, 1947.

55. Friendly, "Taft, Ball Hit Stassen Labor Plan"; Stassen, *Where I Stand*, 73–153, 104, 117.

56. Millis and Brown, *From the Wagner Act to Taft-Hartley*, 281–91; Alfred S. Cleveland, "NAM Spokesman for Industry," *Harvard Business Review* 26 (May 1948): 370–71; *Business Week*, Dec. 7, 1946, p. 19.

57. Millis and Brown, *From the Wagner Act to Taft-Hartley*, 281–91; Christopher L. Tom-

lins, *The State and the Unions* (Cambridge, MA: Cambridge University Press, 1985) 282; AI, *Newsletter*, April 15, 1947, Hubert H. Humphrey Papers, MHS; *Minneapolis Tribune*, n.d., copy in MacKinnon Papers, MHS; *Time*, April 28, 1947, pp. 19, 20.

58. AI, *Newsletter*, July 8, 1947, Humphrey Papers; "A New Deal for America's Employers," *Business Week*, June 28, 1947, p. 15; Millis and Brown, *From the Wagner Act to Taft-Hartley*, 22–28.

59. AI, *Newsletter*, July 8, 1947.

60. Stassen, *Where I Stand*, 139; AI, *Newsletter*, Oct. 16, 1947.

61. AI, *Newsletter*, Oct. 16, 1947.

NOTES TO THE EPILOGUE

1. Minnesota, *Statutes*, Chapters 179.06, 179.07, 179.083, 179.11, 179.13, 179.27, 179.41–179.47.

2. NLRB VS. *MacKay Radio & Telegraph Co.*, 304 U.S. 333 (1938).

3. William B. Gould, *A Primer in American Labor Law* (Cambridge, MA: MIT Press, 1986), 102; Government Accounting Office (GAO), *Labor-Management Relations* (Washington, D.C., Jan. 1991), 12, 13; Aaron Bernstein, "You Can't Bargain with A Striker Whose Job is No More," *Business Week*, Aug. 5, 1991, p. 27; "One for the Rank and File," *Newsweek*, July 19, 1993, pp. 38–39. Union membership dropped from 25.5 percent of the U.S. workforce in 1975 to 16.1 percent in 1990.

4. U.S. Fourth District Court, EA VS. USWA, Plaintiffs' Answers to Defendants' First Set of Interrogatories, March 25, 1992, pp. 10–12, CIV 4-91-947; *Minneapolis Star-Tribune*, June 22, 1983, p. 7B, Aug. 30, 1984, p. M-2, Oct. 30, 1983, p. 1.

5. EA VS. USWA, Interrogatories, 6–8, 10–12; *Minneapolis Star-Tribune*, April 11, 1991, p. 1A; *Minneapolis Star-Tribune*, April 19, 1991, p. 8D; *St. Paul Pioneer Press*, Jan. 23, 1991, p. 7C.

6. Minnesota House File 304, Minnesota Senate File 597; MNCC, "Legislative Alert," April 5, 1991, copy in EA legal files; EA, "Issue Brief," EA files, at Employers Association, Inc., Minneapolis. The Minnesota Employers' Association (MEA) became the Minnesota Association of Commerce and Industry (MACI) in May

1968, the Chamber of Commerce and Industry in Jan. 1987, and, finally, the Minnesota Chamber of Commerce in Jan. 1988; MACI Papers.

7. EA, "Action Alert!!!," May 31, 1991, copy in EA files; *Minneapolis Star-Tribune*, Aug. 10, 1991, p. 1A; David Warner, "Labor Targets the States," *Nation's Business*, Aug. 1991, pp. 22–25.

8. *Minneapolis Star-Tribune*, Aug. 10, 1991, p. 1A; EA, *Newsletter*, Aug. 1993, p. 2; folder cover in EA membership package; EA, "Membership Options," in membership package; EA vs. USWA, Affidavit of Thomas Rinne, May 22, 1992; EA's Labor Relations membership provides direct staff representation in labor relations and collective bargaining issues for annual minimum dues of $1,700 to $2,260; U.S. District Court, Interrogatories, March 25, 1992, pp. 6–8.

9. Memo, Tom Rinne to Tom Ebert, Oct. 4, 1991, EA legal files; EA vs. USWA, Order, Oct. 1, 1992, and Interrogatories, March 25, 1992, both Case 4-91-947.

10. EA vs. USWA, Order, Oct. 1, 1992, and Interrogatories, March 25, 1992, both Case 4-

91-947; *Minneapolis Star-Tribune*, Dec. 9, 1991, p. 6D; Telephone interview of Tom Rinne by author, Dec. 18, 1996; EA, *Newsletter*, April 1994, p. 1. In the 1940s, Henry Halladay and Leavitt R. Barker, both members of the Dorsey and Whitney law firm, sat on the AI board of directors and helped draft the secondary boycott legislation presented to the legislature by the MEA in 1945 and 1947.

11. EA vs. USWA, Civil Docket, Order; *Minneapolis Star-Tribune*, Dec. 9, 1991, p. 6D; interview of Tom Rinne, Dec. 18, 1996; *Wall Street Journal*, Feb. 1, 1995, p. A14. The Labor Policy Association represented 220 large firms, including Honeywell, formerly of Minneapolis, which is also represented on the EA board of directors. The *Wall Street Journal* suggested that the Labor Policy Association was influential regarding labor-management relations in Newt Gingrich's inner circle.

12. EA, *Newsletter*, "1993 in Review," Feb. 1994; *Newsletter*, April 1994; interview of Rinne; *St. Paul Pioneer Press*, March 11, 1994; *St. Paul Pioneer Press*, Aug. 20, 1994, p. G2.

13. *St. Paul Pioneer Press*, Aug. 20, 1994, p. G2.

Index

A Union Against Unions was designed by Will Powers at the Minnesota Historical Society Press. Typesetting was done by Judy Gilats, Peregrine Graphics Services, St. Paul, Minnesota, in Photina and Metro typefaces. This book was printed by Sheridan Books, Chelsea, Michigan.